Studies in Economic Theory

Editors

Charalambos D. Aliprantis
Department of Mathematics
IUPUI
1125 E 38th Street
Indianapolis, IN 46205-2810
USA

Nicholas C. Yannelis
Department of Economics
University of Illinois
Champaign, IL 61820
USA

M. Ali Khan · Nicholas C. Yannelis (Eds.)

Equilibrium Theory in Infinite Dimensional Spaces

With 10 Figures

Springer-Verlag Berlin Heidelberg New York London
Paris Tokyo Hong Kong Barcelona Budapest

Prof. Dr. M. Ali Khan
The Johns Hopkins University
Baltimore, MD 21218, USA

Prof. Dr. Nicholas C. Yannelis
University of Illinois at Urbana-Champaign
Champaign, IL 61820, USA

ISBN 3-540-54480-1 Springer-Verlag Berlin Heidelberg New York Tokyo
ISBN 0-387-54480-1 Springer-Verlag New York Heidelberg Berlin Tokyo

Printing: Weihert-Druck GmbH, Darmstadt
Bookbinding: J. Schäffer GmbH u. Co. KG, Grünstadt
2142/7130-543210 - Printed on acid - free paper

Preface

Apart from the underlying theme that all the contributions to this volume pertain to models set in an infinite dimensional space, they differ on many counts. Some were written in the early seventies while others are reports of ongoing research done especially with this volume in mind. Some are surveys of material that can, at least at this point in time, be deemed to have attained a satisfactory solution of the problem, while others represent initial forays into an original and novel formulation. Some furnish alternative proofs of known, and by now, classical results, while others can be seen as groping towards and exploring formulations that have not yet reached a definitive form. The subject matter also has a wide leeway, ranging from solution concepts for economies to those for games and also including representation of preferences and discussion of purely mathematical problems, all within the rubric of choice variables belonging to an infinite dimensional space, interpreted as a commodity space or as a strategy space. Thus, this is a collective enterprise in a fairly wide sense of the term and one with the diversity of which we have interfered as little as possible.

Our motivation for bringing all of this work under one set of covers was severalfold. Even allowing for the superficiality of the cliché that economic modeling done in the context of an infinite dimensional space enables us to deal with time or uncertainty or location or quality or information, we strongly feel that fruitful and seminal formulations of these issues very quickly reduce to a basic core of material that substantially overlaps with the basic corpus of general equilibrium theory on the one hand, and with the theory of normal-form games on the other. Furthermore, the analytic core of this theory is, in the first instance, functional analysis, and secondarily, the three subjects on which it draws, namely topology, measure theory, and linear algebra. A general overview of all of this material is our primary motivation for this volume.

Such an overview is presented in this volume not in the form of a comprehensive introduction, self-contained and progressing linearly from the less to the more difficult, but rather with different voices and different styles. Thus, this is very much a monograph with a collective authorship rather than a text in the standard use of the term. Whereas we are sure that the material presented here will eventually cohere into a text, we are far from clear whether a text is warranted at this stage of its development, laying aside the question of our competence to write one. What makes this plunge a viable enterprise for the student-researcher of economic theory revolves, in our view, around a book that has attracted to economic theory a steady stream of talented scholars — we have in mind, of course, Gerard Debreu's *Theory of Value.* It is our considered opinion that once one has acquired the technical maturity to appreciate and enjoy this book, a criterion now fulfilled in most of the better graduate programs in both the US and the Continent, a fruitful way to proceed is to get to the frontier of a particular and well-specified problem. The economic and technical insights gained from an in-depth study of one particular problem yield handsome rewards in the context of problems which, to begin with, may seem unrelated and dissimilar. The various sections of this book represent several such directions for the reader. As such, they also can be read independently of each other.

A secondary motivation behind this volume is to exhibit how much progress has been made since particular problems were first formulated and tackled. Thus, the work of Bewley on the existence of competitive equilibrium with an infinite number of commodities and a finite number of agents dates to a 1973 CORE Working Paper, and with an infinite number of agents to his 1970 Ph.D. dissertation; the work of Gabszewicz on the equivalence between the core and competitive equilibria of an atomless economy with an infinite number of commodities derives from his 1971 Ph.D. dissertation; that of Mertens on the same problem to a 1970 CORE Working Paper; the work of Mas-Colell on large anonymous games dates to a 1978 Stanford Working Paper; and, finally, that of Nachman-Kertz on temporary equilibria to 1976. This work has remained unpublished in its original form, and by re-reading it along with current research efforts, one gets a deeper appreciation of the genius of the original contributions; but more importantly, such a re-reading gives important perspectives on the problems themselves. Has the question been posed in too much generality? Is a particular technical alley a dead-end? What was essential and what was inessential in more specific and particular formulations of the problem? In passing, we would like to mention that all of this work, which has remained unpublished until now, was solicited by us for this volume.

Yet another motivation behind our collection is to emphasize the substantial technical overlap between game theory and general equilibrium analysis. Of course, von-Neumann's 1928 paper and his subsequent book with Morgenstern was the first vindication of this point of view and this was subsequently underscored by Kakutani in 1941, by Debreu, Nash, Ky Fan and Glicksberg in 1950–52, and then, finally in 1954, by the Arrow-Debreu proof of the existence of competitive equilibrium. We feel that this point deserves some prominence especially in our time.

A word about technical prerequisites. The basic concepts of functional analysis play a starring role in all of the papers. The reader will need the elements of Banach space theory; in particular, the Hahn-Banach theorem and the interplay between and the basic properties of the weak and weak* topologies. With a little more effort, these results can be recast into the more general terminology of locally convex spaces in which is set the basic Fan-Glicksberg fixed point theorem. There are by now several excellent treatments of this basic material and we leave it to each reader to pick an author with whose style he or she is at ease. However, beyond this general material, each paper furnishes the relevant mathematical references. Of course, it is only fair to mention that a study of classical equilibrium notions such as a *Walrasian equilibrium* or a *core* or a *Nash equilibrium* in the context of an infinite dimensional commodity or strategy space not only requires novel technical arguments and a modification and correction of much of our finite-dimensional intuition about these concepts, but this point also goes the other way; a successful formulation of the outstanding questions has also necessitated the creation of new mathematics. Some of the contributions in this volume also present a flavor of these technical advances that have been made in the last twenty years.

Finally, we would like to express our deep gratitude to Werner Müller, editor of Springer-Verlag, for his sustained encouragement and patience of this project. We are also thankful to Mike Schneider of the University of Illinois for his conscientious and careful typing of difficult material.

M. A. K. *Baltimore, Maryland*
N. C. Y. *Urbana-Champaign, Illinois*

February 8, 1991

TABLE OF CONTENTS

PART 1

MATHEMATICAL BACKGROUND

Integration of Banach-Valued Correspondences

Nicholas C. Yannelis

Abstract. We study the basic properties of the integral of a Banach-valued correspondence. In particular, we examine the convergence, compactness and convexity properties of the Bochner and Gel'fand integrals of a set-valued function. The above properties are applied to prove the existence of an equilibrium for an abstract economy with a continuum of agents.

1. Introduction

The classical model of exchange under perfect competition known as the "Arrow-Debreu-McKenzie model" was formulated in terms of a finite set of agents taking prices as given and engaging in sale and purchase of commodities. Aumann (1966) argued that the classical model is clearly at odds with itself as the finitude of agents means that each individual is able to exercise some influence and therefore the assumption of price taking behavior is not sensible. In a path breaking paper, Aumann (1966) resolves this problem by assuming that the set of agents is an atomless measure space and consequently the influence of each agent in the economy as a whole is "negligible." Hence, the "Aumann economy," that is, an economy with an atomless measure space of agents, captures precisely the meaning of perfect competition.

In order to prove the existence of a competitive equilibrium in a perfectly competitive economy, Aumann (1966) faced the following fundamental problem. What is the definition of the aggregate demand set if the set of agents is an atomless measure space? For instance, if we denote the set of agents by T and denote by $D(t,p)$ the demand set of agent $t \in T$, at prices p, we know that if T is finite, the aggregate demand set is given by the summation of the individual demand sets, i.e., $\sum_{t \in T} D(t,p)$. However, if T is an atomless measure space, then we have to integrate the set $D(t,p)$. But what does it mean to integrate a set-valued function? In a seminal paper Aumann (1965) introduced the notion of the integral of a set-valued function (or correspondence) and proved some basic results needed to tackle the problem of the existence of a competitive equilibrium in an economy with an atomless measure space of agents, and with a finite dimensional commodity space.

However, if one wishes to allow for perfectly competitive economies with an infinite dimensional commodity space, then an extension of the work of Aumann (1965) is required. In particular, from the integration of finite dimensional-valued correspondences we must now pass to integration of Banach-valued correspondences.

The main purpose of this paper is to study the integral of a Banach-valued correspondence and prove some basic theorems needed in general equilibrium and game theory. Results due to Debreu (1967), Datko (1972), Diestel (1977), Hiai-Umegaki (1977), Khan (1982, 1984, 1985), Papageorgiou (1985), Khan-Majumdar (1986), Balder (1988), Yannelis (1988, 1989, 1990), Rustichini (1989), and Castaing (1988) have drastically influenced the present paper which in a way may be considered as a synthesis of the work of the above authors.

2. Preliminaries

2.1 Notation.

$\mathbb{R}^n$ denotes the n-fold Cartesian product of the set of real numbers $\mathbb{R}$.

con A denotes the convex hull of the set A.

$\overline{\text{con}}A$ denotes the closed convex hull of the set A.

2^A denotes the set of all nonempty subsets of the set A.

$\emptyset$ denotes the empty set.

/ denotes the set of theoretic subtraction.

dist denotes the distance.

proj denotes the projection.

If $A \subset X$, where X is a Banach space, cl A denotes the norm closure of A.

If X is a linear topological space, its dual is the space X^* of all continuous linear functionals on X, and if $p \in X^*$ and $x \in X$ the value of p at x is denoted either by $\langle p, x\rangle$ or $p \cdot x$.

If $\{F_n : n = 1, 2, \ldots\}$ is a sequence of nonempty subsets of a Banach space X, we will denote by s-Ls F_n and s-Li F_n the set of its (strong) limit superior and (strong) limit inferior points respectively, i.e.,

$$\text{s-Ls}\, F_n = \{x \in X : x = s - \lim_{k\to\infty} x_{n_k},\ x_{n_k} \in F_{n_k},\ k = 1,2,\ldots\}$$
$$\text{s-Li}\, F_n = \{x \in X : x = s - \lim_{n\to\infty} x_n,\ x_n \in F_n,\ n = 1,2,\ldots\}.$$

A w in front of $\text{Ls}\, F_n$ ($\text{Li}\, F_n$) will mean limit superior (limit inferior) with respect to the weak topology $\sigma(X, X^*)$.

2.2 Definitions. Let X and Y be sets. The *graph* of the set-valued function (or correspondence), $\phi : X \to 2^Y$ is denoted by $G_\phi = \{(x,y) \in X \times Y : y \in \phi(x)\}$. Let (T, τ, μ) be a complete, finite measure space, and X be a separable Banach space. The correspondence $\phi : T \to 2^X$ is said to have a *measurable graph* if $G_\phi \in \tau \otimes \beta(X)$, where $\beta(X)$ denotes the Borel σ-algebra on X and $\otimes$ denotes product σ-algebra. The correspondence $\phi : T \to 2^X$ is said to be *lower measurable* if for every open subset V of X, the set $\{t \in T : \phi(t) \cap V \neq \emptyset\}$ is an element of τ. Recall [see for instance Debreu (1966), p. 359 or Yannelis (1990a), Lemma 3] that if $\phi : T \to 2^X$ has a measurable graph, then ϕ is lower measurable. Furthermore, if $\phi(\cdot)$ is closed valued and lower measurable then $\phi : T \to 2^X$ has a measurable graph. A well-known result of Aumann (1967) which will be of fundamental importance in this paper says that if (T, τ, μ) is a complete, finite measure space, X is a separable metric space and $\phi : T \to 2^X$ is a nonempty valued correspondence having a measurable graph, then $\phi(\cdot)$ admits a *measurable selection*, i.e., there exists a measurable function $f : T \to X$ such that $f(t) \in \phi(t)$ μ-a.e.

We now define the notion of a Bochner integrable function. We will follow closely Diestel-Uhl (1977). Let (T, τ, μ) be a finite measure space and X be a Banach space. A function $f : T \to X$ is called *simple* if there exist $x_1, x_2, \ldots, x_n$ in X and $\alpha_1, \alpha_2, \ldots, \alpha_n$ in τ such that $f = \sum_{i=1}^n x_i \chi_{\alpha_i}$, where $\chi_{\alpha_i}(t) = 1$ if $t \in \alpha_i$ and $\chi_{\alpha_i}(t) = 0$ if $t \notin \alpha_i$. A function $f : T \to X$ is said to be *μ-measurable* if there exists a sequence of simple functions $f_n : T \to X$ such that $\lim_{n\to\infty} \|f_n(t) - f(t)\| = 0$ for almost all $t \in T$. A μ-measurable function $f : T \to X$ is said to be *Bochner integrable* if there exists a sequence of simple functions $\{f_n : n = 1,2,\ldots\}$ such that

$$\lim_{n\to\infty} \int_T \|f_n(t) - f(t)\| d\mu(t) = 0.$$

In this case we define for each $E \in \tau$ the integral to be $\int_E f(t)d\mu(t) = \lim_{n\to\infty} \int_E f_n(t)d\mu(t)$. It can be shown [see Diestel-Uhl (1977), Theorem 2, p. 45] that, if $\phi : T \to X$ is a μ-measurable function then f is Bochner integrable if and only if $\int_T \|f(t)\|d\mu(t) < \infty$. It is important to note that the *Dominated Convergence Theorem* holds for Bochner integrable functions, in particular, if $f_n : T \to X$ $(n = 1, 2, \dots)$ is a sequence of Bochner integrable functions such that $\lim_{n\to\infty} f_n(t) = f(t)$ μ-a.e., and $\|f_n(t)\| \leq g(t)$ μ-a.e., where $g \in L_1(\mu, \mathbb{R})$, then f is Bochner integrable and $\lim_{n\to\infty} \int_T \|f_n(t) - f(t)\|d\mu(t) = 0$.

For $1 \leq p < \infty$, we denote by $L_p(\mu, X)$ the space of equivalence classes of X-valued Bochner integrable functions $x : T \to X$ normed by

$$\|x\|_p = \left(\int_T \|x(t)\|_p d\mu(t)\right)^{1/p}.$$

It is a standard result that normed by the functional $\|\cdot\|_p$ above, $L_1(\mu, X)$ becomes a Banach space [see Diestel-Uhl (1977), p. 50]. We denote by S^p_ϕ the *set of all selections from* $\phi : T \to 2^X$ that belong to the space $L_p(\mu, X)$, i.e.,

$$S^p_\phi = \{x \in L_p(\mu, X) : x(t) \in \phi(t)\ \mu\text{-a.e.}\}.$$

We will also consider the set $S^1_\phi = \{x \in L_1(\mu, X) : x(t) \in \phi(t)\ \mu\text{-a.e.}\}$, i.e., S^1_ϕ is the *set of all Bochner integrable selections from* $\phi(\cdot)$. Using the above set and following Aumann (1965) we can define the *integral of the correspondence* $\phi : T \to 2^X$ as follows:

$$\int_T \phi(t)d\mu(t) = \left\{\int_T x(t)d\mu(t) : x \in S^1_\phi\right\}.$$

In the sequel we will denote the above integral by $\int \phi$. Recall that the correspondence $\phi : T \to 2^X$ is said to be *integrally bounded* if there exists a map $h \in L_1(\mu, \mathbb{R})$ such that $\sup\{\|x\| : x \in \phi(t)\} \leq h(t)$ μ-a.e. Moreover, note that if T is a complete measure space, X is a separable Banach space and $\phi : T \to 2^X$ is an integrably bounded, nonempty valued correspondence having a measurable graph, then by the Aumann measurable selection theorem we can conclude that S^1_ϕ is nonempty and therefore $\int_T \phi(t)d\mu(t)$ is nonempty as well. It should be noted that the measurability of ϕ is a sufficient condition for the nonemptiness of $\int \phi$, but it is not necessary. In fact, $\int \phi$ may be nonempty even if ϕ does not have a measurable graph [see Schechter (1989) for an example to that effect].

A Banach space X has the *Radon-Nikodym Property with respect to the measure space* (T, τ, μ) if for each μ-continuous vector measure $G : \tau \to X$ of bounded variation there exists $g \in L_1(\mu, X)$ such that $G(E) = \int_E g(t)d\mu(t)$ for all $E \in \tau$. A Banach space X has the *Radon-Nikodym Property* (RNP) if X has the RNP with respect to every finite measure space. Recall now [see Diestel-Uhl (1977, Theorem 1, p. 98)] that if (T, τ, μ) is a finite measure space $1 \leq p < \infty$, and X is a Banach space, then X^* has the RNP if and only if $(L_p(\mu, X))^* = L_q(\mu, X^*)$ where $\frac{1}{p} + \frac{1}{q} = 1$.

Let A_n $(n = 1, 2, \ldots)$ be a sequence of nonempty subsets of a Banach space. Following Kuratowski (1966, p. 339) we say that A_n *converges* in A (written as $A_n \to A$) if and only if $\text{s-Li}\, A_n = \text{s-Ls}\, A_n = A$. Also, we say that A_n *converges in the Kuratowski-Mosco sense to* A (written as $A_n \xrightarrow{\text{K-M}} A$) if and only if $\text{s-Li}\, A_n = \text{w-Ls}\, A_n = A$. It may be useful to remind the reader that $\text{Li}\, A_n$ and $\text{Ls}\, A_n$ are both closed sets and that $\text{s-Li}\, A_n \subset \text{s-Ls}\, A_n$ [see Kuratowski (1966), pp. 336–338].

Let X be a metric space and Y be a Banach space. The correspondence $\phi : X \to 2^Y$ is said to be *upper semicontinuous* (u.s.c.) at $x_0 \in X$, if for any neighborhood $N(\phi(x_0))$ of $\phi(x_0)$, there exists a neighborhood $N(x_0)$ of x_0 such that for all $x \in N(x_0)$, $\phi(x) \subset N(\phi(x_0))$. We say that ϕ is u.s.c. if ϕ is u.s.c. at every point $x \in X$. Recall that this definition is equivalent to the fact that the set $\{x \in X : \phi(x) \subset V\}$ is open in X for every open subset V of Y [see for instance Kuratowski (1966), Theorem 3, p. 176].

Let ν be a small positive number and let B be the open unit ball in Y. The correspondence $\phi : X \to 2^Y$ is said to be *quasi upper-semicontinuous* (q.u.s.c.) at $x \in X$, if whenever the sequence x_n $(n = 1, 2, \ldots)$ in X converges to x, then for some n_0, $\phi(x_n) \subset \phi(x) + \nu B$ for all $n \geq n_0$. We say that ϕ is q.u.s.c. if ϕ is q.u.s.c. at every point $x \in X$. It can be easily checked that if ϕ is compact valued, quasi upper-semicontinuity implies upper-semicontinuity and vice-versa.

Let now P and X be metric spaces. The correspondence $F : P \to 2^X$

is said to be *lower semicontinuous* (l.s.c.) if the sequence p_n $(n = 1, 2, \ldots)$ in P converges to $p \in P$, then $F(p) \subset \operatorname{Li} F(p_n)$. Finally recall that the correspondence $F : P \to 2^X$ is said to be *continuous*, if and only if it is u.s.c. and l.s.c.

3. Weak Compactness in $L_p(\mu, X)$

The result below has found several applications in general equilibrium and game theory [see for example Khan (1986), Yannelis (1987, 1990b) and Yannelis-Rustichini (1990, 1991)] and it is known in the literature of economic theory as Diestel's theorem on weak compactness in $L_1(\mu, X)$.

Theorem 3.1. *Let (T, τ, μ) be a complete finite measure space, X be a separable Banach space and $\phi : T \to 2^X$ be an integrally bounded, convex, weakly compact and nonempty valued correspondence. Then S^1_ϕ is weakly compact in $L_1(\mu, X)$.*

Proof. First note that $(L_1(\mu, X))^* = L_\infty(\mu, X^*_{w^*})$ [see for instance Tulcea-Tulcea (1969)]. Pick an arbitrary $x \in L_\infty(\mu, X^*_{w^*})$. If we show that x attains its supremum on S^1_ϕ the result will follow from James's theorem [James (1964)]. To this end, let

$$\sup_{f \in S^1_\phi} f \cdot x = \sup_{f \in S^1_\phi} \int_{t \in T} (f(t) \cdot x(t)) d\mu(t).$$

By Lemma 1 in Debreu-Schmeidler (1972) or Theorem 2.2 in Hiai-Umegaki (1977) we have that

$$\sup_{f \in S^1_\phi} \int_{t \in T} (f(t) \cdot x(t)) d\mu(t) = \int_{t \in T} \sup_{g \in \phi(t)} (g \cdot x(t)) d\mu(t).$$

Define the correspondence $\theta : T \to 2^X$ by

$$\theta(t) = \{y \in \phi(t) : y \cdot x = \sup_{g \in \phi(t)} g \cdot x\}.$$

Since the correspondence $\phi : T \to 2^X$ is weakly compact valued we have that $\theta(t) \neq \emptyset$ for all $t \in T$. Define the function $F : T \times X \to [-\infty, \infty]$ by $F(t, y) = y \cdot x - \sup_{g \in \phi(t)} g \cdot x$. Note that for each fixed $t \in T$, $F(t, \cdot)$

is continuous and for each fixed $y \in X$, $F(\cdot, y)$ is measurable. Hence by a standard result [see for instance Yannelis (1990a, Proposition 3.1)], $F(\cdot,\cdot)$ is jointly measurable and consequently the set

$$F^{-1}(0) = \{(t,y) \in T \times X : F(t,y) = 0\} \quad \text{belongs to } \tau \otimes \beta(X).$$

Since $\phi(\cdot)$ has a measurable graph, the set $G_\phi = \{(t,y) \in T \times X : y \in \phi(t)\}$ is an element of $\tau \otimes \beta(X)$. Observe that

$$G_\theta = F^{-1}(0) \cap G_\phi.$$

Since $F^{-1}(0)$ and G_ϕ belong to $\tau \otimes \beta(X)$ so does G_θ, i.e., $\theta(\cdot)$ has a measurable graph. By the Aumann measurable selection theorem, there exists a measurable function $z : T \to X$ such that $z(t) \in \theta(t)$ μ-a.e. Hence $z \in S^1_\phi$ and

$$\sup_{g \in S^1_\phi} g \cdot x = \int_{t \in T} (z(t) \cdot x(t)) d\mu(t) = z \cdot x.$$

Since $x \in L_\infty(\mu, X^*_{w^*})$ was arbitrary, we can conclude that every element of $(L_1(\mu, X))^* = L_\infty(\mu, X^*_{w^*})$ attains its supremum on S^1_ϕ. This completes the proof of the Theorem.

Remark 3.1. Note that if (T, τ, μ) is a finite measure space, and X is a Banach space then $(L_p(\mu, X))^* = L_q(\mu, X^*_{w^*})$ where $1 \le p < \infty$, $\frac{1}{p} + \frac{1}{q} = 1$ [see Tulcea-Tulcea (1969)]. Hence, in Theorem 3.1 we can replace the fact that S^1_ϕ is weakly in $L_1(\mu, X)$ with the statement that S^p_ϕ, $(1 \le p < \infty)$ is weakly compact in $L_p(\mu, X)$.

Bibliographical notes. Theorem 4.1 was proved by Diestel (1977) in a less general form [see also Byrne (1978)]. However, it should be noted that Castaing had earlier proved a related result to that of Diestel's. Also, Datko (1973) proved a version of Diestel's theorem for a reflexive separable Banach space. The proof of Theorem 4.1 is based on the celebrated theorem of James (1964) and it is patterned after that of Khan (1982, 1987) and Papageorgiou (1985). Recently, Balder (1990) has given an alternative proof of Diestel's theorem using a.e. convergence of arithmetic averages.

4. Weak Sequential Convergence in $L_p(\mu, X)$

We begin by proving the following result:

Theorem 4.1. *Let (T, τ, μ) be a finite measure space and X be a separable Banach space. Let $\{f_\lambda : \lambda \in \Lambda\}$ (Λ is a directed set), be a net in $L_p(\mu, X)$, $1 \leq p < \infty$ such that f_λ converges weakly to $f \in L_p(\mu, X)$. Suppose that for all $\lambda \in \Lambda$, $f_\lambda(t) \in F(t)$ μ-a.e., where $F : T \to 2^X$ is a weakly compact, integrably bounded, convex, nonempty valued correspondence. Then we can extract a sequence $\{f_{\lambda_n} : n = 1, 2, \ldots\}$ from the net $\{f_\lambda : \lambda \in \Lambda\}$ such that:*

(i) f_{λ_n} converges weakly to f, and
(ii) $f(t) \in \overline{\text{con}}\, \text{w-Ls}\{f_{\lambda_n}(t)\}$ μ-a.e.

Proof. We begin the proof of Theorem 4.1 by stating the following result of Artstein (1979, Proposition C, p. 280).

Proposition 4.1. *Let (T, τ, μ) be a finite measure space and let $f_n : T \to R^\ell$ ($n = 1, 2, \ldots$) be a uniformly integrable sequence of functions converging weakly to f. Then,*

$$f(t) \in \text{con}\, \text{w-Ls}\{f_n(t)\} \ \mu\text{-}a.e.$$

Using Artstein's result we can prove the following proposition.

Proposition 4.2. *Let (T, τ, μ) be a finite measure space and X be a separable Banach space whose dual X^* has the RNP. Let $\{f_n : n = 1, 2, \ldots\}$ be a sequence in $L_p(\mu, X), 1 \leq p < \infty$ such that f_n converges weakly to $f \in L_p(\mu, X)$. Suppose that for all n ($n = 1, 2, \ldots$), $f_n(t) \in F(t)$ μ-a.e. where $F : T \to 2^X$ is a weakly compact, nonempty valued correspondence. Then*

$$f(t) \in \overline{\text{con}}\, \text{w-Ls}\{f_n(t)\} \ \mu\text{-}a.e.$$

Proof. Since f_n converges weakly to f and X^* has the RNP, for any $\psi \in (L_p(\mu, X))^* = L_q(\mu, X^*)$ (where $\frac{1}{p} + \frac{1}{q} = 1$), we have that $\langle \psi, f_n \rangle = \int_T \langle \psi(t), f_n(t) \rangle d\mu(t)$ converges to $\langle \psi, f \rangle = \int_T \langle \psi(t), f(t) \rangle d\mu(t)$. Define the functions $h_n : T \to R$ and $h : T \to R$ by $h_n(t) = \langle\psi(t), f_n(t)\rangle$ and $h(t) = \langle(t), f(t)\rangle$ respectively. Since for each n, $f_n(t) \in F(t)$ μ-a.e. and $F(\cdot)$ is weakly compact, h_n is bounded and uniformly integrable. Also, it is easy to check that h_n converges weakly to h. In fact, let $g \in L_\infty(\mu, \mathbb{R})$ and let $M = \|g\|_\infty$, then

$$\begin{aligned}\left|\int_T g(t)(h_n(t) - h(t))d\mu(t)\right| = \Big|\int_T g(t)(\langle\psi(t), f_n(t)\rangle \\ - \langle\psi(t), f(t)\rangle)d\mu(t)\Big| \\ \leq M|\langle\psi, f_n\rangle - \langle\psi, f\rangle|\end{aligned} \tag{4.1}$$

and (4.1) can become arbitrarily small since as it was noted above $\langle\psi, f_n\rangle$ converges to $\langle\psi, f\rangle$.

By Proposition 4.1, we have that $h(t) \in \text{con}\,\text{w-Ls}\{h_n(t)\} \subset \overline{\text{con}}\,\text{w-Ls}\{h_n(t)\}$ μ-a.e., i.e., $\langle\psi(t), f(t)\rangle \in \overline{\text{con}}\,\text{w-Ls}\{\langle\psi, f_n(t)\rangle\} = \langle\psi(t), \overline{\text{con}}\,\text{w-Ls}\{f_n(t)\}\rangle$ μ-a.e. and consequently,

$$\int_T \langle\psi(t), f(t)\rangle d\mu(t) \in \int_T \langle\psi(t), x(t)\rangle d\mu(t), \tag{4.2}$$

where $x(\cdot)$ is a selection from $\overline{\text{con}}\,\text{w-Ls}\{f_n(\cdot)\}$. It follows from (4.2) that:

$$f \in S^p_{\overline{\text{con}}\,\text{w-Ls}\{f_n\}}. \tag{4.3}$$

To see this, suppose by way of contradiction that $f \notin S^p_{\overline{\text{con}}\,\text{w-Ls}\{f_n\}}$, then by the separating hyperplane theorem,[1] there exists $\psi \in (L_p(\mu, X))^* = L_q(\mu, X^*)$, $\psi \neq 0$ such that $\langle\psi, f\rangle > \sup\{\langle\psi, x\rangle : x \in S^p_{\overline{\text{con}}\,\text{w-Ls}\{f_n\}}\}$, i.e., $\int_T\langle\psi(t), f(t)\rangle d\mu(t) > \int_T\langle\psi(t), x(t)\rangle d\mu(t)$, where $x(\cdot)$ is a selection from $\overline{\text{con}}\,\text{w-Ls}\{f_n(\cdot)\}$, a contradiction to (4.2). Hence, (4.3) holds and we can conclude that $f(t) \in \overline{\text{con}}\,\text{w-Ls}\{f_n(t)\}$ μ-a.e. This completes the proof of Proposition 4.2.

---

[1] Note that the set $S^p_{\overline{\text{con}}\,\text{w-Ls}\{f_n\}}$ is nonempty. In fact, since w-Ls$\{f_n\}$ is lower measurable and nonempty valued, so is $\overline{\text{con}}\,\text{w-Ls}\{f_n\}$. So, $\overline{\text{con}}\,\text{w-Ls}\{f_n\}$ admits a measurable selection (recall the Kuratowski and Ryll-Nardzewski measurable selection theorem). Obviously the measurable selection is also integrable since $\overline{\text{con}}\,\text{w-Ls}\{f_n\}$ lies in a weakly compact subset of X. Therefore, we can conclude that $S^p_{\overline{\text{con}}\,\text{w-Ls}\{f_n\}}$ is nonempty.

Remark 4.1. Proposition 4.2 remains true without the assumption that X^* has the RNP. The proof proceeds as follows: Since f_n converges weakly to f we have that $\langle \phi, f_n \rangle$ converges to $\langle \phi, f \rangle$ for all $\phi \in (L_p(\mu, X))^*$. It follows from a standard result [see for instance Dinculeanu (1973, p. 112)] that ϕ can be represented by a function $\psi : T \to X^*$ such that $\langle \psi, x \rangle$ is measurable for every $x \in X$ and $\|\psi\| \in L_q(\mu, \mathbb{R})$. Hence, $\langle \psi, f_n \rangle = \int_T \langle \psi(t), f_n(t) \rangle d\mu(t)$ and $\langle \psi, f \rangle = \int_T \langle \psi(t), f(t) \rangle d\mu(t)$. Define the functions $h_n : T \to R$ and $h : T \to R$ by $h_n(t) = \langle \psi(t), f_n(t) \rangle$ and $h(t) = \langle \psi(t), f(t) \rangle$ respectively. One can now proceed as in the proof of Proposition 4.2 to complete the argument.

We are now ready to complete the proof of Theorem 4.1. Denote the net $\{f_\lambda : \lambda \in \Lambda\}$ by B. Since by assumption for all $\lambda \in \Lambda$, $f_\lambda(t) \in F(t)$ μ-a.e. where $F : T \to 2^X$ is an integrably bounded, weakly compact, convex, nonempty valued correspondence we can conclude that for all $\lambda \in \Lambda$, f_λ lies in the weakly compact set S_F^p (recall Diestel's theorem on weak compactness, Theorem 3.1). Hence, the weak closure of B, i.e., $w - \operatorname{cl} B$, is weakly compact. By the Eberlein-Smulian Theorem [see Dunford-Schwartz (1958, p. 430)], $w - \operatorname{cl} B$ is weakly sequentially compact. Obviously the weak limit of f_λ, i.e., f, belongs to $w - \operatorname{cl} B$. From Whitley's theorem[2] [Aliprantis-Burkinshaw (1985, Lemma 10.12, p. 155)], we know that if $f \in w - \operatorname{cl} B$, then there exists a sequence $\{f_{\lambda_n} : n = 1, 2, \ldots\}$ in B such that f_{λ_n} converges weakly to f. Since the sequence $\{f_{\lambda_n} : n = 1, 2, \ldots\}$ satisfies all the assumptions of Proposition 4.2 and Remark 4.1 we can conclude that $f(t) \in \overline{\text{con}}\, \text{w-Ls}\{f_{\lambda_n}(t)\}$ μ-a.e. This completes the proof of Theorem 4.1.

An immediate conclusion of Theorem 4.1 is the following useful corollary.

Corollary 4.1. *Let (T, τ, μ) be a finite measure space and X be a separable Banach space. Let $\{f_n : n = 1, 2, \ldots\}$ be a sequence of functions in $L_p(\mu, X)$, $1 \le p < \infty$ such that f_n converges weakly to $f \in L_p(\mu, X)$. Suppose that for all n $(n = 1, 2, \ldots)$, $f_n(t) \in F(t)$ μ-a.e., where $F : T \to 2^X$ is a weakly compact, integrably bounded, nonempty valued correspondence. Then*

$$f(t) \in \overline{\text{con}}\, \text{w-Ls}\{f_n(t)\} \ \mu\text{-a.e.}$$

[2] See also Kelley-Namioka (1963, exercise L, p. 165).

Bibliographical Notes. Theorem 4.1 and its proof are due to Yannelis (1989). Corollary 4.1 generalizes previous results of Artstein (1979) and Khan-Majumdar (1986). A related result to Corollary 4.1 has also been obtained by Balder (1988) and Castaing (1988). Ostroy-Zame (1988) have used Corollary 4.1 in order to prove the existence of an equilibrium in economies with a continuum of agents and commodities.

5. Properties of the Set of Integrable Selections from a Correspondence

We begin by proving s-Li and w-Ls versions of Fatou's Lemma for the set of integrable selections.

Theorem 5.1. *Let (T,τ,μ) be a complete, finite measure space and let X be a separable Banach space. If $\phi_n : T \to 2^X$ $(n = 1,2,\dots)$ is a sequence of integrably bounded correspondences having a measurable graph, i.e., $G_{\phi_n} \in \tau \otimes \beta(X)$, then*

$$S^1_{\text{s-Li}\,\phi_n} \subset \text{s-Li}\, S^1_{\phi_n}.$$

Proof. Let $x \in S^1_{\text{s-Li}\,\phi_n}$, i.e., $x(t) \in \text{s-Li}\,\phi_n(t)$ μ-a.e., we must show that $x \in \text{s-Li}\, S^1_{\phi_n}$. First note that $x(t) \in \text{s-Li}\,\phi_n(t)$ μ-a.e. implies that there exists a sequence $\{x_n : n = 1,2,\dots\}$ such that $s - \lim_{n\to\infty} x_n(t) = x(t)$ μ-a.e. and $x_n(t) \in \phi_n(t)) = 0$ μ-a.e. For each n $(n = 1,2,\dots)$, define the correspondence $A_n : T \to 2^X$ by

$$A_n(t) = \left\{ y \in \phi_n(t) : \|y - x(t)\| \le \text{dist}(x(t), \phi_n(t)) + \frac{1}{n} \right\}.$$

Clearly for all n $(n = 1,2,\dots)$ and for all $t \in T$, $A_n(t) \ne \emptyset$. Moreover, $A_n(\cdot)$ has measurable graph. Indeed, the function $g : T \times X \to [-\infty,\infty]$ defined by $g(t,y) = \|y - x(t)\| - \text{dist}(x(t),\phi_n(t))$ is measurable in t and continuous in y and therefore by a standard result [see Yannelis (1990a, Proposition 3.1)], $g(\cdot,\cdot)$ is jointly measurable with respect to the product σ-algebra $\tau \otimes \beta(X)$. It is easy to see that:

$$\begin{aligned} G_{A_n} &= \left\{ (t,y) \in T \times X : g(t,y) \le \frac{1}{n} \right\} \cap G_{\phi_n} \\ &= g^{-1}\left(\left[-\infty, \frac{1}{n} \right] \right) \cap G_{\phi_n}. \end{aligned}$$

Since $\phi_n(\cdot)$ has a measurable graph and $g(\cdot,\cdot)$ is jointly measurable, we can conclude that G_{A_n} belongs to $\tau \otimes \beta(X)$, i.e., $A_n(\cdot)$ has a measurable graph. By the Aumann measurable selection theorem there exists a measurable function $f_n : T \to X$ such that $f_n(t) \in A_n(t)$ μ-a.e. Since $x(t) \in \text{s-Li}\,\phi_n(t)$ μ-a.e., $\lim_{n\to\infty} \text{dist}(x(t), \phi_n(t)) = 0$ μ-a.e. which implies that $\lim_{n\to\infty} \|f_n(t) - x(t)\| = 0$ μ-a.e. Since $f_n(t) \in \phi_n(t)$ μ-a.e. and $\phi_n(\cdot)$ is integrably bounded, by the dominated convergence theorem [see Diestel-Uhl (1977, p. 45)], $f_n(\cdot)$ is Bochner integrable, i.e., $f_n \in L_1(\mu, X)$. Hence, $x \in \text{s-Li}\,S^1_{\phi_n}$ and this completes the proof of Theorem 5.1.

Theorem 5.2. *Let (T, τ, μ) be a finite measure space, X be a separable Banach space and let $\phi_n : T \to 2^X$ $(n = 1, 2, \ldots)$ be a sequence of nonempty, closed valued correspondences such that:*

(i) For all n $(n = 1, 2, \ldots)$, $\phi_n(t) \subset F(t)$ μ-a.e., where $F : T \to 2^X$ is an integrably bounded, weakly compact, convex, nonempty-valued correspondence.

Then

$$\text{w-Ls}\, S^1_{\phi_n} \subset S^1_{\overline{\text{con}}\, \text{w-Ls}\, \phi_n}.$$

Moreover, assume that w-Ls $\phi_n(\cdot)$ *is closed and convex valued.*

Then,

$$\text{w-Ls}\, S^1_{\phi_n} \subset S^1_{\text{w-Ls}\, \phi_n}.$$

Proof. Let $x \in \text{w-Ls}\, S^1_{\phi_n}$, i.e., there exists $x_k \in S^1_{\phi_{n_k}}$ $(k = 1, 2, \ldots)$ such that x_k converges weakly to x. We wish to know that $x \in S^1_{\overline{\text{con}}\, \text{w-Ls}\, \phi_n}$. Since x_k converges weakly to x and x_k lies in a weakly compact set, it follows from Proposition 4.2 that $x(t) \in \overline{\text{con}}\, \text{w-Ls}\{x_k(t)\}$ μ-a.e. and therefore $x(t) \in \overline{\text{con}}\, \text{w-Ls}\, \phi_n(t)$ μ-a.e. Since by assumption for each n, $\phi_n(\cdot)$ lies in the integrably bounded, convex set $F(\cdot)$, we can conclude that $x \in S^1_{\overline{\text{con}}\, \text{w-Ls}\, \phi_n}$. This completes the proof of the fact that:

$$\text{w-Ls}\, S^1_{\phi_n} \subset S^1_{\overline{\text{con}}\, \text{w-Ls}\, \phi_n}. \tag{5.1}$$

Since w-Ls $\phi_n(\cdot)$ is closed and convex (hence weakly closed), we have that $\text{w-Ls}\, \phi_n(\cdot) = \overline{\text{con}}\, \text{w-Ls}\, \phi_n(\cdot)$ and therefore,

$$S^1_{\text{w-Ls}\, \phi_n} = S^1_{\overline{\text{con}}\, \text{w-Ls}\, \phi_n}. \tag{5.2}$$

Combining now (5.1) and (5.2) we can conclude that $\text{w-Ls}\, S^1_{\phi_n} \subset S^1_{\text{w-Ls}\, \phi_n}$. This completes the proof of the theorem.

Combining Theorems 5.1 and 5.2 we can obtain the following dominated convergence result for the set of integrable selections from a correspondence.

Corollary 5.1. *Let (T, τ, μ) be a complete finite measure space and X be a separable Banach space. Let $\phi_n : T \to 2^X$ $(n = 1, 2, \ldots)$ be a sequence of closed valued and lower measurable correspondences such that:*

(i) For each n $(n = 1, 2, \ldots)$, $\phi_n(t) \subset F(t)$ μ-a.e., where $F : T \to 2^X$ is an integrably bounded, weakly compact, convex, nonempty valued correspondence,

(ii) $\phi_n(t) \xrightarrow{\text{K-M}} \phi(t)$ μ-a.e., and

(iii) $\phi(\cdot)$ is convex valued.

Then

$$S^1_{\phi_n} \xrightarrow{\text{K-M}} S^1_\phi.$$

Proof. First note that since for each n $(n = 1, 2, \ldots)$, $\phi_n(\cdot)$ is closed valued and lower measurable, $G_{\phi_n} \in \tau \otimes \beta(X)$, i.e., $\phi_n(\cdot)$ has a measurable graph and so does s-Li $\phi_n(\cdot)$. Now if $\phi(t) = \text{s-Li}\,\phi_n(t) = \text{w-Ls}\,\phi_n(t)$ μ-a.e., it follows from Theorems 5.1 and 5.2 that:

$$S^1_\phi = S^1_{\text{s-Li}\,\phi_n} \subset \text{s-Li}\, S^1_{\phi_n} \subset \text{w-Ls}\, S^1_{\phi_n} \subset S^1_{\text{w-Ls}\,\phi_n} = S^1_\phi.$$

Therefore

$$S^1_\phi = \text{s-Li}\, S^1_{\phi_n} = \text{w-Ls}\, S^1_{\phi_n},$$

and we can conclude that $S^1_{\phi_n} \xrightarrow{\text{K-M}} S^1_\phi$. This completes the proof of the Corollary.

The lemma below will be used to prove Theorem 5.3.

Lemma 5.1. *Let (T, τ, μ) be a complete finite measure space, X be a separable Banach space and $F : T \to 2^X$ be a nonempty closed valued and lower measurable correspondence. Let $\{f_i : i = 1, 2, \ldots\}$ be a sequence in S^p_F, $(1 \le p < \infty)$ such that $F(t) = \text{cl}\{f_i(t) : i = 1, 2, \ldots\}$ μ-a.e. Then, for each $f \in S^p_F$ and $\delta > 0$, there exists a finite measurable partition $\{A_1, A_2, \ldots, A_m\}$ of (T, τ) such that*

$$\left\| f - \sum_{i=1}^m \chi_{A_i} f_i \right\|_p < \delta.$$

Proof. Consider a strictly positive $v \in L_1(\mu, \mathbf{R})$ such that $\int_{t\in T} v(t)d\mu(t) < \frac{\delta^p}{3}$. We can find a countable measurable partition $\{B_i\}$ of (T, τ) such that

$$\|f(t) - f_i(t)\|_p < v(t), \qquad \text{for almost all } t \in B_i,\ i \geq 1.$$

Pick an integer m so that

$$\sum_{i=m+1}^{\infty} \int_{B_i} \|f(t)\|_p d\mu(t) < \frac{(\delta/2)^2}{3},$$
$$\sum_{i=m+1}^{\infty} \int_{B_i} \|f_1(t)\|_p d\mu(t) < \frac{(\delta/2)^2}{3},$$

and define a measurable partition $\{A_1, \ldots, A_m\}$ as follows:

$$A_1 = B_1 \cup \left(\bigcup_{i=m+1}^{\infty} B_i \right), \qquad A_j = B_j \text{ for } j = 2, \ldots, m.$$

Then it can be easily seen that:

$$\left\| f - \sum_{i=1}^{m} \chi_{A_i} f_i \right\|_p = \sum_{i=1}^{m} \int_{B_i} \|f(t) - f_i(t)\|_p d\mu(t)$$
$$+ \sum_{i=m+1}^{\infty} \int_{B_i} \|f(t) - f_1(t)\|_p d\mu(t)$$
$$= \int_T v(t)d\mu(t) + \sum_{i=m+1}^{\infty} 2^p \int_{B_i} (\|f(t)\|_p$$
$$+ \|f_1(t)\|_p) d\mu(t) < \delta.$$

Theorem 5.3. *Let (T, τ, μ) be a complete finite measure space, X be a separable Banach space and $F : T \to 2^X$ be a closed, nonempty valued and lower measurable correspondence. Suppose that S_F^p, $(1 \leq p < \infty)$ is nonempty. Then*

$$S^p_{\overline{\text{con}}F} = \overline{\text{con}} S^p_F.$$

Proof. Define the correspondence $\tilde{F} : T \to 2^X$ by $\tilde{F}(t) = \overline{\text{con}}F(t)$. It can be easily checked that $\tilde{F}(\cdot)$ is lower measurable and obviously closed and convex valued. Moreover, $S^p_{\tilde{F}}$ is closed and convex. Clearly, $\overline{\text{con}} S^p_F \subset S^p_{\overline{\text{con}}F}$ since $S^p_F \subset S^p_{\overline{\text{con}}F}$. To prove that $S^p_{\overline{\text{con}}F} \subset \overline{\text{con}} S^p_F$, consider the sequence $\{f_i : i = 1,2,\ldots\}$ in S_F^p where $\mathrm{cl}\{f_i(t) : i = 1,2,\ldots\} = F(t)$ μ-a.e. Define the set

$$U = \left\{ g : \sum_{i=1}^{n} \lambda_i f_i,\ \lambda_i \geq 0, \text{ rational}, \sum_{i=1}^{n} \lambda_i = 1,\ n \geq 1 \right\}.$$

Observe that U is a countable subset of $S^p_{\overline{\mathrm{con}}F}$ and $\overline{\mathrm{con}}F(t) = \mathrm{cl}\{g(t) : g \in U\}$ μ-a.e. It follows from Lemma 5.1 that for each $f \in S^p_{\overline{\mathrm{con}}F}$ and for each $\delta > 0$ we can find a finite measurable partition $\{A_1, A_2, \ldots, A_m\}$ of (T,τ) and functions $g_1, g_2, \ldots, g_m$ in U such that:

$$\left\| f - \sum_{k=1}^{m} \chi_{A_k} g_k \right\|_p < \lambda.$$

We can now find an integer n so that, for

$$1 \leq k \leq m,\ g_k = \sum_{i=1}^{n} \lambda_{ki} f_i \text{ where } \lambda_{ki} \geq 0,\ \sum_{i=1}^{n} \lambda_{ki} = 1.$$

Observe that:

$$\begin{aligned} \sum_{k=1}^{m} \chi_{A_k} g_k &= \sum_{k=1}^{m} \chi_{A_k} \left(\sum_{i=1}^{n} \lambda_{ki} f_i \right) \\ &= \sum_{(i_1,\ldots,i_m)} (\lambda_{1i_1}, \ldots, \lambda_{mi_m}) \left(\sum_{k=1}^{m} \chi_{A_k} f_{i_k} \right), \end{aligned}$$

where $(i_1, \ldots, i_m)$ is taken for $1 \leq i_k \leq n$, $k = 1,2,\ldots,m$. Therefore, $\sum_{k=1}^{m} \chi_{A_k} g_k$ is a convex combination of functions in S_F^p and we can conclude that $f \in \overline{\mathrm{con}} S_F^p$. This completes the proof of Theorem 5.3.

Below we consider correspondences of two variables and assume that they are measurable in the one variable and u.s.c. or l.s.c. in the other. We then ask the question as to whether the set of all integrable selections of the correspondence is either u.s.c. or l.s.c.

Theorem 5.4. *Let (T,τ,μ) be a complete, finite measure space, P be a metric space and X be a separable Banach space. Let $\psi : T \times P \to 2^X$ be a nonempty valued, integrably bounded correspondence, such that for* *each fixed $t \in T$, $\psi(t,\cdot)$ is q.u.s.c. and for each fixed $p \in P$, $\psi(\cdot,p)$ has a measurable graph. Then*

$$S^1_\psi(\cdot) \text{ is q.u.s.c.}$$

Proof. Let $\tilde{B}$ be the open unit ball in $L_1(p,X)$ and ν be a small positive number. We must show that if $\{p_n : n = 1,2,\dots\}$ is a sequence in p converging to $p \in P$, then for a suitable n_0, $S^1_\psi(p_n) \subset S^1_\psi(p) + \nu\tilde{B}$ for all $n \geq n_0$.

We begin by finding the suitable n_0. Since for each fixed $t \in T$, $\psi(t,\cdot)$ is q.u.s.c. we can find a minimal M_t such that

$$\psi(t,p_n) \subset \psi(t,p) + \delta B \text{ for all } n \geq M_t, \tag{5.3}$$

where $\delta = \frac{\nu}{3\mu(T)}$ (and B is the open unit ball in X).

We now show that M_t is a measurable function of t. However, first we make a few observations. By assumption for each fixed p and n, $G_{\psi(\cdot,p_n)+\delta B} \in \tau\otimes\beta(X)$ and so does $(G_{\psi(\cdot,p_n)+\delta B})^c$, (where S^c denotes the complement of the set S). It is easy to see that $G_{\psi(\cdot,p)} \cap (G_{\psi(\cdot,p_n)+\delta B})^c \in \tau \otimes \beta(X)$. Therefore, the set

$$U = \{(t,x) \in T \times X : (t,x) \in G_{\psi(\cdot,p)} \cap (G_{\psi(\cdot,p_n)+\delta B})^c\}$$

belongs to $\tau \otimes \beta(X)$.

It follows from the projection theorem [see for instance Yannelis (1990a)] that

$$\text{proj}_T(U) \in \tau.$$

Notice that,

$$\begin{aligned}\text{proj}_T(U) &= \{t \in T : \psi(t,p) \not\subset \psi(t,p_n) + \delta B\}\\ &= \{t \in T : \psi(t,p)/(\psi(t,p_n) + \delta B) \neq \emptyset\}.\end{aligned}$$

By virtue of the measurability of the above set we can now conclude that M_t is a measurable function of t. In particular, simply notice that,

$$\begin{aligned}\{t \in T : M_t = m\} = &\bigcap_{n\geq m} \{t \in T : \psi(t,p_n) \subset \psi(t,p) + \delta B\}\\ &\cap \{t \in T : \psi(t,p_{m-1}) \not\subset \psi(t,p) + \delta B\}.\end{aligned}$$

We are now in a position to choose the desired n_0. Since $\psi(\cdot,\cdot)$ is integrably bounded there exists $h \in L_1(\mu, \mathbb{R})$ such that for almost all $t \in T$, $\sup\{\|x\| : x \in \psi(t,p\} \leq h(t)$ for each $p \in P$.

Choose δ_1 such that if $\mu(S) < \delta_1$, $(S \subset T)$, then $\int_S h(t)d\mu(t) < \frac{\nu}{3}$. Since M_t is a measurable function of t, we can choose n_0 such that $\mu(\{t \in T : M_t \geq n_0\}) < \delta_1$. This is the desired n_0. Let $n \geq n_0$ and $y \in S^1_\psi(p_n)$. We must show that $y \in S^1_\psi(p) + \nu\tilde{B}$.

By assumption, for each fixed $p \in P$, $\psi(\cdot,p)$ has a measurable graph and $\psi(\cdot,\cdot)$ is nonempty valued. Hence, by the Aumann measurable selection theorem there exists a measurable function $f_1 : T \to X$ such that $f_1(t) \in \psi(t,p)$ μ-a.e. Define the correspondence $\phi : T \to 2^X$ by $\theta(t) = (\{y(t)\} + \delta B) \cap \psi(t,p)$. It follows from (5.3) that for all $t \in T_0 = \{t : M_t \leq n_0\}$, $\theta(t) \neq \emptyset$. Moreover, $\theta(\cdot)$ has a measurable graph. Another application of the Aumann measurable selection theorem allows us to guarantee the existence of a measurable function $f_2 : T \to X$ such that $f_2(t) \in \theta(t)$ μ-a.e. Define $f : T \to X$ by

$$f(t) = \begin{cases} f_1(t) & \text{for } t \notin T_0 \\ f_2(t) & \text{for } t \in T_0. \end{cases}$$

Then $f(t) \in \psi(t,p)$ μ-a.e. and since $\psi(\cdot,\cdot)$ is integrably bounded we can conclude that $f \in S^1_\psi(p)$. If we show that $\|f - y\| < \nu$ then $y \in S^1_\psi(p) + \nu\tilde{B}$ and we will be done. But this is easy to see. We have

$$\begin{aligned} \|f - y\| &= \int_{T/T_0} \|f_1(t) - y(t)\| d\mu(t) + \int_{T_0} \|f_2(t) - y(t)\| d\mu(t) \\ &< 2\int_{T/T_0} h(t)d\mu(t) + \int_{T_0} \delta d\mu(t) \\ &< \frac{2\nu}{3} + \delta\mu(T) = \frac{2\nu}{3} + \frac{\nu}{3\mu(T)} \cdot \mu(T) = \nu. \end{aligned}$$

This completes the proof of the theorem.

Remark 5.1. If in addition to the assumptions of Theorem 5.4, it is assumed that $S^1_\psi(\cdot)$ is compact valued, then we can conclude that $S^1_\psi(\cdot)$ is u.s.c. Moreover, by adding in Theorem 5.3 the assumption that $\psi(\cdot,\cdot)$ is convex valued and that for all $(t,p) \in T \times P$, $\psi(t,p) \subset K$ where K is a weakly compact, convex, nonempty subset of X, then it follows from Theorem 3.1 that $S^1_\psi(\cdot)$ is weakly compact valued and we can conclude that $S^1_\psi(\cdot)$ is weakly u.s.c., i.e., the set $\{p \in P : S^1_\psi \subset V\}$ is open in P for every weakly open subset V of X.

Theorem 5.5. *Let (T, τ, μ) be a complete, finite separable measure space, P be a metric space and X be a separable Banach space. Let $\psi : T \times P \to 2^X$ be a nonempty, closed, convex valued correspondence such that:*

(i) for each fixed $t \in T$, $\psi(t, \cdot)$ is weakly u.s.c.

(ii) for all $(t,p) \in T \times P$, $\psi(t,p) \subset K(t)$ where $K : T \to 2^X$ is an integrably bounded, weakly compact and nonempty valued correspondence.

Then

$$S^1_\psi(\cdot) \quad \textit{is weakly u.s.c.}$$

Proof. First note that by Theorem 3.1 S^1_K is weakly compact in $L_1(\mu, X)$. Since for each $p \in P$, $S^1_\psi(p)$ is a weakly closed subset of S^1_K, it is weakly compact. Since the measure space (T, τ, μ) is separable and X is a separable Banach space, $L_1(\mu, X)$ is separable. Hence, S^1_K is metrizable as it is a weakly compact subset of $L_1(\mu, X)$ [Dunford-Schwartz (1958, Theorem V.6.3, p. 434)]. Consequently, in order to show that $S^1_\psi(\cdot)$ is weakly u.s.c., it suffices that to show that $S^1_\psi(\cdot)$ has a weakly closed graph, i.e., if $\{p_n : n = 1, 2, \dots\}$ is a sequence in P converging to $p \in P$, then

$$\text{w-Ls}\, S^1_\psi(p_n) \subset S^1_\psi(p).x$$

To this end let $x \in \text{w-Ls}\, S^1_\psi(p_n)$, i.e., there exists x_k $(k = 1, 2, \dots)$ in $L_1(\mu, X)$ such that x_k converges weakly to $x \in L_1(\mu, X)$ and $x_k(t) \in \psi(t, p_{n_k})$ μ-a.e. We must show that $x \in S^1_\psi(p)$. It follows Theorem 4.1 that $x(t) \in \overline{\text{con}}\, \text{w-Ls}\{x_k(t)\}$ μ-a.e. and therefore,

$$x(t) \in \overline{\text{con}}\, \text{w-Ls}\, \psi(t, p_n)\ \mu\text{-a.e.} \tag{5.4}$$

Since for each fixed $t \in T$, $\psi(t, \cdot)$ has a weakly closed graph we have that:

$$\text{w-Ls}\, \psi(t, p_n) \subset \psi(t, p)\ \mu\text{-a.e.} \tag{5.5}$$

Combining (5.2) and (5.3) and taking into account the fact that ψ is convex valued we have that $x(t) \in \psi(t,p)$ μ-a.e. Since ψ is integrably bounded, we can conclude that $x \in S^1_\psi(p)$. This completes the proof of Theorem 5.5.

Alternatively, Theorem 5.5 can be proved by means of the Mazur lemma. As noted above, it suffices to show that $S^1_\psi(\cdot)$ has a weakly closed graph. To this end let $(p_n, y_n) \in G_{S^1_\psi}$ be a sequence such that p_n converges (in the metric topology) to p and y_n converges weakly to y. We must show that $y \in S^1_\psi(p)$. Since $y_n \in S^1_\psi(p_n)$, we have that $y_n(t) \in \psi(t, p_n)$ μ-a.e. By Mazur's lemma there exists $z_n(\cdot) \in \operatorname{con} \bigcup_{n_0 \geq n} y_{n_0}(\cdot)$ such that $z_n(\cdot)$ converges in norm to $y(\cdot)$. Without loss of generality we may assume (otherwise pass to a subsequence) that $z_n(t)$ converges in norm to $y(t)$ for all $t \in T/S$, where S is a set of measure zero. Fix $t \in T/S$. Since by assumption $\psi(t, \cdot)$ is weakly u.s.c. for every small positive number δ, there exists n such that for all $n_0 \geq n$, $\psi(t, p_{n_0}) \subset \psi(t,p) + \delta B$, where B is the open unit ball in X. But then $\operatorname{con} \bigcup_{n_0 \geq n} \psi(t, p_{n_0}) \subset \psi(t,p) + \delta B$ which implies that $z(t) \in \psi(t,p) + \delta B$ and consequently, $y(t) \in \psi(t,p) + \delta B$. Hence, $y(t) \in \psi(t,p)$ by letting δ converge to zero. Since t was arbitrary, $y(t) \in \psi(t,p)$ μ-a.e. Finally, since ψ is integrably bounded, we can conclude that $y \in S^1_\psi(p)$. This completes the proof.

Theorem 5.6. *Let (T, τ, μ) be a complete, finite measure space, X be a separable Banach space and P be a metric space. Let $\phi : T \times P \to 2^X$ be an integrably bounded correspondence such that for each fixed $t \in T$, $\phi(t, \cdot)$ is l.s.c. and for each fixed $p \in P$, $\phi(\cdot, p)$ has a measurable graph. Then*

$$S^1_\phi(\cdot) \quad \textit{is l.s.c.}$$

Proof. Let $\{p_n : n = 1, 2, \ldots\}$ be a sequence in P converging to $p \in P$. We must show that $S^1_\phi(p) \subset \operatorname{Li} S^1_\phi(p_n)$. Since by assumption for each fixed $t \in T$, $\phi(t, \cdot)$ is l.s.c. we have that $\phi(t,p) \subset \operatorname{Li} \phi(t, p_n)$ for all $t \in T$, and therefore

$$S^1_\phi(p) \subset S^1_{\operatorname{Li}\phi}(p_n). \tag{5.6}$$

It follows now from Theorem 5.1 that (5.6) can be written as:

$$S^1_\phi(p) \subset S^1_{\operatorname{Li}\phi}(p_n) \subset \operatorname{Li} S^1_\phi(p_n).$$

Hence,

$$S^1_\phi(\cdot) \quad \text{is l.s.c.}$$

The Corollary below follows directly from Theorems 5.4 and 5.6 and Remark 5.1.

Corollary 5.6. *Let (T, τ, μ) be a complete, finite measure space, P be a metric space and X be a separable Banach space. Let $\psi : T \times P \to 2^X$ be an integrably bounded, nonempty valued correspondence such that for each fixed $p \in P$, $\psi(\cdot, p)$ has a measurable graph and for each fixed $t \in T$, $\psi(t, \cdot)$ in continuous. Moreover, suppose that $S^1_\psi(\cdot)$ is compact valued. Then*

$$S^1_\psi(\cdot) \quad \textit{is continuous.}$$

Bibliographical Notes. Theorems 5.1, 5.2 and Corollary 5.1 are taken from Yannelis (1989). Theorem 5.3 and its proof is due to Hiai-Umegaki (1977). Theorems 5.4 and 5.6 are variations of some results given in Yannelis (1990). The proof of Theorem 5.5 is taken from Yannelis (1990). The alternative proof of Theorem 5.5 is due to Khan-Papageorgiou (1988).

6. Properties of the Integral of a Correspondence

In this section we present an infinite-dimensional generalization of the work of Aumann (1965).

Theorem 6.1. *Let (T, τ, μ) be a finite measure space and X be a separable Banach space. Let $\phi : T \to 2^X$ be a correspondence satisfying the following condition:*

(i) $\phi(t) \subset K(t)$ μ-a.e., where $K : T \to 2^X$ is an integrably bounded, weakly compact, convex, nonempty valued correspondence.

Then $\int \overline{\text{con}}\phi$ is weakly compact.

Proof. Note that since $\overline{\text{con}}\phi(\cdot)$ is (norm) closed and convex so is $S^1_{\overline{\text{con}}\phi}$. It is a consequence of the Separation Theorem that the weak and norm topologies coincide on closed convex sets. Thus, $S^1_{\overline{\text{con}}\phi}$ is weakly closed. Since $S^1_{\overline{\text{con}}\phi}$ is a subset of the set S^1_K and the latter set is weakly compact in $L_1(\mu, X)$ (recall Theorem 3.1), we can conclude that $S^1_{\overline{\text{con}}\phi}$ is weakly compact. Define the mapping $\psi : L_1(\mu, X) \to X$ by $\psi(x) = \int_{t \in T} x(t) d\mu(t)$. Certainly ψ is linear and norm continuous. By Theorem 15 in Dunford-Schwartz (1958, p. 422), ψ is also weakly continuous. Hence, $\psi(S^1_{\overline{\text{con}}\phi}) = \{(\psi(x) : x \in S^1_{\overline{\text{con}}\phi}\} = \int \overline{\text{con}}\phi$ is weakly compact. This completes the proof of the Theorem.

Theorem 6.2. *Let (T, τ, μ) be a finite atomless measure space, X be a Banach space and $\phi : T \to 2^X$ be a correspondence. Then* $\mathrm{cl} \int \phi$ *is convex.*

Proof. Let x, y be elements of the set $\mathrm{cl} \int \phi$, we must show that for any $\delta > 0$ and $\lambda \in (0, 1)$ there exists $z \in \mathrm{cl} \int \phi$ such that $\|z - (\lambda x + (1 - \lambda)y\| < \delta$. Fix $\delta > 0$ and choose x_δ, y_δ in $\int \phi$, such that $\|x - x_\delta\| < \frac{\delta}{2}$ and $\|y - y_\delta\| < \frac{\delta}{2}$. By the definition of the integral of the set-valued function ϕ, we have that there exist h, g in S^1_ϕ such that

$$\left(\int h, \int g \right) = (x_\delta, y_\delta).$$

Define the vector measure $V : \tau \to X \times X$ by

$$V(S) = \left(\int_S h, \int_S g \right).$$

Since the measure space (T, τ, μ) is atomless it follows from Uhl's theorem [see for instance Uhl (1969) or Diestel-Uhl (1977, p. 266)][3] that the norm closure of V is convex. Hence, we can find $\Omega \in \tau$ such that

$$\|V(\Omega) - \lambda V(T)\| < \frac{\delta}{2}.$$

Define the function $z : T \to X$ by

$$z(t) = \begin{cases} h(t) & \text{if } t \in \Omega \\ g(t) & \text{if } t \notin \Omega. \end{cases}$$

Then $z = \int z(t) d\mu(t) \in \int \phi$ and it can be easily checked that

$$\begin{aligned} \|z - (\lambda x + (1 - \lambda)y)\| &\leq \|z - (\lambda x_\delta + (1 - \lambda)y_\delta)\| + \lambda \|x_\delta - x\| \\ &\quad + (1 - \lambda)\|y_\delta - y\| \\ &< \delta. \end{aligned}$$

This completes the proof of Theorem 6.2.

---

[3] Note that the assumption X has the RNP is not needed for proving that the norm closure of the vector measure V is convex.

Define the mapping $\pi : T \to X$ by $\pi(x) = \int_{t\in T} x(t)d\mu(t)$. Note that the integral of the correspondence $\phi : T \to 2^X$ is $\pi(S_\phi^1) = \{\pi(x) : x \in S_\phi^1\}$. With this observation in mind the reader can easily see that the result below is an immediate conclusion of Theorems 5.3, 6.1 and 6.2.

Theorem 6.3. *Let (T, τ, μ) be a finite, atomless measure space and X be a separable Banach space. Suppose that the correspondence $\phi : T \to 2^X$ satisfies assumption (i) of Theorem 6.1. Then*

$$\overline{\text{con}} \int \phi = \int \overline{\text{con}} \phi = \text{cl} \int \phi.$$

The results below are w-Ls and s-Li versions of the Fatou lemma and follow directly from Theorems 5.1 and 5.2 respectively.

Theorem 6.4. *Let (T, τ, μ) be a complete, finite measure space and X be a separable Banach space. If $\phi_n : T \to 2^X$ $(n = 1, 2, \dots)$ is a sequence of integrably bounded correspondences having a measurable graph, i.e., $G_{\phi_n} \in \tau \otimes \beta(X)$, then*

$$\int \text{s-Li}\, \phi_n \subset \text{s-Li} \int \phi_n.$$

Theorem 6.5. *Let (T, τ, μ) be a finite measure space, and X be a separable Banach space. Let $\phi_n : T \to 2^X$ $(n = 1, 2, \dots)$ be a sequence of nonempty, closed valued correspondences such that*

(i) For all n $(n = 1, 2, \dots)$, $\phi_n(t) \subset K(t)$ μ-a.e., where $K : T \to 2^X$ is an integrably bounded, weakly compact, convex, nonempty-valued correspondence.

Then

$$\text{w-Ls} \int \phi_n \subset \text{cl} \int \text{w-Ls}\, \phi_n.$$

Furthermore, if w-Ls $\phi_n(\cdot)$ *is closed and convex valued then*

$$\text{w-Ls} \int \phi_n \subset \int \text{w-Ls}\, \phi_n.$$

As a corollary of Theorems 6.4 and 6.5 (or alternatively from Corollary 5.1), we obtain a Lebesgue-Aumann-type dominated convergence result for the integral of a correspondence.

Corollary 6.1. *Let $\phi_n : T \to 2^X$ $(n = 1, 2, \ldots)$ be a sequence of correspondences satisfying all the assumptions of Theorems 6.4 and 6.5. Suppose that*

(i) $\phi_n(t) \xrightarrow{\text{K-M}} \phi(t)$ μ-a.e.

Then,

$$\int \phi_n \xrightarrow{\text{K-M}} \mathrm{cl} \int \phi.$$

Moreover, if $\phi(\cdot)$ is convex valued, then

$$\int \phi_n \xrightarrow{\text{K-M}} \int \phi.$$

It should be noted that Theorems 6.1, 6.3 and 6.5 have been established using stronger assumptions than those adopted by Aumann (1965). However, the following example below will show that Aumann's results are false in infinite-dimensional spaces. In particular, without assumption (i) of Theorems 6.1, 6.3 and 6.5, all these results above become false.

Example 6.1. Let X in Theorem 6.1 be equal to ℓ_2, i.e., the space of real sequences (a_n) for which the norm $\|a_n\| = (\sum |a_n|^2)^{1/2}$ is finite, and let $T = [0, 2\pi]$, τ the Borel sets in $[0, 2\pi]$ and μ the Lebesgue measure on (T, τ). Let $K = \{x \in \ell_2 : \|x\| \leq 4\pi\}$. Since the space $X = \ell_2$ is reflexive the weak and weak* topologies coincide and thus by the Alaoglu theorem we can conclude that K is weakly compact. Choose a complete orthogonal system $\{w_n : n = 0, 1, \ldots\}$ in $L_2(\mu)$ such that each w_n assumes only the valued ± 1, $w_0 = \chi_{[0,2\pi]}$ and $\int_{t \in [0,2\pi]} w_n(t) d\mu(t) = 0$ for $n = 1, 2, \ldots$. For each n and each $E \in \tau$ let

$$\lambda_n(E) = 2^{-n} \int_{t \in E} \left(\frac{1 + w_n(t)}{2} \right) d\mu(t).$$

Define the vector measure $V : \tau \to \ell_2$ by

$$V(E) = (\lambda_0(E), \lambda_1(E), \ldots).$$

Then $\|V(E)\| < 2\mu(E)$ for each $E \in \tau$. Therefore, the vector measure V is countably additive, V is of bounded variation and it is obviously atomless. Clearly, 0 and $V(T)$ are in $V(\tau) = \{x \in \ell_2 : x = V(E),\ E \in \tau\}$ and note that $\frac{1}{2} VT$ is the convex hull of $V(\tau)$. The argument now of

Lyapunov adopted by Diestel-Uhl (1977, p. 262) can be used here to prove that there is no $E \in \tau$ such that $V(E) = \frac{1}{2}V(T)$, i.e., *the ℓ_2-valued atomless vector measure V of bounded variation is nonconvex.*

Observe now that ℓ_2 has the RNP. Hence, there exists a function $g \in L_1(\mu, \ell_2)$ such that for each $E \in \tau$, $V(E) = \int_{t \in T} \chi_E(t) g(t) d\mu(t)$. Since the norm closure of the range of V is convex [Theorem 10, p. 266 in Diestel-Uhl (1977)] we can conclude that $\frac{1}{2}V(T)$ is in the closure. Consequently, there exists a sequence $\{E_n : n = 1, 2, \ldots\}$ in τ such that $\lim_{n \to \infty} V(E_n) = \frac{1}{2}V(T)$. For each n, define $\phi_n : T \to \ell_2$ by $\phi_n(t) = \chi_{E_n}(t) g(t)$. It can be easily checked that w-Ls$\,\phi_n$ is measurable [see for instance Yannelis (1990a, Lemma 3.12 and Remark 3.1)]. We now show that the inclusion w-Ls$\int \phi_n \subset \int$ w-Ls$\,\phi_n$ does not hold. In particular, since s-Ls$\int \phi_n \subset$ w-Ls$\int \phi_n$ we will prove a slightly stronger result, i.e., the inclusion s-Ls$\int \phi_n \subset$ w-Ls$\int \phi_n$ does not hold. Note that for each n, $\phi_n(t) \in \{0, g(t)\}$ μ-a.e. and so w-Ls$\,\phi_n \subset \{0, g(t), \{0, g(t)\}, \emptyset\}$. For any $\phi \in S^1_{\text{w-Ls}\,\phi_n}$ we have that $\phi(t) = \chi_E(t) g(t)$ μ-a.e., for $E \in \tau$. In order now for the inclusion s-Li$\int \phi_n \subset \int$ w-Ls$\,\phi_n$ to hold, we must have that $\frac{1}{2}V(T) \in \int$ w-Ls$\,\phi_n$, i.e., $\frac{1}{2}V(T) = \int_{t \in E} g(t) d\mu(t) = V(E)$. But as it was remarked above no such $E \in \tau$ exists (since the vector measure V is not convex). hence, the w-Ls version of *the Fatou Lemma fails in infinite-dimensional spaces.* Note that the above example also showed that the integral of the closed valued correspondences $F : T \to 2^{\ell_2}$ defined by $F(t) = \{0, g(t)\}$ *is not compact* (in fact it is not even closed!).[4] Finally, note that $\frac{1}{2}V(T) = \frac{1}{2}\int_{t \in T} g(t) d\mu(t) \in \text{con} \int F$ and $\frac{1}{2}V(T) \notin \int F$, i.e., the integral of the correspondence $F : T \to 2^{\ell_2}$ *is not convex.*[5]

The results below follow directly from Theorems 5.4, 5.6 and Corollary 5.3.

Theorem 6.6. *Let (T, τ, μ) be a complete, finite measure space, P be a metric space and X be a separable Banach space. Let $\psi : T \times P \to 2^X$ be a nonempty valued, integrably bounded correspondence, such that for each fixed $t \in T$, $\psi(t, \cdot)$ is q.u.s.c. and for each fixed $p \in P$, $\psi(\cdot, p)$ has a*

---

[4] Recall that Aumann (1965) demonstrated that if X is finite dimensional and $F : T \to 2^X$ is integrably bounded and closed valued, then $\int F$ is compact.

[5] Note that when X is finite dimensional the well-known result of Richter (1963) assures that $\int F$ is convex.

measurable graph. Then

$$\int \psi(t,\cdot) \quad \textit{is q.u.s.c.}$$

Theorem 6.7. *Let (T,τ,μ) be a complete, finite measure space, X be a separable Banach space and P be a metric space. Let $\phi : T \times P \to 2^X$ be an integrably bounded correspondence such that for each fixed $t \in T$, $\phi(t,\cdot)$ is l.s.c. and for each fixed $p \in P$, $\phi(\cdot\,,p)$ has a measurable graph. Then*

$$\int \phi(t,\cdot) \quad \textit{is l.s.c.}$$

Remark 6.1. If in addition to the assumptions of Theorem 6.7, it is assumed that $\int \psi(t,\cdot)$ is compact valued, then we can conclude that $\int \psi(t,\cdot)$ is u.s.c.

Corollary 6.2. *Let (T,τ,μ) be a complete, finite measure space, P be a metric space and X be a separable Banach space. Let $\psi : T \times P \to 2^X$ be a nonempty valued, integrably bounded correspondence, such that for each fixed $p \in P$, $\psi(\cdot\,,p)$ has a measurable graph and for each fixed $t \in T$, $\psi(t,\cdot)$ is continuous. Moreover, suppose that $\int_T \psi(t,\cdot)d\mu(t)$ is compact valued. Then*

$$\int_T \psi(t,\cdot)d\mu(t) \quad \textit{is continuous.}$$

Below we prove a s-Ls version of the Fatou Lemma in infinite dimensions.

Theorem 6.8. *Let (T,τ,μ) be a complete, finite measure space and X be a separable Banach space. Let $\phi_n : T \to 2^X$ $(n = 1,2,\dots)$ be a sequence of nonempty valued, graph measurable correspondences, taking values in a compact, nonempty subset of X, Then*

$$\text{s-Ls} \int_T \phi_n(t)d\mu(t) \subset \text{cl} \int_T \text{s-Ls}\, \phi_n(t)d\mu(t).$$

Moreover, if $\text{Ls}\, \phi_n(\cdot)$ *is convex valued, then*

$$\text{s-Ls} \int_T \phi_n(t)d\mu(t) \subset \int_T \text{s-Ls}\, \phi_n d\mu(t).$$

Proof. Denote by P the interval $[0,1)$. Define the correspondence $\psi : T \times P \to 2^X$ by

$$\psi(t,p) = \begin{cases} \phi_n(t) & \text{if } \frac{1}{n+1} < p < \frac{1}{n} \\ \phi_n(t) \cup \phi_{n+1}(t) & \text{if } p = \frac{1}{n+1} \\ \mathrm{Ls}\,\phi_n(t) & \text{if } p = 0. \end{cases}$$

It can be easily checked that for each fixed $t \in T$, $\psi(t,\cdot)$ is u.s.c. and that for each fixed $p \in P$, $\psi(\cdot\,,p)$ has a measurable graph. Moreover, ψ is integrably bounded. Hence, ψ satisfies all the assumptions of Theorem 6.6 and thus, $\int_T \psi(t,\cdot)d\mu(t)$ is q.u.s.c. Let now $x \in \mathrm{Ls}\int_T \phi_n(t)d\mu(t)$, i.e., there exists x_{n_k} such that $\lim_{n\to\infty} x_{n_k} = x$, $x_{n_k} \in \int_T \phi_{n_k}(t)d\mu(t)$ $(k = 1,2,\ldots)$. We wish to show that $x \in \mathrm{cl}\int \phi_n(t)d\mu(t)$.

Since $\int_T \psi(t,\cdot)d\mu(t)$ is q.u.s.c. (see Section 2 for a definition) it follows that if p_{n_k} converges to 0 then $\int_T \psi(t,p_{n_k})d\mu(t) \subset \int_T(t,0)d\mu(t)+\nu B$ for all sufficiently large k (where ν is a small positive number and B denotes the open unit ball in X). Consequently, $x_{n_k} \in \int_T \psi(t,0)d\mu(t) + \nu B$ for all sufficiently large k and therefore, $x \in \mathrm{cl}\int_T \psi(t,0)d\mu(t) \equiv \mathrm{cl}\int_T \text{s-Ls}\,\phi_n(t)d\mu(t)$ as was to be shown. If now $\mathrm{Ls}\,\phi_n$ is convex valued (recall that s-Ls $\phi_n(\cdot)$ is closed valued as well), it follows from Theorem 6.1 and the first conclusion of Theorem 6.8 that

$$\text{s-Ls}\int_T \phi_n d\mu(t) \subset \mathrm{cl}\int_T \text{s-Ls}\,\phi_n(t)d\mu(t) = \int_T \text{s-Ls}\,\phi_n(t)d\mu(t).$$

This completes the proof of the Theorem.

We close this section by obtaining the following dominated converge result:

Theorem 6.9. *Let (T,τ,μ) be a complete, finite measure space and X be a separable Banach space. Let $\phi_n : T \to 2^X$ $(n = 1,2,\ldots)$ be a sequence of integrably bounded, nonempty valued correspondence having a measurable graph, such that*

(i) For all n $(n = 1,2,\ldots)$, $\phi_n(t) \subset K$ μ-a.e., where K is a compact, nonempty subset of X, and

(ii) $\phi_n(t) \to \phi(t)$ μ-a.e.

Then

$$\int_T \phi_n(t)d\mu(t) \to \mathrm{cl}\int_T \phi(t)d\mu(t).$$

Moreover, if $\phi(\cdot)$ is convex valued then

$$\int_T \phi_n(t)d\mu(t) \to \int_T \phi(t)d\mu(t).$$

Proof. Since by assumption $\phi_n(t) \to \phi(t)$ μ-a.e., i.e., $\phi(t) = \text{s-Li}\,\phi_n(t) = \text{s-Ls}\,\phi_n(t)$ μ-a.e., it follows from Theorems 6.4 and 6.8 that:

$$\int \phi = \int \text{s-Li}\,\phi_n \subset \text{s-Li} \int \phi_n \subset \text{s-Ls} \int \phi_n \subset \text{cl} \int \text{s-Ls}\,\phi_n = \text{cl} \int \phi.$$

Therefore,

$$\text{cl} \int_T \phi(t)d\mu(t) = \text{s-Li} \int_T \phi_n(t)d\mu(t) = \text{s-Ls} \int_T \phi_n(t)d\mu(t),$$

i.e.,

$$\int_T \phi_n(t)d\mu(t) \to \text{cl} \int_T \phi(t)d\mu(t).$$

If now $\phi(\cdot)$ is convex valued, we can conclude (recall the second conclusion of Theorem 6.8) that:

$$\int \phi = \int \text{s-Li}\,\phi_n \subset \text{s-Li} \int \phi_n \subset \text{s-Ls} \int \phi_n \subset \int \text{s-Ls}\,\phi_n = \int \phi.$$

Thus,

$$\int_T \phi(t)d\mu(t) = \text{s-Li} \int_T \phi_n(t)d\mu(t) = \text{s-Ls} \int_T \phi_n(t)d\mu(t),$$

i.e.,

$$\int_T \phi_n(t)d\mu(t) \to \int_T \phi(t)d\mu(t),$$

and this completes the proof of Theorem 6.9.

Bibliographic Notes. A version of Theorem 6.1 is proved by Yannelis (1988). Theorem 6.2 is due to Datko (1973). The proof given here is taken from Khan (1985). It has been useful in general equilibrium theory [see for instance Rustichini-Yannelis (1989, 1991) and Ostroy-Zame (1988)]. It should be noted that Theorem 6.2 is the infinite dimensional version of Theorem 2 of Aumann (1965) [see also Debreu (1967)] and it was first proved by Datko (1973) for X being a reflexive separable

Banach space. The reflexivity assumption was subsequently relaxed by Khan (1985). Rustichini-Yannelis (1990) showed that if the dimensionality of the measure space is bigger than the dimensionality of the space X, then the conclusion of Theorem 6.3 can be strengthened to $\int \overline{\text{con}\phi} = \int \phi$.

The Example 6.1 is due to Lyapunov [see also Diestel-Uhl (1977, p. 262)]. The argument used to prove that several of the properties of the Aumann integral fail in an infinite dimensional setting is due to Rustichini (1989). Theorems 6.6–6.9 are due to Yannelis (1990). Related results to Theorems 6.6–6.9 were obtained by Debreu (1967).

7. The Gel'fand Integral

Let (T, τ, μ) be a finite measure space and X be a Banach space. Let $f : T \to X^*$ be a function such that $\langle f, x\rangle \in L_1(\mu)$ for all $x \in X$, then for each $A \in \tau$ the element x_A^* in X^* is called the *Gel'fand integral of f* over A, where

$$x_A^*(x) = \int_A \langle f(t), x\rangle d\mu(t) \quad \text{for all } x \in X.$$

We denote by $(S_\phi^1)^*$ the *set of all Gel'fand integrable selections from the correspondence* $\phi : T \to 2^{X^*}$, i.e.,

$$\begin{aligned}(S_\phi^1)^* &= \{x \in (L_1(\mu, X))^* : x(t) \in \phi(t)\ \mu\text{-a.e.}\}\\ &= \{x \in L_\infty(\mu, X^*) : x(t) \in \phi(t)\ \mu\text{-a.e.}\}.\end{aligned}$$

The *Gel'fand integral of the correspondence* $\phi : T \to 2^{X^*}$ is defined as follows:

$$\int \phi(t) d\mu(t) = \left\{ \int \langle f(t), x\rangle d\mu(t) : f \in (S_\phi^1)^* \text{ for all } x \in X \right\}.$$

Note that the above integral may be empty unless ϕ admits weak* measurable selections. A very useful result due to Khan (1985) which has found several applications in game theory and general equilibrium is the fact that the weak* closure of the Gel'fand integral of a correspondence is convex. This result can be proved adopting a similar argument used to prove Theorem 6.2 except that instead of using Uhl's Theorem one can now appeal to a result of Kluvalek [Kluvalek (1973, p. 46, Lemma 5)]. We state below a very useful result for the Gel'fand integral of a correspondence.

Theorem 7.1. *Let (T, τ, μ) be a complete, finite measure space, X^* be the dual of a separable Banach space and $\phi : T \to 2^{X^*}$ be a correspondence with a weak* measurable graph (i.e., $G_\phi \in \tau \otimes \beta_{w^*}(X^*)$, where $\beta_{w^*}(X^*)$ are the Borel subsets of X^* in the weak* topology of X^*) such that $\phi(t)$ is weak* closed and bounded for almost all t in T. Then for all $A \in \tau$,*

$$w^* - \mathrm{cl} \int_A \phi = \int_A w^* - \overline{\mathrm{con}}\phi.$$

Moreover, $\int_A w^* - \mathrm{con}\,\phi$ is weak compact and convex.*

Bibliographical Notes. Theorem 7.1 is due to Khan (1985) and it has found important applications in general equilibrium theory [Rustichini-Yannelis (1989, 1991), Ostroy-Zame (1988)], game theory [Cotter (1990), Khan (1986)] and demand theory [Border (1989), Kim (1990)].

8. An Application

In this section we will indicate how some of the results in Yannelis (1990a) as well as theorems of this paper can be used to prove the existence of an equilibrium for an abstract economy with a measure space of agents.

An *abstract economy* Γ is a quadruple $[(T, \tau, \mu), X, P, A]$, where

(1) (T, τ, μ) is the *measure space of agents*,

(2) $X : T \to 2^Y$ is the *strategy correspondence* (where Y is a linear topological space),

(3) $P : T \times S^1_X \to 2^Y$ is a *preferences correspondence* such that $P(t, x) \subset X(t)$ for all $(t, x) \in T \times S^1_X$, and

(4) $A : T \times S^1_X \to 2^Y$ is a *constraint correspondence* such that $A(t, x) \subset X(t)$ for all $(t, x) \in T \times S^1_X$.

The interpretation of the preference correspondence $P : T \times S^1_X \to 2^Y$ is as follows: We read $y \in P(t, x)$ as "agent t strictly prefers y to $x(t)$ if the given strategies of other agents are fixed." Throughout this section we set $Y = \mathbb{R}^n$ and endow S^1_X with the weak topology.

An *equilibrium* for Γ is an $x^* \in S^1_X$ such that for almost all t in T the following conditions hold:

(i) $x^*(t) \in A(t, x^*)$ and

(ii) $P(t,x^*) \cap A(t,x^*) = \emptyset$.

Below we state the assumptions needed for the proof of our equilibrium existence theorem.

(8.1) (T,τ,μ) is a complete finite separable measure space.

(8.2) $X : T \to 2^Y$ is a correspondence such that:

- (a) It is integrably bounded and for all $t \in T$, $X(t)$ is a closed convex nonempty subset of Y;
- (b) $X(\cdot)$ is lower measurable.

(8.3) $A : T \times S_X^1 \to 2^Y$ is a correspondence such that:

- (a) for each fixed $t \in T$, $A(t,\cdot)$ is continuous;
- (b) $A(\cdot,\cdot)$ is closed, convex and nonempty valued;
- (c) for each fixed $x \in S_X^1$, $A(\cdot,x)$ is lower measurable.

(8.4) $P : T \times S_X^1 \to 2^Y$ is a correspondence such that:

- (a) for each fixed $t \in T$, $P(t,\cdot)$ has an open graph in $S_X^1 \times Y$;
- (b) $x(t) \notin \operatorname{con} P(t,x)$ for all $x \in S_X^1$, μ-a.e.;
- (c) for every open subset V of Y, the set $\{(t,x) \in T \times S_X^1 : A(t,x) \cap \operatorname{con} P(t,x) \cap V \neq \emptyset\}$ belongs to $\tau \otimes \beta_w(S_X^1)$, where $\beta_w(S_X^1)$ denotes the Borel σ-algebra for the weak topology on S_X^1.

We are now ready to state the following result:

Theorem 8.1. *Let $\Gamma = [(T,\tau,\mu), X, P, A]$ be an abstract economy satisfying (8.1)–(8.4). Then an equilibrium in Γ exists.*

Proof. Define the set-valued function $\psi : T \times S_X^1 \to 2^Y$ by $\psi(t,x) = \operatorname{con} P(t,x)$. It can be easily checked that for each fixed $t \in T$, $\psi(t,\cdot)$ has an open graph in $S_X^1 \times Y$ [see for instance Lemma 4.1 in Yannelis (1987)]. Define the set-valued function $\phi : T \times S_X^1 \to 2^Y$ by $\phi(t,x) = \psi(t,x) \cap A(t,x)$. It follows from Lemma 4.2 in Yannelis (1987) that for each fixed $t \in T$, $\phi(t,\cdot)$ is weakly u.s.c., i.e., for every open subset V of Y, the set $\{x \in S_X^1 : \phi(t,x) \cap V \neq \emptyset\}$ is weakly open in S_X^1. By assumption (8.4)(c), $\phi(\cdot,\cdot)$ is lower measurable. Let $U = \{(t,x) \in T \times S_X^1 : \phi(t,x) \neq \emptyset\}$. By Theorem 4.2 in Yannelis (1990a) we can guarantee the existence of a Carathéodory-type selection, i.e., there exists a function $f : U \to Y$ such that $f(t,x) \in \phi(t,x)$ for all $(t,x) \in U$ and for each $t \in T$, $f(t,\cdot)$ is continuous on $U_t = \{x \in S_X^1 : \phi(t,x) \neq \emptyset\}$ and for each $x \in S_X^1$, $f(\cdot,x)$ is measurable on $U_x = \{t \in T : \phi(t,x) \neq \emptyset\}$. Moreover, $f(\cdot,\cdot)$ is jointly measurable. Define the set-valued function $F : T \times S^1_X \to 2^Y$ by

$$F(t,x) = \begin{cases} \{f(t,x)\} & \text{if } (t,x) \in U \\ A(t,x) & \text{if } (t,x) \notin U. \end{cases}$$

It follows at once from the l.s.c. of $\phi(t,\cdot)$ that for each $t \in T$ the set $U_t = \{x \in S^1_X : \phi(t,x) \neq \emptyset\}$ is weakly open in S^1_X. Thus, by Lemma 6.1 in Yannelis-Prabhakar (1983) for each fixed $t \in T$, $F(t,\cdot)$ is weakly u.s.c. in the sense that the set $\{x \in S^1_X : F(t,x) \subset V\}$ is weakly open in S^1_X for every open subset V of Y. As in Yannelis (1987) one can easily check that for each $x \in S^1_X$, $F(\cdot,x)$ has a measurable graph. Also, $F(\cdot,\cdot)$ is closed, convex and nonempty valued. Define the set-valued function $\theta : S^1_X \to 2^{S^1_X}$ by

$$\theta(x) = \{y \in S^1_X : y(t) \in F(t,x) \ \mu\text{-a.e.}\}.$$

Note that by Theorem 3.1, S^1_X is weakly compact in $L_1(\mu,Y)$. Since the measure space (T,τ,μ) is separable, $L_1(\mu,Y)$ is a separable Banach space. Since, weakly compact subsets of a separable Banach space are metrizable, we can conclude that S^1_X is metrizable. Hence, it follows from Theorem 5.5 that $\theta(\cdot)$ is weakly u.s.c., i.e., for every weakly open subset V of S^1_X the set $\{x \in S^1_X : \theta(x) \subset V\}$ is weakly open in S^1_X. Appealing to the Aumann measurable selection theorem, we can conclude that $\theta(\cdot)$ is nonempty valued. Similarly, the set S^1_X is nonempty. Obviously $\theta(\cdot)$ is convex valued and so is the set S^1_X. It follows from the Fan-Glicksberg fixed point theorem that there exists $x^* \in S^1_X$ such that $x^* \in F(x^*)$. It can be easily now checked that the fixed point is by construction an equilibrium for the abstract economy Γ.

Bibliographical Notes. This section is based on Yannelis (1987) where we refer the reader for related results. A version of Theorem 8.1 was first proved by Khan-Vohra (1984). It should be noted that the notion of an equilibrium for an abstract economy is due to Debreu (1952) which in turn generalizes the notion of a noncooperative equilibrium for a game in normal form introduced by Nash (1951). For more applications of Carathéodory-type selections theorems as well as recent results on integration of set-valued function we recommend, the papers of Kim-Prikry-Yannelis (1989), Yannelis-Rustichini (1990, 1991), Balder-Yannelis (1990), and Yannelis (1990b). Finally a paper by Debreu (1967a) uses measure theory and measurable selections extensively.

References

Aliprantis, C. D. and Burkinshaw, O., 1985, *Positive Operators*, Academic Press, New York.

Artstein, Z., 1979, "A Note on Fatou's Lemma in Several Dimensions," *J. Math. Econ.* **6**, 277–282.

Aumann, R. J., 1965, "Integrals of Set-Valued Functions," *J. Math. Anal. Appl.* **12**, 1–12.

Aumann, R. J., 1966, "Existence of a Competitive Equilibrium in Markets with a Continuum of Traders," *Econometrica* **34**, 1–17.

Aumann, R. J., 1967, "Measurable Utility and the Measurable Choice Theorem," *La Decision*, CNRS, Aix-en-Provence, 15–26.

Aumann, R. J., 1976, "An Elementary Proof that Integration Preserves Uppersemicontinuity," *J. Math. Econ.* **3**, 15–18.

Balder, E. J., 1984, "A Unifying Note on Fatou's Lemma in Several Dimensions," *Math. Oper. Res.* **29**, 267–275.

Balder, E. J., 1987, "More on Fatou's Lemma in Several Dimensions," *Canadian Math. Bull.* **30**, 334–339.

Balder, E. J., 1988, "Fatou's Lemma in Infinite Dimensions," *J. Math. Anal. Appl.* **136**, 450–465.

Balder, E. J., 1990, "New Sequential Compactness Results for Spaces of Scalarly Integrable Functions," *J. Math. Anal. Appl.* **151**, 1–16.

Balder, E. J. and Yannelis, N. C., 1990, "Equilibria in Random and Bayesian Games with a Continuum of Players," this volume.

Border, K., 1989, "Stochastic Dominance and Choice of Lotteries," mimeo.

Byrne, C. L., 1978, "Remarks on the Set-Valued Integrals of Debreu and Aumann," *J. Math. Anal. Appl.* **62**, 243–246.

Castaing, C., 1988, "Quelques Resultats de Convergence des Suites Apaptees," *Seminaire D'Analyse Convexe*, Montpellier, Vol. 17, Exposés 1 á 12.

Castaing, C. and Valadier, M., 1977, "Convex Analysis and Measurable Multifunctions," *Lect. Notes Math.* **580**, Springer-Verlag, New York.

Cotter, K., 1990, "Correlated Equilibria with Exogenous Uncertainty," mimeo.

Datko, R., 1973, "On the Integration of Set-Valued Mappings in a Banach Space," *Fund. Math.* **78**, 205–208.

Debreu, G., 1952, "A Social Equilibrium Existence Theorem," *Proc. Natl. Acad. Sci. USA* **38**, 886–893.

Debreu, G., 1967, "Integration of Correspondences," *Proc. Fifth Berkeley Symp. Math. Stat. Prob.*, University of California Press, Berkeley, Vol. II, Part I, 351–372.

Debreu, G., 1967a, "Preference Functions on Measure Spaces of Economic Agents," *Econometrica* **35**, 111–122.

Debreu, D. and Schmeidler, D., 1972, "The Radon-Nikodým Derivative of a Correspondence," *Proc. Sixth Berkeley Symp. Math. Stat. Prob.*, Vol. II,

L. Lecam, J. Neyman and E. Scott, eds., University of California Press, 41–56.

Diestel, J., 1977, "Remarks on Weak Compactness in $L_1(\mu, X)$," *Glasgow Math. J.* **18**, 87–91.

Diestel, J. and Uhl, J., 1977, *Vector Measures*, Mathematical Surveys **15**, American Mathematical Society, Providence, Rhode Island.

Dinculeanu, N., 1973, "Linear Operations on L_p-Spaces," in H. Maynard and D. Tucker, eds., *Vector and Operator Valued Measures and Applications*, Academic Press, New York.

Dunford, N. and Schwartz, J. T., 1958, *Linear Operators*, Part I, Interscience, New York.

Hiai, F. and Umegaki, H., 1977, "Integrals Conditional Expectations and Martingales of Multivalued Function," *J. Multivar. Anal.* **7**, 149–182.

Himmelberg, C. J., 1975, "Measurable Relations," *Fund. Math.* **87**, 53–72.

James, R., 1964, "Weakly Compact Sets," *Trans. Amer. Math. Soc.* **113**, 129–140.

Kelley, J. and Namioka, I., *Linear Topological Spaces,* Springer-Verlag, New York.

Khan, M. Ali, 1982, "On the Integration of Set-Valued Mappings in a Reflexive Banach Space," Johns Hopkins University Working Paper.

Khan, M. Ali, 1984, "An Alternative Proof of Diestel's Theorem," *Glasgow Math. J.* **25**, 45–46.

Khan, M. Ali, 1985, "On Extensions of the Cournot-Nash Theorem," in *Advances in Equilibrium Theory*, Lecture Notes in Economics and Mathematical Systems **244**, C. D. Aliprantis et al, eds., Springer-Verlag, New York.

Khan, M. Ali, 1985a, "On the Integration of Set-Valued Mappings in a Nonreflexive Banach Space II," *Simon Stevin* **59**, 257–267.

Khan, M. Ali, 1986, "Equilibrium Points of Nonatomic Games Over a Banach Space," *Trans. Amer. Math. Soc.* **29**, 737–749.

Khan, M. Ali and Majumdar, M., 1986, "Weak Sequential Convergence in $L_1(\mu, X)$ and an Approximate Version of Fatou's Lemma," *J. Math. Anal. Appl.* **114**, 569–573.

Khan, M. Ali and Papageorgiou, N. S., 1987, "On Cournot-Nash Equilibria in Generalized Quantitative Games with an Atomless Measure Space of Agents," *Proc. Amer. Math. Soc.* **100**, 505–510.

Khan, M. Ali and Vohra, R., 1984, "Equilibrium in Abstract Economies without Ordered Preferences and with a Measure Space of Agents," *J. Math. Econ.* **13**, 133–142.

Kim, T., 1990, "The Subjective Expected Utility Hypothesis and Revealed Preference," *Econ. Theory*, to appear.

Kim, T., Prikry, K. and Yannelis, N. C., 1989, "Equilibria in Abstract Economies with a Measure Space of Agents and with an Infinite Dimensional Strategy Space," *J. Approx. Theory* **56**, 256–266.

Kluvalek, I., 1973, "The Range of a Vector-Valued Measure," *Math. Syst. Theory* **7**, 44–54.

Kuratowski, K., 1966, *Topology*, Vol. I, Academic Press, New York.

Lucchetti, R., Papageorgiou, N. S. and Patrone, F., 1987, "Convergence and Approximation Results for Measurable Multifunctions," *Proc. Amer. Math. Soc.* **100**, 551–556.

Nash, J. F., 1951, "Noncooperative Games," *Ann. Math.* **54**, 286–295.

Ostroy, J. and Zame, W. R., 1988, "Non-Atomic Exchange Economies and the Boundaries of Perfect Competition," mimeo.

Papageorgiou, N. S., 1985, "Representation of Set-Valued Operators," *Trans. Amer. Math. Soc.* **292**, 557–572.

Pucci, P. and Vitillaro, G., 1984, "A Representation Theorem for Aumann Integrals," *J. Math. Anal. Appl.* **102**, 86–101.

Ricceri, B., 1982, "Sur l'Approximation des Selections Mesurables," *C. R. Acad. Sc. Paris* **295**, 527–530.

Richter, H., 1963, "Verallgemeinerung eimer in ser Startistik benötigten Satzes der Masstheorie," *Math. Annalen* **150**, 85–90.

Rustichini, A., 1989, "A Counterexample and an Exact Version of Fatou's Lemma in Infinite Dimension," *Archiv der Mathematic* **52**, 357–362.

Rustichini, A. and Yannelis, N. C., 1986, "An Elementary Proof of Fatou's Lemma in Finite Dimensional Spaces," Department of Economics, University of Minnesota, Discussion Paper No. 237.

Rustichini, A. and Yannelis, N. C., 1989, "Commodity Pair Desirability and the Core Equivalence Theorem," University of Illinois at Urbana-Champaign, mimeo.

Rustichini, A. and Yannelis, N. C., 1990, "What is Perfect Competition?" this volume.

Rustichini, A. and Yannelis, N. C., 1991, "Edgeworth's Conjecture in Economies with a Continuum of Agents and Commodities," *J. Math. Econ.*, to appear.

Schecter, E., 1989, "Closure and Other Properties of the Aumann Integral in Infinite Dimensions," mimeo.

Tulcea, A. I. and Tulcea, C. I., 1969, *Topics in the Theory of Lifting*, Springer-Verlag, New York.

Uhl, J., 1969, "The Range of a Vector-Valued Measure," *Proc. Amer. Math. Soc.* **23**, 158–163.

Yannelis, N. C., 1987, "Equilibria in Noncooperative Models of Competition," *J. Econ. Theory* **41**, 96–111.

Yannelis, N. C., 1988, "Fatou's Lemma In Infinite Dimensional *Proc. Amer. Math. Soc.* **102**, 303–310.

Yannelis, N. C., 1989, "Weak Sequential Convergence in $L_p(\mu, X)$," *J. Math. Anal. Appl.* **141**, 72–83.

Yannelis, N. C., 1990, "On the Upper and Lower Semicontinuity of the Aumann Integral," *J. Math. Econ.* **19**, 373–389.

Yannelis, N. C., 1990a, "Set-Valued Functions of Two Variables in Economic Theory," this volume.

Yannelis, N. C., 1990b, "The Core of an Economy with Differential Information," *Econ. Theory*, to appear.

Yannelis, N. C. and Prabhakar, N. D., 1983, "Existence of Maximal Elements and Equilibria in Linear Topological Spaces," *J. Math. Econ.* **12**, 233–245.

Yannelis, N. C. and Rustichini, A., 1990, "On the Existence of Correlated Equilibria," this volume.

Yannelis, N. C. and Rustichini, A., 1991, "Equilibrium Points of Noncooperative Random and Bayesian Games," *Positive Operators, Riesz Spaces, and Economics*, C. D. Aliprantis, K. C. Border and W. A. J. Luxemburg, eds., Springer-Verlag, forthcoming.

Set-Valued Functions of Two Variables in Economic Theory

Nicholas C. Yannelis

Abstract. Several properties of set-valued functions of two variables are studied. Specifically, we study the existence of (i) Carathéodory-type selections, (ii) random fixed points and (iii) random maximal elements. An application to the problem of the existence of a random price equilibrium is also given.

1. Introduction

Research in economic theory [see for example the classical treatise of Debreu (1959)] has necessitated the use of set-valued functions. The basic properties of set-valued functions which have been useful in economics are: the existence of fixed points, the existence of continuous selections and the existence of measurable selections. Before we discuss the main purpose of this paper, it may be instructive to outline a basic argument to describe the above properties.

Let X be a paracompact space, Y be a linear topological space and $\phi : X \to 2^Y$ (where 2^X denotes the set of all nonempty subsets of X) be a set-valued function such that for all $x \in X$, $\phi(x)$ is convex, nonempty and for each $y \in Y$ the set $\phi^{-1}(y) = \{x \in X : y \in \phi(x)\}$ is open in X. We will show that there exists a continuous function $f : X \to Y$ such that $f(x) \in \phi(x)$ for all $x \in X$, i.e., $\phi(\cdot)$ admits a *continuous selection.*

Since for each $y \in Y$, $\phi^{-1}(y)$ is open and $\phi(x)$ is nonempty for all $x \in X$, the collection $\mathbf{F} = \{\phi^{-1}(y) : y \in Y\}$ is an open cover of X. Since X is paracompact there is an open locally finite refinement $\mathbf{F}' = \{V_a : a \in A\}$ of $\mathbf{F}$. We can use a standard result [see for instance Dugundji (1966)] on the existence of a partition of unity subordinated to the above covering, i.e., we can find a set of continuous functions $\{g_a : a \in A\}$ such that $g_a : X \to [0,1], g_a(x) = 0$ for $x \notin V_a$ and $\sum_{a \in A} g_a(x) = 1$ for all $x \in X$. Since $\mathbf{F}'$ is a refinement of $\mathbf{F}$, for each $a \in A$ we may choose $y_a \in Y$ such that $V_a \subset \phi^{-1}(y_a)$. Define the function $f : X \to Y$ by $f(x) = \sum_{a \in A} g_a(x) y_a$. Given the fact that $\mathbf{F}'$ is locally finite and $\phi(\cdot)$ is convex valued, one can easily verify that $f : X \to Y$ in continuous and $f(x) \in \phi(x)$ for all $x \in X$, i.e., $\phi(\cdot)$ admits a continuous selection.

Note now that if X is a compact, convex, nonempty subset of a locally convex linear topological space and $\phi : X \to 2^X$ is a set-valued function such that for all $x \in X, \phi(x)$ is convex, nonempty and for each $y \in X$, $\phi^{-1}(y)$ is open in X, then $\phi(\cdot)$ has a *fixed point*, i.e., there exists an $x^* \in X$ such that $x^* \in \phi(x^*)$. The proof follows directly by combining the above result together with the Tychonoff fixed point theorem [see for instance Dugundji (1966, Theorem 2.2, p. 414)].

Finally, if (X, a) is a measurable space, Y is a complete separable metric space and $\phi : X \to 2^Y$ is a set-valued function such that for each closed subset V of Y the set $\{x \in X : \phi(x) \cap V \neq \emptyset\}$ belongs to a, and $\phi(\cdot)$ is nonempty closed valued, then there exists a measurable function $f : X \to Y$ such that $f(x) \in \phi(x)$ for all $x \in X$, i.e., $\phi(\cdot)$ admits a *measurable selection.*

To see this let $\{y_1, y_2, \ldots\}$ be a countable dense subset in Y. For each i ($i = 1, 2, \ldots$), and for each n ($n = 1, 2, \ldots$), let $B_n(i) = \{x \in Y : \text{dist}(x, y_i) \leq \frac{1}{n}\}$, (where dist $\equiv$ distance). For each $x \in X$ set $\phi_0(x) = \phi(x)$ and define inductively $\phi_{n+1} : X \to 2^Y$ by $\phi_{n+1}(x) = \phi_n(x) \cap B_{n+1}(M_n(x))$, where $M_n(x) = \min\{i : \phi_n(x) \cap B_{n+1}(i) \neq \emptyset\}$. Then $\{\phi_n : n = 1, 2, \ldots\}$ is a decreasing sequence of nonempty closed subsets in X and the diameter of ϕ_n goes to zero. Define $f : X \to Y$ by $f(x) = \bigcap_{n=1}^{\infty} \phi_n(x)$. Then f is a selection from ϕ, and it is easily verified that f is measurable. In fact, it is easy to check that for each n ($n = 1, 2, \ldots$), and for each closed subset V of Y the set $\{x \in X : \phi_n(x) \cap V \neq \emptyset\}$ belongs to a. Since

$$f^{-1}(V) = \{x \in X : f(x) \in V\} = \bigcap_{n=0}^{\infty} \{x \in X : \phi_n(x) \cap V \neq \emptyset\}$$

we can conclude that $f^{-1}(V)$ is an element of a, i.e., f is measurable.

Recent work in economics and game theory [see for instance Yannelis (1987), Kim-Prikry-Yannelis (1989), Balder-Yannelis (1990) and Yannelis-Rustichini (1991)] has necessitated the use of set-valued functions defined either on the product space $T \times X$ (where T is a measure space and X is a topological space), or in an arbitrary subset U of $T \times X$. In particular, if $\phi : T \times X \to 2^Y$ (where Y is a linear topological space), is a set-valued function such that for each fixed $t \in T, \phi(t, \cdot)$ is lower semicontinuous, $\phi(\cdot, \cdot)$ is nonempty, convex, closed valued and lower measurable, one would like to know whether there exists a *Carathéodory-type selection from* ϕ, i.e., a function $f : T \times X \to Y$ such that $f(t,x) \in \phi(t,x)$ for all $(t,x) \in T \times X$ and for each fixed $t \in T$, $f(t,\cdot)$ is continuous and for each fixed $x \in X$, $f(\cdot\,,x)$ is measurable. Thus, the concept of a Carathéodory-type selection combines the notion of a continuous selection and measurable selection, via the setting of a product space.

It turns out that under appropriate conditions one can obtain several Carathéodory-type selection results adopting a similar argument with the one outlined to prove the existence of a continuous selection. Specifically, one can carry out a parametrized version of the above argument [which in turn is based on an idea of Michael (1956)] where the parameter t ranges over the measure space T.

Our main concern in this paper is to study several properties of set-valued maps of two variables. In particular, we will prove the existence of Carathéodory selections, the existence of random fixed points and the existence of random maximal elements. Finally, we will use the above results to prove the existence of a random price equilibrium.

2. Preliminaries

2.1 Notation.

2^A denotes the set of all nonempty subsets of the set A.
con A denotes the convex hull of the set A.
/ denotes the set of theoretic subtraction.
If $\phi : X \to 2^Y$ is a correspondence (a correspondence is a set-valued function for which all image sets are nonempty), then $\phi|_U : U \to 2^Y$ denotes the restriction of ϕ to U.
$\mathbb{R}^\ell$ denotes the ℓ-fold Cartesian product of the set of real numbers $\mathbb{R}$.
$B(x,\varepsilon)$ denotes the open ball centered at x of radius ε.
int A denotes the interior of A.
cl A denotes the closure of A.
dist denotes distance.
diam denotes diameter.
proj denotes projection.
$\emptyset$ denotes the empty set.

If X is a linear topological space, its dual is the space X^* of all continuous linear functionals on X. If $q \in X^*$ and $y \in X$ the value of q at y is denoted by $q \cdot y$.

2.2 Definitions. Let X and Y be sets. The graph G_ϕ of a correspondence $\phi : X \to 2^Y$ is the set $G_\phi = \{(x, y) \in X \times Y : y \in \phi(x)\}$. If X and Y are topological spaces, $\phi : X \to 2^Y$ is said to be *lower-semicontinuous* (l.s.c.) if the set $\{x \in X : \phi(x) \cap V \neq \emptyset\}$ is open in X for every open subset V of Y; $\phi : X \to 2^Y$ is said to be *upper-semicontinuous* (u.s.c.) if the set $\{x \in X : \phi(x) \subset V\}$ is open in X for every open subset V of Y; if Y is a linear topological space, $\phi : X \to 2^Y$ is said to be *upper-demicontinuous* (u.d.c.) if the set $\{x \in X : \phi(x) \subset V\}$ is open in X for every open half space V of Y. Obviously, u.d.c. is a weaker requirement than u.s.c.

If (X, α) and (Y, β) are measurable spaces and $\phi : X \to 2^Y$ is a correspondence, ϕ is said to have a *measurable graph* if G_ϕ belongs to the product σ-algebra $\alpha \otimes \beta$. We are often interested in the situation where (X, α) is a measurable space, Y is a topological space and $\beta = \beta(Y)$ is the Borel σ-algebra of Y. For a correspondence ϕ from a measurable space into a topological space, if we say that ϕ has a measurable graph, it is understood that the topological space is endowed with its Borel σ-algebra (unless specified otherwise). In the same setting as above, i.e., (X, α) a measurable space and Y a topological space, ϕ is said to be *lower measurable* if $\{x \in X : \phi(x) \cap V \neq \emptyset\} \in \alpha$ for every V open in Y. Furthermore, ϕ is said to be *measurable* if $\{x \in X : \phi(x) \cap B \neq \emptyset\} \in \alpha$ for every closed B in Y.

We now define the concept of a Carathéodory selection which combines the notion a of continuous selection and a measurable selection.

Let (X, α) be a measurable space and Y and Z be topological spaces. Let $\phi : X \times Z \to 2^Y$ be a (possibly empty-valued) correspondence. Let $U = \{(x, z) \in X \times Z : \phi(x, z) \neq \emptyset\}$. A *Carathéodory-type selection from ϕ is a function $f : U \to Y$ such that $f(x, z) \in \phi(x, z)$; for each $x \in X$, $f(x, \cdot)$ is continuous on $U_x = \{z \in Z : (x, z) \in U\}$, and for each $z \in Z$, $f(\cdot, z)$ is measurable on $U_z = \{x \in X : (x, z) \in U\}$.*

If (X, α), (Y, β) and $(Z, \mathbf{F})$ are measurable spaces, $U \subseteq X \times Z$ and $f : U \to Y$, we call f *jointly measurable* if for every $B \in \beta$, $f^{-1}(B) = U \cap A$ for some $A \in \alpha \otimes \mathbf{F}$. It is a standard result that if Z is a separable metric space, Y is metric and $f : X \times Z \to Y$ is such that for each fixed $x \in X$, $f(x, \cdot)$ is continuous and for each fixed $z \in Z$, $f(\cdot, z)$ is measurable, then f is jointly measurable [where $\beta = \beta(Y)$, $\mathbf{F} = \beta(Z)$]. It turns out, that in several instances U is a proper subset of $X \times Z$, and this situation is more delicate. However, in this more delicate situation it can be shown (see Proposition 3.1 below) that f is still jointly measurable.

2.3 Basic Theorems. We close this section by recalling some interesting results, [whose proofs can be found in Castaing-Valadier (1977)] which will be of fundamental importance in this paper:

Projection Theorem. *Let (T, τ, μ) be a complete finite measure space and Y be a complete, separable metric space. If H belongs to $\tau \otimes \beta(Y)$, its projection $\text{proj}_T(H)$ belongs to τ.*

Aumann Measurable Selection Theorem. *Let (T, τ, μ) be a complete finite measure space, Y be a complete, separable metric space and $\phi : T \to 2^Y$ be a nonempty valued correspondence with a measurable graph, i.e., $G_\phi \in \tau \otimes \beta(Y)$. Then there is a measurable function $f : T \to Y$ such that $f(t) \in \phi(t)$ μ-a.e.*

Kuratowski and Ryll-Nardzewski Measurable Selection Theorem. *Let (T, τ) be a measurable space, Y be a separable metric space and $\phi : T \to 2^Y$ be a lower measurable, closed, nonempty valued correspondence. Then there exists a measurable function $f : T \to Y$ such that $f(t) \in \phi(t)$ for all $t \in T$.*

Castaing Representation Theorem. *Let (T, τ) be a measurable space, Y be a separable metric space and $\phi : T \to 2^Y$ be a closed, nonempty valued correspondence. Consider the following statements:*

(i) ϕ is lower measurable, and

(ii) there exist measurable functions $f_n : T \to Y$ $(n = 1, 2, \ldots)$ such that $\text{cl}\{f_n(t) : n = 1, 2, \ldots\} = \phi(t)$ for all $t \in T$.

Then (i) is equivalent to (ii).

3. Elementary Measure Theoretic Facts

This Section contains several elementary results of measure theoretic character, which are going to be useful in the sequel.

Proposition 3.1. *Let (T, τ) be a measurable space, Z be a separable metric space, Y be a metric space and $U \subseteq T \times Z$ be such that:*

(i) for each $t \in T$ the set $U^t = \{x \in Z : (t, x) \in U\}$ is open in Z and
(ii) for each $x \in Z$ the set $U_x = \{t \in T : (t, x) \in U\}$ belongs to τ.

Moreover, let $f : U \to Y$ be such that for each $t \in T$, $f(t, \cdot)$ is continuous on U^t and for each $x \in Z$, $f(\cdot, x)$ is measurable on U_x. Then f is relatively jointly measurable with respect to the σ-algebra $\tau \otimes \beta(Z)$, i.e., for every V open in Y,

$$\{(t, x) \in U : f(t, x) \in V\} = U \cap A$$

for some $A \in \tau \otimes \beta(Z)$.

Proof. Let x_n $(n = 0, 1, 2, \ldots)$ be dense in Z. For $p \geq 1$ set $f_p(t, x) = f(t, x_n)$, for $(t, x) \in U$, if n is the smallest integer such that $x \in B(x_n, \frac{1}{p})$ and $(t, x_n) \in U$. It is easy to see that $f_p(t, x) = f(t, x_n)$ if (t, x) belongs to the set

$$\left[U_{x_n} \times \left(B\left(x_n, \frac{1}{p}\right) \Big/ \bigcup_{m<n} B\left(x_m, \frac{1}{p}\right)\right)\right] \cap U.$$

Observe that by assumption (ii), $U_{x_n} \in \tau$. Note that f_p is defined everywhere on U. To see this, let $(t, x) \in U$. By (i), U^t is open. Thus, let $\varepsilon > 0$ be such that $B(x, \varepsilon) \subseteq U^t$. Since x_n $(n = 0, 1, 2, \ldots)$ are dense in Z, there is some n such that $x_n \in B(x, \min(\varepsilon, \frac{1}{p}))$. Thus, $x_n \in U^t$. Consequently, $x \in B(x_n, \frac{1}{p})$ and $(t, x_n) \in U$, and we can conclude that $f_p(t, x)$ is defined.

We will now show that f_p is relatively jointly measurable. To this end let V be open in Y and set

$$S_n = \{t \in U_{x_n} : f(t, x_n) \in V\}.$$

Since $U_{x_n} \in \tau$ and $f(\cdot, x_n)$ is measurable on U_{x_n}, it follows that $S_n \in \tau$. It can be easily checked that

$$f_p^{-1}(V) = \bigcup_{n=0}^{\infty} \left[S_n \times \left(B\left(x_n, \frac{1}{p}\right) \Big/ \bigcup_{m<n} B\left(x_m, \frac{1}{p}\right)\right)\right] \cap U.$$

Thus, f_p is relatively jointly measurable.

Since for each $t \in T$, $f(t,\cdot)$ is continuous on U^t, we conclude that $f_p(t,x)$ converges to $f(t,x)$ as p goes to infinity. Thus $f(t,x)$ is relatively jointly measurable. The fact that a limit of relatively jointly measurable functions is relatively jointly measurable is clear, since relative joint measurability is just the ordinary measurability with respect to an appropriate σ-algebra; in our case, with respect to the σ-algebra of subsets of U which are of the form $U \cap A$ where $A \in \tau \otimes \beta(Z)$.

Lemma 3.1. *Let (T,τ) be a measurable space, X be a separable metric space and $\phi : T \to 2^X$ be a set-valued function. Consider the following statements:*

(a) $\phi(\cdot)$ is lower measurable,

(b) for each $x \in X$, the function $t \to \operatorname{dist}(x,\phi(x))$ is measurable in t, and

(c) the set-valued function $\psi : T \to 2^X$ defined by $\psi(t) = \operatorname{cl}\phi(t)$ has a measurable graph.

Then $a \iff b \iff c$.

Proof. ($a \iff b$). Note that $\phi(\cdot)$ is lower measurable if for each open ball $B(x,\delta)$ in X the set $\phi^{-1}(B(x,\delta)) = \{t \in T : \phi(t) \cap B(x,\delta) \neq \emptyset\}$ belongs to τ. Also note that for each $x \in X$, the function $t \to \operatorname{dist}(x,\phi(t))$ is measurable in t if the set $\{t \in T : \operatorname{dist}(x,\phi(t)) < \delta\}$ belongs to τ for each $\delta > 0$. Since $\{t \in T : \phi(t) \cap B(x,\delta) \neq \emptyset\} = \{t \in T : \operatorname{dist}(x,\phi(t)) < \delta\}$, we can conclude that $a \iff b$.

($b \iff c$) : Define the function $f : T \times X \to [0,\infty]$ by $f(t,x) = \operatorname{dist}(x,\phi(t))$. By Proposition 3.1, $f(\cdot,\cdot)$ is jointly measurable. Hence, we can conclude that:

$$\begin{aligned} f^{-1}(0) = \{(t,x) : \operatorname{dist}(x,\phi(t)) = 0\} &= \{(t,x) : x \in \operatorname{cl}\phi(t)\} \\ &= G_\psi \in \tau \otimes \beta(X), \end{aligned}$$

and this completes the proof of the Lemma.

Lemma 3.2. *Let (T,τ,μ) be a complete finite measure space, and Y be a complete separable metric space. Let $X : T \to 2^Y$ be a set-valued function with a measurable graph. Then there exist $\{f_k : k = 1,2,\ldots\}$ such that:*

(i) for all k, f_k is a measurable function from $\operatorname{proj}_T(G_X)$ into Y, and

(ii) for almost all $t \in \text{proj}_T(G_X), \{f_k(t) : k = 1, 2, \ldots\}$ *is a dense subset of* $X(t)$.

Proof. For each $n = 1, 2, \ldots$, let $\{E_i^n : i = 1, 2, \ldots\}$ be an open cover of Y such that $\text{diam}(E_i^n) < \frac{1}{2^n}$. For each n, $i = 1, 2, \ldots$, define $T_i^n = \{t \in T : X(t) \cap E_i^n \neq \emptyset\}$. Since $T_i^n = \text{proj}_T\{(t, y) \in T \times Y : y \in X(t) \cap E_i^n\}$ and $X(\cdot) \cap E_i^n$ has a measurable graph in $T \times Y$, $T_i^n \in \tau$ by virtue of the projection theorem. It can be easily checked that $\bigcup_{t=1}^{\infty} T_i^n = \text{proj}_T(G_X) \equiv S$.

For each n, $i = 1, 2, \ldots$, define the set-valued function $X_i^n : T \to 2^Y$ by

$$X_i^n(t) = \begin{cases} X(t) \cap E_i^n, & \text{if } t \in T_i^n \\ X(t), & \text{if } t \notin T_i^n. \end{cases}$$

Since the graph of X_i^n is $\{(t, y) \in T_i^n \times Y : y \in X(t) \cap E_i^n\} \cup \{(t, y) \in T/T_i^n \times Y : y \in X(t)\}$, the correspondence X_i^n has a measurable graph. Also, for each $t \in T, X_i^n(t) \neq \emptyset$ if and only if $X(t) \neq \emptyset$, hence the graphs of X_i^n and X have the same projection onto T. By the Aumann measurable selection theorem, for each $n, i = 1, 2, \ldots$, there exists a measurable function $f_i^n : S \to Y$ such that $f_i^n(t) \in X_i^n(t)$ for almost all $t \in T$. Fix t in T. Let $y \in X(t)$. Since for each $n, \{E_i^n : i = 1, 2, \ldots\}$ is an open cover of Y, for each n, there is some i such that $y \in X(t) \cap E_i^n$. Therefore, $\{f_i^n(t) : n, i = 1, 2, \ldots\}$ is dense in $X(t)$. Hence, the sequence f_i^n, after a suitable reindexing, gives the desired sequence f_k. This completes the proof of the lemma.

Lemma 3.3. *Let* (S_i, α_i) *for* $i = 1, 2$ *be measurable spaces,* $h : S_1 \to S_2$ *be a measurable function and* $A \in \alpha_1 \otimes \alpha_2$. *Then*

$$\text{proj}_{S_1}(G_h \cap A) \in \alpha_1.$$

Proof. (a) If $A = A_1 \times A_2$, where $A_i \in \alpha_i, i = 1, 2, \ldots$ then $\text{proj}_{S_1}(G_h \cap A) = A_1 \cap h^{-1}(A_2) \in \alpha_1$.

(b) If $\text{proj}_{S_1}(G_h \cap A) \in \alpha_1$, then $\text{proj}_{S_1}(G_h \cap A^c) \in \alpha_1$, where $A^c = S_1 \times S_2/A$. For, $\text{proj}_{S_1}(G_h \cap A^c) = S_1/\text{proj}_{S_1}(G_h \cap A)$.

(c) If $\text{proj}_{S_1}(G_h \cap A_n) \in \alpha_1$ for all $n = 1, 2, \ldots$, then $\text{proj}_{S_1}(G_h \cap (\bigcup_{n=1}^{\infty} A_n)) \in \alpha_1$. For, $\text{proj}_{S_1}(G_h \cap (\bigcup_{n=1}^{\infty} A_n)) = \bigcup_{n=1}^{\infty} \text{proj}_{S_1}(G_h \cap A_n)$.

Therefore, $\text{proj}_{S_1}(G_h \cap A) \in \alpha_1$ for all $A \in \alpha_1 \otimes \alpha_2$.

Lemma 3.4. *Let (T_i, τ_i) for $i = 1, 2, 3$ be measurable spaces, $y : T_1 \to T_3$ be a measurable function and $\phi : T_1 \times T_2 \to 2^{T_3}$ be a set-valued function with a measurable graph, i.e., $G_\phi \in \tau_1 \otimes \tau_2 \otimes \tau_3$. Let $W : T_1 \to 2^{T_2}$ be defined by*

$$W(t) = \{x \in T_2 : y(t) \in \phi(t, x)\}.$$

Then W has a measurable graph, i.e., $G_W \in \tau_1 \otimes \tau_2$.

Proof. Define $h : T_1 \times T_2 \to T_3$ by $h(t, x) = y(t)$. Let $S_1 = T_1 \times T_2, \alpha_1 = \tau_1 \otimes \tau_2, S_2 = T_3, \alpha_2 = \tau_3$, and $A = G_\phi$. Then $h : S_1 \to S_2$ is a measurable function and $A \in \alpha_1 \otimes \alpha_2$. Hence, by Lemma 3.3,

$$G_W = \{(t, x) : (t, x, h(t, x)) \in A\} \in \alpha_1 = \tau_1 \otimes \tau_2.$$

Lemma 3.5. *Let (T, τ) be a measurable space, Z be an arbitrary topological space and W_n, $n = 1, 2, \ldots$ be correspondences from T into Z with measurable graphs. Then the correspondences $\bigcup_n W_n(\cdot)$, $\bigcap_n W_n(\cdot)$, and $Z/W_n(\cdot)$ have measurable graphs.*

Proof. Obvious.

Lemma 3.6. *Let (T, τ, μ) be a complete finite measure space, Z be a complete separable metric space, and $W : T \to 2^Z$ be a correspondence having a measurable graph. Then for every $x \in Z$, $\mathrm{dist}(x, W(\cdot))$ is a measurable function, where $\mathrm{dist}(x, \emptyset) = \infty$.*

Proof. First observe that $S = \{t \in T : W(t) \neq \emptyset\}$ belongs to τ by virtue of the projection theorem. Now let λ be a positive real number and note that $\{s \in S : \mathrm{dist}(x, W(s)) < \lambda\} = \{s \in S : W(s) \cap B(x, \lambda) \neq \emptyset\} = \mathrm{proj}_T[G_W \cap (T \times B(x, \lambda))]$. Another application of the projection theorem concludes the proof.

Lemma 3.7. *Let (T, τ, μ) be a complete finite measure space, Z be a complete separable metric space, and $W : T \to 2^Z$ be a correspondence having a measurable graph. Then the correspondence $V : T \to 2^Z$ defined by*

$$V(t) = \{x \in Z : \mathrm{dist}(x, W(t)) > \lambda\},$$

(where λ any real number) has a measurable graph, i.e., $G_V \in \tau \otimes \beta(Z)$.

Proof. Define the function $g : T \times Z \to [0, \infty]$ by $g(t, x) = \text{dist}(x, W(t))$. By Lemma 3.6, $g(\cdot, x)$ is measurable for each x, and obviously $g(t, \cdot)$ is continuous for each t. By Proposition 3.1 we have that g is jointly measurable, i.e., measurable with respect to the product σ-algebra $\tau \otimes \beta(Z)$. Hence, $G_V = g^{-1}([\lambda, \infty]) \in \tau \otimes \beta(Z)$, i.e., $V(\cdot)$ has a measurable graph.

Lemma 3.8. *Let (S, α) be a measurable space, X be a separable metric space and $W : S \to 2^X$ be a lower measurable correspondence. Then the set-valued function $V : S \to 2^X$ defined by*

$$V(s) = \{x \in X : \text{dist}(x, W(s)) < \lambda\},$$

(where λ is any real number) has a measurable graph, i.e., G_V belongs to $\alpha \otimes \beta(X)$.

Proof. Define the function $g: S \times X \to [0, \infty]$ by $g(s, x) = \text{dist}(x, W(s))$. Since $W(\cdot)$ is lower measurable, it follows that $g(\cdot, x)$ is measurable for every fixed x, for

$$\{s \in S : \text{dist}(x, W(s)) < \lambda\} = \{s \in S : W(s) \cap B(x, \lambda) \neq \emptyset\}$$

and the latter set belongs to α by the assumption of lower measurability. Obviously, for each fixed $s \in S, g(s, \cdot)$ is continuous. Hence by Proposition 3.1, g is measurable with respect to the product σ-algebra $\alpha \otimes \beta(X)$. Therefore,

$$G_V = \{(s, x) : x \in V(s)\} = g^{-1}((-\infty, \lambda)) \in \alpha \otimes \beta(X),$$

i.e., $V(\cdot)$ has a measurable graph.

Fact 3.1. *Let (T, τ) be a measurable space, $S \subseteq T, S \in \tau$ and Y be a complete, separable metric space. Let $\phi : T \to 2^Y$ be a lower measurable correspondence and $f : S \to Y$ be a measurable function. Then the set-valued function $\psi : T \to 2^Y$ defined by*

$$\psi(t) = \phi(t) \cap (f(t) + B(0, \varepsilon))$$

is lower measurable. (Here we understand that $f(t) + B(0, \varepsilon) = \emptyset$ if $t \notin S$).

Proof. We must show that $\{t \in T : \psi(t) \cap U \neq \emptyset\} \in \tau$ for every open subset U of Y. For each $t \in T$, let $\theta(t) = (\phi(t) \cap U) + B(0, \varepsilon)$. Observe that

$$\begin{aligned}\{t \in T : \psi(t) \cap U \neq \emptyset\} &= \{t \in T : (\phi(t) \cap U) \cap (f(t) + B(0,\varepsilon)) \neq \emptyset\} \\ &= \{t \in S : f(t) \in \theta(t)\} = \mathrm{proj}_T(G_f \cap G_\theta).\end{aligned}$$

Since U is open, $\phi(t) \cap U$ is lower measurable, and since $\theta(t) = \{y \in Y : \mathrm{dist}(y, \phi(t) \cap U) < \varepsilon\}, \theta(\cdot)$ has a measurable graph by Lemma 3.8. Therefore by Lemma 3.3, $\mathrm{proj}_T(G_f \cap G_\theta) \in \tau$. Therefore $\{t \in T : \psi(t) \cap U \neq \emptyset\} \in \tau$, and this completes the proof of the Fact.

Lemma 3.9. *Let (S, α) be a measurable space Y, be a separable metric space and $\psi : S \to 2^Y$ be a lower measurable correspondence. Then the correspondence $\theta : S \to 2^Y$ defined by*

$$\theta(s) = \{y \in Y : \mathrm{dist}(y, \psi(s)) = 0\},$$

has a measurable graph, i.e., $G_\theta \in \alpha \otimes \beta(Y)$.

Proof. Consider the function $g : S \times Y \to [0, \infty]$ defined by $g(s, y) = \mathrm{dist}(y, \psi(s))$. Since $\psi(\cdot)$ is lower measurable it follows that for each fixed $y \in Y, g(\cdot, y)$ is measurable, for

$$\{s \in S : \mathrm{dist}(y, \psi(s)) < \varepsilon\} = \{s \in S : \psi(s) \cap B(y, \varepsilon) \neq \emptyset\}$$

and the latter set belongs to α by the assumption of lower measurability. Obviously for each fixed $s \in S, g(s, \cdot)$ is continuous. Therefore, by Proposition 3.1, $g(\cdot, \cdot)$ is jointly measurable, i.e., g is measurable with respect to the product σ-algebra $\alpha \otimes \beta(Y)$. It can be easily seen that:

$$\begin{aligned}G_\theta = \{(s, y) \in S \times Y : y \in \theta(s)\} &= \{(s, y) \in S \times Y : g(s, y) = 0\} \\ &= g^{-1}(0) \in \alpha \otimes \beta(Y).\end{aligned}$$

Consequently, $\theta(\cdot)$ has a measurable graph as was to be shown.

Lemma 3.10. *Let (S, α) be a measurable space, Y be a separable metric space and $\phi : S \to 2^Y$ be a nonempty compact valued and lower measurable correspondence. Let X be a nonempty subset of Y. Define the correspondence $\theta : S \to 2^X$ by*

$$\theta(s) = \{q \in X : q \cdot \phi(s) > 0\}.$$

Then $G_\theta \in \alpha \otimes \beta(X)$, i.e., $\theta(\cdot)$ has a measurable graph.

Proof. Since $\phi(\cdot)$ is lower measurable and closed valued, there exist measurable functions (Castaing representation) $u_i : S \to Y, i \in I$ (where I is a countable set) such that

$$\mathrm{cl}\{u_i(s) : i \in I\} = \phi(s) \qquad \text{for all } s \in S.$$

We then have that for all $s \in S$

$$\theta(s) = \bigcup_{n=1}^{\infty} g_n(s),$$

where

$$g_n(s) = \left\{ q \in X : \text{ for all } i \in I, q \cdot u_i(s) > \frac{1}{n} \right\}.$$

We now show that $G_{g_n} \in \alpha \otimes \beta(X)$. To this end, for each $i \in I$ define $h_i : S \times X \to [0, \infty]$ by $h_i(s, q) = q \cdot u_i(s)$. It is easily seen that for each $s \in S, h_i(s, \cdot)$ is continuous and for each $q \in X, h_i(\cdot, q)$ is measurable, and therefore by Proposition 3.1 $h_i(\cdot, \cdot)$ is jointly measurable. Consequently, $h_i^{-1}\left((\frac{1}{n}, \infty)\right)$ belongs to $\alpha \otimes \beta(X)$ and so does $\bigcap_{i \in I} h_i^{-1}\left((\frac{1}{n}, \infty)\right)$. It can be easily checked that $G_{g_n} = \bigcap_{i \in I} h_i^{-1}\left((\frac{1}{n}, \infty)\right)$. Therefore, $g_n(\cdot)$ has a measurable graph, i.e., $G_{g_n} \in \alpha \otimes \beta(X)$. It follows from Lemma 3.5 that $\bigcup_{n=1}^{\infty} G_{g_n} \in \alpha \otimes \beta(X)$. Since $G_\theta = \bigcup_{n=1}^{\infty} G_{g_n}$, we conclude that $\theta(\cdot)$ has a measurable graph. This completes the proof of the Lemma.

Lemma 3.11. *Let (S, α) be a measurable space and $\phi : S \to 2^{\mathbb{R}^\ell}$ be a nonempty compact convex valued and lower measurable correspondence. Let B be a compact, convex, nonempty subset of $\mathbb{R}^\ell$. Define $\theta : S \to 2^B$ by*

$$\theta(s) = \{q \in B : q \cdot \phi(s) > 0\}.$$

Then $\theta(\cdot)$ is lower measurable.

Proof. By virtue of Theorem 4.4 in Himmelberg (1975, p. 59), it suffices to show that the correspondence $h : S \to 2^B$ defined by $h(s) = B/\theta(s) = \{q \in B : q \cdot \phi(s) \leq 0\}$ is measurable. Since $\phi(\cdot)$ is lower measurable and compact valued, it is also measurable [Himmelberg (1975, Theorem 3.1, p. 55)]. Hence, it follows from the Castaing representation theorem that there exist measurable functions $u_i : S \to \mathbb{R}^\ell$, $i \in I$, (where I is a countable set) such that for all $s \in S$, $\mathrm{cl}\{u_i(s) : i \in I\} = \phi(s)$. We then have that $h(s) = \{q \in B : \text{ for all } i \in I, q \cdot u_i(s) \leq 0\}$. It can be easily checked that $h(\cdot)$ is measurable, and so is $B/h(\cdot)$. Since $B/h(s) = \theta(s) = \{q \in B : q \cdot \phi(s) > 0\}$ we conclude that $\theta(\cdot)$ is measurable. Since measurability of $\theta(\cdot)$ implies lower measurability of $\theta(\cdot)$, [Proposition 2.1 in Himmelberg (1975, p. 55)] the proof of the Lemma is now complete.

If F_n $(n = 1, 2, \ldots)$ is a sequence of nonempty subsets of a metric space X, we will denote by LsF_n and LiF_n the set of its limit superior and limit inferior points respectively, i.e.,

$$LsF_n = \{x \in X : x = \lim_{k \to \infty} x_{n_k}, x_{n_k} \in F_{n_k}, k = 1, 2, \ldots\}, \quad \text{and}$$
$$LiF_n = \{x \in X : x = \lim_{n \to \infty} x_n, x_n \in F_n, n = 1, 2, \ldots\},$$

Lemma 3.12. *Let (T, τ, μ) be a complete finite measure space and X be a separable metric space. Let $\{F_n : n = 1, 2, \ldots\}$ be a sequence of nonempty valued and lower measurable correspondences. Then $LiF_n(\cdot)$ has a measurable graph, i.e., $G_{LiF_n} \in \tau \otimes \beta(X)$.*

Proof. First notice that $LiF_n(\cdot)$ is closed valued [recall from Kuratowski (1966, pp. 336–337), that if A_n is a sequence of sets, LiA_n and LsA_n are both closed sets]. By definition [see Kuratowski (1966, p. 335)], $LiF_n(t) = \{f \in X : \lim_{n \to \infty} \text{dist}(f, F_n(t)) = 0\}$. Since by assumption the sequence of set-valued functions $F_n(\cdot)$ have a measurable graph and (T, τ, μ) is a complete measure space, $F_n(\cdot)$ are lower measurable. It follows from Lemma 3.1 that $\text{dist}(f, F_n(t))$ is continuous in f and measurable in t, i.e., $\text{dist}(\cdot, \cdot)$ is jointly measurable with respect to the product σ-algebra $\tau \otimes \beta(X)$. Hence, $\lim_{n \to \infty} \text{dist}(f, F_n(t))$ is jointly measurable with respect to the product σ-algebra $\tau \otimes \beta(X)$. Notice that

$$G_{LiF_n} = \{(t, f) \in T \times X : \lim_{n \to \infty} \text{dist}(f, F_n(t)) = 0\}.$$

Since $\lim_{n \to \infty} \text{dist}(f, F_n(t))$ is jointly measurable, the set G_{LiF_n} belongs to $\tau \otimes \beta(X)$, i.e., LiF_n has a measurable graph. This completes the proof of the Lemma.

Remark 3.1. Under the assumptions of Lemma 3.12, $LsF_n(\cdot)$ has a measurable graph as well. Simply notice that [see Kuratowski (1966, p. 337)] $LsF_n(t) = \{f \in X : Li\, \text{dist}(f, F_n(t)) = 0\}$.

Bibliographical Notes. Lemma 3.1 is due to Debreu (1967). Proposition 3.1 generalizes an earlier result of Kuratowski (1966). The argument is in essence that of Kuratowski, [see also Castaing-Valadier (1977) and Himmelberg (1975) for similar arguments]. Lemmata 3.2–3.8 are taken from Kim-Prikry-Yannelis (1987, 1988) and Lemmata 3.8–3.11 are new. Lemma 3.12 is taken from Yannelis (1990).

4. Carathéodory-Type Selection Theorems

Below we state three Carathéodory-type selection theorems. The reader can easily see that neither theorem implies the other.

Theorem 4.1. *Let (T, τ, μ) be a complete finite measure space, Y be a separable Banach space and Z be a complete separable metric space. Let $X : T \to 2^Y$ be a nonempty-valued correspondence having a measurable graph, i.e., $G_X \in \tau \otimes \beta(Y)$, and $\phi : T \times Z \to 2^Y$ be a convex valued correspondence (possibly empty-valued) with a measurable graph, i.e., $G_\phi \in \tau \otimes \beta(Z) \otimes \beta(Y)$, satisfying the following conditions:*

(i) for each $t \in T$, $\phi(t,x) \subset X(t)$ for all $x \in Z$.

(ii) for each t, $\phi(t,\cdot)$ has open lower sections in Z, i.e., for each $t \in T$, and each $y \in Y$, $\phi^{-1}(t,y) = \{x \in Z : y \in \phi(t,x)\}$ is open in Z.

(iii) for each $(t,x) \in T \times Z$, if $\phi(t,x) \neq \emptyset$, then $\phi(t,x)$ has a nonempty interior in $X(t)$.

Let $U = \{(t,x) \in T \times Z : \phi(t,x) \neq \emptyset\}$ and for each $x \in Z, U_x = \{t \in T : (t,x) \in U\}$ and for each $t \in T, U^t = \{x \in Z : (t,x) \in U\}$. Then there exists a Carathéodory-type selection from ϕ, i.e., there exists a function $f : U \to Y$ such that $f(t,x) \in \phi(t,x)$ for all $(t,x) \in U$ and for each $x \in Z, f(\cdot,x)$ is measurable on U_x and for each $t \in T, f(t,\cdot)$ is continuous on U^t. Moreover, $f(\cdot,\cdot)$ is jointly measurable.

Proof. Let $\phi_x(t) \equiv \phi(t,x)$ for all $x \in Z$. Notice that for each $x \in Z, \phi_x(\cdot)$ has a measurable graph in $T \times Y$. Observe that

$$U_x = \{t \in T : \phi_x(t) \neq \emptyset\} = \text{proj}_T(G_\phi).$$

It follows from the projection theorem that $U_x \in \tau$. By Lemma 3.2 there exist measurable functions $\{y_n(\cdot) : n = 1,2\dots\}$ such that for each $t, \{y_n(t)\}$ is a countable dense subset of $X(t)$. For each $t \in T$, let $W_n(t) = \{x \in Z : y_n(t) \in \phi(t,x)\}$. By assumption (ii) $W_n(t)$ is open in Z. Since by (iii) for each $(t,x) \in U, \phi(t,x)$ has nonempty interior in $X(t)$ and $\{y_n(t) : n = 1,2\dots\}$ is dense in $X(t)$, it follows that $\{W_n(t) : n = 1,2\dots\}$ is an open cover of the set U^t. By Lemma 3.5, $W_n(\cdot)$ has a measurable graph. For each $m = 1,2,\dots$, define the operator $(\ )_m$ by

$$(W)_m = \left\{ w \in W : \mathrm{dist}(w, Z/W) \geq \frac{1}{2^m} \right\}.$$

For each $n = 1,2,\dots$ and t in T let $V_n(t) = W_n(t) / \bigcup_{k=1}^{n-1}(W_k(t))_n$. Obviously, $V_n(t)$ is open in Z. It can be easily checked that $\{V_n(t) : n = 1,2,\dots\}$ is a locally finite open cover of the set U^t. Since for each n, $W_n(\cdot)$ has a measurable graph, so does $V_n(\cdot)$ by Lemmata 3.5 and 3.4. Let $\{g_n(t,\cdot) : n = 1,2,\dots\}$ be a partition of unity subordinated to the open cover $\{V_n(t) : n = 1,2,\dots\}$; for instance, for each $n = 1,2,\dots$, let

$$g_n(t,x) = \frac{\mathrm{dist}(x, Z/V_n(t))}{\sum_{k=1}^{\infty} \mathrm{dist}(x, Z/V_k(t))}.$$

Then $\{g_n(t,\cdot) : n = 1,2,\dots$ is a family of continuous functions $g_n(t,\cdot) : U^t \to [0,1]$ such that $g_n(t,x) = 0$ for $x \notin V_n(t)$ and $\sum_{n=1}^{\infty} g_n(t,x) = 1$ for all $(t,x) \in U$. Define $f : U \to Y$ by $f(t,x) = \sum_{n=1}^{\infty} g_n(t,x) y_n(t)$. Since $\{V_n(t) : n = 1,2,\dots\}$ is locally finite, each x has a neighborhood N_x which intersects only finitely many $V_n(t)$. Hence, for each $t \in T, f(t,\cdot)$ is a finite sum of continuous functions on N_x and it is therefore continuous on N_x. Consequently, $f(t,\cdot)$ is continuous. Furthermore, for any n such that $g_n(t,x) > 0, x \in V_n(t) \subset W_n(t) = \{x \in Z : y_n(t) \in \phi(t,z)\}$, i.e., $y_n(t) \in \phi(t,x)$. So $f(t,x)$ is a convex combination of elements $y_n(t)$ from the convex set $\phi(t,x)$. Consequently, $f(t,x) \in \phi(t,x)$ for all $(t,x) \in U$. Since $V_n(\cdot)$ has a measurable graph, $\mathrm{dist}(x, Z/V_n(\cdot))$ is a measurable function by Lemmata 3.5 and 3.6. Hence, for each n and x, $g_n(\cdot,x)$ is a measurable function. Since for each $n, y_n(\cdot)$ is a measurable function, it follows that $f(\cdot,x)$ is measurable for each x, i.e., $f(t,x)$ is a Carathéodory-type selection from $\phi|_U$. Finally, it follows from Proposition 3.1 that $f(\cdot,\cdot)$ is jointly measurable. This completes the proof of the theorem.

Theorem 4.2. *Let (T, τ, μ) be a complete finite measure space, Y be a separable Banach space and Z be a complete, separable metric space. Let $\phi : T \times Z \to 2^Y$ be a convex, closed (possibly empty-) valued correspondence such that:*

(i) $\phi(\cdot, \cdot)$ is lower measurable with respect to the σ-algebra $\tau \otimes \beta(Z)$ and
(ii) for each $t \in T, \phi(t, \cdot)$ is l.s.c.

Then there exists a jointly measurable Carathéodory-type selection from ϕ.

Proof. We begin by proving the existence of an approximate Carathéodory-type selection. To this end, let $U = \{(t, x) \in T \times Z : \phi(t, x) \neq \emptyset\}$. For each $x \in X$, let $U_x = \{t \in T : (t, x) \in U\}$ and for each $t \in T$, let $U^t = \{x \in Z : (t, x) \in U\}$. We will show that there exists an approximate or ε-Carathéodory-type selection from ϕ, i.e., given $\varepsilon > 0$, there exists a function $f^\varepsilon : U \to Y$ such that $f^\varepsilon(t, x) \in \phi(t, x) + B(0, \varepsilon)$, and for each $x \in Z, f^\varepsilon(\cdot, x)$ is measurable on U_x and for each $t \in T, f^\varepsilon(t, \cdot)$ is continuous on U^t. Since Y is separable we may choose $\{y_n : n = 1, 2, \ldots\}$ to be a countable dense subset of Y. For each $t \in T$ and $\varepsilon > 0$, let $W_n^\varepsilon(t) = \{x \in Z : y_n \in [\phi(t, x) + B(0, \varepsilon)]\}$. It follows from (ii) that for each $t \in T$ and $n = 1, 2, \ldots, W_n^\varepsilon(t)$ is open in Z. Since for each $(t, x) \in U, \phi(t, x) \neq \emptyset$, the set $\{W_n^\varepsilon(t) : n = 1, 2, \ldots\}$ is an open cover of U^t. Note that $\phi(t, x) + B(0, \varepsilon) = \{y \in Y : \text{dist}(y, \phi(t, x)) < \varepsilon\}$. Setting $S = T \times Z, X = Y, \alpha = \tau \otimes \beta(Z)$ and $W(s) = \phi(t, x)$ for $s = (t, x) \in S$ in Lemma 3.8 we conclude that $\phi(\cdot, \cdot) + B(0, \varepsilon)$ has a measurable graph. By Lemma 3.4, $W_n^\varepsilon(\cdot)$ has a measurable graph. As in the previous theorem for each $m = 1, 2, \ldots$, define the operator $(\ )_m$ on subsets of Z by

$$(W)_m = \left\{ w \in W : \text{dist}(w, Z/W) \geq \frac{1}{2^m} \right\}.$$

For $n = 1, 2, \ldots$, let $V_n^\varepsilon(t) = W_n^\varepsilon(t) / \cup_{k=1}^{n-1} (W_k^\varepsilon(t))_n$. It can be easily checked that $\{V_n^\varepsilon(t) : n = 1, 2, \ldots\}$ is a locally finite open cover of the set U^t. Since for each $n, W_n^\varepsilon(\cdot)$ has a measurable graph, by Lemmata 3.5 and 3.7, $V_n^\varepsilon(\cdot)$ has a measurable graph. Let $\{g_n^\varepsilon(t, x) : n = 1, 2, \ldots\}$ be a partition of unity subordinated to the open cover $\{V_n^\varepsilon(t) : n = 1, 2, \ldots\}$, for instance, for each $n = 1, 2, \ldots$, let

$$g_n^\varepsilon(t, x) = \frac{\text{dist}(x, Z/V_n^\varepsilon(t))}{\sum_{k=1}^\infty \text{dist}(x, Z/V_k^\varepsilon(t))}.$$

Then $\{g_n^\varepsilon(t,\cdot) : n = 1,2,\dots\}$ is a family of continuous functions $g_n^\varepsilon(t,\cdot) : U^t \to [0,1]$ such that $g_n^\varepsilon(t,x) = 0$ for $x \notin V_n^\varepsilon(t)$ and $\sum_{n=1}^\infty g_n^\varepsilon(t,x) = 1$ for all $(t,x) \in U$. Define $f^\varepsilon : U \to Y$ by $f^\varepsilon(t,x) = \sum_{n=1}^\infty g_n^\varepsilon(t,x) y_n$. Since $\{V_n^\varepsilon(t) : n = 1,2,\dots\}$ is locally finite, each x has a neighborhood N_x which intersects only finitely many $V_n^\varepsilon(t)$. Hence, $f^\varepsilon(t,\cdot)$ is a finite sum of continuous functions on N_x and it is therefore continuous on N_x. Consequently, $f^\varepsilon(t,\cdot)$ is a continuous function on U^t. Moreover, for any n such that $g_n^\varepsilon(t,x) > 0, x \in V_n^\varepsilon(t) \subset W_n^\varepsilon(t) = \{z \in Z : y_n \in [\phi(t,z) + B(0,\varepsilon)]\}$, i.e., $y_n \in \phi(t,x)+B(0,\varepsilon)$. So $f^\varepsilon(t,x)$ is a convex combination of elements from the convex set $\phi(t,x)+B(0,\varepsilon)$. Therefore, $f^\varepsilon(t,x) \in \phi(t,x)+B(0,\varepsilon)$ for all $(t,x) \in U$. Since $V_n^\varepsilon(\cdot)$ has a measurable graph, by Lemmata 3.5 and 3.6, $\mathrm{dist}(x, Z/V_n^\varepsilon(\cdot))$ is a measurable function for every $x \in Z$. Hence, for each $n, x, g_n^\varepsilon(\cdot\,,x)$ is a measurable function. Consequently, $f^\varepsilon(\cdot\,,x)$ is measurable for each x. Therefore f^ε is an approximate or ε-Carathéodory-type selection from $\phi|_U$. Now we can construct inductively, functions $f_l : U \to Y, l = 1,2,\dots$, such that

(a) $f_l(t,\cdot)$ is continuous on U^t and $f_l(\cdot\,,x)$ is measurable on U_x,
(b) $f_l(t,x) \in \phi(t,x) + B\left(0,\frac{1}{2^l}\right), l = 1,2,\dots,$
(c) $f_l(t,x) \in f_{l-1}(t,x) + 2B\left(0,\frac{1}{2^{l-1}}\right), l = 2,3,\dots.$

The existence of f_l satisfying (a) and (b) for $l = 1$, is guaranteed by the above argument. Suppose that we have $f_1,\dots,f_k$ satisfying (a), (b), and (c) for $l = 1,2,\dots,k$. We must find $f_{k+1} : U \to Y$ which satisfies (a), (b), and (c) for $l = k+1$. Now define $\phi_{k+1}(t,x) = \phi(t,x) \cap (f_k(t,x) + B(0,\frac{1}{2^k}))$. Then $\phi_{k+1}(t,x)$ is nonempty, by the induction hypothesis, and it can be easily checked that for each $t \in T, \phi_{k+1}(t,\cdot)$ is l.s.c. It follows from Fact 3.1 that $\phi^{k+1}(\cdot\,,\cdot)$ is lower measurable. By the above argument (the existence of an approximate Carathéodory-type selection) there exists $f_{k+1} : U \to Y$ such that $f_{k+1}(t,x) \in \phi_{k+1}(t,x) + B(0,\frac{1}{2^{k+1}}))$. But then $f_{k+1}(t,x) \in (f_k(t,x) + B(0,\frac{1}{2^k})) + B(0,\frac{1}{2^{k+1}}) \subset (f_k(t,x) + 2B(0,\frac{1}{2^k}))$ which is (c) and $f_{k+1}(t,x) \in \phi(t,x) + B(0,\frac{1}{2^{k+1}})$ which is (b). By (c), $\{f_l : l = 1,2,\dots\}$ is uniformly Cauchy, and therefore converges uniformly to $f : U \to Y$. Since ϕ is closed valued $f(t,x) \in \phi(t,x)$ for all $(t,x) \in U$. Furthermore, for each $t \in T, f(t,\cdot)$ is continuous in U^t and for each $x \in Z, f(\cdot\,,x)$ is measurable on U_x and therefore, by Proposition 3.1, $f(\cdot\,,\cdot)$ is jointly measurable. This completes the proof of the theorem.

Theorem 4.3. *The statement of Theorem 4.2 remains true without closed valueness of* $\phi : T \times Z \to 2^Y$ *if either*

(i) Y *is finite dimensional or*

(ii) $\phi(t,x)$ *has a nonempty interior for all* $(t,x) \in U$.

Proof. We begin by proving the following claim:

Claim. *Under the conditions of Theorem 4.3 there exists a countable collection* $\mathbf{F}$ *of Carathéodory-type selections from* ϕ *such that for every* $(t,x) \in U$, $\{f(t,x) : f \in \mathbf{F}\}$ *is dense in* $\phi(t,x)$.

Proof. Let $\{E^n : n = 1,2,\dots\}$ be a convex open basis of Y. For each $n = 1,2,\dots$, the set $U^n = \{(t,x) \in T \times Z : \phi(t,x) \cap E^n \neq \emptyset\}$ belongs to $\tau \otimes \beta(Z)$. For each $t \in T$ and each n, set $U^n(t) = \{x \in Z : (t,x) \in U^n\}$. Note that for each $t \in T$, $U^n(t)$ is open in Z. Moreover, $U^n(\cdot)$ has a measurable graph. For each $k = 1,2,\dots$, and $t \in T$, let $A^n_k(t) = \{x \in Z : \text{dist}(x, Z/U_n(t)) \geq \frac{1}{2^k}\}$. By Lemma 3.7, $A^n_k(\cdot)$ has a measurable graph. Note that $\bigcup_{k=1}^{\infty} A^n_k(t) = U^n(t)$, and for each $t \in T$, A^n_k is closed in Z. Define $\phi^n_k : T \times Z \to 2^Y$ by

$$\phi^n_k(t,x) = \begin{cases} \text{cl}(\phi(t,x) \cap E^n) & \text{if } x \in A^n_k(t) \\ \phi(t,x) & \text{if } x \notin A^n_k(t). \end{cases}$$

Since for each $t \in T$, $A^n_k(t)$ is closed in Z, $\phi^n_k(t,\cdot)$ is l.s.c. Moreover, since for every open subset V of Y, $\{(t,x) : \phi^n_k(t,x) \cap V \neq \emptyset\} = \{(t,x) : \text{cl}(\phi(t,x) \cap E^n) \cap V \neq \emptyset, x \in A^n_k(t)\} \cup \{(t,x) : \phi(t,x) : \phi(t,x) \cap V \neq \emptyset, x \notin A^n_k(t)\} \in \tau \otimes \beta(Z)$, it follows that $\phi^n_k(\cdot,\cdot)$ is lower measurable. By Theorem 4.2 there exist Carathéodory-type selection $f^n_k(\cdot,\cdot)$ from $\phi^n_k(\cdot,\cdot)$. Let $\mathbf{F}$ be the collection of all $f^n_k(\cdot,\cdot), k, n = 1,2,\dots$. Then $\mathbf{F}$ is a countable collection of Carathéodory-type selections from ϕ, and it can be easily seen that $\{f(t,x) : f \in \mathbf{F}\}$ is dense in $\phi(t,x)$ for all $(t,x) \in U$. This completes the proof of the claim.

We will now need the following notions. If K is a closed, convex subset of a normed linear space, then a *supporting set* of K is a closed convex subset S of K, $S \neq K$, such that if an interior point of a segment in K is in S, then the whole segment is in S. The set of all elements of K which are not in any supporting set of K will be denoted by $I(K)$. The following facts below are due to Michael (1956, p. 372).

Fact 4.1. *If any convex subset K of Y is either closed or has an interior point or is finite dimensional, then $I(\mathrm{cl}\, K) \subset K$.*

Fact 4.2. *Let K be a nonempty, closed, convex separable subset of a Banach space Y, and $\{y_i = 1, 2, \ldots\}$ be a dense subset of K. If*

$$z_i = y_i + \frac{(y_i - y_1)}{\max(1, \|y_i - y_1\|)} \quad \textit{for all } i \textit{ and } z = \sum_{i=1}^{\infty} \left(\frac{1}{2}\right)^i z_i,$$

then $z \in I(K)$.

We are now ready to complete the proof of Theorem 4.3:

Define $\psi : T \times Z \to 2^Y$ by $\psi(t,x) = \mathrm{cl}\, \phi(t,x)$. Since for each $t \in T$, $\phi(t,\cdot)$ is l.s.c. so is $\psi(t,\cdot)$. Moreover, ψ is lower measurable. By the above claim there exist Carathéodory-type selections $\{g_k(t,x) : k = 1, 2, \ldots\}$ dense in $\psi(t,x)$ for all $(t,x) \in U$. For each $k = 1, 2, \ldots$, let

$$f_k(t,x) = g_1(t,x) + \frac{g_k(t,x) - g_1(t,x)}{\max(1, \|g_k(t,x) - g_1(t,x)\|)},$$

$$f(t,x) = \sum_{k=1}^{\infty} \frac{1}{2^k} f_k(t,x).$$

By Fact 4.2, $f(t,x) \in I(\psi(t,x))$ for all $(t,x) \in U$. Since the series defining f converge uniformly, it follows that for each $t \in T$, $f(t,\cdot)$ is continuous and for each $x \in X$, $f(\cdot,x)$ is measurable. By Fact 4.1, $f(t,x) \in I(\psi(t,x)) \subset \phi(t,x)$ if either (i) or (ii) of Theorem 4.3 are satisfied. This completes the proof of the theorem.

Bibliographical Notes. Theorem 4.1–4.3 and their proofs are due to Kim-Prikry-Yannelis (1987, 1988). Less general versions of Theorem 4.2 are given by Castaing (1975), Fryszkowski (1977) and Rybiński (1985). Applications of these theorems in economics and game theory can be found in Yannelis (1987), Kim-Prikry-Yannelis (1989), Yannelis-Rustichini (1991), Balder-Yannelis (1990) and Yannelis (1990a).

5. Random Fixed Point Theorems

Let (T, τ) be a measurable space, X be a metric space and $\phi : T \times X \to 2^X$ be a correspondence. If there exists a measurable function

$f : T \to X$ such that $f(t) \in \phi(t, f(t))$ for all $t \in T$, then we say that ϕ has a *random fixed point.*

We begin by proving a random version of the Kakutani-Fan-Glicksberg fixed point theorem.

Theorem 5.1. *Let (T, τ, μ) be a complete finite measure space and X be a compact, convex, nonempty subset of a locally convex, separable, metrizable linear topological space. Let $\phi : T \times X \to 2^X$ be a nonempty, convex, closed valued correspondence such that:*

(i) $\phi(\cdot\,,\cdot)$ is lower measurable, i.e., for every open subset V of X the set $\{(t,x) \in T \times X : \phi(t,x) \cap V \neq \emptyset\}$ belongs to $\tau \otimes \beta(X)$,
(ii) for each fixed $t \in T, \phi(t,\cdot)$ is u.s.c.

Then ϕ has a random fixed point.

Proof. Define the correspondence $F : T \to 2^X$ by

$$F(t) = \{x \in X : \operatorname{dist}(x, \phi(t,x)) = 0\}.$$

Setting $S = T \times X$, $X = Y$, $\alpha = \tau \otimes \beta(X)$ and $\psi(s) = \phi(t,x)$ for $s = (t,x)$ in Lemma 3.9, we conclude that $F(\cdot)$ has a measurable graph, i.e., $G_F \in \tau \otimes \beta(X)$. It can be easily checked that for each fixed $t \in T$, the correspondence $\phi(t,\cdot) : X \to 2^X$ satisfies all the conditions of the Fan-Glicksberg fixed point theorem [see for instance Glicksberg (1952)]. Hence, for all $t \in T$, $F(t) \neq \emptyset$. Consequently, the correspondence $F : T \to 2^X$ satisfies all the conditions of the Aumann measurable selection theorem and therefore there exists a measurable function $\bar{x} : T \to X$ such that $\bar{x}(t) \in F(t)$ for almost all $t \in T$, i.e., $\operatorname{dist}(\bar{x}(t), \phi(t, \bar{x}(t))) = 0$ for almost all $t \in T$. Since $\phi(\cdot\,,\cdot)$ is closed valued we conclude that $\bar{x}(t) \in \phi(t, \bar{x}(t))$ for almost all $t \in T$, i.e., $\phi(\cdot\,,\cdot)$ has a random fixed point. This completes the proof of the Theorem.

The result below is a random version of Fan's Coincidence Theorem, [Fan (1969)].

Theorem 5.2. *Let X be a compact convex nonempty subset of a locally convex separable and metrizable linear topological space Y and let (T, τ, v) be a complete finite measure space. Let $\gamma : T \times X \to 2^Y$ and $\mu : T \times X \to 2^Y$ be two nonempty, convex, closed and at least one of them compact valued correspondences such that:*

(i) $\mu(\cdot,\cdot)$ *and* $\gamma(\cdot,\cdot)$ *are lower measurable,*

(ii) for each fixed $t \in T$, *the correspondences* $\mu(t,\cdot) : X \to 2^Y$ *and* $\gamma(t,\cdot) : X \to 2^Y$ *are u.s.c.*

(iii) for every $t \in T$ *and every* $x \in X$, *there exist three points* $y \in X$, $u \in \gamma(t,x), z \in \mu(t,x)$ *and a real number* $\lambda > 0$ *such that* $y - x = \lambda(u - z)$.

Then there exists a measurable function $x^* : T \to X$ *such that* $\gamma(t, x^*(t)) \cap \mu(t, x^*(t)) \neq \emptyset$ *for almost all* $t \in T$.

Proof. Define the correspondence $W : T \times X \to 2^Y$ by $W(t,x) = \gamma(t,x) \cap \mu(t,x)$. Since $\gamma(\cdot,\cdot)$ and $\mu(\cdot,\cdot)$ are closed valued and lower measurable and at least one of them is compact valued, it follows from Theorem 4.1 in Himmelberg (1975) that $W(\cdot,\cdot)$ is lower measurable. Define the correspondence $\phi : T \to 2^X$ by

$$\phi(t) = \{x \in X : W(t,x) \neq \emptyset\}.$$

Observe that

$$\begin{aligned} G_\phi &= \{(t,x) \in T \times X : x \in \phi(t)\} \\ &= \{(t,x) \in T \times X : W(t,x) \neq \emptyset\} \\ &= \{(t,x) \in T \times X : W(t,x) \cap Y \neq \emptyset\}, \end{aligned}$$

and the latter set belongs to $\tau \otimes \beta(X)$ since $W(\cdot,\cdot)$ is lower measurable. Therefore, $G_\phi \in \tau \otimes \beta(X)$. It follows from Fan's Coincidence Theorem, that for each $t \in T, \phi(t) \neq \emptyset$. Thus, the correspondence $\phi : T \to 2^X$ satisfies all the conditions of the Aumann Measurable Selection Theorem and consequently, there exists a measurable function $x^* : T \to X$ such that $x^*(t) \in \phi(t)$ for almost all t in T, i.e., $\gamma(t, x^*(t)) \cap \mu(t, x^*(t)) \neq \emptyset$ for almost all t in T. This completes the proof of the Theorem.

An immediate corollary of the above result is Theorem 5.1.

Corollary 5.1. *Let* X *be a compact, convex, nonempty subset of a locally convex, separable and metrizable linear topological space* Y *and let* (T, τ, v) *be a complete finite measure space. Let* $\gamma : T \times X \to 2^X$ *be a nonempty, convex, closed valued correspondence such that for each fixed* $t \in T$, $\gamma(t,\cdot)$ *is u.s.c. and* $\gamma(\cdot,\cdot)$ *is lower measurable. Then* $\gamma(\cdot,\cdot)$ *has a random fixed point.*

Proof. Define the correspondence $\mu : T \times X \to 2^X$ by $\mu(t,x) = \{x\}$. Clearly for each fixed $t \in T, \mu(t,\cdot)$ is u.s.c. and $\mu(\cdot,\cdot)$ is convex, lower measurable, nonempty, compact valued. Let $x \in X$ and $t \in T$. By choosing $u \in \gamma(t,x), z = x \in \mu(t,x)$ and $\lambda \in (0,1)$ assumption (iii) of Theorem 5.2 is satisfied (simply notice that since X is convex $y = x + \lambda(u-z) = \lambda u+(1-\lambda)x \in X$). Hence, by the previous theorem there exists a measurable function $x^* : T \to X$ such that $\gamma(t,x^*(t)) \cap \mu(t,x^*(t)) \neq \emptyset$ for almost all $t \in T$, i.e., $x^*(t) \in \gamma(t,x^*(t))$ for almost all $t \in T$.

Remark 5.1. Theorem 5.2 and Corollary 5.1 remain true if we replace the assumption that (T,τ,v) is a complete finite (or σ-finite) measure space, by the fact that (T,τ) is simply a measurable space. In this case one only needs to observe that in the proof of Theorem 5.2 for each fixed $t \in T, W(t,\cdot)$ is u.s.c. (as it is the intersection of two u.s.c. correspondences) and therefore, the correspondence $\phi : T \to 2^X$ is closed valued. Since $\phi(\cdot)$ is closed valued and it has a measurable graph by Lemma 3.1, $\phi(\cdot)$ is lower measurable. One can now appeal to the Kuratowski and Ryll-Nardzewski measurable selection theorem to complete the proof of Theorem 5.2.

Theorem 5.3. *Let (T,τ,μ) be a complete finite measure space, and X be a nonempty, compact, convex subset of a separable Banach space Y. Let $\phi : T \times X \to 2^X$ be a nonempty, convex, closed valued correspondence such that:*

(i) $\phi(\cdot,\cdot)$ is lower measurable and
(ii) for each $t \in T, \phi(t,\cdot)$ is l.s.c. Then ϕ has a random fixed point.

Proof. It follows from Theorem 4.2 that there exists a function $f : T \times X \to X$ such that $f(t,x) \in \phi(t,x)$ for all $(t,x) \in T \times X$, and for each $x \in X, f(\cdot,x)$ is measurable and for each $t \in T, f(t,\cdot)$ is continuous. Moreover, $f(\cdot,\cdot)$ is jointly measurable.

Define the set-valued function $F : T \to 2^X$ by $F(t) = \{x \in X : g(t,x) = 0\}$. where $g(t,x) = f(t,x) - x$. It follows from the Tychonoff fixed point theorem that for each fixed $t \in T$, the function $f(t,\cdot) : X \to X$ has a fixed point. Therefore, for each $t \in T, F(t) \neq \emptyset$. Since g is jointly measurable, F has a measurable graph. Hence by the Aumann measurable selection theorem there exists a measurable function $x^* : T \to X$ such that for almost all t in T, $x^*(t) \in F(t)$, i.e., $x^*(t) = f(t,x^*(t)) \in \phi(t,x^*(t))$. This completes the proof of the theorem.

Remark 5.2. The statement of Theorem 5.3 remains true without the closed valuedness of $\phi : T \times X \to 2^X$ if either

(i) Y is finite dimensional or
(ii) $\phi(t,x)$ has a nonempty interior for all $(t,x) \in T \times X$.

The argument is similar to that adopted in the proof of Theorem 5.3 except that one must use now Theorem 4.3 instead of Theorem 4.2.

Remark 5.3. The statement of Theorem 5.3 remains true if we replace (i) and (ii) by:

(i) for each fixed $t \in T, \phi(t,\cdot)$ has an open graph in $X \times X$, and
(ii) ϕ has a measurable graph, i.e., $G_\phi \in \tau \otimes \beta(X) \otimes \beta(X)$.

The argument is the same with that adopted for the proof of Theorem 5.3 except that one must now appeal to Theorem 4.1.

We conclude this Section by proving a random fixed point theorem for weakly u.s.c. (w-u.s.c.) set-valued functions, which has found useful applications in economic theory. However, before we state our result we will need some notation.

Let (T,τ,μ) be a finite measure space, X be a separable Banach space and let $L_1(\mu, X)$ denote the space of equivalence classes of X-valued Bochner integrable function on (T,τ,μ). We denote by S_F^1 the set of all Bochner integrable selections from the set-valued function $F : T \to 2^X$, i.e., $S_F^1 = \{x \in L_1(\mu, X) : x(t) \in F(t)\ \mu\text{-a.e.}\}$.

Theorem 5.4. *Let $\phi : T \times X \to 2^X$ be a nonempty, convex, weakly compact valued correspondence such that:*

(i) $\phi(\cdot,\cdot)$ is lower measurable,
(ii) for each $t \in T, \phi(t,\cdot)$ has a weakly closed graph, that is, w-Ls $\phi(t,x_n) \subset \phi(t,x)$, *(where* w-Ls *denotes weak limit superior) whenever the sequence $\{x_n : n = 1,2,\ldots\}$ converges to x,*
(iii) $\phi(t,x) \subset F(t)$ μ-a.e., where $F : T \to 2^X$ is a lower measurable, integrably bounded, weakly compact, convex and nonempty valued correspondence.

Then $\phi(\cdot,\cdot)$ has a random fixed point.

Proof. Define the set-valued operator $\psi : S_F^1 \to 2^{S_F^1}$ by $\psi(x) = S^1_{\phi(\cdot,x(\cdot))}$. In view of assumption(iii) it follows from Diestel's theorem [see for instance Yannelis (1990a), Theorem 3.1] that S^1_F is a weakly compact subset of $L_1(\mu, X)$. Obviously S^1_F is convex and by virtue of the Kuratowski and Ryll-Nardzewski measurable selection theorem we can conclude that S^1_F is nonempty. We now show that ψ is w-u.s.c., i.e., the set $\{x \in S^1_F : \psi(x) \subset V\}$ is open in S^1_F for any weakly open subset V of S^1_F. Since S^1_F is weakly compact and $\psi(\cdot)$ is weakly closed valued, it suffices to show that $\psi(\cdot)$ has a weakly closed graph. To this end let $\{x_n(\cdot) : n = 1, 2, \ldots\}$ be a sequence in S^1_F converging in the $L_1(\mu, X)$ norm to $x(\cdot) \in S^1_F$, we must show that

$$\text{w-Ls}\, S^1_{\phi(\cdot, x_n(\cdot))} = \text{w-Ls}\, \psi(x_n) \subset S^1_{\phi(\cdot, x(\cdot))} = \psi(x). \tag{5.1}$$

(By passing to a subsequence if necessary if may assume that $x_n(t)$ converges to $x(t)$ μ-a.e.) Let $z \in \text{w-Ls}\, \psi(x_n)$, i.e., there exists $\{z_{n_k} : k = 1, 2, \ldots\}$ in S^1_F such that z_{n_k} converges weakly to $z \in S^1_F$ and $z_{n_k} \in \psi(x_{n_k}) = S^1_{\phi(\cdot, x_{n_k}(\cdot))}$, i.e., $z_{n_k}(t) \in \phi(t, x_{n_k}(t))\mu$-a.e. We must show that $z \in \psi(x)$. It follows from Theorem 4.1 in Yannelis (1990b) that $z(t) \in \overline{\text{con}} w - Ls\{z_{n_k}(t)\}$ μ-a.e. and therefore

$$z(t) \in \overline{\text{con}}\, \text{w-Ls}\, \phi(t, x_n(t)) \ \mu\text{-a.e.} \tag{5.2}$$

Since by assumption (ii) for each $t \in T, \phi(t, \cdot)$ has a weakly closed graph we have that:

$$\text{w-Ls}\, \phi(t, x_n(t)) \subset \phi(t, x(t)) \ \mu\text{-a.e.} \tag{5.3}$$

Combining now (5.2) and (5.3) and taking into account that ϕ is convex valued we conclude that $z(t) \in \phi(t, x(t))$ μ-a.e. Since ϕ is weakly compact valued we have that $z \in S^1_{\phi(\cdot, x(\cdot))} = \psi(x)$, and this proves (5.1). Hence, $\psi : S^1_F \to 2^{S^1_F}$ satisfies all the conditions of the Fan-Glicksberg fixed point theorem and consequently there exists $x^* \in S^1_F$ such that $x^* \in \psi(x^*)$, i.e., $x^*(t) \in \phi(t, x^*(t))$ μ-a.e. This completes the proof of the theorem.

Bibliographical Notes. Theorems 5.1 and 5.4 are new. Theorem 5.2 is taken from Yannelis-Rustichini (1991). Theorem 5.3 is a random version of a result in Yannelis-Prabhakar (1983) and it is taken from Kim-Prikry-Yannelis (1987). The literature on random fixed points is growing rapidly, and perhaps one of the basic references is Itoh (1979). Applications of random fixed points in game theory can be found in Yannelis-Rustichini (1991).

6. Random Maximal Elements and Random Equilibria

6.1 Random Maximal Elements. Let X be a nonempty subset of a linear topological space. Let $P : X \to 2^X$ be a *preference correspondence.* We read $y \in P(x)$ as "y is strictly preferred to x." For instance if $>$ is a binary relation on X one may define $P : X \to 2^X$ by $P(x) = \{y \in X : y > x\}$. The correspondence $P : X \to 2^X$ is said to have a *maximal element* if there exists $\bar{x} \in X$ such that $P(\bar{x}) = \emptyset$. Several results on the existence of maximal elements with applications to equilibrium theory have been given in the literature [see for instance Sonnenschein (1971) and Yannelis-Prabhakar (1983) among others.] Notice that the above preference correspondences need not be representable by utility functions. We will now allow our preference correspondence to depend on the states of nature, i.e., we allow for random preferences.

Let (T, τ, μ) be a complete finite measure space. We interpret T as the states of nature of the world, and suppose that T is large enough to include all the events that we consider to be interesting. τ will denote the σ-algebra of events. A *random preference correspondence P* is a mapping from $T \times X$ into X. We read $y \in P(t, x)$ as "y is strictly preferred to x at the state of nature t". We now can introduce the concept of a random maximal element which is the natural analogue of the ordinary (deterministic) notion of a maximal element. The correspondence $P : T \times X \to 2^X$ is said to have a *random maximal element* if there exists a measurable function $\bar{x} : T \to X$ such that $P(t, \bar{x}(t)) = \emptyset$ for almost all t in T.

The following two theorems on the existence of random maximal elements below generalize the ordinary (deterministic) maximal elements results given in Sonnenschein (1971), and Yannelis-Prabhakar (1983). These theorems will also play a key role in proving random price equilibrium theorem in Section 6.2.

Theorem 6.1. *Let (T, τ, μ) be a complete finite measure space and X be a compact, convex, nonempty subset of $\mathbb{R}^\ell$. Let $P : T \times X \to 2^X$ be a correspondence (possibly empty-valued) such that:*

(i) for every open subset V of X, $\{(t, x) \in T : \operatorname{con} P(t, x) \cap V \neq \emptyset\}$ belongs to $\tau \otimes \beta(X)$.

(ii) for each $t \in T, P(t, \cdot)$ is l.s.c.

(iii) for every measurable function $x : T \to X$, $x(t) \notin \text{con}\, P(t, x(t))$ for almost all $t \in T$.

Then there exists a measurable function $\bar{x} : T \to X$ such that $P(t, \bar{x}(t)) = \emptyset$ for almost all t in T.

Proof. Define the correspondence $\psi : T \times X \to 2^X$ by $\psi(t, x) = \text{con}\, P(t, x)$. By Proposition 2.6 in Michael (1956) for all $t \in T$, $\psi(t, \cdot)$ is l.s.c. and by assumption (i) $\psi(\cdot, \cdot)$ is lower measurable. Let $U = \{(t, x) \in T \times X : \psi(t, x) \neq \emptyset\}$. By Theorem 4.3 there exists a Carathéodory-type selection from ψ, i.e., there exists a function $f : U \to X$ such that $f(t, x) \in \psi(t, x)$ for all $(t, x) \in U$ and for each $t \in T$, $f(t, \cdot)$ is continuous on $U^t = \{x \in X : (t, x) \in U\}$ and for each $x \in X$, $f(\cdot, x)$ is measurable on $U_x = \{t \in T : (t, x) \in U\}$. Notice that for each $t \in T$, $U^t = \{x \in X : \psi(t, x) \neq \emptyset\} = \{x \in X : \psi(t, x) \cap X \neq \emptyset\}$ is open in the relative topology of X, since for each $t \in T$, $\psi(t, \cdot)$ is l.s.c. Furthermore, it follows at once from the lower measurability of $\psi(\cdot, \cdot)$ that the set $U = \{(t, x) \in T \times X : \psi(t, x) \cap X \neq \emptyset\}$ belongs to $\tau \otimes \beta(X)$. By virtue of the projection theorem we have that

$$\begin{aligned}\text{proj}_T(U \cap (T \times \{x\})) &= \text{proj}_T(\{(t, x) \in T \times X : \psi(t, x) \neq \emptyset\} \cap (T \times \{x\})) \\ &= \{t \in T : \psi(t, x) \neq \emptyset\} \\ &= U_x \in \tau.\end{aligned}$$

Hence, by Proposition 3.1, $f(\cdot, \cdot)$ is jointly measurable. Define the correspondence $\theta : T \times X \to 2^X$ by

$$\theta(t, x) = \begin{cases} \{f(t, x)\} & \text{if } (t, x) \in U \\ X & \text{if } (t, x) \notin U. \end{cases}$$

By Lemma 6.1 in Yannelis-Prabhakar (1983) we have that for each $t \in T$, $\theta(t, \cdot) : X \to 2^X$ is u.s.c.. Clearly, θ is convex and nonempty valued and it can be easily seen that $\theta(\cdot, \cdot)$ is lower measurable. Hence by Corollary 5.1, $\theta : T \times X \to 2^X$ has a random fixed point, i.e., there exists a measurable function $\bar{x} : T \to X$ such that $\bar{x}(t) \in \theta(t, \bar{x}(t))$ for almost all t in T. Suppose that for a non-null subset S of T, $(t, \bar{x}(t)) \in U$. Then by the definition of $\theta, \bar{x}(t) = f(t, \bar{x}(t)) \in \psi(t, \bar{x}(t)) = \text{con}\, P(t, \bar{x}(t))$ for all $t \in S$, a contradiction to assumption (iii). Hence, for almost all t

in T, $(t, \bar{x}(t)) \notin U$ and consequently $\psi(t, \bar{x}(t)) = \emptyset$ for almost all t in T which implies that $P(t, \bar{x}(t)) = \emptyset$ for almost all t in T. This completes the proof of the Theorem.

Theorem 6.1 can be extended to separable Banach spaces by strengthening the continuity assumption (ii). More formally we can state the following extension of Theorem 6.1.

Theorem 6.2. *Let (T, τ, μ) be a complete finite measure space and X be a compact, convex, nonempty subset of a separable Banach space. Let $P : T \times X \to 2^X$ be a correspondence (possibly empty-valued) such that*

(i) $\{(t, x, y) \in T \times X \times X : y \in \operatorname{con} P(t, x)\} \in \tau \otimes \beta(X) \otimes \beta(X)$.

(ii) for each $t \in T$ and each $y \in X$ the set $P^{-1}(t, y) = \{x \in X : y \in P(t, x)\}$ is open in the relative norm topology of X,

(iii) for each $(t, x) \in T \times X$, if $P(t, x) \neq \emptyset$ then $P(t, x)$ has a nonempty interior in the relative norm topology of X,

(iv) for every measurable function $x : T \to X, x(t) \notin \operatorname{con} P(t, x(t))$ for almost all $t \in T$.

Then there exists a measurable function $\bar{x} : T \to X$, such that $P(t, \bar{x}(t)) = \emptyset$ for almost all $t \in T$.

Proof. The proof is almost identical with the proof of Theorem 6.1. Define $\psi : T \times X \to 2^X$ by $\psi(t, x) = \operatorname{con} P(t, x)$. By virtue of Lemma 5.1 in Yannelis-Prabhakar (1983) for each $t \in T$ and each $y \in X$ the set $\psi^{-1}(t, y) = \{x \in X : y \in \psi(t, x)\}$ is open in the relative norm topology of X. By Theorem 4.1 there exists a Carathéodory-type selection from ψ. One can now proceed as in the proof of Theorem 6.1 to complete the proof.

Below we indicate how versions of Theorems 6.1 and 6.2 can be easily proved by combining the deterministic maximal elements results given in Yannelis-Prabhakar (1983) with the Aumann measurable selection theorem.

Theorem 6.1′. *Theorem 6.1 remains true if one replaces assumption (i) by*

(i′) $P(\cdot, \cdot)$ is lower measurable.

Proof. Define the correspondence $M : T \to 2^X$ by $M(t) = \{x \in X : P(t,x) = \emptyset\}$. It can be easily checked that for each fixed t in T, the correspondence $P(t,\cdot) : X \to 2^X$ satisfies all the assumptions of Theorem 5.2 in Yannelis-Prabhakar (1983, p. 239) and so for each fixed t in T, the correspondence $P(t,\cdot) : X \to 2^X$ has a maximal element, i.e., there exists $\bar{x}_t \in X$ such that $P(t,\bar{x}_t) = \emptyset$ for all t in T. Therefore, for each $t \in T, M(t) \neq \emptyset$. Since by assumption $P(\cdot,\cdot)$ is lower measurable, the set

$$\begin{aligned} A &= \{(t,x) \in T \times X : P(t,x) \neq \emptyset\} \\ &= \{(t,x) \in T \times X : P(t,x) \cap X \neq \emptyset\}, \end{aligned}$$

belongs to $\tau \otimes \beta(X)$, and so does the complement of the set A which is denoted by A^c. Observe now that

$$\begin{aligned} G_M &= \{(t,x) \in T \times X : x \in M(t)\} \\ &= \{(t,x) \in T \times X : P(t,x) = \emptyset\} \\ &= \{(t,x) \in T \times X : P(t,x) \neq \emptyset\}^c \\ &= A^c, \end{aligned}$$

and the latter set belongs to $\tau \otimes \beta(X)$ as it was noted above. Thus, $M(\cdot)$ has a measurable graph. We can not appeal to the Aumann measurable selection theorem to ensure the existence of a measurable function $\bar{x} : T \to X$ such that $\bar{x}(t) \in M(t)$ for almost all t in T, i.e., $P(t,\bar{x}(t)) = \emptyset$ for almost all t in T. This completes the proof of the Theorem.

Theorem 6.2. *Theorem 6.2 remains true if assumption (iii) is dropped and assumption (i) is replaced by*

(i′) $P(\cdot,\cdot)$ is lower measurable.

Proof. The proof is similar with that of Theorem 6.1′. Define $M : T \to 2^X$ by $M(t) = \{x \in X : P(t,x) = \emptyset\}$. Using Theorem 5.1 in Yannelis-Prabhakar (1983, p. 239) we can conclude that $M(t) \neq \emptyset$ for all t in T. Adopting the argument of the previous Theorem one can show that $G_M \in \tau \otimes \beta(X)$. Appeal now to the Aumann measurable selection theorem to complete the proof.

Remark 6.1. Theorems 6.1′ and 6.2′ remain true if we replace the assumption that (T, τ, μ) is a complete finite measure space by the fact that (T, τ) is a measurable space. The proofs remain the same provided that one observes that the correspondence $M : T \to 2^X$ defined by $M(t) = \{X \in X : P(t, x) = \emptyset\}$ is closed valued since for each $t \in T$, $P(t, \cdot)$ is l.s.c. (this is also true if for each $t \in T$ and each $y \in X$, $P^{-1}(t, y)$ is open in X). Since $M(\cdot)$ is closed valued and it has a measurable graph, it is also lower measurable (recall Lemma 3.1). By virtue of the Kuratowski and Ryll-Nardzewski measurable selection theorem, one can assure the existence of a measurable function $x^* : T \to X$ such that $x^*(t) \in M(t)$ for all $t \in T$, i.e., $P(t, x^*(t)) = \emptyset$ for all $t \in T$.

6.2 Random Equilibria. $\overline{\mathbf{E}} = \{(X_i, P_i, e_i) : i = 1, 2, \ldots, N\}$, an *exchange economy*, is a family of ordered triples (X_i, P_i, e_i) where,

(i) $X_i \subset \mathbb{R}^\ell$ is the *consumption set* of agent i ,

(ii) $P_i : X_i \to 2^{X_i}$ is the *preference correspondence* of agent i, and

(iii) e_i is the *initial endowment* of agent i, where $e_i \in X_i$ for all i.

The pair (e_i, P_i) constitutes the characteristics of agent i, i.e., his/her initial endowment and preference correspondence. The interpretation of the preference correspondence P_i is as in Section 6.1, i.e., we read $y_i \in P_i(x_i)$ as "agent i strictly prefers the consumption vector y_i to x_i."

Let $\Delta = \{q \in \Omega : \sum_{i=1}^{l} q_i = 1\}$ (where Ω denotes the positive cone of $\mathbb{R}^\ell$). For $p \in \Delta, B_i(p) = \{x \in X_i : p \cdot x \leq p \cdot e_i\}$ denotes the *budget set* of agent i, and $D_i(p) = \{x_i \in B_i(p) : P_i(x_i) \cap B_i(p) = \emptyset\}$ denotes the *demand set* of agent i.

Define the *aggregate excess demand* $\zeta : \Delta \to 2^{\mathbb{R}^\ell}$ for the economy $\overline{\mathbf{E}}$ by $\zeta(p) = \sum_{i=1}^{N} D_i(p) - \sum_{i=1}^{N} e_i$.

As in Debreu (1959) a *free disposal price equilibrium* is a vector $\bar{p} \in \Delta$ such that $\zeta(\bar{p}) \cap (-\Omega) \neq \emptyset$. A *price equilibrium* is a vector $\bar{p} \in \Delta$ such that $0 \in \zeta(\bar{p})$. conditions which guarantee the existence of either a free disposal price equilibrium or price equilibrium are by now well-known in the literature, see for instance Debreu (1959) and his references. We now amend the deterministic economy described above by introducing randomness.

Let (T, τ, μ) be a complete finite measure space.

A *random exchange economy* $\mathbf{E} = \{(X_i, P_i, e_i) : i = 1, 2, \ldots, N\}$ is a family of ordered triples (X_i, P_i, e_i), where

(i) $X_i \subset \mathbb{R}^\ell$ is the *consumption set* of agent i,

(ii) $P_i : T \times X_i \to 2^{X_i}$ is the *random preference correspondence* of agent i,

(iii) $e_i : T \to \mathbb{R}^\ell$ is the *random initial endowment* of agent i, where $e_i(t) \in X_i$ for all $t \in T$.

Notice that now each agent's characteristics, i.e., preferences and endowments depend on the state of nature. Hence, randomness is explicitly introduced into agents' characteristics. In this framework, $y_i \in P_i(t, x_i)$ means that "agent i strictly prefers y_i to x_i at the state of nature t."

For $p \in \Delta$ and $t \in T$ define the *random budget set* of agent i by $B_i(t,p) = \{x \in X_i : p \cdot x \leq p \cdot e_i(t)\}$ and the *random demand set* of agent i by $D_i(t,p) = \{x_i \in B_i(t,p) : P_i(t,x_i) \cap B_i(t,p) = \emptyset\}$. Define the *aggregate random excess demand* $\zeta : T \times \Delta \to 2^{\mathbb{R}^\ell}$ for the economy $\mathbf{E}$ by $\zeta(t,p) = \sum_{i=1}^N D_i(t,p) - \sum_{i=1}^N e_i(t)$. We now define the natural analogues of the ordinary concepts of price equilibrium.

A *free disposal random price equilibrium* is a measurable function $\bar{p} : T \to \Delta$ such that

$$\zeta(t, \bar{p}(t)) \cap (-\Omega) \neq \emptyset \qquad \text{for almost all } t \text{ in } T.$$

A *random price equilibrium* is a measurable function $\bar{p} : T \to \Delta$ such that

$$0 \in \zeta(t, \bar{p}(t)) \qquad \text{for almost all } t \text{ in } T.$$

Notice that now the equilibrium price (or the market clearing price) depends on the states of nature. Hence, in this framework the market clearing price will change from one state of the environment to another.

The concept of random price equilibria which is obviously a generalization of the ordinary (deterministic) notion of price equilibrium is not new. It can be traced to Bhattacharya-Majumdar (1973 Section IV, p. 45), Hildenbrand (1971, p. 427) and more recently to Weller (1982, p. 75).

Below we provide conditions which guarantee the existence of either a free disposal random price equilibria or a random price equilibria.

Theorem 6.3. *Let $\zeta : T \times \Delta \to 2^{\mathbb{R}^\ell}$ be a random aggregate excess demand correspondence, satisfying the following assumptions:*

(i) *For each* $t \in T, \zeta(t, \cdot)$ *is u.d.c.,*

(ii) $\zeta(\cdot, \cdot)$ *is lower measurable, i.e., for every open subset* V *of* $\mathbb{R}^\ell$, $\{(t,p) \in T \times \Delta : \zeta(t,p) \cap V \neq \emptyset\} \in \tau \otimes \beta(\Delta)$,

(iii) *for all* $(t,p) \in T \times \Delta, \zeta(t,p)$ *is convex, compact and nonempty,*

(iv) *for all measurable* $p : T \to \Delta$ *there exists* $z \in \zeta(t, p(t))$ *such that* $p(t) \cdot z \leq 0$ *for almost all* $t \in T$.

Then there exists a free disposal random equilibrium, i.e., there exists a measurable function $\bar{p} : T \to \Delta$ *such that* $\zeta(t, \bar{p}(t)) \cap (-\Omega) \neq \emptyset$ *for almost all* t *in* T.

Remark 6.2. Observe that Theorem 6.3 gives as a Corollary the ordinary (deterministic) Gale-Nikaido-Debreu (G-N-D) excess demand theorem [see for instance Debreu (1959, p. 82)] simply by fixing $t \in T$ and considering the correspondence $\zeta(t, \cdot) : \Delta \to 2^{\mathbb{R}^\ell}$. Also it is important to note that the argument which is adopted to prove Theorem 6.3 does not use the G-N-D theorem. The proof we give is direct (starts from "scratch") and provides an alternative way to prove the ordinary G-N-D result.

Proof of Theorem 6.3. Define the correspondence $F : T \times \Delta \to 2^\Delta$ by $F(t,p) = \{q \in \Delta : q \cdot z > 0 \text{ for all } z \in \zeta(t,p)\}$. We will show that the correspondence $F : T \times \Delta \to 2^\Delta$ satisfies all the properties of Theorem 6.1 and therefore it has a random maximal element. By construction the random maximal element, will turn out to be a random price equilibria.

(i) *The correspondence* $F : T \times \Delta \to 2^\Delta$ *is convex valued and for all measurable* $p : T \to \Delta, p(t) \notin F(t, p(t))$, *for almost all* t *in* T.

It can be easily checked that for all $(t,p) \in T \times \Delta, F(t,p)$ is convex. Moreover, it follows directly from assumption (iv) that $p(t) \notin \operatorname{con} F(t,p(t)) = F(t,p(t))$ for all measurable $p : T \to \Delta$ and all t in T.

(ii) *For each fixed* $t \in T, F(t, \cdot)$ *is l.s.c.*

By virtue of Proposition 4.1 in Yannelis-Prabhakar (1983) it suffices to show that for each $t \in T$ and each $q \in \Delta$ the set $F^{-1}(t,q) = \{p \in \Delta : q \in F(t,p)\}$ is open in Δ. To this end, let $V_q = \{x : q \cdot x > 0\}$ be an open half space in $\mathbb{R}^\ell$. Since for each t in $T, \zeta(t, \cdot)$ is u.d.c., the set $W = \{p \in \Delta : \zeta(t,p) \subset V_q\}$ is open in Δ. It can be easily checked that $W = F^{-1}(t, q)$. Therefore, for each $t \in T$ and each $q \in \Delta$ the set $F^{-1}(t, q)$ is open in the relative topology of Δ.

(iii) *The correspondence* $F : T \times \Delta \to 2^{\Delta}$ *is lower measurable.*

Setting $S = T \times \Delta, \alpha = \tau \otimes \beta(\Delta), \phi(s) = \zeta(t, p)$ and $\theta(s) = F(t, p)$ for $s = (t, p)$ in Lemma 3.10, we conclude that $F(\cdot, \cdot)$ is lower measurable.

Therefore, the correspondence, $F : T \times \Delta \to 2^{\Delta}$ satisfies all the assumptions of Theorem 6.1 and consequently, there exists a measurable function $\bar{p} : T \to \Delta$ such that $F(t, \bar{p}(t)) = \emptyset$ for all t in T, i.e.,

(6.1) for all $q \in \Delta$ there exists $z \in \zeta(t, \bar{p}(t))$ such that $q \cdot z \leq 0$ for almost all t in T.

We now show that (6.1) implies that

$$\zeta(t, \bar{p}(t)) \cap (-\Omega) \neq \emptyset \text{ for almost all } t \text{ in } T. \tag{6.2}$$

Suppose otherwise, then for all $t \in A$, where A is a non-null subset of $T, \zeta(t, \bar{p}(t)) \cap (-\Omega) = \emptyset$. Since $\zeta : T \times \Delta \to 2^{\mathbb{R}^{\ell}}$ is convex and compact valued and $-\Omega$ is a closed convex cone, the sets $\zeta(t, \bar{p}(t))$ and $-\Omega$ can be strictly separated, i.e., there exist $r \in \mathbb{R}^{\ell}, r \neq 0$ and $b \in R$ such that

$$\sup_{y \in -\Omega} r \cdot y < b < \inf_{x \in \zeta(t, \bar{p}(t))} r \cdot x \tag{6.3}$$

Notice that $b > 0$ and $r \geq 0$. Without loss of generality we may assume that $r \in \Delta$. It follows from (6.3) that $r \cdot z > 0$ for all $z \in \zeta(t, \bar{p}(t))$ and for all $t \in A$, a contradiction to (6.1). Hence, (6.2) holds and this completes the proof of the Theorem.

Notice that the dimensionality of the commodity spaces in Theorem 6.3 is finite. We now provide an extension of Theorem 6.3 to infinite dimensional commodity space and in particular to a separable Banach space whose positive cone has a nonempty norm interior. The Theorem below may be seen as a generalization of the deterministic equilibrium results of Florenzano (1983) and Yannelis (1985), but only if the underlying commodity space is separable.

Theorem 6.4. *Let Y be a separable Banach space, C the closed convex cone of Y, having an interior point $u, C^* = \{p \in Y^* : p \cdot x \leq 0$ for all $x \in C\} \neq \{0\}$ the dual cone of C and $\tilde{\Delta} = \{p \in C^* : p \cdot u = -1\}$ be the* *price space. Let $\zeta : T \times \tilde{\Delta} \to 2^Y$ be an aggregate random excess demand correspondence satisfying the following conditions:*

(i) For each $t \in T, \zeta(t,\cdot) : \tilde{\Delta} \to 2^Y$ is u.d.c., in the weak topology, (i.e., $\zeta(t,\cdot) : (\tilde{\Delta}, w^*) \to 2^Y$ is u.d.c.),*

(ii) $\zeta(\cdot,\cdot)$ is lower measurable, i.e., for every open subset V of $Y, \{(t,p) \in T \times \tilde{\Delta} : \zeta(t,p) \cap V \neq \emptyset\} \in \tau \otimes \beta_{w^*}(\tilde{\Delta})$, where $\beta_{w^*}(\tilde{\Delta})$ is the Borel σ-algebra for the weak topology on $\tilde{\Delta}$,*

(iii) $\zeta(t,p)$ is convex, compact and nonempty for all $(t,p) \in T \times \Delta$,

(iv) for all measurable $p : T \to \tilde{\Delta}$, there exists $x \in \zeta(t, p(t))$ such that $p(t) \cdot x \leq 0$, for all $t \in T$.

Then there exists a measurable function $\bar{p} : T \to \tilde{\Delta}$ such that $\zeta(t, \bar{p}(t)) \cap C \neq \emptyset$ for almost all t in T.

Proof. We begin by proving an elementary fact.

Fact 6.1. *Let X be a Hausdorff linear topological space, C a closed convex cone of X having an interior point u and $C^* = \{p \in X^* : p \cdot x \leq 0$ for all $x \in C\} \neq \{0\}$ be the dual cone of C. Then $r \cdot u < 0$ for any $r \in C^*$.*

Proof. Suppose by way of contradiction that for some $r \in C^*, r \cdot u = 0$. Pick a symmetric neighborhood V of zero with $u + V \subseteq C$. If $x \in X$, then for some $\lambda > 0$ we have that $\pm\lambda x \in V$ and consequently $\pm\lambda r \cdot x = r(u \pm \lambda x) \leq 0$. Hence, $r \cdot x = 0$ for each $x \in X$, i.e., $r = 0$, a contradiction. Therefore, $r \cdot u < 0$ for any $r \in C^*$, and this completes the proof of the Fact.

We now proceed with the proof of Theorem 6.4, whose idea is essentially the same with that of Theorem 6.3. Define the correspondence $F : T \times \tilde{\Delta} \to 2^{\tilde{\Delta}}$ by

$$F(t,p) = \{q \in \tilde{\Delta} : q \cdot z > 0 \text{ for all } z \in \zeta(t,p)\}.$$

First notice that by Alaoglu's theorem $\tilde{\Delta}$ is weak* compact [Jameson (1970, Theorem 3.8, p. 123)]. Moreover, since Y is a separable Banach space, $\tilde{\Delta}$ is a compact metric space. Adopting the arguments used in the proof of Theorem 6.3 one can easily see that $F : T \times \tilde{\Delta} \to 2^{\tilde{\Delta}}$ satisfies all the properties of Theorem 6.2 (of course, one now has to use Lemma 3.9 to show that $G_F \in \tau \otimes \beta_{w^*}(\tilde{\Delta}) \otimes \beta_{w^*}(\tilde{\Delta})$). Hence, there exists a measurable function $\bar{p} : T \to \tilde{\Delta}$ such that $F(t, \bar{p}(t)) = \emptyset$ for almost all t in T, i.e.,

(6.4) for all $q \in \tilde{\Delta}$ there exists $z \in \zeta(t, \bar{p}(t))$ such that $q \cdot z \leq 0$ for almost all t in T.

We show that (6.4) implies that

$$\zeta(t, \bar{p}(t)) \cap C \neq \emptyset \quad \text{for almost all } t \text{ in } T. \tag{6.5}$$

Suppose otherwise, then for all t in a non-null subset A of T, $\zeta(t, \bar{p}(t)) \cap C = \emptyset$. By the separating hyperplane theorem there exist $r \in Y^*/\{0\}$ and $b \in \mathbb{R}$ such that

$$\sup_{y \in C} r \cdot y < b < \inf_{x \in \zeta(t, \bar{p}(t))} r \cdot x. \tag{6.6}$$

Notice that $b > 0$ and $r \in C^*$. Without loss of generality we may assume that $r \in \tilde{\Delta}$. In fact, if $r \notin \tilde{\Delta}$ then $u \in \operatorname{int} C$ implies (recall Fact 6.1) that $r \cdot u < 0$ and we can replace r by $\frac{u}{-r \cdot u}$. It follows from (6.6) that $r \cdot z > 0$ for all $z \in \zeta(t, \bar{p}(t))$ for all $t \in A$, a contradiction to (6.4) Hence, (6.5) holds and this completes the proof of Theorem 6.4.

Remark 6.3. As we noted earlier Theorem 6.4 may be seen as a generalization of the deterministic equilibrium results of Florenzano (1983) and Yannelis (1985). Moreover, our arguments adopted for the proof of Theorem 6.4 provide an alternative way to prove the above deterministic equilibrium results of the above authors. We do wish however to indicate that a version of Theorem 6.4 can be easily obtained by combining the deterministic result in Yannelis (1985) with the Aumann measurable selection theorem as follows:

Theorem 6.4′. *Replace assumption (ii) in Theorem 6.4 by*

(ii′) $\zeta(\cdot, \cdot)$ *is measurable, i.e., for every closed subset* V *of* Y*, the set* $\{(t, p) \in T \times \tilde{\Delta} : \zeta(p, t) \cap V \neq \emptyset\}$ *belongs to* $\tau \otimes \beta_{w^*}(\tilde{\Delta})$.

Suppose that conditions (i), (iii) and (iv) of Theorem 6.4 are satisfied. Then the conclusion of Theorem 6.4 holds.

Proof. Define the correspondence $W : T \to 2^{\tilde{\Delta}}$ by

$$W(t) = \{p \in \tilde{\Delta} : \zeta(t, p) \cap C \neq \emptyset\}.$$

By Theorem 3.1 in Yannelis (1985, p. 597) for each fixed $t \in T$ there exists $\bar{p}_t \in \tilde{\Delta}$ such that $\zeta(t, \bar{p}_t) \cap C \neq \emptyset$. Therefore, $W(t) \neq \emptyset$ for all $t \in T$. Observe that

$$\begin{aligned} G_W &= \{(t,p) \in T \times \tilde{\Delta} : p \in W(t)\} \\ &= \{(t,p) \in T \times \tilde{\Delta} : \zeta(t,p) \cap C \neq \emptyset\}. \end{aligned}$$

It follows, at once from the measurability of $\zeta(\cdot\, ,\cdot)$, [assumption (ii′)] that $G_W \in \tau \otimes \beta_{w^*}(\tilde{\Delta})$, i.e., $W(\cdot)$ has a measurable graph. Appeal now to the Aumann measurable selection theorem to ensure the existence of a measurable function $\bar{p} : T \to \tilde{\Delta}$ such that $\bar{p}(t) \in W(t)$ for almost all t in T, i.e., $\zeta(t, \bar{p}(t)) \cap C \neq \emptyset$ for almost all t in T.

Bibliographical Notes. All the results in this section are new. They generalize the deterministic results on the existence of maximal elements of Sonnenschein (1971), and Yannelis-Prabhakar (1983) as well as the excess demand equilibrium existence theorems of Debreu (1959), Aliprantis-Brown (1983), Florenzano (1983) and Yannelis (1985), among others.

References

Aliprantis, C. D. and Brown, D. J., 1983, "Equilibria in Markets with a Riesz Space of Commodities," *J. Math. Econ.* **11**, 189–207.

Aliprantis, C. D. and Burkinshaw, O., 1985, *Positive Operators*, Academic Press, New York.

Aumann, R. J., 1967, "Measurable Utility and the Measurable Choice Theorem," in *La Decision*, 15–26, CNRS, Aix-en-Provence.

Balder, E. J. and Yannelis, N. C., 1990, "Equilibria in Random and Bayesian Games with a Continuum of Players," this volume.

Bhattacharya, R. N. and Majumdar, M., 1973, "Random Exchange Economies," *J. Econ. Theory* **6**, 37–67.

Browder, F., 1968, "The Fixed Point Theory of Multivalued Mappings in Topological Vector Spaces," *Math. Ann.* **177**, 283–301.

Castaing, C., 1979, "Sur l'existence des Sections Séparément Continues d'une Multi-Application," in *Travaux du Seminaire d'analyse Convexe*, Univ. des. Sci. et Techniques du Languedoc **5**, 14.

Castaing, C. and Valadier, M., 1977, "Convex Analysis and Measurable Multifunctions," *Lecture Notes in Mathematics* **580**, Springer-Verlag, New York.

Debreu, G., 1959, *Theory of Value*, John Wiley and Sons, New York.

Debreu, G., 1967, "Integration of Correspondences," *Proc. Fifth Berkeley Symp. Math. Stat. Prob.*, University of California Press, Berkeley, Vol. II, Part I, 351–372.

Dugundji, J., 1966, *Topology*, Allyn and Bacon, Boston.

Fan, K., 1952, "Fixed Point and Minimax Theorems in Locally Convex Topological Linear Spaces," *Proc. Natl. Acad. Sci. USA* **38**, 131–136.

Fan, K., 1969, "Extensions of Two Fixed Point Theorems of F. E. Browder," *Math. Z.* **112**, 234–240.

Florenzano, M., 1983, "On the Existence of Equilibria in Economies with an Infinite Dimensional Commodity Space," *J. Math. Econ.* **12**, 207–219.

Fryszkowski, A., 1977, "Carathéodory-type Selectors of Set-Valued Maps of Two Variables," *Bull. Acad. Polon. Sci.* **25**, 41–46.

Glicksberg, I. L., 1952, "A Further Generalization of the Kakutani Fixed Point Theorem, with Applications to Nash Equilibrium Points," *Proc. Amer. Math. Soc.* **3**, 170–174.

Hildenbrand, W., 1971, "Random Preferences and Equilibrium Analysis," *J. Econ. Theory* **3**, 414–429.

Himmelberg, C. J., 1975, "Measurable Relations," *Fund. Math.* **87**, 53–72.

Itoh, S., 1979, "Random Fixed Point Theorems with Applications to Random Differential Equations in Banach Spaces," *J. Math. Anal. Appl.* **67**, 261–273.

Jameson, C., 1970, *Ordered Linear Spaces*, Springer-Verlag, New York.

Kim, T., Prikry, K. and Yannelis N. C., 1987, "Carathéodory-Type Selections and Random Fixed Point Theorems," *J. Math. Anal. Appl.* **122**, 393–407.

Kim, T., Prikry, K. and Yannelis, N. C., 1988, "On a Carathéodory-Type Selection Theorem," *J. Math. Anal. Appl.* **135**, 664–670.

Kim, T., Prikry, K. and Yannelis, N. C., 1989, "Equilibria in Abstract Economies with a Measure Space of Agents and with an Infinite Dimensional Strategy Space," *J. Approx. Theory* **56**, 256–266.

Kuratowski, K., 1966, *Topology*, Vol. I, Academic Press, New York.

Kuratowski, K. and Ryll-Nardzewski, C., 1965, "A General Theorem on Selectors," *Bull. Acad. Polon. Sci. Ser. Sci. Marsh. Astronom. Phys.* **13**, 397–403.

Michael, E., 1956, "Continuous Selections I," *Ann. Math.* **63**, 363–382.

Rybiński, L., 1985, "On Carathéodory Type Selections," *Fund. Math.* **125**, 187–193.

Sonnenschein, H., 1971, "Demand Theory without Transitive Preferences with Applications to the Theory of Competitive Equilibrium," in *Preferences, Utility, and Demand*, J. Chipman, L. Hurwicz, M. K. Richter and H. Sonnenschein, eds., Harcourt Brace Jovanovich, New York.

Weller, P. A., 1982, "The Speed of Convergence of Prices in Random Exchange Economies," *J. Econ. Theory* **28**, 71–81.

Yannelis, N. C., 1985, "On a Market Equilibrium Theorem with an Infinite Number of Commodities," *J. Math. Anal. Appl.* **108**, 595–599.

Yannelis, N. C., 1987, "Equilibria in Noncooperative Models of Competition," *J. Econ. Theory* **41**, 96–111.

Yannelis, N. C., 1990, "On the Upper and Lower Semicontinuity of the Aumann Integral," *J. Math. Econ.* **19**, 373–389.

Yannelis, N. C., 1990a, "Integration of Banach-Valued Correspondences," this volume.

Yannelis, N. C. and Prabhakar, N. D., 1983, "Existence of Maximal Elements and Equilibria in Linear Topological Spaces," *J. Math. Econ.* **12**, 233–245.

Yannelis, N. C. and Rustichini, A., 1991, "Equilibrium Points of Noncooperative Random and Bayesian Games," in *Positive Operators, Riesz Spaces, and Economics*, C. D. Aliprantis, K. C. Border and W. A. J. Luxemburg, eds., Springer-Verlag, forthcoming.

PART 2

EQUILIBRIA, CORE, AND PARETO OPTIMALITY

A Theorem on the Existence of Competitive Equilibria in a Market with a Finite Number of Agents and Whose Commodity Space is L_∞ *

Truman F. Bewley

The current effort to develop the theory of markets with an infinite dimensional commodity space has not yet yielded a very general theorem on the existence of competitive equilibria.[1] The absence of such a result is perhaps explained by the great difficulty, if not impossibility, of applying the standard fixed point theorem arguments. The difficulty arises because the key steps in the argument deal with subsets of the commodity space and its dual. But when the commodity space becomes infinite dimensional, these subsets lose many of the nice properties they have when they lie in $\mathbb{R}^n$.

In this circumstance, it is natural to search for a way to prove existence theorems that uses sets whose dimensionality does not depend on that of the commodity space. In this paper, one will find a form of proof for which this dimensionality depends on the number of consumers in the economy rather than on the commodity space. This argument is used to prove the existence of an equilibrium in a market whose commodity space is L_∞ and in which all preference relations are continuous with respect

---

* A short mathematical appendix appears at the end of this paper.

[1] For a result in this direction, see Bezalel Peleg and Menahem Yaari, "Markets with Countably Many Commodities," Research Program in Game Theory and Mathematical Economics, Research Memorandum No. 37, Department of Mathematics, The Hebrew University of Jerusalem, Israel. Profs. Werner Hildenbrand and Gerard Debreu also have an unpublished result on the existence of equilibria in markets with infinite dimensional commodity spaces.

to the Mackey topology for the duality (L_∞, L_1).[2] However, it can be expected that the method of proof used here may be applied to markets with infinite dimensional commodity space other than L^∞.

The economic model and notation used here follow closely those of Gerard Debreu's private ownership economy in *Theory of Value* (Wiley: 1959). For convenience, the commodity space will be denoted by S. Positive linear functionals on S will be called price systems. The economy considered will have a finite number of consumers, denoted $a_1, \ldots, a_n$, and a finite number of producers, denoted $b_1, \ldots, b_m$. The consumption of each a_i is restricted to this consumption set, $X_i \subset S$. Similarly, the production possibilities of b_j are a set, $Y_j \subset S$. Each consumer, a_i, has a preference preordering, $\succsim_i$, defined on X_i. a_i also has certain resources at his disposal, namely, an initial endowment $w_i \in S$, and a share, θ_{ij}, in the profits of the jth producer, where $0 \leq \theta_{ij} \leq 1$, $\forall ij$, and $\sum_{j=1}^m \theta_{ij} = 1$, $\forall i$. A state of the economy, or an allocation, is an $(m+n)$-tuple $(f, y) = (f_1, \ldots, f_n; y_1, \ldots, y_m)$ of points in S such that $f_i \in X_i$, $y_j \in Y_j$, $\forall i, j$. An allocation is said to be feasible if $\sum_{i=1}^n f_i = \sum_{i=1}^n w_i + \sum_{j=1}^m y_j$. A feasible allocation, (f, y), is said to be a Pareto optimum if there exists no other feasible allocation $(\bar{f}, \bar{y})$ such that $\bar{f}_i \succsim_i f_i$, $\forall i$, and $\bar{f}_i \succ_i f_i$ for at least one i. A feasible allocation (f, y) is said to be a competitive equilibrium if and only if there exists a price system, p, such that 1) for each i, f_i is a $\succsim_i$-maximal point in the budget set $\{s \in X_i : p \cdot s \leq p \cdot w + \sum_{j=1}^m \theta_{ij} p \cdot y_j\}$, and 2) for each j, y_j is such that $p \cdot y_j = \sup\{p \cdot s : s \in Y_j\}$.

The theorem proved in this paper is for an economy with no producers. The reason that producers are excluded is that their inclusion complicates the proof without adding any essentially new problems. At the end of the paper one will find a discussion of how the theorem can be extended to include production.

Before continuing, it is necessary to establish a few notational conventions. The spaces that appear in this paper are Euclidean n-space, $\mathbb{R}^n$, and the spaces $L_\infty(B, \mathcal{B}, \nu)$, $L_1(B, \mathcal{B}, \nu)$, and $ba(B, \mathcal{B}, \nu)$, where $(B, \mathcal{B}, \nu)$ is some positive measure space. Each of these is a space of real-valued functions. $\mathbb{R}^n$ is the set of all functions on n indices, $ba(B, \mathcal{B}, \nu)$ is the

[2] See the mathematical appendix for a brief description of this topology.

set of all bounded additive set functions on $\mathcal{B}$, absolutely continuous with respect to ν, and $L_\infty(B,\mathcal{B},\nu)$ and $L_1(B,\mathcal{B},\nu)$ are spaces of functions on B. Let x and y belong to one of these four vector spaces. Then $x \geq y$ means that $x - y$ is a non-negative function and $x > y$ means $x \geq y$ and $x \neq y$. If x and y are in either $\mathbb{R}^n$ or L_∞, then $x \gg y$ means that $x - y > 0$ and is bounded away from zero.

Theorem.[3] *Let $E = (S,(X_i,\succsim_i,w_i),\ i = 1,\ldots,n)$ be an economy which satisfies the following:*

1) *$S = L_\infty(B,\mathcal{B},\nu)$, where $(B,\mathcal{B},\nu)$ is a positive measure space,*
2) *$\forall i$, $X_i = x_i + K$, where $K = \{s \in S : s \geq 0\}$ = the positive cone of S,*
3) *$\forall i$, $w_i \gg x_i$,*
4) *$\forall i$, $\succsim_i$ is*
   a) *Mackey continuous, that is, for each $\underline{s} \in X_i$, the sets $\{s \in X_i : s \succsim_i \underline{s}\}$ and $\{s \in X_i : s \precsim_i \underline{s}\}$ are closed in X_i with respect to the Mackey topology for the duality (L_∞, L_1),*
   b) *weakly convex, that is, for each $\underline{s} \in X_i$, the set $\{s \in X_i : s \succsim_i \underline{s}\}$ is convex,*
   c) *strongly monotone, that is, $s \in X_i$ and $k > 0$ implies that $s + k \succ_i s$,*
   d) *complete, that is, if $s_1, s_2 \in X_i$, then either $s_1 \succsim_i s_2$ or $s_2 \succsim s_1$.*

If all these conditions are satisfied by E, then E has an equilibrium with respect to a price in L_1. That is, there exists a $p \in L_1$ and an $e = (e_1,\ldots,e_n)$ such that $e_i \in X_i$, $\sum_{i=1}^n e_i = \sum_{i=1}^n w_i$, $p > 0$, and e_i is maximal with respect to $\succsim_i$ in the set $\{s \in X_i : p \cdot s \leq p \cdot w_i\}$.

Proof. In Proposition 6 below it is proved that if an allocation, e is an equilibrium with respect to a price in *ba*, then e is an equilibrium with respect to some price in L_1. Thus, it is sufficient to prove that there exists an equilibrium with respect to some price in *ba*.

Before reading the details of the proof that there exists such an equilibrium, it will be helpful to understand in simple terms the basic form of the argument. This form can be understood quite easily by consideration

[3] This theorem was conjectured by Professors Gerard Debreu and Werner Hildenbrand.

of the usual Edgeworth box. A very simple argument, which shows that the market usually represented by an Edgeworth box has an equilibrium, extends directly to a proof of the above theorem.

The Edgeworth box drawn in Figure 1 represents a market with two agents, each of whom chooses positive quantities of two infinitely divisible commodities. Thus, the consumption set for each agent is the positive quadrant of $\mathbb{R}^2$. The consumption set of agent 1 is represented as the quadrant $X_1O_1Y_1$ and that of agent 2 is $X_2O_2Y_2$. Each agent has an initial endowment w_i in the interior of his consumption set, and the representations of w_1 and w_2 coincide at w. The points in the box which is the intersection of the quadrants $X_1O_1Y_1$ and $X_2O_2Y_2$ represent the set of allocations (s_1, s_2) satisfying $s_1 + s_2 = w_1 + w_2$. If s is a point in this box, the value of s in the quadrant $X_iO_iY_i$ will be denoted s_i.

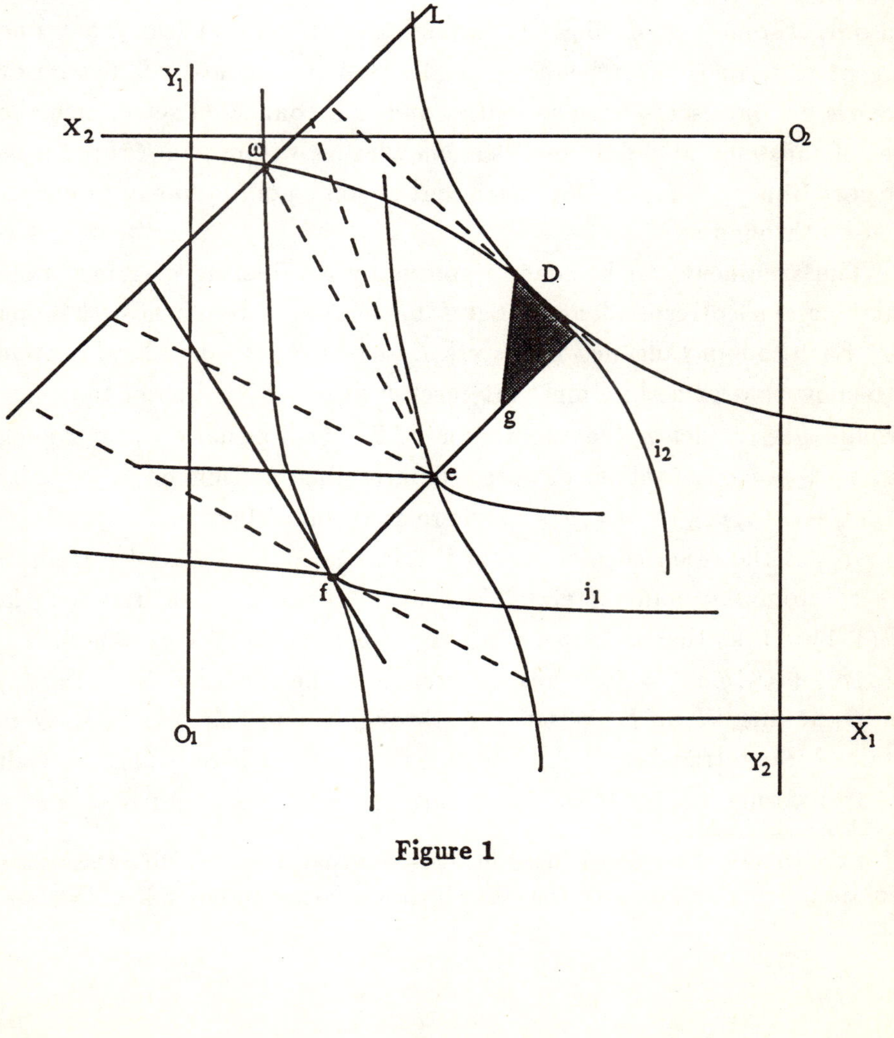

Figure 1

It is assumed that each agent has a convex, continuous, monotone, and complete preference preordering, $\succsim_i$, represented by a utility function u_i satisfying $u_i(w_i) = 0$. The indifference curve of agent j through w is drawn heavily in Figure 1 and labeled i_j.

If a competitive equilibrium exists, it is a Pareto optimum, and the allocation to each agent is at least as desired as his initial endowment. The set of allocations with these two properties, called $\mathcal{O}$ hereafter, is the set of points above i_1 and below i_2 which lie on a point of tangency between an indifference curve of agent 1 and one of agent 2. In Figure 1, $\mathcal{O}$ is represented as the line fg and the shaded area. The method of proof is to obtain a contradiction if $\mathcal{O}$ does not contain an equilibrium.

Clearly, to each $g \in \mathcal{O}$, there corresponds one or more lines through g tangent to the two indifferences curves through g.[4] These lines will be called lines of tangency. It is easy to see that $g \in \mathcal{O}$ is an equilibrium if and only if some line of tangency through g contains w. Clearly, any line tangent to i_1 lines on or below w. and any line tangent to i_2 lies on or above w. $\mathcal{O}$ intersects both i_1 and i_2 and is a connected set. Since the lines of tangency at points in $\mathcal{O}$ somehow move without interruption as one goes from i_1 to i_2, one feels sure that at some point a line of tangency must go through w.

The argument can be made rigorous by considering certain simple functions and correspondences. Let L be the line through w with slope one. Each line of tangency intersects L at one point, and the objective is to show that some line must intersect L at w. If c is line of tangency through $g \in \mathcal{O}$, let p_c be the vector in $\mathbb{R}^2_+$ orthogonal to c and such that $p_1 + p_2 = 1$, that is, the price determining c. Define $\psi_j(g, p_c)$ by $p_c \cdot (w_j + \psi_j(g, p_c)(1,1)) = p_c \cdot g_j$, where a dot indicates a scalar product. $\psi_j(g, p_c)$ is the oriented distance of the intersection of L and c from w as seen from the point of view of agent j. Since p_c is of unit length, $p_c \cdot (1,1) = 1$, so that $\psi_j(g, p_c) = p_c \cdot (g_j - w_j)$. Since $g_1 + g_2 = w_1 + w_2$, $\psi_1(g, p_c) + \psi_2(g, p_c) = 0$. Thus, the range of the function $\psi = (\psi_1, \psi_2)$ lies in the line, H, in $\mathbb{R}^2$ which goes through 0 and has slope -1. H is obtained if one translates L by $-w$ and then rotates it by $-(1/2)\pi$. Call this transformation γ. If ψ_1 maps onto the line O_1X_1 and if ψ_2 maps

[4] Here the word tangent is used in the sense that a straight line through a point on a curve is tangent to the curve if the curve lies on one side of the line.

onto O_1Y_1, then $\psi(g, p_c)$ is simply the image under γ of the intersection of L and c. This geometric description of ψ was not used to define it because it does not generalize easily to the case of markets with more than two agents.

Next, let $\Psi : \mathcal{O} \to H$ be the correspondence defined by $\Psi(g) = \{\psi(g, p_c) : c$ is a line of tangency at $g\}$. Observe that $\Psi(g)$ is always a convex set. A moment's reflection shows that g is a competitive equilibrium if and only if $O \in \Psi(g)$.

Suppose that $0 \notin \cup Ra\Psi$. Then we may compose Ψ with the radial projection $\rho : H \setminus \{0\} \to H$ defined by $\rho(r) = r/||r||$, and one obtains the correspondence $\rho \circ \Psi$ from $\mathcal{O}$ into $S_o = \left\{\left(-\frac{1}{\sqrt{2}}, \frac{1}{\sqrt{2}}\right), \left(\frac{1}{\sqrt{2}}, -\frac{1}{\sqrt{2}}\right)\right\}$. S_o is a zero dimensional sphere and is disconnected. If g lies in the indifference curve i_1 in Figure 1, then, since any tangent line must lie on or below w, $\rho\circ\Psi(g) = \left(\frac{1}{\sqrt{2}}, -\frac{1}{\sqrt{2}}\right)$. Similarly, a point in i_2 maps to $\left(-\frac{1}{\sqrt{2}}, \frac{1}{\sqrt{2}}\right)$. Thus, $\rho \circ \Psi$ maps onto S_o. The fact that Ψ was convex-valued means that $\rho \circ \Psi$ is always either one of the two points in S_o, but never both. Thus, $\rho \circ \Psi$ is a function mapping onto a disconnected set S_o. If we had proved that $\rho \circ \Psi$ were continuous and $\mathcal{O}$ connected, we would have a contradiction, for the continuous image of a connected set is connected. In fact, it is easy to show that $\mathcal{O}$ is connected and that $\rho \circ \Psi$ is continuous, but in order to generalize the argument to the case of more than two agents it is necessary to make further constructions.

Let $u : \mathcal{O} \to \mathbb{R}^2$ be the function defined by $u(g) = (u_1(g_1), u_2(g_2))$. u in fact maps in to $\mathbb{R}^2_+$, since it is assumed that $u_i(w_i) = 0$. Let $\mathcal{U} = u(\mathcal{O})$. It is possible to show that $\phi = \Psi \circ u^{-1}$ is an upper-semi-continuous correspondence.[5] (Consult Figure 2 in order to follow the web of maps described here.) It is also possible to show that $\mathcal{U}$ is homeomorphic to the unit 2-simplex $\Delta_2 = \{r \in \mathbb{R}^2 : r \geq 0, r_1 + r_2 = 1\}$ under the radial projection $h : \mathcal{U} \to \Delta_2$ defined by $h(v) = \left(\frac{v_1}{v_1+v_2} \frac{v_2}{v_1+v_2}\right)$. Finally, Δ_2 is homeomorphic to the interval E_1 whose end points are the two points of S_o. Let $\beta : E_1 \to \Delta_2$ be any homeomorphism. Finally, let $\xi : E_1 \to S_o$ be the composition $\xi = \rho \circ \phi \circ h^{-1} \cdot \beta$. Since ϕ is upper-semi-continuous

[5] Throughout this paper, a correspondence $C : A \to B$ from one topological space, A, into another, B, will be said to be upper-semi-continuous if and only if for every open set $O \subset B$, the set $\{a \in A : C(a) \subset O\}$ is open in A.

and convex valued, and since $\rho \circ \phi$ is onto S_o, ξ is a continuous function from E_1 to S_o, which is impossible since E_1 is connected and S_o is not.

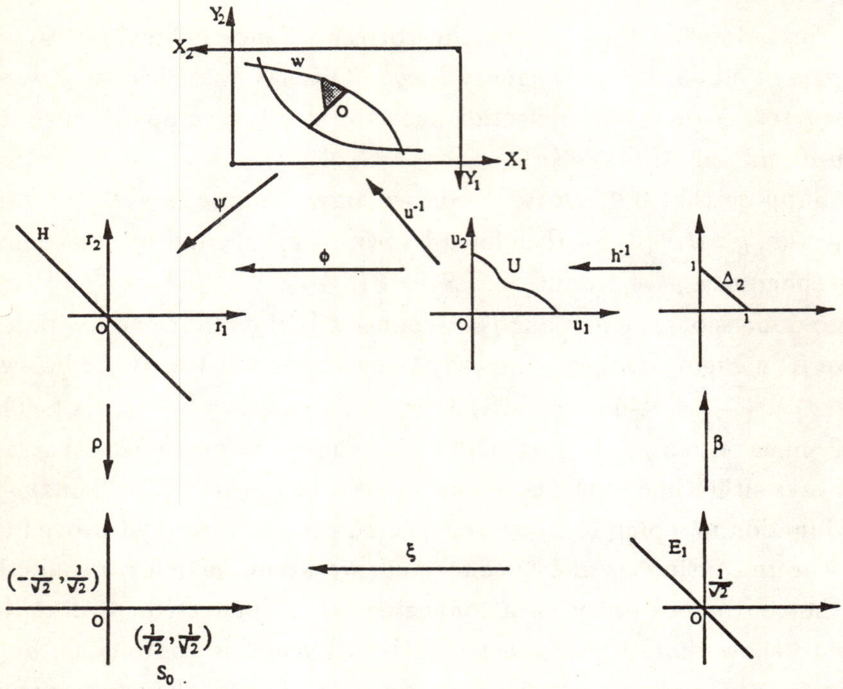

Figure 2

In the case of $n > 2$ agents, one obtains in a parallel fashion an upper-semi-continuous correspondence $\xi : E_{n-1} \to S_{n-2}$, which factors through Δ_n, where E_{n-1} is the $n-1$ dimensional ball $\{r \in \mathbb{R}^n : \sum r_i = 0, \|r\| \leq 1\}$, S_{n-2} is its bounding sphere, and Δ_n is the n-simplex $\{r \in \mathbb{R}^n : r \geq 0, \sum r_i = 1\}$. In constructing ξ, it is important to let the homeomorphism $\beta : E_{n-1} \to \Delta_n$ be such that if r is in the boundary of Δ_n, $\beta^{-1}(r) = \frac{(r-1/n,\ldots,1/n)}{\|r-(1/n,\ldots,1/n)\|}$. Since S_{n-2} is connected if $n \geq 3$, one can no longer use the simple argument made above involving connectedness. However, a more complicated argument is still possible.

Suppose for simplicity that the correspondence ξ is a function. In this case, the upper semi-continuity of ξ implies that it is continuous. Let $a : S_{n-2} \to S_{n-2}$ be the antipodal map, $a(r) = -r$. We will show that $a(r) \neq \xi(r)$, $\forall r \in S_{n-2}$. This is a contradiction for the following reasons.

An elementary result of homotopy theory is that if two maps from a sphere to itself are never equal, one is homotopic to the composition of the other with the antipodal map.[6] Thus, $\xi\ |_{S_{n-2}}$ is homotopic to $a \cdot a = id$, where id is the identity map of S_{n-2}. A second elementary result of homotopy theory is that if a map on a sphere can be extended over the ball in its interior, then the map is homotopic to a constant map. $\xi\ |_{S_{n-2}}$ has the extension ξ, so that it is homotopically trivial. The relation of homotopy is an equivalence relation among maps, so that we have proved that the identity map on S_{n-2} is homotopic to a constant map. But this is impossible for a number of reasons. For instance, the identity map on S_{n-2} induces the identity map on the $n-2^{\text{nd}}$ homology group of S_{n-2}, $H_{n-2}(S_{n-2})$, while a constant map induces the zero map on $H_{n-2}(S_{n-2})$. Since $H_{n-2}(S_{n-2})$ is isomorphic to the group of integers and since homotopic maps induce the same function on $H_{n-2}(S_{n-2})$, we have a contradiction.

To see that $\xi\ |_{S_{n-2}}$ is never equal to the antipodal map, consider the ith face, F_i' of the simplex Δ_n, that is, $F_i' = \{r \in \Delta_n : r_i = 0\}$, and let $F_i = \beta^{-1}(F_i')$. Clearly, $\bigcup_{i=1}^n F_i = S_{n-2}$. The fact that ξ never equals a on F_i follows from the extension to n dimensions of the observation made in Figure 1 that lines tangent to i_1 lie on or below w.

Each Pareto optimum is cost minimizing with respect to some price system in the sense that $g = (g_1, \ldots, g_n)$ is cost minimizing with respect to p if, $\forall i$, $s \succsim_i g_i$ implies that $p \cdot s \geq p \cdot g_i$. In the discussion illustrated by Figure 1, a line of tangency through an optimum g is orthogonal to a price with respect to which g is cost minimizing. The correspondence $\Psi : \mathcal{O} \rightarrow \mathbb{R}^n$ used in the definition of ξ is defined by $\Psi(g) = \{p \cdot (g - w) : g$ is case minimizing with respect to $p\}$.

Now let $r \in F_j$. Then $\xi(r)$ is equal to $\rho \circ \Psi(g)$, where ρ is the radial projection of $\mathbb{R}^n \setminus \{0\}$ on to the unit sphere and where g is an optimum such that $r = \beta^{-1} h(u_1(g_1), \ldots, u_n(g_n))$. But since $r \in F_j$, $u_j(g_j) = 0$, that is, $g_j \sim_j w_j$. Therefore, if g is cost minimizing with respect to p, $p \cdot (g_j - w_j) \leq 0$. This means that the jth component of $\Psi(g)$ is less than or equal to zero, and hence that $\xi(r)$ lies in or below the hyperplane $\{r \in \mathbb{R}^n : r_j = 0\}$. But it is easy to see that if $r \in F_j$, then $a(r)$ lies above

[6] The relation of homotopy between maps is defined in the mathematical appendix.

this hyperplane. Thus, $a(r) \neq \xi(r)\ \forall i \in F_j$.

Many steps in the reasoning sketched above have been left out, but if the reader were to try to fill in these steps, he would find that all arguments involving the commodity space are quite simple and do not depend on the dimensionality of the commodity space. It is the unimportance of the role played by the commodity space that makes it possible to extend the argument to the case of an infinite dimensional commodity space.

To make this extension to the case described in the Theorem, it is first necessary to verify that the preference relation of each agent can be represented by a utility function. That it can be so represented follows from the assumption of strong monotonicity, for choose $k \gg x_i$, where $X_i = x_i + K$. Then, if $s \in X_i$, for some $\alpha > 0$, $\alpha(k - x_i) + x_i > s$. But then, $\alpha(k - x_i) + x_i \succ_i x_i$. Since $O \cdot (k - x_i) + x_i = x_i \precsim_i s$ by monotonicity, it is easy to see that there is a unique $\eta > 0$ such that $\eta(k - x_i) + x_i \sim s$. If u_i is defined by $u_i(s)(k - x_i) + x_i \sim s$, then u_i is continuous with respect to the Mackey topology and is a utility function. By the addition of a constant, it is possible to assume that $u_i(w_i) = O\ \forall i$.

An important step in the proof is the demonstration that if $\mathcal{O}$ is the set of Pareto optima, and if $u : \mathcal{O} \to \mathbb{R}^n$ is the function defined by $u(g) = (u_1(g_1), \ldots, u_n(g_n))$, then the radial projection, h, of $\mathcal{U} = u(\mathcal{O})$ into the standard n-simplex $\Delta_n = \{r \in \mathbb{R}^n : r \geq 0, \sum r_i = 1\}$ is a homeomorphism. Proposition 1 shows that optima actually exist and it also allows us to say enough about these optima to make it possible to prove that h is a homeomorphism.

It will be convenient in the discussion that follows to extend the concept of feasible allocation to include allocations f such that $\sum_{i=1}^n f_i \leq \sum_{i=1}^n w_i$. Let $\mathcal{F} = \{f = (f_1, \ldots, f_n) : \forall i\ f_i \in X_i \text{ and } \sum f_i \leq \sum w_i\}$.

Proposition 1. *Let $\underline{f} \in \mathcal{F}$ be such that $u(\underline{f}) > 0$. Then, there exists a Pareto optimum h such that $u(h) = \alpha u(\underline{f})$, $\alpha > 0$.*

Proof. $\mathcal{F} \subset S^n$, where $S^n = \prod_{j=1}^n S_j$, $S_j = S\ \forall j$. Let $\mathcal{I}$ be the topology on S^n which is the product of the weak-star topologies on the S_j. $\mathcal{F}$ is $\mathcal{I}$-compact, for if $f \in \mathcal{F}$, $f_i \leq \sum_{j=1}^n w_j - \sum_{j \neq i} f_j$. Since $f_i \in X_i = x_i + K$, $f_i \geq x_i$. Therefore, $x_i \leq f_i \leq \sum w_j - \sum_{j \neq i} x_i$, so that $\mathcal{F} = \left(\prod_{j=1}^n \{s \in S : x_i \leq s \leq \sum w_j - \sum_{j \neq i} x_i\}\right) \cap \{f \in S^n : \sum f_j \leq \sum w_j\}$. The first set in this expression is the product of weak-star closed, strongly bounded, and therefore weak-star compact sets. The second set is $\mathfrak{J}$-closed, so that $\mathcal{F}$ is compact.

Let $\tilde{\mathfrak{F}} = \{f \in F : u(f) = \alpha u(\underline{f}), \alpha \in \mathbb{R}\}$, and let $\gtrsim$ be the partial ordering on $\mathcal{F}$ defined by $f \gtrsim g$ if and only if $f_i \gtrsim_i g_i \; \forall i = 1, \ldots, n$. It will be shown that $\tilde{\mathfrak{F}}$ contains an element, h, maximal in $\tilde{\mathfrak{F}}$ with respect to the order $\gtrsim$. Since $h \in \tilde{\mathfrak{F}}$ and $h \gtrsim \underline{f} \in \tilde{\mathfrak{F}}$, $u(h) = \alpha u(\underline{f})$, $\alpha \geq 1$. h is a Pareto optimum, for suppose $g \gtrsim h$ and $h \not\gtrsim g$. Then, there exist $k_1, \ldots, k_n \in K$ such that $g_i - k_i \sim_i h_i$, and $\sum k_i \neq 0$. By adding proportions of $\sum k_i$ onto the g_i, it is possible to obtain $\underline{g} \in \tilde{\mathfrak{F}}$ such that $\underline{g} \gtrsim h$ and $h \not\gtrsim \underline{g}$, contradicting the maximality of h.

To show that $\tilde{\mathfrak{F}}$ contains a $\gtrsim$-maximal element, it suffices, by Zorn's Lemma,[7] to show that every linearly ordered subset has an upper bound. Let G be a linearly ordered subset. By the $\mathfrak{J}$-compactness of $\mathcal{F}$ it follows readily that G has an upper bound in $\mathcal{F}$. In fact, let $P_g = \{f \in \mathcal{F} : f \gtrsim g\}$. Then $P_g = \mathcal{F} \cap \prod_{i=1}^{n} \{s \in S : s \gtrsim_i g_i\}$. But by the convexity and Mackey continuity of the preference relations, $\{s \in S : s \gtrsim_i g_i\}$ is convex and Mackey closed, and therefore weak-star closed. Thus, $\{P_g : g \in G\}$ is a set of $\mathfrak{J}$-closed subsets of $\mathcal{F}$ with the finite intersection property, so that by the compactness of $\mathcal{F}$, $\cap\{P_g : g \in G\} \neq \emptyset$. Any element, $\underline{g}$, of this intersection is an upper bound for G. Clearly, $u_i(\underline{g}_i) \geq \overline{\lim}_{(G,\gtrsim)} u_i(g_i)$ for all i. Since one may subtract elements of K from the components of $\underline{g}$, if necessary, we may assume, w.l.o.g., that $u_i(\underline{g}_i) = \overline{\lim}_{(G,\gtrsim)} u_i(g_i)$. But then, since the vector $\overline{\lim}_{(G,\gtrsim)}$ is proportional to $u(\underline{f})$, $\underline{g} \in \tilde{\mathfrak{F}}$. Q.E.D.

Before continuing, it is necessary to remark that one can assume that the initial allocation, $w = (w_1, \ldots, w_n)$, is not a Pareto optimum, for if it were it would be an equilibrium. By Proposition 3 below, any Pareto optimum is cost minimizing with respect to a price in $ba(B, \mathcal{B}, \nu)$. Using the fact that, for all i, w_i lies in the interior of X_i with respect to the norm topology, it is easy to see that if w were an optimum, it would be a competitive equilibrium with respect to any price for which it was cost minimizing. The next lemma show that if w is not an optimum, as will be assumed henceforth, then the radial projection from $\mathfrak{U}$ into Δ_n is in fact onto.

Lemma 1. *Let $\bar{r}$ be any ray from zero in the positive orthant of $\mathbb{R}^n$.*

---

[7] See John Kelley, *General Topology*, (Van Nostrand: 1955, p. 33).

Then there exists $g \in \mathcal{O}$ *such that* $0 \neq u(g) \in \bar{r}$.

Proof. Since $w \notin \mathcal{O}$, there exists $f \in \mathcal{F}$ such that $f \gtrsim w$ and $w \not\gtrsim f$ in the Pareto ordering, i.e., such that $u(f) > 0$. By use of monotonicity, it is easy to see that without loss of generality we can assume that $u(f) \gg 0$. Again, by the use of monotonicity, it is easy to see that for every point, $r \in \mathbf{R}^n$, such that $0 \leq r \leq u(f)$, there is $g \in \mathcal{F}$ such that $u(g) = r$. But $\{r \in \mathbf{R}^n : 0 \leq r \leq u(f)\}$ is a neighborhood of zero in the positive orthant of $\mathbf{R}^n$. Thus, the statement of the Lemma follows from Proposition 1. Q.E.D.

The next proposition establishes that the projection of $\mathcal{U}$ onto Δ_n is in fact a homeomorphism. Defined precisely, the projection is $h(v) = v[\sum_i v_i]^{-1}$.

Proposition 2. *h is a homeomorphism.*

Proof. h is clearly continuous, and it has already been shown that h is surjective. It follows directly from the definition of a Pareto optimum that h is injective. Since Δ_n is a Hausdorff space, to show that h^{-1} is continuous, it suffices to show that $\mathcal{U}$ is compact. $\mathcal{U}$ is bounded by an argument used in the proof of Proposition 1, so that is suffices to prove that $\mathcal{U}$ is closed.

Let v^k be a sequence in $\mathcal{U}$ converging to v. $v \neq 0$, for by an argument used in the proof of Lemma 1, $\mathcal{U}$ is bounded away from zero. Clearly, v is contained in the positive orthant. Let $\underline{v}$ be the (unique) point in $\mathcal{U}$ on the ray from zero through v. It will be shown that $v = \underline{v}$. If $\underline{v} < v$, eventually $v^k > \underline{v}$, contradicting the optimality of $\underline{v}$. Suppose for the moment that $v \gg 0$. Then, if $\underline{v} > v$, $\underline{v} \gg v$, so that eventually $\underline{v} > v^k$, contradicting the optimality of v^k. Now suppose that $v_1 = \cdots = v_m = 0$, $v_j > 0$ if $m + 1 \leq j \leq n$. Then, if $\underline{v} > v$, $\underline{v}_j > v_j$ if $j > m$, $\underline{v}_j = 0$ if $j \leq m$. Let $g \in \mathcal{O}$ be such that $u(g) = \underline{v}$. Then, for each $j = m+1, \ldots, n$, there exists $k_j \in K$, $k_j \neq 0$ such that $u_j(g_j - k_j) = 1/2(\underline{v}_j + v_j)$. Let $k = \sum_{j=1}^m k_j$, and let $\tilde{\mathcal{F}} = \{f \in S^n : f_j = g_j - k_j$ if $m + 1 \leq j \leq n$ and $f_j = g_j + \alpha_j k$ if $1 \leq j \leq m$, $0 \leq \alpha \leq 1$, $\sum_{j=1}^m \alpha_j = 1\}$. Then, $u(\tilde{\mathcal{F}}) = \{u(f) : f \in \tilde{\mathcal{F}}\}$ covers a neighborhood about $1.2(v + \underline{v})$ in the section of the positive orthant defined by $\{r \in \mathbf{R}^n : r \geq 0, r_j = 1/2(\underline{v}_j + v_j)$ if $m + 1 \leq j \leq n\}$. Eventually, each v^k will be less in all components than some point in

$u(\tilde{\mathcal{F}})$, contradicting the optimality of v^k. Thus, $\underline{v} \leq v \leq \underline{v}$, so that since v and $\underline{v}$ lie on the same ray through the origin, $\underline{v} = v$. Q.E.D.

The next proposition will make it possible to define the correspondence Ψ.

Proposition 3. *Every Pareto optimal allocation in E is cost minimizing with respect to a price in* $ba(B, \mathcal{B}, \nu)$. *That is, if* $f \in \mathcal{O}$, *there exists* $\pi \in ba(B, \mathcal{B}, \nu)$, $\pi \neq 0$, $\pi \geq 0$, *such that for* $i = 1, \ldots, n$, $s \succsim_i f_i$ *implies that* $\pi \cdot s \geq \pi \cdot f_i$.

Proof. Let $P_i = \{s \in X_i : s \succsim_i f_i\}$, and let $Z = \langle \bigcup_{i=1}^n (P_i - f_i) \rangle$.[8] $Z \cap -K = \{o\}$, for suppose $-k = \sum_{i=1}^n \alpha_i(p_i - f_i)$, $0 \leq \alpha_i \leq 1$, $\sum \alpha_i = 1$, $p_i \in P_i$, $k \in K \setminus \{o\}$. Then, if $\underline{f}_i = f_i + \alpha_i(p_i - f_i + k)$, by the convexity of preferences and by monotonicity, $\underline{f}_i \succsim_i f_i$ for all i, and $\underline{f}_i \succ_i f_i$ for all i for which $\alpha_i > 0$. Since $\sum \underline{f}_i = \sum f_i = \sum w_i$, $\underline{f}$ Pareto dominates, so that $f \notin \mathcal{O}$. Since $Z \cap -K = \{o\}$ and $-K$ ha a non-empty interior with respect to the norm topology, there exists $\pi \in ba$ separating $-K$ and Z. Then $\pm\pi$ is the desired price system. Q.E.D.

Let Π be the set of price systems, that is, $\Pi = \{\pi \in ba(B, \mathcal{B}, \nu) : \pi \geq 0, \|\pi\| = \pi(B) = 1\}$. Define $\psi : \mathcal{F} \times \Pi \to \mathbb{R}^n$ by $\psi(f, \pi) = (\pi(f_1 - w_1), \ldots, \pi(f_n - w_n))$. Let $M : \mathcal{O} \to \Pi$ be the correspondence defined by $M(g) = \{\pi \in \Pi : g$ is cost minimizing with respect to $\pi\}$. By Proposition 3, $M(g) \neq \emptyset$, $\forall g \in \mathcal{O}$. Finally, let $\Psi : \mathcal{O} \to \mathbb{R}^n$ be the correspondence defined by $\Psi(g) = \cup\{\psi(g, \pi) : \pi \in M(g)\}$. $g \in \mathcal{O}$ is an equilibrium if $0 \in \Psi(g)$, for suppose $\pi \in M(g)$ is such that $0 = \psi(g, \pi)$. Since g is an optimum, the assumption of monotonicity clearly implies that $\sum g_i = \sum w_i$. Since $\pi \in M(g)$, g is cost minimizing wit respect to π. Thus, $s \succsim_i g_i$ implies $\pi \cdot s \geq \pi \cdot g_i$, i.e., $\pi \cdot s < \pi \cdot g_i$ implies $s \succ_i g_i$. Since, $0 = \psi(g, \pi)$, $\pi \cdot g_i = \pi \cdot w_i$, $\forall i$. Since $w_i \gg x_i$, $\pi \cdot w_i > \pi \cdot x_i$ (where x_i is such that $X_i = x_i + K$). Now suppose that there is $y \in X_i$ such that $\pi \cdot y \leq \pi \cdot w_i$, and $y \succ_i g_i$. Then, for some $1 > \alpha > 0$ sufficiently close to zero, $(1 - \alpha)y + \alpha x_i \succ_i g_i$. This contradiction implies that g_i is a $\succsim_i$-maximal point in the budget set of the ith agent. Thus, g is an equilibrium.

[8] The sign $\langle A \cup B \rangle$, where A and B are subsets of a linear space, means the convex hull of A and B.

Let $\phi = \Psi \circ u^{-1} : \mathcal{U} \to \mathbb{R}^n$. ϕ actually maps into the hyperplane, H, in $\mathbb{R}^n$ defined by $H = \{r \in \mathbb{R}^n : \sum r_i = 0\}$, for, since for every $g \in \mathcal{O}$, $\sum g_i = \sum w_i$, for every $\pi \in \Pi$ and $g \in \mathcal{O}$, $\sum_{j=1}^n \psi_j(g,\pi) = \sum_{j=1}^n \pi(g_j - w_j) = 0$.

The next objectives are to show that ϕ is compact and convex valued and is upper-semi continuous. Since the utility functions are bounded on the set of feasible allocations, by an argument made in the proof of Proposition 1, ϕ maps into a bounded set. By a well-known and easily proved result, this implies that ϕ is upper-semi-continuous iff its graph is closed. Since closed and bounded subsets of $\mathbb{R}^n$ are compact, closedness of the graph of ϕ will also imply that ϕ is compact valued. That ϕ is convex valued will follow immediately from the fact that M is a convex valued correspondence. The next lemma facilitates the discussion of ϕ.

Lemma 2. *M and Ψ are constant on $u^{-1}(v)$ $\forall v \in \mathcal{U}$, so that if $f \in u^{-1}(v)$, $\phi(v) = \Psi(f)$.*

Proof. To say that M is constant on $u^{-1}(v)$ is to say that if $f^1, f^2 \in u^{-1}(v)$, and if f^1 is cost minimizing with respect to π, then so is f^2. Let $P_i = \{s \in S : s \succsim_i f_i^1\} = \{s \in S : s \succsim_i f_i^2\}$, $i = 1, \ldots, n$. Since $\pi \cdot P_i \geq \pi \cdot f_i^1$, $\forall i$, to show that $\pi \in M(f^2)$, it suffices to show that $\pi \cdot f_i^1 = \pi \cdot f_i^2$. Since $f_i^2 \in P_i$, $\pi \cdot f^2 \geq \pi \cdot f^1$, $\forall i$. If for any i, $\pi \cdot f_i^2 > \pi \cdot f_i^1$, $\pi \cdot (\sum f_i^2) > \pi \cdot (\sum f_i^1)$, which contradicts $\sum f_i^2 = \sum w_i = \sum f_i^1$.

Since we have shown that if $f^1, f^2 \in u^{-1}(v)$ and $\pi \in M(f^1)$, then $\pi \cdot f_i^1 = \pi \cdot f_i^2$ $\forall i$, it follows that Ψ is constant on $u^{-1}(v)$. Q.E.D.

Proposition 4. *ϕ is convex valued.*

Proof. If $f \in u^{-1}(v)$, $v \in \mathcal{U}$, we know by Lemma 2 that $\phi(v) = \Psi(f)$. Then, if $r_1, r_2 \in \Psi(f)$, $r^i = \pi^i \cdot (f - w)$, $\pi^i \in M(f)$, $i = 1, 2$. It is now clear that the convexity of $\Psi(f)$ follows from the convexity of $M(f)$. Q.E.D.

Proposition 5. *ϕ has closed graph.*

Proof. Let (v^k, r^k) be in the graph of ϕ and suppose that (v^k, r^k) converges to (v, r). Since $\mathcal{U}$ is closed, $v \in \mathcal{U}$, so that one needs to show only that $r \in \phi(v)$. Let $f^k \in u^{-1}(v^k)$ and $\pi_k \in M(f^k)$ be such that $r^k = \psi(f^k, \pi_k)$, i.e., $r^k = \pi_k \cdot (f^k - w)$, or $\pi_k \cdot f^k = r^k + \pi_k \cdot w$.

Since Π is weak-star compact, a subnet of the π_k, $(\pi_{k(\alpha)})_{\alpha\in D}$, D a directed set, converges in the weak-star topology to $\pi \in \Pi$. We will show that $r = \psi(f, \pi)$, where $f \in u^{-1}(v)$, so that indeed $r \in \phi(v)$.

If $t \in \mathbf{R}$, let $P_i(t) = \{s \in S : u_i(s) \geq t\}$. It is sufficient to prove that $\pi \cdot P_j(v_j) \geq r_j + \pi \cdot w_j \ \forall j$, where $v = (v_1, \ldots, v_n)$, For suppose that this is true. Let $f \in u^{-1}(v)$. Since $f_j \in P_j(v_j)$, $\pi \cdot f_j \geq r_j + \pi \cdot w_j$. We know that $\sum_{j=1}^n r_j^k = 0 \ \forall k$, so that $\sum_{j=1}^n r_j = 0$. Thus, $\sum \pi \cdot f_j = \sum r_j + \sum \pi \cdot w_j$, so that $\pi \cdot f_j = r_j + \pi \cdot w_j \ \forall j$. Thus, $\pi \cdot P_j(v_j) \geq \pi \cdot f_j$ and $r_j = \pi \cdot (f_j - w_j)$, and these two relations show that f is cost minimizing with respect to π and that $r \in \Psi(f) = \phi(v)$.

It will now be shown that $\pi \cdot P_j(v_j) \geq r_j + \pi \cdot w_j \ \forall j$. Let $\delta > 0$ and w.l.o.g. let $j = 1$, Since $r^k(\alpha) \to r$ and $\pi_{k(\alpha)} \cdot w_1 \to \pi \cdot w_1$, there exists $\alpha_1 \in D$ such that $\alpha \geq \alpha_1$ implies that $|r_1^{k(\alpha)} + \pi_{k(\alpha)} \cdot w_1 - (r_1 + \pi \cdot w_1)| < \delta$. Let $s \in P_1(v_1)$. There exists $\alpha_2 \in D$ such that if $\alpha \geq \alpha_2$, $|(\pi_{k(\alpha)} - \pi) \cdot s| < \delta$. Because of the strong monotonicity assumption, the utility maps are open with respect to the norm topology on S. This fact in turn implies that if $t \in \mathbf{R}$ is within some neighborhood of v_1, then $P_1(t) \cap B(s, \delta) \neq \emptyset$.[9] Since $v_1^{k(\alpha)} \to v_1$, there is $\alpha_3 \in D$ such that if $\alpha > \alpha_3$, $P_1(v_1^{k(\alpha)}) \cap B(s, \delta) \neq \emptyset$. Let $\underline{\alpha} \geq (\alpha_1, \alpha_2, \alpha_3)$.

If $\alpha \geq \underline{\alpha}$, there exists $s_\alpha \in P_1(v_1^{k(\alpha)}) \cap B(s, \delta)$, and $|\pi \cdot s - \pi_{k(\alpha} \cdot s_\alpha| \leq |(\pi - \pi_{k(\alpha)}) \cdot s| + |\pi_{k(\alpha)} \cdot (s - s_\alpha)| \leq \delta + \|\pi_{k(\alpha)}\| \|(s - s_\alpha)\| \leq \delta + 1 \cdot \delta = 2\delta$. Since $s_\alpha \in P_1(v_1^{k(\alpha)})$, $\pi_{k(\alpha)} \cdot s_\alpha \geq \pi_{k(\alpha)} \cdot f_1^{k(\alpha)} = r_1^{k(\alpha)} + \pi_{k(\alpha)} \cdot w_1$. But $|r_1^{k(\alpha)} + \pi_{k(\alpha)} \cdot w_1 - (r_1 + \pi \cdot w_1)| < \delta$, so that $\pi \cdot s \geq r_1 + \pi \cdot w_1 - 3\delta$. Since δ is arbitrary, $\pi \cdot s \geq r_1 + \pi \cdot w_1$. Q.E.D.

To recapitulate, it has been shown that the redial projection $h : \mathcal{U} \to \Delta_n$ is a homeomorphism, that the correspondence $\phi : \mathcal{U} \to H$ is upper-semi-continuous and convex and compact valued. It is also known that $0 \in Ra\phi = \cup\{\phi(v) : v \in \mathcal{U}\}$, implies that there is an equilibrium. So let us suppose that $0 \notin \cup Ra\phi$. Then ϕ can be composed with the radial projection of H into the sphere in H of radius one and center 0. Denote this sphere by S_{n-2}, and let $\rho : H \setminus \{0\} \to S_{n-2}$ be the radial projection (defined by $\rho(r) = \frac{r}{\|r\|}$). Next, let E_{n-1} be the ball in H whose surface

[9] Throughout the rest of this paper the notation $B(x, \varepsilon)$ will be used to denote open ball of radius ε about x with respect to the norm of the space containing x.

is S_{n-2}, ($E_{n_1} = \{r \in H : \|r\| \leq 1\}$).

It is now necessary to make the obvious identification between the Euclidean n-spaces in which H and Δ_n are embedded. This identification must be done in such a way the maps $u_j : X_j \to \mathbb{R}$ and $\psi_j : \mathcal{O} \times \Pi \to \mathbb{R}$ map into the same component spaces. Having made this identification, let $\beta : E_{n-1} \to \Delta_n$ be any homeomorphism such that if r is in the boundary of Δ_n, $\beta^{-1}(r) = \frac{r-(1/n,\ldots,1/n)}{\|r-(1/n,\ldots,1/n)\|}$. Now let $\xi = \rho \circ \phi \circ h^{-1} \circ \beta$. This clearly an upper-semi-continuous correspondence from E_{n-1} into S_{n-2}.

It is now possible to carry the argument to the contradiction sketched in the introduction to the proof of the theorem.

Lemma 3. *For every $r \in E_{n-1}$, $\xi(r)$ lies in an open half sphere of S_{n-2}.*

Proof. Since ϕ is convex and compact valued, and since it is assumed that for every $v \in \mathcal{U}$, $0 \notin \phi(v)$, for every $r \in E_{n-1}$, $\phi \circ h^{-1} \circ \beta(r)$ can be strongly separated from zero by a hyperplane. But then $\xi(r) = \rho \circ \phi \circ h^{-1} \circ \beta(r)$ will lie in the same half of this separation as $\phi \circ h^{-1} \circ \beta(r)$. Q.E.D.

Recall that $a : S_{n-2} \to S_{n-2}$ is the antipodal map defined by $a(r) = -r$.

Lemma 4. *For every $r \in S_{n-2}$, $\xi(r)$ lies in an open half sphere, Q_r, of S_{n-2} such that $Q_r \cap B\left(a(r), \frac{1}{n}\right) = \emptyset$.*

Proof. Let $F'_j = \{r \in \Delta_n : r_j = 0\}$, $j = 1, \ldots, n$, be the jth face of Δ_n. Let $F_j = \beta^{-1}(F'_j)$. Since $\bigcup_{j=1}^{n} F_j = S_{n-2}$, it is sufficient to prove the assertion of the lemma for $r \in F_1$. If $v = h^{-1} \circ \beta(r)$, then $v_1 = 0$. Let $t \in \phi(v)$ and let $t = \psi(f, \pi)$, $f \in \mathcal{O}$, $\pi \in \Pi$. Then, since $v = u(f)$, $u_1(f_1) = 0 = u_1(w_1)$, and, since f is cost minimizing with respect to π, $\pi(w_1) \geq \pi(f_1)$. Hence, $t_1 = \psi_1(f, \pi) = \pi(f_1 - w_1) \leq 0$. Thus, $\phi(v)$ lies in the set $Q = \{r \in \mathbb{R}^n : r_1 \leq 0\}$.

It is not hard to see that the first component of any element of F_1 is always less than $-\frac{1}{n}$. From this fact it follows that the distance of the set $a(F_1)$ from the set Q is greater than $\frac{1}{n}$. Hence, if $r \in F_1$, $B\left(a(r), \frac{1}{n}\right) \cap Q = \emptyset$ and hence $\langle \overline{B\left(a(r), \frac{1}{n}\right) \cup \{0\}} \rangle \cap Q = \{0\}$. Using the compactness of $\overline{B\left(a(r), \frac{1}{n}\right)}$ and of ϕ it is easy to see that there exists $\delta > 0$ such that $\langle B\left(a(r), \frac{1}{n}\right) \cup \{0\} \rangle \cap \langle B(\phi \cdot h^{-1} \circ \beta(r), \delta) \cup \{0\} \rangle = \{0\}$. By separating these two sets, one obtains the assertion of the lemma.Q.E.D.

Since, by Lemma 3 for every $r \in E_{n-1}$, $\xi(r)$ lies in an open half sphere, T_r, of S_{n-2}, and since ξ is upper-semi-continuous, for every $r \in E_{n-1}$ there is an open neighborhood O_r of r such that $s \in O_r$ implies that $\xi(r) \subset T_r$. Let δ_1 be a Lebesgue δ for the open cover $\{O_r\}$ of the compact set E_{n-1}.

Similarly, by Lemma 4, for every $r \in S_{n-2}$, $\xi(r)$ lies in an open half sphere, Q_r, of S_{n-2} such that $Q_r \cap B\left(a(r), \frac{1}{n}\right) = \emptyset$, and since ξ is upper-semi-continuous, for every $r \in S_{n-1}$, there is an open ball $B(r, \varepsilon_r)$, $0 < \varepsilon_r < \frac{1}{n}$, such that $s \in B(r, \varepsilon_r)$ implies that $\xi(s) \subset Q_r$. Let δ_2 be a Lebesgue δ for the open cover $\{B(r, \varepsilon_r) \cap S_{n-2}\}$ of the compact set S_{n-2}. Let $0 < \delta < \min(\delta_1, \delta_2)$.

Let $(g_1, \ldots, g_m)$ be a continuous partition of unity for the cover of E_{n-1} by open balls of radius δ. That is, $g_i : E_{n-1} \to [0,1]$ are continuous functions, $\sum_{i=1}^m g_i(r) = 1$, $\forall r \in E_{n-1}$, and each g_i is zero outside some open ball $B(p_i, \delta)$, $p_i \in E_{n-1}$.

For each $i = 1, \ldots, m_m$, let $v_i \in \xi(p_i)$, and let $g : E_{n-1} \to S_{n-2}$ be defined by $g(r) = \rho \sum_{i=1}^m g_i(r) v_i$.

g is clearly continuous whenever it is well-defined, that is, whenever $\sum_{i=1}^m g_i(r) v_i \neq 0$. But in fact, $\sum_{i=1}^m g_i(r) v_i$ is never equal to zero. For since $\delta < \delta_1$, given any $r \in E_{n-1}$, the set of all p_i for which $g_i(r) \neq 0$ are all within the open ball of radius δ_1 about r. But, by the definition of δ_1, this ball is contained within some open set mapped by ξ into an open half sphere of S_{n-2}. Hence, $0 \notin \langle \{\xi(p_i) : g_i(r) \neq \emptyset\} \rangle$.

Next we observe that $g(r) \neq a(r)$, $\forall r \in S_{n-2}$. If $r \in S_{n-2}$, then the set of all p_i such that $g_i(r) \neq 0$ lie within $B(r, \delta_2)$. But by the choice of δ_2, S_{n-2}, $B(r, \delta_2)$ lies within a sphere $B(\underline{r}, \varepsilon)$, where $\underline{r} \in S_{n-2}$ and $\varepsilon < \frac{1}{n}$ is such that $s \in B(\underline{r}, \varepsilon)$ implies that $\xi(s) \subset Q_{\underline{r}}$, where $Q_{\underline{r}}$ is a half sphere of S_{n-2} such that $Q_{\underline{r}} \cap B\left(a(\underline{r}), \frac{1}{n}\right) = \emptyset$. By Lemma 5, below, $B(r, \delta_2) \cap S_{n-2} \subset B(\underline{r}, \varepsilon)$ implies that $B(r, \delta_2) \subset B(\underline{r}, \varepsilon)$. Thus, the set of all v_i such that $g_i(r) \neq 0$ lie within $Q_{\underline{r}}$, so that, since $Q_{\underline{r}}$ is an open half sphere, $g(r) \in Q_{\underline{r}}$. Since $\varepsilon < \frac{1}{n}$, $a(r) \in B\left(a(\underline{r}), \frac{1}{n}\right)$, so that $g(r) \neq a(r)$.

It has been shown that g is a continuous function from E_{n-1} into S_{n-2} such that $g(r) \neq a(r)$ $\forall r \in S_{n-2}$. But, as was pointed out in the introduction to the proof of the theorem, this is impossible. Hence, the proof that there exists an equilibrium with respect to a price in $ba(B, \mathcal{B}, \nu)$

will be complete once the next minor lemma has been proved.

Lemma 5. *Let B be ball in $\mathbb{R}^n$ with positive radius, and let C be its boundary. If B_1 and B_2 are open balls with centers in C and if $B_1 \cap C \subset B_2 \cap C$, then $B_1 \cap B \subset B_2 \cap B$.*

Proof. Let p_1 and p_2 be the centers of B_1 and B_2, respectively, and let C_1 and C_2 be their boundaries. Let $\underline{r}$ be that point in $C \cup B \setminus (B_2 \setminus C_2)$ such that $\|\underline{r} - p_1\| = \inf\{\|r - p_1\| : r - (B \setminus B_2)\}$. It is enough to show that $\underline{r} \in C$. Clearly, $\underline{r} \in C_2 \cap (B \cup C)$. If $\underline{f} \in \operatorname{int} B$, then C_1 and C_2 are tangent at $\underline{r}$, which implies that p_1, p_2, and $\underline{r}$ are colinear. But this is impossible, since $p_1, p_2 \in C$. Q.E.D.

Now that the existence of an equilibrium has been proved, a digression will be made in order to compare this proof with that given by Gerard Debreu in *Theory of Value* for the existence theorem in the finite dimensional case. The essential step in the argument used in this paper could be summarized in the following statement, where Δ_n and H are as above.

Let $\zeta : \Delta_n \to H$ be an upper-semi-continuous, compact, convex valued correspondence. If $r \in \Delta_n$ and $r_i = 0$ implies that the ith component of any point in $\zeta(r)$ is less than or equal to zero, then for some $\underline{r} \in \Delta_n$, $0 \in \zeta(\underline{r})$.

The corresponding step in Debreu's argument is the next statement.

Let $\zeta : \Delta_n \to \mathbb{R}^n$ be an upper-semi-continuous, compact and convex valued correspondence such that $\forall r \in \Delta_n$, no point $s \in \zeta(r)$ satisfies $s < 0$ and, $\forall s \in \zeta(r)$, $r \cdot s \leq 0$. Then for some $\underline{r} \in \Delta_n$, $0 \in \zeta(\underline{r})$.

This second statement is proved in Debreu's book by use of Kakutani's fixed point theorem for correspondences. But the same methods that were used here to prove the first statement can be used to prove the second. To see this, suppose that $0 \notin \cup Ra\zeta$, where ζ satisfies the assumptions of the second assumptions of the second statement. Let $A = \{r \in \mathbb{R}^n : r \not< 0\}$, let $B = \{r \in \mathbb{R}^n : r \leq 0, r \not< 0\}$, and let $\sigma : A \to B$ be the map defined by $\sigma(r) = r - (\max_{i=1,\ldots,n} r_i)e$, where $e = (1, \ldots, 1)$. Let $\dot{\Delta}_n$ be the boundary of Δ_n, and consider $\sigma \circ \zeta \,|_{\dot{\Delta}_n}$. Let $I = \{1, \ldots, n\}$. If $r \in \Delta_n$, then for some non-empty proper subset $J \subset I$, $r_j = 0$, $\forall j \in J$. But since $r \cdot \zeta(r) \leq 0$, $s \in \zeta(r)$ implies that $\sum_{j \in I \setminus J} s_j \cdot r_j \leq 0$. But this means that the statement, $s \in \zeta(r)$ and

$\sigma(s_j) = 0, \forall j \in I \setminus J$, is impossible, for if this statement were true, then one would have $\sum_{j \in I \setminus J} s_j \cdot r_j > 0$.

Now let $\tau : B \setminus \{0\} \to \Delta_n$ be the continuous map defined by $\tau(r) = \frac{r}{\sum_{i=1}^{n} r_i}$, and consider the correspondence $\tau \circ \sigma \circ \zeta$. This is an upper-semi-continuous correspondence with the property that if for any $J \subsetneq I$, F_J is the face of Δ_n defined by $F_J = \{r \in \Delta_n : r_j = 0, j \in J\}$, the $\mathrm{n}\tau \circ \sigma \circ \zeta(F_J) \cap F_{I \setminus J} = \emptyset$. Using the fact that ζ is compact and convex valued, it is possible, by using the techniques used above, to construct a function $g : \Delta_n \to \Delta_n$ with the property that $g(F_J) \cap F_{I \setminus J} = \emptyset \; \forall J \subsetneq I$. That is, g does not carry any point of a fact of Δ_n into the opposite face. Let $\beta : E_{n-1} \to \Delta_n$ be the canonical homeomorphism of the unit ball in $\mathbb{R}^{n-1}$ onto Δ_n. Then, $\beta^{-1} \circ g \circ \beta$ is a continuous function of E_{n-1} onto S_{n-2}, the unit sphere that is the surface of E_{n-1}. Using the fact that g does not carry points of any face to the opposite face, it is possible to construct a homotopy of $\beta^{-1} \circ g \circ \beta|_{S_{n-2}}$ with the identity map on the sphere. But as we showed before, this is impossible.

It is thus seen that both Debreu's proof and the one given above lead by different routes to exactly the same contradiction.

The next proposition completes the proof of the theorem by showing that any equilibrium is an equilibrium with respect to a price in L_1.[10]

Proposition 6. *If f is an equilibrium with respect to $\pi \in ba(B, \mathcal{B}, \nu)$, then $\pi \in L_1(B, \mathcal{B}, \nu)$.*

Proof. Let $f = (f_1, \ldots, f_n)$ be an equilibrium with respect to $\pi \in ba(B, \mathcal{B}, \nu)$. If for any $i = 1, \ldots, n$, f_i is in the strong interior of X_i, the following argument shows that $\pi \in L_1$. W.l.o.g., suppose $f_1 \in \operatorname{int} X_1$. Suppose that $\pi \notin L_1$. Then, there exists $E_n \in \mathcal{B}$ such that $E_n \subset E_{n+1}$ and if $E = \bigcup_{n=1}^{\infty} E_n$, $\lim_n \pi(E_n) < \pi(E)$. Define $0 \leq \alpha < 1$ by $\lim \pi(E_n) = \alpha\pi(E)$.

Since f_1 is in the strong interior of X_1, there exists $\gamma > 0$ such that $B(f_1, \gamma) \subset X_1$. Let $g = f_1 + \gamma\frac{(1-\alpha)}{2}\chi_E$, and let $g_n = g + \gamma(\chi_{E_n} - \chi_E)$.

[10] The reader may have noticed that up to this point the only assumption on the continuity of preferences that has actually been used is that the sets $\{s \in X_i : s \succsim_i \underline{s}\}$ are weak-star closed. It is only in the proof of Proposition 6 that one needs the other half of the continuity assumption, that is that the sets $\{s \in X_i : s \succ_i \underline{s}\}$ are always Mackey open in X_i.

The sequence g_n converges to g in the Mackey topology, for the Mackey topology is the topology of uniform convergence on weakly compact sets of L_1, and weakly compact subsets of L_1 are uniformly absolutely continuous. Thus, g_n converges to g on any weakly compact subset of L_1 and hence in the Mackey topology. Since $g_n, g \in B(f_1, \gamma)$, g_n and g are in X_1. By monotonicity, g is preferred to f_1, so that, since preferences are Mackey continuous, g_n is eventually preferred to f_1. But since f is an equilibrium, $s \succsim_i f_1$ implies that $\pi \cdot s \geq \pi \cdot w_1 = \pi \cdot f_1$. Hence, eventually $\pi \cdot g_n \geq \pi \cdot f_1$. But $\pi \cdot g_n = \pi \cdot f_1 + \gamma \frac{(1-\alpha)}{2} \pi(E) - \gamma\pi(E) + \gamma\pi(E_n) \leq \pi \cdot f_1 + \gamma \frac{(1-\alpha)}{2}\pi(E) - \gamma\pi(E) + \gamma \lim_n \pi(E_n)$, since the E_n form an increasing sequence of sets and π is positive. But then, since $\lim_n \sigma(E_n) = \alpha\pi(E)$, one easily derives that $\pi \cdot g_n \leq \pi \cdot f_1 + \gamma \frac{(\alpha-1)}{2}\pi(E) < \pi \cdot f_1$, $\forall u$. Thus, $\pi \cdot g_n < \pi \cdot f_1$, $\forall n$. This contradiction implies that π is in L_1.

Now suppose that for all i, f_i is in the strong boundary of X_i, that is, that $\operatorname{ess\,inf}(f_i - x_i) = 0$. Since $w_i \gg x_i$ $\forall i$, $\sum(f_i - x_i) = \sum(w_i - x_i) \gg 0$. Let $t_0 = \operatorname{ess\,inf} \sum(w_i - x_i)$, and let $Z_i = \{b \in B : (f_i - x_i)(b) \geq \frac{t_0}{n}\}$. Clearly $\bigcup_{i=1}^n Z_i = B \setminus N$, where N is a ν-null set. Since π is absolutely continuous with respect to ν, $\pi(N) = 0$, and hence, to show that π is countably additive, it is sufficient to show that π is countably additive on Z_i $\forall i$. In order to show that π is countably additive on Z_i, it is first shown that for each i, there is $\pi_i \in L_1$ such that $\pi_i \leq \pi$, $\pi_i \cdot (f_i - x_i) = \pi \cdot (f_i - x_i)$ and $s \succsim_i f_i$ implies that $\pi_i \cdot s \geq \pi_i \cdot f_i$. It then follows quite easily that the existence of such a linear functional implies that π is countably additive on X_i.

W.l.o.g. let $i = 1$. By a translation argument, it can be assumed that $X_1 = K$. Let $P = \{s \in K : s \succsim_1 f_1\}$. Let $C = \{s \in K ; \pi \cdot s \leq \pi \cdot f_1\}$. Let $g \gg 0$ and let $r_0 = \sup\{r : r \geq 0, \langle C \cup rg \rangle \cap \operatorname{st\,int} P = \emptyset\}$, where $\operatorname{st\,int} P$ denotes the interior of P in the norm topology. Since $C \cap \operatorname{st\,int} P = \emptyset$, r_0 exists. Also r_0 is finite, for, since $g \in \operatorname{st\,int} C$, for some $r > 0$, $rg > f_1$ in the vector order of S. But then $rg \succ_1 f_1$, and therefore rg is in the relative Mackey interior of P, and hence $rg \in \operatorname{st\,int} P$. Hence, $r_0 < r$.

Let $D = \langle C \cup r_0 g \rangle$. We will show that D and P can be separated by a positive linear functional in ba, and then that this price system is in fact in L_1. Since D and P are convex, to show that D and P can be separated by a linear functional in ba, it is enough to show that $D \cap \operatorname{st\,int} P = \emptyset$. Supposing the contrary, there are $h \in C$, $\varepsilon > 0$, $0 \leq \alpha < 1$ such that

$B(\alpha h+(1-\alpha)r_0g,\varepsilon)\subset P$. But then, $\alpha h+(1-\alpha)\left(r_0-\frac{\varepsilon}{\|g\|}\right)g\in \operatorname{st}\operatorname{int}P$, which implies that $r_0<r_0-\frac{\varepsilon}{\|g\|}$. So, there exists a non-zero $\pi_1\in ba$ such that $\pi_1(D)\leq\pi(f_1)\leq\pi_1(P)$. Since $f_1+K\subset P$, π_1 is positive.

To show that $\pi_1\in L_1$, we must use the following property of the set $D:\inf\left\{\frac{d(p,D)'}{d(p,S\setminus K)}:p\in\operatorname{st}\operatorname{int}P\right\}=0$, where if T is a subset of S and p a point in S, $d(p,T)=\inf_{s\in T}\|p-s\|$. It will be shown that if D does not have the above property, then there exists $r'>r_0$ such that $\langle C\cup r'g\rangle\cap\operatorname{st}\operatorname{int}P=\emptyset$, contrary to the definition of r_0.

Suppose there exists $1>\varepsilon>0$ such that for all $p\in\operatorname{st}\operatorname{int}P$, $\frac{d(p,D)}{d(p,S\setminus K)}>\varepsilon$. Then, for every $e\in D$, $\frac{d(e,P)}{d(e,S\setminus K)}\geq\varepsilon(1-\varepsilon)$, for suppose $\underline{e}\in D$ is such that $\frac{d(\underline{e},P)}{(\underline{e},S\setminus K)}<\varepsilon(1-\varepsilon)$. Then, there is $\underline{p}\in P$ such that $d(\underline{e},\underline{p})<\varepsilon(1-\varepsilon)d(\underline{e},S\setminus K)$. But $d(\underline{p},S\setminus K)\geq d(\underline{e},S\setminus K)-d(\underline{e},\underline{p})>(1-\varepsilon)d(\underline{e},S\setminus K)$, so that $d(\underline{e},\underline{p})<\varepsilon(1-\varepsilon)d(\underline{e},S\setminus K)<\varepsilon d(\underline{p},S\setminus K)$ or $\frac{d(p,D)}{d(\underline{p},S\setminus K)}<\varepsilon$, contrary to assumption.

Let $\varepsilon'=\varepsilon(1-\varepsilon)$, so that $\inf\left\{\frac{d(e,p)}{d(e,S\setminus K)}:e\in\operatorname{st}\operatorname{int}D\right\}\geq\varepsilon'$. Since $g\in\operatorname{st}\operatorname{int}K$, $d(g,S\setminus K)=\operatorname{ess}\inf g=\gamma>0$. Let $h\in C$. Then, if $0\leq\alpha<1$, $\inf_{p\in P}\|\alpha h+(1-\alpha)r_0g-p\|\geq\varepsilon'd(\alpha h+(1-\alpha)r_0g,S\setminus K)=\varepsilon'\operatorname{ess}\inf(\alpha h+(1-\alpha)r_0g)\geq\varepsilon'r_0(1-\alpha)\operatorname{ess}\inf g=\varepsilon'r_0(1-\alpha)\gamma$. If r_0 is increased to $r'=\frac{\varepsilon'r_0}{2}+r_0$, then

$$\begin{aligned}\inf_{p\in P}\cdot\|\alpha h+(1-\alpha)r'g-p\|&\geq\inf_{p\in P}\|\alpha h+(1-\alpha)r_0g-p\|\\&\quad-(1-\alpha)(r'-r_0)\gamma\\&\geq\varepsilon'\cdot r_0(1-\alpha)\gamma-\frac{(1-\alpha)\varepsilon'r_0\gamma}{2}\\&=\frac{\varepsilon'r_0(1-\alpha)\gamma}{2}\\&>0.\end{aligned}$$

Since $h\in C$ and $0\leq\alpha<1$ were arbitrary, $\langle C\cup r'g\rangle\cap\operatorname{st}\operatorname{int}P=\emptyset$, so that $r_0\geq r'>r_0$.

Let $G=\{s\in K:\pi_1\cdot s\leq\pi_1\cdot f_1\}$. Since $D\subset G$, G also has the property that $\inf\left\{\frac{d(p,G)}{d(p,S\setminus K)}:p\in\operatorname{st}\operatorname{int}P\right\}=0$. If $\pi\notin L_1$, there exists $E_n\uparrow E,E_n,E\in\mathcal{B}$ such that $\lim_n\pi_1(E_n)=\alpha\pi_1(E)$, $0\leq\alpha<1$. Let $\eta>0$ be such that $\|s-t\|<\eta$ implies that $|\pi_1(s)-\pi_1(t)|<\frac{3-3\alpha}{4}\pi_1(E)$. Let $p\in\operatorname{st}\operatorname{int}P$ be such that $\frac{d(p,G)}{d(p,S\setminus K)}<\eta$, and let $0<\gamma\leq d(p,S\setminus K)$.

Then, $B(p,\eta\cdot\gamma)\cap G\neq\emptyset$. Let $g=p+\gamma\frac{(1-\alpha)}{4}\chi_E$. By monotonicity, g is in the relative Mackey interior of P. $g_n=g+\gamma(\chi_{E_n}-\chi_E)\cdot g_n\to g$ in the Mackey topology and $\|g_n-p\|<\gamma$, so that eventually $g_n\succsim_1 f_1$ and hence eventually $\pi_1\cdot g_n\geq\pi_1\cdot f_1$. $\pi_1\cdot g_n\leq\pi_1\cdot p+\gamma\frac{(1-\alpha)}{4}\pi_1(E)-\gamma\pi_1(E)+\gamma\cdot\alpha\pi_1(E)=\pi_1\cdot p+\gamma\frac{(-3+3\alpha)}{4}\pi_1(E)$. But since $B(p,\eta\cdot\gamma)\cap G\neq\emptyset$, $\pi_1\cdot p-\pi_1\cdot f_1<\gamma\frac{(3-3\alpha)}{4}\pi_1(E)$, so that $\pi_1\cdot g_n<\pi_1\cdot f_1$. This contradiction shows that π_1 is countably additive.

To recapitulate, we have shown that it is possible to choose positive $\pi_1,\ldots,\pi_n\in L_1(B,\mathcal{B},\nu)$ such that $\pi_i\cdot P_i\geq\pi_i\cdot f_i\geq\pi_i\cdot C_i$, where $P_i=\{s\in X_i : s\succsim_i f_i\}$, and $C_i=\{s\in X_i:\pi\cdot s\leq\pi\cdot f_i\}$. Clearly, one can choose the π_i such that $\pi_i\cdot(f_i-x_i)=\pi\cdot(f_i-x_i)=\pi(w_i-x_i)>0$. If $s\in K$ and $\pi\cdot s\neq 0$, let $s'=\frac{\pi\cdot(f_i-x_i)}{\pi\cdot s}s$. Since $\pi\cdot s'=\pi\cdot(f_i-x_i)$, $\pi_i\cdot s'\leq\pi_i\cdot(f_i-x_i)=\pi\cdot(f_i-x_i)=\pi\cdot s'$ or $\pi_i\cdot s\leq\pi\cdot s$. By a standard argument, the fact that π is an equilibrium price and the monotonicity of preferences imply that if $s\in K$ and $s\neq 0$ then $\pi\cdot s>0$. Thus, $\pi_i\leq\pi$.

Recall that it is necessary to demonstrate that π is countably additive on $Z_i=\left\{b\in B:(f_i-x_i)(b)\geq\frac{t_0}{n}\right\}$. If π is not countably additive on Z_i, there exist $E_n\uparrow E\subset Z_i$, $E_n,E\in\mathcal{B}$ and such that $\lim_n\pi(E_n)<\pi(E)$. Let $g_n=f_i-x_i-\frac{t_0}{n}\chi_E+\frac{t_0}{n}\chi_E$. Since $E\subset Z_i$, $g_n\geq 0$, so that $\pi\cdot g_n\geq\pi_i\cdot g_n$ $\forall n$. Since π_n is countably additive, $\pi_i\cdot g_n\uparrow\pi_i\cdot(f_i-x_i)=\pi\cdot(f_i-x_i)$. Thus, $\pi\cdot g_n\uparrow\pi\cdot(f_i-x_i)$, contradicting $\lim_n\pi(E_n)<\pi(E)$. Q.E.D.

This completes the proof of the theorem.

The value of this theorem clearly lies chiefly in the method of proof, for the theorem excludes production. There are quite reasonable assumptions that can be made about production sets which make it possible to use the same method to prove the existence of equilibria for economies with production. Unfortunately, this equilibrium would be with respect to a price in $ba(B,\mathcal{B},\nu)$. It is not clear that there are reasonable conditions on productions sets that imply that there exist equilibria with respect to a price in L_1. The proof given above of Proposition 6 depended on the fact that if f is an allocation, then $\sum f_i=\sum w_i\gg 0$. But if the economy includes production, then if (f,y) is an allocation, $\sum_{i=1}^n f_i=\sum_{i=1}^n w_i+\sum_{j=1}^m y_j$, and it is no longer possible to assert that $\sum f_i\gg 0$. (Return to page 2 for an explanation of notation.)

A fundamental step in the proof of the existence theorem was the proof the Pareto optima exist. This latter proof depended on the fact that the set of feasible allocations was bounded. To assure that the set of feasible allocations be bounded when there are producers, it is enough to assume that the intersection of each production set with any translate of the positive cone be a bounded set. But because of resource limitations, this is an acceptable assumption.

In order to understand the effect of resource limitations, consider the case of an economy with an infinite time horizon. It is assumed that each agent lives infinitely long, and that the choices to be made are among programs of production and consumption over an infinite number of discrete time periods. In each time period, there are a finite number, k, of commodities, so that the commodity space is the set of all bounded functions from the positive integers, $\mathbb{N}$, to $\mathbb{R}^k$. This space is actually equal to $\ell_\infty = L_\infty(\mathbb{N})$, but it is important to retain its interpretation as functions into $\mathbb{R}^k$. For each time period, $t \in \mathbb{N}$, let $Y_t \subset (\mathbb{R}^k \times \mathbb{R}^k)$ be a closed convex set such that $y \in Y_t$ and $y \geq 0$ implies $y = 0$. These are normal assumptions about production sets in the finite dimensional case. Inputs of factors in period t result in the output of consumption goods in time t and of capital goods in period $t+1$. These capital goods in time t are available as factors in the next period. Let $Y_t' = (0, \ldots, 0, Y_t, 0, \ldots)$. One may assume that the asymptotic cones of the Y_t' are positively semi-independent.[11] $Y' = \sum_{t=1}^{\infty} Y_t'$ is the set of technically feasible infinite production programs. $Y' \subset \mathbb{R}^{\mathbb{N}}$ and there is no reason to assume that the programs are all bounded and therefore actually lie in ℓ_∞. However, it is reasonable to assume that when resource limitations are taken into account, the set of feasible programs would be uniformly bounded. The limitation on land alone would put an upper bound on any production, no matter how technology changes over time. This limitation is expressed as follows. Let K' be the positive cone orthant of $\mathbb{R}^{\mathbb{N}}$, and let w be any element of K' which is uniformly bounded. Then, $Y' \cap (K' - w)$ is a bounded set, and hence lies in ℓ_∞. Since it is reasonable to assume that the initial endowments of agents are uniformly bounded over time, it is apparent that all relevant programs lie in ℓ_∞. Hence, it seems reasonable to let the commodity space be ℓ_∞, and to

[11] See Gerard Debreu, *Theory of Value*, p. 22.

assume that if $w \in \ell_\infty$ and Y is a production set, then $Y \cap (K + w)$ is bounded in the norm of ℓ_∞, where K is the positive cone. However, in the usual interpretation of decentralized production, it is said that a producer acts so as to maximize profit among all technically possible production programs, feasible or infeasible, bounded or not. But this criticism is not valid if the price system lies in ℓ_1. Let Y' be as above and let $Y = Y' \cap \ell_\infty$ and let π be a positive element of ℓ_1. If y is a maximal element of Y with respect to π, then it is easy to see that it is a maximal point in Y'. This Y also has the important property that it is a weak-star closed subset of ℓ_∞. Weak-star convergence implies pointwise convergence, and Y is closed under pointwise limits, for the sets $\sum_{t=1}^{T} Y_t'$ are closed since the Y_t' are closed and their asymptotic cones are positively semi-independent. (See Gerard Debreu, *Theory of Value*, p. 23 (9).)

In the light of the above discussion, it seems reasonable to say that in the case of markets with an infinite time horizon, ℓ_∞ is a reasonable commodity space, and that the following assumptions are permissible:

(1) each production set, Y_j, $j = 1, \ldots, m$, has the property that $Y \cap (w + K)$ is bounded for all $w \in \ell_\infty$,
(2) $Y_j \cap K = \{0\}$,
(3) $\sum_{j=1}^{m} Y_j$ is convex,
(4) Y_j is weak-star closed.

Another application of models with an infinite dimensional commodity space is to a market involving choice under uncertainty and where commodities are representable as functions on a probability space with infinitely many points. Considerations similar to those made above make the above assumptions reasonable in this case as well.

With the above assumptions it is not hard to fill in the steps of the proof of the existence of an equilibrium. The proof that Pareto optima exist and that the set $\mathcal{U}$ is homeomorphic to Δ_n hold with little change. The next step is to prove that for each Pareto optima, (f, y), there exists a price $\pi \in ba$, such that $\forall j$, $\pi \cdot y = \max \pi \cdot Y_j$, and $\forall i$, $s \succsim_i f_i$ implies that $\pi \cdot s \geq \pi \cdot f_i$. To see this one need only prove that the set $\langle \bigcup_{i=1}^{n} (P_i - f_i) \rangle \cap \cap \sum_{j=1}^{m} (Y_j - y_j)$ does not have strong interior, where $P_i = \{s : s \succsim_i f_i\}$.

The proof of the existence theorem made use of the function $\psi(f, \pi) = \pi(f - w)$. In the case of a market with production, this function becomes

$\psi_i(f, y, \pi) = \pi(f_i - w_i - \sum_{j=1}^{m} \theta_{ij} y_j)$. Let $\phi : \mathcal{U} \to H$ be defined by $\phi(v) = \{\psi(f, y, \pi) : (f, y)$ is a Pareto optimum such that $u(f) = v$; (f, y) is cost minimizing and profit maximizing with respect to $\pi\}$. It is necessary to show that $\phi(v)$ is characterized by the values taken by ψ for one optimum (f, y) such that $u(f) = v$, and then it is necessary to show that ϕ is upper-semi-continuous. Both of these assertions can be proved using slight modifications of the arguments for the case with no producers, provided one exploits the fact that if $\psi(f, y, \pi)$ is an element of $\phi(v)$, then y is profit maximizing with respect to π. For instance, consider the proof that ϕ is upper-semi-continuous. Let (v^n, r^n) be a sequence in the graph of ϕ and suppose that $(v^n, r^n) \to (v, r)$. v is in $\mathcal{U}$ as before. Let (f^n, y^n) and (f, y) be optima such that $u(f^n) = v^n$, $u(f) = v$, and let $r^n = (\psi(f^n, y^n, \pi_n)$. A subset of the π_n converge to a price π. It is necessary to show that $r = (f, y, \pi)$. The key step in the argument is to show that if $u_i(s) \geq v$, then $\pi \cdot s \geq r_i + \pi(w_i + \sum_{j=1}^{m} \theta_{ij} y_j)$. It is known that $\pi_n \cdot f_i^n = r_i^n + \pi_n(w_i + \sum_{j=1}^{m} \theta_{ij} y_j^n)$. But $\pi_n \cdot y_j^n \geq \pi \cdot y_j$, and hence, $\pi_n \cdot f_i^n \geq r_i^n + \pi_n(w_i + \sum_{j=1}^{m} \theta_{ij} y_j)$. From here the proof is exactly as before.

Once it is known that the correspondence ϕ is upper-semi-continuous, no further changes need to be made in the proof that an equilibrium exists with respect to a price in $ba(B, \mathcal{B}, \nu)$.

The problem of finding conditions under which an equilibrium exists with respect to a price in L_1 has not yet been solved in a satisfactory manner. It would be enough to assume that the production sets have non-empty Mackey interior, but this assumption would conflict with the assumption that the intersection of production sets with translates of the positive cone are bounded. It is possible to find a basis of Mackey continuous neighborhoods of zero such that each of the neighborhoods contains the absolute value of any of its elements. Thus, if the intersection of such a neighborhood with the positive cone were bounded, it would be bounded. But then the Mackey topology would be stronger than the norm topology, which would imply that $ba(B, \mathcal{B}, \nu) = L_1(B, \mathcal{B}, \nu)$, which is possible only if $\mathcal{B}$ is a finite set. It might be that production sets have other properties that would assure that equilibria would be equilibria with respect to prices in L_1. It is tempting to hope that under appropriate assumptions, equilibrium consumptions would lie in the interior of each consumer's consumption set. Proposition 6 would then imply that the equilibrium price was countably additive. But, in the case of production over an infinite time period, consumers would never consume capital goods. Capital goods could be suppressed from the model by projecting the production sets onto the components representing all other commodities, but then the prices of capital goods would not be determined by the model.

It would be a great advantage to find reasonable conditions under which the price would lie in L_1, for if it would be possible to do so, one could eliminate the assumption that $w_i \gg x_i$. This assumption makes little sense in the case of production over time. It is only necessary in order to assure that for any non-zero price system, the wealth of every agent be greater than the minimum of the price system on his consumption set. This positivity implies that if (f, y) is a Pareto optimum which is cost minimizing and profit maximizing with respect to π, and if $\psi(f, y, \pi) = 0$, then each f_i is a maximal point in the ith agent's budget set, so that (f, y) is in fact an equilibrium,. If one knew that π would be countably additive, then one could eliminate the assumption that $w_i \gg x_i$ in the case of production over time, in the following way. It is quite reasonable to assume that the sacrifice of any positive amount of any commodity in the first period would make possible an increased production of every other commodity in the first period and of all other commodities in later periods. It is easy to see that this implies that under this assumption any profit maximizing price in ℓ_1 is positive in all components of the first period. Hence, in this case it would be necessary to assume only that w_i was greater than x_i in one component of the first period. Since it is reasonable to suppose that $x_i = 0$, one need only assume that each agent have a positive quantity of some resource, such as labor, in the first period. This assumption is certainly sound.

Mathematical Appendix

The best references for the mathematics used in this paper are John Kelley, *General Topology* (Van Nostrand: 1955), John Kelley and Isaac Namioka, *Linear Topological Spaces* (Van Nostrand: 1963), and Nelson Dunford and Jacob Schwartz,. *Linear Operators, Part I* (Interscience).

I) The spaces L_1, L_∞, and ba. Let $(B, \mathcal{B}, \nu)$ be a positive measure space. $ba(B, \mathcal{B}, \nu)$ is the set of all bounded, finitely additive set functions on $(B, \mathcal{B}, \nu)$ absolutely continuous with respect to ν. $L_1(B, \mathcal{B}, \nu)$ is the set of all countably additive set functions in ba. $L_\infty(B, \mathcal{B}, \nu)$ is the set of all essentially bounded measurable functions on $(B, \mathcal{B}, \nu)$. A function is essentially bounded iff the essential supremum of its absolute value is finite, where the essential supremum is defined by $\operatorname{ess\,sup} f = \inf\{r : \nu\{b \in B : f(b) \geq r\} = 0\}$. ba, L_1, and L_∞ are all normed spaces. The norm on ba and L_1 is defined by $\|\pi\| = \sup \sum_{i=1}^{k} |\pi(E_i)|$, where the supremum is taken over all finite subsets of $\mathcal{B}$. The norm on L_∞ is $|f| = \operatorname{ess\,sup} |f|$. If π is a positive element of ba, $\|\pi\| = \pi(B)$. Each element of ba is a real-valued linear function on L_∞ under the action $\pi \cdot f = \int f d\nu$. ba is in fact the dual of L_∞, that is, it is the space of all real-valued linear functions on L_∞, continuous with respect to the norm topology. The same action makes each element of L_∞ a linear function of L_1, and L_∞ is in fact the dual of L_1.

Let $\mathcal{T}$ and $\mathcal{S}$ be linear topological spaces such that $\mathcal{S}$ is the dual of $\mathcal{T}$ under the action $(t, s) \to s \cdot t$. A net t_α in $\mathcal{T}$ is said to converge weakly to t iff $s \cdot t_\alpha \to s \cdot t \; \forall s \in \mathcal{S}$. The topology derived from this sense of convergence is called the weak topology. It is in fact the weakest topology on $\mathcal{T}$ such that $\mathcal{S}$ is the dual of $\mathcal{T}$ with that topology. Similarly, the weak-star topology on $\mathcal{S}$ is the weakest topology on $\mathcal{S}$ such that $\mathcal{T}$ is the dual of $\mathcal{S}$ with that topology. It is the topology defined by the sense of convergence, $s_\alpha \to s$ iff $t \cdot s_\alpha \to t \cdot s \; \forall t \in \mathcal{T}$.

If $T \subset \mathcal{T}$, then the polar of T in S is $\{s \in S : |s \cdot t| \leq 1 \; \forall t \in T\}$. The Banach-Aloaglu Theorem says that the polar of any neighborhood of zero in a linear topological space is weak-star compact. The unit balls in L_1 and L_∞ are neighborhoods of zero in the norm topologies, and their polars are the unit balls in L_∞ and ba respectively. Thus, the unit balls of L_∞ and ba are weak-star compact. The set of all prices in ba, Π, is defined to be $\{\pi \in ba : \pi \geq 0, \|\pi\| = 1\}$. If $\pi \geq 0$, then $\|\pi\| = \pi(B) = \pi \cdot \chi_B$, where χ_B, the characteristic function of B, is in L_∞. Also, $\pi \geq 0$ if and only if for every positive $f \in L_\infty$, $\pi \cdot f \geq 0$. Thus $\Pi = \{\pi \in ba : \pi \cdot f \geq 0, \; \forall f \in L_\infty \text{ such that } f \geq 0, \; \pi \cdot \chi_B = 1\}$, and hence Π is a weak-star closed subset of the unit ball in ba and is hence weak-star compact.

Returning to the spaces $\mathcal{T}$, $\mathcal{S}$, the Mackey topology on $\mathcal{S}$ is the strongest topology on $\mathcal{S}$ such that $\mathcal{T}$ is the dual of $\mathcal{S}$ when $\mathcal{S}$ is given that topology. Neighborhoods of zero in this topology are characterized by the fact that they contain polars of weakly compact subsets of L_1. In the case of L_∞ and L_1, the Mackey topology on L_∞ is the strongest topology on L_∞ such that L_1 is the dual of L_∞. This topology has a neighborhood base at zero consisting of polars of weakly compact subsets of L_1. Weakly compact subsets of L_1 are characterized by the fact that they are bounded and uniformly σ-additive. That is, $C \subset L_1$ is weakly compact iff $\sup\{\|\pi\| : \pi \in C\} < \infty$, and if for all n, $E_n \in \mathcal{B}$ and $E_{n+1} \supset E_n$, and if $E = \bigcup_{n=1}^{\infty} E_n$, then $\pi(E_n) \to \pi(E)$ uniformly on C.

II) Justification of Use of Mackey Topology. An attempt is made here to reveal some of the significance of the assumption that preferences are continuous with respect to the Mackey topology, by consideration of a few examples.

Suppose that $B = \mathbf{N}$, the positive integers, that $\mathcal{B}$ = the set of all subsets of $\mathbf{N}$, and that ν is the counting measure. Then $L_\infty(B, \mathcal{B}, \nu) = \ell_\infty$. Let $c \in \ell_1$ and suppose $c \geq 0$, that is, $c = \{c_t\}$, where c_t is a non-negative sequence such that c_t converges. For each t, let u_t be a utility function on $\mathbb{R}^n$. We will consider utility functions on L_∞ of the form $u(f) = \sum_{t=1}^{\infty} c_t u_t(f_{nt+1}, \ldots, f_{(n+1)t})$. The assumptions listed below will be of interest.

Assumption 1) $\forall t$, $u_t : \mathbb{R}^n_+ \to [0,1]$ and is continuous.

Assumption 2) $\forall t$, $u_t : \mathbb{R}^n_+ \to \mathbb{R}$ and the u_t are uniformly bounded on balls about 0 in $\mathbb{R}^n$ and are uniformly equicontinuous.

Assumption 3) $\forall t$, $u_t = u_1$ and u_1 is continuous and concave, and maps $\mathbb{R}^n_+$ into $\mathbb{R}$.

Assumption 4) $\forall t$, $u_t : \mathbb{R}^n_+ \to \mathbb{R}$, and the u_t are continuous and are uniformly bounded on balls about 0 in $\mathbb{R}^n_+$.

Assumption 1 implies that if f_n is a positive sequence in ℓ_∞ that converges pointwise to f, then $u(f_n)$ converges to $u(f)$.

Assumptions 2 and 3 imply that if f_n is a positive sequence in ℓ_∞ that converges in the weak-star topology to f, then $u(f_n)$ converges to $u(f)$.

Assumption 4 implies that if f_n is a positive sequence in ℓ_∞ that converges in the Mackey topology to f, then $u(f_n)$ converges to $u(f)$.

The first assertion follows from the Lebesgue Dominated Convergence theorem. The second assertion follows from the fact that Assumptions 2 and 3 imply that the u_t are uniformly dominated by a linear function plus a constant. The third assertion follows from the fact that Mackey convergent sequences in ℓ_∞ are bounded.

III) Homotopy. Two continuous functions $f, g : A \rightarrow B$ are said to be homotopic iff there exists a continuous functions $H : A \times [0,1] \rightarrow B$ such that $H(a,0) = f(a)$, $H(a,1) = g(a)$. A good interpretation of the homotopy relation is that the graph of f can be deformed smoothly into that of g without tearing it.

The Core of an Economy Without Ordered Preferences

Nicholas C. Yannelis*

Abstract. Core existence results are proved for exchange economies with an infinite dimensional commodity space. In particular, the commodity space may be any ordered Hausdorff linear topological space, and agents' preferences need not be transitive, complete, monotone or convex; preferences may even be interdependent. Under these assumptions a quasi equilibrium may not exist.

1. Introduction

During the last decade, contributions in consumer theory [e.g., Sonnenschein (1971), Shafer (1974) and Kim-Richter (1986)] and contributions in equilibrium theory [e.g., Mas-Colell (1974), Gale-Mas-Colell (1975), Shafer-Sonnenschein (1975), Borglin-Keiding (1976), McKenzie (1981), and Yannelis-Prabhakar (1983)] have shown that the transitivity axiom is not only a restrictive assumption but unnecessary as well. In fact, very general competitive equilibrium existence results have been obtained for finite economies where agents' preferences need not be ordered, i.e., need not be transitive or complete (therefore, need not be representable by utility functions), and may be interdependent. These existence results for the competitive equilibrium have been further generalized to economies with infinitely many commodities [see for instance Mas-Colell (1986) or Yannelis-Zame (1986) among others]. Thus, significant progress has been made on the task of establishing very general conditions for the existence of a competitive equilibrium.

The core is an alternative solution concept which has been widely used in game theory and by extension in general equilibrium analysis. It is still not known whether or not core existence results can be obtained

---

* The results of this paper were obtained in 1984. The present version is virtually identical to the Discussion paper No. 214, June 1985, University of Minnesota. The minor changes are due to suggestions made by Charles Holly to whom I am very thankful. It should be noted that Atsumi Kajii has recently obtained α-core existence results for normal form games without ordered preferences.

at the level of generality established for competitive equilibrium existence theorems.

The first core existence result for an economy was proved in Scarf (1967, 1971). He required agents' preferences to be transitive and complete. Border (1984) recently generalized this result to allow for preferences which need not be transitive or complete. Both authors obtain their results for economies with a finite dimensional commodity space, and follow a common argument: First, they establish that the core of a balanced non-side payment game is nonempty; and second, they show the nonemptiness of the core of an economy by showing that the game derived from an economy is balanced.[1]

Recently, several nonexistence core results have been given for infinite dimensional commodity spaces [see for instance Araujo (1985) and Mas-Colell (1986)]. In particular, these authors have shown by means of counter-examples that in an infinite dimensional commodity space, where agents' preferences are representable by very well-behaved utility functions, one can not necessarily even expect individually rational Pareto optimal allocations to exist. Therefore, the question is raised under what conditions can core existence results be obtained in an infinite dimensional commodity space. The purpose of this paper is to show that in any ordered Hausdorff linear topological space, core allocations exist under very mild assumptions. In particular, agents' preferences need not be ordered, monotone or nonsaturated. Indeed, under these assumptions even a quasi-equilibrium need not exist. Moreover, we show that in any ordered Hausdorff linear topological space, individually rational Pareto optimal allocations exist, even if preferences are interdependent and may not be ordered, monotone or nonsaturated.

It may be instructive to comment on the technical aspects of the

---

[1] It should be noted that a different proof of Scarf's result has been given in Shapley (1973). In particular Shapley provides an extension of the Sperner Lemma which is used to obtain a generalized version of the Knaster-Kuratowski-Mazurkiewicz (K-K-M) theorem known in the literature as K-K-M-S. By means of the K-K-M-S theorem Shapley proves that the core of a balanced game is nonempty. Here we must note that an elegant proof of the K-K-M-S theorem was recently given by Ichiichi (1981), by using the coincidence theorem of Fan (1969).

paper. Although the arguments of Scarf (1967, 1971) and Shapley (1973) are based on finite dimensional results, Border's (1984) proof is based on an infinite dimensional fixed point result of Fan (1969). At first glance, it seems that Border's arguments might be extended to cover infinite dimensional commodity spaces; unfortunately, a careful examination of his proof indicates that this is not possible. The problem arises from the fact that the convex hull of an upper-semicontinuous (u.s.c.) correspondence need not be u.s.c. when the dimensionality of the commodity space is infinite [see Schaefer (1971, exercise 27, p. 72)]. Consequently, in order to prove the nonemptiness of the core for an economy with infinitely many commodities and without ordered preferences different arguments than the ones used by Scarf, Shapley and Border seem to be needed. In particular, following Bewley's (1972) ideas we will prove an infinite dimensional core existence result by considering its trace in finite dimensions.

However, a different approach is adopted to prove that with interdependent preferences individually rational Pareto optimal allocations exist. In particular, the main mathematical tool that we use is an existence of maximal elements result which is a corollary of either the Knaster-Kuratowski-Mazurkiewicz (K-K-M) Lemma as extended by Fan (1962) or the Browder (1968) fixed point theorem. In fact, we will show that these two remarkable technical theorems turn out to be equivalent in the sense that each one can be derived from the other. It should be noted that the idea of using maximal elements results to prove optima goes back to Debreu (1959, p. 92). The same idea was also used in Hildenbrand (1974, Theorem 3, p. 230) and Berninghaus (1977, Theorem 1, p. 283). However, the assumption that preferences are transitive and complete and consequently representable by utility functions is crucial to their arguments. It turns out, that allowing simultaneously, preferences to be nonordered and the dimensionality of the commodity space to be infinite, rather powerful fixed point results seem to be needed. It is exactly for this reason that we make use of the theorems of Fan (1962) and Browder (1968).

The paper is organized in the following way. Section 2 contains some notation and definitions. Section 3 shows the equivalence between the K-K-M Lemma as extended by Fan and the Browder fixed point theorem. The main results of the paper, i.e., core existence theorems, are stated in Section 4 and their proofs are given in Section 5. In Section 6 we discuss some pathological examples known in the literature. Finally, some concluding remarks are given in Section 7.

2. Notation and Definitions

2.1 Notation.

2^A denotes the set of all subsets of A.

con A denotes the convex hull of the set A.

$\mathbb{R}^\ell$ denotes the ℓ-fold product of the set of real numbers $\mathbb{R}$.

$|S|$ denotes the number of elements in the set S.

If $\phi : X \to 2^Y$ is a correspondence, $\phi|_A$ denotes the restriction of ϕ to A, i.e., $\phi|_A : A \to 2^Y$.

$\emptyset$ denotes the empty set.

$\setminus$ denotes the set theoretic subtraction.

int A denotes the interior of A.

If X is a linear topological space, its dual is the space X^* of all continuous linear functionals on X.

2.2 Definitions. Let X and Y be two topological spaces. Let $\phi : X \to 2^Y$ be a set-valued function (or correspondence). The set-valued function $\phi^{-1} : Y \to 2^X$ defined by $\phi^{-1}(y) = \{x \in X : y \in \phi(x)\}$ is called the *lower section* of ϕ. We say that $\phi : X \to 2^Y$ has *open lower sections* if for each $y \in Y$ the set $\phi^{-1}(y) = \{x \in X : y \in \phi(x)\}$ is open in X. A binary relation $\mathcal{P}$ on X is a subset of $X \times X$. We read $x\mathcal{P}y$ as "x is strictly preferred to y." Define the correspondence $P : X \to 2^X$ by $P(x) = \{y \in X : y\mathcal{P}x\}$. We call P a *preference correspondence*, and $P(x)$ denotes its *upper section* and $P^{-1}(y)$ its *lower section*. The set-valued function $P : X \to 2^X$ has an *open graph* if the set $\{(x, y) \in X \times X : y \in P(x)\}$ is open in $X \times X$. Moreover, $P : X \to 2^X$ is said to be *lower semicontinuous* if the set $\{x \in X : P(x) \cap V \neq \emptyset\}$ is open in X for every open subset V of X. If there exists $x^* \in X$ such that $P(x^*) = \emptyset$ we say that x^* is a *maximal element* in X.

3. The K-K-M-F Lemma and the Browder Fixed Point Theorem

3.1 Theorems. Fan (1962) extended the powerful Knaster-Kuratowski-Mazurkiewicz (K-K-M) theorem from a Euclidean space to Hausdorff linear topological spaces. Another simple but powerful fixed point theorem was proved by Browder (1968). Both results, in addition to their applications in mathematics, have recently proved extremely useful in economics. In fact, they have become the main technical tools to prove the existence of maximal elements and equilibria in linear topological spaces of arbitrary dimension. As a consequence, generalizations of the results of Debreu (1952), Sonnenschein (1971), Mas-Colell (1974), Gale-Mas-Colell (1975), and Shafer-Sonnenschein (1975) have been obtained [see for instance, Borglin-Keiding (1976), Yannelis-Prabhakar (1983), and Toussaint (1984)]. Since these two theorems will be the main mathematical tools used in the sequel, it is of interest to know the relationship between them. The purpose of this section is to show that Fan's generalization of the K-K-M theorem (called here K-K-M-F) theorem) can be easily derived from Browder's fixed point theorem and that the Browder fixed point theorem can be easily derived from the K-K-M-F theorem. Therefore one may consider these two results as equivalent.

The K-K-M-F theorem proved in Fan (1962) is stated below:

Theorem 3.1 (K-K-M-F). *Let X be an arbitrary convex set in a Hausdorff linear topological space Y. For each $x \in X$, let $F(x)$ be a closed set in Y such that the following two conditions are satisfied:*

(i) the convex hull of any finite subset $\{x_1, \ldots, x_n\}$ of X is contained in $\bigcup_{i=1}^n F(x_i)$, and

(ii) $F(x)$ is compact for at least one $x \in X$.

Then $\bigcap_{x \in X} F(x) \neq \emptyset$.

We now state Browder's (1968) fixed point theorem.

Theorem 3.2 (Browder). *Let X be a compact, convex, nonempty subset of a Hausdorff linear topological space Y and $\phi : X \to 2^X$ be a correspondence such that:*

(1) $\phi(x)$ is nonempty for all $x \in X$,

(2) $\phi(x)$ is convex for all $x \in X$,

(3) for each $y \in X$, the set $\phi^{-1}(y) = \{x \in X : y \in \phi(x)\}$ is open in X, i.e., ϕ has open lower sections.

Then there exists $x^* \in X$ such that $x^* \in \phi(x^*)$.

3.2 Proof of the K-K-M-F Theorem via Browder's Fixed Point Theorem. Since $F(x)$ is closed in Y for each $x \in X$ and compact for at least one $x \in X$, it suffices to prove that $\bigcap_{i=1}^n F(x_i) \neq \emptyset$ for every subset $\{x_1, \ldots, x_n\}$ of X. Suppose otherwise, i.e., $\bigcap_{i=1}^n F(x_i) = \emptyset$ for some finite subset $\{x_1, \ldots, x_n\}$ of X. Let Δ be the finite dimensional simplex spanned by the finite set $\{x_1, \ldots, x_n\}$. Since the topology induced on any finite dimensional subspace of Y by the topology of Y coincides with the Euclidean topology, Δ is homeomorphic to a Euclidean ball (Kelley and Namioka, 1963, Theorem 7.3, p. 59). Define the correspondence $\psi : \Delta \to 2^\Delta$ by $\psi(x) = \{y \in \Delta : x \notin F(y)\}$. Then for each $x \in \Delta$, $\psi(x)$ is nonempty. Indeed, at least one x_i, $(1 \leq i \leq n)$ is in $\psi(x)$, for otherwise $x \in \bigcap_{i=1}^n F(x_i)$, and so $\bigcap_{i=1}^n F(x_i) \neq \emptyset$. Notice that for each $y \in \Delta$, $\psi^{-1}(y) = \{x \in \Delta : y \in \psi(x)\} = \Delta \setminus \{x \in \Delta : x \in F(y)\}$. Observe that $\{x \in \Delta : x \in F(y)\} = \Delta \cap F(y)$, and this is a closed set in Δ. Hence, for each $y \in \Delta$ the set $\psi^{-1}(y)$ is open in Δ. Define the correspondence $\phi : \Delta \to 2^\Delta$ by $\phi(x) = \operatorname{con} \psi(x)$ for all $x \in \Delta$. Then, $\phi(x)$ is convex and nonempty for all $x \in \Delta$. Furthermore, by Lemma 5.1 in Yannelis-Prabhakar (1983) the set $\phi^{-1}(y) = \{x \in \Delta : y \in \phi(x)\}$ is open in Δ for each $y \in \Delta$. Consequently, the correspondence $\phi : \Delta \to 2^\Delta$ satisfies all the assumptions of Theorem 3.2. Hence, there exists $x^* \in \Delta$ such that $x^* \in \phi(x^*) = \operatorname{con} \psi(x^*)$. But, $x^* \in \operatorname{con} \psi(x^*)$ implies that there exist points $y_1, \ldots, y_m$ in Δ and real numbers $a_1, \ldots, a_m$, $a_j \geq 0$, $(1 \leq j \leq m)$, $\sum_{j=1}^m a_j = 1$, such that $x^* = \sum_{j=1}^m a_j y_j$ and $y_j \in \psi(x^*)$ for all j, a contradiction to assumption (i). Indeed, by assumption (i), for any arbitrary collection of points $\{y_1, \ldots, y_m\}$ out of X, we have that $\operatorname{con}\{y_1, \ldots, y_m\} \subset \bigcup_{i=1}^m F(y_i)$. Thus, if $x^* \in \operatorname{con}\{y_1, \ldots, y_m\}$, then $x^* \in \bigcup_{i=1}^m F(y_i)$ which implies that $x^* \in F(y_i)$ for at least one i. The above contradiction establishes that, $\bigcap_{i=1}^n F(x_i) \neq \emptyset$, and this completes the proof of the K-K-M-F theorem.

3.3 Proof of Browder's Fixed Point Theorem via the K-K-M-F Theorem. Suppose otherwise, i.e., for all $x \in X$, $x \notin \phi(x)$. Let for each $y \in X$, $F(y) = X \setminus \phi^{-1}(y)$. Since by assumption (3) for each $y \in X$, $\phi^{-1}(y)$ is open in X, it follows that for each $y \in X$, $F(y)$ is closed in X and obviously closed in Y since X is a compact subset of Y. Moreover, $F(y)$ is compact for each $y \in X$. It is easy to see that for any arbitrary set of points $\{y_1, \ldots, y_n\} \subset X$, we have that $\operatorname{con}\{y_1, \ldots, y_n\} \subset \bigcup_{i=1}^n F(y_i)$. For otherwise, there exists $x \in \operatorname{con}\{y_1, \ldots, y_n\}$ and $x \notin \bigcup_{i=1}^n F(y_i)$ which implies that $x \in \phi^{-1}(y_i)$ for all i or $y_i \in \phi(x)$ for all i and therefore $x \in \operatorname{con}\{y_1, \ldots, y_n\} \subset \operatorname{con}\phi(x) = \phi(x)$, a contradiction to $x \notin \phi(x)$ for all $x \in X$. Hence, by Theorem 3.1 $\bigcap_{y \in X} F(y) \neq \emptyset$. Let $z \in \bigcap_{y \in X} F(y)$. Then for all $y \in X$, $z \notin \phi^{-1}(y)$ which implies that $\phi(z) = \emptyset$, for some $z \in X$. But this contradicts assumption (1). Therefore there exist $x^* \in X$ such that $x^* \in \phi(x^*)$, and the proof of the Browder theorem is now complete.

3.4 Existence of Maximal Elements. It is easy to check that Browder's fixed point theorem is equivalent to the following existence of maximal elements result.

Theorem 3.3. *Let X be a nonempty, compact, convex subset of a Hausdorff linear topological space Y and $P : X \to 2^X$ be a preference correspondence such that:*

(i) $x \notin P(x)$ for all $x \in X$
(ii) $P(x)$ is convex for all $x \in X$
(iii) P has open lower sections.

Then there exists $x^* \in X$ such that $P(x^*) = \emptyset$.

Hence, we can reach the following conclusion:

K-K-M-F $\Leftrightarrow$ *Browder Theorem*
$\Leftrightarrow$ *Existence of Maximal Elements Theorem.*

A direct consequence of the K-K-M-F or Browder theorems is the following result, whose proof can be found in Yannelis and Prabhakar (1983 p. 239, Theorem 5.1).

Theorem 3.4. *Let X be a nonempty, compact, convex subset of a Hausdorff linear topological space and $\phi : X \to 2^X$ be a correspondence having open lower section satisfying the condition that $x \notin \operatorname{con}\phi(x)$ for all $x \in X$. Then there exists $x^* \in X$ such that $\phi(x^*) = \emptyset$.*

By means of Theorem 3.4 one can obtain the following Corollary [see Yannelis and Prabhakar (1983, p. 240, Corollary 5.1)] which is a generalized version of a result of Borglin-Keiding (1976, Corollary 1, p. 314). We first need to introduce a definition.

Definition 3.1. *Let X be a subset of a linear topological space. A correspondence $\phi : X \to 2^X$ is said to be of class $\mathcal{L}$, if*

(i) $x \notin \operatorname{con}\phi(x)$ for all $x \in X$,
(ii) ϕ has open lower sections.

Let $\psi : X \to 2^X$ be a correspondence. The correspondence $\phi_x : X \to 2^X$ is an *$\mathcal{L}$-majorant* of ψ at x if ϕ_x is of class $\mathcal{L}$ and there is an open neighborhood of x denoted by N_x such that for all $z \in N_x$, $\psi(z) \subset \phi_x(z)$. The correspondence $\psi : X \to 2^X$ is *$\mathcal{L}$-majorized* if for each $x \in X$ such that $\psi(x) \neq \emptyset$, there is an $\mathcal{L}$-majorant of ψ at x.

Corollary 3.1. *Let X be a nonempty, compact, convex subset of a Hausdorff linear topological space and $\phi : X \to 2^X$ be an $\mathcal{L}$-majorized correspondence. Then there exists $x^* \in X$ such that $\phi(x^*) = \emptyset$.*

By means of the above Corollary we will prove Theorem 4.1. We would like to emphasize the fact that Corollary 3.1 is a consequence of the Theorems of K-K-M-F and Browder. Moreover, it was pointed out in Borglin-Keiding (1976) that Corollary 3.1 yields an extension of the Kakutani fixed point to Hausdorff locally convex linear topological spaces. With those preliminary mathematical results out of the way we now turn to our core existence theorems.

4. The Main Results

4.1 The Economy. We formalize the notion of an exchange economy in the usual way. Let $I = \{1, \ldots, N\}$ be a finite set of agents. For each $i \in I$, let X_i be a nonempty subset of an ordered Hausdorff linear topological space L. By an *exchange economy with N agents and a commodity space L* (or simply *an economy in L*) we mean the set $\mathcal{E} = \{(X_i, P_i, e_i) : i = 1, \ldots, N\}$ of triples where,

(a) X_i is the *consumption set* of agent i;
(b) $P_i : X \to 2^X$ (where $X = \prod_{i\in I} X_i$) is the *preference correspondence* of agent i;
(c) e_i is the *initial endowment* of agent i, where $e_i \in X_i$ for all $i \in I$.

An *allocation* is a vector $x = (x_1, \ldots, x_N) \in X = \prod_{i\in I} X_i$. An allocation x is said to be *feasible* if $\sum_{i\in I} x_i = \sum_{i\in I} e_i$. Denote by F the *set of all feasible allocations*, i.e., $F = \{x \in X : \sum_{i \in I} x_i = \sum_{i \in I} e_i\}$. Notice that we have allowed for interdependent preferences. In this framework $y \in P_i(x)$ means that agent i strictly prefers the allocation y to x. More simply one may define $P_i : X \to 2^X$ by $P_i(x_1, \ldots, x_N) = \{y \in X : (y_1, \ldots, y_N)\mathcal{P}_i(x_1, \ldots, x_N)\}$.

4.2 The α-Core. If $S \subset I$ then $(y^S, x^{I \setminus S})$ denotes the vector z in X such that:

$$z_i = \begin{cases} y_i & \text{if } i \in S \\ x_i & \text{if } i \notin S. \end{cases}$$

An *α-core allocation* of $\mathcal{E}$ is a vector $x = (x_1, \ldots, x_N) \in X$ such that:

(i) $x \in F$, and

(ii) it is not true that there exist $S \subset I$ and $(y_i)_{i \in S} \in \prod_{i \in S} X_i$ such that $\sum_{i \in S} y_i = \sum_{i \in S} e_i$, and $(y^S, z^{I \setminus S}) \in P_i(x_1, \ldots, x_N)$ for all $i \in S$ and for any $z \in \prod_{i \notin S} X_i$, $\sum_{i \notin S} z_i = \sum_{i \notin S} e_i$.

In other words an α-core allocation for the economy $\mathcal{E}$ must satisfy two conditions. First it must be feasible and secondly, no coalition of agents can redistribute their initial endowments and make all its members better off, once the complementary coalition chooses to redistribute its initial endowment. For a game in normal form, the notion of α-core was introduced in Aumann (1964). It was also used by Scarf (1971) who proved the nonemptiness of the α-core for an n-person game with a finite dimensional strategy space, where each agent's preferences were assumed to be transitive, complete, and continuous.

The *set of all α-core allocations for the economy* $\mathcal{E}$ is denoted by $\mathcal{C}(\mathcal{E})$.

4.3 The Extreme α-Core. If $i \in I$, then (y_i, z^{I^i}) denotes the vector w in X such that:

$$w_j = \begin{cases} y_j & \text{if } j = i \\ z_j & \text{if } j \neq i. \end{cases}$$

An allocation $x \in X$ is said to be *individually rational* if:

(i) $x \in F$, and

(ii) for all $i \in I$, it is not true that $e \in P_i(x)$.

An allocation $x \in X$ is said to be *Pareto optimal* if:

(i) $x \in F$, and

(ii) there is no $y \in F$ such that $y \in P_i(x)$ for all $i \in I$.

An *extreme α-core allocation* of $\mathcal{E}$ is a vector $x = (x_1, \ldots, x_N) \in \prod_{i \in I} X_i$ which satisfies individual rationality and Pareto optimality.

Denote by $\mathcal{C}_e(\mathcal{E})$ the *set of all extreme α-core allocations for the economy* $\mathcal{E}$. Notice that the concept of extreme α-core allocations takes into account only two extreme coalitions, i.e., the grant coalition and the coalitions of one agent alone. Therefore, it is clear that the set of all extreme α-core allocations for $\mathcal{E}$ is bigger than the set of all α-core allocations for $\mathcal{E}$, i.e., $\mathcal{C}(\mathcal{E}) \subseteq \mathcal{C}_e(\mathcal{E})$. However, *it is easy to see that in a two person economy, i.e., when* $|I| = 2$, $\mathcal{C}(\mathcal{E}) = \mathcal{C}_e(\mathcal{E})$.

Finally, if preferences are "selfish," i.e., $P_i : X_i \to 2^{X_i}$ is defined by $P_i(x_i) = \{y_i \in X_i : y_i \mathcal{P}_i x_i\}$, we will call an individually rational Pareto optimal allocation, an *extreme core allocation.*

4.4 The Selfish Core. Let $\mathcal{E} = \{(X_i, \bar{P}_i, e_i) : i = 1, \ldots, N\}$ be an exchange economy, where $\bar{P}_i : X_i \to 2^{X_i}$ is defined by $\bar{P}_i(x_i) = \{y_i \in X_i : y_i \mathcal{P}_i x_i\}$. Notice that preferences are not interdependent. In this framework we may define the notion of selfish core or simply core as follows:

A *selfish core* (or *core*) *allocation* of $\mathcal{E}$ is a vector $x = (x_1, \ldots, x_N) \in X$ such that:

(i) $x \in F$, and
(ii) it is not true that there exist $S \subset I$ and $(y_i)_{i \in S} \in \prod_{i \in S} X_i$ such that $\sum_{i \in S} y_i = \sum_{i \in S} e_i$ and $y_i \in \bar{P}_i(x_i)$ for all $i \in S$.

The above notion of core is the one extensively used in equilibrium analysis. In fact, this is the notion of core used recently in Border (1984) as well. Denote by $\mathcal{C}_s(\mathcal{E})$ the *set of all selfish core allocations for* $\mathcal{E}$.

4.5 Theorems. Before we state our two main results we will need the following definition.

Definition 4.1. *A Hausdorff topology τ, on an ordered Hausdorff linear topological space L, will be called compatible if:*

(a) τ is weaker than the Hausdorff topology of L;
(b) τ is a vector space topology (i.e., the vector space operations on L are continuous in the topology τ);
(c) all order intervals $[0, y] = \{z \in L : 0 \le z \le y\}$ *in L are τ-compact.*

Theorem 4.1. *Let* $\mathcal{E} = \{(X_i, P_i, e_i) : i \in I\}$ *be an exchange economy* *in L, where L is endowed with the compatible topology* τ*, satisfying for each* $i \in I$ *the following assumptions:*

(4.1) $X_i = L^+$, *(L^+ denotes the positive cone of L),*

(4.2) $x \notin \text{con}\, P_i(x)$ *for all* $x \in X$,

(4.3) P_i *has* τ*-open lower sections, i.e., for each* $y \in X$ *the set* $\{x \in X : y \in P_i(x)\}$ *is* τ*-open in* X.

Then there exists an extreme α*-core allocation of* $\mathcal{E}$*, i.e.,* $\mathcal{C}_e(\mathcal{E}) \neq \emptyset$.

Theorem 4.2. *Let* $\mathcal{E} = \{(X_i, \bar{P}_i, e_i) : i \in I\}$ *be an exchange economy in L, where L is endowed with the compatible topology* τ*, satisfying for each* $i \in I$ *the following assumptions:*

(4.4) $X_i = L^+$,

(4.5) $x_i \notin \text{con}\, \bar{P}_i(x_i)$ *for all* $x_i \in X_i$,

(4.6) $\bar{P}_i$ *has a* τ*-open graph, i.e., the set* $\{(x_i, y_i) \in X_i \times X_i : y_i \in \bar{P}_i(x_i)\}$ *is* τ*-open in* $X_i \times X_i$.

Then there exists a selfish core allocation of $\mathcal{E}$*, i.e.,* $\mathcal{C}_s(\mathcal{E}) \neq \emptyset$.

Corollary 4.1. *Let* $\mathcal{E} = \{(X_i, P_i, e_i) : i \in I\}$ *be an exchange economy in L, satisfying the following assumptions:*

(4.7) X_i *is a nonempty, convex, compact subset of L,*

(4.8) $x \notin \text{con}\, P(x)$ *for all* $x \in X$,

(4.9) P_i *has open lower sections.*

Then there exists an extreme α*-core allocation of* $\mathcal{E}$*, i.e.,* $\mathcal{C}_e(\mathcal{E}) \neq \emptyset$.

Corollary 4.2. *Since for* $I = \{1, 2\}$, $\mathcal{C}(\mathcal{E}) = \mathcal{C}_e(\mathcal{E})$ *it follows from Theorem 4.1 that* $\mathcal{C}(\mathcal{E}) \neq \emptyset$.

Remark 4.1. Notice that if in Theorem 4.1 and Corollary 4.1 we had selfish preferences, i.e., $\bar{P}_i : X_i \to 2^{X_i}$ the arguments in the proofs (see Section 5) remain unaffected. In fact, define $P_i : X \to 2^X$ by $P_i(x) = \bar{P}_i(x_i) \times \prod_{j \neq i} X_j$, then the proofs go through with no modification.

4.6 Discussion of the Assumptions. Let us now discuss the assumptions in Theorems 4.1 and 4.2.

First notice that (4.1) is identical with (4.4), and (4.2) is essentially the same with (4.5). Assumption (4.1) is quite standard in equilibrium theory and needs no explanation. Assumption (4.2) is a very weak form of convexity of the upper section. It was first introduced by Shafer-Sonnenschein (1975). Notice that $x \notin \operatorname{con} P_i(x)$ for all $x \in X$ implies that $x \notin P_i(x)$ for all $x \in X$, i.e., P_i is *irreflexive* Of course the same conclusion can be obtained for the selfish preference correspondence $\bar{P}_i$. Assumption (4.3) is a quite weak form of continuity. In fact, if P_i has a τ-open graph in $X \times X$ then both sections (upper and lower) are τ-open. Notice that, (4.3) implies [see Yannelis-Prabhakar (1983, Proposition 4.1, p. 237)] that P_i is τ-lower semicontinuous, i.e., the set $\{x \in X : P_i(x) \cap V \neq \emptyset\}$ is τ-open in X for every τ-open subset V of X.

Finally, since any competitive equilibrium allocation is in the selfish core and obviously in the extreme core it is of interest to know whether or not under the assumptions of either Theorems 4.1 or 4.2 or Corollary 4.1 there exists a competitive equilibrium. However, the example of Mas-Colell (1986), indicates that under the assumptions of either Theorems 4.1 or 4.2 or Corollary 4.1 one should not even expect quasi-equilibria to exist.

It is important to note that in a finite dimensional commodity space if one consumer has a concave, monotone, continuous utility function, strictly positive initial endowments and his/her consumption set is compact, there is always an equilibrium and *a fortiori* the core is nonempty. Contrary to the finite dimensional commodity setting, in an infinite dimensional commodity framework, Mas-Colell's example shows that one should not even expect a quasi equilibrium to exist. Therefore, Theorems 4.1, 4.2 and Corollary 4.1 provide existence core results for economies in which quasi equilibria may not exist.

4.7 Concrete Spaces. In Theorems 4.1 and 4.2 the commodity space L was assumed to be any ordered Hausdorff linear topological space endowed with the compatible topology τ. However, in concrete spaces the topology τ will vary according to the underlying ordered Hausdorff linear topological space L. For instance if the commodity space is the Lebesgue space L_p, $1 \leq p < \infty$ the compatible topology will be the weak topology.

This follows from the fact that the spaces L_p, $1 \leq p < \infty$ are normed vector lattices with order continuous norm, i.e., order intervals are weakly compact [see Aliprantis and Burkinshaw (1985, Theorem 12.9) or Schaefer (1974, Theorem 6.6, p. 100 and Example 6, p. 92)]. If the commodity space is L_∞ or ℓ_∞ the compatible topology will be the weak* topology. Recall that Alaoglou's theorem implies that order intervals are weak* compact [see Aliprantis and Burkinshaw (1985, Theorem 9.20)]. Finally, if the commodity space is the space of real sequences ℓ_p, $1 \leq p < \infty$ the compatible topology will be the norm topology. This follows from the standard result that order intervals in ℓ_p, $1 \leq p < \infty$ are norm compact [see for instance Yannelis and Zame (1984, Theorem 10.1, p. 48)].

It may be instructive to compare our continuity assumption (4.3) with that of Araujo (1985) [or Berninghaus (1977)] whose commodity space is ℓ_∞ (or L_∞), with consumption sets $X = \ell_\infty^+$ (or L_∞^+).

In Araujo (1985), preferences are given by a weak preference relation $\succsim$ which is reflexive, transitive, complete. Assume that $\succsim$ satisfies:

(i) the set $\{y \in X : y \succsim x\}$ is Mackey closed in X and convex for each $x \in X$,

(ii) the set $\{x \in X : y \succsim x\}$ is norm closed in X for each $y \in X$.

If we let P be the strict preference relation induced by $\succsim$, then $P(x) = X \setminus \{y \in X : x \succsim y\}$ and $P^{-1}(y) = \{x \in X : y \in P(x)\} = X \setminus \{x \in X : x \succsim y\}$. Therefore, for each $x \in X$, $P(x)$ is norm open in X and for each $y \in X$, $P^{-1}(y)$ is Mackey open in X. However, since by the Mackey-Arens Theorem [see for instance Bewley (1972, p. 352, (8))] the Mackey topology coincides with the weak* topology on closed convex sets, it follows that the set $\{y \in X : y \succsim x\}$ is weak* closed in X and consequently $P^{-1}(y)$ is weak* open in X. Therefore, since in L_∞ (or ℓ_∞) the compatible topology is the weak* topology, the continuity assumption (4.3) in Theorem 4.1, for $L = L_\infty$ is not stronger than the ones of Araujo's (1985) (or Berninghaus' (1977)) continuity assumptions, who require that the set $\{y \in X : y \succsim x\}$ is Mackey (weak*) closed in X for every $x \in X$. Hence, Theorem 4.1 can be considered as a generalization of the existence results of Araujo (1985) and Berninghaus (1977). Specifically, the commodity space can be any arbitrary ordered linear topological space and preferences need not be transitive, complete or convex and may be interdependent.

5. Proof of the Theorems

5.1 Proof of Theorem 4.1. Suppose otherwise, i.e., $\mathcal{C}_e(\mathcal{E}) = \emptyset$, then for all $x \in F$ either

(5.1) there exists $y \in F$ such that $y \in P_i(x)$ for all i, or

(5.2) for at least one agent i, $e \in P_i(x)$.

For each $i \in I$ define $\psi_i : X \to 2^X$ by $\psi_i(x) = \text{con}\, P_i(x)$. Since by assumption (4.3) P_i has τ-open lower sections it follows from Lemma 5.1 in Yannelis and Prabhakar (1983, p. 239), that ψ_i has τ-open lower sections in X. Let $\psi_{i|F}$ be the restriction of ψ_i to F. It follows from (5.1) that:

(5.3) for all $x \in F$ there exists $y \in F$ such that $y \in P_i(x) \subset \text{con}\, P_i(x) = \psi_{i|F}(x)$ for all $i \in I$.

For each $i \in I$ define $\Phi_i : F \to 2^F$ by $\Phi_i(x) = \psi_{i|F}(x) \cap F$. Define $A = \{w \in F : \text{there exist } z \in F \text{ such that } z \in P_i(w) \text{ for all } i \in I\}$. It can be easily checked that A is open in F. It follows from (5.3) that:

(5.4) for all $x \in A$, $\Phi_i(x)$ is nonempty for all $i \in I$.

Notice that from assumption (4.2) we have that $x \notin \text{con}\, \Phi_i(x) = \Phi_i(x)$ for all $x \in F$. Moreover, it can be easily seen that Φ_i has τ-open lower sections in F, i.e., Φ_i is of class $\mathcal{L}$. For $x \in F$, let $S_x = \{i \in I : e \in P_i(x)$. It follows from (5.2) that

(5.5) for all $x \in F$ and all $i \in S_x$, $\Phi_i(x) \neq \emptyset$.

Indeed, from (5.2) we can conclude that for all $x \in F$ and all $i \in S_x$, $e \in P_i(x) \subset \text{con}\, P_i(x) = \psi_{i|F}(x)$. Consequently, for all $x \in F$ and all $i \in S_x$, $e \in \Phi_i(x)$.

Define the correspondence $\theta : F \to 2^F$ by

$$\theta(x) = \begin{cases} \bigcap_{i \in I} \Phi_i(x) & \text{if } x \in A \\ \bigcap_{i \in S_x} \Phi_i(x) & \text{if } x \in F \setminus A. \end{cases}$$

It follows from (5.4) and (5.5) that

(5.6) for all $x \in F$, $\theta(x) \neq \emptyset$.

Notice that F is nonempty, convex, bounded and τ-closed. Moreover, F lies on the order interval $[0, Ne]^N = \{x \in X : 0 \leq x_j \leq Ne \text{ for all } j \in I\}$ which is τ-compact. Therefore, F is a τ-compact subset of X. If we show that θ is $\mathcal{L}$-majorized we can then appeal to Corollary 3.1. To this end let $x \in F$. Then either (a) $x \in A$, or (b) $x \in F \setminus A$. If (a) holds then $\theta(x) = \bigcap_{i \in I} \Phi_i(x) \neq \emptyset$. Choose $w \in \theta(x)$. Then $w \in \Phi_i(x)$ for all i. Fix an agent j in I. Since A is an open set in F, and Φ_j has τ-open lower sections in F, then $\theta(z) = \bigcap_{i \in I} \Phi_i(z) \subset \Phi_j(z)$ for all $z \in A$. If (b) holds then $\theta(x) = \bigcap_{i \in S_x} \Phi_i(x) \neq \emptyset$. Choose $e \in \theta(x)$. Then $e \in \Phi_i(x)$ for all $i \in S_x$ which implies that $e \in P_i(x)$ for all $i \in S_x$. Fix an agent j in S_x. Since P_j has τ-open lower sections in F there exists a neighborhood of x, N_x such that $e \in P_j(z)$ for all $z \in N_x$. But then $j \in S_z$ for all $z \in N_x$. Consequently, $\theta(z) = \bigcap_{i \in S_z} \Phi_i(z) \subset \Phi_j(z)$ for all $z \in N_x$. Therefore, θ is $\mathcal{L}$-majorized. By Corollary 3.1 there exists $x^* \in F$ such that $\theta(x^*) = \emptyset$, a contradiction to (5.6). Since we have obtained a contradiction to our supposition that $\mathcal{C}_e(\mathcal{E}) = \emptyset$ the proof of the Theorem is complete.

5.2 Proof of Theorem 4.2. Let $\mathfrak{F}$ be the set of all finite dimensional subspaces of L containing the initial endowments. For each $f \in \mathfrak{F}$ and for each $i \in I$ define the consumption set X_i^f and the preference correspondence $\bar{P}_i^f : X_i^f \to 2^{X_i^f}$ by

$$X_i^f = X_i \cap f$$

$$\bar{P}_i^f(x_i) = \bar{P}_i(x_i) \cap f.$$

We now have an economy $\mathcal{E}^f = \{(X_i^f, \bar{P}_i^f, e_i) : i = 1, \ldots, N\}$, in a finite dimensional commodity space. It can be checked that each economy $\mathcal{E}^f$ satisfies all the conditions of Border's Proposition (1984, p. 1540), and consequently for each $f \in \mathfrak{F}$, $\mathcal{C}_s(\mathcal{E}^f) \neq \emptyset$, i.e., there exists $x^f = (x_1^f, \ldots, x_N^f)$ in $\prod_{i \in I} X_i^f$ such that:

(5.7) $\sum_{i \in I} x_i^f = \sum_{i \in I} e_i$, and

(5.8) it is not true that there exist $S \subset I$ and $(y_i)_{i \in S} \in \prod_{i \in S} X_i^f$ such that $\sum_{i \in S} y_i = \sum_{i \in S} e_i$ and $y_i \in \bar{P}_i^f(x_i^f)$ for all $i \in S$.

From (5.7) it follows that for each $f \in \mathfrak{F}$

$$0 \leq \sum_{i \in I} x_i^f = \sum_{i \in I} e_i = e \leq Ne.$$

Hence for each $f \in \mathfrak{F}$ the vectors x_i^f lie on the order interval $[0, Ne]$, which is τ-compact. Direct the set $\mathfrak{F}$ by inclusion so that $\{(x_1^f, \ldots, x_N^f) : f \in \mathfrak{F}\}$ forms a net in $L \times L \times \cdots \times L$. Since all the vectors x_i^f belong to the order interval $[0, Ne]$ which is τ-compact, the net $\{(x_1^f, \ldots, x_N^f) : f \in \mathfrak{F}\}$ has a subnet which converges in the compatible topology τ, to some vector $x_1^*, \ldots, x_N^*$ in $[0, Ne]$. We must show that $x_1^*, \ldots, x_N^*$ is a core allocation for the economy $\mathcal{E}$.

Denote the convergent subnet by $\{(x_1^{f(m)}, \ldots, x_N^{f(m)}) : m \in M\}$ where M is a set directed by "$\geq$." First of all we know that $\sum_{i\in I} x_i^{f(m)} = \sum_{i\in I} e_i$ for all $m \in M$. Since the vectors $x_i^{f(m)}$ converge to x_i^* in the compatible topology τ, and τ is a vector space topology we conclude that $\sum_{i\in I} x_i^* = \sum_{i\in I} e_i$, i.e., $x^* = (x_1^*, \ldots, x_N^*)$ is a feasible allocation for the economy $\mathcal{E}$. To complete the proof we must show that:

(5.9) it is not true that there exist $S \subset I$ and $(y_i)_{i\in S} \in \prod_{i\in S} X_i$ such that $\sum_{i\in S} y_i = \sum_{i\in S} e_i$ and $y_i \in \bar{P}_i(x_i^*)$ for all $i \in S$.

Suppose otherwise, i.e., there exist $S \subset I$ and $(y_i)_{i\in S} \in \prod_{i\in S} X_i$ such that $\sum_{i\in S} y_i = \sum_{i\in S} e_i$ and $y_i \in \bar{P}_i(x_i^*)$ for all $i \in S$. Since $x_i^{f(m)}$ converges to x_i^* in the compatible topology τ and by assumption (4.6) $\bar{P}_i$ has a τ-open graph, there exists $m_1 \in M$ such that $y_i \in \bar{P}_i(x_i^{f(m)})$ for all $m \geq m_1$ and all $i \in S$. Choose $m_2 \geq m_1$ so that, if $m \geq m_2$, $y_i \in X_i^{f(m)}$ for all $i \in S$. Then $y_i \in \bar{P}_i^{f(m)}(x_i^{f(m)})$ for all $m \geq m_2$, all $i \in S$, and clearly $\sum_{i\in S} y_i = \sum_{i\in S} e_i$. But this contradicts the fact that $x^{f(m)}$ is a core allocation of the economy $\mathcal{E}^{f(m)}$. Hence (5.9) is satisfied and this completes the proof of the theorem.

5.3 Proof of Corollary 4.1. It follows from assumption (4.7) that the set of all feasible allocations F is compact. Therefore, an identical argument with that used in Theorem 4.1 can be adopted to complete the proof of the Corollary.

6. Examples

We can now turn to some known pathological examples in the literature and see what goes wrong in infinite dimensions. In particular, Araujo (1985), Mas-Colell (1986) and Jones (1986) illustrated by means of simple examples the difficulties in obtaining existence of extreme core allocations in an infinite dimensional commodity setting. The following simple example due to Jones (1986) may be used to illustrate these difficulties.

Example 6.1. *Consider an economy with two agents, i.e.,* $I = \{1, 2\}$. *The commodity space is* $L = C[0,1]$, *i.e., the space of continuous functions on the interval* $[0,1]$ *under the supnorm. The consumption sets* *are* $X_1 = X_2 = C[0,1]^+$, *i.e., the positive cone of* $C[0,1]$. *Their utility functions and their initial endowments are given as follows:*

$$u_1(x) = \int_0^1 tx(t)\,dt,$$

$$u_2(x) = \int_0^1 (1-t)x(t)\,dt,$$

and

$$e_1 = e_2 = \frac{1}{2}.$$

Notice that utility functions are norm continuous, concave, and monotone. However, there is no individually rational Pareto optimal allocation, i.e., the extreme core which coincides with the selfish core is empty. (Of course there are two Pareto optimal allocations which are not individually rational, i.e., give all the initial endowment to either agent 1 or agent 2.) The non-existence of extreme core allocations lies on the fact that the set of all feasible allocations (which is norm closed and bounded) is not norm compact (notice that consumption sets are not norm compact). Thus, the proofs of Theorems 4.1 and 4.2 or Corollary 4.1 do not go through. The same difficulty occurs in the Araujo-Mas-Colell example [see for instance Araujo (1974, Theorem 3)]. In particular there are two agents whose preferences are norm continuous monotone convex but consumption sets are not norm compact. Hence, the above examples have violated assumption (4.7) of Corollary 4.1 and assumptions (4.3) and (4.6) of Theorems 4.1 and 4.2 respectively. Consequently, the conclusion to be drawn is that if the set of all feasible allocations is compact in a topology which is at least as strong as the topology in which preferences are continuous, then extreme α-core allocations always exist.

The intuition behind the above conclusion is quite simple. In particular, the maximal elements result (Theorem 3.3) is used to prove the existence of extreme α-core allocations (Theorem 4.1). However, if in Theorem 3.3 the preference correspondence $P: X \to 2^X$ has open lower sections in a topology which is stronger than the topology in which the set X is compact, then Theorem 3.3 fails and a fortiori Corollary 3.1 fails as well. The following example illustrates this.

Example 6.2. *Let Y be a Banach space. Denote by $\|\cdot\|$ the norm on Y. Let X be equal to the set $\{x \in Y^* : \|x\| \leq 1\}$. Notice that by the Alaoglou theorem [see Aliprantis and Burkinshaw (1985, Theorem 9.20)] X is weak* compact, and it is obviously convex and nonempty. Let $f : X \to X$ be a norm continuous mapping which does not have the fixed point property, i.e., $x \neq f(x)$ for any $x \in X$. Let $S((f(x), \frac{\|x-f(x)\|}{2})$ be an open ball in Y centered at $f(x)$ with radius $\frac{\|x-f(x)\|}{2}$. Define the preference correspondence $P : X \to 2^X$ by $P(x) = S(f(x), \frac{\|x-f(x)\|}{2}) \cap X$. It can be easily checked that P has norm open lower sections, is convex valued and irreflexive, i.e., P is of class $\mathfrak{L}$ and consequently $\mathfrak{L}$-majorized. Notice, that for all $x \in X$, $f(x) \in P(x)$, i.e., P has no maximal element in X.*

7. Remarks

Remark 7.1. A careful examination of Theorem 4.1 shows that its proof remains unaffected if the set of agents I is any countable set, provided that we assume that the aggregate initial endowment is finite.

Remark 7.2. Theorem 4.2 can be extended in a straightforward manner to coalition production economies as in the Border (1984) framework. One needs to impose in addition to balanced technology [see for instance Border (1984)], the standard assumptions on the production side of the economy, which guarantee that the set of all feasible allocations is compact in the compatible topology. The proof of Theorem 4.2 remains essentially unchanged.

Remark 7.3. Ichiichi and Schaffer (1983) have obtained core existence results, for games in characteristic function form, with a measure space of agents, and with a strategy space which is L_∞. Although our framework is entirely different than theirs, it is still of interest to know whether Theorems 4.1 and 4.2 can be extended to a measure space of agents. It seems to us that there are serious technical difficulties.

Remark 7.4. Recently the work of Kim and Richter (1986) in consumer and equilibrium theory showed that the strict preference relations which need not be transitive or complete can be replaced by weak preference relations which need not be transitive or complete. Using their methods one can obtain core existence results for weak preference relations which need not be transitive or complete.

Remark 7.5. A rather more natural definition of the core with interdependent preferences is what Aumann (1964) calls strong equilibrium. One may define a *strong equilibrium allocation* of $\mathcal{E} = \{(X_i, P_i, e_i) : i \in I\}$ as a vector $x = (x_1, \ldots, x_N) \in X$ such that

(i) x is feasible, and

(ii) it is not true that there exist $S \subset I$ and $(y_i)_{i \in S} \prod_{i \in S} X_i$ such that for all $i \in S$, $\sum_{i \in S} y_i = \sum_{i \in S} e_i$, $\sum_{i \notin S} x_i = \sum_{i \notin S} e_i$, and $(y^S, x^{I \setminus S}) \in P_i(x_1, \ldots, x_N)$.

However, Scarf (1967, p. 180) showed that even with stronger conditions than those used in Theorem 4.2, the β-core (recall that the set of strong equilibrium allocations is a subset of the β-core) may be empty and therefore the set of strong equilibrium allocations may be empty as well.

Appendix

Fan's (1962) extension of the K-K-M Lemma to Hausdorff linear topological spaces was based on the finite dimensional K-K-M result. This way of proving an infinite dimensional result by considering its trace on finite dimensions, sometimes simplifies the arguments considerably. Indeed this method of proof was adopted by Fan (1952) to extend the Kakutani fixed point to Hausdorff locally convex linear topological spaces. We now provide an alternative proof of the K-K-M-F theorem which is similar in spirit with that of Fan but makes use of the Brouwer fixed point theorem. In addition to the fact that our proof is very intuitive it turns out to be elementary. Notice that in finite dimensions the Brouwer fixed point can be used to derive the K-K-M theorem,[3] the Sperner Lemma and the Kakutani fixed point theorem. In that sense Brouwer's result may be considered as a milestone in Fixed Point Theory.

[3] A proof that the Brouwer fixed point theorem implies the K-K-M Lemma is $\mathbf{R}^\ell$ is given by Ichiichi (1981a) who attributes the argument to K. C. Border and E. Green. Although our proof is more involved than that in Ichiichi (1981) the idea is essentially the same.

Proof of Theorem 3.1. It suffices to prove that $\bigcap_{i=1}^n F(x_i) \neq \emptyset$ for every finite subset $\{x_1, \ldots, x_n\}$ of X. Suppose otherwise; i.e., $\bigcap_{i=1}^n F(x_i) = \emptyset$ for some finite subset $\{x_1, \ldots, x_n\}$ of X. Let Δ be the simplex spanned by the finite set $\{x_1, \ldots, x_n\}$. Since the topology induced on any finite dimensional subspace by the topology of Y is equivalent to the Euclidean topology, Δ is homeomorphic to a Euclidean ball [Kelley and Namioka (1963, Theory 7.3, p. 49)]. Denote by d the Euclidean metric in the finite dimensional subspace spanned by $\{x_1, \ldots, x_n\}$. Define $\psi : \Delta \to 2^\Delta$ by $\psi(x) = \{y \in \Delta : x \notin F(y)\}$. Then for each $x \in \Delta$, $\psi(x) \neq \emptyset$. Indeed at least one x_i, $(1 \leq i \leq n)$ is in $\psi(x)$, for otherwise $x \in \bigcap_{i=1}^n F(x_i)$. For each $y \in \Delta$ let $\psi^{-1}(y) = \{x \in \Delta : y \in \psi(x)\} = \Delta \setminus \{x \in \Delta : x \in F(y)\}$. Since $\{x \in \Delta : x \in F(y)\} = \Delta \cap F(y)$ is closed in Δ, the set $\psi^{-1}(y)$ is open in Δ for each $y \in \Delta$. Define $\phi : \Delta \to 2^\Delta = \operatorname{con} \psi(x)$. Then ϕ is convex and nonempty valued. Moreover, ϕ has open lower sections in Δ [Yannelis and Prabhakar (1983, Lemma 5.1)]. Nonempty valueness of ϕ implies that for every $x \in \Delta$ there is a $y \in \Delta$ such that $x \in \phi^{-1}(y)$. Hence, the collection $\{\phi^{-1}(y) : y \in \Delta\}$ is an open cover of Δ. But Δ compact implies that there exists a finite set of points $\{y_1, \ldots, y_n\}$ such that $\Delta \subseteq \bigcup_{i=1}^n \phi^{-1}(y_i)$. Define $\alpha_i : \Delta \to \mathbb{R}_+$ by $\alpha_i(x) = d(x, \Delta \setminus \phi^{-1}(y_i))$, $1 \leq i \leq n$. Set $g_i(x) = (\alpha_i(x))/(\sum_{j=1}^n \alpha_j(x))$ for all $x \in \Delta$, $1 \leq i \leq n$. Then, $g_i(x) = 0$ for $x \notin \phi^{-1}(y_i)$, $0 \leq g_i(x) \leq 1$ and $\sum_{i=1}^n g_i(x) = 1$ for all $x \in \Delta$. Define $f : \Delta \to \Delta$ by $f(x) = \sum_{i=1}^n g_i(x) y_i$. Clearly f is continuous and for each i such that $g_i(x) \neq 0$, $x \in \phi^{-1}(y_i)$ or $y_i \in \phi(x)$. Hence, $f(x)$ is a convex combination of points y_i in the convex set $\phi(x)$ and so $f(x) \in \phi(x)$ for all $x \in \Delta$. By Brouwer's fixed point theorem there exists $x^* \in \Delta$ such that $x^* = f(x^*) \in \phi(x^*) = \operatorname{con} \psi(x^*)$. But $x^* \in \operatorname{con} \psi(x^*)$ implies that there exist points $y_1, \ldots, y_m$ in Δ and real numbers $a_1, \ldots, a_m$, $a_j \geq 0$, $(1 \leq j \leq m)$, $\sum_{j=1}^m a_j = 1$ such that $x^* = \sum_{j=1}^m a_j y_j$ and $y_j \in \psi(x^*)$ for all j. But $y_j \in \psi(x^*)$ implies that $x^* \notin F(y_j)$ for all j, a contradiction to assumption (i). Therefore $\bigcap_{i=1}^n F(x_i) \neq \emptyset$, and this completes the proof.

References

Aliprantis, C. D. and Burkinshaw, O., 1985, *Positive Operators*, Academic Press, New York.

Araujo, A., 1985, "Lack of Pareto Optimal Allocations in Economies with Infinitely Many Commodities: The Need for Impatience," *Econometrica* **53**, 455–461.

Aumann, R. J., 1964, "The Core of a Cooperative Game Without Side Payments," *Trans. Amer. Math. Soc.*, 539–552.

Bewley, T., 1972, "Existence of Equilibria in Economies with Infinitely Many Commodities," *J. Econ. Theory* **64**, 514–540.

Berninghaus, S., 1977, "Individual and Collective Risks in Large Economies," *J. Econ. Theory* **15**, 279–294.

Border, K. C., 1984, "A Core Existence Theorem for Games Without Ordered Preferences," *Econometrica* **52**, 1537–1542.

Borglin, A. and Keiding, H., 1976, "The Existence of Equilibrium Actions and of Equilibrium: A Note on the 'New' Existence Theorems," *J. Math. Econ.* **3**, 313–316.

Browder, F., 1968, "The Fixed Point Theory of Multivalued Mappings in Topological Vector Spaces," *Math. Ann.* **177**, 283–301.

Debreu, G., 1952, "A Social Equilibrium Existence Theorem," *Proc. Natl. Acad. Sci. USA* **38**, 886–893.

Debreu, G., 1959, *Theory of Value*, John Wiley and Sons, New York.

Fan, K., 1952, "Fixed Point and Minimax Theorems in Locally Convex Topological Linear Spaces," *Proc. Natl. Acad. Sci. USA* **38**, 131–136.

Fan, K., 1962, "A Generalization of Tychonoff's Fixed Point Theorem," *Math. Ann.* **143**, 305–310.

Fan, K., 1969, "Extensions of Two Fixed Point Theorems of F. E. Browder," *Math. Z.* **112**, 234–240.

Gale, D. and Mas-Colell, A., 1975, "An Equilibrium Existence Theorem for a General Model without Ordered Preferences," *J. Math. Econ.* **2**, 9–15.

Hildenbrand, W., 1974, *Core and Equilibrium of a Large Economy*, Princeton University Press, Princeton, New Jersey.

Ichiichi, T., 1981, *Game Theory for Economic Analysis*, Academic Press, New York.

Ichiichi, T., 1981a, "On the Knaster-Kuratowski-Mazurkiewicz-Shapley Theorem," *J. Math. Anal. Appl.* **81**, 297–299.

Ichiichi, T. and Schaffer, S. T., 1983, "The Topological Core of a Game without Side Payments," *Econ. Stud. Q.* **34**, 1–8.

Jones, L. E., 1986, "Special Problems Arising in the Study of Economies with Infinitely Many Commodities," in *Models of Economic Dynamics*, H. F. Sonnenschein, ed., Springer-Verlag Lecture Notes in Economics and Mathematical Systems #264, Berlin-New York, 184–205.

Kajii, A., 1989, "A Generalization of Scarf's Theorem: An α-Core Existence Theorem without Transitivity," Harvard University, mimeo.

Kelley, J. and Namioka, I., 1963, *Linear Topological Spaces,* Springer, New York.

Kim, T. and Richter, M. K., 1986, "Nontransitive, Nontotal Consumer Theory," *J. Econ. Theory* **38**, 324–363.

McKenzie, L. W., 1981, "The Classical Theorem on Existence of Competitive Equilibrium," *Econometrica* **49**, 819–841.

Mas-Colell, A., 1974, "An Equilibrium Existence Theorem Without Complete or Transitive Preferences," *J. Math. Econ.* **1**, 237–246.

Mas-Colell, A., 1986, "The Price Equilibrium Existence Problem in Topological

Vector Lattices," *Econometrica* **54**, 1039–1054.

Scarf, H., 1967, "The Core of an *N*-Person Game," *Econometrica* **35**, 50–69.

Scarf, H., 1971, "On the Existence of a Cooperative Solution for a General Class of *N*-Person Games," *J. Econ. Theory* **3**, 169–181.

Schaefer, H. H., 1971, *Topological Vector Spaces*, Springer-Verlag, Berlin.

Schaefer, H. H., 1974, *Banach Lattices and Positive Operators*, Springer-Verlag, Berlin.

Shafer, W. J., 1974, "The Nontransitive Consumer," *Econometrica* **42**, 913–919.

Shafer, W. J. and Sonnenschein, H., 1975, "Equilibrium in Abstract Economies Without Ordered Preferences," *J. Math. Econ.* **2**, 345–348.

Shapley, L. S., 1973, "On Balanced Games without Side Payments," in *Mathematical Programming*, T. C. Hu and S. M. Robinson, eds., Academic Press, New York.

Sonnenschein, H., 1971, "Demand Theory without Transitive Preferences with Applications to the Theory of Competitive Equilibrium," in *Preferences, Utility, and Demand*, J. Chipman, L. Hurwicz, M. K. Richter and H. Sonnenschein, eds., Harcourt Brace Jovanovich, New York.

Toussaint, S., 1984, "On the Existence of Equilibria in Economies with Infinitely Many Commodities and without Ordered Preferences," *J. Econ. Theory* **33**, 98–115.

Yannelis, N. C. and Prabhakar, N. D., 1983, "Existence of Maximal Elements and Equilibria in Linear Topological Spaces," *J. Math. Econ.* **12**, 233–245.

Yannelis, N. C. and Zame, W. R., 1984, "Equilibria in Banach Lattices without Ordered Preferences," Preprint no. 71, Institute for Mathematics and Its Applications, University of Minnesota, Minneapolis, MN, (a shortened version appeared in the *J. Math. Econ.* **15**, 1986, 85–110).

Fundamental Theorems of Welfare Economics in Infinite Dimensional Commodity Spaces

Robert A. Becker*

1. Introduction

The fundamental theorems of classical welfare economics state conditions for a competitive equilibrium allocation to be a Pareto optimal allocation and conversely. The first modern treatments of this equivalence between competitive and optimal allocations may be found in the seminal papers of Arrow [1951] and Debreu [1951]. They presented an axiomatic framework for the characteristics and properties of economies with a finite number of agents and commodities. The separating hyperplane theorem from convex analysis was the key to their demonstration of the second classical welfare theorem.

The problem of optimal economic growth over an infinite horizon defines a family of model economies with infinite dimensional commodity spaces. The voluminous literature on this question dating to the classic paper of Ramsey [1928] attests to the importance of optimal growth theory. The optimum growth problem has been reinterpreted as the basis for solving representative agent dynamic competitive equilibrium models in both the cases of perfect foresight equilibrium under certainty (Becker [1981]) and recursive competitive equilibrium in the presence of uncertainty (Prescott and Mehra [1980]). This explicit recognition of the important link between rational expectations equilibrium paths and optima is a statement of the fundamental welfare theorems for the economies under study. The first and second welfare theorems in infinite dimensional commodity spaces have since played an important role in the development

* I would like to thank Kerry Back, John H. Boyd, Christian Gilles, and Nicholas Yannelis for comments leading to several improvements in the drafts of this paper. The usual caveat applies.

of dynamic competitive analysis and its applications to asset pricing and macrodynamics.[1]

Debreu [1954] was the first to examine the analogs of the welfare theorems in infinite dimensional commodity spaces. He proposed that a dual pair of linear spaces formally express the commodity-price duality relationship. He argued that if preferences were strictly convex, then every price supported allocation where no consumer was satiated was a Pareto optimum (the first fundamental welfare theorem). In the converse direction, he showed that if the previous convexity hypothesis was maintained, a mild continuity assumption was met by agents preference relations, and the interior of the aggregate production set had a non-empty interior or the commodity space was finite dimensional, then every Pareto optimum allocation where some agent was not satiated could be supported by a price system (the second fundamental welfare theorem). He applied his results to the case where the commodity space was the space of bounded sequences of real numbers, l_∞, endowed with the supremum norm topology. The positive cone of this space has a non-empty interior; by assuming free disposal of commodities, the production set in this space possessed a non-empty interior. The commodity space l_∞ arose naturally in Malinvaud's [1952] study of efficient capital accumulation programs. Subsequently, Bewley [1990], [1969], and [1972] studied equilibrium problems in L_∞ spaces. His paper, [1969], included a discussion of the price support problem for economies modelled on L_∞ and having a finite number of agents.[2] Later researchers investigating intertemporal exchange economies, asset pricing models, differentiated commodity models, and location problems devised economies with infinite dimensional commodity spaces whose positive cones lacked an interior.[3] Another strand of research examined overlapping generations models with a double infin-

---

[1] The text by Harris [1987] illustrates the role of the welfare theorems in dynamic competitive analysis. See Brock [1982] and Mehra [1988] for applications of the welfare theorems to asset pricing theory. The link to competitive business cycles may be found in King, Plosser and Rebelo [1988].

[2] Following Bewley, Berninghaus [1977] utilized L_∞ to explore the support property and the optimal allocation of collective and individual risk in an exchange economy.

[3] See Peleg and Yaari [1970], Mas-Colell [1975, 1986a, 1986b], Jones [1984, 1986] for references.

ity of traders and commodities. Samuelson [1958] showed that the first fundamental theorem did not extend to those economies.

Research in the 1980's on infinite dimensional versions of the welfare theorems emphasized the price support problem for economies with a finite number of agents. The order structure of the commodity space was placed at the forefront of the analysis. New concepts (e.g., proper preferences) were introduced in order to obtain the support property. Moreover, an approximate support property was found in cases failing to satisfy the new sufficient conditions for the exact support property to obtain.

The purpose of this paper is to survey the recent developments on the existence of price supports for Pareto optimal allocations following Debreu's seminal contribution. Some proofs will be included in the body of the paper in order to illustrate the methods used to demonstrate the second fundamental welfare theorem as well as its approximate versions. The economic model and Debreu's versions of both welfare theorems are reviewed in Section 2. The extensions of the second welfare theorem exploiting the order properties of the commodity space as well as the properness conditions are the subject of Section 3. The approximate support theory in the absence of properness or an order structure are surveyed in Section 4. Concluding comments are offered in Section 5.

2. Valuation Equilibrium and Pareto Optimality: Debreu's Framework

Debreu's [1954] contribution is developed in this section along with some comments and illustrative examples.

2.1 The Economic Model. The commodity space is a real linear space E. The economic model is described by the consumers, producers and relations between them.

The ith consumer ($i = 1, 2, \ldots, m$) chooses a point x_i, his consumption, in a given subset X_i of E called his *consumption set.* The set X_i describes all the possible consumption points potentially available to the consumer. Positive coordinates of x_i denote goods actually consumed and negative coordinates represent goods or services supplied (for example, labor services). Each agent has a complete *preference order* on X_i; the *(weak) preference relation* is denoted by R_i and the corresponding *strict preference relation* is denoted by P_i. A point x_i^s is a saturation point of X_i, if $x_i^s R_i x_i$ for all $x_i \in X_i$.

Producer j ($j = 1, 2, \ldots, k$) chooses a point y_j, his production, in a given subset Y_j of E, called the *production set.* A positive coordinate of y_j denotes an output for producer j and a negative coordinate is taken to be an input for producer j. The set Y_j incorporates the limitations of the available technology. The set $Y = Y_1 + \cdots + Y_k$ is called the *aggregate production set.* Denote $x = \sum_{i=1}^{m} x_i$, $y = \sum_{j=1}^{k} y_j$ and let $\omega \in E$ denote the vector of initial resources in this economy. A $(m+k)$-tuple $[(x_i),(y_j)]$ is called a *state* of the economy. A state $[(x_i),(y_j)]$ is an *attainable allocation* (or simply an *allocation*) provided $x_i \in X_i$ for all $i, y_j \in Y_j$ for all j, and $x - y = \omega$.[4] The set of all attainable allocations will be denoted by $\mathcal{A}$, i.e.,

$$\mathcal{A} = \{[(x_i),(y_j)] : x_i \in X_i,\ y_j \in Y_j \text{ and } x - y = \omega\}.$$

A *price system* or *valuation functional* is a real valued linear functional p defined on E. This means that p is taken to be an element of the algebraic dual of E, denoted E'. The statements of Debreu's theorems will include the appropriate topological restrictions needed to insure that p is in the topological dual of E. Given a point z in E, $p(z)$ denotes the "value" assigned to the commodity basket z by the price system p. It is important to point out that there is no guarantee that p may be represented by a linear form with an economic interpretation.[5]

A state $[(x_i),(y_j)]$ is a *valuation equilibrium* with respect to p if:

(2.1) $[(x_i),(y_j)]$ is attainable;

(2.2) for every i:

$x_i \in X_i$, $p(x_i) \geq p(z_i)$ implies $x_i R_i z_i$ (best satisfaction of preferences subject to a budget constraint);

(2.3) for every j:

---

[4] It should be noted that he does not assume free disposal in the definition of the model.

[5] For example, $p(z) = pz$, an inner product.

$h_j \in Y_j$ implies $p(y_j) \geq p(h_i)$ (profit maximization subject to technological constraints).

A valuation equilibrium is also known as an *valuation equilibrium with transfer payments.*[6] An attainable state $[(x_i), (y_j)]$ is said to be *supported* by a non-zero price $p \in E'$ whenever (2.3) holds for each j, and

(2.4) for every i:

$z_i R_i x_i$ implies $p(z_i) \geq p(x_i)$ (expenditure minimization).

In applications, E is a topological vector space and support prices are generally sought in the topological dual of E.[7]

An attainable allocation $[(x_i), (y_j)]$ is said to be:

(2.5) *Pareto optimal*, whenever no other attainable allocation $[(z_i, h_j)]$ satisfies $z_i R_i x_i$ for all i and $z_i P_i x_i$ for at least one i;

(2.6) *weakly Pareto optimal*, whenever there exists no other allocation $[(z_i), (h_j)]$ satisfying $z_i P_i x_i$ for all i.

Clearly, every Pareto optimal allocation is weakly Pareto optimal.[8]

2.2 A Valuation Equilibrium is a Pareto Optimum.

Debreu [1954] assumes two conditions (given below) are met by the consumption sets of agents.

(I) For every i, X_i is convex.

(II) For every i: $x_i \in X_i$, $z_i \in X_i$, and $z_i P_i x_i$ implies $(1-t)x_i + tz_i P_i x_i$ for all t, $0 < t < 1$.

---

[6] The definition of the economy does not utilize an *a priori* specification of the initial endowments of agents or claims on profits since the focus of the discussion is on Pareto optimal allocations. Hence, the definition of valuation equilibrium uses $p(x_i)$ to denote the ith agent's income. For this reason, a valuation equilibrium also differs from the concept of a *quasiequilibrium* (e.g., see Aliprantis, Brown and Burkinshaw [1989, p. 135]).

[7] Duffie [1986, p. 16] establishes the existence of support prices in the algebraic dual for a Pareto optimal allocation. In the infinite dimensional commodity space context, the economic interpretation of a possibly *discontinuous* supporting functional is problematic. Hence, the interest in conditions yielding a continuous supporting price system.

[8] A converse is true with further restrictions on preferences. For an exchange economy, the converse is true when preferences are continuous and monotone. See Aliprantis, Brown and Burkinshaw [1989, p. 40].

Axiom (I) expresses the convexity hypotheses for consumption sets. Assumption II is a strict convexity requirement for the *strict upper contour set* $P_i(x_i)$ *associated with* x_i, where $P_i(x_i) = \{z_i \in X_i : z_i P_i x_i\}$. The *strict lower contour set*, $P_i^{-1}(x_i)$, *associated with* x_i is defined by $P_i^{-1}(x_i) = \{z_i \in X_i : x_i P_i z_i\}$. The *upper (lower) contour set*, $R_i(x_i)$ ($R_i^{-1}(x_i)$), *associated with* x_i is defined by $R_i(x_i) = \{z_i \in X_i : z_i R_i x_i\}$ ($R_i^{-1}(x_i) = \{z_i \in X_i : x_i R_i z_i\}$).

Theorem 2.1. *Under Assumptions I and II, every valuation equilibrium* $[(x_i),(y_j)]$ *where no* x_i *is a saturation point, is a Pareto optimum.*

This result expresses the first fundamental theorem of welfare economics. The proof of Theorem 2.1 will not be repeated here since it is basically identical to arguments in the finite dimensional commodity case (c.f., Arrow [1951]). Notice that convexity axioms are not placed on producers. Moreover, the range of possible commodity spaces is not limited by either topological or partial order assumptions. The nonsatiation assumption simply states that no consumer is at a "bliss" level of consumption — a hypothesis that is independent of any topological or partial order structures that might be imposed on E. This is necessary since neither the topological concept of local nonsatiation nor the partially ordered space notion of global nonsatiation due to monotonicity of preferences apply in this general framework. The combination of Debreu's nonsatiation assumption and convexity hypotheses built on the primitive linear space properties of E substitute for the local nonsatiation axiom in the essentially algebraic proofs of the first welfare theorem familiar from the finite dimensional commodity space literature where convexity assumptions are notably absent.

2.3 A Pareto Optimum is a Valuation Equilibrium.

The second fundamental welfare theorem states conditions under which a Pareto optimal state is supported by a non-zero continuous linear functional. The introduction of continuity considerations means that a topological structure must be assigned to E. Additional conditions are invoked to deduce that a price supported Pareto optimal state is in fact a valuation equilibrium.

Debreu [1954] required E to be a topological vector space. All commodity spaces are understood to be Hausdorff without further mention.

Let F denote the topological dual of E. Additional restrictions on the economy are stated below.

Let w_i, z_i be consumption points in X_i. Define $I(w_i, z_i) = \{t \in \mathbb{R} : (1-t)w_i + tz_i \in X_i\}$. If X_i is convex, then $I(w_i, z_i)$ is an interval in $\mathbb{R}$.

(III) For every i, x_i, w_i, z_i in X_i, the sets

a) $\{t \in I(w_i, z_i) : (1-t)w_i + tz_i R_i x_i\}$

and

b) $\{t \in I(w_i, z_i) : x_i R_i (1-t)w_i + tz_i\}$

are closed in $I(w_i, z_i)$.

A preference relation R_i satisfying Assumption (III) is said to be *continuous along line segments.*[9] A preference relation R_i is said to be *continuous* if $R_i(x_i)$ and $R_i^{-1}(x_i)$ are closed sets in X_i for each $x_i \in X_i$. The preference relation R_i is *regular* if $R_i(x_i)$ is closed for each $x_i \in X_i$. If R_i is continuous, then it is also continuous along line segments.

The next assumptions restrict the aggregate production set Y.

(IV) Y is convex.

(V) E is finite dimensional and/or Y has an interior point.

If E is an infinite dimensional space, the requirement that Y have a non-empty interior limits the range of possible commodity spaces.

The second fundamental welfare theorem in Debreu's paper is given below.

Theorem 2.2. *Under the assumptions I–V, every Pareto optimum $[(x_i), (y_i)]$, where some x_i is not a saturation point, is supported by a non-zero continuous linear functional p on E.*

The central argument in Debreu's proof of Theorem 2.2 is a separation argument; it is sketched below. Let i^* be a value of i for which x_i is not a saturation point. Define the set

$$Z = P_{i^*}(x_{i^*}) + \sum_{i \neq i^*} R_i(x_i) - Y.$$

The definition of a Pareto optimum $[(x_i), (y_j)]$ implies $\omega \notin Z$. Debreu uses assumptions I–III to show for all i the sets $R_i(x_i)$ and $P_i(x_i)$ are

---

[9] In the finite dimensional case, it is easy to see that the lexicographic order on $\mathbb{R}^2_+$ violates the continuity along line segments axiom.

convex. Since Y is convex by assumption IV, it follows that Z is a convex set. $P_{i^*}(x_{i^*})$ is non-empty, since agent i^* is not satiated at the given optimum, hence Z is non-empty. The way has now been prepared to separate $\{\omega\}$ and Z. The following variant of the Hahn-Banach theorem is the main mathematical tool used in the proof of Theorem 2.2.

Separation Theorem. *Suppose that A and B are non-empty convex subsets of a linear topological space E and that the interior of A is non-empty. Then there is a continuous linear functional p on E separating A and B if and only if B is disjoint from the interior of A.*[10]

A proof of this result may be found in Kelly, Namioka, et al [1963, p. 118]. Application of the Separation theorem to the sets Z and $\{\omega\}$ yields the existence of a (nontrivial) continuous linear functional p on E such that $p(z) \geq p(\omega)$ for all $z \in Z$. By an argument analogous to the finite dimensional case (c.f., Arrow [1951]), one can see that p supports the Pareto optimum. This Pareto optimum is also an equilibrium with transfer payments, if there is, for every i, a $w_i \in X_i$ such that $p(w_i) < p(x_i)$. This extra property is called the *cheaper point condition.*[11]

2.4 Comments and Examples.

The standard discounted one-sector optimal growth model associated with Ramsey [1928] is defined by the programming problem:

$\sup \sum_{t=1}^{\infty} \delta^{t-1} u(c_t)$ by choice of $\{c_t, k_t\}$ subject to the constraints $c_t + k_{t+1} \leq f(k_t)$, $c_t \geq 0$, $k_t \geq 0$, $t = 1, 2, \ldots$, and $k_1 \leq k$.

In this model, c_t is the consumption at t, k_t is the capital at t, f is the production function, u the one period reward or felicity function, δ is the discount factor, and k is the initial capital. The interpretation of the model is that there is a single consumption-capital good. At each time t, the output, $f(k_t)$ must be divided between consumption and a stock for next period's production.

Typically, u and f are taken to be $C^{(2)}$, monotone strictly concave functions, and $0 < \delta < 1$. There is a maximum sustainable stock, b, if $f(b) = b$ for some $b > 0$. In this case, it is easy to show that any

---

10 Recall, a linear functional p is said to *separate* A and B if and only if p is not identically zero and $\sup\{p(x) : x \in A\} \leq \inf\{p(x) : x \in B\}$.

11 See Debreu's Remark, pp. 103, of the reprinted version of the paper.

program $\{c_t, k_t\}_{t=1}^{\infty}$ meeting the constraints must be bounded from above by $\max\{k, b\}$.

This standard optimal growth model may be recast in Debreu's framework.[12] Set $E = \{\mathbf{x} = \{x_t\} : x_t \in \mathbb{R}^3 \text{ and } \|\mathbf{x}\|_\infty < \infty\}$.[13] A point $\mathbf{x} \in E$ has three components: $\mathbf{x} = (\mathbf{x}_1, \mathbf{x}_2, \mathbf{x}_3)$ and $\mathbf{x}_l = \{x_{lt}\}_{t=1}^{\infty}$ $(l = 1, 2, 3)$.

There is a representative consumer and aggregate production technology. The consumer is characterized by a consumption set, X, and a utility function, U. The production sector is characterized by a production set, Y.

The consumption set of the consumer, X, is defined by:

$$X = \{\mathbf{x} \in E : x_{2t+1} + x_{3t} \geq 0,\ -x_{21} \leq k,\ x_{1t} \geq 0,\ x_{2t} \leq 0,\ x_{3t} \geq 0\}$$

where x_{1t} is the quantity of the consumption good arranged at date 1 to be delivered and consumed at date t, $-x_{2t}$ is the quantity of the capital good the agent agrees to deliver to the production sector *before* production at date t, and x_{3t} is the quantity of the capital good the agent arranges at time 1 to take delivery of after production at date t. The constraint $x_{2t+1} + x_{3t} \geq 0$ merely records the fact that capital to be delivered to the production sector before production at $t + 1$ must not exceed the capital delivered to the agent after production takes place at time t.[14] The constraint $-x_{21} \leq k$ says the initial capital stock is exogenously given to the agent and free disposal of that stock is possible. The obvious nonnegativity and nonpositivity constraints complete the specification of X.

The consumer's preference order is defined in terms of the utility function $U : X \to \mathbb{R}$ defined by the formula

$$U(\mathbf{x}) = \sum_{t=1}^{\infty} \delta^{t-1} u(x_{1t}),$$

[12] See Harris [1987, pp. 64–73] for a generalized version of this model and a bond contract interpretation of the model.

[13] $\|\mathbf{x}\|_\infty = \sup\{|x_t| : t = 1, 2, \ldots \text{ for } x_t = (x_{1t}, \ldots, x_{nt}) \in \mathbb{R}^n\}$ where $\|\cdot\|$ is a fixed norm on $\mathbb{R}^n$.

[14] An optimal allocation will satisfy this constraint with equality.

where $u \in C^{(2)}(\mathbb{R}_+, \mathbb{R})$ is bounded, $u' > 0$ and $u'' < 0$. The relation R is then defined by $\mathbf{x}R\mathbf{w}$ if and only $U(\mathbf{x}) \geq U(\mathbf{w})$ for any $\mathbf{x}$, $\mathbf{w}$ in X.

The aggregate production set for this economy, Y, is defined by

$$Y = \{\mathbf{y} \in E : y_{1t} + y_{3t} \leq f(-y_{2t}),\ y_{1t} \geq 0,\ y_{2t} \leq 0,\ y_{3t} \geq 0 \text{ for all } t\}.$$

The initial endowment of the economy is the zero vector in E. Clearly, a state $[(\mathbf{x}), (\mathbf{y})]$ is an attainable allocation in this model if and only if $\mathbf{x} - \mathbf{y} = 0$, $\mathbf{x} \in X$ and $\mathbf{y} \in Y$. Therefore, a state $[(\mathbf{x}), (\mathbf{y})]$ is a Pareto optimum if and only if it solves the optimal growth problem with $c_t = x_{1t}$, $k_t = -x_{2t}$, $k_{t+1} = x_{3t}$, and $k_1 = k$. In fact, there is a unique Pareto optimum for this economy. The assumptions of Theorem 2.2 are met for this economy given the optimal allocation.[15] It follows that the Pareto optimum $[(\mathbf{x}), (\mathbf{y})]$ is supported by a non-trivial continuous linear functional p on E. In addition, if $0 \in X$ and $0 \in Y$, a space specific argument may be used to show the optimum is a valuation equilibrium.[16]

The remaining question is to prove that p can be represented as a sequence of prices. This means $p = (p_1, p_2, p_3)$ with $p \in l$ for $l = 1, 2, 3$, where l is the positive cone in l. As is well known, the supremum norm dual of $l_\infty \equiv l_\infty(S, \Sigma, \mu)$ is $ba \equiv ba(S, \Sigma, \mu)$, the space of *charges* (or bounded additive scalar functions) defined on Σ, where S is the set of integers, Σ the set of all subsets of S, and μ is the counting measure, i.e., $\mu(G)$ gives the cardinality of the set $G \in \Sigma$. The spaces l_∞ and ba are paired by means of the bilinear functional πz defined by $\pi(z) = \int z(s)d\pi$. If $\pi \in ba$ is a countably additive charge then the Radon-Nikodym theorem (Dunford and Schwartz [1958, p. 181]) implies there exists a unique $\pi \in l_1$, such that $\pi(z) = \sum_{t=1}^{\infty} p_t z_t$ for each $z \in l_\infty$. The countably additive elements of ba have price representations. However, there may be linear functionals on l_∞ which are not identifiable with price systems in this fashion. A charge failing to have a countably additive part is known as a *pure charge*.[17] In general, a charge may be uniquely decomposed into a maximally countably additive measure and a pure charge; this is the

[15] This is a consequence of free disposal.

[16] See Harris [1987, pp. 68–70]. The key step is to show int $(X \cap Y) \neq \emptyset$.

[17] See Bhaskara Rao and Bhaskara Rao [1983] for details on the properties of ba.

Yosida and Hewitt Decomposition theorem (Bhaskara Rao and Bhaskara Rao [19, p. 241]). Put differently, *ba* is the direct sum of *ca*, the space of bounded countably additive measures, and *pch*, the space of pure charges.

The economic interpretation of prices which are charges originated in the work of Radner [1967] on the existence of efficiency prices for production plans in infinite horizon capital theoretic production models. Bewley [16, 17] added further intuition in his presentation of sufficient conditions for support (and equilibrium) prices to be countably additive. Subsequently, Richard [1986] argued for the use of the order continuous dual of l_∞ as the price space in order to exclude pure charges as price systems. Gilles and Leroy [1989] argued that the Yosida-Hewitt decomposition of a price system in *ba* could be interpreted as a decomposition of the price system into a "market fundamental" component represented by a measure in ca and a "price bubble" component represented by an element of *pch*. All of these authors have observed that the "tail" of a consumption sequence in l_∞ determined the valuation of that bundle when the price system included a bubble. Various "myopia" hypotheses have been introduced as sufficient conditions to rule out bubbles as components of support (or equilibrium) prices. In the Ramsey case, the myopia of the preference relation implies the supporting valuation functional is countably additive and therefore based on market fundamentals alone.[18]

A modification in the objective function may be used to illustrate the importance of the continuity along line segments assumption as well as the possibility for support prices in *ba* to be pure charges. Consider the Rawls maximin utility function: $U(\mathbf{x}) = \inf_t x_{1t}$. It can be shown that U is upper semi-continuous in the supremum norm topology on l_∞, hence R is regular but not continuous since U is not lower semi-continuous. On the other hand, R is continuous along line segments. Debreu's result implies the Pareto optimum allocation with the Rawls maximin criterion may be supported by some non-trivial linear functional in *ba*. Is the supporting functional necessarily countably additive?[19] Suppose that k equals the

[18] See Prescott and Lucas [1972] and Harris [1987, pp. 68–73].

[19] The myopia assumption (IV) in Prescott and Lucas [1972, p. 417] is not satisfied by the maximin criterion: This utility function does not discount sufficiently distant consumption.

Golden-rule stock g, where $g = \text{argmax}[f(x) - x]$. In this case, the supporting price system must be a pure charge. The optimal program given the Golden-rule initial stocks is the stationary plan found by consuming $f(g) - g$ in every period and maintaining the stocks g. Suppose π is the supporting price system in ba and its Yosida-Hewitt decomposition is given by $\pi = p + \nu$, where p is countably additive and ν is a pure charge. Condition (2.4) holds for any positive price system in ba: in order to increase utility by ε over the Golden-rule level consumption must rise by at least ε in every period. On the other hand, profit maximization (2.3) implies that $p_{t+1}f'(g) = p_t$ for all t; $f'(g) = 1$ implies $p_{t+1} = p_t$ for all t. Thus $p = 0$ and $\pi = \nu$ obtains.[20] Finally, the one sector-model with the Rawls objective function highlights the importance of the interiority properties of Y in the separation argument rather than further restricting preferences to obtain the second welfare theorem. Subsequent researchers have strengthened the continuity along line segments hypothesis by assuming continuous preference orders.

There are other examples of applications of Debreu's second theorem in dynamic competitive analysis. One sector optimal growth models under uncertainty (Harris [1987], Prescott and Mehra [1980]), asset pricing (Mehra [1988]), multi-agent heterogeneous capital goods models (Bewley [1982], Coles [1985, 1986], Yano [1984], and Marimon [1989]) may be placed into this framework. However, Debreu's result does have limitations.

First, Debreu's hypotheses on the existence of a non-empty interior for the aggregate production set may not be met in reasonable models. In the one sector case, this happens when a maximum sustainable stock fails to exist. For example, take $f(k) = rk$ with $r > 1$ or $f(k) = \sqrt{k} + 2k$. The commodity space is now $E = \{\mathbf{x} = \{x_t\}_{t=1}^{\infty} : x_t \in \mathbb{R}^3\}$, a component

[20] I am indebted to Christian Gilles for this argument (private communication) in response to a conjecture stated in a draft of the paper. His letter also contains a proof that if $k > g$, the supporting price is a pure charge and it is countably additive in the case $0 < k < g$, but never a mixture. For $k > g$, the intuition is that the optimal path eventually equals the Golden-rule state. In the second case, the optimum is the stationary path maintaining initial consumption at the level $f(k) - k$. Since $f'(k) > 1$, the profit conditions induce discounting into the supporting price system and force $\nu = 0$.

$\mathbf{x}_l \in s$, the space of all real sequences, and the interior of s^+ is empty in the topology of coordinate- wise convergence or its equivalent topologies (that is, the Frechet metric topology and weak $\sigma(s, s_0)$-topology where s_0 is the space of sequences which are eventually zero).

The question of existence of Pareto optimal allocations for L_∞-spaces was first examined by Bewley [1990] in an exchange economy setup. Magill [1981] later extended Bewley's result to the production case. Bewley's existence proof anticipated many of the subsequent technical developments in the literature. The heart of his existence argument was based on showing the weak* compactness of the set of feasible allocations and the weak* continuity of agents preference relations. The former property utilized the fact that the order intervals in L_∞ are weak* compact by Alaoglu's theorem (see Aliprantis and Burkinshaw [1985, p. 141]). The later property followed from the combination of the Mackey-Arens theorem (see Schaeffer [1986, p. 130]) with the maintained assumptions that preference orders were convex and Mackey continuous. An argument based on Zorn's lemma then led to the existence of an optimal allocation. The proof is basically a translation of the classical Weierstrass existence theorem for one agent constrained optimization problems to the many agent model. The assumption that agents preference orders were complete, transitive, and had utility representations therefore played a non-trivial role in his existence argument.

However, establishing the existence of Pareto optimal allocations by means of *direct methods* may not be possible for l_∞-spaces endowed with the sup norm topology in the above manner. In the one sector case, Majumdar [1975] showed if there is a positive maximum sustainable stock, then the set of attainable allocations is sup norm bounded but is not sup norm compact. Araujo [1985] presented examples of economies on l_∞-spaces endowed with the sup norm topology without Pareto optima. He then weakened the topology on l_∞ and reconsidered the existence question. He proved that a topology for which preferences are continuous and non-trivial Pareto optimal allocations exist is necessary and sufficient for agents preferences to exhibit impatience in the sense of Brown and Lewis [1981]. The existence of optima could be obtained from Bewley's proof with either the Mackey or strict topologies for the dual pair (l_∞, l_1).

Yannelis [1990] demonstrated the existence of individually rational

Pareto optima as well as core allocations in a very general exchange economy framework. He required the commodity space to have a compatible Hausdorff topology τ. This means that τ is weaker than the Hausdorff topology of E, τ is a vector space topology, and all order intervals are τ-compact. The consumption set of each agent is taken to be the positive cone of E. Agents are assumed to have τ-continuous preference relations and satisfy a weak irreflexivity property. This topology need not be locally convex and the interior of the positive cone may be empty. Agents need not have convex, complete, or transitive preferences; utility functions may not exist. Consequently, Yannelis replaced the use of Zorn's lemma in Bewley's [1990] proof by a fixed point argument. It is interesting to note that in the case of l_∞, the compatible topology is the weak* topology $\sigma^*(l_\infty, l_1)$. In this case the order interval generated by the social endowment vector is weak* compact; Yannelis' existence theorem clearly generalizes Bewley's [1990] result.[21] Moreover, Yannelis' theorem also says that a nonempty interior of the positive cone of E is only critical for establishing the price support property of optima and hence the existence of competitive equilibrium.

Araujo's [1985] characterization of economies with non-trivial Pareto optima suggests that a form of the second welfare theorem might be conjectured for the dual pair (l_∞, l_1) with the Mackey topology $m(l_\infty, l_1)$. One advantage of selecting this dual pair is that the supporting prices have an economically meaningful representation in terms of market fundamentals. Unfortunately, Debreu's theorem cannot be used since l_∞^+ has an empty interior in the $m(l_\infty, l_1)$-topology; free disposal does not imply the aggregate production set has a non-empty interior. A new form of the second welfare theorem is needed to handle this space as well as other spaces whose positive cones have an empty interior.

Of course, one could try to describe sufficient conditions for an aggregate production set to possess a non-empty interior. Khan and Peck [1989] do this for ordered Banach spaces. Specifically, they showed that a particular formalization of the requirement that Y have "bounded marginal rates of substitution" implies a closed, convex-production set with "free

---

[21] See Section 3.5 below for a related discussion in the case of the Peleg-Yaari economy.

disposal" has a non-empty interior.[22] They also give examples showing this will fail in locally convex spaces such as s.

3. Weak Pareto Optimality and the Support Property

Ordered linear spaces form the natural framework for most economic models. As noted, there are many examples of models whose commodity spaces have positive cones lacking an interior. The new results and methods introduced for the analysis of the support problem in those spaces are surveyed next.

Before getting into the detailed development of the support theory, it is useful to recall a well known example due to Jones [1986, ex. 9, p. 196]. This example shows that continuity of preferences by itself is insufficient for the support property to obtain in a model where the positive cone has an empty interior. The commodity space is l_2, the space of square summable sequences, and the price space is also l_2. These spaces are placed in duality with the weak topology, $\sigma(l_2, l_2)$. There is a representative agent with utility function U defined by

$$U(\mathbf{x}) = \sum_{t=1}^{\infty} u(x_t, t)$$

where $u(\chi, t) = t^{-2}(1 - e^{-t^2 \chi})$, for $t = 1, 2, \ldots$. The endowment vector is ω; it is defined coordinate-wise by $\omega = 1/t^2$. It can be shown that U is $\sigma(l_2, l_2)$-continuous. The endowment vector is the Pareto optimal allocation. However there is no supporting price system in l_2. The only price candidates are $p_t = u'(w_t, t) = e^{-1}$ for all t. This trial price sequence is not square summable. The implication of this example is that prices measure marginal valuations of goods and the continuity of preferences, by itself, does not restrict the sequence of marginal utilities to lie in the dual of the commodity space.

---

[22] It is also worth observing here that Debreu does not require X_i to be closed or open.

3.1 The Economic Model and Riesz Spaces. The economic models of Bewley [1972], Peleg and Yaari [1970], and others where placed in an abstract setting in Aliprantis and Brown [1983] by the introduction of a Riesz dual system representation of the commodity-price duality. Riesz space concepts may be found in Aliprantis and Burkinshaw [1978, 1985]. The connection between Riesz spaces and infinite dimensional commodity spaces is elaborated on in the monograph by Aliprantis, Brown and Burkinshaw [1989]. I will follow their terminology and setup for the most part.

The commodity-price duality is described by a Riesz dual system $\langle E, F\rangle$, where the Riesz space E is the commodity space and the Riesz space F is the price space. As usual, $\geq$ is the partial order relation on E^+ (the positive cone of E) and the evaluation $p(x)$ will now be denoted by px for all $x \in E$ and $p \in F$.[23]

The social endowment vector is ω. There are m consumers indexed by i as in Part II. The consumption set of i is taken to be E^+. The preference relation R_i is assumed to be continuous, strictly convex in the sense of (II), and monotone. Monotonicity means that $x > y$ in E^+ implies xP_iy.[24] There is a locally convex topology τ on E consistent with the dual system $\langle E, F\rangle$ for which every preference order is τ-continuous.[25]

There are k producers indexed as before by j with production sets Y_j. An element $y_j \in Y_j$ is a production plan for the producer. The Riesz space structure of E permits y_j to be written as the difference between its positive part, y_j^+, and its negative part, y_j^-. The positive part of y is interpreted as the output vector and the negative part of y is the input vector. Each production set is assumed to be a weakly closed convex set and $Y_j \cap E^+ = \{0\}$ (irreversibility). The definitions of the aggregate production set and attainable allocations are as in Part II.

An *exchange economy* $\mathcal{E}$ is a 3-tuple

$$\mathcal{E} = (\langle E, F\rangle, [R_i], \omega);$$

---

23 Another standard notation for $p(x)$ is $\langle x, p\rangle$, which is used in Section 4.3.2.

24 $x > y$ means $x \geq y$, $x \neq y$.

25 If the preference of an agent i is represented by a utility function u_i, then that utility function is τ-continuous. This implies that the utility function is Mackey continuous (see Aliprantis, Brown and Burkinshaw [1989, p. 179]).

a *production economy* $\mathcal{E}$ is a 4-tuple

$$\mathcal{E} = (\langle E, F\rangle, [R_i], [Y_j], \omega),$$

where the Riesz dual system represents the commodity-price duality in both cases and each consumer i and producer j have the previously described characteristics. In either case ω is unrestricted in the sense that $\omega = 0$ is admissible (as in the one-sector optimal growth model).

3.2 Proper Preferences and Technologies.

The Jones example given above shows the need to find further restrictions on preferences that will lead to support prices in the chosen dual of the commodity space. Mas-Colell [1986] introduced the concept of proper preferences to express the new restrictions needed for the support property to obtain in an exchange economy. The analogous proper technology condition for production economies appeared in Mas-Colell [1986].

3.2.A Proper Preferences.

Mas-Colell [1986] introduced the concept of proper preferences as a restriction on preferences which could be used to prove that a Pareto optimum enjoyed the support property. His motivation for doing this was to use the support property as a step in demonstrating the existence of a quasi- equilibrium for the economy using the welfare maximization technique of Negishi [1960]. The role of the properness assumption is to compensate for the lack of interior points in the positive cone.[26] In the remainder of this subsection, indices indicating individual consumers and producers are suppressed since the meaning is clear.

Definition 3.1. *Let E be a Riesz space, τ a linear topology on E and R a preference relation on E^+.*

1) *The preference relation R is said to be τ-**proper** at some point $x \in E^+$ whenever there exists some $v > 0$ and some τ-neighborhood V of zero such that $x - \alpha v + zRx$ in E^+ with $\alpha > 0$ implies $z \notin \alpha V$.*
2) *The preference relation R is said to be **uniformly τ-proper** whenever there exists some $v > 0$ and some τ-neighborhood V of zero such*

[26] Bewley [1990] initiated the use of the Negishi approach in L_∞ where the interior of the positive cone is non-empty. Magill [1981] published the first proof of existence of an equilibrium following the Negishi approach in L_∞.

that for any arbitrary $x \in E^+$ satisfying $x - \alpha v + zRx$ in E^+ with $\alpha > 0$ it follows that $z \notin \alpha V$.

Any vector v that satisfies property (2) is called a *vector* or *direction of uniform properness for R.* If it is necessary to indicate the v in the definitions, then R is said to be a v-uniformly τ-proper preference relation. A uniformly proper preference relation is the formal implementation of the idea that any loss of consumption along the direction of v cannot be substituted for by a "small" basket of goods. Speaking heuristically, uniform properness bounds marginal rates of substitution (c.f., Yannelis and Zame [1986]). Mas-Colell [1986] characterized proper preference relations as follows.[27]

Theorem 3.1. *Let τ be a locally convex topology on a Riesz space E and let R be a preference relation of E^+. Then R is uniformly τ-proper if and only if there exists a non-empty τ-open convex cone Γ such that*

a) $\Gamma \cap (-E^+) \neq \emptyset$; *and*
b) $(x + \Gamma) \cap P(x) = \emptyset$ *for all* $x \in E^+$.

The τ-uniform proper preference condition is designed to prepare for the use of the Separation theorem. Indeed, if R is a convex τ-proper preference relation at $x \in E$, then there is a $p \in F$, $p \neq 0$, such that $pz \geq px$ for all $z \in R(x)$.[28]

Definition 3.2. *Let R be a preference relation defined on a subset X of the commodity space E. Then a vector $v \in E$ is said to be an* **extremely desirable bundle** *(or* **vector***) for R whenever*

1. $x + \alpha v \in X$ *holds for all* $x \in X$ *and all* $\alpha > 0$; *and*
2. $x + \alpha v P x$ *holds for all* $x \in X$ *and all* $\alpha > 0$.[29]

If R is a monotone preference relation on E^+ and E^+ has a non-empty interior or E is an AM-space with unit and there is an extremely desirable bundle, then R is uniformly proper. Properness is a strength-

---

[27] Yannelis and Zame [1986, p. 91] also derived this result.

[28] See Mas-Colell [1986a, p. 1043].

[29] Yannelis and Zame [1986, pp. 90–91] introduced a variant of extreme desirability in their marginal rate of substitution hypothesis on preferences.

ening of the monotonicity axiom in those cases.[30]

Back [1988] extended the concept of τ-uniformly proper preferences for exchange economies modelled on a vector lattice E equipped with a locally convex topology, and where agents consumption sets may be strictly contained in E^+. His definition requires an agent's consumption set X_i to be comprehensive, that is, $X_i + E^+ \subset X$. He then restricts the notion of proper preferences to those points lying in the order interval $[0, \omega]$ generated by the social endowment. I will give an example of an economy that is constructed in the spirit of Back's framework (see Section 3.5).

3.2.B Proper Technologies.

Mas-Colell [1986] introduced the analogous notion of τ-properness for production sets. Richard [1986] proposed a weaker formulation of a proper technology set; it is the definition followed in this paper. His definition is along the lines of the characterization Theorem 3.1.[31]

Definition 3.3. *A production set Y contained in a locally convex-solid Riesz space E is said to be uniformly τ-proper whenever there exists a vector $w > 0$ and a convex τ-neighborhood W of zero such that the convex cone $\Gamma = \{\alpha(w + x : \alpha > 0$ and $x \in W\}$ satisfies*

$$(z + \Gamma) \cap \{y \in Y : y^+ \geq z^+\} = \emptyset$$

for all $z \notin Y$.

The point w is called a *vector* or *direction of uniform properness* for the producer.

It will be seen in the next section that some models will not have locally solid commodity spaces. Consequently another definition of proper technology will be necessary for that class of commodity spaces than the locally convex-solid Riesz space family. A definition for that case is

---

30 See Aliprantis, Brown and Burkinshaw [1989, p. 118] for a discussion of the Am-space with unit case and Mas-Colell [1986a, p. 1043] on the L_∞ case.

31 Yannelis and Zame [1986] and Zame [1987] proposed different definitions of proper technologies. Zame [1987] required the aggregate production set to meet his version of the properness condition, whereas Mas-Colell's [1986] assumption was in force for each producer's technology set. Zame [1987] also assumes E is a Banach lattice, a condition not required for the Richard [1986] definition of a τ-proper technology set.

delayed until Section 3.4 in order to motivate the economic reasons for looking at those commodity spaces in the first place.

3.3 Exchange Economies.

3.3.1 Mas-Colell's Theorem for Locally Convex-Solid Riesz Spaces.

Let $\mathcal{E}$ be an exchange economy for which the commodity space is a locally convex-solid Riesz space, that is, there is a basis at zero consisting of convex and solid sets. This topology τ on E is assumed consistent with the dual system $\langle E, F \rangle$ and every preference relation R_i is τ-continuous. The order structure on E and τ-uniform properness conditions on the preference relation permit a separation argument proof of the second welfare theorem. The form and proof of this result is due to Mas-Colell [1986]. The proof turns on the Riesz Decomposition Property and the properness conditions.[32] Hence, the order structure of the commodity space plays an essential role.

Theorem 3.2. *Let $\mathcal{E}$ be an exchange economy defined on a locally convex-solid Riesz space with monotone, convex and uniformly τ-proper preferences. Then every weak Pareto optimal allocation has the support property.*

If V_i is a convex solid τ-neighborhood of zero and $v_i > 0$ is a direction of uniform properness for agent i, then any weakly Pareto optimal allocation has the support property with price system $p > 0$ satisfying $pv = 1$ and $|pz| \leq 1$ for all $z \in V = \bigcap_{i=1}^m V_i$ where $v = \sum_{i=1}^m v_i$.

The proof of this theorem follows from some preliminary remarks and lemmas. First, given a weak Pareto optimum $[(x_i)]$ define the set

$$Z = \sum_{i=1}^{m} R_i(x_i) - \omega.$$

Z is a convex set and $0 \in Z$. The next result is an immediate consequence of the uniform properness hypothesis.

---

[32] The Riesz Decomposition Property states: If x, y_1 and y_2 are three positive points in a Riesz space satisfying $0 \leq x \leq y_1 + y_2$, then there exist positive points x_1 and x_2 such that $0 \leq x_1 \leq y_1$, $0 \leq x_2 \leq y_2$ and $x = x_1 + x_2$. For a proof, see Aliprantis, Brown and Burkinshaw [1989, p. 89].

Lemma 3.3. *If $v_i > 0$ is a direction of uniform properness for agent i and V_i is a convex solid τ-neighborhood of zero such that $x - \alpha v_i + zR_i x$ in E^+ implies $z \in \alpha V_i$, then $V = \bigcap_{i=1}^m V_i$ is a convex solid neighborhood of zero.*

Set $v = \sum_{i=1}^m v_i$ and let Γ be the convex cone generated by $v + V$. The order structure of the commodity space and the proper preference hypothesis are combined in the next result which is preparation for the application of the Separation theorem. This lemma also utilizes the locally solid property of the topology τ.

Lemma 3.4. $Z \cap (-\Gamma) = \emptyset$.

Proof. Suppose $Z \cap (-\Gamma) \neq \emptyset$. Then there exist $z_i \in R_i(x_i)$ $(i = 1, \ldots, m)$, $\alpha > 0$ and $w \in V$ such that $\sum_{i=1}^m (z_i - x_i) = -\alpha(v + w)$. Let $z = \sum_{i=1}^m z_i$, $x = \sum_{i=1}^m x_i$. Then we may write

$$z - x + \alpha v = -\alpha w.$$

Let $y = z - x + \alpha v$ and observe $y \leq z + \alpha v$. Hence $y^+ \leq z + \alpha v$. By the Riesz Decomposition Property, there exist $y_i \in E$ $(i = 1, \ldots, m)$ with $0 \leq y_i \leq z + \alpha v$ and $y^+ = \sum_{i=1}^m y_i$. Set $h_i = z_i + \alpha v_i - y_i \geq 0$ and observe that $h_i P_i z_i$ $(i = 1, \ldots, m)$. Since v_i is a vector of uniform properness for each agent i $(i = 1, \ldots, m)$, if $h_i - \alpha v_i + y_i R_i h_i$, then $y_i \notin \alpha V_i$. But $0 \leq y_i \leq y^+ \leq |y| = \alpha |w| \in \alpha V$ implies $y_i \in \alpha V$ and so $y_i \in \alpha V_i$, a contradiction. Hence $h_i P_i z_i$ and $z_i R_i x_i$, so transitivity of R_i implies $h_i P_i x_i$ as well. Now adding over i and using $[(x_i)]$ is an allocation:

$$\begin{aligned} h \equiv \sum_{i=1}^m h_i &= \sum_{i=1}^m (z_i + \alpha v_i - y_i) \\ &= \sum_{i=1}^m (z_i - x_i + \alpha v_i) + \omega - \sum_{i=1}^m y_i \\ &= y - y^+ + \omega \leq \omega \end{aligned}$$

The state $[(h_i^*)]$ defined by setting $h_1^* = h_1 + \omega - h$ and $h_i^* = h_i$ $(i = 2, \ldots, m)$ is an allocation satisfying $h_i^* P_i x_i$ for all i, which is impossible since $[(x_i)]$ is a weak Pareto optimum. Q.E.D.

Lemma 3.5. *There is a linear functional p which separates Z and* $(-\Gamma)$. *The separating functional p supports the weak Pareto optimum. Moreover, p may be normalized so that* $pv = 1$ *and* $|pz| \leq 1$ *for all* $z \in V$.

Proof. The interior of $-\Gamma$ is non-empty as $-v + V \subseteq \Gamma$. Lemma 3.4 implies $Z \cap (-\Gamma) = \emptyset$. The Separation theorem implies there is a $p \neq 0$, $p \in E'$, and a constant c such that $pz \geq c \geq -pg$ for all $z \in Z$ and $g \in \Gamma$. As G is a cone, $c \geq 0$; as $0 \in Z$, $c \leq 0$, so $c = 0$.

If $x \in R_i(x_i)$, then $x - x_i \in Z$ and $px > px_i$ must hold. Therefore $[(x_i)]$ has the support property with this price system. Moreover, $p \geq 0$ holds and $pv \geq 0$.

Suppose $pv = 0$. Since $w \in V$ implies $-v \pm w \in -\Gamma$, the separation property implies $p(-v \pm w) = \pm pw \leq 0$ for all $w \in V$ and p must be zero, which is impossible. Therefore, $pv > 0$ and p may be chosen so that $pv = 1$. For $z \in V$, it follows that $|pz| \leq 1$ since $pv = 1$, $-v \pm z \in V$, and $p(-v \pm z) \leq 0$. Q.E.D.

3.3.2 Extensions of Mas-Colell's Theorem.

There are several notable extensions of Mas-Colell's theorem. The first result is due to Back [1988] who provides the analog of the second welfare theorem for consumption sets contained in E^+ and satisfying his modification of the uniform properness condition. The second result is due to Araujo and Monteiro [1989] who weaken the uniform properness hypothesis to a pointwise properness property on individual preference orders in a class of exchange economies with locally convex-solid commodity spaces. However, an example due to Richard and Zame [1986] suggests that, in general, it will not be possible to weaken uniform properness to pointwise properness and still obtain an exact support theorem.[33]

Interestingly, Back as well as Araujo and Monteiro use related ideas: Back requires his properness condition on the order interval $[0, \omega]$ and Araujo and Monteiro require their pointwise condition to obtain on the intersection of the principal ideal generated by the endowment vector and the positive cone of the commodity space. In both cases, the properness hypothesis is assumed on the economically relevant portion of the

---

[33] The Richard and Zame [1986] example is for the commodity space l_2. It is related to the Jones example quoted at the start of 4.1. However, the Jones example of a commodity space is not a locally convex-solid Riesz space.

commodity space. The idea of concentrating the assumptions on an economically relevant part of the commodity space will be illustrated by a new example of a Peleg and Yaari [1970] economy in Section 3.5.

Economies with Riesz commodity spaces which are not locally solid were constructed by Huang and Kreps [1987].[34] They considered a class of economies motivated by intertemporal resource allocation questions whose simplest realization was the commodity space defined by the set of right continuous real-valued functions of bounded variation defined on $[0,1]$ with the $\|\cdot\|_1$−norm and positive cone $E^+ = \{x \in E : x \geq 0$ and nondecreasing$\}$. The positive cone is "too small" for the lattice operations to be continuous: The topology is not locally solid. However, the dual space is $L_\infty([0,1])$ which is a Riesz space for the induced order. Jones's [1984] version of the differentiated commodity model takes $M([0,1])$, the space of measures on the interval $[0,1]$, and the price space is $C([0,1])$, the space of continuous functions on $[0,1]$. There is no topology compatible with this dual pair which turns the commodity space of measures into a locally convex-solid Riesz space. However, the dual space in this example is also a Riesz space. The recognition that these examples shared the feature that their dual spaces were lattices lead Mas-Colell and Richard [1987] to propose analogs of the properness conditions for exchange economies with a Riesz space of commodities and dual space enjoying a lattice structure. They were then able to demonstrate a form of the second fundamental welfare theorem. I will not go any further into the details of their results since Richard [1989] has published a price support theorem for weak Pareto optima in a production economy. His results will be presented in Section 3.4. It should also be noted here that Back's [1988] version of the price support theorem fits into the broader framework proposed by Mas-Colell and Richard.

Optimal growth theorists dating back to Ramsey have studied a preference ranking known as the overtaking criterion. This preference relation is a partial order on the consumption stream without discounting future

---

[34] The product differentiation models of Jones [1984] and Mas-Colell [1975] also fail to have locally convex-solid Riesz commodity spaces. However, Jones gave existence results based on space specific arguments. Mas-Colell and Richard [1987] make it clear that the Huang and Kreps model stimulated their research into the price support problem in Riesz spaces.

utilities. Yi [1989] showed that an exchange economy with each consumer following the overtaking criterion cannot be cast in Debreu's [1954] framework. Moreover, he argued, for example, if $E = s$, then the topology making the preference relations continuous was so strong that the commodity space was no longer a **topological vector space.**[35] However, he was able to obtain versions of the first and second welfare theorems by means of a structure specific argument. Interestingly, he had to utilize two budget constraint concepts that differed in their requirements for repayment of debt.

3.4 Production Economies. Using the modified version of the proper technology hypothesis, Aliprantis, Brown and Burkinshaw [1989, pp. 220-223] obtained the following variant of Mas-Colell's [1986] production economy second welfare theorem. The commodity space is taken to be a locally convex-solid Riesz space.

Theorem 3.6. *Let $\mathcal{E} = (\langle E, F\rangle, [R_i], [Y_j], \omega)$ be an economy defined for the Riesz dual system $\langle E, F\rangle$. Assume the topology τ is locally convex-solid. If preferences and production sets are uniformly τ-proper, then every weakly Pareto optimal allocation has the support property.*

If $V_i(W_j)$ is a convex solid neighborhood of zero and $v_i(w_j) > 0$ is a direction of uniform properness for $i(j)$, then any weakly Pareto optimal allocation has the support property with price system $p > 0$ and $|pz| \leq 1$ for all $z \in V_1 \cap \cdots \cap V_m \cap W_1 \cap \cdots \cap W_k$ and $pu = 1$ for $u \equiv \sum_{i=1}^m v_i + \sum_{j=1}^k w_j$.

The proof of Theorem 3.6 is analogous to the argument for Theorem 3.2, so it will not be given below.

As previously noted some economic models cannot be cast in a locally solid commodity space framework. One important characteristic of a locally convex-solid topology is that the positive cone, E^+, is τ-closed.[36] Richard [1989] observed the second welfare theorem could be deduced for production economies if the E^+ closure property was combined with the requirement that the dual space be a vector sublattice of the order dual of the commodity space. The definition of a uniformly τ-proper preference

---

[35] Yi [1989, p. 63].

[36] Aliprantis and Burkinshaw [1985, p. 163].

relation does not require a locally solid topology. However, the definition of a proper technology set must be modified along the lines of the definition originally proposed by Mas-Colell [1986]. Richard's [1989] conception of a proper technology appropriate for commodity spaces without uniformly continuous lattice operations is introduced below.

Let Y be a production set (dropping j labels). Assume that $Y \subset E$, $0 \in Y$, Y is convex, has the free disposal property ($Y - E^+ \subset Y$), and E^+ is τ-closed. A set $\mathcal{Y}$ is a *pre-technology set* for Y if $\mathcal{Y}$ is a convex lattice satisfying free disposal ($\mathcal{Y} - E^+ \subset \mathcal{Y}$) and if $(1+\varepsilon)\mathcal{Y} \subset \mathcal{Y}$ for some $\varepsilon > 0$.[37] Richard's [1989] definition of a proper technology is given below.

Definition 3.4. *The pair $(Y, \mathcal{Y})$ has uniformly τ-proper production if there exists a vector $w > 0$ and an open neighborhood of zero $W \subset E$ such that the open cone Γ generated by $\{w\} + W$ satisfies $(y - \Gamma) \cap \mathcal{Y} \subset Y$ for all $y \in Y$.*

The point w is a direction of vector of uniform properness for the technology set Y. Richard [1989] assumed that the technology set of each producer was uniformly τ-proper and the aggregate endowment was a direction of uniform properness for all producers and consumers.[38] Define a set Z by

$$Z = \{[(x_i'), (y_j')] : x_i' \in E^+ \ (i = 1, \ldots, m), y_j' \in Y \ (j = 1, \ldots, k)$$

and

$$\sum_{i=1}^{m} x_i' \leq \omega + \sum_{j=1}^{k} y_j'\}.$$

Notice that $\mathcal{A} \subset Z$. Let E_{m+k} denote $m + k$ copies of E. Given a weakly compact convex set $\mathcal{K}$ in F_{m+k}^+, where F_{m+k} is the dual space of E_{m+k}, and an allocation $[(x_i), (y_j)]$, define another set $\mathcal{P}([(x_i), (y_j)]$ by

$$\mathcal{P}([(x_i), (y_j)] = \Big\{ (p, q) = (p_1, \ldots, p_m; q_1, \ldots, q_k) \in \mathcal{K} : p_i x_i' \geq p_i x_i \text{ for}$$

$$\text{all } x_i' \in R_i(x_i) \ (i = 1, \ldots, m), q_j y_j \geq q_j y_j' \text{ for all } y_j' \in Y_j, \text{ and}$$

---

37 See Mas-Colell [1986] and Richard [1989].

38 Hence $\omega \neq 0$. Recall, the one sector optimal growth model as reformulated in Section 2.4 does not enjoy this characteristic.

$$\left.\sum_{i=1}^{m} p_i x_i - \sum_{j=1}^{k} q_j y_j \geq \sum_{i=1}^{m} p_i x_i' - \sum_{j=1}^{k} q_j y_j' \text{ for all } [(x_i'), (y_j')] \in Z \right\} .$$

Suppose that the state $[(x_i), (y_j)]$ is a weak Pareto optimum allocation for the economy $\mathcal{E}$ and E^+ is a τ-closed set. The next result was obtained by Richard [1989, pp. 46-47] as preparation for his statement and proof of the second fundamental welfare theorem.

Lemma 3.7. *There is a weakly compact, convex set $\mathcal{K} \subset F^+_{m+k}$, such that $\sum_{i=1}^{m} p_i\omega + \sum_{j=1}^{m} q_j\omega = 1$ for all $(p,q) \in \mathcal{K}$ and such that for any weak Pareto optimal allocation $[(x_i), (y_j)]$, the set $\mathcal{P}([(x_i), (y_j)])$ is a non-empty, convex and weakly compact set.*

The proof of this Lemma utilizes the proper preference and technology properties to construct a particular set $\mathcal{K}$ with the desired characteristics. Alaoglu's theorem is the basis for the weak compactness of $\mathcal{K}$. Richard then shows that Z may be separated from another set constructed using the proper preference axiom and the structure of production sets. The separation argument gives rise to the non-empty, convex and weakly compact set $\mathcal{P}([(x_i), (y_j)])$.

The lattice property of the dual space F implies $\pi = (\bigvee_i p_i) \vee (\bigvee_j q_j)$ is a continuous linear functional on E whenever $(p,q) \in F_{m+k}$. This is used to get a supporting price system for a weak Pareto optimum which is the supremum of the prices supporting the individual weakly preferred sets and production sets.

Theorem 3.8. *Suppose $\mathcal{E}$ is an economy defined on the Riesz dual system $\langle E, F\rangle$. Assume that E^+ is τ-closed and F is a sublattice of the order dual of E. Let $[(x_i), (y_j)]$ be a weak Pareto optimal allocation for $\mathcal{E}$. If $\pi = (\bigvee_i p_i) \vee (\bigvee_j q_j)$ for $(p,q) \in \mathcal{P}([(x_i), (y_j)])$, then $\pi \in F$ has the support property, $\pi\omega \geq (m+k)^{-1}$, $\pi x_i = p_i x_i$ $(i = 1, \ldots, m)$, and $\pi y_j = q_j y_j$ $(j = 1, \ldots, k)$.*

The proof of Richard's theorem follows by verifying that the functional π (which exists by Lemma 3.7) has the desired properties. The whole point of Richard's proof is to show that this linear functional supports the weakly preferred sets of all agents and the production sets of all producers at the optimal allocation. Richard [1989] also established the existence of non-trivial weak Pareto optimum allocations with the same hypotheses on $\mathcal{E}$ used in Theorem 3.8. Finally, Richard observes [1989, p. 46] that the "best theorem" obtains for the Mackey topology of the dual pair. In this sense, his work confirms the intuition of Bewley [1972] who first proposed (in L_∞) that the Mackey topology was the appropriate one for infinite dimensional space models.

Khan and Vohra [1988] also gave sufficient conditions for a production economy defined on a dual pair of linear spaces $\langle E, F\rangle$ to enjoy the support property. Their condition amounts to a statement that marginal rates of substitution be uniformly bounded for any production set and requires the dual of the commodity space to have a norm.[39]

3.5 The Peleg-Yaari Economy: An Example. The second welfare theorem may illustrated for a class of economies in the framework of the Peleg and Yaari [1970] exchange economy. The commodity space is s with the $\sigma(s, s_0)$-topology. This economy is not covered by Debreu's theorem since s^+ has an empty interior. Preferences in the Peleg-Yaari economy are not, in general, uniformly proper. In fact, there are no utility functions on s which are strictly monotone, quasi-concave, $\sigma(s, s_0)$-continuous, and uniformly $\sigma(s, s_0)$-proper.[40]

Therefore, welfare theorems based on proper preferences do not apply to this economy. However, the order properties of the commodity space may be used in some cases to concentrate the analysis on the principal ideal A_ω generated by the social endowment vector ω. Aliprantis, Brown and Burkinshaw [1989, p.142; 3] observed that if $\mathcal{E}$ is an exchange economy with Riesz dual system $\langle E, F\rangle$, then the characteristics of $\mathcal{E}$ — when restricted to A_ω — define a new exchange economy with Riesz dual system $\langle A_\omega, A'_\omega\rangle$. Underlying every exchange economy with Riesz dual system $\langle E, F\rangle$, there is an exchange economy with the same preferences and endowments and with $\langle A_\omega, A'_\omega\rangle$ as the commodity-price duality. The space A_ω may be topologized in a manner suitable for application of Mas-Colell's [1986] theorem.

The restriction of the model to A_ω is also in the spirit of Back's [1988] exchange economy model. Beals and Koopmans [1969] gave an example ((B1) below) of a utility function that is not continuous on s^+. However,

[39] See their Condition M (p. 155).

[40] See Aliprantis, Brown and Burkinshaw [1989, p. 174].

the Beals and Koopmans example is continuous on a subset of s^+ containing the principal ideal A_ω generated by the endowment vector. This suggests that hypotheses on preferences need only hold the economically relevant part of the commodity space formalized by the principal ideal A_ω.

Assume: $\omega = (\alpha, \alpha^2, \alpha^3, \ldots)$ for $\alpha > 1$.

$$A_\omega = \{\mathbf{x} \equiv \{x_t\} \in s : |\mathbf{x}| \leq \lambda|\omega| \text{ for some } \lambda \geq 0\}.$$

A_ω is the principal ideal generated by the aggregate endowment vector. Observe that the order interval $[0, \omega]$ is a weakly compact subset of s by Tychonoff's Compactness Theorem.

Let $\beta \geq \alpha$ and define the β-weighted l_∞ norm (or β-norm), $|\cdot|_\beta$, by

$$|\mathbf{x}| = \sup_t |x_t/\beta_t|.$$

The β-topology on A_ω is the norm topology induced by the β-norm. The α-topology refers to the case $\alpha = \beta$. It can be shown that $A_\omega \subseteq \{\mathbf{x} \in s : |\mathbf{x}|_\beta < \infty\}$ and consequently A_ω may be embedded in the Banach space l_∞ with the supremum norm.[41] Hence the dual space of A_ω, denoted A'_ω, is *ba*. The pair $\langle A_\omega, A'_\omega\rangle$ is a Riesz dual system and the β-norm topology is a locally convex-solid topology on A_ω. Denote the positive cone of A_ω by A^+_ω.

Let R be a preference relation on A^+_ω and let u denote the corresponding utility function representing R (provided it exists). I will say that R is a **β-myopic preference relation** (u is a **β-myopic utility function**) if $R(u)$ is a continuous preference relation (utility function) on A^+_ω endowed with the β-norm topology. Boyd [1986, 1990] developed a general method for constructing β-myopic utility functions for models arising in capital theory. For example, he shows the following functions are β-myopic when $\beta > \alpha$:

(B1) $u(\mathbf{x}) = \sum_{t=1}^{\infty} \delta^{t-1} x_t^\mu$, for $\delta, \mu \in (0,1)$, $\delta\alpha^\mu \leq \delta\beta^\mu < 1$;
(B2) $u(\mathbf{x}) = \sum_{t=1}^{\infty} \delta^{t-1} \arctan(x_t^\mu)$, for $\delta, \mu \in (0,1)$;

---

41 If $\omega = (1,1,1,\ldots)$, then $A_\omega = l_\infty$. For $\beta > \alpha$, A_ω may be embedded in c_0, the space of sequences convergent to 0. Given the sup norm topology, this space has dual l_1.

(B3) $u(\mathbf{x}) = -\sum_{t=1}^{\infty} \exp[-\sum_{s=1}^{t} v(x_s)]$ where $v(0) > 0$, v is monotone increasing and concave.

Examples (B1)–(B3) are members of the class of recursive utility functions. Boyd's theory supplies a general method for constructing these utility functions on a fixed principal ideal in a Riesz space. It turns out that strictly monotone β-myopic utility functions are proper in the sense of Mas-Colell [1986].[42] Moreover, ω is a vector of uniform properness for those preference relations.[43] In particular, R is uniformly proper in the α-norm topology in the case where u obeys a classical Inada condition at 0 (as is the case in examples (B1–B2). Notice that example (B2) is not uniformly proper in the $m(l_\infty, l_1)$-topology (see Back [1988]). Preference relations are assumed to be strictly monotonic in the remainder of this section.

Boyd [1990, Lemma 2] showed that the β-norm topology and the relative product topology coincide on A_ω provided $\beta > \alpha$. In particular, this implies that the order interval $[0, \omega]$ is compact in the β-norm topology.[44] This is the main observation needed to show the existence of Pareto optimal allocation for an exchange economy $\mathcal{E}$ modelled with commodity-price dual system $\langle A_\omega, A'_\omega \rangle$. Economically, the $\beta > \alpha$ is a joint hypothesis on preferences and endowments necessary for the development of the existence and support theory.

The set of attainable allocations is $\mathcal{A}$; assume that $\mathcal{A}$ exhibits a free disposal property:

$$\mathcal{A} = \{(x'_1, x'_2, \ldots, x'_m) : x'_i \in A^+_\omega \text{ and } \sum_i x'_i \leq \omega\}.$$

---

42 This follows by observing that A^+_ω has a non-empty α-norm interior, the β-norm is a lattice norm for $\beta > \alpha$, and preferences are monotonic (see Aliprantis, Brown and Burkinshaw [1989, p. 118] and Mas-Colell [1986a, p. 1043]).

43 The strict monotonicity and continuity requirements exclude the Rawls utility function from consideration in this framework.

44 The sequence $\{\alpha^t/\beta^t\} \to 0$ as $t \to \infty$, hence the order interval $[0, \Omega]$ is weakly compact in l_∞ where $\Omega_t = \alpha^t/\beta^t$. Indeed, the order interval $[0, \Omega]$ is norm compact (see Aliprantis, Brown and Burkinshaw [1989, p. 103]). The fact that $\beta > \alpha$ is crucial for this to hold. The requirement that $\beta > \alpha$ is also analogous to the hypothesis $a \geq \omega$ in Theorem 3.5.15 of Aliprantis, Brown and Burkinshaw [1989, p. 164].

Pareto optimal allocations exist for economies with β-myopic utility functions defined on A_ω^+: just mimic the existence argument in Aliprantis, Brown and Burkinshaw [1989, pp. 40-41] replacing ω_i by 0.[45]

Let $[(x_i)]$ denote a Pareto optimal allocation.[46]

Theorem 3.9. *Let $\mathcal{E}$ be an exchange economy for which each agent has β-myopic, strictly monotone and strictly concave preferences on A_ω^+ where $\omega = (\alpha, \alpha^2, \alpha^3, \ldots)$ and $\alpha \geq 1$. If $[(x_i)]$ is a Pareto optimal allocation and $\beta > \alpha$, then $[(x_i)]$ has the support property for some non-zero $p \in l_1$. If $px_i > 0$, then $x_i R_i x_i'$ holds for all $x_i' \in A$ satisfying $px_i' \leq px_i$.*

Proof. Theorem 3.2 implies there exists a non-zero $p \in ba$ such that $w_i R_i x_i$ implies $pw_i \geq px_i$ for each i. Clearly $p \geq 0$ and for each i having $px_i > 0$, $x_i R_i w_i$ for all w_i satisfying $pw_i \leq px_i$. The normalization $p(\sum_i v_i) = 1$ follows where v_i is the vector of uniform properness for agent i. In this model, we have $v_i = \omega$ for each i. Therefore, we may take $p(m\omega) = 1$; again by renormalizing, we have $p\omega = 1$. Let p support the Pareto optimal allocation $[(x_i)]$. Since each agent has strictly monotone preferences, it follows that $p > 0$. Since ω is extremely desirable for each i, we may use Aliprantis, Brown and Burkinshaw's Theorem 3.4.21 [1989, p. 147] to show that p is order continuous on A_ω. Therefore, $p \in l_1$.Q.E.D.

The use of Mas-Colell's theorem rather than Debreu's yields additional information about the properties of the supporting price system. First, the argument that strictly monotone β-myopic preferences are sufficient for the support prices to lie in l_1 exploits the order structure of the problem. The key facts are that $\alpha > 0$ bounds the endowment strictly away from the origin, the endowment ω is extremely desirable for each consumer, and A_ω is embedded in c_0 with *order continuous dual* $(c_0)_n^\sim = l_1$.[47] Second, $p \in l_1$ and $p\omega = 1$ imply $p_t \to 0$ faster than $\alpha^t \to \infty$

[45] The existence problems raised by Araujo [1985] for the sup norm topology do not arise in economies with β-myopic utility and weakly compact order interval $[0, \omega]$.

[46] For this exchange economy, an allocation is Pareto optimal if and only if it is a weak Pareto optimal allocation since preferences are strictly monotonic. See Aliprantis, Brown and Burkinshaw [1989, p. 153].

[47] The comments of Aliprantis, Brown and Burkinshaw [1989, pp. 172–173, Example 3.6.5 and Richard [1986] on the economic significance of the order continuous dual motivate this point. In terms of the Yosida-Hewitt decompo-

whenever $\alpha > 1$.

4. Pareto Optimality and the Approximate Support Property

Proper preferences and technologies are critical for the establishment of the support property in economies where the interior of the positive cone is empty. There are many interesting economic problems naturally failing to satisfy the uniform properness conditions. As previously noted, preferences in the Peleg and Yaari [1970] model are not proper on s^+. The approximate support theory yields approximate support prices in their model.[48] The purpose of this section is to review the approximate versions of the fundamental welfare theorems and link the question of the existence of approximate support prices to the mathematical literature on the Helly problem.

If the properness hypotheses are not met, then it turns out that the best one can expect is that a weakly Pareto optimal allocation has an approximate system of support prices. This was first shown in Khan and Vohra [1985]. Aliprantis, Brown and Burkinshaw [1987] introduced the idea of supporting allocations approximately by prices. Khan and Vohra [1988] examined the approximate price supportability of weakly Pareto optimal allocations in locally convex spaces. Aliprantis and Burkinshaw [1988] characterized the weakly Pareto optimal allocations in a symmetric Riesz space setup. They also presented an example of an exchange economy defined on a symmetric Riesz space with the approximate support property but without support prices. Becker, Bercovici and Foias [1989] generalized the result of Aliprantis and Burkinshaw to a locally convex commodity space model.

---

sition of ba, the pure charges are not order continuous linear functionals. Also, see Schaeffer [1986, pp. 89–92].

[48] Of course, there may be Peleg and Yaari models where exact supportability obtains because the commodity space can be chosen as a subset of s in the manner of the example in Section 3.5. However, economies with β-myopic utility functions and $\beta \leq \alpha$ will not fall into that category; in those cases, exact supportability could fail.

4.1 Examples. Jones [1986] constructed the first examples of a weak Pareto optimum failing to have the support property. His one consumer example was given previously in Part 3. In that case, the upper contour set of the agent at the optimum could not be supported by any non-zero linear functional in the dual space. Aliprantis and Burkinshaw [1988] presented an example of an exchange economy model inspired by Mas-Colell [1986] that could only be approximately supported. Their example will be covered in Section 4.2.

Becker, Bercovici and Foias [1989] constructed an example of a production economy without the support property. In their case, the commodity-price duality is given by the dual pair (l_2, l_2) endowed with the weak topology. The production set lies in the kernel of a functional which is l_1 continuous, but not l_2 continuous: the production set is not proper at the origin. Moreover, their production set does not exhibit free disposal. The social production set is defined by

$$Y = \{y = (\eta_1, \eta_2, \dots) \in l_2 : |\eta_j| \leq 2^{-j} \ (j = 1, 2, \dots), \sum_{j=1}^{\infty} \eta_j = 0\}.$$

There is a single consumer with consumption set l_2^+. The preference relation is defined by the order relation $\geq$, i.e., xRw if and only if $x \geq w$. The aggregate endowment vector is $\omega = (2^{-1}, 2^{-2}, \dots, 2^{-j}, \dots)$. Notice that $R(\omega) = \{x = (\xi_1, \xi_2, \dots) \in l_2^+ : \xi_j \geq 2^{-j} \ (j = 1, 2, \dots)\}$. It is easy to show that $(\omega, 0)$ is a weak Pareto optimal allocation. If $(\omega, 0)$ is supported by prices, then there is a non-zero $p \in l_2$ such that $px \geq p\omega$ for all $x \in R(\omega)$, and $py \leq p0 = 0$ for all $y \in Y$. By taking $y = \pm y^{(n)}$, where $y^{(n)} = (0, 0, \dots, 0, -2^{-n-1}, 2^{-n-1}, 0, 0, \dots)$, we obtain $-p_n + p_{n+1} = 0$. Since $p \in l_2$, $p = 0$ follows. Therefore, any price system which "supports" this weak Pareto optimum must be zero.

Jones [1986] also constructed a second example of a weak Pareto optimum without the support property. This time, there were two agents inhabiting an exchange economy. At the weak Pareto optimum allocation, each agent's preferred set has a price support, but there is not a common set of prices in the dual space supporting both agent's preferred sets at that optimum. Richard and Zame [1986] and Back [1988] also gave similar examples. I will present the Jones [1986, pp. 196–197] example to illustrate the nature of the problem.

Let $E = L_\infty$, $F = C^1(0,1)$, the continuous functions on $(0,1)$ which have continuous and bounded derivatives. Assign this dual pair the weak topology, $\sigma(E,F)$. There are two agents with utility functions

$$U_1(x(t)) = \int_0^1 tx(t)dt, \qquad U_2(x(t)) = \int_0^1 (1-t)x(t)dt.$$

These preferences are continuous since they are linear. The social endowment vector is $\omega = \chi_{(0,1)}$ where χ denotes the characteristic function.

The allocation $x_1 = \chi_{(0,1/2)}$ and $x_2 = \chi_{(1/2,1)}$ is a weak Pareto optimum. The price system defined by $p(t) = t$ is an element of F and supports the allocation x_1 assigned to agent one. Similarly, the price system $p(t) = (1-t)$ supports the allocation x_2 assigned to agent two. However, there is no price system in the dual space F which simultaneously supports both agents optimal allocations.[49] It turns out that there are prices in the dual that approximately support this Pareto optimum in the sense that consumers approximately minimize expenditure and profits are approximately maximized by producers. The next two subsections present the precise notion of approximation used to resolve the non-existence question raised by this and other examples.

4.2 Approximate Welfare Theorems in Riesz Spaces. The economy is described by the Riesz space model defined in Section 3.1. An attainable state $[(x_i),(y_j)]$ is said to be approximately supported by prices whenever for each $\varepsilon > 0$ and each $a \in E^+$, there exists a $p \in F$ such that

(4.1) $p\omega = 1$;

(4.2) xR_ix_i in X_i implies $px \geq px_i - \varepsilon$; and

(4.3) $py_j \geq \sup\{py : y \in Y \text{ and } y \leq a\} - \varepsilon$ for all j.

The constraint $y \leq a$ in (4.3) expresses the limitations on producers imposed by limited resources when $a = \omega$. Technically, the constraint plays the role of requiring approximate profit maximization over the set of possible input-output vectors that could be achieved with the economy's resources.

[49] The "price system" $p(t) = \max\{t,(1-t)\}$ supports the allocations, but it is not an element of the dual space. The problem is the dual is not a lattice; the conditions of Richard's [1989] theorem are not met.

Prices are not normalized to have unit norm since the commodity space is not required to be a normed linear space. In the case of a Banach lattice, the normalization in (4.1) is not the same as the normalization $||p|| = 1$ and $p\omega = 1$.[50]

In the case of a finite dimensional commodity space, if the production sets exhibit free disposal and ω is strictly positive, then an allocation is price supported if and only if it is approximately price supported.[51] Consequently, given free disposal, approximate price supportability can only arise in infinite dimensional commodity space models. Aliprantis and Burkinshaw [1988, pp. 46-49] gave an example of a two-person pure exchange economy modelled on the symmetric Riesz dual system (l_1, l_∞). The aggregate initial endowment is the vector

$$\omega = \left[\frac{1}{2}^2, \frac{1}{2}^4, \ldots, \frac{1}{2}^n, \ldots\right],$$

which is a strictly positive element of l_1. Both agents have the Mas-Colell [1986] utility function $U : l_1 \to \mathbb{R}$ defined by

$$U(\mathbf{x}) = \sum_{t=1}^{\infty} u_n(x_n),$$

where $u_n : \mathbb{R} \to \mathbb{R}$ is defined for each natural number n by the formulas

$$u_n(t) = \begin{cases} 2^n(t) & \text{if } t \leq (1/2^{2n}) \\ (1/2^n) - (1/2^{2n}) + t & \text{if } t > (1/2^{2n}). \end{cases}$$

The utility function U is concave, strictly monotone and norm continuous. Aliprantis and Burkinshaw [1988] established that the equal division allocation $x_i = \frac{1}{2}\omega$ is Pareto optimal and cannot be supported by non-zero prices in l_∞. The novel step in their example compared to previous examples is that they show this Pareto optimum may be approximately supported by prices in l_∞. Specifically, for any $\varepsilon > 0$, and k fixed such that $\sum_{n=k}^{\infty} 2^{-n} < \varepsilon/2$, they show the price system $p \equiv q/qw$ approximately supports this Pareto optimal allocation where $q = (2, 2^2, \ldots, 2^k, 1, 1, 1, \ldots) \in l_\infty$.

---

[50] See Aliprantis and Burkinshaw [1988, Lemma 1].

[51] Aliprantis and Burkinshaw [1988, Lemma 1].

Aliprantis and Burkinshaw [1988, Theorem 4] give a complete characterization of a weakly Pareto optimal allocation. Their main result is quoted below. Recall that a Riesz dual system $\langle E, F\rangle$ is symmetric if all the order intervals of E are weakly compact. The Riesz dual system $\langle s, s_0\rangle$ is symmetric, so this commodity space is a rich source of economic models with the approximate support property (e.g., the Peleg and Yaari [1970] model).[52]

Theorem 4.1. *Assume that the Riesz dual system for the economy is symmetric and that the aggregate endowment is strongly desirable by each consumer. Then an allocation is weakly Pareto optimal if and only if it is approximately supported by prices.*

The proof of Theorem 4.1 has two natural parts corresponding to each welfare theorem. I will concentrate my remarks on the proof of the approximate second welfare theorem, contained in Theorem 4.1. The Separation theorem and order structure of the model are used to obtain the result.

For $a \in E^+$, define

$$Y_j^a = \{y \in Y_j : y \leq a\} \quad (j = 1, \ldots, k)$$

and

$$Y^a = Y_1^a + \cdots + Y_k^a.$$

Let $[(x_i), (y_j)]$ be a weak Pareto optimal allocation. The following technical result is the crucial step in Aliprantis and Burkinshaw's [1988] proof of the approximate second welfare theorem. Recall τ is the given locally convex topology on E consistent with the dual system $\langle E, F\rangle$.

Lemma 4.2. *Assume the Riesz dual system for the economy is symmetric. If $R_i \equiv R_i(x_i)$, then for each $a \in E^+$ the convex set*

$$R = R_1 + \cdots + R_m - Y^a$$

is weakly closed.

---

[52] For a Peleg and Yaari [1970] exchange economy modelled on $\langle s, s_0\rangle$ with the weak topology, the closure of $\mathcal{A}_\omega$ is s. This is one of the conditions in the Araujo and Monteiro [1989] exact support theorem without uniform σ-proper preferences. However, the preference relations on s_+ fail to meet the pointwise uniform condition assumed in their support theorem.

Proof.[53] Fix $a \in E^+$, and let z be in the weak closure of R. Since R is convex, Z also belongs to τ-closure of R. Thus, there exists a net $\{z_\alpha\}$ of R with $z_\alpha \xrightarrow{\tau} z$. Write

$$z_\alpha = \sum_{i=1}^{m} x_\alpha^i - \sum_{j=1}^{k} y_\alpha^j, \tag{4.4}$$

where $x_\alpha^i \in R_i$, and $y_\alpha^j \in Y_j^a$.

Clearly, $(y_\alpha^j)^+ \leq a$ and so, since $[0,a]$ is weakly compact, every subnet of $\{(y_\alpha^j)\}$ has a weakly convergent subnet. From

$$0 \leq \sum_{i=1}^{m} x_\alpha^i + \sum_{j=1}^{k} (y_\alpha^j)^- = z_\alpha + \sum_{j=1}^{k} (y_\alpha^j)^+ \leq z_\alpha + ka,$$

we see that $0 \leq x_\alpha^i \leq z_\alpha + ka$ and $0 \leq (y_\alpha^j)^- \leq z_\alpha + ka$ holds for all i and j. By the Riesz Decomposition Property, we can write $x_\alpha^i = w_\alpha^i + v_\alpha^i$ with $0 \leq w_\alpha^i \leq z_\alpha^i$ and $0 \leq v_\alpha^i \leq ka$ for all α. Then $w_\alpha^i \xrightarrow{\tau} w^i$, and since $[0,ka]$ is weakly compact, it follows that $\{v_\alpha^i\}$ has a weakly convergent subnet. Therefore, $\{x_\alpha^i\}$ has a weakly convergent subnet, i.e., we can assume $x_\alpha^i \xrightarrow{w} x_i$ (where $\xrightarrow{w}$ stands for weak convergence). By an analogous argument, we can assume $y_\alpha^j \xrightarrow{w} y_j$ holds for all j. Since the R_i and Y_j^a are weakly closed sets, it follows that $x_i \in R_i$ for all i and $y_j \in Y_j^a$ for all j.

By taking weak limits in (4.4), we see that

$$z = \sum_{i=1}^{m} x_i - \sum_{j=1}^{m} y_j \in R.$$

Q.E.D.

Proof (Theorem 4.1).[54] Let $[(x_i),(y_j)]$ be a weak Pareto optimum, let $a \in E^+$, and fix $\varepsilon > 0$. Set $b = a + \sum_{k=1}^{m} |y_j|$ and $R_i = R_i(x_i)$ as before. Choose $0 < t < 1$ such that $0 < 1 - t < \varepsilon$ and $(1-t)/t < \varepsilon$. Lemma 4.2 implies the convex set

$$R = R_1 + \cdots R_m - Y^b - t\omega$$

[53] This proof is a combination of the arguments in Lemmas 2 and 3 of Aliprantis and Burkinshaw [1988].

[54] This discussion is based on Aliprantis and Burkinshaw's paper [1988, Theorem 3].

is weakly closed, hence τ-closed as well (Schaeffer [1986, p. 130]). Since ω is an extremely desirable bundle for each consumer i, and $[(x_i),(y_i)]$ is a weak Pareto optimum, it can be shown that $0 \notin R$.

Let V be a circled, convex τ-neighborhood of zero with $V \cap R = \emptyset$. Since 0 is an interior point of V, and R is τ-closed, we may invoke the Separation theorem and separate $\{0\}$ and R. Hence there exists a price $q \in F$ satisfying $qf > 0$ for each $f \in R$. For $e \equiv \sum_{i=1}^{m} x_i = \omega + \sum_{j=1}^{k} y_j$, it follows that $(1-t)e \in R$ and $qe > 0$. Put $p = q/pe$; note $p \in F$ and $pf > 0$ holds for all $f \in R$. Evidently $pe = 1$. The rest of the argument proves (4.2) and (4.3).

The verification of (4.2) proceeds as follows: Fix agent r, choose $x \in R_r(x_r)$ and define $z_i \in E^+$ by $z_i = x$ if $i = r$ and $z_i = x_i$ if $i \neq r$. An elementary computation reveals that $x = x_r + (1+t)e \in R$, so $p[x - x_r + (1-t)e] > 0$. Rearranging the inequality yields property (4.2). An analogous argument may be used to deduce (4.3) from the inequality $pf > 0$ for all $f \in R$. Q.E.D.

The proof of Theorem 4.1 exploits the order structure of the commodity space to show the set R is weakly compact (Lemma 4.2) and hence τ-closed. A natural question is to determine whether or not approximate versions of the second welfare theorem hold in locally convex spaces.

4.3 Approximate Welfare Theorems in Locally Convex Commodity Spaces.

The first approximate welfare theorems for locally convex spaces were obtained by Khan and Vohra [1988]. They assumed the space enjoyed an order structure. The important point of their work is that neither the commodity or price spaces were assumed to be lattices. Subsequently, Becker, Bercovici and Foias [1989] demonstrated approximate forms of the welfare theorems for locally convex commodity spaces were not necessarily partially ordered by a binary relation.

4.3.1 The Khan and Vohra Approximate Welfare Theorems.

Khan and Vohra [1988] employ the same basic setup as in Debreu's [1954] paper with one exception: the commodity space, E, is assumed to be a partially ordered space with order relation $\geq$. The induced order on the dual space, F, is also denoted by $\geq$.

For any real number $\varepsilon > 0$ and any $z \in E^-$, $z \neq 0$, a (α, z)-

approximate valuation equilibrium for the economy consists of a pair $(p, [(x_i), (y_j)])$ such that

(1) $p \in F$, $p > 0$, and $p(z) = -1$;

(2) $[(x_i), (y_i)]$ is an attainable allocation such that

  (a) $zR_i x_i$ implies $p(z) \geq p(x_i) - \varepsilon$ for all i, and

  (b) $z \in Y_j$ implies $p(z) \leq p(y_j) + \varepsilon$ for all j.

Aliprantis and Burkinshaw [1988] required producers to know more than just the prices and their own technology set. The Khan and Vohra [1988] definition of approximate valuation equilibrium does not agree with the one in Aliprantis and Burkinshaw [1988] in the case E is a Riesz space. First, Khan and Vohra use a different normalization for the approximate supporting linear functional p. If ω is a non-zero element of E^+, then setting $z = -\omega$ would yield the Aliprantis and Burkinshaw normalization. It is important to note that the hypotheses of Theorem 4.1 imply that $\omega \in E^+$ and $\omega \neq 0$.[55] The requirement that ω be extremely desirable in Theorem 4.1 therefore precludes the application of that result to the optimal growth model where $\omega = O$.

Khan and Vohra propose several axioms for their economic model:

(KV1)(a) *X_i is a closed convex subset of E.*

(b) *There exists a convex set $K \subset E$ and K has a lower bound for $\geq$.*

(KV2) *For each i, R_i is a reflexive, regular, and convex preference relation.*

(KV3)(a) *For each j, Y_j is a closed convex subset of E.*

(b) *For all j, $0 \in Y_j$, $(E^-) \subset Y_j$, $\bar{Y} \cap (-\bar{Y}) = \{0\}$ where Y is the aggregate technology set and $\bar{Y}$ is the closure of Y.*

(KV4) *There exists an agent i such that $x > y$ and $yP_i z$ implies $xP_i y$.*

Khan and Vohra do *not* assume R_i is either complete or transitive. Moreover, they do not make *any* assumptions about R^{-1}. They do require inaction to be a possible input-output vector and free disposal possible for each producer. The closure requirement in the irreversibility axiom is necessary because Y need not be a closed set even though each Y_j is

[55] Recall the Aliprantis and Burkinshaw result (Theorem 4.1) assumes ω is an extremely desirable bundle. This implies $\omega \neq 0$, otherwise P_i would not be irreflexive.

assumed closed. Indeed, the closure of Y is one of the key properties necessary for a successful separation agreement. As we saw, Aliprantis and Burkinshaw [1988] exploited the Riesz space structure in their framework to show the crucial set R derived from consumers upper contour sets and the "truncated" technology set Y^a is a τ-closed set.

Khan and Vohra [1988] proposed two alternative conditions for the model that were basically sufficient conditions for the crucial set W (defined below) to be closed as preparation for the application of a separation theorem. Their conditions are:

Choquet Condition. *The set K in (KV1)(b) and Y are $\sigma(E,F)$-complete. Here, $\sigma(E,F)$ is the weak topology for the dual pair.*

Dieudonné Condition. *The set K in (KV1)(b) and Y are locally compact.*

Their main approximate second welfare theorem is stated next.

Theorem 4.3. *If the economy satisfies (KV1)–(KV4) and if either the Choquet or the Dieudonné Condition is fulfilled, then for any $\varepsilon > 0$, $z \in E^-$, $z \neq 0$, a Pareto optimal allocation is a (ε, z)-approximate valuation equilibrium for the economy.*

Let $[(x_i),(y_j)]$ and set $W = \sum_{i=1}^{m} R_i(x_i) - \sum_{j=1}^{k} Y_j - \omega$. The difficult task is to show W is a closed set. Khan and Vohra [1988] demonstrate this when either the Choquet or Dieudonne conditions hold.[56] Axioms (KV2) and (KV3) imply W is a nonempty, convex set. Axiom (KV4) and the assumed Pareto optimality of the state $([x_i],[y_j])$ implies $W \cap E^- = \{0\}$. Given any $z \in E^-$, $z \neq 0$, Khan and Vohra apply a separation theorem due to Phelps [1964] in order to find the valuation functional that yields the approximate valuation equilibrium result.

4.3.2 The Becker, Bercovici and Foias Approximate Welfare Theorems.

The economic model used by Becker, Bercovici and Foias [1989] is similar to the one employed by Khan and Vohra [1988]. The commodity-price duality is described by the dual

[56] They also present some other hypotheses motivated by the same question. The conditions quoted in the text are illustrative of their approach. See their paper for the detailed arguments showing W is closed in the various cases.

pair (E,F) placed in duality by the bilinear form $\langle x,p\rangle$ for $x \in E$ and $p \in F$. Use $\sigma(E,F)$ $[\sigma(F,E)]$ to denote the weak topology on E $[F]$ determined by the duality of $E \times F$. The neighborhood system of the zero vector in F endowed with the $\sigma(F,E)$ topology is denoted by $\mathcal{N}_F(0)$. For $V \subset F$, the polar of V in E is the set

$$^\circ V = \{x \in E : |\langle x,p\rangle| \leq 1 \text{ for all } p \in V\}.$$

Recall that a convex subset A of E is absolutely convex if $\lambda A \subseteq A$ whenever $|\lambda| \leq 1$. The polar $^\circ V$ is a $\sigma(F,E)$-closed absolutely convex subset of E.

The economic model is identical to Debreu's [1954] setup with respect to the specification of agents consumption and production sets. The aggregate endowment is ω. The specific hypotheses made by Becker, Bercovici and Foias [1989] are:

(BBF1) For each i and for each $x \in X_i$, $R_i(x)$ is a non-empty, convex and $\sigma(E,F)$-closed subset of E.

(BBF2) For each i and for each $x \in X_i$, $P_i(x)$ is not empty and for every t, $0 < t < 1$, $tR_i(x) + (1-t)P_i(x) \subset P_i(x)$.

(BBF3) For each j, Y_j is a non-empty $\sigma(E,F)$-closed convex subset of E.

E is not assumed to be partially ordered. Hence, irreversibility and free disposal cannot, in general, be formulated in this framework. Typically, $O \in Y_j$, but this is not essential for the results. The preference relations of agents are convex, regular and monotone. Axiom (BBF2) implies Debreu's second axiom. As in Khan and Vohra's paper, preference relations are not assumed to be either complete or transitive.

Becker, Bercovici and Foias [1989] introduced a new definition of price supportability that reflects the lack of an order structure in the commodity space.

An allocation $[(x_i),(y_j)]$ is said to have the *approximate support property* if for all $\varepsilon > 0$, for all $V \in \mathcal{N}(0)$, and for all $(x'_1, x'_2, \ldots, x'_m) \in P_1(x_1) \times P_2(x_2) \times \cdots \times P_m(x_m)$, there exists a $p = p(\varepsilon, V, x'_1, x'_2, \ldots, x'_m) \in F$, such that

(1) $\langle x' - x, p\rangle = 1$, $x = \sum_i x_i$, $x' = \sum_i x'_i$;

(2) $\langle x''_i, p\rangle \geq \langle x,p\rangle - \varepsilon$ for all $x''_i \in R_i(x_i) \cap V$ $(i = 1,2,\ldots,m)$;

(3) $\langle y''_j, p\rangle \leq \langle y,p\rangle + \varepsilon$ for all $y''_j \in Y_j \cap V$ $(j = 1,2,\ldots,k)$.

An allocation $[(x_i), (y_j)]$ is said to have the *support property* if for all $(x'_1, x'_2, \ldots, x'_m) \in P_1(x_1) \times P_2(x_2) \times \cdots \times P_m(x_m)$, there exists a $p \in F$, such that

(4) $\langle x' - x, p\rangle = 1$, $x = \sum_i x_i$, $x' = \sum_i x'_i$;
(5) $\langle x''_i, p\rangle \geq \langle x, p\rangle$ for all $x''_i \in R(x_i)$ $(i = 1, 2, \ldots, m)$;
(6) $\langle y''_j, p\rangle \leq \langle y_j, p\rangle$ for all $y''_j \in Y$ $(j = 1, 2, \ldots, k)$.

Becker, Bercovici and Foias show their notion of approximate price supportability characterizes the weakly Pareto optimal allocations in a general model of an abstract economy. Their first result is a version of the second fundamental welfare theorem.

Theorem 4.4. *A weak Pareto optimum allocation* $[(x_i), (y_j)]$ *has the approximate support property.*

Proof. Let $V \in \mathcal{N}_F(0)$ and $x'_i \in P_i(x_i)$, $i = 1, \ldots, m$. V may be taken to be absolutely convex and closed if necessary; also, we can assume that x_i, x'_i, y, y'_j, $x = \sum x_i$, $x' = \sum x'_i$, $y = \sum y_j$, and $y' = \sum y'_j$ belong to ${}^\circ V$. Fix $x'_i \in P_i(x_i)$; clearly $x'_i \neq x_i$ for all i. For any $t \in (0, 1)$, define a subset $A(t)$ of E by

$$A(t) = (tR_1(x_1) + (1-t)\{x'_i\}) \cap^\circ V + \cdots +$$
$$(tR_m(x_m) + (1-t)\{x'_m\}) \cap^\circ V + (-Y_1 \cap^\circ V + \cdots + (-Y_k)) \cap^\circ V.$$

Obviously $A(t)$ is not empty. Each of the sets $(tR_i(x_i) + \{x'_i\}) \cap^\circ V$ and $(-Y_j) \cap^\circ V$ are weakly compact by Alaoglu's theorem. Therefore, $A(t)$ is weakly compact for each t, $0 < t < 1$. Moreover, $A(t)$ is convex by (BBF1).

I claim $\omega \notin A(t)$ for any $t \in (0, 1)$. Suppose $\omega \in A(t)$ for some $t \in (0, 1)$. Then there are $x''_i \in R_i(x_i)$ and $y''_j \in Y_j$ such that

$$\omega = tx'' + (1-t)x' - y''$$

where $x'' = \sum_{i=1}^m x''_i$, $y'' = \sum_{j=1}^k y''_j$. But this would imply that $[(tx''_i + (1-t)x'_i), (y''_j)]$ is an allocation. Moreover (BBF3) implies $tx''_i + (1-t)x'_i P_i x_i$, which contradicts the assumption that $[(x_i), (y_j)]$ is a weak Pareto optimum.

For fixed $t \in (0, 1)$, the Separation theorem (Dunford and Schwartz [1958, Corollary 11, p. 418] implies there exists a $p \in F$, $p \neq 0$, and an

$\alpha \in R$ such that for all $a \in A(t)$

$$\langle \omega, p\rangle < \alpha < \langle a, p\rangle. \tag{4.5}$$

Note that this p depends on the choices of t, V, and the x_i'.

Proof of (1). Let $a = tx + (1-t)x' - y$. Clearly $a \in A(t)$; then (4.5) implies

$$\langle \omega, p\rangle < \alpha \leq -(1-t)\langle x, p\rangle + (1-t)\langle x', p\rangle + \langle \omega, p\rangle,$$

since $-y = \omega - x$ (because $[(x_i),(y_j)]$ is an allocation). Hence

$$0 < [\alpha - \langle \omega, p\rangle]/(1-t) \leq \langle x' - x, p\rangle.$$

Without loss of generality, we can now choose p such that

$$\langle x' - x, p\rangle = 1. \tag{4.6}$$

Proof of (2). Let $x_i'' \in R(x_i) \cap {}^\circ V$ and for some i, let $a = tx + (1-t)x' + t(x_i'' - x_i) - y$. Obviously $a \in A(t)$ since $(x_1, x_2, \ldots, x_{i-1}, x_i'', x_{i+1}, \ldots, x_m) \in R_1(x_1) \times R_2(x_2) \times \cdots \times R_m(x_m)$

By the separation property (1) and $-y = \omega - x$,

$$\langle \omega, p\rangle < \alpha \leq \langle a, p\rangle = t\langle x, p\rangle + (1-t)\langle x', p\rangle + t\langle x'' - x_i, p\rangle + \langle \omega, p\rangle - \langle x, p\rangle.$$

By (1), $0 < t < \langle x_i'' - x_i, p\rangle + (1-t)$, or

$$-[(1-t)/t] < \langle x_i'' - x_i, p\rangle.$$

Rearranging, we have $\langle x_i'', p\rangle \geq \langle x_i, p\rangle - (1-t)/t$. Now choose t such that $\varepsilon = (1-t)/t$.

Proof of (3). Now for some j put $a = tx + (1-t)x' - y + (y_j - y'')$, where $y'' \in Y_j$. Again $a \in A(t)$ since $(y_1, y_2, \ldots, y_{j-1}, y_j'', y_{j+1}, \ldots, y_k) \in Y_1 \times \cdots \times Y_k$.

Therefore, by the separation property (4.5),

$$\langle \omega, p\rangle < \alpha \leq t\langle x, p\rangle + (1-t)\langle x', p\rangle - \langle y, p\rangle + \langle y_j, p\rangle - \langle y_j'', p\rangle.$$

As $-y = \omega - x$,

$$0 < t\langle x, p\rangle + (1-t)\langle x', p\rangle - \langle x, p\rangle + \langle y_j, p\rangle - \langle y_j'', p\rangle,$$

or

$$\langle y_j'', p\rangle < (1-t)\langle x' - x, p\rangle + \langle y_j, p\rangle = (1-t) + \langle y_j, p\rangle$$

by (4.6). As $0 < t < 1$, $\varepsilon = (1-t)/t > (1-t)$. Thus, $\langle y_j'', p\rangle \leq \langle y_j, p\rangle + \varepsilon$. Q.E.D.

If $\sum_i R_i(x_i)$ is closed, then in condition (2) one can take $x_i'' \in R_i(x_i)$ $(1 \leq i \leq m)$. The Riesz structure on E assumed by Aliprantis and Burkinshaw [1988] assures this condition is met. Here the polar $^\circ V$ is used to show that $R_i(x_i) \cap {}^\circ V$ is weakly compact. Therefore the weak neighborhood system of 0 in F may be replaced by the Mackey system of 0 in F in the definition of approximate price supportability. The compactness arguments in the proof of Theorem 4.4 will remain valid, hence Theorem 4.4 may be strengthened in this direction.

The Becker, Bercovici and Foias analog of the first fundamental welfare theorem is given below.

Theorem 4.5. *An allocation $[(x_i), (y_j)]$ having the approximate support property is a weak Pareto optimum.*

Proof. If $[(x_i), (y_j)]$ is not a weak Pareto Optimum, then there is an allocation $([x_1', \ldots, x_m'], [y_1', \ldots, y_k'])$ with $x_i' \in P_i(x_i)$. Take $V \in \mathcal{N}_F(0)$ such that $^\circ V$ contains each of the points x_i, x_i', y_j, and y_j' $(i = 1, \ldots, m; j = 1, \ldots, k)$. Choose $\varepsilon = 1/2k$. Let p be the price system from the approximate support property corresponding to this choice of ε, V, $(x_1', \ldots, x_m')$. Then

$$\langle x_i', p\rangle \geq \langle x_i, p\rangle - \varepsilon \text{ for all } i,$$

and

$$\langle y_j', p\rangle \leq \langle y_j, p\rangle + \varepsilon \text{ for all } j.$$

Adding over i and j respectively, we have

$$\langle x', p\rangle \geq \langle x, p\rangle - m\varepsilon,$$

and

$$\langle y', p\rangle \leq \langle y, p\rangle + k\varepsilon.$$

But $([x_i'],[y_j'])$ and $([x_i],[y_j])$ are allocations, so $x' = \omega + y'$ and $x = \omega + y$. Thus $\langle x', p\rangle = \langle \omega, p\rangle + \langle y', p\rangle$ and $\langle x, p\rangle = \langle \omega, p\rangle + \langle y, p\rangle$. Therefore, eliminating $\langle \omega, p\rangle$, we have (using (1)):

$$1 = \langle x' - x, p\rangle = \langle y' - y, p\rangle \leq k\varepsilon = 1/2, \tag{4.7}$$

but (4.7) is impossible. Q.E.D.

The proof of Theorem 4.5 also shows that only the normalization property and the profit property from the production sector are needed to show that the approximate support property implies the allocation is a weak Pareto optimum. This means that a weaker form of the approximate support property can be used to obtain a weak Pareto optimum allocation.

An allocation $[(x_i),(y_j)]$ is said to have the weak approximate support property if for all $\varepsilon > 0$, for all $V \in \mathcal{N}_F(0)$, and for all $(x_1', x_2', \ldots, x_m') \in P_1(x_1) \times \cdots \times P_m(x_m)$ there exists a $p = p(\varepsilon, V, x_1', x_2', \ldots) \in F$, such that

(7) $\langle x' - x, p\rangle = 1$, $x = \sum_i x_i$, $x' = \sum_i x_i'$;
(8) $\langle y_j'', p\rangle \leq < y_j, p > +\varepsilon$ for all $y_j'' \in Y_j \cap^\circ V$ $(j = 1, 2, \ldots, k)$.

Corollary 4.6. *An allocation $[(x_i),(y_j)]$ having the weak approximate support property is a weak Pareto optimum.*

In view of this Corollary and Theorem 4.4, the properties weak Pareto optimum, approximate support property, and weak approximate support property are equivalent. Moreover, in an exchange economy, the approximate support property reduces to the normalization property (7) above. In this case, one may also conclude that any allocation preferred to the given optimal allocation by every agent is not a feasible allocation. Mas-Colell and Richard [1987] observed that in Jones' example (see Section 4.1) the dual of the commodity space is not a lattice. They argue that this is the structural feature of the model responsible for the failure of the support property. However, Theorem 4.4 does apply to Jones' example.

4.3.3 The Helly Problem.

The generality of the approximate support property result rather than the support property for a weak Pareto optimum appears to be the economic analog of the *Helly problem.*

The Helly problem is concerned with conditions needed to solve a finite number of linear equations defined on the dual of a locally convex topological vector space. In general, only an approximate solution to those equations exists. Helly's Theorem may be found, for example, in Hille and Phillips [1957, p. 31], Dunford and Schwartz [1958, p. 86] or Yosida [1980, pp. 109–110]. The analogy to the price support problem is clear: a weak Pareto optimum determines a finite number of points in E. The support property holds when a finite system of *inequalities* defined over the dual has a solution $p \in F$. The Helly theorem suggests that an exact solution will generally fail to exist. Indeed, this is the implication of Fan's [1956] consistency theorem for a system of linear inequalities. Fan's result applies to infinite systems as well as finite systems.[57] I will state his result for finite systems in order to focus attention on the analogy to the price support problem.

Fan's Theorem. *Let $x_1, \ldots, x_m$ be a finite number of elements of a real normed linear space E, and let $\alpha_1, \ldots, \alpha_m$ be a corresponding family of real numbers. Then, for any $\rho > 0$, the following two conditions are equivalent:*

(A) There exists a continuous linear functional p on E with $\|p\| < \rho$ such that

$$\langle x, p\rangle \geq \alpha_i \quad (i = 1, \ldots, m).$$

(B) For any m positive numbers $\beta_1, \beta_2, \ldots, \beta_m$, the inequality

$$\rho \| \sum_{i=1}^{m} \beta_i x_i \| \geq \sum_{i=1}^{m} \beta_i \alpha_i$$

holds.

Proof.[58] (A) clearly implies (B), so we need to prove that (B) implies (A).

Assuming (B), consider the point $\alpha \in \mathbb{R}^m$, $\alpha = (\alpha_1, \ldots, \alpha_m)$. Let $\mathbb{R}^m_+$ be the positive cone in $\mathbb{R}^m$ and let F be the dual of E. The set

$$S_\rho = \{p \in F : \|p\| \leq \rho\}$$

---

[57] See Fan [1956, Theorem 12]. See his Theorem 13 for other necessary and sufficient conditions for the existence of a solution to system (4.8).

[58] The argument is a repackaging of Fan's proof.

is compact with respect to the weak*-topology of F by Alaoglu's theorem. Let $K = \{(\langle x_1, p\rangle, \ldots, \langle x_m, p\rangle) \in \mathbb{R}^m : p \in S_\rho\}$. K is a compact subset of $\mathbb{R}^m$ since S_ρ is compact. Suppose no $p \in S_\rho$ satisfies all of the inequalities of (A). Then $K \cap (\mathbb{R}^m_+ + \alpha) = \emptyset$. These two sets may be strictly separated by a hyperplane in $\mathbb{R}^m$. Hence, there exist $m+1$ numbers $\beta_0, \beta_1, \ldots, \beta_m$ such that

$$\sum_{i=1}^{m} \beta_i \langle x_i, p\rangle < \beta_0 \text{ for } p \in S_\rho$$

and

$$\sum_{i=1}^{m} \beta_i (z_i + \alpha_i) > \beta_0 \text{ whenever } z_i \geq 0.$$

The first inequality implies

$$\rho \left\| \sum_{i=1}^{m} \beta_i x_i \right\| \leq \beta_0;$$

the second one implies

$$\sum_{i=1}^{m} \beta_i \alpha_i > \beta_0 \text{ and } \beta_i \geq 0.$$

But the $\beta_1, \ldots, \beta_m$ must, by assumption, satisfy (B) with the opposite inequality, which is impossible. Therefore (A) must follow from (B). Q.E.D.

The crucial point of this proof is the role played by compactness of the ρ-unit sphere in the dual space. In approximate support results obtained by Becker, Bercovici and Foias [1989], compactness entered the separation argument in place of properness or interiority hypotheses since $A(t)$ is weakly compact. This step uses the Alaoglu theorem in much the same way as in Fan's result. Put differently, the Becker, Bercovici and Foias [1989] proof exploits Alaoglu's theorem to show that the intersection of a polar of $V \in \mathcal{N}_F(0)$ with the sets $\{tR_i(x_i) + (x')\}$ or $(-Y_j)$ is weakly compact. This use of the polar and the choice of the crucial scalar t in their proof then opens the path for a separation argument and an approximate price support result. Consequently, it is the general failure of compactness of sets of the form $\sum_{i=1}^{m} R_i(x_i) - Y$ which leads to the approximate support property rather than the exact support property in the absence of either Debreu's interiority hypothesis or the Mas-Colell properness conditions.[59]

5. Conclusion

The fundamental theorems of welfare economics have been demonstrated for a large class of classical economic environments cast in infinite dimensional commodity spaces. Several extensions of this theory might prove interesting and draw on the new approaches opened by the work on commodity spaces whose positive cone lacks an interior.

At present, only approximate support theorems have been obtained for economies with regular preference orders defined on a locally convex commodity space. One extension of the existing exact support property results could be to the case of regular preference relations. This would necessitate a generalization of properness to upper semi-continuous utility functions. More generally, it would be interesting to extend the notion of properness to locally convex spaces that may not be partially ordered and thereby obtain exact support results for those general spaces. The extension characterization of proper preferences found in Richard and Zame [1986] might be the basis for a general definition of properness in locally convex spaces. Another possible area for generalization of the exact support theorems would be to economies without ordered preferences.

Convexity assumptions play a natural role in the work derived from Debreu's seminal paper. Recently, the possibility of extending the welfare theorems to nonclassical environments has been raised by a number of researchers. Bonnisseau and Cornet [1988] showed that a form of the second welfare theorem is available in an environment with non-convex technologies arising from increasing returns to scale. Their results are the analogs of Debreu's classical theory in so far as the production sets must have non-empty interiors in the infinite dimensional case. Khan and Vohra [1985] consider a public goods economy in a locally convex commodity space setup. The objective of both papers is to demonstrate the "marginal rule" in a nonclassical model. Both papers also introduce various notions of "tangent cones" drawn from recent work in nonlinear

[59] A related discussion may be found in Jones [1987].

analysis. Further investigation of public goods, increasing returns to scale and externality models in the locally convex case would seem to offer one interesting line of problems. In particular, Khan and Vohra require (as a sufficient condition for non-trivial examples) the positive cone of the commodity space to have a non-empty interior. It is also reasonable to conjecture that an approximate version of the marginal rule exists for general locally convex spaces, but this remains for future work to answer.

Khan and Vohra [1985] do not use a lattice structure for the commodity space, so it is natural to wonder if their results would hold up in an economy with a Riesz dual system structure. In particular, what is the linkage, if any, between the alternative concepts of "tangent cones" and proper preferences? First steps in this direction have been taken by Khan [1987].[60] He proves a version of the second fundamental welfare theorem by using the Ioffe normal cone. His result applies to a local concept of Pareto optimality in which an "optimal" allocation is not dominated by some nearby allocation. He requires the commodity space to be locally convex, have a lattice structure and closed positive cone.

References

Aliprantis, C. D. and Brown, D. J., 1983, "Equilibria in Markets with a Riesz Space of Commodities," *J. Math. Econ.* **11**, 189–207.

Aliprantis, C. D., Brown, D. J. and Burkinshaw, O., 1987, "Edgeworth Equilibria", *Econometrica* **55**, 1109–1138.

Aliprantis, C. D., Brown, D. J. and Burkinshaw, O., 1989, *Existence and Optimality of Competitive Equilibria*, Springer-Verlag, New York.

Aliprantis, C. D. and Burkinshaw, O., 1978, *Locally Solid Riesz Spaces*, Academic Press, New York.

---

[60] Khan [1988] shows by means of an example constructed on the space c_0 consisting of sequences converging to zero endowed with the supremum norm that there is an economy which has a production set without free disposal and for which the Ioffe normal cone at the Pareto optimum is the entire dual space (l_1), but the Clarke normal cone is a strict subset of the dual. In this case, he argues the later cone may be the economically more appealing construct. Khan also points out that it is possible to repackage some examples in the mathematics literature to construct economies in which either concept of normal cone at the Pareto optimal production and consumption plans have intersections consisting of the zero vector. These optima cannot be price supported.

Aliprantis, C. D. and Burkinshaw, O., 1985, *Positive Operators*, Academic Press, New York.

Aliprantis, C. D. and Burkinshaw, O., 1988, "The Fundamental Theorems of Welfare Economics without Proper Preferences," *J. Math. Econ.* **17**, 41–54.

Araujo, A., 1985, "Lack of Pareto Optimal Allocations in Economies with Infinitely Many Commodities: The Need for Impatience," *Econometrica* **53**, 455–461.

Araujo, A. and Monteiro, P. K., 1989, "Equilibrium without Uniform Conditions," *J. Econ. Theory* **48**, 416–427.

Arrow, K. J., 1951, "An Extension of the Basic Theorems of Classical Welfare Economics," in *Proc. Second Berkeley Symp. Math. Stat. Probab.*, J. Neyman, ed., University of California Press, Berkeley and Los Angeles, 507–532.

Back, K., 1988, "Structure of Consumption Sets and Existence of Equilibria in Infinite Dimensional Commodity Spaces," *J. Math. Econ.* **17**, 88–99.

Beals, R. and Koopmans, T. C., 1969, "Maximizing Stationary Utility in a Constant Technology," *SIAM J. Appl. Math.* **17**, 1001–1015.

Becker, R. A., 1981, "The Duality of a Dynamic Model of Equilibrium and an Optimal Growth Model: the Heterogeneous Capital Goods Case," *Q. J. Econ.* **96**, 271–300.

Becker, R. A., Bercovici, H. and Foias, C., 1989, "Weak Pareto Optimality and the Approximate Support Property," working paper, Indiana University.

Berninghaus, S., 1977, "Individual and Collective Risks in Large Economies, *J. Econ. Theory* **15**, 279–294.

Bewley, T., 1990, "A Theorem on the Existence of Equilibria in a Market with a Finite Number of Agents and whose Commodity Space is L_∞," this volume.

Bewley, T., 1969, "Equilibrium Theory with an Infinite Dimensional Commodity Space," working paper, CORE.

Bewley, T., 1972, "Existence of Equilibria in Economies with Infinitely Many Commodities," *J. Econ. Theory* **4**, 514–540.

Bewley, T., 1982, "An Integration of Equilibrium Theory and Turnpike Theory," *J. Math. Econ.* **10**, 233–267.

Bhaskara Rao, K. P. S. and Bhaskara Rao, M., 1983, *Theory of Charges*, Academic Press, New York.

Bonnisseau, J. M. and Cornet, B., 1988, "Valuation Equilibrium and Pareto Optimality in Non-Convex Economies," *J. Math. Econ.* **17**, 293–308.

Boyd III, J. H., 1986, *Preferences, Technology and Dynamic Equilibria*, Ph.D. Dissertation, Indiana University.

Boyd III, J. H., 1990, "Recursive Utility and the Ramsey Problem," *J. Econ. Theory* **50**, 326–345.

Brock, W. A., 1982, "Asset Prices in a Production Economy," *The Economics of Information and Uncertainty*, J. McCall, ed., University of Chicago Press, Chicago, 1–42.

Brown, D. J. and Lewis, L. M., 1981, "Myopic Economic Agents," *Econometrica* **49**, 359–368.

Coles, J., 1985, "Equilibrium Turnpike Theory with Constant Returns to Scale and Possibly Heterogeneous Discount Factors," *Int. Econ. Rev.* **26**, 671–679.

Coles, J., 1986, "Equilibrium Turnpike Theory with Time-Separable Utility," *J. Econ. Dyn. Control* **10**, 367–394.

Debreu, G., 1951, "The Coefficient of Resource Utilization," *Econometrica* **19**, 273–292, reprinted in *Mathematical Economics: Twenty Papers of Gerard Debreu*, Cambridge University Press, New York, 1983, 30–49.

Debreu, G., 1954, "Valuation Equilibrium and Pareto Optimum," *Proc. Natl. Acad. Sci. U.S.A.* **40**, 588–592. Reprinted in *Mathematical Economics: Twenty Papers of Gerard Debreu*, Cambridge University Press, New York, 1983, 98–104.

Duffie, D., 1986, "Competitive Equilibria in General Choice Spaces," *J. Math. Econ.* **14**, 1–23.

Dunford, N. and Schwartz, J. T., 1958, *Linear Operators Part I: General Theory*, Wiley Interscience Publishers, New York.

Fan, K., 1956, "On Systems of Linear Inequalities," in *Linear Inequalities and Related Systems*, H. W. Kuhn and A. W. Tucker, eds., Princeton University Press, 99–156.

Gilles, C. and Leroy, S. T., 1989, "Bubbles and Charges," working paper, University of California at Santa Barbara.

Harris, M., 1987, *Dynamic Economic Analysis*, Oxford University Press, New York-Oxford, UK.

Hille, E. and Phillips, R. S., 1957, *Functional Analysis and Semi-Groups*, American Mathematical Society, Providence.

Huang, C. and Kreps, D., 1987, "On Intertemporal Preferences with a Continuous Time Dimension I: The Case of Certainty," working paper, Massachusetts Institute of Technology.

Jones, L. E., 1984, "A Competitive Model of Commodity Differentiation," *Econometrica* **52**, 507–530.

Jones, L. E., 1986, "Special Problems Arising in the Study of Economies with Infinitely Many Commodities," in *Models of Economic Dynamics*, H. F. Sonnenschein, ed., Springer-Verlag Lecture Notes in Economics and Mathematical Systems #264, Berlin-New York, 184–205.

Jones, L. E., 1987, "Existence of Equilibria with Infinitely Many Commodities: Banach Lattices Reconsidered," *J. Math. Econ.* **16**, 89–104.

Kelly, J. L., Namioka, I., et al, 1963, *Linear Topological Spaces*, Van Nostrand and Co., Princeton.

Khan, M. Ali, 1987, "Ioffe's Normal Cone and the Foundations of Welfare Economics: The Infinite Dimensional Theory," working paper, University of Illinois.

Khan, M. Ali, 1988, "Ioffe's Normal Cone and the Foundations of Welfare Economics: An Example," *Econ. Lett.* **28**, 15–19.

Khan, M. Ali and Peck, N. T., 1989, "On the Interiors of Production Sets in Infinite Dimensional Spaces," *J. Math. Econ.* **18**, 29–39.

Khan, M. Ali and Vohra, R., 1985a, "Approximate Equilibrium Theory in Economics with Infinitely Many Commodities," working paper, University of Illinois.

Khan, M. Ali and Vohra, R., 1985b, "Pareto Optimal Allocations of Non-Convex Economies in Locally Convex Spaces," working paper, University of Illinois, published in *Nonlinear Analysis* **12**, 943–950, 1988.

Khan, M. Ali and Vohra, R., 1988, "On Approximate Decentralization of Pareto Optimal Allocations in Locally Convex Commodity Spaces," *J. Ap-*

prox. Theory **52**, 149–161.

King, R. G., Plosser, C. I. and Rebelo, S. T., 1988, "Production, Growth and Business Cycles I: The Basic Neoclassical Model," *J. Monetary Econ.* **21**, 195–232.

Magill, M., 1981, "An Equilibrium Existence Theorem," *J. Math. Anal. Appl.* **84**, 162–169.

Majumdar, M., 1975, "Some Remarks on Optimal Growth with Intertemporally Dependent Preferences," *Rev. Econ. Stud.* **42**, 147–153.

Malinvaud, E., 1952, "Capital Accumulation and Efficient Allocation of Resources," *Econometrica* **30**, 233–268.

Marimon, R., 1989, "Stochastic Turnpike Property and Stationary Equilibrium, *J. Econ. Theory* **47**, 282–306.

Mas-Colell, A., 1975, "A Model of Equilibrium with Differentiated Commodities," *J. Math. Econ.***2**, 263–296.

Mas-Colell, A., 1986a, "The Price Equilibrium Problem in Topological Vector Lattices," *Econometrica* **54**, 1039–1053.

Mas-Colell, A., 1986b, "Valuation Equilibrium and Pareto Optimality Revisited, in *Contributions to Mathematical Economics*, W. Hildenbrand and A. Mas-Colell, eds., North-Holland, New York, 317–331.

Mas-Colell, A. and Richard, S. F., 1987, "A New Approach to the Existence of Equilibria in Vector Lattices," working paper, Harvard University.

Mehra, R., 1988, "On the Existence and Representation of Equilibrium in an Economy with Growth and Nonstationary Consumption," *Int. Econ. Rev.* **29**, 131–135.

Negishi, T., 1960, "Welfare Economics and Existence of an Equilibrium for a Competitive Economy," *Metroeconomica* **12**, 92–97.

Peleg, B. and Yaari, M. E., 1970, "Markets with Countably Many Commodities, *Int. Econ. Rev.* **11**, 369–377.

Phelps, R. R., 1964, "Weak* Support Points of Convex Sets in E^*," *Isr. J. Math.* **2**, 177–182.

Prescott, E. C. and Lucas Jr, R. E., 1972, "A Note on Price Systems in Infinite Dimensional Space," *Int. Econ. Rev.* **13**, 416–422.

Prescott, E. C. and Mehra, R., 1980, "Recursive Competitive Equilibrium: The Case of Homogeneous Households," *Econometrica* **48**, 1365–1379.

Radner, R., 1967, "Efficiency Prices for Infinite Horizon Production Programs, *Rev. Econ. Stud.* **34**, 51–66.

Ramsey, F., 1928, "A Mathematical Theory of Saving," *Econ. J.* **38**, 543–559.

Richard, S. F., 1986, "Competitive Equilibrium in Riesz Spaces," working paper, Carnegie-Mellon University.

Richard, S. F., 1989, "A New Approach to Production Equilibria in Vector Lattices," *J. Math. Econ.* **18**, 41–56.

Richard, S. F. and Zame, W. R., 1986, "Proper Preferences and Quasi-Concave Utility Functions," *J. Math. Econ.* **15**, 231–247.

Samuelson, P. A., 1958, "An Exact Consumption-Loan Model of Interest with or without the Social Contrivance of Money," *J. Pol. Econ.* **66**, 467–482.

Schaeffer, H. H., 1986, *Topological Vector Spaces*, Springer-Verlag, New York.

Yannelis, N. C., 1990, "The Core of an Economy without Ordered Preferences, this volume.

Yannelis, N. C. and Zame, W. R., 1986, "Equilibria in Banach Lattices without Ordered Preferences," *J. Math. Econ.*, **15**, 85–110.

Yano M., 1984, "Competitive Equilibrium on Turnpikes in a McKenzie Economy, I: A Neighborhood Turnpike Theorem," *Int. Econ. Rev.* **25**, 695–718.

Yi, G., 1989, "Classical Welfare Theorems in Economies with the Overtaking Criterion," *J. Math. Econ.* **18**, 57–75.

Yosida, K., 1980, *Functional Analysis*, Sixth Edition, Springer-Verlag, New York.

Zame, W. R., 1987, "Competitive Equilibria in Production Economies with an Infinite Dimensional Commodity Space," *Econometrica* **55**, 1075–1108.

PART 3

CORE EQUIVALENCE

A Limit Theorem on the Core of an Economy with a Continuum of Commodities

Jean Jaskold Gabszewicz

Abstract. The Edgeworth-Scarf-Debreu [see Debreu-Scarf (1963)] theorem on the core of a pure exchange economy is extended to allow for a continuum of commodities.

1. Introduction

In view of suggesting a direct interpretation of this continuum, we submit the extension of a model recently developed for the treatment of economic equilibrium under uncertainty [see Arrow (1953)]; in this model, each trader starts out with an initial endowment (point in n-dimensional commodity space) the value of which depends upon which one of S (S finite) mutually exclusive states of the world would obtain. Then, in place of trading commodities, participants exchange *claims* to commodities, to be delivered if, and only if, a particular state s obtains. Instead of a finite set of states of the world, we will consider a set S of mutually exclusive states s which is a *continuum* (for instance, an interval of points on a line). To simplify, we will assume that initial endowments, if state s obtains, are defined in terms of only one commodity (money, for instance) so that a plan over uncertainty appears as a real-valued function f defined on S, that assigns, to each state s in S, the amount $f(s)$ of contingent claims to that commodity made available by the program f. Each trader comes to the markets for contingent claims with such an initial program and then exchange of claims contingent on the states s takes place, before it is known what state really obtains. After trading, each participant is endowed with a final program over the states s. Interpretation of a continuum of commodities is presumably not confined to the preceding one. Another extension could be immediately obtained by working with consumption programs defined over a continuous time and applying the foregoing reasoning to the problem of intertemporal allocation of resources.

In a similar way, continuous models could also be used for the treatment of equilibrium in economies that include some commodities, the quality of which is allowed to vary continuously. Another application would be the analysis of economic equilibrium over space, when treating the space as a continuous variable.

Since programs appear as functions on S, the set of programs must be represented by a subset of some functional space. We have chosen for this representation the set of positive functions in $L^\infty(S, \Sigma, \mu)$, where S is the set of states, Σ a σ-algebra of subsets of S, μ a finite and positive measure defined on Σ and $L^\infty(S, \Sigma, \mu)$ the set of all μ-essentially bounded real valued functions defined on S, normed by $\|f\| = \mu \operatorname{ess\,sup}_{s \in S} |f(s)|$. Though there is always some arbitrariness in the choice of a particular space, it seems however that $L^\infty(S, \Sigma, \mu)$ is the best-adapted model for the treatment of exchange when a continuum of commodities is introduced as a basic assumption.

With the sole exception that the set of commodities is a continuum, the model follows, point by point, that of Scarf-Debreu. A major difference in the interpretation will appear however, as a consequence of the fact that the price system is defined as an element in the conjugate space of $L^\infty(S, \Sigma, \mu)$, i.e., as a bounded additive set function defined on Σ, the set of "events." We plan however to publish details on this interpretation in a subsequent paper, this one being essentially devoted to the model itself and the proof of the limit theorem.

It seems also a very interesting question to analyze whether the continuum of commodities will entail significant consequences when a continuum of traders is simultaneously introduced in the picture. It is well-known that, if a continuum of traders is allowed to participate to the exchange of a finite set of different commodities, an equivalence theorem between the set of competitive allocations and the core is available; e.g., Aumann (1964). It remains to show whether this theorem is still valid under the same assumptions, when the field of exchange is extended to a continuum of different commodities. On this question also we plan to publish a subsequent paper with other authors.

Section II is devoted to the mathematical model; the theorems and their proofs are presented in section III.

2. The Mathematical Model

Let μ be a finite and positive measure defined on a σ-field Σ of subsets of a set S. Let Σ^* be the Lebesgue extension of the σ-field Σ and (S, Σ^*, μ) the Lebesgue extension of the measure space (S, Σ, μ). Let $L^\infty(S, \Sigma^*, \mu)$ consist of all μ-essentially bounded real valued functions defined on S, with the norm[1]

$$\|f\| = \mu - \text{ess sup}_{s \in S} |f(s)| \tag{2.1}$$

For two vectors f and g in L^∞ define $f \gg g$ if $f(s) > g(s)$ for μ-almost all $s \in S$, $f \geq g$ if $f(s) \geq g(s)$ for μ-almost $s \in S$, $f > g$ if $f \geq g$ and there exists a μ-nonnull subset $E \in \Sigma^*$ with $f(s) > g(s)$ for all s in E. Define also $L^\infty_+ = \{f \mid f \in L^\infty; f \geq 0\}$ and $L^\infty_- = \{f \mid f \in L^\infty; f < 0\}$. Let $ba(S, \Sigma^*, \mu)$ be the set of x for those bounded real-valued additive set functions defined on Σ^* which vanish on sets of μ-measure zero. For two elements π and σ in $ba(S, \Sigma^*, \mu)$ define $\pi \geq \sigma$ if and only if $\pi(E) \geq \sigma(E)$ for all $E \in \Sigma^*$ and $\pi > \sigma$ if and only if $\pi \geq \sigma$ and there exists $E \in \Sigma^*$ with $\pi(E) > \sigma(E)$. Let S be the *set of states.* An *event* is a subset in Σ^*. We consider a pure exchange economy, involving m *agents*, indexed by i, $i = 1, \ldots, m$, exchanging claims contingent on states s. A *program* is a point of L^∞_+, the set of programs. Each agent i starts out with an *initial* assignment, ω_i, a point of L^∞_+; thus $\omega_i(s)$ represents the amount of claims contingent on state s, held by agent i before any exchange on the markets. One assumes

$$\omega_i \gg 0; \quad i = 1, \ldots, m. \tag{2.2}$$

An *allocation* x is an m-tuple of vectors $(x_1, \ldots, x_m)$ in L^∞_+ with $\sum_{i=1}^m (x_i(s) - \omega_i(s)) = 0$ for μ-almost all s in S. For each agent i there is defined a relation $\succsim_i$ on L^∞_+, the preference-indifference relation, which satisfies the following conditions:

(2.3) the relation $\succsim_i$ is a *quasi-order.* i.e., it is complete, reflexive and transitive.

---

[1] Strictly speaking, an elements f in $L(S, \Sigma^*, \mu)$ is not a function, but a class of functions, two functions in the same class differing only on a set of S of μ-measure zero. We shall however follow the usual practice that assimilates two functions whose values differ only on a μ-null set of S.

For f and g in L_+^∞, the relations $>_i$ (preference) and $\sim_i$ (indifference) are then defined by

$$f >_i g \Longleftrightarrow f \succsim_i g \quad \text{but not} \quad g \succsim_i f;$$

$$f \sim_i g \Longleftrightarrow f \succsim_i g \quad \text{and} \quad g \succsim_i f.$$

(2.4) *Weak desirability*: $f \gg g \Rightarrow f >_i g$ and $f \geqq g \Rightarrow f \succsim_i g$.

(2.5) *Continuity*: for all $g \in L_+^\infty$, the sets $\{f \mid f >_i g\}$ and $\{f \mid g >_i f\}$ are open (relative to L_+^∞) for distance associated with the norm (2.1).

(2.6) *Strong convexity*: let f and g be arbitrary programs with $f \succsim_i g$ and let $\alpha \in]0,1[$; then

$$\alpha f + (1-\alpha)g >_i g.$$

Let $x = (x_1, \ldots, x_m)$ be a given allocation and let I be an arbitrary set of agents. The allocation x is *blocked* by I if it is possible to find programs y_i for all i in I such that $\sum_{i \in I}(y_i(s) - \omega_i(s)) = 0$ for μ-almost all s in S and $y_i \succsim_i x_i$ for all i in I with strict preference for at least one member of I. The *Core* is the set of all allocations which cannot be blocked by any set I.

A *price system* is an element $\pi \in ba(S, \Sigma^*, \mu)$ with $\pi > 0$.

The *budget set* for an agent i, determined by the price system π, is the set defined as $B_i = \{f \mid f \in L_+^\infty; \int_S f(s)\pi(ds) \leqq \int_S \omega_i(s)\pi(ds)\}$.[2,3]

A *competitive equilibrium* is a pair (π, x) consisting of a price system π and an allocation x, such that, for all $i \in \{1, \ldots, m\}$, x_i is in B_i and $B_i \cap \{f \mid f >_i x_i\} = \emptyset$.

A *competitive allocation* is an allocation x for which there exists a price system π such that (π, x) is a competitive equilibrium.

3. Theorems and Proofs

[2] The definition and properties of integrals with respect to a bounded additive set function—as used here for defining price systems, budget sets, etc.—can be found in Dunford and Schwartz (1958, III.2, pp. 101–119).

[3] The fact that any element $f \in L^\infty(S, \Sigma^*, \mu)$ is integrable with respect to any $\pi \in ba(S, \Sigma^*, \mu)$ is proved as the first part of Theorem 16, IV.8, Dunford and Schwartz (1958, p. 296).

Theorem I. *A competitive allocation is in the core.*

Proof. Let $x = (x_1, \ldots, x_m)$ be a competitive allocation and π such that (π, x) is a competitive equilibrium. Assume that there exists a set of agents I and an allocation y with

$$\sum_{i \in I} (y_i(s) - \omega_i(s)) = 0 \tag{3.1}$$

for μ-almost all $s \in S$, $y_i \succsim_i x_i$ for all $i \in I$ and $y_j \succ_j x_j$ for some $j \in I$. Then

(i) $y_j \succ_j x_j \Rightarrow \int_S y_j(s)\pi(ds) > \int_S \omega_j(s)\pi(ds)$, for, otherwise, $B_j \cap \{f \mid f \succ_j x_j\} \neq \emptyset$ and (π, x) is not a competitive equilibrium.

(ii) $y_i \succsim_i x_i \Rightarrow \int_S y_i(s)\pi(ds) \geqq \int_S \omega_i(s)\pi(ds)$.

Suppose on the contrary, that

$$\int_S y_i(s)\pi(ds) < \int_S \omega_i(s)\pi(ds). \tag{3.2}$$

Define then z by

$$z(s) = y_i(s) + \frac{\delta}{\pi(S)} \quad \text{for all } s \in S,\ \delta > 0.$$

Since $\pi \in ba(S, \Sigma^*, \mu)$, $\pi(S) < \infty$ and since π is a price system, $\pi(S) > 0$. Then, clearly $z \gg y$, so weak desirability implies $z \succ_i y_i$ and, from transitivity (2.3), $z \succ_i x_i$. Moreover

$$\int_S z(s)\pi(ds) = \int_S y_i(s)\pi(ds) + \delta.$$

Assumption (3.2) implies that, for a sufficiently small $\delta > 0$,

$$\int_S z(s)\pi(ds) < \int_S \omega_i(s)\pi(ds).$$

Finally, $z \succ_i x_i$ and (i) together imply $\int_S z(s)\pi(ds) > \int_S \omega_i(s)\pi(ds)$ and the contradiction follows.

By (i) and (ii),

$$\sum_{i \in I} \left[\int_S (y_i(s) - \omega_i(s))\pi(ds) \right] = \int_S \left[\sum_{i \in I} (y_i(s) - \omega_i(s) \right] \pi(ds) > 0. \tag{3.3}$$

Any μ-null set is a π-null set so that, by (3.1),

$$\pi \left[\left\{ s / s \in S; \sum_{i \in I} (y_i(s) - \omega_i(s)) \neq 0 \right\} \right] = 0$$

and (3.3) contradicts $\sum_{i \in I} (y_i(s) - \omega_i(s)) = 0$ for μ-almost all $s \in S$.

Q.E.D.

We shall now follow the procedure used by Debreu and Scarf for enlarging the market and we quote them almost verbatim:
"We imagine the economy to be composed of m types of agents, with r agents of each type. For two agents to be of the same type, we require them to have precisely the same preferences and precisely the same initial assignment. The economy therefore consists of mr agents, whom we index by the pair of numbers (i, q) with $i = 1, \ldots, m$ and $q = 1, 2, \ldots, r$. The first index refers to the type of individuals of the same type. An allocation is described by a collection of mr programs x_{iq} such that

$$\sum_{i=1}^{m} \sum_{q=1}^{r} x_{iq}(s) - r \sum_{i=1}^{m} \omega_i(s) = 0$$

for μ-almost all s in S.

"The following theorem makes for the simplicity of our study:

Theorem II. *An allocation in the core assigns the same program to all agents of the same type.*

Proof. For any particular type i, let x_i represent the least desired of the programs x_{iq} according to the common preferences for agents of this type and assume that for some type i' two agents have been assigned different programs (i.e., programs differing on at least a μ-nonnull set of S). Then

$$\frac{1}{r} \sum_{q=1}^{r} x_{iq} \succsim_i x_i \quad \text{for all } i$$

with strict preference holding for i'. However,

$$\sum_{i=1}^{m} \left(\frac{1}{r} \sum_{q=1}^{r} x_{iq}(s) - \omega_i(s) \right) = 0 \quad \mu\text{-almost everywhere}$$

and therefore the set consisting of one agent of each type, each of whom receives a least desired program, would block. Q.E.D.

"This theorem implies that an allocation in the core for the repeated economies considered here may be described by a collection of m programs $(x_1, \ldots, x_m)$ with $\sum_{i=1}^{m} (x_i(s) - \omega_i(s)) = 0$ μ-almost everywhere. The particular collections of programs in the core will, of course, depend on r.

It is easy to see that the core for $r+1$ is contained in the core for r, for a coalition which blocks in the economy with r repetitions will certainly be available for blocking in the economy with $(r+1)$ repetitions.

"If we consider a competitive allocation consisting of one agent of each type and repeat the allocation when we enlarge the economy to r agents of each type, the resulting allocation is competitive for the large economy and consequently is in the core. We see, therefore, that as a function of r, the cores form a nonincreasing sequence of sets, each of which contains the collection of competitive allocations for the economy of one agent of each type."

To obtain a result which parallels Theorem 3 of Debreu and Scarf (1963), i.e., that no other allocations than the competitive one are in the core for all r, we shall first prove a sequence of lemmas. To this end, let $x = (x_1, \ldots, x_m)$ in the core for all r and define $F_i = \{f \mid f \in L^\infty_+; f >_i x_i\}$ and $G_i = \{f \mid f \in L^\infty; f + \omega_i >_i x_i\}$. Let Γ be the convex hull of the union of the sets G_i. Since, for every i, G_i is convex and non empty, Γ consists of the set of all vectors which may be written as $\sum_{i=1}^m \alpha_i z_i \geqq 0$, $\sum_{i=1}^m \alpha_i = 1$ and $z_i \in G_i$.

Lemma 1. $L^\infty_- \cap \Gamma = \emptyset$.

Proof. Suppose on the contrary that there exists a point $-x^* = \sum_{i=1}^m \alpha_i z_i < 0$ with $\sum_{i=1}^m \alpha_i = 1$, $\alpha_i \geqq 0$ and $z_i + \omega_i \in F_i$.

Select an integer k, which will eventually tend to $+\infty$, and let a_i^k be the smallest integer greater than or equal to $k\alpha_i$. Also let I be the set of i for which $\alpha_i > 0$. For each i in I we define y_i^k by

$$y_i^k(s) = \frac{k\alpha_i}{a_i^k} z_i(s) + \frac{k}{a_i^k N} x^*(s) \quad \text{for all } s \in S,$$

where N is the cardinality of I. We notice that

$$\sum_{i \in I} a_i^k y_i^k(s) = k \left(\sum_{i \in I} \alpha_i z_i(s) + x^*(s) \right) = 0$$

for μ-almost all s in S.

For each $i \in I$, the sequence

$$\left\{ \frac{k\alpha_i}{a_i^k} z_i + \omega_i \right\}_{k \in N^*}$$

converges uniformly μ-almost everywhere to $z_i + \omega_i \in F_i$ and the continuity assumption (2.5) implies

(i) $\frac{k\alpha_i}{a_i^k} z_i + \omega_i >_i x_i$ for sufficiently large k. Since for all $k \in N^*$, $\frac{k}{a_i^k N} x^* > 0$, the weak desirability assumption (2.4) implies that

(ii) $\frac{k\alpha_i}{a_i^k} z_i + \frac{k}{a_i^k N} x^* + \omega_i = y_i^k + \omega_i \gtrsim_i \frac{k\alpha_i}{a_i^k} z_i + \omega_i$.

Finally, (i), (ii) and transitivity (2.3) together imply $y_i^k + \omega_i >_i x_i$ for sufficiently large k. Consider the coalition made of a_i^k agents of type of i to each one of whom we assign $\omega_i + y_i^k$ where i runs over the set I. Such a coalition blocks the allocation $(x_1, \ldots, x_m)$ repeated a number of times equal to $\max_{i \in I} a_i^k$. This contradicts the assumption that x is in the core for all r. Q.E.D.

Clearly both Γ and L_-^∞ have interior points in the considered topology. Since they are both convex, they can be separated by a nonzero continuous linear functional ϕ,[4] i.e.,

$$\phi(f_1) \leqq M \leqq \phi(f_2), \quad \text{for all } f_1 \in L_-^\infty,\ f_2 \in \Gamma.$$

By the analytic representation theorem of functionals on L^∞,[5] there is a unique bounded additive set function $\pi \in ba(S, \Sigma^*, \mu)$ such that

$$\int_S f_1(s)\pi(ds) \leqq M \leqq \int_S f_2(s)\pi(ds), \quad f_1 \in L_-^\infty,\ f_2 \in \Gamma. \tag{3.4}$$

Lemma 2. $M \geqq 0$.

Proof. Suppose $M < 0$; since $\phi \neq 0$, $\pi \neq 0$, i.e., there exists some $E \in \Sigma^*$ for which $\pi(E) \neq 0$. Suppose first that there exists some $E \in \Sigma^*$ for which $\pi(E) > 0$. Define then a sequence $\{f_n\}_{n \in N^*}$ by

$$f_n(s) = \begin{cases} -\frac{1}{n\pi(E)}, & \text{if } s \in E \\ = 0 & \text{if } s \in S \setminus E. \end{cases}$$

Since $\pi \in ba(S, \Sigma^*, \mu)$, $\pi(E) < \infty$; furthermore, if E were a μ-null set, then E would be a π-null set, and it is not the case, so that $\mu(E) > 0$.

[4] Dunford and Schwartz (1958, V.2.8, p. 417).

[5] Dunford and Schwartz (1958, IV.8.16, p. 296).

Consequently, $f_n \in L^{\infty}_{-}$ for all $n \in N^*$ and, for n sufficiently large, $\int_S f_n(s)\pi(ds) = -\frac{1}{n} > M$, contradicting (3.4).

Suppose now that there exists no set $E \in \Sigma^*$ with $\pi(E) > 0$; then, from $\pi \neq 0$, there exists some $E \in \Sigma^*$ for which $\pi(E) < 0$. Define then f by

$$f(s) = \begin{cases} \frac{1}{\pi(E)} & \text{if } s \in E, \\ = 0 & \text{if } s \in S \setminus E. \end{cases}$$

By the same reasoning as before, $|\pi(E)| < \infty$, $\mu(E) > 0$ and $f \in L^{\infty}_{-}$. But clearly, $\int_S f(s)\pi(ds) = 1 > M$, contradicting again (3.4). Consequently, $M \geqq 0$. Q.E.D.

By the preceding lemma and (3.4)

$$\int_S f(s)\pi(ds) \geqq 0 \tag{3.5}$$

for all $f \in \Gamma$ and thus, for all $f \in G_i$. By definition of F_i we get

$$\int_S f(s)\pi(ds) \geqq \int_S \omega_i(s)\pi(ds) \tag{3.6}$$

for all $f \in F_i$.

Lemma 3. $\pi > 0$.

Proof. Suppose first that there exists a subset $E \in \Sigma^*$ such that $\pi(E) < 0$. Choose then a program $f \in F_i$ for some i. For each finite integer n, define the program g_n by

$$g_n(s) = \begin{cases} f(s) + \frac{1}{n} & \text{for } s \in S \setminus E \\ f(s) + n & \text{for } s \in E. \end{cases}$$

By weak desirability, $g_n >_i f$ for all n; by transitivity, $g_n >_i x_i$ and, by (3.6)

$$\int_S g_n(s)\pi(ds) \geqq \int_S \omega_i(s)\pi(ds). \tag{3.7}$$

However,

$$\int_S g_n(s)\pi(ds) = \int_S f(s)\pi(ds) + \frac{1}{n}\pi(S \setminus E) + n\pi(E).$$

It follow from $\pi(E) < 0$, that, for a finite integer n^*,

$$\int_S g_n^*(s)\pi(ds) < \int_S \omega_i(s)\pi(ds)$$

contradicting (3.7). Since there is no set E such that $\pi(E) < 0$ and since $\pi \neq 0$, there is a set $E \in \Sigma^*$ such that $\pi(E) > 0$. This proves the lemma. Q.E.D.

Lemma 4. *For all agents i, x_i is in the budget set B_i determined by π.*

Proof. We have to prove

$$\int_S x_i(s)\pi(ds) \leqq \int_S \omega_i(s)\pi(ds), \quad i = 1, \ldots, m. \tag{3.8}$$

Assume on the contrary that there exists some i' such that $\int_S x_i(s)\pi(ds) > \int_S \omega_i(s)\pi(ds)$. Because of weak desirability (2.4) there are for all i programs arbitrarily close to x_i that i prefers to x_i; therefore x_i is in the closure of F_i and by (3.6)

$$\int_S x_i(s)\pi(ds) \geqq \int_S \omega_i(s)\pi(ds)$$

for all $i = 1, \ldots, m$. Then

$$\sum_{i=1}^{m}\left[\int_S x_i(s)\pi(ds) - \int_S \omega_i(s)\pi(ds)\right] = \int_S \left[\sum_{i=1}^{m}(x_i(s) - \omega_i(s))\right]\pi(ds) > 0,$$

contrary to the assumption that x is in the core and hence an allocation.

Q.E.D.

Lemma 5. *For all $i = 1, \ldots, m$, $B_i \cap F_i = \emptyset$.*

Proof. Let $f \in F_i$ for some i. From $\pi > 0$ and $\omega_i \gg 0$, $\int_S \omega_i(s)\pi(ds) > 0$ so that, by (3.6) $\int_S f(s)\pi(ds) > 0$. Hence there is a set $E \in \Sigma^*$, with $\pi(E) > 0$, and a number $\delta > 0$ such that $f(s) > \delta$ for all $s \in E$.

Suppose now, contrary to the lemma, $\int_S f(s)\pi(ds) \leqq \int_S \omega_i(s)\pi(ds)$. Define then $\{f_n\}$ by

$$f_n(s) = \begin{cases} f(s) - \frac{1}{n\pi(E)} & \text{for all } s \in E; \\ f(s) & \text{for all } s \in S \setminus E. \end{cases}$$

For a sufficiently large n, $\frac{1}{n\pi(E)} < \delta$ so that $f_n \in L_+^\infty$ and $f_n >_i x_i$ (by the continuity assumption (2.5)). Consequently $f_n \in F_i$ and $f_n - \omega_i \in G_i$. However

$$\begin{aligned}\int_s (f_n - \omega_i)(s)\pi(ds) &= \int_S f_n(s)\pi(ds) - \int_s \omega_i(s)\pi(ds) \\ &= \int_S f(s)\pi(ds) - \int_S \omega_i(s)\pi(ds) - \frac{1}{n} \\ &< 0,\end{aligned}$$

contradicting (3.5). Q.E.D.

By Lemma 3, π is a price system; by Lemma 4, x_i is in the budget set B_i for all i; by Lemma 5, $B_i \cap \{f \mid f >_i x_i\} = \emptyset$. We have thus proved:

Theorem 3. *"If $(x_1, \ldots, x_m)$ is in the core for all r then it is a competitive allocation."*

References

Arrow, K. J., 1953, "Le Rôle des Valeurs Boursières pour la Répartition la meilleure des Risques," *Econometrie*, CNRS, Paris, 41–47.

Aumann, R. J., 1964, "Markets with a Continuum of Traders," *Econometrica* **32**, 39–50.

Debreu, G. and Scarf, H., 1963, "A Limit Theorem on the Core of an Economy," *Int. Econ. Rev.* **4**, 235–246.

Dunford, N. and Schwartz, J. T., 1958, *Linear Operators Part I: General Theory*, Wiley Interscience Publishers, New York.

An Equivalence Theorem for the Core of an Economy with Commodity Space $\mathbf{L}_\infty - \tau(\mathbf{L}_\infty, \mathbf{L}_1)$

Jean-François Mertens[1,2]

Abstract. The equivalence of the core and the set of competitive equilibrium is proved, for an economy with an atomless measure space of agents and with a commodity space which is L_∞ endowed with the Mackey-topology $\tau(L_\infty, L_1)$.

1. Introduction

An equivalence theorem for the core of an economy is known when the commodity space is of the type $C(S)$, where $C(S)$ is the set of bounded continuous functions on a topological space[3] S, or when it is L_∞ endowed with the strong topology.[4]

In fact, one could use more generally an ordered Banach space whose positive cone has an interior point—Gabszewicz's proof shows this in the separable case, but already in July 1968 it was well known to him how easily that restriction could be dispensed with.

But existence—even for finitely many agents—is known only for L_∞ with the Mackey topology τ. Further, when one has to consider L_∞ as commodity space, the Mackey topology τ seems much more natural than the strong topology β: the Mackey topology rules out a family of

---

[1] I am greatly indebted to R. Aumann for a very stimulating conversation on this subject.

[2] Note added in proof (1990): This is basically [i.e., except for some clarifications] an unaltered copy of CORE DP 7028 (1970). If I remember correctly that conversation with R. Aumann, he was stressing the importance of going beyond the separable case (strong measurability), to check really whether equivalence did not depend on there being (many) more traders than commodities.

[3] See J. J. Gabszewicz, *Coeurs et Allocations concurrentielles dans des économies d'échange avec un continu de biens*, Librairie Universitaire, Louvain, 1968.

[4] See T. Bewley, *An Equivalence Theorem in the Case Where the Commodity Space is Infinite Dimensional*, CORE DP 6821.

pathological preferences orderings, while the strong topology rules out the intuitively most acceptable allocations.

This paper aims at filling this gap.

The main question which remains open in this paper is whether one can dispense with the assumption that $i(a)$ is the limit of an increasing sequence of step functions. Besides this, there remain two other open questions in the paper:

The first one is whether one could drop the assumption "$\forall a\ i(a)$ is an interior point of the positive orthant of L^{β}_{∞}" requiring only "$\forall a$, $i(a)(s) > 0$ a.e., and $\int_A i(a)d\mu$ is an interior point of the positive orthant of L^{β}_{∞}."

It is easily seen from the proof that this is possible when $i(a)$ is measurable with respect to the strong topology of L_{∞}. [Or, slightly more generally, when there exists a step function $g \leq i$ such that $\int_A g(a)d\mu \geq \varepsilon$.] But in general it seems not too difficult to construct a counter-example.

The other open question concerns the assumption of separability of (S, Σ, σ).

As soon as we will be able to describe a good topology on the space of closed subsets L^{τ}_{∞}, for which, when (S, Σ, σ) is separable, the measurable maps are exactly the maps whose graph is measurable in the product, we will probably also be able to overcome easily this difficulty, by defining an economy as a τ-smooth measure—and using, together with the remark at the end of the proof here, the increasing net of separable subspaces.

2. The Model

Let $(A, \mathcal{A}, \mu)$ be a totally σ-finite positive non-atomic measure space, the space of economic agents.

Let (S, Σ, σ) be a totally σ-finite separable positive measure space.

The space of commodities will be the positive orthant of $L_{\infty} = L_{\infty}(S, \Sigma, \sigma)$. $ba = ba(S, \Sigma, \sigma)$ will denote the space of all bounded additive set functions on (S, Σ) which vanish on the σ-null sets.

L^{β}_{∞} will denote L_{∞} endowed with the strong topology. L^{τ}_{∞} will denote L_{∞} endowed with the Mackey-topology $\tau(L_{\infty}, L_1)$.

Let, for each agent a, $i(a)$ be his initial endowment, and $\succ_a$ be a monotonic (i.e., $x \succ_a y$, $z \geq x \Rightarrow z \succ_a y$, and $x + \varepsilon \succ_a x$) preference relation on the positive orthant of L_{∞}. Assume:

1) $\forall a \in A$, $i(a)$ is an interior point of the positive orthant of L^{β}_{∞};
2) $i(a)$ is a Pettis-integrable function from $(A, \mathcal{A}, \mu)$ into L^{τ}_{∞};
3) $\forall a\ \forall x \in L_{\infty,+}$, $\{y \mid y \succ_a x\}$ is open in $L^{\tau}_{\infty,+}$;
4) The graph of $(\succ)$ is measurable in $(A, \mathcal{A}, \mu) \otimes L^{\tau}_{\infty} \otimes L^{\tau}_{\infty}$.

An allocation is a Pettis-integrable function from $(A, \mathcal{A}, \mu)$ into L^{τ}_{∞}. Definitions of the Core of this economy and of price-equilibria—with prices in $L_1(S, \Sigma, \sigma)$—are as usual.

Preliminary Remarks. 1) L^{τ}_{∞} is a Lusin space.

A Polish space is a separable topological space, the topology of which can be derived from a complete metric. A Lusin space is a regular topological space, for which there exists a stronger Polish topology.

Now, on the bounded subsets of L^{τ}_{∞}, the Mackey topology coincides with the topology of convergence in measure on each subset of finite measure. It follows that the bounded subsets are complete, metric and separable, and thus L^{τ}_{∞} is a Lusin space, as a countable union of Polish spaces.

It follows that the Baire subsets and the Borel subsets coincide, and that they are the same for each regular coarser topology. All measures are tight: so there is no ambiguity in defining measurability concept.

L^{τ}_{∞} endowed with its Borel σ-algebra is thus a standard Borel space.

2) Pettis integrability of the map $i(a)$ means that for each π, $\pi \in L_1$ (or: π price system): $\pi \cdot i(a)$ in an integrable function on $(A, \mathcal{A}, \mu)$, and that there exists an element $\int i(a) d\mu \in L_{\infty}$ s.t. for each $\pi \in L_1$ (or: for each price system) $\pi \int i(a) du = \int \langle \pi \cdot i(a) \rangle d\mu$.

Using the fact that L^{τ}_{∞} is a Lusin space, it is easily seen that this implies that the map $i(a)$ is measurable (in the usual sense) with values in L^{τ}_{∞}.

Further, it can be checked that the measurable maps $i(a)$ with values in L^{τ}_{∞} are exactly the maps representable by a measurable function, $i(a, s)$ on the product $(A, \mathcal{A}, \mu) \times (S, \Sigma, \sigma)$, such that $\forall a$, $i(a) \in L_{\infty}$.

Fubini's theorem implies then that, when $i(a)$ is positive and L^{τ}_{∞}-measurable, then it is Pettis-integrable as soon as $\int i(a, s) d\mu(a)$ is a bounded function of s.

3) When preferences are in addition complete, transitive, and continuous ($\{y \mid x \succ y\}$ is open in $L^{\tau}_{\infty,+}$ for each x), the assumption that

the graph of $\succ$ is measurable in $A \otimes L^{\tau}_{\infty} \otimes L^{\tau}_{\infty}$ is equivalent with the assumption that, for each x, y, $\{a \mid x \succ_a y\}$ is measurable (Aumann-measurability) or that the map $a \to \succ_a$ is measurable with respect to the Kannai-topology. (Consider the utility representation where the constant function $u_a(x) \sim_a x$.)

3. Theorem

Theorem. *If $i(a)$ is the limit of an increasing sequence of step functions, then the core is equal to the set of competitive equilibria.*

Proof. It is well known that an equilibrium-allocation is in the Core.

Let $x(a)$ be an allocation in the Core.

In this proof we mean by "simple function" a measurable function with countably many values.

Let $C = \{\int_E f(a)d\mu \mid E \in \mathcal{A},\ f$ Pettis integrable simple function from $(E, \mathcal{A}_E, \mu_E)$ into L^{τ}_{∞}; a.e. in E, $i(a) + f(a) \succ_a x(a)$, $\mu(E) \neq 0\}$.

Since $(A, \mathcal{A}, \mu)$ is atomless, C is convex, and since x is in the Core, $C \cap L_{\infty,-} = \phi$. $L_{\infty,-}$ being also convex and having an interior point in the strong topology of L_{∞}, there exists by the Hahn-Banach theorem an element

$$\pi \in ba(S, \Sigma, \sigma), \quad \pi \geq 0,\ \pi \neq 0 \text{ s.t. } \forall y,\ y \in C \Rightarrow \pi(y) \geq 0.$$

Let us now show that $\pi \in L_1(S, \Sigma, \sigma)$.

There exists a unique decomposition $\pi = \pi_c + \pi_f$ of π into a countably additive part π_c and a purely finitely additive part π_f, with $\pi_c \geq 0$ and $\pi_f \geq 0$.

Further there exists a sequence $\cdots \subseteq B_i \subseteq B_{i+1} \subseteq \cdots$, $B_i \in \Sigma$, $\bigcup_i B_i = S$, such that

$$\forall i \quad \pi_f(B_i) = 0.$$

We will show $\pi_f = 0$.

Let $E \in \mathcal{A}$, $0 < \mu(E) < +\infty$, f Pettis integrable simple function from $(E, \mathcal{A}_E, \mu_E)$ into L^{τ}_{∞}; a.e. in E, $i(a) + f(a) \succ_a x(a)$.

Let $\psi_i(a) = [i(a) + f(a)] \cdot I(B_i)$.

Then, for each $a \in E$, $\psi_i(a) \xrightarrow{\tau(L_\infty, L_1)} i(a) + f(a)$, and thus $\exists n_0 : \forall i$, $i \geq n_0$, $\psi_i(a) \succ_a x(a)$.

Let $E_n = \{a \mid a \in E, \forall i, i \geq n, \psi_i(a) \succ_a x(a)\}$. Then, $E_i \subseteq E_{i+1} \subseteq \cdots$, $\bigcup_i E_i = E$. So we can suppose $\mu(E_i) > 0$.

By assumption the function $h(a) = \operatorname{ess\,inf}_{s \in S} i(a,s)$ is strictly positive and it is integrable. Thus there exists a strictly positive integrable simple function $g(a)$ such that $g(a) \leq h(a) \leq i(a,s)$.

Let now

$$\chi_i(a) = \psi_i(a) - i(a) \cdot I(B_i) - g(a) \cdot (1 - I(B_i)).$$

Then $\chi_i(a) \geq \psi_i(a) - i(a)$; thus a.e. in E_i: $i(a) + \chi_i(a) \succ_a x(a)$. Further $\chi_i(a) = f(a) \cdot I(B_i) - g(a) \cdot (1 - I(B_i))$. So $\chi_i(a)$ is a Pettis integrable simple function. Thus $\int_{E_i} \chi_i(a) d\mu \in C$, and thus

$$\pi \int_{E_i} [f(a) \cdot I(B_i) - g(a) \cdot (1 - I(B_i))] d\mu \geq 0$$

$$\pi \left(I(B_i) \cdot \int_{E_i} f(a) d\mu \right) \geq \pi \left((1 - I(B_i)) \int_{E_i} g(a) d\mu \right).$$

Since $\pi_f = 0$ on B_i, we can replace π by π_c in the left hand member, and since $\pi \geq \pi_f$ we can replace π by π_f in the right hand member. So

$$\pi_c \left(I(B_i) \int_{E_i} f(a) d\mu \right) \geq \pi_f \left((1 - I(B_i)) \int_{E_i} g(a) d\mu \right).$$

Since $\pi_f = 0$ on B_i, the right hand member is equal to

$$\pi_f \int_{E_i} g(a) d\mu = \pi_f(S) \cdot \int_{E_i} g(a) d\mu \text{ since } g(a) \text{ is constant}$$

and thus, when $i \to +\infty$, the right hand member converges to

$$\pi_f(S) \cdot \int_E g(a) d\mu.$$

Similarly the left hand member, when $i \to +\infty$, converges to $\pi_c \int_E f(a) d\pi$ by Lebesgue's monotone convergence theorem (π_c is countably additive and $f \geq -i$). So

$$\pi_c \left[\int_E f(a) d\mu \right] \geq \pi_f(S) \cdot \int_E g(a) d\mu \geq 0. \tag{1}$$

Assume now $E \subseteq A_K = \{a \mid \|i(a)\| \leq K, \|x(a)\| \leq K\}$, and let $f_i(a)$ be a sequence of Pettis-integrable simple functions converging a.e. on E to $x(a) - i(a) + \varepsilon$ in L^{τ}_{∞}, such that $i(a) + f_n(a) \geq 0$ (assumption on i), and $\|f_n(a)\| \leq K + \varepsilon$.

Let $E_i = \{a \in E \mid \forall j, j \geq i, i(a) + f_j(a) \succ_a x(a)\}$. Then $E_i \subseteq E_{i+1} \subseteq \cdots, \cup E_i = E$.

Thus, replacing in (1) E by E_i and f by f_i, $\pi_c \int_{E_i} f_i d\mu \geq 0$, and, passing to the limit,

$$\pi_c \int_E (x(a) - i(a) + \varepsilon) d\mu \geq 0,$$

thus

$$\pi_c \int_E x(a) d\mu \geq \pi_c \int_E i(a) d\mu,$$

or, by Fubini's theorem

$$\forall E \subseteq A_K, \qquad \int_E \pi_c(x(a)) d\mu \geq \int_E \pi_c(i(a)) d\mu.$$

It follows that

$$\pi_c(x(a)) \geq \pi_c(i(a)) \quad \text{a.e. on } A_K, \text{ hence on } A.$$

But since $\int x(a) d\mu \leq \int i(a) d\mu$, we have

$$\pi_c(x(a)) = \pi_c(i(a)).$$

So

$$\lim_{i \to \infty} \pi_c \int_{E_i} f_i d\mu = \pi_c \int_E (x(a) - i(a) + \varepsilon) d\mu = \varepsilon \cdot \mu(E) \cdot \pi_c(S).$$

Now

$$\pi_c \int_{E_i} f_i d\mu \geq \pi_f(S) \cdot \int_{E_i} g d\mu$$

by (1). So

$$\lim_{i \to \infty} \pi_c \int_{E_i} f_i d\mu \geq \pi_f(S) \cdot \int_E g d\mu \geq 0.$$

It follows that

$$\varepsilon \cdot \mu(E) \cdot \pi_c(S) \geq \pi_f(S) \cdot \int_E g d\mu \geq 0.$$

Since ε is arbitrary, and $\int_E g d\mu > 0$, we have $\pi_f(S) = 0$, and $\pi_c = \pi$: π is countably additive, and thus in $L_1(S, \Sigma, \sigma)$. Further we have proved that

$$\langle \pi \cdot x(a) \rangle = \langle \pi \cdot i(a) \rangle \quad \text{a.e.}$$

which implies $x(a)$ is a.e. in the budget set.

Let us finally prove that (π, x) is a competitive equilibrium. There remains to be shown that $x(a)$ is a.e. maximal in the budget set.

Consider the correspondence

$$a \to P(a) = \{y \mid y \in L_\infty, \pi(y) \leq \pi(i(a)), y \succ_a x(a)\}.$$

This correspondence is obviously measurable in $(A, a, \mu) \otimes L_\infty^\tau$. Since L_∞^τ is Lusin, it follows that the set $E = \{a \mid P(a) \neq \emptyset\}$ is measurable. We have to show that $\mu(E) = 0$.

Because $\pi(i(a)) > 0$, if $P(a)$ is nonempty, the set

$$P'(a) = \{y \in L_\infty \mid \pi(y) < \pi(i(a)), y \succ_a x(a)\}$$

is obviously also nonempty, and this correspondence is also measurable. If $\mu(E) > 0$, since L_∞^τ is a Lusin space, there would exist a measurable selection $y(a)$ of $P'(a)$ on E. Restricting ourselves to some subset of positive measure E' of E, we can even assume $y(a)$ to be Pettis-integrable.

Consider now a sequence $f_n(a)$ of Pettis-integrable simple functions from $(E', \mathcal{A}, \mu)$ to L_∞^τ, which converges a.e. in the Mackey topology to $y(a) - i(a)$, and s.t. $f_n(a) + i(a) \geq 0$.

Since $\forall a$, $P'(a)$ is Mackey open, there exists n_0 s.t.

$$\forall n,\ n \geq n_0 : \quad i(a) + f_n(a) \in P'(a).$$

Let $E_n = \{a \mid a \in E' : \forall j, j \geq n, i(a) + f_j(a) \in P'(a)\}$. We have $E_n \subseteq E_{n+1} \subseteq \cdots, \bigcup_n E_n = E'$. So we can assume $\mu(E_n) > 0$.

Thus

$$\int_{E_n} f_n(a) d\mu(a) \in C,$$

and so

$$\pi \cdot \int_{F_n} f_n(a) d\mu(a) \geq 0 \quad \forall F_n \subseteq E_n$$

by Fubini's theorem ($f_n \geq -i$)

$$\int_{F_n} < \pi \cdot f_n(a) > d\mu(a) \geq 0,$$

and so, on E_n

$$\pi \cdot f_n(a) \geq 0 \quad \text{a.e.}$$

Passing the limit in n, we obtain that:

$$\pi \cdot (y(a) - i(a)) \geq 0,$$

so that

$$\pi \cdot y(a) \geq \pi \cdot i(a),$$

which contradicts out assumption.

So (π, x) is a competitive equilibrium. This completes the proof of the theorem.[3]

---

[3] It follows from our definition of the price system π in the beginning of this proof that any weak limit in $ba(S, \Sigma, \sigma)$ of price systems π is again a competitive price system with respect to x. We have also shown that any competitive price system so defined is in fact in $L_1(S, \Sigma, \sigma)$. So it follows that the set of all price systems with respect to x is weakly compact (and convex) in $L_1(S, \Sigma, \sigma)$—when normalized.

The Principle of Equivalence

Harrison H. C. Cheng*

Abstract. A general principle of obtaining equivalence of core and quasi-Walrasian allocations in nonatomic markets with an infinite number of commodities is formulated through four ingredients: the set of arbitrage, the coalitional representation, the space of allocations and the (weak) Lyapunov Convexity Theorem.

1. Introduction

In his Frisch Memorial Lecture at the Fifth World Congress of the Econometric Society at MIT in 1985, Debreu (see the article, Debreu (1986)) credited Karl Vind as the first person to give a coalitional representation of the economy and derive the Core-Walras equivalence result as a direct consequence of Lyapunov's theorem on the range of a nonatomic vector measure (see Lyapunov (1940)).

Since the contributions of Scarf (1962), Aumann (1964) and Vind (1964), there has developed a substantial amount of literature on the subject. There has also been important contributions to extend the Core-Walras equivalence result to the case of nonatomic markets with infinitely many commodities (Gabszewicz (1968), Peleg and Yaari (1970), Bewley (1973), Mas-Colell (1975), Ostroy (1984), Gretsky and Ostroy (1985), Aliprantis, Brown and Burkinshaw (1985, 1986), Ostroy and Zame (1986), Rustichini and Yannelis (1991)).

At the same time there are significant improvements in the equivalence result for the finite dimensional theory. An important development for this paper is the works of Brown and Robinson (1975), Khan (1974b), Rashid (1979), Brown and Khan (1980) and Anderson (1978). Anderson (1978) and Khan (1974b) obtain approximation results for core and Walrasian allocations in a finite large economy using only free disposal

---

* Special thanks are due to T. Armstrong for correcting an error in definitions; to A. Khan for helping me in the literature; to N. Yannelis for showing me his unpublished work; and to W. Zame and J. Ostroy for fruitful discussions I had with them. Thanks are also due to the referee for correcting many errors. All remaining errors are my responsibility.

arguments. The equivalence version of Anderson has been obtained by Cheng (1986) in a nonatomic market with finitely many commodities under the same assumptions. (A nonstandard version of this result is in Khan (1974b).) The equivalence result in this general framework is between core allocations and quasi-Walrasian allocations (Debreu 1962)). In fact, for the finite dimensional theory, the free disposal assumption can also be dropped as in the very general result of Hildenbrand (1968).

Another important development for the purpose of this paper is the work of Armstrong and Richter (1984). Armstrong and Richter (1984) take the coalitional approach of Vind (1964) and obtain a very comprehensive equivalence result for the finite dimensional case. An often unnoticed innovation in Armstrong and Richter (1984) is an abstract and axiomatic formulation of the space of allocations. (The terminology they use is the "spliceable cone" of allocations. In our case it is a linear space.) There are a variety of spaces of allocations we can consider (see Armstrong and Richter (1984) for a rich collection), and a variety of equivalence results can be obtained accordingly. Through an axiomatic formulation of the space of allocations, a more unified *Principle of Equivalence* will emerge.

The equivalence result in Armstrong and Richter (1984) has been modified in Cheng (1986) in two respects. Firstly, the assumptions on preferences in Armstrong and Richter (1984) are different from those of Khan (1974b) and Anderson (1978), and the arguments are more than the free disposal ones used by Khan and Anderson. Since the free disposal arguments have great intuitive appeal and are generalizable to the infinite dimensional case, Cheng (1986) modified the result of Armstrong and Richter (1984) by using only the free disposal arguments. Secondly, the axiomatic formulation of the space of allocations in Armstrong and Richter (1984) has been adapted in Cheng (1986) in a form that can be used in the infinite dimensional case (See Remark 1 in section 2). We are now ready to take the big step from the finite dimensional world of Cheng (1986) into the infinite dimensional one of this paper.

There are four basic ingredients in our analysis: (1) the set of arbitrage, (2) the coalitional representation, (3) the axiomatic formulation of the space of allocations, and (4) the (weak) Lyapunov Convexity Theorem. We will now describe their respective roles in the formulation of the

Principle of Equivalence.

1.1 The Set of Arbitrage. When all goods are desirable, a positive net trade vector is universally desirable in the sense that it is desirable for every trader in the economy whatever the current consumption. More generally, a set of arbitrage is a collection of net trade vectors which are universally desirable. The positive cone (with 0 deleted) is an obvious example of a set of arbitrage. The term "arbitrage" is borrowed from the arbitrage pricing theory (see Harrison-Kreps (1979), Kreps (1981), and Cheng (1987d)). In Cheng (1986), we took the strictly positive cone as the set of arbitrage. When the commodity space is infinite dimensional, the set of arbitrage is an open convex cone containing the positive cone (with 0 deleted). The existence of an extremely desirable commodity (see Yannelis and Zame (1986)) implies the existence of an open convex cone of arbitrage, which in turn implies the uniform properness condition in Mas-Colell (1986).

The existence of an open convex set of arbitrage constitutes the only assumption on the preferences in our analysis. A quite general existence result for the open convex cone of arbitrage has been obtained in the securities trading model (see Remark 2 in section 2). Through the set of arbitrage, we can carry out an analysis similar to the free disposal arguments of Khan (1974b), Anderson (1978), and Cheng (1986). The quasi-Walrasian allocations and core allocations can be characterized using the set of arbitrage. The open convex property of the set of arbitrage makes it easy to apply the separation theorem to obtain a Walrasian price system. The openness of the set of arbitrage also makes it sufficient to use a weak form of Lyapunov Convexity Theorem.

1.2 The Coalitional Representation. An exchange economy is usually described by individual consumption constraints, preferences and endowments. We call this an individual representation of the economy. The best way to understand the Core-Walras equivalence is, however, through the coalitional representation. In the coalitional representation, allocations are described by vector measures and coalitions rank allocations through unanimity. For nonatomic markets, the transformation from an individual representation to a coalitional one involves an integration procedure. There are different concepts of integration in infinite dimensional spaces, the simplest one being Bochner integral. As long as a coalitional representation satisfying the prescribed properties is obtained, whatever integration concept used is acceptable. An illustration of this transformation is shown in section 6 using Bochner integration.

A coalitional representation of the economy can be given without any regard to the individual representation. There are coalitional representations which have no counterpart in the individual ones. In this sense, a coalitional representation can be a more general way of describing an economy. We use the coalitional representation as a tool for understanding the Core-Walras equivalence and as a convenient vehicle for the formulation of the Principle of Equivalence, not just for the sake of generality.

The coalitional representation of the economy allows us to give simple characterizations of Walrasian and Core allocations that bring out the close connection between the two concepts. It becomes immediately clear from the characterizations that the gap between the two concepts is an appropriate form of Lyapunov Convexity Theorem.

1.3 The Axiomatic Formulation of the Space of Allocations. The axiomatic properties (H.1)~(H.5) in section 2 for the space of allocations say that it is a linear space of vector measures containing the endowment measure, the uniform measure, and the restriction of every vector measure in the space to any coalition. The axiomatic approach gives a unified treatment to various restrictions on allocations we want to impose. There is a huge variety of infinite dimensional spaces and vector measures taking values in such spaces. In order to apply the Lyapunov Convexity Theorem, different technical restrictions are often needed for different commodity spaces. The axiomatic approach is actually indispensable in the formulation of the Principle of Equivalence for this reason.

The restrictions on allocations can be technical as well as economic. For instance, we envision the restriction of trades through money (Mas-Colell (1982)) and the informational restrictions on trades in the dynamic trading model (Radner (1972)), Duffie-Huang (1985)). These potential applications have yet to be explored.

1.4 The Lyapunov Convexity Theorem. We say that

the space of allocations H (with range in $(X, \mathfrak{X})$) has the (weak) Lyapunov Convexity Property if for all $f, g \in H$, the closure of the range of (f, g) (with range in $(X^2, \mathfrak{X}^2)$) is convex. Whenever H has the (weak) Lyapunov Convexity Property, a convexification theorem can be established (Theorem 5 in section 3) which bridges the gap between core allocations and quasi-Walrasian allocations.

Having described all the ingredients, we can now state the *Principle of Equivalence* informally as follows: Let the economy be nonatomic. Suppose there exits an open convex cone of arbitrage, and the space of allocations has the (weak) Lyapunov Convexity Property, then every core allocation is a quasi-Walrasian allocation.

In this paper, we do not impose any constraints on consumption, and the consumption set is taken to be the whole space. This is acceptable in the securities trading model where unlimited short sales are allowed (see Hart (1975) and Cheng (1987c)). For trading in real commodities, we should at least impose positive constraints. The positive constraints can be handled (see an interesting result of Rustichini and Yannelis (1987)), but the technical machinery and the functional analytic tools that we need to deal with the problem are quite substantial. These constraint problems can easily overwhelm the basic ideas I am trying to present in this paper. The nature of the problem of positive constraints is also quite different from the issue I am addressing here and is best treated in a separate paper.

The examples in section 5 give flesh to the Principle of Equivalence. They are also designed for the following purpose: To give various specifications of the space of allocations in various commodity spaces so that the principle of equivalence is applicable. Example 1 deals with Fréchet spaces endowed with the weak topology. Example 2 deals with general Banach spaces, while example 3 deals with more special types of Banach spaces. The commodity space in example 4 is also a general Banach space, but vector measures are allowed to be finitely additive. Example 5 deals with a general infinite dimensional space. There are finitely many types of endowments, but the preference distribution can be quite arbitrary. The space of allocations is more specialized than the foregoing examples. Example 6 deals with the case when the strong Lyapunov convexity property holds (see also Remark 4 in section 3). In this case, the topology can also be quite arbitrary. Example 7 considers the commodity space studied in Bewley (1972, 1973). Our specification of the space of allocations is different from Bewley (1973), therefore results are not directly comparable. Our choice is motivated by the way in which a simple application of the Principle of Equivalence is readily available. Example 8 looks at the commodity space of Mas-Colell (1975) and Jones (1983, 1984). For a comparison between the equivalence results of Example 8 and Mas-Colell (1975), see section 7. Example 9 utilizes the basis structure of the Banach space.

Production is not treated in this paper. But it can be incorporated quite easily. Cheng (1987a) contains a treatment of the production sector. The existence problem in the coalitional framework has been studied in Armstrong and Richter (1986) and Zame (1986). An existence result for models without constraints is obtained in Cheng (1987c). The relationship between coalitional representation and individual representation is studied in Debreu (1967) and Zame (1986). The machinery for handling the constraint problem has been employed in Cheng (1987b). The characterizations of Walrasian and Core allocations in section 2 have been implicitly used in almost all the works in this area and are given an explicit treatment in Gretsky and Ostroy (1985) under a stronger set of conditions.

There is another aspect of the *Principle of Equivalence* we do not address here. This is the robustness of the equivalence result with respect to various types of restrictions on the coalitional formation. (See Edgeworth (1881), Schmeidler (1972), Mas-Colell (1978, 1982), Armstrong and Richter (1984), Cheng (1986, 1987a), Hansen (1969), Vind (1973), Grodal (1972), Champsaur-Laroque (1971) and Khan (1974a).) We hope to have a more systematic treatment of the subject in the future.

In section 7, a more careful comparison of our result with the existing literature can be found. It should be noted that many of the ideas in this paper are also present in Gretsky and Ostroy (1985) to which I am heavily indebted.

2. Characterizations of Walrasian and Core Allocations

In this section we want to show that the coalitional representation of the economy allows us to give simple characterizations of Walrasian and core allocations that bring out the close connection between the two concepts. These characterizations will be carried out in a very general setting in which the space of agents can be either finite or infinite and the commodity space is either finite dimensional or any (real) Hausdorff locally convex topological vector space.

We will only consider the case of pure exchange. For the case of production economy, the reader is referred to Cheng (1987a). Surprisingly, it is possible to give similar characterizations when there is consumption externality, and the concept of Walrasian allocations is replaced by strong Walrasian allocations. This can also be found in Cheng (1987a). Here we will confine ourself to the case of no externality.

Let A be the set of all individual agents. The set A can be quite arbitrary and can be either a finite set or an infinite set. Let $\mathcal{A}$ be a field of subsets of A, and μ be a nonnegative finitely additive real valued measure on $\mathcal{A}$. An element $a \in \mathcal{A}$ is called a coalition, and $\mu(a)$ represents the proportion of agents in the coalition a. We therefore assume $\mu(A) = 1$.

Let X be the commodity space endowed with a topology $\mathcal{X}$ so that $(X, \mathcal{X})$ becomes a Hausdorff locally convex topological vector space. Let X^* be the topological dual of X. A price system can be represented by an element $p \in X^*$.

An allocation can be represented by a finitely additive function from $\mathcal{A} \to X$. Such a function will be called a vector measure in accordance with the usual mathematical terminology. We will require all allocations to be absolutely continuous with respect to μ, *i.e.*, the vector measure $f : \mathcal{A} \to X$ satisfies

$$\lim_{\mu(a) \to 0} f(a) = 0$$

We also call such vector measures μ-continuous. Intuitively, this means we only consider allocations giving small total amount of commodities to small coalitions. An element $x \in X$ can be regarded as an allocation in the following natural way:

$$a \to \mu(a)x$$

This vector measure is of course μ-continuous, and will be denoted by $\hat{x}$. Such vector measures represent uniform allocations.

The endowment is represented by a vector measure $w : \mathcal{A} \to X$. We do not impose any restriction on $w(a)$ in this section, except that w is μ-continuous.

When A is infinite, it is often desirable to impose various regularity conditions on vector measures. For this reason, we adopt the following general formulation. Let the space of allocations be a set H of μ-continuous vector measures satisfying the following properties:

(H.1) $w \in H$ and $\hat{x} \in H$ for all $x \in X$.
(H.2) If $f, g \in H$, then $f + g \in H$.
(H.3) If $f \in H$, $t \in R$, $t \geq 0$, then $tf \in H$.
(H.4) If $f \in H$, $a_0 \in \mathcal{A}$, then the vector measure $f|a_0 = g : a \to f(a \cap a_0)$ belongs to H.
(H.5) If $f \in H$ then $-f \in H$.

Remark 1. If A is a finite set, then $H = X^{\#A}$. The conditions (H.1)∼(H.4) together are similar to the concept of spliceable cone in Armstrong and Richter (1984). With the addition of (H.5), H becomes a linear space. There are some differences between the above formulation and that of Armstrong and Richter (1984) (abbreviated as A & R). In A & R, there are finitely many commodities. Let the component measures of w be denoted by $w^1, \ldots, w^\ell$ and let $\tilde{w} = w^1 + w^2 + \cdots + w^\ell$. The negligible traders in A & R are defined with respect to $\mu = \tilde{w}$. A & R include vector measures which may not be absolutely continuous with respect to $\tilde{w}$, while we only consider μ-continuous vector measures. There are also differences in the assumptions on preference relations and in the equivalence results obtained. An adequate comparison requires a relatively long digression, and cannot be done here. The reader is referred to Cheng (1986) for detailed discussions.

For each $a \in \mathcal{A}$, $\mu(a) > 0$, we assign a partial ordering $\succ_a \in H \times H$ defined on the space of allocations. The coalitional preference $\succ_a$ has the following interpretation: $f \succ_a g$ if and only if every member of the coalition regarded f as better than g. This interpretation is embodied in the first two properties below. The third property rules out the consumption externality.

(P.1) If $f \succ_a g$ and $f \succ_b g$ then $f \succ_{a \cup b} g$.

(P.2) If $f \succ_a g$ and $b \subset a$, $\mu(b) > 0$, then $f \succ_b g$.

(P.3) If $f|a = f'|a$, $g|a = g'|a$ then $f \succ_a g$ if and only if $f' \succ_a g'$.

We shall assume the existence of a set V representing universally desirable directions of trades. The following assumptions embody this idea:

(V.1) V is an open convex cone

(V.2) For all $f \in H$, $a \in \mathcal{A}$, $k \in V$, $\mu(a) > 0$, we have $f + \hat{k} \succ_a f$.

(V.3) If $f \succ_a g$ then $f + \hat{k} \succ_a g$ for all $k \in V$.

Remark 2. In the asset market equilibrium of the securities trading model, a commodity is a random return represented by a real-valued random variable. Let $u : R \rightarrow R$ be the Von-Neumann Morgenstein utility function of the trader. Assume that u is concave and strictly increasing with marginal utilities bounded away from 0 and infinity. Let (Ω, F, μ) be a probability space and $X = L^p(\Omega, F, \mu)$ be the set of all real-valued random variables with a finite L^p-norm, $1 \leq p \leq \infty$. Let K be the positive cone in X with 0 deleted. Then there exists an open convex cone V containing K satisfying $x + v \succ x$ for all $x \in X$ and $v \in V$ (see Cheng (1987c)). This property can then be translated into (V.2), (V.3), as shown in section 6 at the end of this paper.

The economy is represented by $(A, \mathcal{A}, \mu)$, w, H, V, and $\mathcal{A} \xrightarrow{\succ} 2^{H \times H}$ satisfying the above properties.

An allocation $f \in H$ is called feasible if $f(A) = w(A)$. A feasible allocation $f \in H$ is called a Walrasian allocation if there exists $p \in X^*$ such that (i) $p \cdot k > 0$ for all $k \in V$, (ii) $p \cdot f(a) = p \cdot w(a)$ for all $a \in \mathcal{A}$, $\mu(a) > 0$, and (iii) $p \cdot f'(a) > p \cdot w(a)$ whenever $f' \succ_a f$, $a \in \mathcal{A}$. A feasible allocation $f \in H$ is called a quasi-Walrasian allocation if there exists $p \in X^*$ such that (i) $p \cdot k > 0$ for all $k \in V$, (ii) $p \cdot f(a) = p \cdot w(a)$ for all $a \in \mathcal{A}$, $\mu(a) > 0$, and (iii) $pf'(a) \geq p \cdot w(a)$ whenever $f' \succ_a f$, $a \in \mathcal{A}$.

Remark 3. In the above definitions of Walrasian and quasi-Walrasian allocations, the condition $p \cdot k > 0$ for all $k \in V$ is a consequence of equilibrium conditions (ii) and (iii). To see this, let $k \in V$. We have $f + \hat{k} \succ_a f$ for all $a \in \mathcal{A}$, $\mu(a) > 0$. By property (iii) $p \cdot (f(a) + \mu(a)k) \geq p \cdot w(a)$. By property (ii), $\mu(a)p \cdot k \geq 0$ *i.e.*, $\rho \cdot k \geq 0$ for all $k \in V$. Since

V is an open set, we must have $\rho \cdot k > 0$ for all $k \in V$. Hence property (i) is proved. We explicitly list property (i) because of its importance in our analysis.

In addition to the mild form of continuity implicit in (V.1), we may add the following weak form of lower continuity (C). Condition (C) is not made unless explicitly stated.

(C) If $f \succ_a g$, then there exists $h \in H$ such that $h(a) \in V$ and $f - h \succ_a g$.

It is obvious that a Walrasian allocation is also quasi-Walrasian. When the condition (C) is made, the two concepts are identical. This is the content of the following proposition:

Proposition 1. *Under (C), a quasi-Walrasian allocation is a Walrasian allocation.*

Proof. Let $f \in H$ be a quasi-Walrasian allocation, and $p \in X^*$ an associated price. If for some $a \in \mathcal{A}$, $\mu(a) > 0$, we have $f' \in H$ such that $f' \succ_a f$ and $pf'(a) = pw(a)$, we can find $h \in H$ such that $h(a) \in V$ and $f' - h \succ_a f$. Then $p\big(f'(a) - h(a)\big) < pf'(a) = pw(a)$ violating the quasi-Walrasian property. □

Given $f \in H$, the set of all desirable net trades for $a \in \mathcal{A}$ is denoted by $N(f,a) = \{x : x = f'(a) - w(a) \text{ for some } f' \in H,\ f' \succ_a f\}$. The set of all possible desirable net trades for the economy is denoted by $N(f) = \bigcup_{a \in \mathcal{A}} N(f,a)$. The closed convex hull of a set $S \subset X$ will be denoted by $\overline{co}(S)$. The following Walrasian separation property will be used to give a price-free characterization of quasi-Walrasian allocations:

(W) $\quad \overline{co}\, N(f) \cap (-V) = \emptyset.$

Theorem 1. *The allocation $f \in H$ is quasi-Walrasian if and only if property (W) holds.*

Proof. Let $f \in H$ be a quasi-Walrasian allocation with an associated price $p \in X^*$. Define $M = \{x : px \geq 0\}$. Let $x \in N(f,a)$, with $x = f'(a) - w(a)$, $f' \succ_a f$. Then $px = p\big(f'(a) - w(a)\big) \geq 0$ and $x \in M$. Therefore $N(f,a) \subset M$ for all $a \in \mathcal{A}$ and $N(f) \subset M$. Since M is closed and convex, we immediately have $\overline{co}\ N(f) \subset M$. From the condition $-pV < 0$, we have $(-V) \cap M = \emptyset$, therefore $\overline{co}\ N(f) \cap (-V) = \emptyset$ and property (W) is proved.

Conversely, assume that (W) is satisfied for some $f \in H$. We want to show that f is quasi-Walrasian. The set $\overline{co}\, N(f)+V$ is open and does not contain 0. Therefore by Hahn-Banach Theorem (Schaefer (1980), p. 46) there is $p \in X^*$ such that $p[\overline{co}\, N(f) + V] > 0$. Since $f + \hat{k} \succ_A f$, we have $k = f(A) + k - w(A) \in N(f, A) \subset N(f)$ and $p(k + V) > 0$ for all $k \in V$. Hence $p(k+k) > 0$ or $pk > 0$ for all $k \in V$. Since 0 is a boundary point of V, $\sup p(-V) = 0$ and $\inf p\, \overline{co}\, N(f) \geq \sup -pV = 0$. Hence for any $f' \succ_a f$ we have $p\big(f'(a) - w(a)\big) \geq 0$. Finally to verify the budget constraint, we take $f + \hat{k} \succ_a f$, hence $p\big(f(a) + \mu(a)k - w(a)\big) \geq 0$ for all $a \in \mathcal{A}$, $\mu(a) > 0$. Let $k \to 0$, we have $p\big(f(a) - w(a)\big) \geq 0$ for all $a \in \mathcal{A}$, $\mu(a) > 0$. Therefore the real-valued measure $p\big(f(a) - w(a)\big)$ is nonnegative when $\mu(a) > 0$, and $p\big(f(a) - w(a)\big) = 0$. Hence we must have $p\big(f(a) - w(a)\big) = 0$ for all $a \in \mathcal{A}$, $\mu(a) > 0$. □

A feasible allocation $f \in H$ is called a core allocation if there does not exist $f' \in H$, $a \in \mathcal{A}$, $\mu(a) > 0$ such that $f' \succ_a f$ and $f'(a) = w(a)$.

Theorem 2. *If $f \in H$ is a core allocation, then $N(f) \cap (-V) = \emptyset$.*

Proof. Suppose for some $k \in V$, $-k = f'(a) - w(a)$, $f' \succ_a f$. Then we have $f'(a) + k = w(a)$. The allocation $f + \frac{1}{\mu(a)}\hat{k}$ has the following properties: $f' + \frac{1}{\mu(a)}\hat{k} \succ_a f$ and $(f' + \frac{1}{\mu(a)}\hat{k})(a) = f'(a) + k = w(a)$. This violates the core property. □

Theorem 3. *Under (C), $N(f) \cap (-V) = \emptyset$ implies that f is a core allocation.*

Proof. If not, there exists $f' \in H$, $a \in \mathcal{A}$ such that $f' \succ_a f$ and $f'(a) = w(a)$. By assumption (C), there exists $h \in H$ such that $h(a) \in V$ and $f' - h \succ_a f$. This implies that $f'(a) - h(a) - w(a) \in N(f, a) \subset N(f)$ or $-h(a) \in N(f)$. Hence $-h(a)k \in N(f) \cap (-V)$, contradicting our assumption.

Theorem 4. *Under (C), a quasi-Walrasian allocation is a core allocation.*

Proof. If f is a quasi-Walrasian allocation, by Theorem 1, $\overline{co}N(f) \cap (-V) = \emptyset$ hence $N(f) \cap (-V) = \emptyset$. By Theorem 3, f is a core allocation. □

3. The Convexification Theorem in Nonatomic Markets

This section is devoted to the convexification effect of a large economy and the role of the Lyapunov Convexity Theorem in the nonatomic market. The Lyapunov Convexity Theorem is the basis of the convexification theorem which in turn is the essence of the Core-Walras Equivalence.

First, we begin with the definition of nonatomicity of a vector measure. We say that $f : \mathcal{A} \to X$ is nonatomic if for any $a \in \mathcal{A}$, $\mu(a) > 0$ and any neighborhood U of 0 in X, there exists a finite partition $a = \bigcup_{i=1}^{n} b_i$ such that $f(b_i) \in U$ for all $i = 1, 2, \ldots, n$. It is easy to see that if μ is nonatomic (as a real-valued measure) and f is μ-continuous, then f is nonatomic. For countably additive vector measures, we have the following alternative definition (see Kluvánek (1973)): We call $a \in \mathcal{A}$ an atom if $f(a) \neq 0$, and if $b \in \mathcal{A}$, $b \subset a$ implies $f(b) = 0$ or $f(b) = f(a)$. We call f nonatomic if there exists no atom of f.

Let $(A, \mathcal{A}, \mu)$ be the agents' space with μ nonatomic. Let H be a space of allocations from $\mathcal{A}$ to $(X, \mathfrak{X})$ satisfying (H.1)~(H.5). We say that H has the (weak) *Lyapunov Convexity Property if for every $f \in H$, the $\mathfrak{X}$-closure of the range $R(f) = \{f(a) : a \in \mathcal{A}\}$ is convex, and for every f, $g \in H$ the closure of the range of the vector measure $a \to \big(f(a), g(a)\big)$ with respect to the product topology is also convex.*

Remark 4. The Lyapunov Convexity Property is a *weak* one, because it only requires the closure of the range to be convex, while the range itself may not be convex. The strong Lyapunov Convexity Property refers to the case when the range itself is convex. The characterization of vector measures with the strong Lyapunov Convexity Property is given by Kingman and Robertson (1968) and Knowles (1974). An example of this is given in example 6 of section 5.

Remark 5. A closed convex set in $(X, \mathfrak{X})$ is also closed with respect to any topology $\mathfrak{X}'$ consistent with the duality (X, X^*) (Schaefer (1980), p. 130). Hence if H has the Lyapunov Convexity Property with respect to $(X, \mathfrak{X})$ it also has the property with respect to any topology $\mathfrak{X}'$ on X weaker than $\mathfrak{X}$ and stronger than the weak topology on X. For a Fréchet space $(F, \mathfrak{F})$, the Lyapunov Convexity Property always holds in

H with respect to the weak topology in F (See Kluvánek (1973) and Cheng (1987a)). Hence there exists a finest topology $\mathfrak{X}^0$ consistent with the duality (F, F^*) such that the Lyapunov Convexity Property always holds in H with respect to $(F, \mathfrak{X}^0)$. Section 5 contains more examples in which the Lyapunov Convexity Property holds with respect to the norm topology in a Banach space.

Theorem 5. *(The Convexification Theorem) Let μ be nonatomic and H be a space of allocations consisting of μ-continuous vector measures from $\mathcal{A}$ to X satisfying (H.1)$\sim$(H.5). If the Lyapunov Convexity Theorem holds in H with respect to $(X, \mathfrak{X})$, then for all $f \in H$, we have*

$$\overline{N(f)} = \overline{co}\, N(f)$$

where the closure is taken with respect to the $\mathfrak{X}$-topology.

Proof. The proof will proceed in several steps.

Step 1. $\overline{N(f,a)} = \overline{co}\, N(f,a)$ for all $a \in \mathcal{A}$.
Let $x_1, x_2 \in N(f,a)$ and $\lambda \in (0,1)$, then there exists $f_1, f_2 \in H$ such that $x_1 = f_1(a) - w(a)$, $x_2 = f_2(a) - w(a)$ and $f_1 \succ_a f$, $f_2 \succ_a f$. Applying the Lyapunov Convexity Theorem to the vector measure $b \to (f_1(b), f_2(b)) \in X^2$, we can then choose a net $a_n \subset a$ such that $\lim (f_1(a_n), f_2(a_n)) = \lambda(f_1(a), f_2(a))$. Define f_n by $f_n = f_1|a_n + f_2|a - a_n$, then $f_n|a_n = f_1|a_n \succ_{a_n} f$ and $f_n|a-a_n = f_2|a-a_n \succ_{a-a_n} f$. Hence $f_n \succ_a f$. Moreover $f_n(a) - w(a) = f_1(a_n) + f_2(a - a_n) - w(a) = f_1(a_n) - f_2(a_n) + f_2(a) - w(a) \to \lambda f_1(a) - \lambda f_2(a) + f_2(a) - w(a) = \lambda f_1(a) + (1-\lambda) f_2(a) - \lambda w(a) - (1-\lambda) w(a) = \lambda(f_1(a) - w(a)) + (1-\lambda)(f_2(a) - w(a)) = \lambda x_1 + (1-\lambda) x_2$. Therefore $\lambda x_1 + (1-\lambda) x_2 \in \overline{N(f,a)}$ and $co\, N(f,a) \subset \overline{N(f,a)}$ which implies $\overline{co}\, N(f,a) \subset \overline{N(f,a)}$. The other inclusion direction is obvious. Hence step 1 is proved.

Step 2. $\lambda N(f,a) \subset \overline{N(f)}$ for all $a \in \mathcal{A}$, $\lambda \in [0,1]$.
The proof is very similar to step 1, hence we shall be brief. Let $x \in N(f,a)$, there exists $f' \in H$ such that $x = f'(a) - w(a)$, $f' \succ_a f$. Define the vector measure $b \to (f'(b), w(b))$ and choose a net $a_n \subset a$ such that $\lim (f'(a_n), w(a_n)) = \lambda(f'(a), w(a))$. Define $f_n = f'|a_n$ then $\lambda x = \lim (f_n(a_n) - w(a_n))$ with $f_n \succ_{a_n} f$. Hence $f_n(a_n) - w(a_n) \in N(f, a_n)$ and $\lambda x \in \overline{N(f)}$.

Step 3. $\overline{N(f,a)} + \overline{N(f,b)} \subset \overline{N(f)}$ when $a \cap b = \emptyset$.
Let $x_1 = \lim_n \big(f_1^n(a) - w(a)\big)$ with $f_1^n \succ_a f$ and $x_2 = \lim_n \big(f_2^n(b) - w(b)\big)$ with $f_2^n \succ_a f$, then we can define $f^n = f_1^n|a + f_2^n|b$, then $x_1 + x_2 = \lim_n \big(f^n(a \cup b) - w(a \cup b)\big)$ and $f^n \succ_{a\cup b} f$, hence $x_1 + x_2 \in \overline{N(f)}$.

Step 4. $co\, N(f) \subset \overline{N(f)}$.
The proof of this step is a "convex" mixture of arguments used in steps 1, 2 and 3. Let $x_1 \in N(f,a)$ and $x_2 \in N(f,b)$, $\lambda \in (0,1)$. If $a \cap b = \emptyset$, then step 2 shows that $\lambda x_1 = \lim_n y_n$, $y_n \in N(f,a_n)$, $a_n \subset a$ and $(1-\lambda)x_2 = \lim_n z_n$, $z_n \in N(f,b_n)$, $b_n \subset b$. Then the arguments in step 3 show that $\lambda x_1 + (1-\lambda)x_2 \in \overline{N(f)}$. Hence assume that $a \cap b \neq \emptyset$. Without loss of generality, we can assume that $\mu(a \cap b) > 0$, $\mu(a \setminus b) > 0$ and $\mu(b \setminus a) > 0$. Let $x_1 = f_1(a) - w(a)$, $f_1 \succ_a f$ and $x_2 = f_2(b) - w(b)$, $f_2 \succ_b f$. Then $\lambda x_1 + (1-\lambda)x_2 = \lambda\big(f_1(a \setminus b) - w(a \setminus b)\big) + (1-\lambda)\big(f_2(b \setminus a) - w(b \setminus a)\big) + \lambda\big(f_1(a \cap b) - w(a \cap b)\big) + (1-\lambda)\big(f_2(a \cap b) - w(a \cap b)\big)$. Step 2 shows that $\lambda\big(f_1(a \setminus b) - w(a \setminus b)\big)$ and $(1-\lambda)\big(f_2(b \setminus a) - w(b \setminus a)\big)$ are limits of some $\{y_n : y_n \in N(f,a_n),\ a_n \subset a \setminus b\}$ and $\{z_n : z_n \in N(f,b_n),\ b_n \subset b\}$ respectively. Also step 1 shows that $\lambda\big(f_1(a \cap b) - w(a \cap b)\big) + (1-\lambda)\big(f_2(a \cap b) - w(a \cap b)\big) \in N(f, a \cap b)$. Therefore, arguments in step 3 show that $\lambda x_1 + (1-\lambda)x_2 \in \overline{N(f)}$.

The proof of the theorem is complete by noting that $\overline{co}\, N(f) \subset \overline{N(f)}$ follows from step 4, and we clearly have $\overline{N(f)} \subset \overline{co}\, N(f)$. Hence $\overline{N(f)} = \overline{co}\, N(f)$. □

4. The Principle of Equivalence

We now combine all the elements into a formal description of the *Principle of Equivalence.*

Theorem 6. *Let $(A, \mathcal{A}, \mu)$ be the agents' space with μ nonatomic and finitely additive. Let $(X, \mathfrak{X})$ be the commodity space, H be a space of allocations consisting of μ-continuous vector measures satisfying (H.1)~(H.5). let $\succ_a$ be the coalitional preferences satisfying (P.1)~(P.3).*

Assume that there exists a set V satisfying (V.1)~(V.3) and that H has the (weak) Lyapunov Convexity Property with respect to $(X, \mathfrak{X})$. The conclusion is that every core allocation is a quasi-Walrasian allocation.

Proof of the Principle. By Theorem 2, if f is a core allocation, then $N(f) \cap (-V) = \emptyset$. let $(-V)^c$ be the complement of $(-V)$, then $(-V)^c$ is a closed set containing $N(f)$ hence $\overline{N(f)} \subset (-V)^c$, and we have $\overline{N(f)} \cap (-V) = \emptyset$. By *Theorem 5*, $\overline{N(f)} = \overline{co}\, N(f)$, hence $\overline{co}\, N(f) \cap (-V) = \emptyset$. The Walrasian Separation Property is satisfied, and by Theorem 1, f is a quasi-Walrasian allocation. □

We now give some general comments about the Principle:

(1) The bigger the space H is, the more requirements we impose on the core allocations. The equilibrium we get is also correspondingly stronger.

(2) The stronger the topology is, the larger the class of preference relations we can admit. The price system we get, however, also tends to be less well-behaved.

(3) If the Lyapunov Convexity Property holds in H with respect to $(X, \mathfrak{X})$, it also holds in H with respect to $(X, \mathfrak{X}')$, $\mathfrak{X}'$ weaker than $\mathfrak{X}$, and $(X, \mathfrak{X}')$ a Hausdorff locally convex topological vector space.

5. Examples of the Principle

The following is a collection of applications of the Principle of Equivalence. Example 1 uses the weak topology and is studied in Cheng (1987a). Examples 2, 3 and 4 use the norm topology. Example 5 is inspired by the commodity arbitrage literature, the vector measures correspond to the simple trading strategies in Harrison-Kreps (1979). Example 6 applies the characterization of convexity of the range of vector measures by Kingman and Robertson (1968) and Knowles (1974). The topology can be quite arbitrary. Example 7 looks at the commodity space of Bewley (1972, 1973). Example 8 looks at the commodity space of Mas-Colell (1975) and Jones (1983, 1984). Example 9 utilizes the basis structure of the Banach space.

Example 1. This example is the case studied in Cheng (1987a). We refer the reader to that paper for more details. The agents' space is $(A, \mathcal{A}, \mu)$, where $\mathcal{A}$ is a field of subsets, μ is a nonnegative finitely additive nonatomic measure. The commodity space X is a Fréchet space (*i.e.*, a complete metrizable locally convex topological vector space). Take the topology $\mathcal{X}$ to be the weak topology in X. The space of allocations H is the set of *all* μ-continuous vector measures from $\mathcal{A}$ to X.

It can be shown that the Lyapunov Convexity Property holds in H with respect to $(X, \mathcal{X})$, see Cheng (1987a). Note that vector measures in H need not have bounded variation.

Example 2. The agents' space $(A, \mathcal{A}, \mu)$ is a finite measure space, *i.e.*, $\mathcal{A}$ is a σ-field on A and $\mu : \mathcal{A} :\to R_+$ is countably additive. The commodity space is a Banach space X, $\mathcal{X}$ is the norm topology. If $f : \mathcal{A} \to X$ is a μ-continuous vector measure, then clearly f is also countably additive. Furthermore, in this case, μ-continuity can be characterized as: $\mu(a) = 0$ implies $f(a) = 0$ (DU, p. 10).

A vector measure is of bounded variation if $\sup_\pi \sum_{a\in\pi} \|f(a)\| < \infty$, where the supremum is taken over all finite partitions of A into pairwise disjoint members of A. The following condition will be imposed on vector measures:

(BVC) $f : \mathcal{A} \to X$ is a μ-continuous vector measure of bounded variation.

There are various types of restrictions or regularity conditions we can impose on vector measures. Consider the following version for motivation:

(GWC) $\{\frac{1}{\mu(a)} f(a) : a \in \mathcal{A} \text{ and } \mu(a) > 0\}$ is relatively weakly compact *i.e.*, the weak closure is weakly compact.

When $A = [0,1]$, $\mathcal{A}$ is the Borel σ-field, μ is the Lebesgue measure, and $X = R^{¶}$, and f is defined by $f(E) = \int_E g d\mu$, $E \in \mathcal{A}$, g is an integrable function on $[0,1]$, the condition (GWC) means that g is essentially bounded, *i.e.*, $\|g(t)\| \leq M$ *a.e.* in $[0,1]$ for some M. Hence the name GWC refers to the global version of the relative weakly compact range of the corresponding *individual* allocations. Consider then, the following local version of the property:

(LWC) For all $a \in \mathcal{A}$, $\mu(a) > 0$, there exists $a' \subset a$, $a' \in \mathcal{A}$, $\mu(a') > 0$ such that $\{\frac{1}{\mu(b)} f(b) : b \in \mathcal{A}, b \subset a', \mu(b) > 0\}$ is relatively weakly compact.

For $A = [0,1]$, $\mathcal{A} =$ the Borel σ-field in $[0,1]$, $\mu =$ the Lebesgue measure, $X = R^{¶}$, and f defined by $f(E) = \int_E g d\mu$ for an integrable $g : [0,1] \to R^{¶}$, condition (LWC) is always satisfied. Therefore the condition has no teeth in the finite dimensional context. For $X = L_1[0,1]$ the condition (LWC) need not be satisfied for μ-continuous vector measures of bounded variation satisfying $\sup\{\frac{\|f(b)\|}{\mu(b)} : b \in \mathcal{A}, \mu(b) > 0\} < +\infty$. For example, consider the following vector measure $f(E)$ = the characteristic function on E for $E \in \mathcal{A}$. Clearly f is μ-continuous and of bounded variation. For any $E \in \mathcal{A}$, $\mu(E) > 0$, we have $\|\frac{1}{\mu(E)} f(E)\| = 1$ hence $\{\frac{1}{\mu(E)} f(E) : E \in \mathcal{A}, \mu(E) > 0\}$ is a subset of the unit sphere in $L_1[0,1]$. To show that (LWC) does not hold it is sufficient to show that for any $\bar{E} \in \mathcal{A}$, $\mu(\bar{E}) > 0$ the collection $\{\frac{1}{\mu(E)} f(E) : E \in \mathcal{A}, \mu(E) > 0, E \subset \bar{E}\}$ of functions in $L_1[0,1]$ is not uniformly integrable (DU, p. 76). The uniform integrability fails because $\lim_{\mu(E)\to 0} \int \frac{1}{\mu(E)} \chi_E = 1 \neq 0$.

We now let the space of allocations H to be the set of all vector measures $f : \mathcal{A} \to X$ satisfying (BVC) and (LWC). By Diestel and Uhl (1977, p. 77), for each $f \in H$, there exists a Bochner integrable function $g : A \to X$ such that $f(a) = \int_a g d\mu$ for all $a \in \mathcal{A}$. By Uhl (1969, see the concluding remark), the norm closure of the range of f is convex (and norm compact). Hence H has the Lyapunov Convexity Property.

Example 3. The agents space $(A, \mathcal{A}, \mu)$ is a finite measure space, with μ nonatomic. We shall take X to be a Banach space having the Radon-Nikodým property, and $\mathfrak{X}$ is the norm topology. The definition is given in the following.

A Banach space X has the Radon-Nikodým property with respect to a finite measure space if for every μ-continuous vector measure of bounded variation, there exists a Bochner integrable function $g : A \to X$ such that $f(a) = \int_a g d\mu$ for all $a \in \mathcal{A}$.

A Banach space X has the Radon-Nikodým property if X has the Radon-Nikodým property with respect to every finite measure space. The most well-known examples of Banach spaces with the Radon-Nikodým property are the reflexive spaces and the separable dual spaces (see DU, p. 79, section 3). The space, c_0, of infinite sequences converging to 0 endowed with the sup norm does not have the Radon-Nikodým property (DU, p. 60), and $L_\infty(A, \mathcal{A}, \mu)$ contains a copy of c_0, hence does not have the Radon-Nikodým property (DU, p. 81). The space $L_\infty(A, \mathcal{A}, \mu)$ is a dual space but is not separable. The space $L_1(A, \mathcal{A}, \mu)$, μ nonatomic, does not have the Radon-Nikodým property (DU, p. 61). It is separable but not a dual space.

We now take H to be the set of all vector measures $f : \mathcal{A} \to X$ satisfying (BVC). Then H has the Lyapunov Convexity Property. This should be clear from the discussions in Example 2. (See also DU, p. 266).

Example 4. The agents' space is $(A, \mathcal{A}, \mu)$, where $\mathcal{A}$ is a field of subsets of A, μ is finitely additive and nonatomic. The commodity space X is a Banach space, $\mathfrak{X}$ is the norm topology. Let H be the set of all vector measures $f : \mathcal{A} \to X$ satisfying (GWC). The Lyapunov Convexity Theorem holds in H with respect to $(X, \mathfrak{X})$. We shall offer no proof here, since it is too long.

Example 5. The agents' space is $(A, \mathcal{A}, \mu)$, where $\mathcal{A}$ is a field of subsets of A, μ is finitely additive and nonatomic. The commodity space $(X, \mathfrak{X})$ is any (real) Hausdorff locally convex topological vector space. Let H be the set of all vector measures $f : \mathcal{A} \to X$ such that there exists a finite subset $\{x_1, \ldots, x_n\} \subset X$ and a corresponding finite partition of $A = a_1 \cup a_2 \ldots \cup a_n$, satisfying $f(a) = \sum_{i=1}^n \mu(a \cap a_i) x_i$ for all $a \in \mathcal{A}$. We call $f \in H$ simple vector measures. The range of f is contained in a finite dimensional subspace of X. Hence H has the Lyapunov Convexity Property.

Example 6. The agents' space is a finite measure space $(A, \mathcal{A}, \mu)$ with μ nonatomic. The commodity space is a Banach space X, the topology $\mathfrak{X}$ is any topology consistent with the duality (X, X^*).

For any μ-continuous vector measure $f : \mathcal{A} \to X$, we can define for any $p \in X^*$, $\nu(a) = p \cdot f(a)$, then ν is a countably additive real valued measure on $(A, \mathcal{A}, \mu)$. Let $M_f = \{\nu :$ there exists $p \in X^*$, $\nu(a) = p \cdot f(a)$ for all $a \in \mathcal{A}\}$. Let $L^\infty(\mu)$ be the set of all μ-essentially bounded real valued function on A. We say that M_f is a thin set (as a subset of the set of all countably additive real valued measures on $(A, \mathcal{A}, \mu)$) if for any $a \in \mathcal{A}$, $\mu(a) > 0$, there exists $h \in L_\infty(\mu)$, $h \neq 0$, h vanishing outside a such that $\int h d\nu = 0$ for all $\nu \in M_f$. We shall let H be a linear space of vector measures satisfying (H.1)~(H.5) such that for any $f, g \in H$, $M_f \cup M_g$ is a thin set, *i.e.*, for any $a \in \mathcal{A}$, $\mu(a) > 0$, there exists $h \in L_\infty(\mu)$, $h \neq 0$, h vanishing outside a such that $\int h d\nu = 0$ for all $\nu \in M_f \cup M_g$.

If f is a simple vector measure defined in example 5, M_f is a thin set (see the proof in Holmes (1975, p. 106) for finite dimensional vector measures. The same proof applies to simple vector measures). Hence the space of all simple vector measures satisfies the condition that $M_f \cup M_g$ is a thin set for all $f, g \in H$.

The property that M_f is a thin set characterizes the convexity of the range of f on each $a \in \mathcal{A}$ (Kingman and Robertson (1968), see also DU, p. 263, and Knowles (1974)). Hence for all $f, g \in H$, the vector measure $a \to (f(a), g(a))$ has convex range and H has the strong Lyapunov Convexity Property. For an example of H bigger than the space of simple vector measures, let $A = \{(t_1, t_2) : 0 \le t_1 \le 1, 0 \le t_2 \le 1\}$, $\mathcal{A}$ be the Borel σ-field, μ be the two-dimensional Lebesgue measure. Let $X = L_1[0,1]$, define the vector measure $f : \mathcal{A} \to X$ by $f(a) = \int_0^1 \mathcal{X}_a(\cdot, t_2)dt_2$, then $f(a) \in L_1[0,1]$. Then M_f is a thin set and $R(f)$ is weakly compact convex (see DU, p. 265). Let H be the linear space spanned by the simple vector measures and $\{f|a,\ a \in \mathcal{A}\}$. To show that H satisfies our requirement, it is sufficient to show that for all simple vector measures g, $M_f \cup M_g$ is a thin set. We shall do this by following Lindenstrauss's (1966) proof. It is sufficient to show that if $\bar{\nu}$ is a real valued measure on $(A, \mathcal{A}, \mu)$ absolutely continuous with respect to μ, then for any $a \in \mathcal{A}$, $\mu(a) > 0$, there exists $h \in L_\infty(\mu)$ vanishing outside a such that $\int h d\nu = 0$ for all $\nu \in M_f$ and $\int h d\bar{\nu} = 0$. The rest follows by induction. Since $R(f)$ is convex, there exists $b \subset a$ such that $f(b) = \frac{1}{2} f(a)$. Without loss of generality, we can assume $\bar{\nu}(b) > 0$. We further choose $b_1 \subset b$ such that $f(b_1) = \frac{1}{2} f(b)$. If $\bar{\nu}(b_1) = \frac{1}{2}\bar{\nu}(b)$, we can let $h = 1$ on b_1 and $h = -1$ on $b \setminus b_1$, $h = 0$ outside b then $\int h d\bar{\nu} = 0$, and $\int hd(p \cdot f) = \frac{1}{2} p \cdot f(b) - \frac{1}{2} p \cdot f(b) = 0$. Hence h has all the properties. If $\bar{\nu}(b_1) \neq \frac{1}{2}\bar{\nu}(b)$, let $b_2 = b - b_1$, then $\bar{\nu}(b_1) \neq \bar{\nu}(b_2)$. Let $k = \frac{\bar{\nu}(a-b) - 2\bar{\nu}(b_2)}{\bar{\nu}(b_1) - \bar{\nu}(b_2)}$ define $h = k$ on b_1, $h = (2-k)$ on b_2, $h = -1$ on $a - b$, $h = 0$ outside a, then $\int h d\bar{\nu} = 0$, and $\int hd(p \cdot f) = kp \cdot f(b_1) + (2-k)p \cdot f(b_2) - p \cdot f(a-b) = p \cdot f(b) - p \cdot f(a-b) = 0$, *i.e.*, $\int h d\nu = 0$ for all $\nu \in M_f$. Therefore we have shown that H can be bigger than the space of simple vector measures.

Example 7. The agents' space $(A, \mathcal{A}, \mu)$ is a finite measure space. The commodity space X is $L_\infty(M, \mathcal{M}, \nu)$, where ν is a σ-finite measure. This is the commodity space considered by Bewley (1972, 1973). Let H be the space of all vector measures $f : \mathcal{A} \to X$ satisfying (BVC) and (LWC) as defined in example 2. Let V be open with respect to the Mackey topology of the duality $(L_\infty(M, \mathcal{M}, \nu),\ L_1(M, \mathcal{M}, \nu))$. As explained in example 2, H has the Lyapunov Convexity Property with respect to X

with the norm topology. Since the norm topology is stronger than the Mackey topology, it is easily seen that the Lyapunov Convexity Property also holds in H with respect to X with the Mackey topology. Hence a core allocation must be a quasi-Walrasian allocation with a price system which is Mackey continuous, *i.e.*, the price system belongs to $L_1(M, \mathcal{M}, \nu)$.

Example 8. The agent's space is $(A, \mathcal{A}, \mu)$, $\mathcal{A}$ is a field of subsets of A and μ is finitely additive and nonnegative. Let K be a compact metric space, X be the set of all bounded signed Borel measures on K endowed with the variation norm. Then X is a Banach space under the variation norm. Let $\mathcal{X}_1$ be the weak topology in X and $\mathcal{X}_2$ be the weak star topology under the duality $(C(K), X)$, where $C(K)$ is the space of continuous functions on K with the sup norm. The commodity space X with the topology $\mathcal{X}_2$ is studied by Mas-Colell (1975), Jones (1983, 1984). Let H be the set of all μ-continuous vector measures from $\mathcal{A} \to X$. By example 1, the Lyapunov Convexity Property holds in H with respect to $(X, \mathcal{X}_1)$ as well as $(X, \mathcal{X}_2)$. If V is open with respect to $\mathcal{X}_2$, then the price system we obtain for a core allocation is also weak star continuous, hence the price system can be represented by a continuous function on K.

Example 9. The agents' space $(A, \mathcal{A}, \mu)$ is a finite measure space. The commodity space X is a Banach space. A sequence $\{x_n\} \subset X$ is called a Schauder basis if each $x \in X$ has a unique representation,

$$x = \sum_{n=1}^{\infty} \alpha_n x_n.$$

A Schauder basis $\{x_n\}$ is called boundedly complete if for each scalar sequence $\{\alpha_n\}$ such that

$$\sup_n \left\| \sum_{k=1}^{n} \alpha_k x_k \right\| < \infty$$

then $\sum_{n=1}^{\infty} \alpha_n x_n$ converges.

We assume that X has a boundedly complete Schauder basis. By DU (p. 64), X has the Radon-Nikodým Property. Hence if we let H be the set of all μ-continuous vector measures of bounded variation, then H has the Lyapunov Convexity Property (a special case of example 3). This example can be applied to the space ℓ_1.

6. Individualistic Representation

Let $(A, \mathcal{A}, \mu)$ be a finite measure space, X be a Banach space. An allocation is specified by a Bochner integrable function $g : A \to X$. Let IH be the space of all such Bochner integrable functions. The individual endowment is represented by $e : A \to X$, $e \in IH$. A generic element of A will be denoted by $t \in A$. Hence $e(t)$ or e_t refers to the value of e at t. For each $x \in X$, we can define the constant function, denoted by $\tilde{x} : t \to x$.

For each $t \in A$, we assign a partial ordering $\succ_t \in X \times X$ satisfying the following properties

(R.1) V is an open convex set having 0 as a boundary point.
(R.2) For all $t \in A$, $x \in X$, $k \in V$, we have $x + k \succ_t x$.
(R.3) If $x \succ_t y$ then $x + k \succ_t y$ for all $t \in A$, $k \in V$.

The continuity assumption can be rephrased as:

(C′) If $x \succ_t y$ then there exists $\varepsilon > 0$ such that $x - k \succ_t y$ for all $k \in V$, $\|k\| < \varepsilon$.

The above descriptions completely specify an individualistic representation of an economy. To obtain a coalitional representation, we can define H to be the space of all vector measures defined by $f(a) = \int_a g d\mu$ for some $g \in IH$. There is a one-to-one correspondence between IH and H. Define w by $w(a) = \int_a e d\mu$. For $\tilde{x} \in IH$, we have $\hat{x}(a) = \int_a \tilde{x} d\mu$. Let $g \in IH$ and $f \in H$ is defined by $f(a) = \int_a g d\mu$, then $f|a_0$ is defined by $a \to \int_{a \cap a_0} g d\mu$. Hence $f|a_0 \in H$. It is easy to see that H satisfies all the conditions (H.1)~(H.5) in section 2.

For each $f \in H$, we denote the corresponding $g \in IH$ by df. Given $a \in \mathcal{A}$, $\mu(a) > 0$, define $\succ_a \in H \times H$ by $f \succ_a g$ if and only if $df(t) \succ_t dg(t)$ μ *a.e* in a. Then clearly all conditions (P.1)~(P.3) in section 2 are satisfied, and we have specified a system of coalitional preferences. Moreover (V.1)~(V.3) are also satisfied, and (C) is satisfied if (C′) is satisfied.

Now all results in section 2, 3 and 4 apply to our economy with H as the space of coalitional allocations, μ nonatomic, and X can be any Banach space with the norm topology, and we obtain the Core-Walras equivalence results in the individualistic representation. See also example 2 in section 5.

7. A Discussion of the Literature

This is a vast subject. I can only be illustrative here. In the following comparisons, we should remember that the paper deals with models without consumption constraints, while all the works cited below deal with models with constraints. The comparisons are subject to this qualification. However, this qualification will be removed in the future.

For the finite dimensional commodity space, the result here reduces to the result in Cheng (1986). By comparison, our analysis does not use the continuity assumptions in Aumann (1964), Armstrong and Richter (1984). However we do rely on the free disposal assumption which is not needed in Hildenbrand (1968).

For the infinite dimensional commodity space, Bewley's (1973) result can be phrased in the terminology here as follows: He uses the individualistic representation; the integration he uses is more similar to the Pettis Integral; he assumes Mackey-continuity of preferences. The measurability assumptions he uses can be interpreted as restrictions on the allocations. For an alternative result, see example 7 in section 5.

For the model of Mas-Colell (1975), the result can be rephrased as follows: He represents the economy as a probability measure on the space of consumer characteristics which is taken to be a compact metric space. He uses the weak star topology (induced by the space of continuous functions on the characteristics space) which is even weaker than the weak topology, and assumes preference relations to be weak star continuous. V is taken to be weak star open and contains the axis of the divisible commodity. The set of allocations is uniformly bounded, hence is more restrictive and is only a subset of a linear space. For an alternative result, see example 8 in section 5.

The paper by Gretsky and Ostroy (1985) is most similar to our framework. There is a similar price-free characterization of Walrasian allocations, but the two sets being separated are different. The major difference is explained by our assumption that V is an open set. We should emphasize again that this does not mean that we are dealing only with positive cones with a nonempty interior. In the presence of positive constraints, this only means that there exists an open V such that whenever x, y are in the positive cone, $x - y \in V$ then x is preferred to y by all agents. Another major difference is our use of an axiomatic treatment of the space of allocations. This allows us to formulate a general *Principle of Equivalence.* Example 9 is an alternative formulation of the equivalence result in Ostroy (1984), which also contains an existence result.

Zame (1986) allows the space of allocations to include vector measures of unbounded variation. But additional complicated assumptions are made to obtain the equivalence result. He also provides many interesting examples of the existence problem. There is also a more extensive discussion of the relationship between individualistic and coalitional representations.

Aliprantis, Brown and Burkinshaw (1985, 1986) investigate the relationship between core allocations and equilibria in the replicated case in pure exchange as well as production economies.

References

Aliprantis, C. D., Brown, D. J., and Burkinshaw, O., 1985, "Edgeworth Equilibria," Cowles Foundation Discussion paper.

Aliprantis, C. D., Brown, D. J. and Burkinshaw, O., 1986, "Edgeworth Equilibria in Production Economies," Cowles Foundation Discussion paper.

Anderson, R., 1978, "An Elementary Core Equivalence Theorem," *Econometrica* **46**, 1483–1487.

Armstrong, T. and Richter, M. K., 1984, "The Core-Walras Equivalence," *J. Econ. Theory* **33**, 116–151.

Armstrong, T. and Richter, M. K., 1986, "Existence of Non-atomic Core-Walras Allocations," *J. Econ. Theory* **38**, 137–159.

Aumann, R., 1964, "Markets with a Continuum of Traders," *Econometrica* **32**, 39–50.

Bewley, T., 1972, "Existence of Equilibria in Economies with Infinitely Many Commodities," *J. Econ. Theory* **4**, 514–540.

Bewley, T., 1973, "The Equality of the Core and the Set of Equilibria in Economies with Infinitely Many Commodities and Continuum of Agents," *Int. Econ. Rev.* **14**, 383–393.

Brown, D. J. and Khan, M. A., 1980, "An Extension of the Brown-Robinson Equivalence Theorem," *Appl. Math. Comp.* **6**, 167–175.

Brown, D. J. and Robinson, A., 1975, "Nonstandard Exchange Economies," *Econometrica* **43**, 41–55.

Champsaur, P. and Laroque, G., 1971, "Notes Sur Les Mechanismes de Blocage," unpublished manuscript, Paris.

Cheng, Harrison H. C., 1986, "The Coalitional Approach to the Core Theory," *J. Math. Econ.*, forthcoming.

Cheng, Harrison H. C., 1987a, "Arbitrage Theory and Equilibrium: The Case of Unconstrained Consumption," MRG Working Paper M8719, Department of Economics, University of Southern California.

Cheng, Harrison H. C., 1987b, "The Existence of Arbitrage-Free Equilibria in Banach Spaces," MRG Working Paper M8712, Department of Economics, University of Southern California.

Cheng, Harrison H. C., 1987c, "Asset Market Equilibrium in Infinite Dimensional Economies," *J. Math. Econ.*, to appear.

Cheng, Harrison H. C., 1987d, "Dynamic Hedging, Arbitrage Pricing, and the Efficient Market Hypothesis: An Axiomatic Approach," Department of Economics, University of Southern California.

Debreu, G., 1962, "New Concepts and Techniques for Equilibrium Analysis," *Int. Econ. Rev.* **3**, 257–273.

Debreu, G., 1967, "Preference Functions on Measure Spaces of Economic Agents," *Econometrica* **35**, 111–122.

Debreu, G., 1986, "Theoretic Models: Mathematical Form and Economic Content," *Econometrica* **54**, 1259–1270.

Diestel, J. and Uhl, J. J., 1977, *Vector Measures*, Amer. Math. Soc., Math. Surveys **15**, Providence, Rhode Island.

Duffie, D. and Huang, C. F., 1985, "Implementing Arrow-Debreu Equilibria by Continuous Trading of Few Long-lived Securities," *Econometrica* **53**, 1337–1357.

Edgeworth, F., 881, *Mathematical Psychics*, Kegan Paul, London.

Gabszewicz, J., 1968, "Coeurs et Allocations Concurrentielles dans des Economies d'Echange avec un Continu de Biens," Librarie Universitair, Louvain.

Gretsky, N. and Ostroy, J., 1985, "Thick and Thin Market Non-Atomic Exchange Economies" in *Advances in Equilibrium Theory*, C. D. Aliprantis, O. Burkinshaw and N. J. Rothman, eds., Springer-Verlag, New York.

Grodal, B., 1972, "A Second Remark on the Core of an Atomless Economy," *Econometrica* **40**, 581–583.

Hansen, T., 1969, "A Note on the Limit of the Core of an Exchange Economy," *Int. Econ. Rev.* **10**, 479–483.

Harrison, J. M. and Kreps, D., 1979, "Martingales and Arbitrage in Multiperiod Securities Markets," *J. Econ. Theory* **20**, 381–408.

Hart, O., 1974, "On the Existence of Equilibrium in a Securities Model," *J. Econ. Theory* **9**, 293–311.

Hildenbrand, W., 1968, "The Core of an Economy with a Measure Space of Economic Agents," *Rev. Econ. Stud.* **35**, 443–452.

Holmes, R., 1975, *Geometric Functional Analysis and Its Applications*, Springer-Verlag, New York.

Jones, L., 1983, "Existence of Equilibria with Infinitely Many Consumers and Infinitely Many Commodities," *J. Math. Econ.* **12**, 119–138.

Jones, L., 1984, "A Competitive Model of Product Differentiation," *Econometrica* **52**, 507–530.

Khan, M. Ali, 1974a, "Some Remarks on the Core of a 'Large Economy'," *Econometrica* **42**, 633–642.

Khan, M. Ali, 1974b, "Some Equivalence Theorems," *Rev. Econ. Stud.* **41**, 549–565.

Kingman, J. and Robertson, A., 1968, "On a Theorem of Lyapunov," *J. London Math. Soc.* **43**, 347–351.

Kluvánek, I., 1973, "The Range of a Vector Valued Measure," *Math. Sys. Theory* **7**, 44–54.

Knowles, G., 1974, "Lyapunov Vector Measures," *SIAM J. Control* **13**, 294–

303.

Kreps, D., 1981, "Arbitrage and Equilibrium in Economies with Infinitely Many Commodities," *J. Math. Econ.* **8**, 15–36.

Lindenstrauss, L., 1966, "A Short Proof of Lyapunov's Convexity Theorem," *J. Math. Mech.* **15**, 971–972.

Lyapunov, A. A., 1940, " Sur les Fonctions-Vecteurs Complèment Additives," *Izvestija Akademii Nauk SSSR*, 465–478.

Mas-Colell, A., 1975, "A Model of Equilibrium with Differentiated Commodities," *J. Math. Econ.* **2**, 263–295.

Mas-Colell, A., 1978, "A Note on the Core Equivalence Theorem: How Many Blocking Coalitions Are There?" *J. Math. Econ.* **5**, 207–215.

Mas-Colell, A., 1982, "Perfect Competition and the Core," *Rev. Econ. Stud.* **49**, 15–30.

Mas-Colell, A., 1986, "The Price Equilibrium Existence Problem in Topological Vector Lattices," *Econometrica* **54**, 1039–1054.

Ostroy, J., 1984, "The Existence of Walrasian Equilibrium in Large-Square Economies," *J. Math. Econ.* **13**, 143–163.

Peleg, B. and Yaari, M., 1970, "Markets with Countably Many Commodities," *Int. Econ. Rev.* **11**, 369–377.

Radner, R., 1972, "Existence of Equilibrium of Plans, Prices, and Price Expectations in a Sequence of Markets," *Econometrica* **40**, 289–303.

Rashid, S., 1979, "The Relationship Between Measure-Theoretic and Non-Standard Exchange Economies," *J. Math. Econ.* **6**, 195–202.

Richter, M. K., 1971, "Coalitions, Core and Competition," *J. Econ. Theory* **3**, 323–334.

Rustichini, A. and Yannelis, N. C., 1991, "Edgeworth's Conjecture in Economies with a Continuum of Agents and Commodities," *J. Math. Econ.*, to appear.

Scarf, H., 1962, "Analysis of Markets with a Large Number of Participants," *Recent Advances in Game Theory*, Princeton University Press, Princeton, NJ.

Schaefer, H., 1980, *Topological Vector Spaces*, Springer-Verlag, New York.

Schmeidler, D., 1972, "A Remark on the Core of an Atomless Economy," *Econometrica* **40**, 579–580.

Uhl, J., 1969, "The Range of a Vector-Valued Measure," *Proc. Amer. Math. Soc.* **23**, 158–163.

Vind, K., 1964, "Edgeworth Allocations in an Exchange Economy with Many Traders," *Int. Econ. Rev.* **5**, 165–177.

Vind, K., 1973, " A Third Remark on the Core of an Atomless Economy," *Econometrica* **40**, 585–586.

Yannelis, N. C. and Zame, W. R., 1986, "Equilibria in Banach Lattices without Ordered Preferences," *J. Math. Econ.* **15**, 85–110.

Zame, W., 1986, "Markets with a Continuum of Traders and Infinitely Many Commodities," Department of Mathematics, SUNY at Buffalo.

PART 4

THE EXISTENCE OF AN EQUILIBRIUM IN ECONOMIES WITH A CONTINUUM OF AGENTS

A Very Weak Theorem on the Existence of Equilibria in Atomless Economies with Infinitely Many Commodities

Truman F. Bewley

Abstract. The equilibrium existence theorem we obtain resembles Robert Aumann's (1966) Auxiliary Theorem, in which he assumes that preferences are commodity-wise saturated. Our result may therefore be looked upon as a first step towards a satisfactory existence theorem for l_∞ (if such a theorem exists).

1. Introduction

It is by no means clear that a satisfactory equilibrium existence theorem exists in the case where there are both infinitely many commodities and infinitely many participants in an economy. We list three of the main mathematical difficulties involved.

(1) There exists no infinite dimensional version of Fatou's Lemma, similar to Schmeidler's version in the finite dimensional case. Such a theorem would enable one to prove at least that Pareto optima exist in economies with infinitely many agents and commodities. One might then search among the Pareto optima for an equilibrium.

(2) Budget sets in $\mathcal{L}_\infty$ are typically not norm bounded and hence not weak-star compact, even when they are defined by price systems in $\mathcal{L}_1$. Hence, budget sets need contain no maximal points for weak-star upper-semicontinuous preference orderings (counter-examples are easy to construct). It would be acceptable to assume that preference orderings are convex and Mackey continuous and hence weak-star upper-semicontinuous, but we see that in this case demand functions with respect to price systems in $\mathcal{L}_1$ need not be defined.

(3) The evaluation function $\pi \cdot x$ is not jointly continuous on $\mathcal{L}_\infty \times ba$ or on $\mathcal{L}_\infty \times \mathcal{L}_1$ when $\mathcal{L}_\infty$ is given the $\sigma(\mathcal{L}_\infty, \mathcal{L}_1)$ topology, ba the $\sigma(ba, \mathcal{L}_\infty)$ topology, and $\mathcal{L}_1$ the $\sigma(\mathcal{L}_1, \mathcal{L}_\infty)$ topology. This means that if some agent's demand function ξ were defined on a certain set of price systems, ξ would

not necessarily be $\sigma(\mathcal{L}_\infty, \mathcal{L}_1)$ continuous there. For suppose that π_λ were a net converging to π in the appropriate weak topology. Let ω be the agent's initial endowment and suppose that $\xi_{\pi_\lambda} \to x$ in the $\sigma(\mathcal{L}_\infty, \mathcal{L}_1)$ topology. Then, we would know that $\pi_\lambda \cdot \xi_{\pi_\lambda} = \pi_\lambda \cdot \omega \to \pi \cdot \omega$, but we would not know that $\pi_\lambda \cdot \xi_{\pi_\lambda} \to \pi_\lambda \cdot x$. Hence, we would not even know if x satisfied the budget constraint $\pi \cdot x \leq \pi \cdot \omega$, so that we certainly would not know that $x = \xi_\pi$. It would be very convenient to have the demand function be continuous with respect to the $\sigma(\mathcal{L}_\infty, \mathcal{L}_1)$ and $\sigma(ba, \mathcal{L}_1)$ or $\sigma(\mathcal{L}_1, \mathcal{L}_\infty)$ topologies, since these are the only topologies with respect to which one may hope to make compactness arguments.

We are able to prove an equilibrium existence theorem for pure trade economies by making highly restrictive assumptions which remove difficulties 1–3. We will assume that consumption sets are norm bounded and hence $\sigma(\mathcal{L}_\infty, \mathcal{L}_1)$ compact. This will remove difficulty (2) and make possible a compactness argument that removes difficulty (1). We will also assume that the commodity space is ℓ_∞. It happens that the Mackey topology coincides with the $\sigma(l_\infty, \ell_1)$ topology on bounded subsets of l_∞, and it is also true that if Π is a $\sigma(\ell_1, \ell_\infty)$ compact subset of ℓ_1 and if ℓ_∞ is given the Mackey topology, then the evaluation function is jointly continuous on $\ell_\infty \times \Pi$. These two facts remove difficulty (3).

2. Notation, Definitions, and Mathematical Results

We will make use of the concept of a topological space of economic agents introduced by Gerard Debreu in [1959]. Since we assume that there is no production, each agent will be described by his preferences and initial endowment. The *set of all possible economic agents will be* $A = \mathcal{P} \times l_\infty$, where $\mathcal{P}$ is the set of all subsets of $l_\infty \times l_\infty$. We will give $\mathcal{P}$ the topology of the uniformity $\mathcal{U}_p$ derived from the Mackey topology. We given A the product of this topology on $\mathcal{P}$ and the Mackey topology on l_∞.

$\omega : A \to l_\infty$ and $P : A \to \mathcal{P}$ will be the projections. If $a \in A$, $X(a) = \{x \in l_\infty : (x, y) \in P(a) \text{ or } (y, x) \in P(a) \text{ for some } y \in l_\infty\}$. If $(x, y) \in P(a)$, we will write $x \succsim_a y$. If $\pi \in ba$, $\beta_\pi(a) = \{x \in X(a) : \pi \cdot x \leq \pi \cdot \omega(a)\}$ and $\xi_\pi(a) = \{x \in \beta_\pi(a) : \text{if } y \in \beta_\pi(a), x \succsim_a y\}$.

$\omega_i(a)$ will denote the ith component of $\omega(a)$. Similarly, if $\pi \in \ell_1$, π_i will denote the ith component of π.

Following Werner Hildenbrand [1970], we will define an *economy* to be a positive Borel probability measure on A with compact support. By the Borel σ-field on A, we mean the σ-field generated by the open sets of A. By a Borel measure we mean one on the Borel sets. A *support* for a measure ν on A is defined to be a closed set $\operatorname{supp}\nu$ with the property that if U is open in A and $U \cap \operatorname{supp}\nu \neq \emptyset$, then $\nu(U) > 0$.

An economy ν will be said to be atomless if $\nu(\{a\}) = 0, \forall a \in A$.

An allocation for an economy ν will be a function $f : \operatorname{supp}\nu \to l_\infty$ such that $f(a) \in X(a), \forall a$ and measurable in the sense that is the limit in measure of a sequence of simple functions, the limit in ℓ_∞ being with respect to the supremum norm. An equilibrium is then an allocation f and a price system $\pi \in ba$ such that $\int f d\nu = \int \omega d\nu$ and $f(a) \in \xi_\pi(a)$, $\forall a \in \operatorname{supp}\nu$. The integral $\int f d\nu$ is defined to be a vector $x \in \ell_\infty$ such that $\pi \cdot x = \int \pi \cdot f d\nu$, for all $\pi \in \ell_1$. In our case, ξ_π will be a continuous function, so that it will simply be necessary to find a $\pi \in ba$ such that $\int \xi_\pi d\nu = \int \omega d\nu$.

The following simple fact is the reason for our choice of l_∞ as the commodity space.

F1. On norm bounded subsets of l_∞, the Mackey topology equals the product topology. The product topology is, of course, the topology of componentwise convergence.

Since by the Tychonoff Theorem [Kelley, 1955, p. 143], bounded subsets of l_∞ are compact in the product topology, F1 implies that

F2. Norm bounded subsets of l_∞ are Mackey relatively compact.

Let B be a bounded subset of l_∞ and let $\hat{\mathcal{P}} = \{P \in \mathcal{P} : P \subset B \times B\}$. Since the product topology is metrizable, it follows that the restriction of the uniformity $\mathfrak{U}_p$ to $\hat{\mathcal{P}}$ is also metrizable. It follows that

F3. If $\hat{A}$ is a subset of A such that P and ω are uniformly bounded on $\hat{A}$, then the restriction of the topology on A to $\hat{A}$ is metrizable.

Let ev be the function on $\ell_\infty \times \ell_1$ defined by $ev(x, \pi) = \pi \cdot x$. We have already mentioned the fact that

F4. If Π is a $\sigma(\ell_1, \ell_\infty)$ compact subset of ℓ_1, then ev is jointly continuous on $\ell_\infty \times \Pi$ with respect to the product of the Mackey topology on ℓ_∞ and the $\sigma(\ell_1, \ell_\infty)$ topology on Π.

F4 follows from the fact that the Mackey topology is the topology of uniform convergence on convex, circled, $\sigma(\ell_1, \ell_\infty)$ compact subsets of ℓ_1 [Schaefer, 1966, p. 131]. Let $x_l \to x \in \ell_\infty$ in the Mackey topology and $\pi_\lambda \to \pi$ in the $\sigma(\ell_1, \ell_\infty)$ topology. $|\pi_l \cdot x_\lambda| \leq |\pi_\lambda \cdot (x_\lambda - x)| + |(\pi_\lambda - \pi) \cdot x|$. The first term goes to zero since the $\{\pi_\lambda\}$ belong to a weakly compact set in ℓ_1, and the second term goes to zero because $\pi_\lambda \to x$ weakly.

3. The Existence Theorem and Its Proof

Theorem. *Let the commodity space be l_∞ and let the set of agents A be as in the previous section. Let ν be an atomless measure on A with compact support. Suppose that $\forall a \in \operatorname{supp} \nu$,*

(i) $X(a) = \hat{X} = \{x \in l_\infty^+ : \|x\|_\infty \leq c\}$, *where* $c > 2$,

(ii) $1 \leq \omega_j \leq c - 1$, $j = 1, \ldots, \infty$,

(iii) $P(a)$ *defines a transitive, reflexive, and complete preference ordering,*

(iv) (continuity) $P(a)$ *is closed,*

(v) (strong monotonicity) if $x, z \in \hat{X}$ *and* $x > z$, *then* $x \succsim_a z$,

(vi) (strict convexity) if $x, z \in \hat{X}$ *and if* $x \succsim_a z$, *then* $\alpha x + (1-\alpha) z >_a z$, $\forall 0 < \alpha < 1$.

Then, ν has an equilibrium with price system in ℓ_1.

We will find an equilibrium for ν by taking the limit of equilibria for finite economies approximating ν. First we need to check that any finite economy whose agents are in $\operatorname{supp} \nu$ has an equilibrium with respect to a price system in *ba*.

If $a \in \operatorname{supp} \nu$, we extend $\succsim_a$ to a preference ordering, on l_∞^+. Let Δ be the ray $\{r\vec{l} : r \geq 0\}$, where $\vec{l}$ is the vector $(1, 1, \ldots)$. We extend $\succsim_a$ to $\hat{X} \cup \Delta$ by letting $r'\vec{l} \succsim_a r\vec{l}$ if and only if $r' \geq r$. Define $S : l_\infty^+ \to \hat{X} \cup \Delta$ by

$$S(x) = \begin{cases} x, & \text{if } x \in \hat{X} \cup \Delta \\ (\inf_j x_j)\vec{l}, & \text{if } x \geq c\vec{l} \\ x \wedge c\vec{l}, & \text{otherwise,} \end{cases}$$

where $x \wedge c\vec{l}$ is the vector whose jth component is $\min(x_j, c)$. If $x, x' \in l_\infty^+$, let $x \succsim_a x'$ if and only if $S(x) \succsim_a S(x')$.[1] It is easy to verify that the resulting preordering is $\sigma(l_\infty, \mathcal{L}_1)$ upper-semi-continuous and norm lower-semi-continuous. Thus, any finite economy drawn from $\operatorname{supp}\nu$ and with the extended preorderings satisfies the assumptions of Theorem 1 of Bewley [1972], so that the extended economy has an equilibrium with a non-negative price system in ba. Clearly, the equilibrium consumptions must lie in $\hat{X}$, so that we in fact have an equilibrium for the original economy.

Let $\Pi_e = \{\pi \in ba : \|\pi\| = 1$ and π is an equilibrium price system for some finite economy whose participants lie in $\operatorname{supp}\nu\}$. Since Π_e is contained in the positive cone of ba, zero does not lie in its closure. In fact, much more is true.

Lemma 1. *The $\sigma(ba, l_\infty)$ closure of Π_e is a $\sigma(\ell_1, l_\infty)$ compact subset of ℓ_1.*

Proof. Since Π_e is $\sigma(ba, l_\infty)$ relatively compact, it suffices to show that the $\sigma(ba, l_\infty)$ closure of Π_e is contained in ℓ_1. So let π_λ be a net in Π_e converging in the $\sigma(ba, l_\infty)$ topology to $\bar{\pi}$. Let $\bar{\pi} = \bar{\pi}_c + \bar{\pi}_p$, as in Yosida-Hewitt [1956] Theorem A. It suffices to show that $\bar{\pi}_p = 0$. Before doing so, we show that

$$\bar{\pi}_c \neq 0 \tag{1}$$

Clearly (1) follows from

(2) there exists N such that $\pi(E_N) < \frac{c-1}{c}$, $\forall \pi \in \Pi_e$, where $E_N = \{N, N+1, \ldots\}$.

We now prove (2). Let $\hat{X}' = \{x \in \hat{X} : x_1 \leq c-1\}$. Clearly, $\hat{X}'$ is compact. Let $T_n : \hat{X}' \to \hat{X}$ be defined by $T_n(x) = (\min(x_1 + 1, c), x_2, \ldots, x_n, 0, 0, \ldots)$. T_n is continuous. By the monotonicity and continuity of preferences, we see that for each $a \in \operatorname{supp}\nu$ and $x \in \hat{X}'$, there exists $N(a, x)$ such that if $n \geq N(a, x)$, then $T_n(x) \succ_a x$. By the compactness of $(\operatorname{supp}\nu) \times \hat{X}'$, it follows that there exists N such that if $n \geq N$, then $T_n(x) \succ_a x$, $\forall (a, x) \in (\operatorname{supp}\nu) \times \hat{X}'$.

---

[1] This method of extending a preference relation defined on a truncated consumption set is the natural extension of the method used by Robert Aumann [1966].

Suppose that $\pi \in \Pi_e$ and $\pi(E_N) \geq \frac{c-1}{c}$. Then, for any $(a,x) \in (\operatorname{supp}\nu) \times \hat{X}'$, $\pi \cdot T_N(x) \leq \frac{1}{c}c = 1 \leq \pi \cdot \omega(a)$, where the last inequality follows from assumption (ii). Thus, for no a does $\xi_\pi(a)$ lie in $\hat{X}'$. Hence, if $\mathcal{E}$ is a finite subset of A, $\sum_{a\in\mathcal{E}} \xi_1(a,\pi) > (\#\mathcal{E})(c-1)$, where $\#\mathcal{E}$ is the number of of elements in $\mathcal{E}$. But by assumption (ii), $\sum_{a\in\mathcal{E}} \omega_1(a) \leq (\#\mathcal{E})(c-1)$. This implies that π cannot be an equilibrium price system for $\mathcal{E}$, and hence that $\pi \notin \Pi_e$. This proves (2).

Now suppose that $\bar{\pi}_p \neq 0$. Let $0 < \varepsilon < \min\left(\frac{\|\bar{\pi}_p\|}{2}, \frac{\|\bar{\pi}_c\|}{2}\right)$. Choose N_1 so that

$$\bar{\pi}_c(E_{N_1}) < \frac{\varepsilon}{4c}. \tag{3}$$

Let $n \geq N_1$. We define a function $T_n(a,\cdot) : \beta_{\bar{\pi}_c}(a) \to \hat{X}$. If $x \in \beta_{\bar{\pi}_c}(a)$, if $1 \leq i \leq n$, and if $0 \leq \alpha \leq 1$, let $x^{i,\alpha}$ be defined by

$$x_j^{i,\alpha} = \begin{cases} c, & \text{if } 1 < j < i, \\ \alpha c + (1-\alpha)x_i, & \text{if } j = i, \\ x_j, & \text{if } i < j \leq n, \\ 0, & \text{if } j > n. \end{cases}$$

There exists an i and an α such that

$$\bar{\pi}_c \cdot x^{i,\alpha} = \bar{\pi}_c \cdot \omega(a) + \frac{\varepsilon}{4}, \tag{4}$$

for $\bar{\pi}_c \cdot x^{i,\alpha}$ is non-decreasing in i and α, $\bar{\pi}_c \cdot x^{1,0} = \bar{\pi}_c \cdot x \leq \bar{\pi}_c \cdot \omega(a)$, and

$$\begin{aligned} \bar{\pi}_c \cdot x^{n,1} &\geq c \sum_{i=1}^{N_1} \bar{\pi}_{c_i} \\ &\geq c \sum_{i=1}^{\infty} \bar{\pi}_{c_i} - \frac{\varepsilon}{4} \\ &\geq (c-1) \sum_{i=1}^{\infty} \bar{\pi}_{c_i} + 2\varepsilon - \frac{\varepsilon}{4} \\ &\geq \bar{\pi}_c \cdot \omega(a) + \frac{7\varepsilon}{4} \\ &> \bar{\pi}_c \cdot \omega(a) + \frac{\varepsilon}{4}. \end{aligned}$$

Let $(\underline{i}, \underline{\alpha})$ be the smallest i and then the smallest α such that (4) holds and then let $T_n(a,x) = x^{\underline{i},\underline{\alpha}}$.

T_n is continuous in a and x. For each a and x, there is $N_2(a,x)$ such that if $n \geq N_2(a,x)$, then $T_n(a,x) \succ_a x$. By an easy compactness argument, it follows that there exists $N_2 \geq N_1$ such that if $n \geq N_2$, then $T_n(a,x) \succ_a x$, $\forall a \in \operatorname{supp} \nu$, $x \in \beta_{\bar{\pi}_c}(a)$.

Choose λ_1 so that if $\lambda \geq \lambda_1$, then

$$\left|\pi_i^\lambda - \bar{\pi}_{c_i}\right| < \frac{\varepsilon}{4cN_2}, \quad i = 1, \ldots, N_2, \tag{5}$$

and

$$\left|\pi^\lambda(E_{N_2}) - \bar{\pi}(E_{N_2})\right| < \varepsilon. \tag{6}$$

Such a λ_1 exists since $\pi^\lambda \to \bar{\pi}$ in the $\sigma(ba, l_\infty)$ topology.

If $x \in \beta_{\bar{\pi}_c}(a)$ and $\lambda \geq \lambda_1$, then

$$\begin{aligned}
\pi^\lambda \cdot T_{N_2}(a,x) &= \sum_{i=1}^{N_2} \pi_i^\lambda \cdot T_{N_2}(a,x)_i \\
&\leq \sum_{i=1}^{N_2} \bar{\pi}_{c_i} T_{N_2}(a,x)_i + \frac{\varepsilon}{4} \qquad \text{(by (5))} \\
&\leq \bar{\pi}_c \omega(a) + \frac{\varepsilon}{2} \qquad \text{(by the definition of } T_{N_2}(a,x)) \\
&\leq \sum_{i=1}^{N_2} \pi_{c_i} \cdot \omega_i(a) + \frac{3\varepsilon}{4} \qquad \text{(by (3) and because } N_2 \geq N_1) \\
&\leq \sum_{i=1}^{N_2} \pi_i^\lambda \cdot \omega_i(a) + \varepsilon \qquad \text{(by (5))} \\
&\leq \sum_{i=1}^{N_2} \pi_i^\lambda \cdot \omega_i(a) + \pi^\lambda(E_{N_2}) \qquad \begin{array}{l}\text{(by (6) and because} \\ \text{by the choice of } \varepsilon, \\ \bar{\pi}(E_{N_2}) > 2\varepsilon)\end{array} \\
&\leq \pi^\lambda \cdot \omega(a).
\end{aligned}$$

We must see that if $\lambda \geq \lambda_1$, $T_{N_2}(a,x) \in \beta_{\pi^\lambda}(a)$, $\forall a \in \operatorname{supp} \nu$ and $\forall x \in \beta_{\bar{\pi}_c}(a)$. Hence, $\xi_{\pi^\lambda}(a) \notin \beta_{\bar{\pi}_c}(a)$, $\forall a$. But this is impossible, for if $\pi_c \cdot \xi_{\pi^\lambda}(a) > \bar{\pi}_c \cdot \omega(a)$, $\forall a$, there can exist no finite set $\mathcal{E} \subset \operatorname{supp} \nu$ such that $\sum_{a \in \mathcal{E}} \xi_{\pi^\lambda}(a) = \sum_{a \in \mathcal{E}} \omega(a)$ and hence, $\pi^\lambda \notin \Pi_e$. This contradiction proves that $\bar{\pi}_p = 0$. Q.E.D.

Let $\bar{\Pi}_e$ be the $\sigma(\mathcal{L}_1, l_\infty)$ closure of Π_e and let $\bar{\Pi}_e$ have the $\sigma(\ell_1, l_\infty)$ topology. The compactness of $\bar{\Pi}_e$ has the following consequence.

Lemma 2. $\xi : \operatorname{supp} \nu \times \bar{\Pi}_e \to X$ *is uniformly continuous.*

Proof. Since $(\operatorname{supp} \nu) \times \bar{\Pi}_e$ is compact, it is enough to show that ξ is continuous on $A \times \bar{\Pi}_e$. Let (a_λ, π^λ) be a net in $A \times \bar{\Pi}_e$ converging to (a, π). Since $\hat{X}$ is compact, it suffices to show that every cluster point of $\xi_{\pi^\lambda}(a_\lambda)$ is equal to $\xi_\pi(a)$. Let x be such a cluster point. A subnet of $\xi_{\pi^\lambda}(a_\lambda)$ converges to x, call it $\xi_{\pi^\lambda}(a_\lambda)$.

We show that $x \succsim_a \xi_\pi(a)$. Let $z \in \hat{X}$ be such that $\pi \cdot z < \pi \cdot \omega(a)$. Since $\bar{\Pi}_e$ is weakly compact and ω is Mackey continuous, it follows from F4 that

$$\pi^\lambda \cdot \omega(a_\lambda) \to \pi \cdot \omega(a), \tag{1}$$

so that for sufficiently large λ, $\pi^\lambda \cdot z \leq \pi^\lambda \cdot \omega(a_\lambda)$. But then, for these λ, $\xi_{\pi^\lambda}(a_\lambda) \succsim_{a_\lambda} z$. Since $\xi_{\pi^\lambda}(a_\lambda) \to x$ and $a_\lambda \to a$, it follows that $x \succsim_a z$. Since $\omega(a) \gg 0$, $\{z \in x : \pi \cdot z < \pi \cdot \omega(a)\}$ is dense in $\beta_\pi(a)$. Hence, $x \succsim_a \xi_\pi(a)$.

Since by F4, $\pi^\lambda \cdot \xi_{\pi^\lambda}(a_\lambda) \to \pi \cdot x$, it follows from (1) that $\pi \cdot x \leq \pi \cdot \omega(a)$. Hence, by strong convexity, $x = \xi_\pi(a)$. Q.E.D.

Lemma 2 implies $\{\xi_\pi(\cdot) : \pi \in \bar{\Pi}_e\}$ is uniformly equicontinuous. This fact makes the proof of the Theorem almost trivial.

Proof of Theorem. By F3, we may choose a metric d for the topology on $\operatorname{supp} \nu$. For each positive integer n, there exists a partition of $\operatorname{supp} \nu$ into sets $F_{n,1}, \ldots, F_{n,N_n}$ such that $\nu(F_{n,i}) = \frac{1}{N_n}$, $\forall i$, and such that $\operatorname{diam} F_{n,i} = \operatorname{supp}\{d(a, a') : a, a' \in F_{n,i}\} < \frac{1}{n}$, $\forall i$. The existence of such a partition follows from an inductive argument using the fact that atomless measures have convex range.

Let $a_{n,i} \in F_{n,u}$ and $\mathcal{E}_n$ be the economy $(a_{n,i}, \ldots, a_{n,N_n})$. $\mathcal{E}_n$ has an equilibrium price system $\pi_n \in \Pi_e$. Let $\pi \in \ell_1$ be a cluster point of the sequence π_n and let $\pi_{n(\lambda)}$ be a subnet converging to π.

Let $\hat{\xi}_n : \operatorname{supp} \nu \to \hat{X}$ be defined by $\hat{\xi}_n(a) = \sum_{i=1}^{N_n} \chi_{F_{n,i}}(a) \xi_{\pi_n}(a_{n,i})$, where $\chi_{F_{n,i}}$ is the indicator function of $F_{n,i}$. Clearly $\int \hat{\xi}_n d\nu = \frac{1}{N_n} \sum_{i=1}^{N_n} \xi_{\pi_n}(a_{n,i}) = \frac{1}{N_n} \sum \omega(a_{n,i})$. Since the diameters of the $F_{n,i}$'s decrease to zero uniformly and since the $\xi(\cdot, \pi_n)$ are uniformly equicontinuous, it follows that $\left| \int \hat{\xi}_{n(\lambda)} d\nu - \int \xi_{\pi_n(\lambda)} d\nu \right| \to 0$. Similarly, $\sum \frac{1}{N_n} \omega(a_{n(\lambda),i}) \to \int \omega d\nu$. Hence, $\int \xi_\pi d\nu = \int \omega d\nu$ and π is an equilibrium price system for ν. Q.E.D.

References

Aumann, R., 1966, "Existence of Competitive Equilibria in Markets with a Continuum of Traders," *Econometrica* **34**, 1–17.

Bewley, Truman, 1972, "Existence of Equilibria in Economies with Infinitely Many Commodities," *J. Econ. Theory* **4**, 514–540.

Debreu, G., 1959, *Theory of Value*, John Wiley and Sons, New York.

Hildenbrand, W., 1970, "On Economies with Many Agents," *J. Econ. Theory* **2**, 161–168.

Kelley, J. L., 1955, *General Topology*, van Nostrand, New York.

Schaefer, H. H., 1971, *Topological Vector Spaces*, Springer, New York and Berlin.

Yosida, K. and Hewitt, E., 1956, "Finitely Additive Measure," *Amer. Math. Soc. Trans.* **72**, 46-66.

Equilibria in Markets with a Continuum of Agents and Commodities

M. Ali Khan and Nicholas C. Yannelis

Abstract. We prove the existence of an equilibrium for an exchange economy with a measure space of agents and with an infinite dimensional commodity space.

1. Introduction

The purpose of this paper is to prove the existence of a competitive equilibrium for an economy with a measure space of agents and with an infinite dimensional commodity space.

The principle ways our result differs from that of Bewley (1990) are: (a) we assume that the consumption set of each agent is a weakly compact subset of either the space of continuous functions on a compact metric space $C(X)$, or the Lebesgue space L_∞; (b) the measure space of agents need not be atomless; and (c) we provide a direct proof, i.e., we do not need to use the Aumann (1966) existence result as Bewley does.

The paper proceeds as follows: Section 2 contains some notation and definitions. In Section 3 the main result of the paper is stated. An auxiliary result is stated in Section 4 and its proof is given in Section 5. Section 6 contains the proof of the main theorem. Finally some concluding remarks are given in Section 7.

2. Notation and Definitions

2.1 Notation.

2^A denotes the set of all nonempty subsets of the set A;
con A denotes the convex hull of the set A;
$\overline{\text{con}}A$ denotes the closed convex hull of the set A;
$\setminus$ denotes the set theoretic subtraction;
$\mathbb{R}^\ell$ denotes the ℓ-fold Cartesian product of the set of real numbers $\mathbb{R}$;
$\emptyset$ denotes the empty set.

2.2 Definitions. Let X, Y be two topological spaces. A set-valued function (or correspondence) $\phi : X \to 2^Y$ is said to be *upper semicontinuous* (u.s.c.) if the set $\{x \in X : \phi(x) \subset V\}$ is open in X for every open subset V of Y. Throughout the paper we will consider the setting where X is a metric space and Y is a Banach space. In this setting we will say that ϕ is *norm* u.s.c., if the set $\{x \in X : \phi(x) \subset V\}$ is open in X for every norm open subset V of Y. Furthermore, we will say that ϕ is *weakly* u.s.c., if the set $\{x \in X : \phi(x) \subset V\}$ is open in X for every weakly open subset V of Y.

Let X and Y be sets. The *graph* of the correspondence $\phi : X \to 2^Y$ is denoted by $G_\phi = \{(x, y) \in X \times Y : y \in \phi(x)\}$.

We now define the notion of a Bochner integrable function. Let (T, τ, μ) be a finite measure space, and X be a Banach space. A function $f : T \to X$ is called *simple* if there exist $x_1, x_2, \ldots, x_n$ in X and $\tau_1, \tau_2, \ldots, \tau_n$ in τ such that $f = \sum_{i=1}^n x_i \chi_{\tau_i}$, where

$$\chi_{\tau_i}(t) = \begin{cases} 1 & \text{if } t \in \tau_i \\ 0 & \text{if } t \notin \tau_i. \end{cases}$$

A function $f : T \to X$ is said to be *μ-measurable* if there exists a sequence of simple functions $f_n : T \to X$ such that $\lim_{n\to\infty} \|f_n(t) - f(t)\| = 0$ for almost all $t \in T$. A μ-measurable function $f : T \to X$ is said to be *Bochner integrable* if there exists a sequence of simple functions $\{f_n : n = 1, 2, \ldots\}$ such that

$$\lim_{n\to\infty} \int_T \|f_n(t) - f(t)\| d\mu(t) = 0.$$

In this case we define for each $E \in \tau$ the integral to be $\int_E f(t) d\mu(t) = \lim_{n\to\infty} \int_E f_n(t) d\mu(t))$. It is a standard result [see Diestel-Uhl (1977, Theorem 2, p. 45)] that, if $f : T \to X$ is a μ-measurable function then ϕ is Bochner integrable if and only if $\int_T \|f(t)\| d\mu(t) < \infty$.

Let (T, τ, μ) be a complete finite measure space, i.e., μ is a real-valued, non-negative countably additive measure defined on a complete σ-field τ of subsets of T such that $\mu(T) < \infty$. Let X be a Banach space. We denote by $L_1(\mu, X)$ the space of equivalence classes of X-valued Bochner integrable functions $f : T \to X$ normed by

$$\|f\| = \int_T \|f(t)\| d\mu(t).$$

Normed by the functional $\|\cdot\|$ above, $L_1(\mu, X)$ becomes a Banach space [(see Diestel-Uhl (1977, p. 50)]. A correspondence $\phi : T \to 2^X$ is said to have a *measurable graph* if $G_\phi \in \tau \otimes \beta(X)$ where $\beta(X)$ denotes the Borel σ-algebra on X and $\otimes$ denotes product σ-algebra. The correspondence $\phi : T \to 2^X$ is said to be *lower measurable* if for every open subset V of X the set $\{t \in T : \phi(t) \cap V \neq \emptyset\}$ belongs to τ. The correspondence $\phi : T \to 2^X$ is said to be *integrably bounded* if there exists a map $h \in L_1(\mu, \mathbb{R})$ such that for almost all $t \in T$, $\sup\{\|x\| : x \in \phi(t)\} \leq h(t)$. A *measurable selection* for the correspondence $\phi : T \to 2^X$ is a measurable function $f : T \to X$ such that $f(t) \in \phi(t)$ for almost all $t \in T$. A well-known result of Aumann (1967) says that if ϕ is a correspondence from a complete finite measure space to a separable metric space such that ϕ has a measurable graph and it is nonempty valued, then ϕ has a measurable selection. Following Aumann (1965) we now define the notion of the Aumann integral. Let T be a finite measure space, X be a Banach space and $\phi : T \to 2^X$ be a correspondence. We denote by S^1_ϕ the set of all X-valued Bochner integrable selections for $\phi(\cdot)$, i.e., $S^1_\phi = \{x \in L_1(\mu, X) : x(t) \in \phi(t)$ for almost all $t \in T\}$. In the sequel we will call the above set, *the set of integrable selections.* We are now ready to define the integral of the correspondence $\phi(\cdot)$ as follows:

$$\int_T \phi(t) d\mu(t) = \left\{ \int_T x(t) d\mu(t) : x(\cdot) \in S^1_\phi \right\}.$$

We will denote the above integral as $\int \phi(\cdot)$, and call it the *Aumann integral.* We now state a result which will play a crucial role in the sequel. This is *Diestel's Theorem* [Diestel (1977)], which says that if $K : T \to 2^Y$ (here T is a finite measure space and Y is a separable Banach space) is an integrably bounded, convex, nonempty weakly compact valued correspondence, then S^1_K is weakly compact in $L_1(\mu, Y)$.

3. The Main Theorem

3.1 The Model. We now turn to the main result of the paper, i.e., the existence of a competitive equilibrium in economies with infinitely many commodities and agents.

Denote by E the *commodity space*, where E is an ordered separable Banach space whose positive cone E_+ has an *interior point* u. An *economy* $\mathcal{E}$ is a quadruple $[(T,\tau,\mu), X, \succsim, e]$ where

(1) (T,τ,μ) is a measure *space of agents*;
(2) $X : T \to 2^{E_+}$ is the *consumption correspondence*,
(3) $\succsim_t \subset X(t) \times X(t)$ is the *preference relation* of agent t,
(4) $e : T \to E_+$ is the *initial endowment* where for all $t \in T$, $e(t) \in X(t)$ and for all $t \in T$, $e(t)$ belongs to a norm compact subset of $X(t)$.

Denote the *budget set* of agent t at prices p by $B(t,p) = \{x \in X(t) : p \cdot x \leq p \cdot e(t)\}$. The *demand set* of agent t at prices p is defined as $D(t,p) = \{x \in B(t,p) : \text{for all } y \in B(t,p), x \succsim_t y\}$.

A *competitive equilibrium* for $\mathcal{E}$ is a price-consumption pair (p,f), $p \in E_+^*/\{0\}$, $f \in L_1(\mu, E_+)$ such that:

(i) $f(t) \in D(t,p)$ for almost all t in T, and
(ii) $\int_T f(t)d\mu(t) \leq \int_T e(t)d\mu(t)$.

3.2 Assumptions. The following assumptions which are standard in equilibrium analysis will be needed to prove our Main Theorem.

(3.1) (T,τ,μ) is a complete finite measure space.

(3.2) The correspondence $X : T \to 2^{E_+}$ is integrably bounded, closed, convex, nonempty, weakly compact valued, and it has a measurable graph, i.e., $G_X \in \tau \otimes \beta(E_+)$.

(3.2′) The correspondence $X : T \to 2^{E_+}$ is closed, convex, nonempty, norm compact valued and it has a measurable graph.

(3.3) (a) For each $t \in T$ and each $x \in X(t)$ the set $R(t,x) = \{y \in X(t) : y \succsim_t x\}$ is convex, and norm closed and the set $R^{-1}(t,x) = \{y \in X(t) : x \succsim_y\}$ is norm closed, (b) $\succsim_t$ is measurable in the sense that the set $\{(t,x,y) \in T \times E_+ \times E_+ : y \succsim_t x\}$ belongs to $\tau \otimes \beta(E_+) \otimes \beta(E_+)$.

(3.4) For all $t \in T$, there exists $z(t) \in X(t)$ such that $e(t) - z(t)$ belongs to the norm interior of E_+.

3.3 The Main Result. We are now ready to state our main result:

Main Theorem. *Let $\mathcal{E}$ be an economy satisfying (3.1)–(3.4). Then a competitive equilibrium exists in $\mathcal{E}$.*

A couple of comments are in order. Note that at a first glance, assumption (3.2) seems quite strong. In particular, traditionally the consumption sets are bounded from below *only*. However, in economies with a continuum of agents and commodities it has been shown by Zame (1987) that without the upper bound on the consumption sets, an equilibrium may not exist. Hence, if positive results need to be obtained the bound on the consumption sets must be imposed. Of course, once the bound on the consumption sets is imposed we are automatically in a world of either weakly compact or weak* compact consumption sets. For instance if the commodity space in any ordered (reflexive) Banach space and the consumption sets are norm bounded and (weakly) weak* closed, we can directly conclude by virtue of Alaoglu's Theorem [see Dunford-Schwartz (1966)] that the consumption sets are (weakly) weak* compact.

The weak compactness of consumption sets is needed to ensure that the set of all feasible allocations, i.e., $F = \{x \in S^1_X : \int_T x(t)d\mu(t) \leq \int_T e(t)d\mu(t)\}$ is weakly compact. In particular, under assumption (3.2) it follows from Diestel's Theorem that S^1_X is weakly compact and from this we can conclude that F is weakly compact as well. Notice that in economies with finitely (or even countably) many agents and infinitely many commodities the set of feasible allocations belongs to an order interval. Since order intervals are typically compact in the "compatible" topology that the commodity space is endowed with, the set of feasible allocations is always compact in the "compatible" topology. For instance if E is an ordered (reflexive) Banach space endowed with the (weak) weak* topology, one can easily see that order intervals are norm bounded and (weakly) weak* closed, hence, by Alaoglu's Theorem (weakly) weak* compact.

Since with a continuum of agents F does not belong to an order interval such an argument cannot be followed. However, one can replace assumption (3.2) by the fact that the set of all feasible allocations, i.e., F, is weakly compact. The proof of the Main Theorem remains unchanged in this case.

It is worth noting that even with a finite dimensional commodity space and a continuum of agents the set of all feasible allocations F is not compact in any topology. Nevertheless the use of the Fatou Lemma in several dimensions enables one to dispense with the bound on the consumption sets [see for instance Aumann (1966) or Schmeidler (1969)]. However, since Fatou's Lemma fails in infinite dimensional spaces [see for instance Rustichini (1989) or Yannelis (1990a)] a similar argument with that of Aumann or Schmeidler cannot be adopted. At this point we should mention that the coalitional approach adopted by Zame does not require the bound or the consumption set. In particular in this approach each allocation is always in an order internal which is compact typically in the topology that the commodity space is endowed with. However, as it was noted by Zame (1987) the existence of a competitive equilibrium for the conditional approach does not imply the existence of a competitive equilibrium for the Aumann individualistic approach adopted in this paper, *unless* the consumption sets are bounded. A more elaborate discussion of the connection of the two approaches can be found in Zame.

We now briefly discuss the assumption of convexity of preferences. One may wonder why the convexity assumption on preferences is needed. In particular, one of the nice features of the Aumann economy is that one can dispense with the assumption of convexity of preferences. In fact as Aumann (1966) showed, the Lyapunov Theorem will enable us to convexify the aggregate demand set and this makes applicable the standard fixed point argument. However, in infinite dimensional spaces Lyapunov's Theorem fails [see Diestel-Uhl (1977)] and consequently without convexity of preferences the aggregate demand set need not be convex. Hence, again if positive results need to be obtained the assumption of convexity of preferences must be imposed. [For further remarks on this issue see Rustichini-Yannelis (1990).]

4. An Auxiliary Theorem

As in Aumann (1966) in order to prove our Main Theorem, we first establish an auxiliary result. Recall that Aumann compactifies the economy and he proves a result for compact consumption sets [a similar auxiliary result was proved by Schmeidler (1969), as well]. Then using his auxiliary result (which is indeed the heart of the proof) he is able to complete the proof of his main theorem. A similar idea will be adopted here. In particular, we first establish an Auxiliary Theorem where consumption sets are norm compact. Once this result is available we proceed to complete the proof of the Main Theorem as follows. We construct a suitable family of truncated subeconomies each of which satisfies the assumptions of the Auxiliary Theorem. By appealing to the Auxiliary Theorem we can conclude that a competitive equilibrium exists in each subeconomy. Therefore, we obtain a net of equilibrium consumption-price pairs for the truncated subeconomies. The proof then is completed by extracting converging subnets whose limit is a competitive equilibrium for the original economy.

Below we state our Auxiliary Theorem which may be seen as the infinite dimensional extension of Aumann's (1966) Auxiliary Theorem.

Auxiliary Theorem. *Let $\mathcal{E}$ be an economy satisfying (3.1), (3.2')–(3.4). Then a competitive equilibrium exists in $\mathcal{E}$.*

5. Proof of the Auxiliary Theorem

We begin by stating the following generalization of the Gale-Nikaido-Debreu Lemma proved in Yannelis (1985).

Main Lemma. *Let Y be a Hausdorff locally convex linear topological space whose positive cone Y_+ has an interior point u. Let $\Delta = \{p \in Y_+^* : p \cdot u = 1\}$. Suppose that the correspondence $\zeta : \Delta \to 2^Y$ satisfies the following conditions:*

(i) For all $p \in \Delta$ there exists $z \in \zeta(p)$ such that $p \cdot z \leq 0$,
(ii) $\zeta : \Delta \to 2^Y$ is weak u.s.c., (i.e., $\zeta : (\Delta, w^*) \to 2^Y$ is u.s.c.),*
(iii) for all $p \in \Delta$, $\zeta(p)$ is nonempty, convex and compact.

Then there exists $\bar{p} \in \Delta$, such that $\zeta(\bar{p}) \cap (-Y_+) \neq \phi$.

The Theorem below will be of fundamental importance for the proof of our equilibrium existence theorem. It should also be noted that results of the same nature with the Theorem below have found applications to equilibrium points of non-cooperative models of competition [see for instance Schmeidler (1973), Khan (1986), Khan-Papageorgiou (1987), and Yannelis (1987, 1990a)].

Theorem 5.1. *Let (T, τ, μ) be a complete, finite, separable measure space, Y be a separable Banach space, P be a metric space and $X : T \to 2^Y$ be an integrably bounded, convex, weakly compact, nonempty valued correspondence. Let $D : T \times P \to 2^Y$ be a nonempty, norm closed, convex valued correspondence such that:*

(i) for all $(t,p) \in T \times P$, $D(t,p) \subset X(t)$,
(ii) for each fixed $t \in T$, $D(t,\cdot)$ is norm u.s.c., and
(iii) for each fixed $p \in P$, $D(\cdot\,,p)$ has a measurable graph.

Then the correspondence $\phi : P \to 2^X$ defined by $\phi(p) = \{x \in S^1_X : x(t) \in D(t,p)$ for almost all $t \in T\}$ is nonempty valued and weakly u.s.c.

Proof. (a) Since for each fixed $p \in P$, $D(\cdot\,,p)$ has a measurable graph and it is nonempty valued, it follows from the Aumann measurable selection theorem that there exists a measurable function $f : T \to Y$ such that $f(t) \in D(t,p)$ for almost all t in T. Since $D(\cdot\,,\cdot)$ is integrably bounded, f is integrable and therefore $f \in \phi(p)$ for each $p \in P$. Hence, ϕ is nonempty valued.

(b) We now show that ϕ is weakly u.s.c. First, notice that by virtue of Diestel's Theorem, S^1_X is compact in the weak topology. Since by assumption (T, τ, μ) is a separable measure space, $L_1(\mu, Y)$ is separable [Dunford-Schwartz (1958, p. 381)]. Since S^1_X is a weakly compact subset of the separable Banach space $L_1(\mu, Y)$, by Theorem V.6.3 in Dunford-Schwartz (1958, p. 334), S^1_X is metrizable. Given that S^1_X with the weak topology is a compact metrizable space, in order to prove that ϕ is weakly u.s.c., it suffices to show that G_ϕ is closed in $P \times S^1_X$, where S^1_X is endowed with the weak topology. To this end let p_n, $(n = 1, 2, \ldots)$ be a sequence in P converging to p (in the metric topology), let y_n, $(n = 1, 2, \ldots)$ be a sequence in S^1_X converging weakly to y, and let $y_n \in \phi(p_n)$. We must show that $y \in \phi(p)$. Let $A_i = \operatorname{con} \bigcup_{j>i} y_j$ for $i = 1, 2, \ldots$. Since y_n converges weakly to y by Mazur's Theorem [see for instance Dunford-Schwartz (1958), Corollary 14, p. 422)] for each $i = 1, 2, \ldots$, there exists a sequence $\{z^i_n\}$ in A_i converging in norm to y. For any $\delta > 0$, we can find n_1 such that $\|z^1_{n_1} - y\| < \delta$. Similarly for $m > 1$, we can find n_m such that $\|z_{n_m} - y\| < \frac{\delta}{m}$. Continuing this process we can construct a sequence, appropriately relabeled $\{z_n\}$, such that $z_n \in \operatorname{con} \bigcup_{j \geq n} y_j$, and z_n converges in norm to y. Without loss of generality we can assume that

$z_n(t)$ converges in norm to $y(t)$ (otherwise pass to a subsequence) for all $t \in T/S$, where $S \subset T$, $\mu(S) = 0$. Fix t in T/S. Since for each fixed $t \in T$, $D(t, \cdot)$ is norm for u.s.c., for every $\delta > 0$ we can find n, $(n = 1, 2, \ldots)$ such that for all $n_0 \geq n$ we have $D(t, p_{n_0}) \subset D(t, p) + \delta B$, (where B is the open unit ball in Y). Hence

$$\operatorname{con} \bigcup_{n_0 \geq n} D(t, p_{n_0}) \subset D(t, p) + \delta B \Rightarrow z_n(t) \in D(t, p) + \delta B$$

$$\Rightarrow y(t) \in D(t, p) + \delta B.$$

By letting δ go to zero, we conclude that $y(t) \in D(t, p)$. Since $t \in T/S$ was arbitrary, $y(t) \in D(t, p)$ for almost all t in T. Finally since $D(t, p) \subset X(t)$ for all $t \in T$ and $D(\cdot, \cdot)$ is integrably bounded, we can conclude that $y \in \phi(p)$. This completes the proof of the Theorem.

Corollary 5.1. *Let $D : T \times P \to 2^Y$ be a correspondence satisfying all the assumptions of Theorem 5.1. Then,*

(i) $\int D(\cdot, p)$ is nonempty, and
(ii) $\int D(t, \cdot)$ is weakly u.s.c.

Proof. (i) Since for each $p \in P$, $\psi(p) \neq \phi$, it follows that $\int D(\cdot, p)$ is nonempty.

(ii) We now show that $\int D(t, \cdot)$ is weakly u.s.c. Define $\psi : P \to 2^{S^1_X}$ by $\psi(p) = \{y \in S^1_X : y(t) \in D(t, p)$ for almost all t in $T\}$. Let $f : S^1_X \to Y$ be a mapping defined by $f(\psi(p)) = \int D(t, p)$. Clearly f is norm continuous and linear. It is a standard result [see for instance Aliprantis-Burkinshaw (1985, Theorem 9.16, p. 139) or Dunford-Schwartz (1958, Theorem 15, p. 422)] that f is also weakly continuous. By Theorem 5.1, ψ is weakly u.s.c. and so is $f(\psi)$. Hence, $\int D(t, \cdot)$ is weakly u.s.c. and this completes the proof of the Corollary.

Remark 5.1. The separability assumption on the measure space (T, τ, μ) in Theorem 5.1 and Corollary 5.1 is not needed provided the reader follows the argument in Yannelis (1990a, Theorem 5.4 and Remark 5.1).

Observe that conclusions (i) and (ii) of the above corollary have been proved by Aumann (1965, 1976) for $Y = \mathbb{R}^\ell$. Hence the above corollary may be seen as an extension of Aumann's result. Conclusion (ii) of

Corollary 5.1 can be also obtained as a corollary of the infinite dimensional version of Fatou's Lemma proven in Yannelis (1988). For a further discussion on this see Yannelis (1990a).

The following result proved in Yannelis (1988, Lemma 3.1) is the infinite dimensional extension of Theorem 4 in Aumann (1965).

Lemma 5.1. *Let (T, τ, μ) be a complete finite measure space and Y be a separable Banach space. Let $\phi : T \to 2^Y$ be a closed, convex valued correspondence such that $\phi(t) \subset X(t)$ for all $t \in T$, where $X : T \to 2^Y$ is an integrably bounded, nonempty, weakly compact, convex valued correspondence. Then,*

$$\int_T \phi(t)d\mu(t) \quad \textit{is weakly compact.}$$

Notice that Aumann (1965) does not require $\phi(\cdot)$ to be convex valued. However, it can be easily shown that the above result is false without the convex valuedness of ϕ [see Rustichini (1989) or Yannelis (1990a)].

We now state a recent result proved in Khan-Vohra (1985, Theorem B, p. 331).

Lemma 5.2. *Let $\{z_k : k \in K\}$ be a net in B, where B is a weakly compact subset of a Banach space, and suppose that z_k converges weakly to z. Then we can extract a sequence $\{z_n : n = 1, 2, \ldots\}$ from the net $\{z_k : k \in K\}$ which converges weakly to z.*

With all these preliminary results out of the way, we can now complete the proof of the Auxiliary Theorem.

Let $\Delta = \{p \in E^*_+ : p \cdot u = 1\}$ be the price space. It follows from Alaoglu's Theorem [Jameson (1970, p. 123)] that Δ is weak* compact. Moreover, since E is a separable Banach space, Δ is metrizable, [Dunford-Schwartz (1958, p. 426)]. For $p \in \Delta$ and $t \in T$, let the budget set be $B(t,p) = \{x \in X(t) : p \cdot x \leq p \cdot e(t)\}$. Since for each $t \in T$, $X(t)$ is norm compact and Δ is weak* compact, the bilinear form $(p, x) \to p \cdot x$ is jointly continuous [see for instance Yannelis-Zame (1986) Lemma A, p. 107]. Hence, it follows from assumption (3.4) that for each fixed $t \in T$, $B(t, \cdot)$ is continuous and a standard argument can be adopted to show that for each fixed $t \in T$, $D(t, \cdot)$ is u.s.c. in the sense that the set $\{p \in \Delta : D(t,p) \subset V\}$ is weak* open in Δ for every norm space subset V of E_+.

Since $\succsim_t$ is convex, transitive and complete, a standard argument shows that $D(\cdot,\cdot)$ is convex and nonempty valued. We will show that for each fixed $p \in \Delta$, $B(\cdot,p)$ has a measurable graph. To see this for $p \in \Delta$, define $g_p : T \times E \to [-\infty,\infty]$ by $g_p(t,x) = p \cdot x - p \cdot e(t)$. Clearly, g_p is measurable in t and continuous in x, and hence by a standard result [see for instance Yannelis (1990, Proposition 3.1)], $g_p(\cdot,\cdot)$ is jointly measurable. Therefore, $g_p^{-1}([-\infty,0]) \in \tau \otimes \beta(E)$. It can be easily checked that

$$\begin{aligned} G_{B(\cdot,p)} &= \{(t,x) \in T \times X(t) : p \cdot x \leq p \cdot e(t)\} \\ &= g_p^{-1}([-\infty,0]) \cap G_X. \end{aligned}$$

Since by assumption $X(\cdot)$ has a measurable graph it follows that for each fixed $p \in \Delta$, $G_{B(\cdot,p)} \in \tau \otimes \beta(E)$. Since (T,τ,μ) is a complete measure space and $B(\cdot,\cdot)$ is closed valued, it follows [see for instance Yannelis (1990, Lemma 3.1)] that for each fixed $p \in \Delta$, $B(\cdot,p)$ is lower measurable. Hence, by Castaing's Representation Theorem [see Yannelis (1990)] there exists a family $\{f_n : n = 1,2,\dots\}$ of measurable functions $f_n : T \to E$ such that for all $t \in T$, $\mathrm{cl}\,\phi\{f_n(t) : t \in T\} = B(t,p)$ (where cl denotes norm closure). For $n = 1,2,\dots$ let

$$D_n(t,p) = \{y \in B(t,p) : y \succsim_t f_n(t)\}.$$

Since $\succsim_t$ and $B(\cdot,p)$ have measurable graphs so does $D_n(\cdot,p)$. We wish to show that $D(t,p) = \bigcap_{n=1}^{\infty} D_n(t,p)$. Obviously, $D(t,p) \subset D_n(t,p)$ for each n, $(n = 1,2,\dots)$. We now show that $\bigcap_{n=1}^{\infty} D_n(t,p) \subset D(t,p)$. Suppose otherwise, i.e., there exists $z \in \bigcap_{n=1}^{\infty} D_n(t,p)$ and $z \notin D(t,p)$, i.e., there exists $y \in B(t,p)$ such that $y \succsim_t x$. Notice that by assumption the set $\{w \in B(t,p) : w \succsim_t z\}$ is norm closed in $B(t,p)$. Since the family $\{f_n(t) : n = 1,2,\dots\}$ is norm dense in $B(t,p)$ we can find an n_0 such that $f_{n_0}(t) \succsim_t z$, a contradiction. Hence, $D(t,p) = \bigcap_{n=1}^{\infty} D_n(t,p)$ and since for each fixed $p \in \Delta$, $D_n(\cdot,p)$ $(n = 1,2,\dots)$ have measurable graph so does $D(\cdot,p)$.

Define the excess demand correspondence $\zeta : \Delta \to 2^E$ for the economy $\mathcal{E}$ by

$$\zeta(p) = \int_T D(t,p)d\mu(t) - \int_T e(t)d\mu(t).$$

We must show that ζ satisfies all the conditions of the Main Lemma. Clearly, for each $p \in \Delta$, $\zeta(p)$ convex valued and $p \cdot \zeta(p) \leq 0$. Since for each fixed $p \in \Delta$, $D(\cdot, p)$ has a measurable graph and is nonempty valued, the first conclusion of Corollary 4.1 assures that $\int D(\cdot, p)$ is nonempty and therefore, $\zeta(p)$ is nonempty for each $p \in \Delta$. Since for each fixed $t \in T$, $D(t, \cdot)$ is u.s.c. and $D(\cdot, \cdot)$ is convex, closed valued and $D(t,p) \subset X(t)$ for all $t \in T$, where $X : T \to 2^{E_+}$ is integrably bounded, norm compact, convex, nonempty valued, it follows from the second conclusion of Corollary 5.1 that $\int D(t, \cdot)$ is weakly u.s.c. and so ζ is weakly u.s.c. as well. Finally, it follows from Lemma 5.1 that $\int_T D(t,p)d\mu(t)$ is weakly compact, and hence, $\zeta(p)$ is weakly compact for each $p \in \Delta$. Consequently, ζ satisfies all the assumptions of the Main Lemma and therefore that there exist $(\bar{p}, \bar{x})$ such that $\bar{x} \in \zeta(\bar{p})$ and $\bar{x} \leq 0$, i.e., $\bar{x} = \int_T f(t)d\mu(t) - \int_T e(t)d\mu(t) \leq 0$ and $f(t) \in D(t,p)$ for almost all $t \in T$. Hence $(\bar{p}, f)$ is a competitive equilibrium and this completes the proof of the Auxiliary Theorem.

6. Proof of the Main Theorem

Let $\mathcal{F}$ be a family of all nonempty, norm compact, convex subsets of E_+ containing the initial endowments. For each $F \in \mathcal{F}$ define the consumption correspondence $X^F : T \to 2^{E_+}$ by

$$X^F = F \cap X(t).$$

Moreover, for each $F \in \mathcal{F}$ let $\succsim_t^F$ be the preference relation of agent t induced on F. Let $S^1_{X^F} = \{x \in L_1(\mu, E_+) : x(t) \in X^F(t)$ for almost all t in $T\}$.

We now have a truncated economy $\mathcal{E}^F = [(T, \tau, \mu), X^F, \succsim^F, e]$ which is easily seen that satisfies all the assumptions of the Auxiliary Theorem. Consequently, a competitive equilibrium in $\mathcal{E}^F$ exists, i.e., there exist (p_F, x_F), $p_F \in E^*_+/\{0\}$, $x_F \in S^1_X F$ such that:

(i) $x_F(t) \in D(t, p_F)$ for almost all t in T, and
(ii) $\int_T x_F(t)d\mu(t) \leq \int_T e(t)d\mu(t)$.

Since for each X is weakly compact, nonempty, and convex valued, by Diestel's Theorem, S^1_X is weakly compact in $L_1(\mu, E_+)$. Observe that for each $F \in \mathcal{F}$, $x_F \in A = \{y \in S^1_X : \int_T y(t)d\mu(t) \leq \int_T e(t)d\mu(t)\}$. It can be easily checked that A is convex and norm closed and as a consequence of the Separation Theorem weakly closed. Since S_X^1 is weakly compact, we can conclude that A is weakly compact as well. Notice that for each $F \in \mathcal{F}$, $x_F \in A$, and $\mathcal{F}$ is net directed by inclusion. Hence, the net $\{x_F : F \in \mathcal{F}\}$ has a subset, still denoted by x_F which converges weakly to $\bar{x} \in A$. Moreover, for each $F \in \mathcal{F}$, p_F lies in $\Delta = \{q \in Y_+^* : q \cdot u = 1\}$ and the latter set is weak* compact. Hence, from the equilibrium net $\{(p_F, x_F) : F \in \mathcal{F}\}$ we can always extract convergent subnets. It is clear that $\int_T \bar{x}(t)d\mu(t) \leq \int_T e(t)d\mu(t)$, i.e., $\bar{x}$ is a feasible allocation. We must now show that the limiting allocation $\bar{x}(t)$ is maximal in the budget set, for almost all t in T, in order to complete the proof. We know that for each $F \in \mathcal{F}$, $x_F(t) \in D(t, p_F)$ for almost all t in T, and x_F converges weakly to $\bar{x}$. Since the net $\{x_F : F \in \mathcal{F}\}$ lies in the weakly compact set A, by Lemma 5.2 we can extract a sequence x_n, $(n = 1, 2, \ldots)$ from the net $\{x_F : F \in \mathcal{F}\}$ which converges weakly to $\bar{x} \in A$. Corresponding to the sequence x_n, $(n = 1, 2, \ldots)$ we can also extract a sequence p_n, $(n = 1, 2, \ldots)$ from the net $\{p_F : F \in \mathcal{F}\}$. Obviously, p_n belongs to Δ, and p_n has a subsequence still denoted by p_n which converges weak* to $\bar{p}$.

Therefore, we have a sequence $\{(p_n, x_n) : n = 1, 2, \ldots\}$ such that p_n converges weak* to $\bar{p}$ and x_n converges weakly to $\bar{x}$. Since $x_n(t) \in D(t, p_n)$ for almost all $t \in T$ and $D(t, p_n)$ is contained in $X(t)$ we have that $x_n \in \phi(p_n) = \{y \in S_X^1 : y(t) \in D(t, p_n)$ for almost all t in $T\}$. By Theorem 5.1 the correspondence $\phi : \Delta \to 2^{S_X^1}$ is weakly u.s.c. and closed valued and thus we can conclude that $\bar{x} \in \phi(\bar{p})$, i.e., $\bar{x}(t) \in D(t, \bar{p})$ for almost all t in T. Hence, $\bar{x}(t)$ is maximal in the budget set for almost all t in T and this completes the proof of the Theorem.

7. Concluding Remarks

Remark 7.1. As in Aumann (1965), we assumed that agents' preferences are complete. Schmeidler (1969) showed that the completeness assumption can be dropped from the Aumann model. However, this is not the case with infinitely many commodities. Specifically, without the completeness assumption on preferences, Mas-Colell (1974) showed that even if preferences are convex, the demand set may not be convex and therefore the aggregate demand set may not be convex. Of course such a problem does not arise in Schmeidler's framework since with an atomless measure space of agents and finitely many commodities the aggregate demand set is always convex as a consequence of the Lyapunov Theorem. [This is also the case in Rustichini-Yannelis (1990) where the economy has "many more" agents than commodities and there is a convexifying effect on aggregation.]

Remark 7.2. If the convexity assumptions on preferences is relaxed from our model, once we assume that the measure space of agents is atomless, then we can easily prove the existence of an approximate or δ-competitive equilibrium. In particular, one can convexify the demand set $D(t,p)$ by taking its closed convex hull, i.e., $\overline{\text{con}}D(t,p)$. [Notice that for each fixed $t \in T$, $\overline{\text{con}}D(t,p)$ is u.s.c. and for each fixed $p \in \Delta$, $\overline{\text{con}}D(\cdot,p)$ has a measurable graph.] Note that by Theorem 1 in Khan (1986) [see also Yannelis (1990a, Theorem 6.3)] we have that

$$\text{cl} \int_T D(t,p)d\mu(t) = \int_T \overline{\text{con}}D(t,p)d\mu(t).$$

Proceeding now as in the proof of the Auxiliary Theorem one can easily show that $x(t) \in D(t,p)$ for almost all t in T and $\| \int_T x(t)d\mu(t) - \int_T e(t)d\mu(t)\| < \delta$. Note that now the completeness assumption on preferences is not needed (recall Remark 7.1).

Remark 7.3. The space $C(X)$, i.e., the space of continuous functions on the compact metric space X with the sup norm is an ordered separable Banach space whose positive cone has a nonempty norm interior. Hence, the Main Theorem covers $C(X)$. It is important to note that in this space even if the set of agents is finite one cannot relax the bound from the consumption sets. In particular, since order intervals are not compact in any topology, one cannot conclude that the set of all feasible allocations (which always lie in an order interval) is compact. Finally, it is important to note that our Main Theorem covers $L_\infty(\Omega)$, i.e., the space of essentially bounded measurable functions on the measure space Ω, with the sup norm. This is due to the fact that weakly compact subsets of L_∞ are norm separable [see for instance Diestel-Uhl (1977, Theorem 13, p. 252)].

References

Aliprantis, C. D. and Burkinshaw, O., 1985, *Positive Operators*, Academic Press, New York.

Aumann, R. J., 1965, "Integrals of Set-Valued Functions," *J. Math. Anal. Appl.* **12**, 1–12.

Aumann, R. J., 1966, "Existence of a Competitive Equilibrium in Markets with a Continuum of Traders," *Econometrica* **34**, 1–17.

Aumann, R. J., 1967, "Measurable Utility and the Measurable Choice Theorem," *La Decision*, CNRS, Aix-en-Provence, 15–26.

Aumann, R. J., 1976, "An Elementary Proof that Integration Preserves Uppersemicontinuity," *J. Math. Econ.* **3**, 15–18.

Bewley, T. F., 1990, "A Very Weak Theorem on the Existence of Equilibrium in Atomless Economies with Infinitely Many Commodities," this volume.

Castaing, C. and Valadier, M., 1977, "Convex Analysis and Measurable Multifunctions," *Lect. Notes Math.* **580**, Springer-Verlag, New York.

Debreu, G., 1959, *Theory of Value*, John Wiley and Sons, New York.

Diestel, J., 1977, "Remarks on Weak Compactness in $L_1(\mu, X)$," *Glasgow Math. J.* **18**, 87–91.

Diestel, J. and Uhl, J., 1977, *Vector Measures*, Mathematical Surveys **15**, American Mathematical Society, Providence, Rhode Island.

Dunford, N. and Schwartz, J. T., 1958, *Linear Operators*, Part I, Interscience, New York.

Jameson, G., 1970, *Ordered Linear Spaces*, Springer-Verlag, New York.

Khan, M. Ali, 1976, "On the Integration of Set-Valued Mappings in a Nonreflexive Banach Space II," *Simon Stevin* **59**, 257–267.

Khan, M. Ali, 1986, "Equilibrium Points of Nonatomic Games Over a Banach Space," *Trans. Amer. Math. Soc.* **29**, 737–749.

Khan, M. Ali and Papageorgiou, N. S., 1987, "On Cournot-Nash Equilibria in Generalized Quantitative Games with an Atomless Measure Space of Agents," *Proc. Amer. Math. Soc.* **100**, 505–510.

Khan, M. Ali and Vohra, R., 1985, "On the Existence of Lindahl Equilibria in Economies with a Measure Space of Nontransitive Consumers," *J. Econ. Theory* **36**.

McKenzie, L. W., 1959, "On the Existence of General Equilibrium for a Competitive Market," *Econometrica* **27**, 54–71.

Mas-Colell, A., 1974, "An Equilibrium Existence Theorem Without Complete or Transitive Preferences," *J. Math. Econ.* **1**, 237–246.

Rustichini, A., 1989, "A Counterexample and an Exact Version of Fatou's Lemma in Infinite Dimension," *Archiv der Mathematic* **52**, 357–362.

Rustichini, A. and Yannelis, N. C., 1990, "What is Perfect Competition?" this volume.

Schmeidler, D., 1969, "Competitive Equilibrium in Markets with a Continuum of Traders and Incomplete Preferences," *Econometrica* **37**, 578–585.

Schmeidler, D., 1970, "Fatou's Lemma in Several Dimensions," *Proc. Amer. Math. Soc.* **24**, 300–306.

Schmeidler, D., 1973, "Equilibrium Points of Non-Atomic Games," *J. Stat. Phys.* **7**, 295–300.

Vind, K., 1964, "Edgeworth Allocations in an Exchange Economy," *Int. Econ. Rev.* **5**, 165–177.

Yannelis, N. C., 1985, "On a Market Equilibrium Theorem with an Infinite Number of Commodities," *J. Math. Anal. Appl.* **108**, 595–599.

Yannelis, N. C., 1987, "Equilibria in Noncooperative Models of Competition," *J. Econ. Theory* **41**, 96–111.

Yannelis, N. C., 1988, "Fatou's Lemma in Infinite Dimensional Spaces," *Proc. Amer. Math. Soc.* **102**, 303–310.

Yannelis, N. C., 1990, "Set-Valued Functions of Two Variables in Economic Theory," this volume.

Yannelis, N. C., 1990a, "Integration of Banach-Valued Correspondences," this volume.

Yannelis, N. C. and Zame, W. R., 1986, "Equilibria in Banach Lattices without Ordered Preferences," *J. Math. Econ.* **15**, 85–110.

Zame, W. R., 1987, "Markets with a Continuum of Traders and Infinitely Many Commodities," mimeo.

What is Perfect Competition?

Aldo Rustichini and Nicholas C. Yannelis*

Abstract. We provide a mathematical formulation of the idea of perfect competition for an economy with infinitely many agents and commodities. We conclude that in the presence of infinitely many commodities the Aumann (1964, 1966) measure space of agents, i.e., the interval $[0,1]$ endowed with Lebesgue measure, is not appropriate to model the idea of perfect competition and we provide a characterization of the "appropriate" measure space of agents in an infinite dimensional commodity space setting. The latter is achieved by modeling precisely the idea of an economy with "many more" agents than commodities. For such an economy the existence of a competitive equilibrium is proved. The convexity assumption on preferences is not needed in the existence proof.

1. Introduction

Perfect competition prevails in an economy if no individual can influence the price at which goods are bought and sold.

In order to model rigorously the idea of perfect competition, Aumann (1964, 1965, 1966) assumed that the set of agents in the economy is an atomless measure space. As a consequence of the non-atomicity assumption, each agent in the economy is negligible and therefore will take prices as given.

A special feature of the Aumann model is that the number of commodities in the economy is finite. In particular the commodity space in his model is the positive cone of the Euclidean space $\mathbb{R}^n$. This is quite important because given the fact that the measure space of agents is atomless and the dimension of the commodity space is finite, it turns out that the convexity assumption on preferences is not needed to prove the existence of a competitive equilibrium. In particular, the Lyapunov theorem is used to convexify the aggregate demand set and make the standard fixed point argument applicable.

However, the situation is quite different when the commodity space is not finite dimensional. Indeed, the Lyapunov theorem fails in infinite dimensional spaces [see for instance Diestel-Uhl (1977)] and one loses

* We wish to thank Tom Armstrong for useful comments. As always we are responsible for any remaining errors.

the nice convexifying effect on the aggregate demand set. (Here, it is important to note that all the basic results of Aumann (1965) which constitute the main technical tools to model the idea of perfect competition fail in infinite dimensional spaces [see for instance Rustichini (1989) or Yannelis (1990)].)

Moreover, as it is known from the work of Aumann (1964), in the presence of finitely many commodities, core allocation characterize competitive equilibrium allocations. However, contrary to the Aumann core equivalence theorem, in infinite dimensional commodity spaces in general, core allocations do not characterize competitive equilibrium allocations. In particular, Rustichini-Yannelis (1991) showed that even if the measure space of agents is atomless, preferences are (weakly) continuous, strictly convex, monotone, and initial endowments strictly positive, the core equivalence theorem ceases to be true. Does this then suggest that the nonatomicity assumption may not be enough in infinite dimensional commodity spaces in order to model the idea of perfect competition?

It may be useful, before we proceed, to put aside for a moment the strictly mathematical nature of the problem, and look more closely at the economic significance of the nonatomicity condition, and its implications in the case where the commodity space is finite dimensional. By definition, any subset of the space of agents, that is any coalition, must have positive measure in order not to be insignificant. We may think of this as a "critical mass" condition on any coalition.

On the other hand, thanks to the nonatomicity condition, any coalition of nonzero measure will have a set of possible subcoalitions (still of positive measure) which is so large that it makes any collusive behavior arduous.

The previous discussion suggests that one should not look for a characterization of perfect competition (or more generally of a strategic situation where each single player has an insignificant influence) in the space of agents or players by itself, but in the relation of the dimension of the measure space of agents and the dimension of the commodity (or strategy) space. The concept of dimension, of course, has to be given a rigorous formulation. Simply and informally stated, the characterization of perfect competition that we introduce in this paper does not just specify how many agents there are, but how many agents (or players) deal with how many commodities (or strategy choices). To put it differently, the assumption which is introduced in this paper is that the economy needs to have "many more" agents than commodities. Such an assumption (see Sections 3 and 6 for a rigorous definition) is stronger than the nonatomicity condition of the measure space of agents in an infinite dimensional commodity space setting and it is equivalent to the nonatomicity assumption in finite dimensional commodity spaces. In essence, this is the hidden assumption in the Aumann model which drives his results.[1]

The main contribution of this paper is to provide a rigorous formulation of the idea of perfect competition, and derive the analogous results to those of Aumann for separable Banach spaces. Moreover, we characterize the measure space of agents which satisfy the condition that the dimensionality of the measure space of agents is bigger than that of the commodity space. As it may be expected, the Aumann (1964, 1966) measure space of agents, i.e., the $[0,1]$ interval endowed with Lebesgue measure is not "large enough" to model the idea of perfect competition in the presence of infinitely many commodities.

The rest of the paper is organized as follows: Section 2 contains definitions and some mathematical preliminaries. Section 3 contains the main result, i.e., the integral of a Banach-valued correspondence is convex provided that the dimensionality of the measure space is greater than the dimensionality of the Banach space. This result is interpreted as the convexifying effect on the aggregate demand set. Section 4 characterizes the measure space whose dimensionality is bigger than that of the Banach space of commodities. Some important corollaries of the main result are collected in Section 5. Section 6 uses the main result of this paper to prove the existence of the competitive equilibrium. Finally, Section 7 contains an application of our main theorem to the problem of the existence of a pure strategy Nash equilibrium in games with a continuum of players and

[1] It should be noted that several authors have already made remarks of this nature [see for example, Mertens (1990), Mas-Colell (1975), Gretsky-Ostroy (1985), Ostroy-Zame (1988)], but they did not provide a precise mathematical modeling of the idea of "many more" agents than commodities. The only exemption is the work of Lewis (1977) which uses nonstandard analysis. In particular, she makes use of a nonstandard analog of the Lyapunov theorem proved by Loeb (1971).

with an infinite dimensional strategy space.

2. Definitions and Preliminaries

The space X is a Banach space over the field $\mathbb{R}$ of real numbers; it is assumed to be separable. The norm of an element $x \in X$ will be denoted by $\|x\|$. Unless otherwise specified, the topology on X will be the norm topology.

A special importance will be assumed by a fixed weak compact subset K of X. We recall that (Dunford-Schwartz [1958], V. 6.3) the weak topology of K is a metric topology. As usual for a set $A \subset X$ we denote by $\mathrm{co}\,A$ and $\overline{\mathrm{co}}A$ the convex hull and the closed convex hull of A, respectively. For a subset $A \subseteq X$, we denote by $P(A)$ or 2^A the set of all nonempty subsets of A, and $P_f(A)$ the set of all closed subsets of A.

The Banach space topology on X induces a natural structure of measure space on it if we denote by $\beta(X)$ the set of norm Borel subsets of X (and for any $A \in \beta(X)$, $\beta(A)$ are the Borel subsets of A). If $\beta_w(X)$ denotes the Borel σ-algebra generated by the weak topology of X, then from Masani [1978], Theorem 2.5(b), we have $\beta(X) = \beta_w(X)$.

We now proceed to describe our measure space. T will be a measurable space, with a σ-algebra τ, and a measure μ; we shall always assume (T, τ, μ) to be complete and finite. We do not assume nonatomicity, since such a condition will be contained in an assumption which we will introduce later.

$L_\infty(\mu)$ is the space of real valued, measurable, essentially bounded functions defined on T. For any $E \in \tau$, the measure space (E, τ_E, μ_E) is naturally defined; and so is the space $L_{\infty,E}(\mu) \equiv \{f : E \to \mathbb{R},\ f$ is τ_E-measurable and μ_E-essentially bounded$\}$.

In this paper a *set-valued function* (or *correspondence*) F is defined to be a map from T to a set of all the nonempty subsets of X, $P(X)$. We denote the *graph* of F by $G_F = \{(t,x) \in T \times X : x \in F(t)\}$. For a given correspondence F, the new correspondence $\mathrm{co}\,F$ and $\overline{\mathrm{co}}F$ are defined by $(\mathrm{co}\,F)(t) \equiv \mathrm{co}(F(t))$, and analogously for $\overline{\mathrm{co}}F$.

Various notions of measurability are discussed in Himmelberg [1957]. In the case where the measure space T is complete, X is Souslin (conditions which are satisfied in our case) and F is closed valued they turn out to be equivalent [Himmelberg [1957], Theorem 3.5]. We adopt the following:

Definition. *The correspondence $F : T \to P(X)$ is said to be measurable if the graph of F, $\{(t,x) \in T \times X : x \in F(t)\}$ is an element of the product measure space $\tau \otimes \beta(X)$. The $\overline{\text{co}}$ operation preserve measurability [Himmelberg [1975], Theorem 9.1].*

K is now a compact Hausdorff space (in the weak topology). Let $C(K)$ be the space of continuous functions on K, and $C(K)^*$ its dual space. It is well known [Dunford-Schwartz [1957] Theorem IV.6.3] that this last space is (isometrically isomorphic to) the space rca(K), the space of all regular, countably additive real valued set functions, defined on the σ-field of the Borel (norm) subsets of K; rca$^+(K)$ are the nonnegative elements of rca(K). For any Borel subset A, rca(A) and rca$^+(A)$ are defined in the natural way. For any Borel subset A of K, we denote M_A the unit ball of rca$^+(A)$; that is:

$$M_A \equiv \{\mu \in \text{rca}^+(A) : \mu(A) \leq 1\}.$$

If $\mu(A) = 1$, we refer to μ as usual as a *probability measure*. Among the probability measures over a Borel set we single out those having unit mass concentrated at one point:

Definition. *For any Borel subset A, the set of Dirac measures on A, denoted D_A, is the subset of M_A of elements δ_a, with $a \in A$, such that*

$$(\delta_a, \phi) = \phi(a) \quad \textit{for every} \quad \phi \in C(K).$$

For any $m \in$ rca(K), its norm $|m|$ is the total variation. We shall consider on the following measurable functions defined on T and with values in the space M_K. More precisely we introduce $L_\infty^{w^*}(\mu, M_K)$, the set of M_K-valued functions f which satisfy: (i) $\|f\| \in L^\infty(\mu)$; (ii) $t \mapsto (f(t), \phi)$ is a measurable (real valued) function for every $\phi \in C(K)$; [see Ionescu-Tulcea, A. and C., (1969), p. 99]. Also we let

$$L_\infty^{w^*}(\mu, M_F) \equiv \{\gamma \in L_\infty^{w^*}(\mu, M_K) : \nu(t) \in M_{F(t)} \ \mu\text{-a.e.}\}$$
$$L_\infty^{w^*}(\mu, D) \equiv \{\gamma \in L_\infty^{w^*}(\mu, M_K) : \nu(t) \in D \ \mu\text{-a.e.}\}$$
$$L_\infty^{w^*}(\mu, D_F) \equiv \{\gamma \in L_\infty^{w^*}(\mu, D) : \nu(t) \in D_{F(t)} \ \mu\text{-a.e.}\}.$$

Also for $\nu \in M$, F a closed subset of K, we define $(\nu, F) \equiv \int_K x\chi_F(x)d\nu(x)$ where χ_F is the indicator function of the set F. If X is a Banach space, we will denote by $L_1(\mu, X)$ the space of equivalence classes of X-valued Bochner integrable functions $f : T \to X$ normed by

$$\|f\| = \int_T \|f(t)\| d\mu(t).$$

The *integral of the set-valued function* $F : T \to 2^X$ is as usual:

$$\int_T F(t)d\mu(t) = \left\{ \int_T x(t)d\mu(t) : x(t) \in F(t) \ \mu\text{-a.e.} \right\}.$$

We will denote the above integral by $\int F$ or $\int F d\mu$.

3. The Main Theorem
(Convexifying Effect on Aggregation)

The following simple lemmata will be used later.

Lemma 1. *Let $\nu \in M_A \setminus D_A$. Then there exist two measures $\nu_\pm$ which satisfy:*

$$\nu_\pm = \nu \pm \nu_2 \in M_A \quad \textit{with:} \quad \nu_2 \neq 0,\ \nu_2 \in \mathrm{rca}(A).$$

Remark. Note ν_2 may *not* be an element of M_A.

Proof. Since ν is not Dirac, there exist two disjoint Borel subsets of A, S and B say, such that

$$0 < \nu(S) \leq \nu(B) < 1. \tag{1}$$

We denote with $\nu(S)$, ν_B the restriction of ν to the two set S, B. Define now $\theta \equiv \nu(S)/\nu(B)$: from (1) above follows that $\theta \in (0, 1]$; also define: $\nu_2 \equiv -\nu_S + \theta\nu_B$ (clearly $\nu_2 \neq 0$); and $\nu_\pm \equiv \nu \pm \nu_2$. It is now an easy computation to check that $\nu_\pm \in M_A$.

Lemma 2. *Let $E \in \tau$ with $\mu(E) > 0$, and $\nu \in L_\infty^{w^*}(\mu, M_F)$ with $\nu(t) \in M_{F(t)} \setminus D_{F(t)}$ for every $t \in E$. Then there exists a measurable function $\nu_2(t) \in \mathrm{rca}(F(t))$, $\nu_2 \neq 0$ and $\nu \pm \nu_2 \in M_{F(t)}$, μ-a.e.*

Proof. The function ν_2 will result as a measurable selection from a correspondence. We recall $M_{F(t)}$ is a w^*-compact, convex subset of M_K. Define now: $\hat{\theta} = \max\{\theta \geq 0 : B(\nu(t), \theta) \subset M_{F(t)}\}$. From Lemma 1, $\hat{\theta} > 0$ for every $t \in E$; also $\hat{\theta}$ is a measurable function.

Now the correspondence $N(t) \equiv B(\gamma(t)), \hat{\theta}(t))$ is measurable [see Castaing and Valadier, (1977), III-41] with complete values, and takes values in M_K, a separable space (because this space is compact and metric). The result follows from the previous lemma and the Kuratowski and Ryll-Nardzewski (1962) measurable selection theorem.

Recall now that for any vector space over the real field an algebraic (Hamel) basis exists. The cardinality of any Hamel basis is the same, and we denote, for any vector space X, $\dim X$ the cardinality of any of its bases.

We introduce the following condition.

(A1) For the pair $((T, \tau, \mu), X)$, if E belongs to τ, $\mu(E) > 0$, then $\dim L_{E,\infty}(\mu) > \dim X$.

Remark 1. This is the condition that there are "many more" agents than commodities. In section 4 we shall characterize the measure spaces that satisfy the above condition.

Remark 2. The assumption implies that for any linear map T from $L_{E,\infty}(\mu)$ to X there exists a function f such that $f \neq 0$, $T(f) = 0 \in X$. This is the condition which will be actually used in the proof of the main theorem and its corollaries.

Remark 3. When X is finite dimensional, the assumption that the measure space (T, τ, μ) is non-atomic implies the assumption (A1) above. Of course, the reverse is also true. Hence the Main Theorem below, as well as the corollaries of the section 5 imply the analogous results in Aumann (1965).

Remark 4. We recall here that a Banach space is of second category and so (since every finite dimensional proper subspace is closed and with empty interior) it cannot have, if it is infinite dimensional, a countable Hamel basis. On the other hand such a space, as being a separable metric space, has cardinality at most $2^{\aleph_0}$. We conclude (under the continuum hypothesis) $\dim X = 2^{\aleph_0}$.

Remark 5. Readers familiar with the proof by Lindenstrauss (1966) of Lyapunov's convexity theorem, or Knowles' theorem [see Knowles (1974) or Kluvanek-Knowles (1975)] will recognize the main idea of the proof.

Main Theorem. *Let K be a weakly compact, nonempty subset of X and let $F : T \to 2^K$ be a measurable, closed valued correspondence. Assume that the pair $((T, \tau, \mu), X)$ satisfy (A1). Then*

$$\int F = \int \overline{\text{co}} F.$$

Proof. Fix $t \in T$. Define

$$I(M_{F(t)}) \equiv \{x \in X : x = \int_K a d\mu(a), \quad \text{with} \quad \mu \in M_{F(t)}\}.$$

Clearly

$$\text{co}\, F(t) \subset I(M_{F(t)}).$$

Also, since $M_{F(t)}$ is w^*-compact convex, and the map $\mu \to \int_K a d\mu(a)$ is linear, and w^* to w-continuous, $I(M_F)$ is closed and convex, and therefore

$$\overline{\text{co}} F \subset I(M_F).$$

Clearly

$$\int_T F d\mu = \{x \in X : x = \int_T (\delta(t), F(t)) d\mu(t), \quad \delta \in D_F\}.$$

Obviously, $\int_T F d\mu \subset \int_T \overline{\text{co}} F d\mu$. We will now prove the converse inclusion. From $\overline{\text{co}} F(t) \subset I(M_{F(t)})$ it follows that

$$\int_T \overline{\text{co}} F d\mu \subset \int I(M_{F(t)}) d\mu(t).$$

We will now prove that

$$\int_T I(M_{F(t)}) d\mu(t) \subset \int_T F d\mu,$$

and this will complete the proof of the theorem.

For any $x \in \int_T F d\mu$, define

$$H_x \equiv \{\nu \in L_\infty^{w^*}(\mu, M_F) : \int_T (\nu, F) d\mu = x\}.$$

The set H_x is convex, and w^*-compact [see Castaing and Valadier, (1977), V-2]. We will now prove that the set of extreme points of H_x (denoted by extH_x) are contained in $L_\infty^{w^*}(\mu, D_F)$. From the representation formula for $\int_T F d\mu$, this will prove our claim. Let $\nu \in \text{ext}H$; we assume, arguing by contradiction that $\nu \notin L_\infty^{w^*}(\mu, D_F)$, i.e., that for a set E of μ-measure nonzero: $\nu(t) \notin D_{F(t)}$, $t \in E$.

From Lemma 2 we derive the existence of a rca(K) valued τ-measurable function ν_2 such that $\nu(t) \pm \nu_2(t) \in M_{F(t)}$ and $\nu_2 \neq 0$. Now from (A1) we deduce the existence of an $f \in L_{E,\infty}(\mu)$ such that

$$\int_T (f\nu_2, F) d\mu(t) = 0; \quad \|f\|_{L_{E,\infty}(\mu)} > 0.$$

Now extend f to a function $\bar{f} \in L_{\infty(\mu)}$ setting $\bar{f}(t) = 0$, for every $t \notin E$. We conclude:

$$\nu_1 \pm f\nu_2 \in H, \quad \nu_1 + f\nu_2 \neq \nu_1 - f\nu_2$$

so that ν_1 is *not* an extreme points of H, a contradiction. This completes the proof of the Main Theorem.

The above result tells us the following: Suppose that (T, τ, μ) is interpreted as the measure space of agents and X is the commodity space. Let P be a separable metric space denoting the price space. Denote by $D(t,p)$ the demand set of agent t at prices p, i.e., D is a set-valued function from $T \times P$ to K. If (A1) is satisfied (i.e., if there are "many more" agents than commodities), then it follows from our Main Theorem that the aggregate demand set $\int_{t \in T} D(t,p) d\mu(t)$ is convex (see also Corollary 1 in Section 5). In other words there is a convexifying effect on aggregation despite the fact that we have infinitely many commodities [compare with Khan-Yannelis (1990) or Ostroy-Zame (1988)].

4. Models of Agents' Spaces

We now take a closer look at the possible variety of measure spaces of agents. Our main purpose is to describe those spaces for which the assumption (A1) holds, when X is an (infinite dimensional) separable Banach space.

In the following we shall say that two measure spaces (T_i, τ_i, μ_i), $i = 1, 2$, are *isomorphic* if there exists a *measure preserving set isomorphism* between them. A set isomorphism is a one to one mapping $\phi : \tau_1 \to \tau_2$ such that $\phi(T_1 \setminus E) = T_2 \setminus \phi(E)$, $\phi(\bigcup_{i=1}^{\infty} E_i) = \bigcup_{i=1}^{\infty} \phi(E_i)$ if $E_i \notin \tau_1$ for $i = 1, 2, \ldots$. ϕ is said to be measure preserving if $\mu_2(\phi(E)) = \mu_1(E)$ for every $E \in \tau_1$; we consider here the equivalence classes of measurable sets modulo the ideal of sets of measure zero.

Consider now the unit interval $I = [0, 1]$, with β the Borel subsets of I, and λ the Lebesgue measure. For every ordinal number α we now define that product

$$T^\alpha = \prod_{\gamma > \alpha} I_\alpha, \quad \text{with } I_\alpha \equiv I \text{ for every } \alpha.$$

The measure theoretic product space, a complete finite measure space, is denoted $(T^\alpha, \tau^\alpha, \mu^\alpha)$. Recall that a measurable rectangle is a set of the form $\prod_{\gamma<\alpha} A_\gamma$, where $A_\gamma = I$ for all but a finite number of indices, and $A_\gamma \in \beta$ otherwise. The σ-algebra τ^α is the σ-algebra generated by the clan of all measurable rectangles. The measure μ^α satisfies

$$\mu^\alpha\left(\prod_{\gamma<\alpha} A_\gamma\right) = \prod_{i=1}^{m} \lambda(A_{\gamma i})$$

for every measurable rectangle where the sides $\{A_{\gamma i} \mid i = 1, \ldots, m\}$ are different from I (for details, see for instance von Neumann (1950)).

When $\alpha \leq \omega$ the measure space $(T^\alpha, \tau^\alpha, \mu^\alpha)$ is (isomorphic to) the unit interval with Borel subsets and Lebesgue measure. Note that by the isomorphism theorem of Halmos and von Neumann (1948) every *separable* and nonatomic measure space of total measure one is isomorphic to it.

For cardinals of cardinality higher than ω a complete classification of the measure spaces is possible thanks to Maharam's Theorem [Maharam (1942)]. For a σ-algebra τ, let $\bar{\tau}$ be the least cardinal number which is the power of a basis of τ. The σ-algebra is called homogeneous if $\bar{\lambda} = \bar{\tau}$ for any principal ideal $\lambda \leq \tau$ which is not the null ideal. Maharam's theorem now states that every homogeneous measure algebra of total one is isomorphic to a $(T^\alpha, \tau^\alpha, \mu^\alpha)$, as previously described for some cardinal α. We may therefore restrict our attention to such product spaces.

For any ordinal number $\bar\gamma$, $\bar\gamma < \alpha$, and every set $A \in \beta$ we define the function:

$$f_{A,\bar\gamma}(x) = \begin{cases} 1 & \text{if } x_{\bar\gamma} \in A; \\ 0 & \text{if } x_{\bar\gamma} \notin A_\gamma \end{cases}$$

where $x_{\bar\gamma}$ is the coordinate of the point x in the measure space which corresponds to the ordinal $\bar\gamma$. Clearly, every such function is measurable (note $\{f_{\bar\gamma} > 1/2\} = \prod_{\gamma<\bar\gamma} D_\gamma \times A \times \prod_{\bar\gamma<\gamma<\alpha} D_\gamma$) and essentially bounded. The set of functions $\{f_\gamma\}_{\gamma<\alpha}$ is a set of linearly independent functions, and has cardinality $\aleph(\alpha)$. Setting $\alpha = \omega_1$ is clearly enough to satisfy (A1). We have proved the following result:

Theorem 4.1. *For every separable Banach space X, there exists a measure space (T_1, τ_1, μ_1) such that the assumption (A1) is satisfied. This measure space can be taken to be the product measure space with factors (I, β, λ) and $\alpha = \omega_1$.*

The conclusion to be drawn from the above result is that the $[0,1]$ interval endowed with Lebesgue measure [as Aumann (1964, 1966) formulated his model] is not "large enough" to model perfect competition in infinite dimensional commodity spaces.

5. Some Corollaries

Suppose that the correspondence $F : T \to 2^K$ satisfies all the assumptions of the Main Theorem. Then we can deduce the following Corollaries.

Corollary 1. *$\int_T F d\mu$ is convex.*

Proof. Directly from the fact that $\int_T F d\mu = \int_T \overline{\text{co}} F d\mu$, and that $\int_T \overline{\text{co}} F d\mu$ is convex because it is the linear image of the convex set $S_{\overline{\text{co}}F} = \{y \in L_1(\mu, X) : y(t) \in \overline{\text{co}} F(t)\ \mu\text{-a.e.}\}$.

Corollary 2 (Fatou's Lemma, exact version). *If $F_n(\cdot) : T \to 2^K$ $(n = 1, 2, \ldots)$ are measurable correspondences, then*

$$\text{w-Ls} \int_T F_n(t) d\mu \subset \int_T \text{w-Ls}\, F_n(t) d\mu.$$

Proof. The proof is the following chain of inclusions:

$$\begin{aligned}\text{w-Ls} \int_T F_n(t)d\mu &\subset \text{cl} \int_T \text{w-Ls}\, F_n(t)d\mu \\ &= \int_T \overline{\text{co}}\, \text{w-Ls}\, F_n(t)d\mu \\ &= \int_T \text{w-Ls}\, F_n(t)d\mu.\end{aligned}$$

The first inclusion is the approximate version of Fatou's lemma in infinite dimensional spaces [see Yannelis (1988)], the second is the Datko-Khan theorem [Khan (1985)]. Finally the third inclusion follows from our Main Theorem.

Corollary 3 (integration preserves u.s.c.). *Let Δ be a metric space and $F : \Delta \times T \to 2^K$ be a correspondence such that for each fixed $t \in T$, $F(\cdot, t)$ is weakly u.s.c. (w-u.s.c.), i.e., if the sequence p_n converges to p, then* w-Ls $F(p_n, t) \subset F(p, t)$. *Then $\int_T F(\cdot, t)d\mu$ is w-u.s.c.*

Proof. Since for each $t \in T$, $F(\cdot, t)$ is w-u.s.c., we have that

$$\text{w-Ls}\, F(p, t) \subset F(p_0, t), \quad \text{whenever} \quad p_n \to p_0. \tag{5.1}$$

We show that $\int_T F(\cdot, t)d\mu(t)$ is w-u.s.c., i.e., if $p_n \to p_0$ then

$$\text{w-Ls} \int_T F(p_n, t)d\mu(t) \subset \int_T F(p_0, t)d\mu(t).$$

It follows from Corollary 2 that

$$\text{w-Ls} \int_T F(p_n, t)d\mu(t) \subset \int_T \text{w-Ls}\, F(p_n, t)d\mu(t). \tag{5.2}$$

From (5.1) it follows that

$$\int \text{w-Ls}\, F(p_n, t)d\mu(t) \subset \int F(p_0, t)d\mu(t). \tag{5.3}$$

Combining now (5.2) and (5.3) we can conclude that

$$\text{w-Ls} \int F(p_n, t)d\mu(t) \subset \int F(p_0, t)d\mu(t),$$

i.e., $\int F(\cdot, t)d\mu(t)$ is w-u.s.c.

Note that Corollary 1 is the infinite dimensional generalization of Theorem 1 in Aumann (1965) or Debreu (1967, p. 369) known as the Lyapunov-Richter theorem. Corollary 2 is an exact version of the Fatou Lemma in infinite dimensional spaces. It is worth pointing out that the sequence of set-valued functions $F_n(\cdot)$ need not be convex valued contrary to the related results obtained in Yannelis (1988) and Rustichini (1989). The latter is also true for Corollary 3, i.e., no convexity assumption is needed to show that integration preserves w-u.s.c. It is important to note that all the above Corollaries are false in infinite dimensional spaces [see for instance Rustichini (1989) or Yannelis (1990) for a counterexample] even if the measure space is atomless. What seems to drive the above results is condition (A1).

6. The Existence of a Competitive Equilibrium

Let X denote the *commodity space* where X is an ordered, separable Banach space whose positive cone X_+ has an interior point u. An economy $\mathcal{E}$ is a quadruple $[(T,\tau,\mu),Y,\succsim,e]$ where

(1) (T,τ,μ) is the measure space of agents;
(2) $Y : T \to 2^{X_+}$ is the *consumption set-valued function* of each agent;
(3) $\succsim_t \subset Y(t) \times Y(t)$ is the *preference relation* of agent t;
(4) $e : T \to X_+$ is the *initial endowment* of agent t, where $e(t) \in Y(t)$ μ-a.e., and for all $t \in T$, $e(t)$ belongs to a norm compact subset of $Y(t)$;
(5) the pair $[(T,\tau,\mu),X]$ satisfies the assumption (A1).

Denote the *budget set* of agent t at prices p by $B(t,p) = \{x \in Y(t) : p\cdot x \leq p \cdot e(t)\}$. The *demand set* of agent t at prices p is $D(t,p) = \{x \in B(t,p) : x \succsim_t y \text{ for all } y \in B(t,p)\}$. A *competitive equilibrium* for $\mathcal{E}$ is a pair (p,f), $p \in X_+ \setminus \{0\}$, $f \in L_1(\mu, X_+)$ such that:

(i) $f(t) \in D(t,p)$ μ-a.e., and
(ii) $\int_T f(t)d\mu(t) \leq \int_T e(t)d\mu(t)$.

We now introduce the following assumptions:

(a.1) (T,τ,μ) is a complete finite measure space.

(a.2) The correspondence $Y : T \to 2^{X_+}$ is integrably bounded, closed, convex, nonempty, weakly compact valued, and it has a measurable graph, i.e., $G_Y \in \tau \otimes \beta(X_+)$.

(a.3)(a) For each $t \in T$ and each $x \in Y(t)$ the set $R(t,x) = \{t \in Y(t) : y \succsim_t x\}$ is weakly closed and the set $R^{-1}(t,x) = \{y \in Y(t) : x \succsim_t y\}$ is norm closed,

(b) $\succsim_t$ is measurable in the sense that the set $\{(t,x,y) \in T \times X_+ \times X_+ : y \succsim_t x\}$ belongs to $\tau \otimes \beta(X_+) \otimes \beta(X_+)$,

(c) $\succsim_t$ is transitive, complete, and reflexive.

(a.4) For all $t \in T$, there exists $z(t) \in Y(t)$ such that $e(t) - z(t)$ belongs to the norm interior of X_+.

Theorem 6.1. *Let $\mathcal{E}$ be an economy satisfying (a.1)–(a.4). Then a competitive equilibrium exists in $\mathcal{E}$.*

Proof. It follows by combining the main existence result in Khan-Yannelis (1990) together with the Main Theorem and its corollaries.

Note that Theorem 6.1 above is the counterpart of the Main Existence Theorem of a competitive equilibrium in Khan-Yannelis (1990). It should be emphasized, that contrary to the Khan-Yannelis (1990) or Bewley (1990) setting, the economy that we considered in this paper has "many more" agents than commodities [recall (5) above] and this allows us to drop the convexity assumption on preferences.

It is worth pointing out that for the core equivalence theorem [see for instance Rustichini-Yannelis (1989, 1991)] the convexity assumption on preferences is also not needed regardless as to whether the economy has "many more" agents than commodities. The reason is that for the proof of the core equivalence theorem, one has to separate an open set from the closure of the "aggregate net trade preferred set." By virtue of the approximate Lyapunov theorem we will have that the norm closure of the "aggregate net trade preferred set" is convex [see Rustichini-Yannelis (1989, 1991)] and this will enable us to apply the standard separating hyperplane argument.

However, despite the fact that without convexity of preferences both sets coincide (i.e., the core and the set of competitive equilibrium allocations are the same), they may be empty unless of course we have "many more" agents than commodities, as the above theorem indicates.

Finally it should be noted that the preference relation $\succsim$ in Theorem 6.1 need not be complete, contrary to the Khan-Yannelis (1990) existence theorem.

7. The Existence of a Pure Strategy Nash Equilibrium

We now indicate how from our main theorem one can obtain a generalization of Schmeidler's (1973) result on the existence of a pure strategy Nash equilibrium for a game with a continuum of players with a finite dimensional strategy space. In particular, in view of the failure of the Lyapunov theorem in infinite dimensional spaces, as it was shown by Khan (1986), one can only now obtain an approximate pure strategy Nash equilibrium once the dimensionality of the strategy space is allowed to be infinite. However, by applying our main theorem, we show that one can still obtain an exact pure strategy Nash equilibrium for a game with a continuum of players and with an infinite dimensional strategy space, provided that the game has "many more" players than strategies. We outline the details below:

A *game* G is a quadruple $\langle (T, \tau, \mu), X, Y, u \rangle$ where

(1) (T, τ, μ) is a complete finite *measure space of players*,
(2) X is the *strategy space* which is assumed to be a separable Banach space,
(3) $Y : T \to 2^X$ is a measurable function denoting the *strategy set* of player t,
(4) $u : T \times X \times L_1(\mu, Y) \to \mathbb{R}$ is the *utility function* of player t, where for each fixed x, $u(\cdot, \cdot, x)$ is a Borel measurable function on $\{(t, y) : y \in Y(t)\}$,
(5) the pair $((T, \tau, \mu), X)$ satisfies the condition (A.1).

Note that the above definition of a game is identical with that of Khan (1986) with the addition of (5), i.e., we have replaced the nonatomicity assumption in Khan (1986), with the condition that we have "many more" players than strategies.

Denote by $\text{ext}Y(\cdot)$ the extreme points of the set $Y(\cdot)$. We are now ready to state the following result.

Theorem 7.1. *Let $G = \langle (T, \tau, \mu), X, Y, u \rangle$ be a game satisfying the following assumptions:*

(7.1) $Y : T \to 2^X$ is a nonempty, closed, convex, weakly compact and integrably bounded correspondence;

(7.2) $u : T \times X \times L_1(\mu, Y) \to \mathbb{R}$ is linear on X;

(7.3) $u : T \times X \times L_1(\mu, Y) \to \mathbb{R}$ is weakly continuous on $X \times L_1(\mu, Y)$.

Then G has a pure strategy Nash equilibrium, i.e., there exists $x^* \in L_1(\mu, \text{ext}Y)$ such that for almost all t in T,

$$u(t, x^*(t), x_T^*) = \max_{y \in Y(t)} u(t, y, x_T^*) \quad \textit{where} \quad x_T^* = \int_{t \in T} x^*(t) d\mu(t).$$

Proof. Combine Khan's (1986) theorem together with our Main Theorem.

References

Aumann, R. J., 1964, "Markets with a Continuum of Traders," *Econometrica* **32**, 39–50.

Aumann, R. J., 1965, "Integrals of Set-Valued Functions," *J. Math. Anal. Appl.* **12**, 1–12.

Aumann, R. J., 1966, "Existence of a Competitive Equilibrium in Markets with a Continuum of Traders," *Econometrica* **34**, 1–17.

Bewley, T., 1990, "A Very Weak Theorem on the Existence of Equilibria in Atomless Economies with Infinitely Many Commodities," this volume.

Castaing, C. and Valadier, M., 1977, "Convex Analysis and Measurable Multifunctions," *Lect. Notes Math.* **580**, Springer-Verlag, New York.

Debreu, G., 1967, "Integration of Correspondences," *Proc. Fifth Berkeley Symp. Math. Stat. Prob.*, University of California Press, Berkeley, Vol. II, Part I, 351–372.

Diestel, J. and Uhl, J., 1977, *Vector Measures*, Mathematical Surveys, No. 15, American Mathematical Society, Providence, Rhode Island.

Dunford, N. and Schwartz, J. T., 1958, *Linear Operators*, Part I, Interscience, New York.

Gretsky, N. E. and Ostroy, J., 1985, "Thick and Thin Market Nonatomic Exchange Economies," in *Advances in Equilibrium Theory*, C. D. Aliprantis et al, eds., Springer-Verlag.

Halmos, P. R. and Von Neumann, J., 1941, "Operator Methods in Classical Mechanics, II," *Ann. Math.* **43:2**.

Himmelberg, C. J., 1975, "Measurable Relations," *Fund. Math.* **87**, 53–72.

Ionescu-Tulcea, A. and C., 1969, *Topics in the Theory of Lifting*, Springer-Verlag, Berlin.

Khan, M. Ali, 1976, "On the Integration of Set-Valued Mappings in a Nonreflexive Banach Space II," *Simon Stevin* **59**, 257–267.

Khan, M. Ali, 1986, "Equilibrium Points of Nonatomic Games over a Banach Space," *Trans. Amer. Math. Soc.* **293:2**, 737–749.

Khan, M. Ali and Yanelis, N. C., 1990, "Existence of a Competitive Equilibrium in Markets with a Continuum of Agents and Commodities," this volume.

Kluvanek, I. and Knowles, G., 1975, "Vector Measures and Control System," *Math. Stud.* **20**, North Holland.

Knowles, G., 1974, Liapunov Vector Measures, *SIAM J. Control* **13**, 294–303.

Kuratowski, K. and Ryll-Nardzewski, C., 1962, "A General Theorem on Selectors," *Bull. Acad. Polon. Sci. Ser. Sci. Marsh. Astronom. Phys.* **13**, 397–403.

Lewis, L., 1977, Ph.D. Thesis, Yale University.

Loeb, P., 1971, "A Combinatorial Analog of Lyapunov's Theorem for Infinitesimal Generated Atomic Vector Measures," *Proc. Amer. Math. Soc.* **39**, 585–586.

Lindenstrauss, J., 1966, "A Short Proof of Lyapunov's Convexity Theorem," *J. Math. Mech.* **15**, 971–972.

Maharam, D., 1942, "On Homogeneous Measure Algebras," *Proc. Natl. Acad. Sci.* **28**, 108–111.

Masani, P., 1978, "Measurability and Pettis Integration in Hilbert Spaces," *J. Reine Angew. Math.* **297**, 92–135.

Mas-Colell, A., 1975, "A Model of Equilibrium with Differentiated Commodities," *J. Math. Econ.* **2**, 263–295.

Mertens, J.-F., 1990, "An Equivalence Theorem for the Core of an Economy with Commodity Space $L_\infty - \tau(L_\infty, L_1)$," this volume.

Ostroy, J. and Zame, W. R., 1988, "Non-Atomic Exchange Economies and the Boundaries of Perfect Competition," mimeo.

Robertson, A. P. and Kingman, J. F. C., 1968, "On a Theorem of Lyapunov," *J. London Math. Soc.* **43**, 347–351.

Rustichini, A., 1989, "A Counterexample and an Exact Version of Fatou's Lemma in Infinite Dimensions," *Archiv der Mathematic*, **52**, 357–362.

Rustichini, A. and Yannelis, N. C., 1989, "Commodity Pair Desirability and the Core Equivalence Theorem," mimeo.

Rustichini, A. and Yannelis, N. C., 1991, "Edgeworth's Conjecture in Economies with a Continuum of Agents and Commodities," *J. Math. Econ.*, to appear.

Schmeidler, D., 1973, "Equilibrium Points of Non Atomic Games, *J. Stat. Phys.* **7:4**, 295–300.

Von Neumann, J., 1950, "Functional Operators," *Ann. Math. Stud.* **22**, Princeton University Press.

Yannelis, N. C., 1988, "Fatou's Lemma In Infinite Dimensional Spaces," *Proc. Amer. Math. Soc.* **102**, 303–310.

Yannelis, N. C., 1990, "Integration of Banach-Valued Correspondences," this volume.

PART 5

CORRELATED EQUILIBRIA

On the Existence of Correlated Equilibria

Nicholas C. Yannelis and Aldo Rustichini

Abstract. We provide sufficient conditions which guarantee the existence of correlated equilibria in noncooperative games with finitely many players.

1. Introduction

A basic solution for noncooperative games which has found several applications in economics is that of a Nash equilibrium [see Nash (1951)]. Recently, Aumann (1974, 1987) introduced the idea of a correlated equilibria as an extension of the Nash equilibrium in order to allow for correlation between the player's randomizations. This notion can be described as follows: Let Ω denote the set of states of nature of the world and consider the game $\Gamma = \{(X_i, u_i, S_i, \mu_i) : i = 1, 2, \ldots, m\}$ where X_i is the *strategy set* of player i, $u_i : \prod_{j=1}^{m} X_j \to \mathbb{R}$ is the *payoff* of player i, S_i is a partition of Ω denoting the *private information* of player i and μ_i is the *prior* of player i—a probability measure on Ω. For simplicity we assume that players have the same prior, i.e., $\mu_i \equiv \mu$ for all i. A *strategy* of player i is an S_i-measurable function $x_i : \Omega \to X_i$. An m-tuple of strategies $(x_1^*, x_2^*, \ldots, x_m^*)$ is said to be a *correlated equilibrium* for the game Γ, if for all i, $(i = 1, 2, \ldots, m)$

$$\sum_{\omega\in\Omega} u_i(x_i^*(\omega), \ldots, x_m^*(\omega))\mu(\omega) \geq \sum_{\omega\in\Omega} u_i(x_i^*(\omega), \ldots, x_i, \ldots, x_m^*(\omega))\mu(\omega)$$

for every strategy x_i.

A fundamental question which arises is under what conditions the game Γ has a correlated equilibrium. The purpose of this paper is to provide an answer to this question. In particular, we show that if Ω is a probability measure space, X_i is a (Banach) set-valued function defined on Ω whose values are convex and weakly compact and u_i is weakly continuous, integrably bounded and concave in the ith coordinate, then the game Γ has a correlated equilibrium.[1] Moreover, adopting an idea of Khan (1986) [see also Schmeidler (1973)], i.e., by viewing the extreme points of the set X_i as pure strategies we also prove a pure strategy correlated equilibrium existence result for the game Γ.[2]

The proofs of our results require arguments of a rather novel-type. However, it should be noted that the techniques which have been used in the literature of the existence of a Nash equilibrium in games with a continuum of players [e.g., Schmeidler (1973), Khan (1986), Yannelis (1987) and Yannelis-Rustichini (1991)] will turn out to be useful. Moreover, some theorems of Aumann (1965) on the integration of set-valued functions as well as extensions of Aumann's results given by Datko (1973), Khan (1986), Rustichini (1989) and Yannelis (1988) will play an important role.

The paper is organized in the following way: Section 2 contains notation and definitions. The main results of the paper are stated in Section 3 and their proofs are collected in Section 4 and 5. Finally, some concluding

---

[1] Note that the convexity of the strategy set of each player amounts to a mixed strategy correlated equilibrium result and this may be objectionable; to quote Aumann (1987, p. 11) "In view of the fact that players may wish to use mixed strategies, the reader may question the assumption that each player knows his own action. There is no problem if, as usual, one thinks of a mixed strategy simply as a random device for helping the player make up his mind, so that in the end he does know which action he takes." Also, it is important to note that whenever Nash-type equilibrium existence results are applied to exchange economies the assumption of convexity of the strategy set of each player constitutes no real economic restriction. In particular, exchange economies are converted to abstract economies and the consumption set of each agent in the exchange economy (which is interpreted as the strategy set of each player in the abstract economy) is typically assumed to be convex [see for instance Arrow-Debreu (1954) or more recently Yannelis (1987)].

[2] It should be noted that recently, Hart-Schmeidler (1987) have obtained correlated equilibrium results different from ours. In particular, they do not consider the case of asymmetric information. It should be noted that the existence of a correlated equilibrium in a less general setting than ours can be obtained by showing that Nash equilibria are correlated and therefore the classical equilibrium existence result of Nash is directly applicable [see for instance Aumann (1974)]. Moreover, a different correlated equilibrium concept and its existence has been examined in Nowak (1990).

remarks are given in Chapter 6.

2. Notation and Definitions

2.1 Notation.

2^A denotes the set of all nonempty subsets of the set A.
con A denotes the convex hull of the set A.
$\overline{\text{con}}A$ denotes the closed convex hull of the set A.
$\mathbf{R}^\ell$ denotes the ℓ-fold Cartesian product of the set of real numbers $\mathbf{R}$.
$\emptyset$ denotes the empty set.
If X is linear topological space, its dual is the space X^* of all continuous linear functionals on X, and if $p \in X^*$ and $x \in X$ the value of p at x is denoted by $\langle p, x \rangle$.

2.2 Definitions. Let X, Y be topological spaces. The correspondence[3] $\phi : X \to 2^Y$ is said to be *upper semicontinuous* (u.s.c.) if the set $\{x \in X : \phi(x) \subset V\}$ is open in X for every open subset V of Y. The *graph* of the correspondence $\phi : X \to 2^Y$ is denoted by $G_\phi = \{(x, y) \in X \times Y : y \in \phi(x)\}$.

Let $(\Omega, \mathcal{T}, \mu)$ be a complete finite measure space and X be a separable Banach space. The correspondence $\phi : \Omega \to 2^X$ is said to have a *measurable graph* if $G_\phi \in \mathcal{T} \otimes \mathcal{B}(X)$, where $\mathcal{B}(X)$ denotes the Borel σ-algebra on X and $\otimes$ denotes product σ-algebra. The correspondence $\phi : T \to 2^X$ is said to be *lower measurable* if for every open subset V of X the set $\{\omega \in \Omega : \phi(\omega) \cap V \neq \emptyset\}$ is an element of $\mathcal{T}$. It is well known that if $\phi : \Omega \to 2^X$ has a measurable graph it is also lower measurable [Himmelberg (1975, p. 47)]. Furthermore, if $\phi(\cdot)$ is closed valued and lower measurable then $\phi(\cdot)$ has a measurable graph.

Below we define the notion of a Bochner integrable function. We will follow the treatment of Diestel-Uhl (1977). Let $(\Omega, \mathcal{T}, \mu)$ be a finite measure space and X be a Banach space. A function $f : \Omega \to X$ is called *simple* if there exist $x_1, x_2, \ldots, x_n$ in X and $\sigma_1, \sigma_2, \ldots, \sigma_n$ in $\mathcal{T}$ such that $f = \sum_{i=1}^n x_i \chi_{\sigma_i}$, where $\chi_{\sigma_i} = 1$ if $\omega \in \sigma_i$ and $\chi_{\sigma_i}(\omega) = 0$ if $\omega \notin \sigma_i$. A function $f : \Omega \to X$ is said to be *μ-measurable* if there exists a sequence of

[3] A correspondence is a set-valued function for which all image sets are nonempty.

simple functions $f_n : \Omega \to X$ such that $\lim_{n\to\infty} \|f_n(\omega) - f(\omega)\| = 0$ μ-a.e. A μ-measurable function $f : \Omega \to X$ is said to be *Bochner integrable* if there exists a sequence of simple functions $\{f_n : n = 1, 2, \dots\}$ such that

$$\lim_{n\to\infty} \int_\Omega \|f_n(\omega) - f(\omega)\| d\mu(\omega) = 0.$$

In this case we define for each $A \in \mathcal{T}$ the integral to be $\int_A f(\omega)d\mu(\omega) = \lim_{n\to\infty} \int_A f_n(\omega)d\mu(\omega)$. It is a standard result [Diestel-Uhl (1977, Theorem 2, p. 45)] that if $f : \Omega \to X$ is a μ-measurable function then f is Bochner integrable if and only if $\int_\Omega \|f(\omega)\|d\mu(\omega) < \infty$. We denote by $L_1(\mu, X)$ the space of equivalence classes of X-valued Bochner integrable functions $x : \Omega \to X$ normed by $\|x\| = \int_\Omega \|x(\omega)\|d\mu(\omega)$. It is well known that normed by the functional $\|\cdot\|$ above, $L_1(\mu, X)$ becomes a Banach space [Diestel-Uhl (1977, p. 50)]. We denote by S_ϕ the *set of all X-valued Bochner integrable selections from the correspondence* $\phi : \Omega \to 2^X$, i.e.,

$$S_\phi = \{y \in L_1(\mu, X) : y(\omega) \in \phi(\omega) \ \mu\text{-a.e.}\}.$$

Following Aumann (1965) the *integral of the correspondence* $\phi : \Omega \to 2^X$ is defined as follows:

$$\int_\Omega \phi(\omega)d\mu(\omega) = \left\{\int_\Omega y(\omega)d\mu(\omega) : y \in S_\phi\right\}.$$

We will denote the above integral by $\int \phi$. A correspondence $\phi : \Omega \to 2^X$ is said to be *integrably bounded* if there exists a map $g \in L_1(\mu, \mathbb{R})$ such that $\sup\{\|x\| : x \in \phi(\omega)\} \le g(\omega)$ μ-a.e. Note that if Ω is a complete finite measure space, and X is a separable Banach space and $\phi : \Omega \to 2^X$ is a nonempty-valued correspondence with a measurable graph (or equivalently $\phi(\cdot)$ is lower measurable and closed valued), then $\phi : \Omega \to 2^X$ admits a *measurable selection*, i.e., there exists a measurable function $f : \Omega \to X$ such that $f(\omega) \in \phi(\omega)$ μ-a.e. By virtue of this result and provided that the correspondence $\phi : \Omega \to 2^X$ is integrably bounded, we can conclude that S_ϕ is nonempty and hence $\int \phi$ is nonempty as well.

A Banach space X has the *Radon-Nikodym Property* with respect to the measure space $(\Omega, \mathcal{T}, \mu)$ if for each μ-continuous vector measure $G : \mathcal{T} \to X$ of bounded variation there exists $g \in L_1(\mu, X)$ such that

$G(E) = \int_E g(\omega)d\mu(\omega)$ for all $E \in \mathcal{T}$. A Banach space X has the *Radon-Nikodym Property* (RNP) if X has the RNP with respect to every finite measure space. It is a standard result [Diestel-Uhl (1977, Theorem 1, p. 98)] that if $(\Omega, \mathcal{T}, \mu)$ is a finite measure space $1 \leq p < \infty$, and X is a Banach space, then X^* has the RNP if and only if $(L_p(\mu, X))^* = L_q(\mu, X^*)$ where $\frac{1}{p} + \frac{1}{q} = 1$.

We conclude this section by noting that if X is a separable Banach space, $(\Omega, \mathcal{T}, \mu)$ is a finite positive measure space and $\phi : \Omega \to 2^X$ is an integrably bounded, nonempty, weakly compact, and convex valued correspondence then by *Diestel's Theorem* [see for instance Yannelis (1990)], we have that S_ϕ is weakly compact in $L_1(\mu, X)$.

3. The Main Theorems

Let Y be a separable Banach space whose dual Y^* has the RNP and $(\Omega, \mathcal{T}, \mu)$ be a complete probability measure space. As usual, we interpret Ω as the states of nature of the world and assume that Ω includes all the events that we consider to be interesting, $\mathcal{T}$ will denote the σ-algebra of events and obviously μ is the measure on $(\Omega, \mathcal{T})$.

A *game* $\Gamma = \{(X_i, u_i, S_i) : i = 1, 2, \ldots, m\}$ is a set of triplets (X_i, u_i, S_i) where,

(1) $X_i : \Omega \to 2^Y$ is the *strategy correspondence* of player i,

(2) $u_i : \prod_{j=1}^m Y_j \to \mathbb{R}$ is the *payoff function* of player i, and

(3) S_i is the *private information* of player i, where S_i is a partition of $(\Omega, \mathcal{T})$. (Note that the probability measure μ on $(\Omega, \mathcal{T})$ can be interpreted as the common prior of each player.)

Denote by L_{X_i} the set of all Bochner integrable and S_i-measurable selections from the strategy set X_i of player i, i.e., $L_{X_i} = \{x_i \in L_1(\mu, Y) : x_i : \Omega \to Y$ is S_i-measurable and $x_i(\omega) \in X_i(\omega)$ μ-a.e.$\}$. Let $L_X = \prod_{i=1}^m L_{X_i}$. Moreover, let $L_{\tilde{X}_i} = \prod_{j \neq i} L_{X_j}$ and denote the points of $L_{\tilde{X}_i}$ by $\tilde{x}_i$.

The *expected payoff* of player i is a function $g_i : L_X \to \mathbb{R}$ defined by

$$g_i(x) = \int_{\omega \in \Omega} u_i(x(\omega))d\mu(\omega).$$

A strategy $x^* \in L_X$ is said to be a *correlated equilibrium* for the game Γ, if for all i, $(i = 1, 2, \ldots, m)$,

$$g_i(x^*) = \max_{x_i \in L_{X_i}} g_i(x_i, \tilde{x}_i^*).$$

We are now ready to state the following result.

Theorem 3.1. *Let* $\Gamma = \{(X_i, u_i, S_i) : i = 1, 2, \ldots, m\}$ *be a game satisfying for all i the following assumptions:*

(a.3.1) $X_i : \Omega \to 2^Y$ *is an integrably bounded, weakly compact, convex, nonempty valued and* S_i*-lower measurable correspondence,*

(a.3.2) u_i *is weakly continuous and integrably bounded,*

(a.3.3) u_i *is concave in the* i^{th} *coordinate, i.e., for each* $\tilde{x}_i \in \tilde{X}_i = \prod_{j \neq i} X_j$, $u_i(x_i, \tilde{x}_i)$ *is a concave function of* x_i *on* X_i.

Then Γ *has a correlated equilibrium.*

We now turn to the existence of a pure strategy correlated equilibrium. From now on until the end of this section we set $Y = \mathbb{R}^\ell$. Hence, for the game Γ described above X_i is a correspondence from Ω into $\mathbb{R}^\ell$. Moreover, we assume that for each i, S_i is a sub σ-algebra of $\mathcal{T}$ and the restriction of μ to S_i is still denoted by μ. We denote by X_i^e the *extreme points* of X_i.

A *pure strategy correlated equilibrium* for the game Γ is an $x^* : \Omega \to \prod_{i=1}^m X_i^e$ such that each $x_i^*(\cdot)$ is S_i-measurable and for all i, $(i = 1, 2, \ldots, m)$,

$$\int_{\omega \in \Omega} u_i(x^*(\omega)) d\mu(\omega) \geq \int_{\omega \in \Omega} u_i(x_i(\omega), \tilde{x}_i^*(\omega)) d\mu(\omega)$$

for any S_i-measurable function $x_i : \Omega \to X_i^e$.

We are now ready to state our second main result.

Theorem 3.2. *Let* $\Gamma = \{(X_i, u_i, S_i) : i = 1, 2, \ldots, m\}$ *be a game satisfying for each i the following assumptions:*

(a.3.4) (Ω, S_i, μ) *is a complete, atomless probability measure space,*

(a.3.5) $X_i : \Omega \to 2^{\mathbb{R}^\ell}$ *is an integrably bounded, compact, convex, nonempty valued and* S_i*-lower measurable correspondence,*

(a.3.6) u_i *is continuous, integrably bounded, and linear on* $\prod_{j=1}^m Y_j$.

Then Γ *has a pure strategy correlated equilibrium.*

The next two sections are devoted to the proofs of our theorems.

4. Proof of Theorem 3.1

Let $L_{\tilde{X}_i} = \prod_{j \neq i} L_{X_j}$. For each i define the correspondence $\phi_i : L_{\tilde{X}_i} \to 2^{L_{X_i}}$ by

$$\phi_i(\tilde{x}_i) = \{y_i \in L_{X_i} : g_i(y_i, \tilde{x}_i) = \max_{x_i \in L_{X_i}} g_i(x_i, \tilde{x}_i)\}.$$

Also define the correspondence $\Phi : L_X \to 2^{L_X}$ by

$$\Phi(x) = \prod_{i=1}^{m} \phi_i(\tilde{x}_i).$$

We must show that the set valued function $\Phi : L_X \to 2^{L_X}$ satisfies all the conditions of the Fan-Glicksberg fixed point theorem [Fan (1952), Glicksberg (1952), see also Berge (1963, p. 251)]. Clearly, a fixed point of Φ is a correlated equilibrium for the game Γ. We begin by proving the following fact:

Fact 4.1. *L_X is weakly compact, nonempty, and convex.*

Proof. It follows directly from Diestel's theorem that L_{X_i} is weakly compact and therefore L_X is weakly compact as well. Obviously, since each $X_i(\cdot)$ is convex valued, L_{X_i} is convex and so is L_X. Since $X_i(\cdot)$ is closed valued and S_i-lower measurable (assumption (a.3.1)) it follows from the Kuratowski and Ryll-Nardzewski measurable selection theorem [Himmelberg (1975, p. 60)] that there exists an S_i-measurable function $f_i : \Omega \to Y$ such that $f_i(\omega) \in X_i(\omega)$ μ-a.e. Since X_i is integrably bounded f_i is also Bochner integrable, i.e., $f_i \in L_1(\mu, Y)$ and therefore we can conclude that $f_i \in L_{X_i}$. Consequently, L_{X_i} is nonempty and so is $L_X = \prod_{i=1}^{m} L_{X_i}$. This completes the proof of the claim.

Fact 4.2. *For each i, $(i = 1, 2, \ldots, m)$, $g_i(\cdot)$ is weakly continuous.*

Proof. Let $\{x_n : n = 1, 2, \ldots\}$ be a sequence in $L_X = \prod_{i=1}^m L_{X_i}$ converging weakly[4] to $x \in L_X$, i.e., for each i, $(i = 1, 2, \ldots, m)$ the sequence $\{x_n^i : n = 1, 2, \ldots\}$ in L_{X_i} converges weakly to x^i in L_{X_i}. If we show that for all i, x_n^i converges pointwise in the weak topology of X_i to x^i, then given the fact that u_i is integrably bounded and weakly continuous the result will follow from the Lebesgue dominated convergence theorem. Note that since for each i the partition S_i is countable, i.e., $S_i = \{\alpha_i^1, \alpha_i^2, \alpha_i^3, \ldots\}$ the fact that x_n^i and x^i are elements of L_{X_i} implies that

$$x_n^i = \sum_{k=1}^{\infty} x_n^{i,k} \chi_{\alpha_i} k$$

and

$$x^i = \sum_{k=1}^{\infty} x^{i,k} \chi_{\alpha_i} k$$

for $x_n^{i,k}$, $x^{i,k}$ in X_i and therefore we can conclude that x_n^i converges pointwise in the weak topology of X_i to x^i. This completes the proof of the claim.

It follows from Berge's maximum theorem [Berge (1963, p. 116)] that for each i, $\phi_i(\cdot)$ is weakly u.s.c. Moreover, since for each i, u_i is concave in the ith coordinate it follows that for each i and each $\tilde{x}_i \in L_{\tilde{X}_i}$, $g_i(x_i, \tilde{x}_i)$ is a quasi-concave function of x_i on L_{X_i} and consequently for each i, $\phi_i(\cdot)$ is convex valued. Since $g_i(\cdot)$ is weakly continuous and L_{X_i} is weakly compact, $\phi_i(\cdot)$ is nonempty valued. Thus, $\phi_i : L_{\tilde{X}_i} \to 2^{L_{X_i}}$ is a weakly u.s.c., closed, convex, nonempty valued correspondence and so is $\Phi : L_X \to 2^{L_X}$ defined by $\Phi(x) = \prod_{i=1}^m \phi_i(\tilde{x})$, [Berge (1963, Theorem 4', p. 114)]. Consequently, the set-valued function $\Phi : L_X \to 2^{L_X}$ satisfies all the conditions of the Fan-Glicksberg fixed point theorem and therefore exists $x^* \in L_X$ such that $x^* \in \Phi(x^*)$. It can be easily checked that the fixed point is by construction a correlated equilibrium for the game Γ. This completes the proof of Theorem 3.1.

---

[4] Let $\{f_n : n = 1, 2, \ldots\}$ be a sequence in $L_1(\mu, Y)$. Then f_n converges weakly to f if and only if $\langle f_n, p\rangle$ converges to $\langle f, p\rangle$ for any $p \in L_\infty(\mu, Y^*)$ (recall that Y^* has the RNP), which is equivalent to the fact that $\langle f_n \chi_A, p\rangle = \langle f_n, \chi_A p\rangle$ converges to $\langle f, \chi_A p\rangle = \langle f\chi_A, p\rangle$ for any $p \in L_\infty(\mu, Y^*)$, $A \in \mathcal{T}$, and each condition above implies that $\langle f_n \chi_A, x^*\rangle = \langle f_n, \chi_A x^*\rangle$ converges to $\langle f\chi_A, x^*\rangle = \langle f, \chi_A x^*\rangle$ for any $x^* \in Y^*$, $A \in \mathcal{T}$.

5. Proof of Theorem 3.2

Denote by $L_{X_i^e}$ the set of all Bochner integrable and S_i-measurable selections from the strategy set X_i^e of player i, that is, $L_{X_i^e} = \{x_i \in L_1(\mu, \mathbb{R}^\ell) : x_i : \Omega \to \mathbb{R}^\ell$ is S_i-measurable and $x_i(\omega) \in X_i^e(\omega)$ μ-a.e.$\}$. Let $L_{X^e} = \prod_{i=1}^m L_{X_i^e}$. Define the mapping $\pi : L_1(\mu, \mathbb{R}^\ell) \to \mathbb{R}^\ell$ by $\pi(y) = \int_{\omega\in\Omega} y(\omega)d\mu(\omega)$. The integral of the set-valued function X_i^e is $\int_{\omega\in\Omega} X_i^e(\omega)d\mu(\omega) = \pi(L_{X_i^e}) = \{\pi(y) : y \in L_{X_i^e}\}$. We denote the above integral by $\int X_i^e$. let $\int X^e = \prod_{i=1}^m \int X_i^e$, $\int \tilde{X}_i^e = \prod_{j\neq i} \int X_j^e$ and denote the points of $\int \tilde{X}_i^e$ by $\tilde{x}_i$.

Note that since by assumption (a.3.6) u_i is linear on $\prod_{j=1}^m Y_j$ the domain of the expected utility $g_i(x) = \int_{\omega\in\Omega} u_i(x(\omega))d\mu(\omega)$ is now $\int X$ and this latter set will turn out to be equal to $\int X^e$. Since for each i, X_i is compact and convex valued, by the Krein-Milman-Minkowski theorem we have that:

$$\operatorname{con} X_i^e(\omega) = X_i(\omega) \ \mu\text{-a.e.} \tag{5.1}$$

Integrating (5.1) we obtain:

$$\int \operatorname{con} X_i^e = \int X_i. \tag{5.2}$$

Since the measure space (Ω, S_i, μ) is atomless, it follows from Theorem 3 in Aumann (1965) that:

$$\int \operatorname{con} X_i^e = \int X_i^e. \tag{5.3}$$

Combining (5.2) and (5.3) we have that $\int X_i^e = \int X_i$ and therefore $\int X^e = \int X$.

For each i, $(i = 1, 2, \ldots, m)$ define the set-valued function $F_i : \int \tilde{X}_i^e \to 2^{\int X_i^e}$ by

$$F_i(\tilde{x}_i) = \{y_i \in \int X_i^e : g_i(y_i, \tilde{x}_i) = \max_{x_i \in \int X_i} g_i(x_i, \tilde{x}_i)\}.$$

Moreover, define the correspondence $F : \int X^e \to 2^{\int X^e}$ by

$$F(x) = \prod_{i=1}^m F_i(\tilde{x}_i).$$

We will show that the set-valued function $F : \int X^e \to 2^{\int X^e}$ satisfies all the conditions of the Kakutani fixed point theorem. It can be easily seen that a fixed point of the set-valued function F is by construction a pure strategy correlated equilibrium for the game Γ. We begin by proving the following claim.

Claim 5.1. *$\int X^e$ is compact and nonempty.*

Proof. Since for each i, X_i is lower measurable and closed valued, it has a measurable graph [Himmelberg (1975, p. 47)]. Furthermore, since for each i, X_i is integrably bounded it follows from Theorem 4 in Aumann (1965) that $\int X_i$ is compact and so is $\int X^e = \int X$. We now show that $\int X^e$ is nonempty. Since for each i, X_i is S_i-lower measurable and closed valued, by the Kuratowski and Ryll-Nardzewski measurable selection theorem that there exists an S_i-measurable function $f_i : \Omega \to \mathbb{R}^\ell$ such that $f_i(\omega) \in X_i(\omega)$ μ-a.e. Since X_i is integrably bounded f_i is integrable, i.e., $f_i \in L_1(\mu, \mathbb{R}^\ell)$ and therefore $f_i \in L_{X_i}$. Hence, L_{X_i} is nonempty and so is $L_X = \prod_{i=1}^m L_{X_i}$. The latter enable us to conclude that $\int X$ is nonempty as well. Consequently, $\int X^e$ is compact and nonempty as was to be shown.

Note that since for each i, u_i is integrably bounded and continuous by virtue of the Lebesgue dominated convergence theorem we can conclude that for each i, g_i is continuous. As in the proof of Theorem 3.1, it can be easily now checked that for each i, F_i is an u.s.c. closed convex valued correspondence and so is F. By the Kakutani fixed point theorem there exists $x^* \in \int X^e$ such that $x^* \in F(x^*)$, which implies that for all i, $(i = 1, 2, \ldots, m)$, $g_i(x^*) = \max_{x_i \in \int X_i^e} g_i(x_i, \tilde{x}_i^*)$, i.e., x^* is a pure strategy correlated equilibrium for the game Γ. This completes the proof of Theorem 3.2.

6. Concluding Remarks

Remark 6.1. Note that Theorem 3.2, i.e., the existence of a pure strategy correlated equilibrium is based heavily on the Lyapunov theorem. In particular, Theorem 3 in Aumann (1965) which enabled us to obtain (5.3), i.e., $\int \operatorname{con} X_i^e = \int X_i^e$, is proved by means of the Lyapunov theorem [see also Schmeidler (1973) for a similar argument with the one used to prove Theorem 3.2].

Remark 6.2. In Theorem 3.2 we assumed that the strategy set of each player is a subset of a finite dimensional Euclidean space. The reason for this is that we needed Lyapunov's theorem (as noted above), a result which is false in infinite dimensional spaces [see for instance Diestel-Uhl (1977, p. 262)]. The question which arises is whether the argument used to prove Theorem 3.2 remains valid if the strategy set of each player satisfies (a.3.1). The answer is a qualified yes. In particular, note that the key step in the proof of Theorem 3.2 was to show that $\int X^e = \int X$. The latter statement was obtained by using the Krein-Milman-Minkowski Theorem and Theorem 3 of Aumann (1965). However, in an infinite dimensional setting, (5.1) in the proof of Theorem 3.2 becomes

$$\overline{\text{con}} X_i^e(\omega) = X_i(\omega) \ \mu\text{-a.e.} \tag{5.1'}$$

Therefore,

$$\int \overline{\text{con}} X_i^e = \int X_i. \tag{5.2'}$$

By a Theorem of Datko (1973) [see also Khan (1986) for a more general statement], we have that:

$$\int \overline{\text{con}} X_i^e = \text{cl} \int X_i^e, \text{(where cl denotes norm closure).}^5$$

Combining (5.2′) and (5.3′) we can conclude that the aggregate set of pure strategies is dense in the aggregate set of mixed strategies, i.e, $\text{cl} \int X^e = \int X$. Furthermore, $\text{cl} \int X^e$ is convex [Khan (1986, p. 261)], and by Lemma 3.1 in Yannelis (1988), $\int X$ is weakly compact. Finally it is easy to show that $g_i(\cdot)$ is weakly continuous. In fact, since by assumption (a.3.6) u_i is (norm) continuous and integrably bounded it follows from the Lebesgue dominated convergence theorem that g_i is (norm) continuous. Since u_i is linear so is g_i and by Theorem 15 in Dunford-Schwartz (1958, p. 422) we can conclude that g_i is weakly continuous.

[5] Rustichini (1989) showed that in the extensions of Theorem 3 of Aumann (1965) given in Datko (1973) and Khan (1986) the norm closure cannot be removed (i.e., in expression (5.3′) the norm closure cannot be dispensed with).

The rest of the argument is now similar with that adopted for the proof of Theorem 3.2. However, in this case since cl $\int X^e = \int X$ one can only obtain an approximate pure strategy correlated equilibrium for the game Γ. Nevertheless, one can still prove the existence of an exact pure strategy correlated equilibrium for a game with an infinite dimensional strategy space provided that the game has "many more" states than strategies, i.e., the dimension of the state space (Ω, S_i, μ) is bigger than the dimension of the strategy space Y. Of course the concept of dimension has to be given a rigorous formulation. We refer the reader to the work of Rustichini-Yannelis (1990) for an extensive discussion of this point. In particular, Rustichini-Yannelis show that the (norm) closure can be removed and have that $\int X^e = \int X$.

Remark 6.3. Theorems 3.1 and 3.2 remain true if the utility function of each player u_i is allowed to be state dependent, i.e., u_i is now defined on $\Omega \times \prod_{j=1}^{m} Y_j$.

Remark 6.4. Theorems 3.1 and 3.2 remain valid if one allows players to have different priors.

Remark 6.5. Our results can be easily extended to abstract economies as defined in Debreu (1952) and Arrow-Debreu (1954).

References

Arrow, K. and Debreu, G., 1954, "Existence of an Equilibrium for a Competitive Economy," *Econometrica* **22**, 265–290.

Aumann, R. J., 1965, "Integrals of Set-Valued Functions," *J. Math. Anal. Appl.* **12**, 1–12.

Aumann, R. J., 1974, "Subjectivity and Correlation in Randomized Strategies," *J. Math. Econ.* **1**, 67–96.

Aumann, R. J., 1987, "Correlated Equilibrium as an Expression of Bayesian Rationality," *Econometrica* **55**, 1–18.

Balder, E. J., 1988, "Generalized Equilibrium Results for Games with Incomplete Information," *Math. Oper. Res.* **13**, 265–276.

Berge, C., 1963, *Topological Spaces*, Oliver and Boyd, Edinburgh and London.

Datko, R., 1973, "On the Integration of Set-Valued Mappings in a Banach Space," *Fund. Math.* **78**, 205–208.

Debreu, G., 1952, "A Social Equilibrium Existence Theorem," *Proc. Natl. Acad. Sci. USA* **38**, 886–893.

Diestel, J., 1977, "Remarks on Weak Compactness in $L_1(\mu, X)$," *Glasgow Math. J.* **18**, 87–91.

Diestel, J. and Uhl, J., 1977, *Vector Measures*, Mathematical Surveys **15**, American Mathematical Society, Providence, Rhode Island.

Dunford, N. and Schwartz, J. T., (1958), *Linear Operators*, Part I, Interscience, New York.

Fan, K., 1952, "Fixed Point and Minimax Theorems in Locally Convex Topological Linear Spaces," *Proc. Natl. Acad. Sci. USA* **38**, 131–136.

Glicksberg, I. L., 1952, "A Further Generalization of the Kakutani Fixed Point Theorem, with Applications to Nash Equilibrium Points," *Proc. Amer. Math. Soc.* **3**, 170–174.

Hart, S. and Schmeidler, D., 1987, "Existence of Correlated Equilibria," CARESS Working Paper No. 87-14, University of Pennsylvania.

Himmelberg, C. J., 1975, "Measurable Relations," *Fund. Math.* **87**, 53–72.

Khan, M. Ali, 1976, "On the Integration of Set-Valued Mappings in a Nonreflexive Banach Space II," *Simon Stevin* **59**, 257–267.

Khan, M. Ali, 1986, "Equilibrium Points of Nonatomic Games Over a Banach Space," *Trans. Amer. Math. Soc.* **29**, 737–749.

Nash, J., 1951, "Non-Cooperative Games," *Ann. Math.* **54**, 286–295.

Nowak, A. S., 1990, "Existence of Correlated Weak Equilibria in Discontinuous Games," this volume.

Rustichini, A., 1989, "A Counterexample and an Exact Version of Fatou's Lemma in Infinite Dimensions," *Archiv der Mathematic* **52**, 357–362.

Rustichini, A. and Yannelis, N. C., 1990, "What is Perfect Competition?" this volume.

Schmeidler, D., 1973, "Equilibrium Points of Non-Atomic Games," *J. Stat. Physics* **7**, 295–300.

Yannelis, N. C. and Rustichini, A., 1991, "Equilibrium Points of Noncooperative Random and Bayesian Games," forthcoming in *Positive Operators, Riesz Spaces, and Economics*, C. D. Aliprantis, K. C. Border and W. A. J. Luxemburg, eds., Springer-Verlag.

Yannelis, N. C., 1987, "Equilibria in Noncooperative Models of Competition," *J. Econ. Theory* **41**, 96–111.

Yannelis, N. C., 1988, "Fatou's Lemma in Infinite Dimensional Spaces," *Proc. Amer. Math. Soc.* **102**, 303–310.

Yannelis, N. C., 1990, "Integration of Banach-Valued Correspondences," this volume.

Existence of Correlated Weak Equilibria in Discontinuous Games

Andrzej S. Nowak

Abstract. This paper treats of non-zero-sum discontinuous games with compact Hausdorff strategy spaces. It is assumed that the payoff function of each player in the game is bounded, Borel measurable and is upper semicontinuous on his strategy space, for all fixed actions of the remaining players. It is shown that for each $\varepsilon > 0$, such games possess correlated weak ε-equilibria introduced by Moulin and Vial as extension of correlated equilibria in the sense of Aumann. The existence of Nash or correlated ε-equilibria is an open problem.

1. Introduction

Correlated weak equilibria were introduced by Moulin and Vial [1978] as "simple extensions" of correlated equilibria in the sense of Aumann [1974, 1987]. They are known to exist in non-zero-sum compact continuous games where the pure strategy spaces are given compact Hausdorff topologies and the payoff functions are continuous. This is a corollary to the well-known Nash equilibrium theorem [Glicksberg, 1952] or the correlated equilibrium theorem due to Hart and Schmeidler [1989, Theorem 3] because (as it immediately follows from the definitions) the set of correlated weak equilibria in a compact-continuous game always contains the set of correlated equilibria and the latter set contains the convex hull of Nash equilibria. For details we refer the reader to Moulin [1981], Moulin and Vial [1978], Aumann [1974], Aumann [1987], and Hart and Schmeidler [1989]. In Gerard-Varet and Moulin [1978], Moulin [1981], and Moulin and Vial [1978], the reader can also find some interesting examples of correlated weak equilibria.

The paper is devoted to studying the existence of correlated weak ε-equilibria ($\varepsilon > 0$) in some discontinuous non-zero-sum m-person games. (We deal with countably additive mixed strategies.) Our main objective is to prove that correlated weak ε-equilibria do exist in very general games, where the pure strategy spaces are endowed with compact Hausdorff topologies and the payoff function of each player is a bounded Borel measurable function (on the Cartesian product of the strategy spaces) and is upper semicontinuous in his strategies, for all fixed actions of the remaining players (see the Equilibrium Theorem in §2). Both Nash equilibria and correlated equilibria in the sense of Aumann are not known to exist in such games. The Nash equilibrium theorems due to Dasgupta and Maskin and others do not concern discontinuous games that are studied in this paper; see Dasgupta and Maskin [1989a, 1989b] and the references therein.

Our proof of the existence result in §2 does not use any fixed point argument. It refers to Fan's minimax theorem instead [Fan, 1953, Theorem 2], which can be deduced from the von Neumann minimax theorem or the standard linear duality theorem; see [Owen, 1982], [Sion, 1958, §4]. A correlated weak ε-equilibrium for a given game and for a given $\varepsilon > 0$ is obtained as an ε-supmin mixed strategy in some auxiliary zero-sum game. A related approach to Aumann's correlated equilibria in matrix games was recently taken by Hart and Schmeidler [1989]. Correlated equilibria are also studied in [Yannelis and Rustichini, 1990], but from a different point of view. The results obtained in [Yannelis and Rustichini, 1990] are of a different nature.

2. The Equilibrium Theorem

We begin with some preliminaries. Let X be a compact Hausdorff space. By $\mathcal{B}(X)$ we denote the σ-algebra of all Borel subsets of X. $\mathcal{B}_0(X)$ means the Baire σ-algebra in X; that is, the smallest σ-algebra in X for which all continuous real valued functions $f : X \to \mathbb{R}$ are measurable. Clearly, $\mathcal{B}_0(X) \subset \mathcal{B}(X)$. A nonnegative Radon measure on X is a nonnegative bounded countably additive regular measure on $\mathcal{B}(X)$ [Meyer, 1966, II.37]. By $M(X)$ we denote the set of all nonnegative Radon measures p on X such that $p(X) \leq 1$. Clearly, every $p \in M(X)$ is a regular measure on $\mathcal{B}_0(X)$. It is also true that every countably additive regular measure p on $\mathcal{B}_0(X)$ such that $p(X) \leq 1$ has a unique extension to a Radon measure in $M(X)$ [Meyer, 1966, II.T 35]. Let $P(X)$ denote the set of all probability measures from $M(X)$. Assume that $P(X)$ and $M(X)$ are given the weak*-topology [Dunford and Schwartz, 1958; Edwards, 1965]. Then by the Riesz Representation Theorem [Dunford and Schwartz, 1958, Theorem IV, 6.3] and the Banach-Alaoglu Theorem [Dunford and Schwartz, 1958, Theorem V.4.2], both $M(X)$ and $P(X)$ are compact spaces.

Let $f : X \to \mathbb{R}$ be an upper semicontinuous function. Then f is Borel measurable. Moreover, the function $p \longmapsto \int f(x)p(dx)$ defined on $M(X)$ is upper semicontinuous as well; see [Edwards, 1965, Chapter 0.2.10] and [Meyer, 1966, II.T.36].

Let $N = \{1, 2, \ldots, m\}$ and let X^n, $n \in N$, be a sequence of compact Hausdorff spaces. The Cartesian product of X^n's is denoted by $X = \prod_{n \in N} X^n$. We assume that X is endowed with the product topology. Then, by Tychonoff's Theorem [Edwards, 1965], X is a compact Hausdorff space. Moreover, we know that $\mathcal{B}_0(X) = \prod_{n \in N} \mathcal{B}_0(X^n)$, the product of σ-algebras $\mathcal{B}_0(X^n)$, $n \in N$ [Meyer, 1966, II.T30]. (In general, it is not true that $\mathcal{B}(X) = \prod_{n \in N} \mathcal{B}(X^n)$. However, when X^n's are metrizable spaces, the equality holds.)

Let $q_n \in M(X^n)$, $n \in N$. By $q_1 \times q_2 \times \cdots \times q_m$ we denote the Radon measure from $M(X)$ obtained as the unique extension to $\mathcal{B}(X)$ of the usual product measure $q_1 \times \cdots \times q_m$ [Dunford and Schwartz, 1958] defined on the product σ-algebra $\prod_{n \in N} \mathcal{B}_0(X^n)$ which as already noted coincides with $\mathcal{B}_0(X)$.

An *m-person game* that we consider in this paper is defined by a sequence of objects $(S^n, u^n)_{n \in N}$ where

(A_1) $N = \{1, \ldots, m\}$ is the *set of players*,
(A_2) S^n is a compact Hausdorff space of *pure strategies* for player $n \in N$,
(A_3) $u_n : S \to \mathbb{R}$ is a bounded Borel measurable *payoff function* for player $n \in N$, defined on $S = \prod_{n \in N} S^n$, the set of all sequences $(s^n)_{n \in N}$ of strategies played by the players, endowed with the product topology and the Borel σ-algebra $\mathcal{B}(S)$.

Define S^{-n} as $\prod_{\substack{k \in N \\ k \neq n}} S_k$. Thus S^{-n} is the set of all strategies played by everyone except player n. Denote by π^{-n} the projection mapping from S to S^{-n}. For each Borel set $B \in \mathcal{B}(S^{-n})$ we put $B \times S^n = (\pi^{-n})^{-1}(B)$. Then $B \times S^n$ is a Borel subset of S. Let $p \in P(S)$. Associated with p and any $n \in N$ is the marginal distribution p^{-n} on $\mathcal{B}(S^{-n})$. Namely for each $B \in \mathcal{B}(S^{-n})$, $p^{-n}(B) = p(B \times S^n)$. It is easy to prove that p^{-n} is a probability Radon measure on S^{-n} [Hart and Schmeidler, 1989, the proof of Theorem 3, footnote 16]. Following Aumann [1974, 1987], we call any $p \in P(S)$ a *correlated strategy* for the players. The expected payoff for player $n \in N$ with respect to $p \in P(S)$ is denoted by $u_n(p)$.

Let $p \in P(S)$ and $q_n \in M(S^n)$, $n \in N$. By $u_n(p^{-n}q_n)$ we denote the integral of u_n with respect to the Radon measure $p^{-n}q_n \in M(S)$. (Here $p^{-n}q_n$ means the unique extension to $\mathcal{B}(S)$ of the usual product measure $p^{-n} \times q_n$ defined on $\mathcal{B}_0(S^{-n}) \times \mathcal{B}_0(S^n)$, which coincides with $\mathcal{B}_0(S)$.) The construction of $p^{-n}q_n$ and Fubini's Theorem (see [Edwards, 1965, Theorem 4.17.4] or [Federer, 1969, Theorem 2.6.2]) imply that

$$\begin{aligned} u_n(p^{-n}q_n) &= \iint u_n(s^{-n}, s^n)p^{-n}(ds^{-n})q_n(ds^n) \\ &= \iint u_n(s^{-n}, s^n)q_n(ds^n)p^{-n}(ds^{-n}), \end{aligned}$$

where (s^{-n}, s^n) means $(s^n)_{n \in N}$.

Let $\varepsilon \geq 0$ be given. A *correlated weak ε-equilibrium* (see [Moulin, 1981; Moulin and Vial, 1978]) is a Radon measure $p \in P(S)$ such that

$$u_n(p) + \varepsilon \geq u_n(p^{-n}q_n) \tag{2-1}$$

for all

$$q_n \in P(S^n) \text{ and } n \in N.$$

A measure $p \in P(S)$ is a *correlated weak equilibrium* if p satisfies (2-1) with $\varepsilon = 0$.

The interpretation is as follows: At first a correlated strategy p is fixed during a preplay communication process between the players. Then p is sent to a neutral arbiter who realizes the game. It is assumed that after choosing p but before starting the game every player has the right to change his mind (revise his previous decision) and he may ask the arbiter for using some of his private (pure or mixed) strategies. (No communication is allowed between the players at this stage.) The game starts after everyone has made his final decision. If player n insists on using his strategy $q_n \in P(S^n)$ while the remaining players decide to correlate their pure actions according to $p \in P(S)$, fixed at the beginning, then the expected income for player n will be $u_n(p^{-n}q_n)$. In view of the above, (2.1) says that if p is a correlated weak ε-equilibrium (ε is small), then unilateral deviations from it are not profitable.

Equilibrium Theorem. *Suppose a game satisfies A_1–A_3 and the function $u_n(s^{-n}, \cdot)$ is upper semicontinuous on S^n, for every player $n \in N$ and $s^{-n} \in S^{-n}$. Then, for each $\varepsilon > 0$, the game has a correlated weak ε-equilibrium with finite support. If all the payoff functions are continuous on S, then the game has a correlated weak equilibrium.*

Proof. Let $Q = \{(q_1, \ldots, q_m) : q_n \in M(S^n), n \in N, \text{and } \sum_{n \in N} q_n(S^n) = 1\}$. Assume that each $M(S^n)$ is given the weak* topology. Then Q can be recognized as a compact convex subset of $\prod_{n \in N} M(S^n)$, endowed with the product topology. Consider a zero-sum game where the strategy space for Player I is given by

$$\begin{aligned} r(p, q) &= r(p, (q_1, \ldots, q_m)) \\ &= \sum_{n=1}^{m} (q_n(S^n) u_n(p) - u_n(p^{-n} q_n)), \end{aligned} \tag{2-2}$$

where $p \in P = P(S)$, $q = (q_1, \ldots, q_m) \in Q$ and $u_n(p^{-n} q_n) = \int u_n dp^{-n} q_n$.

(Here $p^{-n} q_n$ is the Radon measure on S determined by p^{-n} and q_n. Clearly $p^{-n} q_n$ need not be a probability measure.)

Let $\underline{v}$ ($\bar{v}$) be the lower (and upper) value for the zero-sum game. Clearly $\underline{v} \leq \bar{v}$ and

$$\underline{v} \geq \sup_{p \in FP} \inf_{q \in Q} r(p, q),$$

where FP is the set of all probability measures from $P(S)$ having finite support. It is clear that FP is convex and $r(\cdot, q)$ is affine on FP, for each $q \in Q$. Also, $r(p, \cdot)$ is affine on Q for each $p \in FP$. Moreover, from our semicontinuity assumption and (2-2), it follows that for each $p \in FP$, $r(p, \cdot)$ as a function of q is lower semicontinuous on Q. Since Q is compact and convex by Ky Fan's Theorem [1953, Theorem 2], we get

$$\underline{v} \geq \sup_{p \in FP} \inf_{q \in Q} r(p, q) = \inf_{q \in Q} \sup_{p \in FP} r(p, q) = \inf_{q \in Q} \sup_{p \in P} r(p, q) = \bar{v}.$$

Hence

$$\sup_{p \in P} \inf_{q \in Q} r(p, q) = \sup_{p \in FP} \inf_{q \in Q} r(p, q) = \bar{v}. \tag{2-3}$$

We will show that $\bar{v} \geq 0$. Let $q = (q_1, \ldots, q_m) \in Q$, $K_q = \{n : q_n(S^n) = 0\}$. Clearly, $N - K_q \neq \emptyset$. Let $p = p_1 \times p_2 \times \cdots \times p_m$ be the product of the measures defined on S where $p_n = \frac{q_n}{q_n(S^n)}$ if $n \in N - K_q$ and p_n arbitrary probability measure on S^n if $n \in K_q$. Then by Fubini's Theorem [Federer, 1969, Theorem 2.6.2], $r(p,q) = 0$. Hence $\sup_{p \in P} r(p,q) \geq 0$, for each $q \in Q$, and consequently $\bar{v} \geq 0$. Applying this observation and (2-3), for each $\varepsilon > 0$, we can find some $p_\varepsilon \in FP$ such that

$$\varepsilon + r(p_\varepsilon, q) \geq 0, \quad \text{for all } q \in Q. \tag{2-4}$$

Let $n \in N$ and $q = (q_1, \ldots, q_m)$ where $q_k = 0$ for $k \neq n$, q_n is an arbitrary probability measure on S^n. Then from (2-4), we infer that $\varepsilon + u_n(p_\varepsilon) - u_n(p_\varepsilon^{-n} q_n) \geq 0$, for each $n \in N$, and $q_n \in P(S^n)$. Thus, p_ε is a correlated weak ε-equilibrium. Moreover, we know that p_ε has a finite support. If all u_n's are continuous on S, then the function r defined by (2-2) is continuous on P and the existence of a correlated weak equilibrium is obvious. The proof is finished.

Open problem. Do Nash or correlated equilibria exist in discontinuous non-zero-sum games studied in this paper?

Acknowledgement. The author wishes to thank Professor T. E. S. Raghavan for some useful discussions on the topic of this paper.

References

Aumann, R. J., 1974, "Subjectivity and Correlation in Randomized Strategies," *J. Math. Econ.* **1**, 67–96.

Aumann, R. J., 1987, "Correlated Equilibrium as an Expression of Bayesian Rationality," *Econometrica* **55**, 1–18.

Dasgupta, P. and Maskin, E., 1986, "The Existence of Equilibrium in Discontinuous Economic Games, I: Theory," *Rev. Econ. Stud.* **53**, 1–26.

Dasgupta, P. and Maskin, E., 1986, "The Existence of Equilibrium in Discontinuous Economic Games, II: Applications," *Rev. Econ. Stud.* **8**, 27–41.

Dunford, N. and Schwartz, J. T., 1958, *Linear Operators*, Interscience Publishers, New York.

Edwards, R. E., 1965, *Functional Analysis: Theory and Applications*, Holt, Rinehart and Winston, New York.

Fan, K., 1953, "Minimax Theorems," *Proc. Natl. Acad. Sci. USA* **39**, 42–47.

Federer, H., 1969, *Geometric Measure Theory*, Springer-Verlag, New York.

Gerard-Varet, L. A. and Moulin, H., 1978, "Correlation and Duopoly," *J. Econ. Theory* **19**, 123–149.

Glicksberg, I. L., 1952, "A Further Generalization of the Kakutani's Fixed Point Theorem with Application to Nash Equilibrium Points," *Proc. Amer. Math. Soc.* **3**, 170–174.

Hart, S. and Schmeidler, D., 1989, "Existence of Correlated Equilibria," *Math. Oper. Res.* **14**, 18–25.

Meyer, P. A., 1966, *Probability and Potentials*, Blaisdell Publishing Company, Waltham, London.

Moulin, H., 1981, *Theorie des Jeux pour l'Economie et la Politique*, Herman, Paris.

Moulin, H. and Vial, J. P., 1978, "Strategically Zero-Sum Games: The Class of Games Whose Completely Mixed Equilibria Cannot be Improved Upon," *Int. J. Game Theory* **7**, 201–221.

Owen, G., 1982, *Game Theory*, Academic Press, New York.

Sion, M., 1958, "On General Minimax Theorems," *Pacific J. Math.* **8**, 171–176.

Yannelis, N. C. and Rustichini, A., 1990, "On the Existence of Correlated Equilibria," this volume.

Communication Equilibria with Large State Spaces

Kevin D. Cotter

Abstract. A definition of communication equilibrium of games for which players may have arbitrary [rather than finite] type spaces is examined. The revelation principle is proven, and the set of equilibria is compared with the sets of strategy and action correlated equilibria. The equilibrium correspondence is shown to be discontinuous with respect to the information structure of the game, in contrast with previous continuity results for strategy and action correlated equilibrium.

1. Introduction

Some recent progress in game theory has been made on characterizing the set of outcomes which follow from the common knowledge of rationality of players. Aumann (1974, 1987) first explained that there exist plausible equilibria of nonstochastic games which are not Nash equilibria. Players may rationally base their actions on a correlation device, which is a set of signals not defined *a priori* as part of the game. If the signals of different players are correlated, then their resulting actions may also be correlated, leading to outcomes which are not Nash equilibria. A correlated equilibrium is then a set of beliefs about the actions of players which can be sustained by some correlation device.

The use of a correlation device can be extended to games with uncertainty and asymmetric information about payoffs. Since the information of players is generally a source of correlation of actions, which is permitted in a Bayesian-Nash equilibrium, the focus is on equilibria which rely on an additional correlation device. One question which arises is to what extent this correlation device may depend on the prior information of players. Two extreme cases have been studied previously by this author. An equilibrium which relies only on an additional correlation device that is independent of the prior information of players is known as a strategy correlated equilibrium [Cotter (1990a)], while permitting the use of any correlation device leads to an action correlated equilibrium [Cotter (1989)].

In this paper an equilibrium concept which falls between strategy and action correlated equilibrium is constructed. A communication equilibrium relies on a correlation device which depends only on the information of players which is freely and rationally provided by them. This equilibrium allows for all possible forms of direct and noisy communication between players, and generalizes communication equilibrium as defined in the mechanism design literature [e.g., Myerson (1983)] by allowing players to have an arbitrary [rather than finite] set of possible states of information. One of the most important results in mechanism design, the revelation principle, is proven for this more general model. In addition, any strategy correlated equilibrium is shown to be a communication equilibrium with a "deaf" mediator, and any communication equilibrium is an action correlated equilibrium.

The model in this paper is presented in Section 2, along with a brief review of equilibrium concepts which depend on correlation but not communication. The definition of communication equilibrium, along with a proof of the revelation principle, is given in Section 3, and an alternate model with parallel results is presented in Section 4. Section 5 compares communication equilibria with other equilibrium concepts. The continuity of the communication equilibrium correspondence is examined in Section 6.

2. The Model

Consider a game with uncertainty and a finite set of players $I \equiv \{1, \ldots, I\}$. To economize notation I denotes both the set and the number of players, and $i \in I$ is a generic player. Each player I has the following characteristics.

action space	A_i, a compact metric space.
privately observed type	$t_i \in T_i$, a complete separable metric space.
payoff function	$u_i : T \times A \to \mathbb{R}$, where $A = \prod_{i \in I} A_i$ and $T = \prod_{i \in I} T_i$.

For any metric space X, let $\Delta(X)$ be the set of probability[1] measures on X with the usual topology of weak convergence. By Theorem II.6.2

[1] When no other qualification is stated, all measures are Borel, and measurability of sets and functions refers to Borel measurability.

and II.6.4 of Parthasarathy (1967), $\Delta(X)$ is a compact [resp. separable] metric space if and only if X is compact [resp. separable]. The information of players about the types of others is given by an information structure $\nu \in \Delta(T)$. Let ν_i be the marginal of ν on T_i. The assumptions about the payoff function are straightforward.

Assumption 2.1. For each i,

(a) the mapping $t \to u_i(\cdot, a)$ is measurable for each $a \in A$,
(b) the mapping $a \to u_i(t, \cdot)$ is continuous for each $t \in T$,
(c) the mapping $t \to \sup_{a \in A} |u_i(\cdot, a)|$ is integrable.

The standard method for defining an equilibrium for this games has been to transform the game into a nonstochastic game in behavioral [or distributional] strategies. Let $S_i = \{s_i : T_i \to \Delta(A_i) \mid s_i \text{ is measurable}\}$ be the set of player i's behavioral strategies and $S^p = \prod_{i \in I} S_i$. Using the convention that for any $s \in S^p$ [resp. $a \in A$, $t \in T$], s_{-i} [resp. a_{-i}, t_{-i}] is the profile of strategies [resp. actions, types] of players other than i, player i's payoff function in the transformed game is the expected payoff function $U_i : S^p \to \mathbb{R}$, where

$$U_i(s_i, s_{-i}) = \int_t \int_{A_{-i}} \int_{A_i} u_i(t_i, t_{-i}, a_i, a_{-i}) s_i(t_i)(da_i) s_{-i}(t_{-i})(da_{-i}) \nu(dt). \tag{1}$$

Most definitions of equilibrium for Bayesian games have been constructed by applying standard equilibrium concepts to the transformed game. A *Bayesian-Nash Equilibrium* (BNE) [Milgrom and Weber (1985), Radner and Rosenthal (1982)] is a Nash equilibrium for the transformed game, i.e., $s^* \in S^p$ such that for each i and $s_i \in S_i$, $U_i(s^*) \geq U_i(s_i, s^*_{-i})$. A *strategy correlated equilibrium* (SCE) [Cotter (1990b)] is a correlated equilibrium [Aumann (1987)] for the transformed game, i.e., a probability distribution $\eta \in \Delta(S^p)$ such that for each i and measurable $\delta_i : S_i \to S_i$,

$$\int_{S^p} U_i(s) \eta(ds) \geq \int_{S^p} U_i(\delta_i(s_i), s_{-i}) \eta(ds). \tag{2}$$

As explained by Cotter (1989), an SCE only allows correlation based on devices or signals which are independent of the type space T. Let $S = \{s : T \to \Delta(A) \mid s \text{ is measurable}\}$ be the set of *joint strategies.* Permitting correlation based on arbitrary correlation devices leads to an *action correlated equilibrium* (ACE), which is a joint behavioral strategy $s \in S$ such that for each i and measurable function $\alpha_i T_i \times A_i \to A_i$,

$$\int_{T\times A} u_i(t,a)s(t)(da)\nu(dt) \geq \int_{T\times A} u_i(t,\alpha_i(t_i,a_i),a_{-i})s(t)(da)\nu(dt). \quad (3)$$

An ACE uses the correlation device s which "knows" t. The device recommends an action to each player, with the profile of recommendations to all players following the probability distribution $s(t)$. Each player i optimally chooses to follow the recommendation given t_i, his own recommended action, and the belief that all other players will follow their recommendations.

Note that any BNE or SCE generates a joint strategy, so they are also ACEs.

3. Representation of Communication Strategies and Equilibria

The problem with the definition of an ACE is that is does not explain how the correlation device comes to "know" t. Such a correlation device is best interpreted as a profile of common beliefs about the behavior of the players. If, however, the correlation device is interpreted as an explicit mechanism, then it should also satisfy the condition that is somehow receives t from the players. Imposing such a condition leads to a communication equilibrium, which is defined below.

According to Myerson (1983), a mediator is a device which collects information about the state of nature via confidential messages from each player, then transmits a recommended action to each player based on the messages. Each player then takes an action based on the mediator's suggestion. There is no mechanism to insure than players will transmit all of their information correctly or follow the mediator's recommendation. Therefore, an equilibrium must satisfy incentive compatibility conditions which takes account of the player's ability to deceive or disobey the mediator.

In this section, Myerson's definition is extended to games for which the type and action spaces of players need not be finite, and the mediator and players may transmit arbitrary messages to each other. Define a *communication game* to be profiles of message spaces $X = (X_1, \ldots, X_I)$ and $M = (M_1, \ldots, M_I)$, with each X_i and M_i complete separable metric spaces, and a measurable *communication function* $r : X \to \Delta(M)$. In a communication game, player i observes t_i and sends a message $x_i \in X_i$ to the communication function, following the distribution $\sigma_i(t_i) \in \Delta(X_i)$. The communication function receives the messages $x \equiv (x_1, \ldots, x_I)$ and sends a profile of messages $m = (m_1, \ldots, m_I) \in M$ to the players, following the distribution $r(x) \in \Delta(M)$. Player i then receives the message m_i and chooses a mixed strategy $\delta_i(t_i, m_i) \in \Delta(A_i)$. Let $\sum_i(X_i) = \{\alpha_i : T_i \to \Delta(X_i) \mid \sigma_i \text{ is measurable}\}$ and $D_i = \{\delta_i : T_i \times M_i \to \Delta(A_i) \mid \delta_i \text{ is measurable}\}$ be the sets of *message functions* and *reaction functions* for player i respectively.

Note the above definition of communication equilibrium permits arbitrary forms of communication. Special cases include noiseless as well as noisy communication between individual players and groups of players.

The following technical result will be needed.

Lemma 3.1. *Let Y be a complete separable metric space and let $\phi : T \to \Delta(Y)$ be measurable. Then for any measurable function $b : Y \to \mathbb{R}$, the function $t \to \int_Y b(y)\phi(t)(dy)$ is measurable.*

Proof. Let $\{b^n\}$ be a sequence of simple functions on Y which increase to b. For each n, the function $t \to \int_Y b^n(y)\phi(t)(dy)$ is measurable by Theorem 3.2(b) of Cotter (1989). For each t, the sequence $\left\{\int_Y b^n(y)\phi(t)(dy)\right\}$ converges to $\int_Y b(y)\phi(t)(dy)$ by the monotone convergence theorem, proving the result.

The next result states that the combination of messages, recommendations, and reactions is mathematically tractable.

Theorem 3.2. *For each i let $(\sigma_i, \delta_i) \in \sum_i(X_i) \times D_i$. Then there exists a unique profile of players' actions $s \in S$ that is the outcome of the communication game, such that for any $f : T \times A \to \mathbb{R}$ satisfying Assumption 2.1,*

$$\int_T \int_A f(t,a)s(t)(da)\nu(dt) = \int_T \int_X \int_M \int_A f(t,a)\delta_1(t_1, m_1)(da_1) \ldots \delta_I(t_I, m_I)(da_I)r(x)(dm)\sigma_1(t_1)(dx_1) \ldots \sigma_I(t_I)(dx_I)\nu(dt). \tag{4}$$

Proof. The first step is to show that the right-hand side of (4) is defined. The function $(t,m) \to \int_A f(t,a)\delta_1(t_1,m_1)(da_1)\ldots\delta_I(t_I,m_I)(da_I)$ is measurable since each δ_i is measurable. By Lemma 3.1, $(t,x) \to \int_M \int_A f(t,a)\delta_1(t_1,m_1)(da_1)\ldots\delta_I(t_I,m_I)(da_I)r(x)(dm)$ is measurable, so the right-hand side of (4) is defined by repeated use of Lemma 3.1.

The right-hand side of (4) defines a real function $\phi : L[C(A)] \to \mathbb{R}$, where $L[C(A)] = \{f : T \to C(A) \mid f$ is measurable with respect to the supremum norm on $C(A)\}$, and ϕ is easily verified to be linear and continuous with respect to the norm topology on $L[C(A)]$. Letting $M(A)$ be the space of signed measures on A with the weak convergence topology, $\phi \in L[C(A)]^* = \{s : T \to M(A) \mid s$ is measurable with respect to the weak topology on $M(A)\}$. Therefore, there exists $s : T \to M(A)$ satisfying (4). To show s maps into $\Delta(A)$, note that (4) is nonnegative for nonnegative f, and for a.e. t,

$$\begin{aligned}
&\left|\int_A f(t,a)s(t)(da)\right| \\
&= \left|\int_X \int_M \int_A f(t,a)\delta_1(t_1,m_1)(da_1)\ldots\delta_I(t_I,m_I)(da_I)r(x)(dm)\right. \\
&\qquad \left.\times\, \sigma_1(t_1)(dx_1)\ldots\sigma_I(t_I)(dx_I)\right| \\
&\leq \int_X \int_M \int_A \sup_{a\in A} |f(t,a)|\delta_1(t_1,m_1)(da_1)\ldots\delta_I(t_I,m_I)(da_I)r(x)(dm) \\
&\qquad \times\, \sigma_1(t_1)(dx_1)\ldots\sigma_I(t_I)(dx_I) \\
&= \sup_{a\in A} |f(t,a)|
\end{aligned}$$

proving the result. □

Corollary 3.3. *Equation (4) holds for any Borel-measurable function $f : T \times A \to \mathbb{R}$.*

Proof. Follows from Lemmas 3.1 and 3.2. □

Replacing f with u_i in equation (4) yields the payoff function $V_i : \prod_{i\in I}(\Sigma_i(X_i) \times D_i) \to \mathbb{R}$. A *communication equilibrium* (CE) is a communication game $\{(X_1,\ldots,X_I),(M_1,\ldots,M_I),r^*\}$ and a profile of messages and reactions $((\sigma_1^*,\delta_1^*),\ldots,(\sigma_I^*,\delta_I^*)) \in \prod_{i\in I}(\Sigma_i(X_i) \times D_i)$ which is a Nash equilibrium for the game where each player's payoff function is V_i and strategy set is $\sum_i(X_i) \times D_i$.

One well-known problem with this definition of CE is that permitting arbitrary messages and reactions creates an intractably large set of possible equilibria. For any CE there exist a continuum of communication games with equilibria which differ only in the message structure used by the players, though the information conveyed by the players' messages is the same. The solution to this problem is the well-known revelation principle, which states that for any CE, there exists an equivalent CE in which the player accurately transmits her information to the communication function and obeys it recommendation. Define a *direct revelation game* to be a communication game for which $X_i = T_i$ and $M_i = A_i$ for each i. For each i define the truthful message function $\bar{\sigma}_i \in \sum_i(T_i)$ such that for a.e. t_i, $\bar{\sigma}_i(t_i)$ is the point mass on t_i, and the obedience function $\bar{\delta}_i \in D_i$ such that $\bar{\delta}_i(t_i, \alpha_i)$ is the point mass on α_i for a.e. t_i and all α_i.

Earlier proofs of the revelation principle have assumed a finite number of player types and a finite action space for each player.

Theorem 3.4. *For any CE which yields the joint behavioral strategy $s^* \in S$, the direct revelation game with communication function s^* has the CE $((\bar{\delta}_1, \bar{\sigma}_1), \ldots, (\bar{\delta}_I, \bar{\sigma}_I))$.*

Proof. Let $((\delta_1^*, \sigma_1^*), \ldots, (\delta_I^*, \sigma_I^*))$ be a CE for the communication game and $\bar{r}^* \in S$ be the joint behavioral strategy generated by $(r^*, \delta^*, \sigma^*)$ as given in Theorem 3.2. Consider the direct revelation game for which the communication function is $\bar{r}^*$. Suppose player i were to play (δ_i, σ_i) while every other player j played $(\bar{\delta}_j, \bar{\sigma}_j)$. Without loss of generality suppose $\delta_i : T_i \times A_i \to A_i$ and $\sigma_i : T_i \to T_i$. The resulting payoff to player i would be

$$\int_T \int_A u_i(t, \delta_i(t_i, a_i), a_{-i}) \bar{r}^*(\sigma_i(t_i), t_{-i})(da) \nu(dt) \tag{6}$$

which equals, by Corollary 3.3,

$$\begin{aligned} &\int_T \int_X \int_M \int_A u_i(t, \delta_i(t_i, a_i), a_{-i}) \\ &\quad \times \delta_i^*(t_i, m_i)(da_i) \delta_{-i}^*(t_{-i}, m_{-i})(da_{-i}) r(x)(dm) \\ &\quad \times \sigma_i^*(\sigma_i(t_i))(dx_i) \sigma_{-i}^*(\sigma_{-i}(t_{-i}))(dx_{-i}) \nu(dt). \end{aligned} \tag{7}$$

This is the payoff that would result in the original game if player i chose the message function $\sigma_i^*(\sigma_i(\cdot))$ and the reaction function induced by the composition of δ_i and δ_i^*. Since the original game is a CE, (7) is dominated by

$$\int_T \int_A \int_A u_i(t,a)\delta_i^*(t_i,m_i)(da_i)\delta_{-i}^*(t_{-i},m_{-i})(da_{-i})$$
$$\cdot\, r^*(\sigma_i^*(\sigma_i(t_i)),\sigma_i^*(t_{-i}))(dm)\nu(dt) = \int_T \int_A u_i(t,a)\bar{r}^*(t)(da)\nu(dt) \quad (8)$$

which is the payoff in the direct revelation game if player i chooses (δ_i^*, σ_i^*). This completes the proof. □

A consequence of the revelation principle is that every CE can be identified with the joint strategy it generates, as given by Lemma 3.2. Therefore, the set of CE is a subset of S.

4. Communication Equilibria and the Partition Model

The results of the previous section are now stated in terms of the partition model of a game with incomplete information. In the partition model a single underlying probability space $(\Omega, \mathcal{F}, \mu)$ models all prior uncertainty in the game, where Ω is a complete separable metric space and $\mathcal{F}$ its Borel sets. Each player has the following characteristics:

action space	A_i, a compact metric space. Let $A = \prod_{i\in I} A_i$.
information field	$\mathcal{G}_i$, a sub-σ-field of $\mathcal{F}$.
payoff function	$u_i : \Omega \times A \to \mathbb{R}$.

The assumptions regarding u_i are analogous to Assumption 2.1.

Assumption 4.1. For each i,

(a) the mapping $\omega \to u_i(\omega, a)$ is measurable for each $a \in A$,
(b) the mapping $a \to u_i(\omega, a)$ is continuous for each $\omega \in \Omega$,
(c) the mapping $\omega \to \sup_{a\in A} |u_i(\omega, a)|$ is integrable.

The advantage of the partition model over the type model described previously is that each player's information is a parameter $\mathcal{G}_i$ which is distinct from the underlying uncertainty in the game. Given a communication game $\{(X_1, \ldots, X_I), (M_1, \ldots, M_I), r\}$, player i chooses a message function $\sigma_i \in \sum_i(\mathcal{G}_i; X_i) = \{\sigma_i : \Omega \to \Delta(X_i) \mid \sigma_i \text{ is } \mathcal{G}_i\text{-measurable}\}$ and a deviation function $\delta_i \in D_i(\mathcal{G}_i) = \{\delta_i : \Omega \times M_i \to \Delta(A_i) \mid \delta_i \text{ is } \mathcal{G}_i \times \mathcal{M}_i\text{-measurable}\}$. A communication equilibrium for this game is a profile of messages and deviations $((\sigma_1^*, \delta_1^*), \ldots, (\sigma_I^*, \delta_I^*)) \in \prod_{i \in I}(\sum_i(\mathcal{G}_i; X_i) \times D_i(\mathcal{G}_i))$ such that for any i and any $(\sigma_i, \delta_i) \in \sum_i(\mathcal{G}_i; X_i) \times D_i(\mathcal{G}_i)$,

$$\begin{aligned}
&\int_\Omega \int_X \int_M \int_A u_i(\omega, a)\delta_i^*(\omega, m_i)(da_i)\delta_{-i}^*(\omega, m_{-i})(da_{-i})r^*(x)(dm) \\
&\quad \times \sigma_i^*(\omega)(dx_i)\sigma_{-i}^*(\omega)(dx_{-i})\mu(d\omega) \\
&\geq \int_\Omega \int_X \int_M \int_A u_i(\omega, a)\delta_i(\omega, m_i)(da_i)\delta_{-i}^*(\omega, m_{-i})(da_{-i})r^*(x)(dm) \\
&\quad \times \sigma_i(\omega)(dx_i)\sigma_{-i}^*(\omega)(dx_{-i})\mu(d\omega).
\end{aligned} \tag{9}$$

The expressions in Equation (9) are defined in Theorem 3.2.

With respect to a partition model, a direct revelation game is a communication game for which $X_i = \Omega$ and $M_i = A_i$ for each i. For each i define the truthful message function $\bar{\sigma}_i^{\mathcal{G}_i} \in \sum_i(\mathcal{G}_i; \Omega)$ such that for a.e. $\bar{\sigma}_i^{\mathcal{G}_i}(\omega) = P[\cdot \mid \mathcal{G}_i](\omega)$,[2] and obedience $\bar{\delta}_i^{\mathcal{G}_i} \in D_i(\mathcal{G}_i)$ such that $\bar{\delta}_i^{\mathcal{G}_i}(t_i, \alpha_i)$ is the point mass on α_i for a.e. ω and all α_i.

For any partition model there exists an equivalent type model. For each i let $(T_i, \mathcal{T}_i)$ be a copy of $(\Omega, \mathcal{G}_i)$, and $\mathcal{Z} = \prod_{i \in I} Z_i$. Assume without loss of generality that $\mathcal{F} = \vee_{j \in I}\mathcal{G}_i$, the smallest σ-field containing each $\mathcal{F}_i$. By Theorem 9 of Cotter (1990b), there exists a unique measure ν on $(T, \mathcal{T})$ and a set isomorphism $\Phi : \mathcal{G} \to \mathcal{T}$ such that $\nu(B) = \mu(\Phi^{-1}(G))$ for $G \in \mathcal{G}$ and for each i and $G_i \in \mathcal{G}_i$, $\Phi(G_1 \cap \cdots \cap G_I) = G_1 \times \cdots \times G_I$. There does not generally exist a corresponding point function from Ω to T, but there do exist [Cotter (1990b, Lemma 3, Theorem 4.4, Lemma 4.5, Theorem 4.8)] isomorphisms $\mathbf{T} : L[\Omega; C(A)] \to L[T; C(A)]$, $\mathbf{T} : \sum_i(\mathcal{G}_i; X_i) \to \sum_i(X_i)$, and $\mathbf{T} : D_i(\mathcal{G}_i) \to D_i$ which preserve players' expected playoff functions. It is also easy to verify that $\mathbf{T}(\bar{\sigma}_i^{\mathcal{G}_i}) = \bar{\sigma}$ and $\mathbf{T}(\bar{\delta}_i^{\mathcal{G}_i}) = \bar{\delta}$. Therefore, Theorem 3.4, the revelation principle applies to the partition model.

---

[2] Since Ω is a complete separable metric space, regular conditional probabilities such as the latter expression exist [Parthasarathy (1967, Theorem V.8.1)].

5. Comparisons with Other Equilibria

The sets of BNE, ACE, and CE are subsets of the joint behavioral strategy space S. While an SCE is not an element in S, it does generate a joint strategy. This mapping from SCEs to joint strategies is many-to-one [Cotter (1990b), Example 2.2].

In this section the sets of joint behavioral strategies generated by these four equilibrium concepts are compared.

Theorem 5.1. *Define the sets BNE, CE, and ACE⊂S to be the sets of BNE's, CE's, and ACEs, respectively, and let SCE⊂S be the set of joint behavioral strategies generated by the set of SCEs. Then* $BNE \subset SCE \subset CE \subset ACE$.

Proof. By Theorem 4.4 of Cotter (1989), BNE⊂SCE⊂ACE since by Lemma 6.2 of Cotter (1989), any ACE is a CE without the communication of types to the communication function. It remains only to be shown that SCE⊂CE.

Let $\eta^* \in \Delta(S^p)$ be an SCE generating $s^* \in S$. Consider the communication game with $M_i = S_i$ and $r^*(x) \equiv \eta^*$ for all x. Since the mediation function does not depend on x, the communication of players is irrelevant. Let δ_i^* be defined by $\delta_i^*(t_i, m_i) = m_i(t_i)$. The profile $((\bar{\sigma}_1, \delta_i^*), \dots, (\bar{\sigma}_I, \delta_I^*))$ generates the joint behavioral strategy s^*. Suppose player i were to choose any other (σ_i, δ_i). Then it would be choosing a strategy outside the profile η^*, while the profiles of other players would be unaffected since r^* does not respond to players' messages. Therefore, player i's payoff would be reduced since η^* is an SCE. This completes the proof. □

The proof of Theorem 5.1 shows that an SCE is a CE with a "deaf" mediator, i.e., a communication function r^* which does not depend on x. Conversely, if r^* is a CE which does not depend on x, then the definition of CE reduces to that of SCE.

Corollary 5.2. *The set of CE is nonempty.*

Proof. The set of SCE is nonempty by Corollary 4.9 of Cotter (1990a), so the result follows from Theorem 5.1. □

6. Continuity of the Equilibrium Correspondence

It is useful to know the extent to which the equilibria of the game depend on its underlying characteristics. Let G be the set of parameters of the game, and $\Delta(T \times A)$ the set of possible outcomes, where each $(s, \mu) \in S \times \Delta(T)$ is identified with the corresponding measure on $T \times A$ [Cotter (1989, Theorem 3.2)]. The dependence of the game on its parameters can be posed in terms of the equilibrium correspondence $\xi \longrightarrow \Delta(T \times A)$. The most important such properties are upperhemicontinuity and nonempty-valuedness. Though many possible definitions of G exist, in this section attention will be restricted to $G = \Delta(T)$, the set of information structures ν on T, with the weak topology. Consider a sequence $\{\mu^n\} \subset \Delta(T)$. The action equilibrium correspondence was shown to be continuous [Cotter (1989, Theorem 5.2)] provided each player's payoff function is continuous on $T \times A$. Unfortunately, this result does not hold for communication equilibria.

Example 6.1. Consider a two person game. Their action sets are $A_1 = \{U, D\}$ and $A_2 = \{L, R\}$, and type spaces are $T_1 = T_2 = [0,1]$. The payoff function, which does not depend on the type space, is

x	L	R
U	$(1,1)$	$(0,0)$
D	$(0,0)$	$(2,2)$

Let $s \in S$ be given by

$$s(t_1, t_2) = \begin{cases} (U, L) & \text{if } t_1 = t_2 \\ (D, R) & \text{if } t_1 \neq t_2 \end{cases}$$

Given the profile of signals received by the communication device, the messages sent to the players are always obeyed regardless of the probability distribution on T. If player 1 receives U, she knows that player 2 received L and should optimally play U, while if player 1 receives D, she knows that player 2 received R and should optimally play D. Similarly, player 2 will always optimally choose to obey the communication device's recommendation.

Now let $\{\mu^n\}$ be a sequence of probability distributions on T, where μ^n is given by the density function $f^n(t_1,t_2) = 1/[(t_1-t_2)^n(1-n)(1-2n)]$. It is easily verified that μ^n converges weakly to μ, which is the uniform distribution on the diagonal of T. For each n and any t_i observed by player i, the conditional probability that player $-i$ will transmit $\tau_{-i} = t_i$ is zero. Therefore, $s \in \xi(\mu^n)$. However, $s \notin \xi(\mu)$, since if player i observes t_i, the conditional probability that player $-i$ will transmit $\tau_{-i} = t_i$ is one, so player i should transmit anything but t_i. Therefore with the weak topology on $\delta(T)$, ξ is not upperhemicontinuous for *any* topology on S.□

References

Aumann, R., 1974, "Subjectivity and Correlation in Randomized Strategies," *J. Math. Econ.* **1**, 67–96.

Aumann, R., 1987, "Correlated Equilibrium as an Expression of Bayesian Rationality," *Econometrica* **55**, 1–18.

Cotter, K., 1990a, "Correlated Equilibria in Games with Type-Dependent Strategies," *J. Econ. Theory*, to appear.

Cotter, K., 1990b, "Similarity of Games with Incomplete Information," *J. Math. Econ.*, to appear.

Cotter, K., 1989, "Correlated Equilibria with Payoff Uncertainty," CMSEMS Discussion Paper #840, Northwestern University.

Milgrom, P. and Weber, R., 1985, "Distributional Strategies for Games with Incomplete Information," *Math. Oper. Res.* **10**, 619–632.

Myerson, R., 1983, "Bayesian Equilibrium and Incentive Compatibility: An Introduction," CMSEMS Discussion Paper #548, Northwestern University.

Parthasarathy, K., 1967, *Probability Measures on Metric Spaces*, Academic Press, New York.

Radner, R. and Rosenthal, R., 1982, "Private Information and Pure Strategy Equilibria," *Math. Oper. Res.* **7**, 410–409.

PART 6

GAMES WITH A CONTINUUM OF PLAYERS

An Axiomatic Approach to the Efficiency of Non-Cooperative Equilibrium in Economies with a Continuum of Traders

Andreu Mas-Colell*

Preface (1991). This is a reprint of Technical Report 274, IMSSS, Stanford, 1978. Substantial parts of it have appeared in P. Dubey, A. Mas-Colell, and M. Shubik: "Efficiency Properties of Strategic Market Games: An Axiomatic Approach," *J. Econ. Theory* **22**, 1980, and in A. Mas-Colell: "On a Theorem of Schmeidler," *J. Math. Econ.*, 1984. Needless to say, the author is gratified and thankful that the editors have found enough valuable left to request its publication in this volume.

1. Introduction

In this paper we shall attempt an axiomatization of a central theme of economic theory, namely the idea that the non-cooperative equilibria of market-like economies with many relatively small traders, are Walrasian (Hence efficient) or, in other words, that price-taking behavior is, in a mass market, the natural consequence of "action (or message) taking" behavior. The classical partial equilibrium reference is, of course, Cournot's [1938]. Recently, the seminal paper of Shubik [1972] has stimulated the development of a whole class of general equilibrium models where the validity or not of the theme can be precisely discussed. Another general equilibrium version of Cournot's model is represented by Gabszewicz-Vial [1971], Hart [1977] and Novshek-Sonnenschein [1978]. Our own contribution will also be general equilibrium and to the extent

* This work was supported by National Science Foundation Grant SOC77-06000 at the Institute for Mathematical Studies in the Social Sciences, Stanford University. I am indebted to Mr. Ch. Kahn for detecting a gap in the proof of an earlier version and, for useful discussion and suggestions, to P. Dubey, W. Heller, L. Hurwicz, A. Postlewaite, M. Shubik, W. Thomson, and the participants of the IMSSS seminar where this paper was presented in July 1978. The usual caveat applies.

that the set-up will not explicitly incorporate quoted prices it is more in the line of Shubik's.

The main difficulty for the non-cooperative analysis of economies, and specially for the general equilibrium analysis, is the need to model the economy in game theoretic terms. There is not a unique, somehow given, way to do so. The game begin played in real economic life is a complicated one and the theoretician can only hope to build an interesting gallery of models emphasizing different important features. This provides the motivation for our work: since a wide variety of specifications lead to the conclusion that the non-cooperative equilibria of extensive economies are Walrasian it seems justified to engage in axiomatics. The modelling problem is sidestep by assuming (and, admittedly, this is quite a lot to assume) that a sort of trading game is given to us in an abstract manner. We then try to identify general principles yielding the desired conclusions. A similar program is begin pursued by Dubey and Shubik [1978] on the basis of their previous in-depth analysis of particular models.

Our axiomatization will be fairly transparent and, from the mathematical point of view, trivial. The basic principles turn out to be:

(i) *convexity*: traders have available a convex set of messages or actions.

(ii) *anonymity*: from the point of view of the market, only the message sent by the trader matters.

(iii) *non-degeneracy*: it must be possible for individual players to influence to a substantial extent their trading possibilities in the market.

(iv) *neutrality*: the trading possibilities of any player are influenced by the actions of the other players only through the *mean* of those actions (and not, say, through the variance).

The present exercise does not attempt to offer palatable and attractive axioms. It is done rather in the spirit of capturing general features of an important theoretical phenomenon. Thus, we do not intend to give any normative significance to our results. This is definitely not a paper in the designing of resource allocations mechanisms tradition (we refer to the substantial literature growing out of Hurwicz [1959] pioneer contribution).

As in Aumann [1963] for "large number of small traders" we shall adopt the idealization of the continuum. We do this merely for convenience since a completely parallel asymptotic version could undoubtedly be worked out, although we suspect it would be somewhat messier. It is a fortunate fact that the consideration of a large number of small traders (in the limit a continuum) has simplifying implications for the non-cooperative analysis. Indeed, under general conditions if individual players are, in whichever is the relevant sense, very small relative to the size of the game the only sensible expectations (at "equilibrium" or at "disequilibrium" plays) of individual players is that the rest of the players will not react (or react very little) to changes of their actions. Thus, in contrast to games among few, simple Cournot-Nash equilibria emerges as the natural non-cooperative solution. Our treatment of Cournot-Nash equilibrium in the continuum builds on a paper of Schmeidler [1973] which deserves to be better known.

It can be asked which is the relation of the results here and the Core equivalences theorem (see Hildenbrand [1974] and his references). The conclusions are of the same nature: in the continuum a certain game theoretic solution concept yields the same outcome than the Walrasian equilibrium. A departure is that Cournot-Nash is non-cooperative while the Core is cooperative. This, we feel, is not a very important difference. If one does not worry about informational constraints to view the Core as a cooperative or a non-cooperative concept is largely a matter of taste. An important distinction is that here market institutions are given (albeit in an abstract manner) while they are not in Core theory.

Sections 2 to 10 develops the model up to the statement of the main theorem in Section 10. Section 11 deals with an aspect of the Cournot-Nash concept in the presence of the anonymity axiom. Section 12 dwells in the general topic of games with a continuum of players.

2. The Economic Model and Basic Definitions

The commodity space is $\mathbb{R}^\ell$.

A *trader* is characterized by:

(i) a closed, convex, non-empty set $X \subset \mathbb{R}$ of *feasible net trades*, interpreted as the set of contracts the trader can honor, and

(ii) a preferences ordering $\succsim \subset X \times X$ on X.

Every X is assumed to satisfy *free disposability*, i.e., if $x \in X$ then $x + \mathbf{R}^\ell_+ \subset X$. Preferences $\gtrsim$ are taken to be *continuous*, *convex*, and *monotone*. The set of characteristics is $\mathcal{A} = \{(X, \gtrsim)\}$. As in Hildenbrand [1974], one can view $\mathcal{A}$ as a measurable space by endowing it with the σ-field derived from the closed convergency topology on the closed subsets of $\mathbf{R}^\ell$.

We define the economy à la Aumann [1963], i.e., as a (measurable) map $\mathcal{E} : I \equiv [0, 1] \to \mathcal{A}$; of course, I is equipped with Lebesgue measure. We denote $\mathcal{E}(t)$ by $(X_t, \gtrsim_t)$.

An *assignment* is an integrable map $\underset{\sim}{x} : I \to \mathbf{R}^\ell$ such that

$$\int \underset{\sim}{x}(t)dt = 0.$$

An assignment $\underset{\sim}{x}$ is *feasible* if $\underset{\sim}{x}(t) \in X_t$ for a.e. $t \in I$.

A feasible assignment $\underset{\sim}{x}$ is *efficient* if there is no other feasible assignment $\underset{\sim}{x}'$ such that $\underset{\sim}{x}'(t) \gtrsim x(t)$ for a.e. $t \in [0, 1]$ and $\underset{\sim}{x}'(t) \succ_t x(t)$ for a set of t's of positive measure.

A feasible assignment $\underset{\sim}{x}$ is *Walrasian* if there is $p \in \mathbf{R}^\ell$ such that, for a.e. $t \in I$,

$$\underset{\sim}{x}(t) \text{ is } \gtrsim_t \text{-maximal on } \{x \in X_t : p \cdot x \leq 0\}.$$

It is of course, well known that with the hypothesis made a Walrasian assignment is efficient.

Remark 1. The previous set-up allows for production if production sets are owned by individual traders. The difficulty for the treatment of firms collectively owned is that one would like an institution free formalization of the basic entities of the economy while the usual approaches (using "shares," etc.) are market dependent.

Remark 2. Notice, and this distinction is basic to all of our treatment, that there are two kinds of constraints in the trading problem, i.e., *public constraints* embodied in the fact that the sum of net trades must be zero (i.e., markets should clear) and the *private constraints* requiring that individual net trades belong to the individual trading sets. As a matter of interpretation we take that the private constraints are not publicly observable. Thus, assignments, which can be thought as public information, need not satisfy the private constraints.

Remark 3. With the exception of the results, which hold only in the continuum case, the model and concepts of this paper apply without modification of economies with atoms and therefore to economies with a finite number of participants. One only needs to interpret I as an appropriate measure space.

3. Abstract Trading Games

Let the set of traders $I = [0, 1]$ be given.

There is given a non-empty set A called the *message* or *action space.* We assume that *A is a convex subset of a separable Banach space.* It will be conceptually simpler if the reader thinks of A as finite dimensional, i.e., a subset of some $\mathbb{R}^m$. It should be emphasized that it is crucial to our approach that A be convex.

A *play* is an integrable function $\underset{\sim}{a} : I \to A$.

A trading game is specified by the action space A and an outcome rule which associates with every play $\underset{\sim}{a}$ an assignment $\underset{\sim}{x}_{\underset{\sim}{a}} : I \to \mathbb{R}^\ell$.

For the measure theoretic treatment to be a sensible one we should require that the outcome rule satisfies the following property (for which formulation I am indebted to Sergiu Hart): *if* $[\underset{\sim}{a}] = [\underset{\sim}{a}']$ *then* $[\underset{\sim}{x}_{\underset{\sim}{a}}] = [\underset{\sim}{x}_{\underset{\sim}{a}'}]$. The symbol [ ] denotes the equivalence class of the function. Informally speaking, this property has the implication that individual actions do have individual but not social consequences (benefit or damages) which is a well known heuristic requirement for a competitive process to yield efficient outcomes (i.e., no externalities).

Remark 4. In the case where A is infinite dimensional (which, we repeat, shall not be emphasized) "integrable" can be taken to mean Pettis integrable (see, for example, Yosida [1971]).

Remark 5. Since plays $\underset{\sim}{a}$ are integrable they are, a fortiori, measurable. We do not feel that the confinement of our interest to measurable plays is restrictive. In the first place, the class of measurable functions is quite broad (to exhibit a non-measurable function one has to appeal to the Axiom of Choice). In the second place one has to keep in mind that the continuum of players is only an idealization. If one were to explicitly regard it as a limit of games with a finite number of players then there would never be any need to leave the class of measurable functions. But since we have not worked out the details of an asymptotic theory, we must leave the previous point as a tentative one.

Remark 6. We could in the definition of a play require that $\underset{\sim}{a}$ be only measurable, thus allowing for non-integrable players. This however would not be very useful and since at an important point we shall have to integrate we prefer to impose the condition now. If A is bounded then every measurable $\underset{\sim}{a} : I \to A$ is, of course, integrable.

Remark 7. In our approach the outcomes of a player need not be feasible assignments. This is in keeping with the modelling of market institutions as blind to private characteristics. Any player is free to send any message to the market but the assignment which is the outcome of the play can become a reality only if almost every trader can honor the proposed contract without going bankrupt. Thus, our model is in the nature of a tâtonnement one and the use of the term "game" is abusive. We hope not too much. Still, if one insisted in contemplating only outcomes which are privately and publicly feasible it would be possible to model the whole set-up in terms of Debreu's Generalized Games (see Debreu [1952]). See Remark 10 for this. The present situation can be contrasted with the well-known Walrasian price tâtonnement. Here public constraints are always satisfied but private ones need not. There private constraints do hold but the public ones need not (i.e., at given arbitrary prices there may be excess demand or supply).

In general equilibrium version of Cournot model proposed by Shubik [1972] provides an example of an abstract game.

Example 1. *There are two commodities $\ell = 1, 2$. Trading sets are of the form $X_t = \mathbb{R}^2_+ - \{w_t\}$ where w_t represents trader t initial endowments of commodities. The action space is $[0, r] \times [0, r]$ where r is a large number. An action (a_1, a_2) is to be interpreted as follows: a_1 (resp. a_2) is the amount of commodity 1 (resp. 2) a trader proposes to deliver in exchange for some quantity (to be determined) of commodity 2 (resp. 1). Let $\underset{\sim}{a}$ be a play; then the outcome is given by*

$$\underset{\sim}{x}_{\underset{\sim}{a}}(t) = \left(a_2(t)\frac{\int \underset{\sim}{a}_1}{\int \underset{\sim}{a}_2} - a_1(t),\ a_1(t)\frac{\int \underset{\sim}{a}_2}{\int \underset{\sim}{a}_1} - a_2(t) \right).$$

If either $\int \underset{\sim}{a}_1 = 0$ or $\int \underset{\sim}{a}_2 = 0$, we put $\underset{\sim}{x}_{\underset{\sim}{a}} \equiv 0$.

Multicommodity versions of the Shubik model have been presented in Shapley [1974], Jaynes, Okuno and Schmeidler [1976], Pazner and Schmeidler [1976], Postlewaite and Schmeidler [1978], Dubey and Shapley [1977]. Jaynes et al and Dubey et al are continuum of traders models.

In the next two examples the messages-actions are whole demand-supply functions.

Example 2. *There are two commodities* $\ell = 1, 2$. *Trading sets are of the form* $X_t = \mathbf{R}^2_+ - \{w_t\}$ *where* w_t *represents trader* t *initial endowments of commodities. The message space is* $A = \{f \in C([0,r]) : f$ *is* $f(0) \geq 0$ *and* $f(r) \geq 0\}$ *where* r *is a large number and for* $p \in [0,r]$ $f(p)$ *is to be interpreted as a proposal to buy ("sell" if negative)* $f(p)$ *units of the second commodity in exchange for* $pf(p)$ *units of the first commodity. Let* $\underset{\sim}{a}$ *be a play. Define* $p\underset{\sim}{a} = \max\{p \in [0,r] : \left(\int \underset{\sim}{a}\right)(p) = 0\}$. *Then the outcome is given by* $x_{\underset{\sim}{a}}(t) = (-p\underset{\sim}{a}(t), \underset{\sim}{a}(t))$.

Example 3. *Identical to Example 2 except that now* $A = \{f \in C([0,r]) : f(0) \geq 0, f(r) \geq 0$ *and* f *is decreasing*$\}$.

Example 4. *Identical to Example 2 except that now* $A = \{f \in C([0,r]) : f(0) \geq 0, f(r) \leq 0, f([0,r]) \subset [-s,s]$ *and* f *is decreasing*$\}$, *where* s *is a large number.*

Remark 8. Example 2 shows there is teeth in our hypothesis that to envy play $\underset{\sim}{a}$ there corresponds a unique assignment. If an arbitrary rule has not been chosen to select one of the market clearing prices, the market mechanism of the example could have possibly generated several equilibrium prices.

4. Non-Cooperative Equilibria

Let an economy $\mathcal{E} : I \to \mathcal{A}$ and a trading game with action space A be given.

Definition. *A play* $\underset{\sim}{a}$ *is a Cournot-Nash (CN) equilibrium if* $\underset{\sim}{x}_{\underset{\sim}{a}}$ *is feasible and for almost every* $t \in I$, $\underset{\sim}{x}_{\underset{\sim}{a}}(t)$ *is* $\succsim_t$ *maximal on* $X_t \cap \{\underset{\sim}{x}_{\underset{\sim}{a}'}(t) : \underset{\sim}{a}'(t') = \underset{\sim}{a}(t')$ *for all* $t' \neq t\}$.

Since we will very quickly specialize our model we shall not dwell in any extension on a discussion of the previous general definition.

Remark 9. The definition as well as our whole treatment of the continuum of trades game has taken inspiration in D. Schmeidler [1973] work on CN equilibria for games with a continuum of players.

Remark 10. It is possible to arrive at the same notion of CN equilibrium by using the Generalized Game concept of Debreu [1952]. Indeed, for every play $\underset{\sim}{a}$ and $t \in I$ let $A(\underset{\sim}{a}, t) = \{a \in A : \underset{\sim}{x}_{\underset{\sim}{a}'}(t) \in X_t, \underset{\sim}{a}'(t) = a, \underset{\sim}{a}'(t) = \underset{\sim}{a}(t') \text{ for } t' \neq t\}$. A play $\underset{\sim}{a}$ is *admissible* if $\underset{\sim}{a}(t) \in A(\underset{\sim}{a}, t)$ for a.e. $t \in I$. The restriction of the abstract game to admissible plays defines a Generalized Games since now every play yields fully feasible outcomes. An admissible play $\underset{\sim}{a}$ is then a CN equilibrium of the generalized game if for a.e. $t \in I$ $\underset{\sim}{a}_{\underset{\sim}{a}}(t)$ is $\succsim_t$ maximal on $\{\underset{\sim}{x}_{\underset{\sim}{a}'}(t) : \underset{\sim}{a}'(t) \in A(\underset{\sim}{a}, t), \underset{\sim}{a}'(t') = \underset{\sim}{a}(t')$ for $t' \neq t\}$. But this is precisely the definition we gave above.

5. The Anonymity Axiom

We will now restrict our consideration to games where outcomes depend only on the actions played and not on the names of the players. More precisely: (i) if two traders choose the same action, they get assigned the same net trade, i.e., trader discrimination is not possible, and (ii) for a given fixed action of a trader the net trade assigned depends only on the distribution of the actions of all traders. Those are particular conditions, but they adequately embody the anonymity principles of well functioning markets: the trading possibilities of any particular economic agent are limited *only* by their availability of commodities to trade.

As already hinted at our wish to impose an anonymity axiom explains two particular aspects of the treatment of abstract games in Section 3: the strategy sets of different traders were assumed equal and the outcome of a play was not required to satisfy the private feasibility constraints.

Let $\mathcal{M}$ be the set of probability measures on A with finite mean. To every play $\underset{\sim}{a} : I \to A$ there corresponds a $\nu_{\underset{\sim}{a}} = \gamma \circ \underset{\sim}{a}^{-1} \in \mathcal{M}$.

Anonymity Axiom. *There is a function $G : A \times \mathcal{M} \to \mathbb{R}^\ell$ such that for all players $\underset{\sim}{a} : \underset{\sim}{x}_{\underset{\sim}{a}}(t) = G(\underset{\sim}{a}(t), \nu_{\underset{\sim}{a}})$ for a.e. $t \in I$.*

We will require that the G function be continuous.

Continuity Axiom. *The function G given by the anonymity axiom is jointly continuous when $\mathcal{M}$ is endowed with the topology of the weak convergence (see Hildenbrand [1974], p. 48 for a definition).*

We have:

Proposition 1. *Under the anonymity and the Continuity Axiom there is only one function that satisfies the Anonymity Axiom.*

Proof. Let $G, G' : A \times \mathcal{M} \to \mathbb{R}^\ell$ satisfy the axiom. Take any $v \in \mathcal{M}$ and $a \in A$. There is some sequence $\nu_n \to \nu$ such that $\text{supp}(\nu_n) = A$. We can also find $\underset{\sim}{a}_n, \underset{\sim}{a}$ such that $\nu_n = \gamma \cdot \underset{\sim}{a}_n^{-1}$, $\nu = \gamma \cdot \underset{\sim}{a}^{-1}$. (This is Skorohod theorem, see Hildenbrand [1974]). Since $\text{supp}(\nu_n) = A$, we have $\gamma \{t \in I : \|\underset{\sim}{a}_n(t) - a\| \leq \frac{1}{n}\} > 0$. Hence by the axiom there is $t_n \in I$ such that $\|\underset{\sim}{a}_n(t_n) - a\| \leq \frac{1}{n}$ and $G'(\underset{\sim}{a}_n(t_n), \nu_n) = x_{\underset{\sim}{a}_n}(t_n) = G(\underset{\sim}{a}_n(t_n), \nu_n)$. Since $\underset{\sim}{a}_n(t_n) \to a$ and $\nu_n \to \nu$ we conclude $G'(a, \nu) = G(a, \nu)$ by the continuity axiom. Q.E.D.

Note that under the anonymity axiom, a play $\underset{\sim}{a} : I \to A$ is a Cournot-Nash equilibrium if $G(\cdot, \nu_{\underset{\sim}{a}}) : I \to \mathbb{R}^\ell$ is a feasible assignment and for almost all $t \in I$, $G(\underset{\sim}{a}(t), \nu_{\underset{\sim}{a}})$ is $\gtrsim_t$ maximal on $X_t \cap \{G(a, \nu_{\underset{\sim}{a}}) : a \in A\}$. We say then that $\nu_{\underset{\sim}{a}}$ is a CN action distribution.

Examples 1–4 satisfy the anonymity axiom. Example 4 satisfies the continuity axiom while Examples 1 to 3 do not. In Example 3 the lack of continuity is due to the unboundedness of A. In Example 2 to this and to the potential multiplicity of equilibria. Example 1 can fail to be continuous only exceptionally (i.e., when $\int \underset{\sim}{a}_1 = 0$ or $\int \underset{\sim}{a}_2 = 0$). We should remark here that the continuity axiom plays only as minor role in the proof of the main theorem and that, at any rate, it suffices that it hold a neighborhood of the CN action distributions.

Remark 11. Even if we could formally dispense with the Continuity Axiom it is not clear that we would wish to do so. The continuum of traders is an idealization of a finite-but-large situation and there is no doubt that if our results are to imply anything for the latter some form of limit continuity will be required. Otherwise the continuum and the finite-but-large versions of the same model may behave in radically different ways. For example, it is not difficult to adapt Hurwicz's greed process (see [1959]) into our abstract trading game set-up in such a manner that for the finite-but-large version every Pareto optimal individually rational assignment can be obtained from some CN play while for the continuum version every CN play yields Walrasian assignments. The problem is that in building up G it is inescapable to make it discontinuous.

Also in the context of the designing of mechanisms problem, Thomson [1978] has examples which once viewed as abstract trading games satisfy all our axioms except continuity and which have an asymptotic behavior differing markedly from our conclusions for the continuous case (see Green [1978] for a discussion of this continuity problem in a different but related context).

We may also mention that the problems raised by mechanism yielding several possible assignments for the same play (see Remark 8) is not really its multiplicity. This could be handled easily. It is more serious than that fact that the Continuity Axiom will no longer be tenable, at least as an "everywhere" axiom. Possibly this could be tackled by referring only to generic cases but a very careful and somewhat complex analysis would be needed. We opt to keep things simple.

6. Interior Equilibria

Our aim is to specify conditions implying that the assignment of a Cournot-Nash equilibrium is Walrasian and therefore efficient. The anonymity axiom assumed, the next two figures illustrate situations where this is not so.

Let an action distribution $\nu \in \mathcal{M}$ be given and let $B_\nu = G(A, \nu)$ be the "public budget set." Then $B_\nu \cap X_t$ is the choice set faced by trader t. A given play $\underset{\sim}{a} : I \to A$ will be Cournot-Nash if for a.e., $t \in I$, $G(\underset{\sim}{a}(t), \nu_{\underset{\sim}{a}}) \in B_\nu \cap X_t$ is $\succsim_t$ maximizing in $B_\nu \cap X_t$.

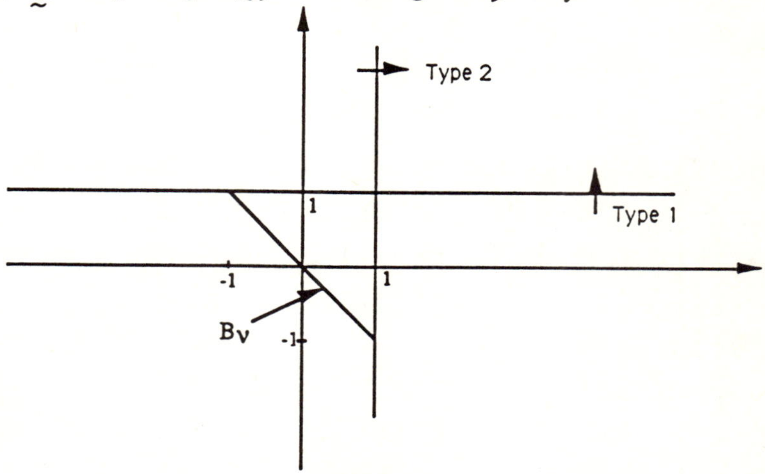

Figure 1

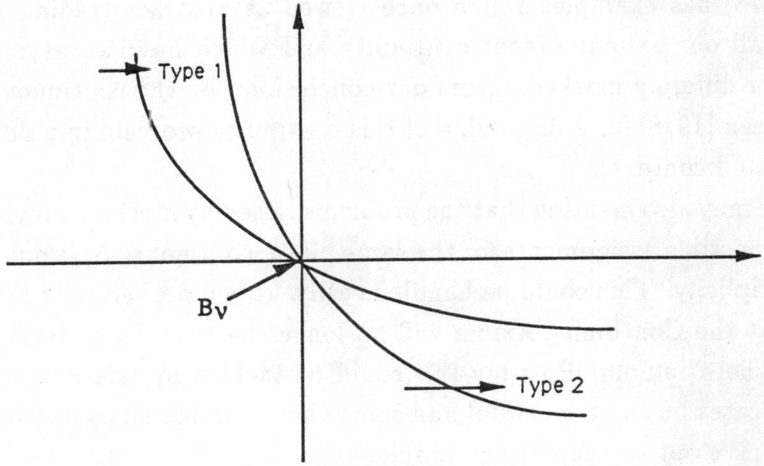

Figure 2

Figures 1 and 2 do schematically represent Cournot-Nash equilibria of abstract trading games which are not Walrasian. They can be supported by trivial examples of abstract games.

In the following two examples $X_t = \mathbb{R}^2$ and there are two types of traders with measure 1/2 each. Preferences of the types are as in Figure 1 for Example 5 and Figure 2 for Example 6.

Example 5. *$G(a,\nu) = \left(\int i d\nu - a, a - \int i d\nu\right)$ where i is the identity map in A. Now let ν be such that $\nu(\{-1\}) = \nu(\{1\}) = 1/2$. For this ν, $B_\nu = \{(-a,a) : a \in [-1,1]\}$. So, type 1 will choose $a = 1$ leading to the net trade $(-1,1)$ while type 2 will choose $a = -1$ leading to the net trade $(1,-1)$. Hence the induced action distribution is compatible with ν.*

Example 6. *Let A be arbitrary and for any ν put $G(a,\nu) = 0$.*

The problem in Figure 1 is that the traders preference maximization net trade is at the boundary of B_ν. In Figure 2, B_ν is too small, i.e., there is not enough responsiveness of possible net trades to individual actions. In fact given any ℓ an example in the nature of Figure 2 can be constructed provided B_ν is of dimension less than $\ell - 1$.

Examples 4 and 5 prompt us to regard as a desirable property of a Cournot-Nash equilibria $\underset{\sim}{a}$ that for a.e., $t \in I$ there be enough room in $B_{\nu_{\underset{\sim}{a}}}$ around $G(\underset{\sim}{a}(t), \nu_{\underset{\sim}{a}})$ where "enough" means the possibility of moving in at least $(\ell - 1)$ independent directions. This sounds a familiar theme, if one wants that the outcome of a decentralized competitive process be efficient then there should be a "full set of markets."

Definition. *Given an abstract game, a Cournot-Nash equilibria* $\underset{\sim}{a} : I \to A$ *shall be called interior, if, for a.e. t, a neighborhood of* $\{G(\underset{\sim}{a}(t), \nu_{\underset{\sim}{a}})\}$ *in* $B_{\nu_{\underset{\sim}{a}}}$ *is homeomorphic to* $\mathbb{R}^n$, $n \geq \ell - 1$.

Note that the notion of interior equilibrium is compatible with traders being at the boundary of their *private* budget sets $B_\nu \cap X_t$.

Our main theorem to be stated in Section 7 will be of the form: "Under a number of axioms on the abstract games every interior equilibrium yields a Walrasian assignment." One could of course give conditions under which every equilibrium is interior. This would be the case if, for example, (i) $A \subset \mathbb{R}^n$ is open, (ii) for every ν, $G(\cdot, \nu) : A \to \mathbb{R}^\ell$ is continuously differentiable, and (iii) for every a, $D_aG(a, \nu)$ has rank $= \ell - 1$, or if (iii) holds and B is closed and unbounded or if B_ν is a boundaryless $(\ell - 1)$ topological manifold. Those conditions, however, would be somewhat limiting on the class of allowable abstract games. As an instance, they are not quite satisfied in Example 1 (the problem being the situation where $\int \underset{\sim}{a}_1 = 0$ or $\int \underset{\sim}{a}_2 = 0$). So, we prefer not to impose them and to restrict ourselves to making claims about interior equilibria only. In concrete example it appears to be an easy matter to check whether a given equilibrium is interior or not.

7. The Neutrality Axiom

An interior NC equilibrium need not yield a Walrasian assignment.

Example 7. *There are two types of traders each with measure* $1/2$. *Trading sets equal* $\mathbb{R}^2$. *The action set is* $A = [0, 25]$. $G : A \times \mathcal{M} \to \mathbb{R}^2$ *has the form*

$$G(a, \nu) = \left(\int i d\nu - a, a^{1/2} - \int i^{1/2} d\nu \right).$$

Preferences will be specified later on. Take the distribution ν *given by* $\nu(\{4\}) = (\{16\}) = 1/2$. *Then* $B_\nu = \{(10 - a, a^{1/2} - 3) : a \in [0, 25]\}$

is as represented in Figure 3. The points in B_ν corresponding to $a = 4$ and $a = 16$ are, respectively, $(6,-1)$ and $(-6,1)$. Obviously we can draw types 1 and 2 indifference curves as in Figure 3. Here half the measure of traders will choose $a = 4$ and the other half $a = 16$. So, we are at an interior Nash-Cournot equilibrium which is not Walrasian (nor, for that matter, efficient).

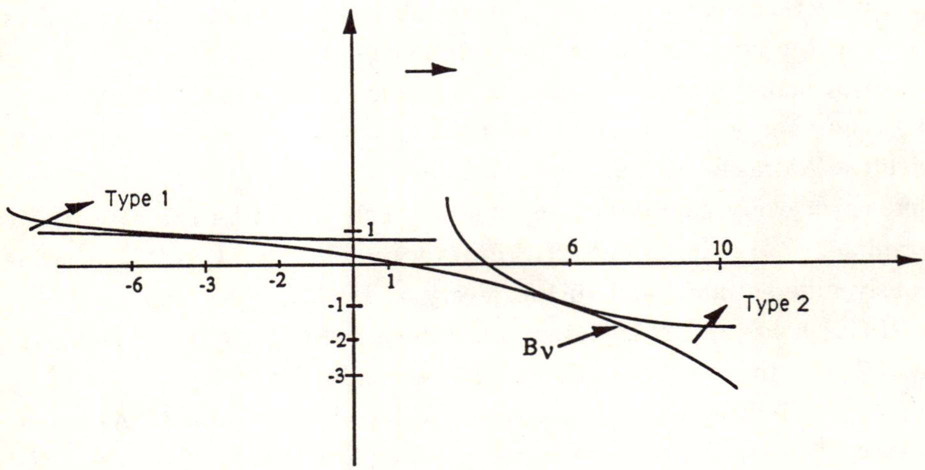

Figure 3

In the previous example it may seem unnatural that the origin (i.e., the possibility of no trade) does not belong to B_ν and that $B_\nu \cap \mathbb{R}^\ell_{++} \neq \emptyset$. This can be easily taken care of.

Example 8. *Let $g : \mathbb{R} \to \mathbb{R}$ be any continuous function going through the origin and $\bar{\nu}$ a probability measure on $\mathbb{R}$ such that $\int id\bar{\nu} = 0$ and $\int gd\bar{\nu} = 0$. Then it is possible to find an abstract trading game with $A = \mathbb{R}$ such that at $\bar{\nu}$, $B_{\bar{\nu}} =$ Graph g and for any ν one has $0 \in B_\nu$. Indeed, define*

$$G(a,\nu) = \left(a - \frac{|a|}{\int |a| d\nu} \int id\nu, g(a) - \frac{|a|}{\int |a| d\nu} \int gd\nu\right).$$

If $\int |a| d\nu = 0$ put $G(a,\nu) = 0$. Then we can generate "public budget sets" as the ones in Figure 4 and 5. If g is strictly monotone then preferences can be constructed such that the even distribution between the two types of traders indicated in the figures becomes a CN distribution.

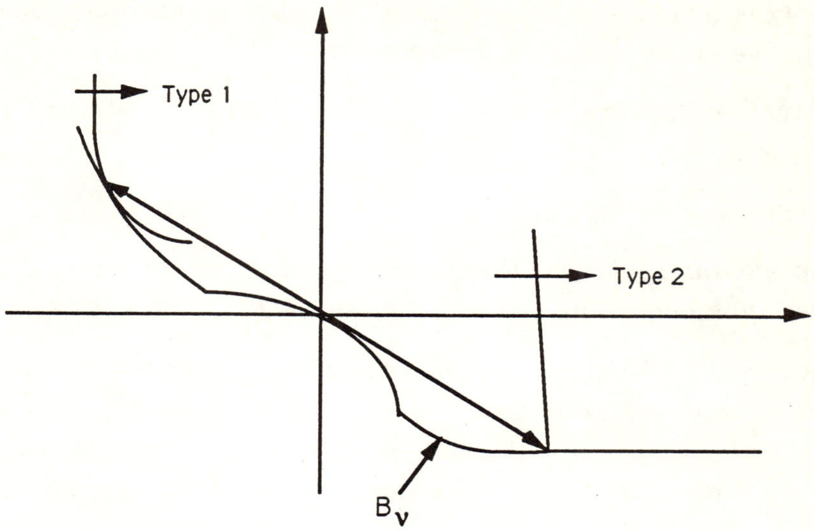

Figure 4

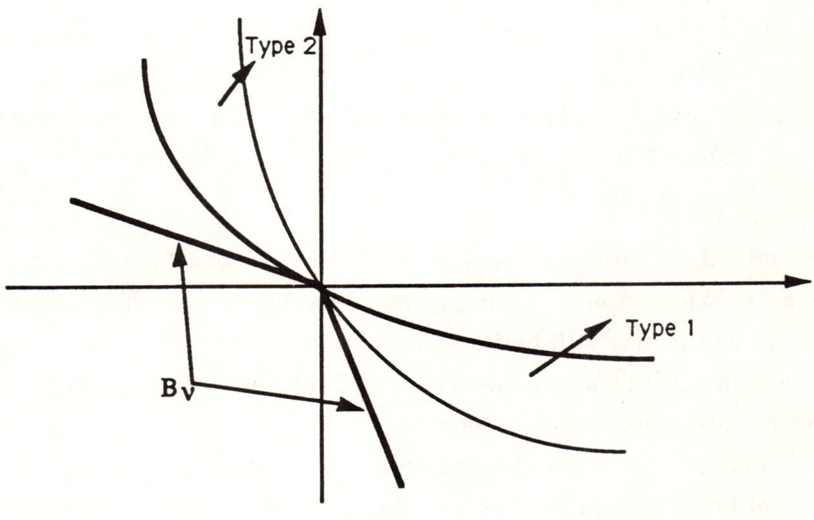

Figure 5

We should conclude that what goes wrong in Examples 7 and 8 is that B_ν is not a linear manifold. It is clear that the source of the non-linearity is that $G(a,\nu)$ depends on ν through moments other than the mean. The following axiom suggests itself:

Neutrality Axiom. *For any ν, $\nu' \in \mathcal{M}$, if $\int id\nu = \int id\nu'$ then $G(\cdot,\nu) = G(\cdot,\nu')$.*

Then we have:

Proposition 2. *Assume the Anonymity and Continuity Axioms. If the Neutrality Axiom is satisfied, then for any $\nu \in \mathcal{M}$, B_ν is a convex set.*

Proof. Let $\bar{\nu}$ be given. By the continuity condition we can assume without loss of generality that $\int id\bar{\nu}$ belongs to the relative interior of A. We proceed to show that $G(\cdot,\bar{\nu}) : A \to \mathbb{R}^\ell$ is then linear. Let $g_\nu : A \to \mathbb{R}$ be any of the coordinate functions of $G(\cdot,\nu)$. We know that for any $\nu \in \mathcal{M} \int g_\nu d\nu = 0$ and that g_ν depends on ν only through $\int id\nu$. If $g_{\bar{\nu}}$, which is continuous, is not linear, then an easy argument shows the existence of $a_1, a_2 \in A$ and $0 \le \alpha \le 1$ such that $\alpha g_{\bar{\nu}}(a_1) + (1-\alpha)g_{\bar{\nu}}(a_2) \neq g_{\bar{\nu}}(\alpha a_1 + (1-\alpha)a_2)$. Since $\int id_{\bar{\nu}}$ is the relative interior of A, we can, without loss of generality assume that $\bar{\nu}(\{a_1\}), \bar{\nu}(\{a_2\}) > 0$ (i.e., we can give to $\{a_1\}$ and $\{a_2\}$ a positive measure without altering $\int id_{\bar{\nu}}$). Now let ν' be equal to $\bar{\nu}$ except for a small $\varepsilon > 0$ am amount of mass equal to $\alpha\varepsilon$ (resp. $(1-\alpha)\varepsilon$) is transferred from $\{a_1\}$ (resp. $\{a_2\}$) to $\alpha a_1 + (1-\alpha)a_2$. We still have $\int id\bar{\nu} = \int id\nu'$, which implies $g_{\bar{\nu}} = g_{\nu'}$, but $0 = \int g_{\bar{\nu}} d\bar{\nu} \neq \int g_{\nu'} d\nu'$, a contradiction. Q.E.D.

Remark 12. Examples 1 to 4 satisfy the Neutrality Axiom. It can well happen that an economic trading game be naturally given in a form which does not. But it may still be possible in many cases to find an equivalent trading game, with an expanded but still convex action-message space, for which the axiom does indeed hold. For example, we may have a typical competition problem among many firms with the strategies of the individual firm being prices and qualities of goods (suppose there are only m possible qualities). The concept of mean quality is then irrelevant to the equilibrium problem. It may not even be defined. So, the Neutrality Axiom is not satisfied. On the other hand if we view as the set of actions the much larger set of supply (and demand) functions for the m quality good (with arguments the m vector of prices), then the neutrality axiom will hold because only the aggregate demand and supply matters.

Remark 13. It is important to notice the interplay between the neutrality axiom and the convexity hypothesis on the action-message space A. It is the latter which gives teeth to the first. Indeed, it is always formally possible, by expanding A, to satisfy, at least approximately, the neutrality axiom. The problem is that the expanded A will fail to be convex. For example, if $A = [0,1]$ and the outcome net trades depend on plays through the mean and the variance of the action distribution we could extend the action space to $A' = \{(s, s^2) : s \in [0,1]\} \subset [0,1]^2$ and regard the neutrality axiom as satisfied. Of course A' is not convex.

8. The Theorem

We are now ready for the main theorem.

Theorem 3. *Suppose the Anonymity, Neutrality and the Continuity Axioms hold. Then every interior Cournot-Nash equilibrium yields a Walrasian assignment.*

Proof. Let a be the Cournot-Nash equilibrium. Put $B = B_{\nu_{\underset{\sim}{a}}}$, $x_t = \underset{\sim}{x}_{\underset{\sim}{a}}(t)$.

By interiority of Proposition 2, B must be a convex set of dimension $\geq \ell - 1$. Also, for a.e. $t \in I$, x_t should belong to the relative interior of B.

Take $p \in \mathbb{R}$ such that $\{v \in \mathbb{R}; pv = 0\}$ is parallel to the linear space spanned by B_ν. Pick a t with x_t interior, since x_t is $\succsim_t$ maximizing in B and $x_t + z \succ x_t$ whenever $z \gg 0$ we can choose $p \geq 0$, $p \neq 0$. So, $\dim B = \ell - 1$. Since $px_t = px_{t'}$ for a.e. t, $t' \in I$ and $\int x_t dt = 0$ we have $pB = 0$.

Take any t with x_t interior. Suppose that $z \in X_t$, $pz \leq 0$ and $z \succ_t xt$. Pick $z' \gg x$, then $pz' > 0$ and $z' \succ_t x_t$. Hence, by convexity of preferences there is $z'' \in [z, z']$ with $z'' \succ_t x_t$ and $pz'' = 0$. Also, $z''' \succ_t x_t$ for any $z''' \in [z'', x_t)$. But x_t belongs to the relative interior of B which is of full dimension in $\{v \in \mathbb{R} : pv = 0\}$. Hence we can assume $z''' \in B$. But this contradicts the fact that x_t is $\succsim_t$ maximizing in B_ν. Hence no such z exists and we are done. Q.E.D.

Remark 14. One may wonder if we do not get too strong a result, in the sense that obtaining an efficient, not necessarily Walrasian, assignment would be good enough. However, under quite general circumstances (although not always) it is the case that if the assignment derived from an anonymous continuum trading game is efficient then it is competitive. See Hammond [1976] for a related issue.

Remark 15. Some of the multicommodity models which build on Shubik's initial contribution exhibit non-efficient CN equilibria even in the continuum (see, for example, Jaynes, Okuno and Schmeidler [1976] or Dubey and Shapley [1977]). To understand why this is formally possible in models which superficially seem to satisfy all our axioms we must go back to the issue of the feasibility of the assignments obtained as outcomes of plays. As indicated in Remark 7 our plays have a definite tâtonnement character. This is not the case in the models referred to which are games in the proper sense, i.e., every play must yield a feasible outcome. In our context, every player t would be restricted to send messages guaranteeing that, no matter which are the messages of the rest of the population, the net trade assigned to t is feasible. Therefore, the effective message space of t is $A_t = \{a \in A : G(a, \mathcal{M}) \subset X_t\}$ (A_t will be non-empty if, for example, there exists a no-trade option). Given a play $\underset{\sim}{a}$, the effective private budget of t is $G(A_t, \nu_{\underset{\sim}{a}})$ which will typically be smaller than $B_{\nu_{\underset{\sim}{a}}} \cap X_t$. If it is "much" smaller we would not expect efficiency. In particular it may well happen that a CN equilibrium of the proper game is not a CN equilibrium of the original tâtonnement game.

In a more substantive vein the difference can be traced to our abstract treatment assuming away any problems related to the technology of transactions. In the Shubik type models one usually has $\ell - 1$ markets exchanging goods against some money and the nature of the game is such that purchases can only be made with money in hand and not with the receipts of sales. Note that the problem is one of timing not of quantity constraints self-fulfilling expectations. At any rate, if not much money is available the equilibria may well be efficient. Typically the inefficiency will disappear with a well developed credit system, a point emphasized by Shubik. We have proceeded in our formulation as if we really were in such a situation, i.e., money receipts are fully available for purchases.

9. On the Concept of Strict Nash-Cournot Equilibrium

Suppose we have given an economy $\mathcal{E} : I \to \mathcal{A}$ and an anonymous trading game $G : A \times \mathcal{M} \to \mathbb{R}^\ell$. From a non-cooperative game theoretic standpoint a CN play $\underset{\sim}{a} : I \to A$ will be rather fragile if there were traders (strictly speaking, a non-null set of traders) that could obtain a better net trade by pretending to be n different players (infinite but otherwise arbitrary). Indeed, in an anonymous mass market there can be nothing to present an individual trader from entering it several times. This observation prompts the following

Definition. *A play* $\underset{\sim}{a} : I \to A$ *is a strict Nash-Cournot equilibrium if* $x_{\underset{\sim}{a}}$ *is feasible and for a.e.,* $t \in [0,1]$. $(G(\underset{\sim}{a}(t), \nu_{\underset{\sim}{a}})$ *is* $\succsim_t$ *maximal on* $X_t \tilde{\cap} \bigcup_{n=1}^{\infty} nB_{\nu_{\underset{\sim}{a}}}$.

It is obvious from Proposition 2 and the proof of Theorem 3 that

Proposition 4. *If the Anonymity, Continuity and Neutrality axioms are satisfied then every CN equilibrium is strict.*

Without the neutrality axiom a CN equilibrium needs not to be strict. For example, if at a CN distribution ν we have that $B_\nu \cap \mathbb{R}^\ell_{++} \neq \emptyset$ (as in Example 6) then by the monotonicity of preferences the distribution cannot be a strict CN.

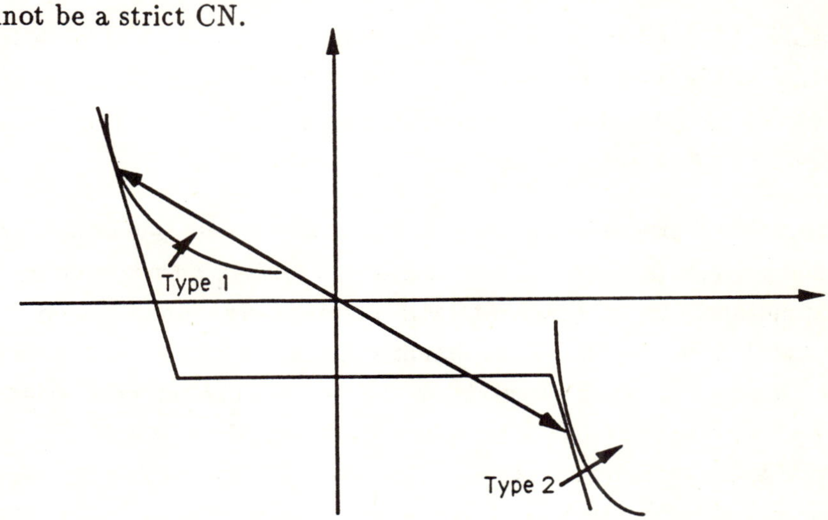

Figure 6

Without the neutrality axiom, is every strict Cournot-Nash equilibrium Walrasian? Not necessarily. In Figures 5 and 6 there are two situations where the CN equilibria are interior and strict but not Walrasian (the two types indicated have the same weight). By using the technique of Example 7 we can without difficulty formally construct economies and trading games supporting both figures so that they become valid example. In Figure 6 the origin does not belong to B_ν. In Figure 5, B_ν fails to be smooth. In fact we have

Proposition 5. *Suppose that the anonymity axiom holds. Let a be a strict CN equilibrium. If* $0 \in B_{\nu_{\underset{\sim}{a}}}$ *and* $B_{\nu_{\underset{\sim}{a}}}$ *is a* $(\ell - 1)$ C^1 *manifold, then the equilibrium is Walrasian.*

Proof. Let T be the $(\ell - 1)$ tangent plane to $B_{\nu_{\underset{\sim}{a}}}$ at 0.

It is easy to verify that for any $z \in T$, $\bigcup_{n=1}^{\infty} nB_{\nu_{\underset{\sim}{a}}}$ contains net trades arbitrarily close to z. Henceforth by the continuity of preferences, for a.e., $t \in [0,1]$, $\underset{\sim}{x}_a(t) \succsim_t z$ for any $z \in T$. Because of monotonicity of preferences, $T \cap \mathbb{R}^\ell_{++} = \emptyset$. Hence we can pick $p \geq 0$ such that $T = \{z \in \mathbb{R}^\ell : pz = 0\}$. With p as the candidate Walrasian price the proof proceeds from this point on as in Theorem 3. Q.E.D.

As Example 7 and Figure 4 show, Proposition 5 holds for strict NC equilibria but not for ordinary ones.

Remark 16. Given an anonymous trading game $G : A \times \mathcal{M} \to \mathbb{R}^\ell$ it is possible to build a new one $G^* : A^* \times \mathcal{M}^* \to \mathbb{R}^\ell$ so that the concept of ordinary and strict CN equilibria coincide in G^* and the ordinary equilibria of G^* correspond to the strict equilibria of G.

One would proceed as follows. Let A be a complete, separable subset of a Banach space. Denote by A^* the set of finite, non-negative integer valued measures on A. Endow A^* with the weak-star topology and Borel sets. Let $\mathcal{M}^*$ be the (Borel) probability measures on A^* with bounded mean. A play is now an integrable $\underset{\sim}{a}^* : I \to A^*$. The integral is defined by $\left(\int \underset{\sim}{a}^*\right)(V) = \int \underset{\sim}{a}^*(t)(V)$ for every Borel set $V \subset A$. It is a non-negative finite measure on A (see Mas-Colell [1975], Section 3.1 for the mathematical technicalities of this remark). Given $\underset{\sim}{a}^*$ we let $\nu^*_{\underset{\sim}{a}^*} \in \mathcal{M}^*$ be the Borel probability measure induced by $\underset{\sim}{a}^*$ on A^*. An element $\nu^* \in \mathcal{M}^*$

induces a distribution ν on A by letting

$$\nu(V) = \frac{1}{\int a^*(A)d\nu^*} \int a^*(V)d\nu^*.$$

Given a play $\underset{\sim}{a}^*$ one lets $\nu_{\underset{\sim}{a}^*}$ be the measure in A corresponding to $\nu^*_{\underset{\sim}{a}^*}$. Clearly,

$$\nu_{\underset{\sim}{a}^*} = \frac{1}{(\int \underset{\sim}{a}^*)(A)} \left(\int \underset{\sim}{a} \right).$$

Finally, one defines

$$G^*(a^*, \nu^*) = \int G(a, \nu) da^*.$$

Note that in this new game the neutrality axiom is satisfied but A^* is not convex. Also, an interior strict Nash-Cournot equilibrium of G is an ordinary NC equilibrium of G^* but not necessarily an interior one (see Figure 5 where B_{ν^*} is the convex hull of B_ν).

10. Nash-Cournot Equilibria of Non-Atomic Games

This section is independent of the rest of the paper. It does deal with general games rather than with particular trading ones.

We have informally argued, as a justification of our work, that the notion of CN equilibrium is a good non-cooperative concept in the continuum of traders situation. It may, therefore, be worthwhile to describe a class of continuum games where there is no difficulty whatsoever in defining CN equilibrium plays and where a quite satisfactory existence theory is available. The class is the natural general analog of the anonymous trading games studied in the previous sections. The results amount to a slight generalization of Schmeidler's Theorem 2 in [1973]. The treatment owes much to Hildenbrand [1974] and Hart, Hildenbrand and Kohlberg [1974] approach to the study of economies and Walrasian allocations.

Let A be a non-empty, compact metric space of *actions* and the set of (Borel) probability measures on A endowed with the weak convergence topology. The space $\mathcal{M}$ is compact and metrizable.

A *player* is characterized by a continuous utility function $u : A \times \mathcal{M} \to \mathbb{R}$. Given the action $a \in A$ taken by a player with characteristics u and the action distribution of all traders ν, $u(a,\nu)$ represents the utility enjoyed by the player. We should remark that a treatment via preference relations rather than utility functions could be carried out without difficulty.

Let $\mathcal{U}_A$ be the space of continuous utility functions $u : A \times \mathcal{M} \to \mathbb{R}$ endowed with the supremum norm. It will be denoted as the space of *players' characteristics.*

A continuum game (strictly speaking, an anonymous game with action space A) is then characterized by a (Borel) measure on μ with compact support.

Definition. *Given a game μ, a (Borel) measure τ on $\mathcal{U}_A \times A$ is a Cournot-Nash distribution if, denoting by $\tau_{\mathcal{U}}$, τ_A the marginals of τ on $\mathcal{U}_A$ and A respectively, we have:*

(i) $\tau_{\mathcal{U}} = \mu$ *and*
(ii) $\tau(\{(u,a) : u(a,\tau_A) \geq u(A,\tau_A)\}) = 1.$

By use of the concept of CN equilibrium distribution (modelled after Hart, Hildenbrand and Kohlberg [1974]), the existence theorem of Schmeidler [1973] can be straightforwardly extended to cases where A is not finite.

Theorem 6. *Given a game μ on $\mathcal{U}_A$ there exists a CN equilibrium distribution.*

Proof. Since the support of μ is compact, A is compact and the functions in $\mathcal{U}_A$ are continuous, it suffices to prove the theorem for A finite and μ non-atomic (indeed, let $A_n \to A$ in the Hausdorff metric and $\mu_n \to \mu_{A_n}$ in the weak convergence plus Hausdorff metric convergence of the supports, $\mu_n \in \mathcal{U}_{A_n}$. Then if τ_n is a CN equilibrium for μ_n, $\{\tau_n\}_1^\infty$ has a weak convergence accumulation point τ which is easily checked to be a CN distribution for μ).

Let $A = \{a_1, \ldots, a_n\}$. We can identify $\mathcal{M}$ with the $n-1$ simplex. For any $1 \leq i \leq n$ let $e_i \in \mathbb{R}^n$ be the vector with $e_i^i = 1$ and $e_i^j = 0$ for $i \neq j$. Denote $\mathcal{F} = \operatorname{supp} \mu$ and define the correspondence $\phi : \mathcal{F} \times \mathcal{M} \to \mathbb{R}^n$ by

$$\phi(u,\nu) = \{e_i : u(a_i,\nu) \geq u(A,\nu)\}.$$

It is non-empty and upper hemicontinuous. Now let $\Phi : \mathcal{M} \to \mathcal{M}$ be defined by

$$\Phi(\nu) = \int \phi(u, \nu) d\mu(u).$$

Since μ is non-atomic, Φ is non-empty convex valued and upper-hemicontinuous (see Hildenbrand [1974], pp. 64 and 73]). By Kakutani fixed point theorem there is $\bar{\nu} \in \Phi(\bar{\nu})$, i.e., there is a (measurable) function $g : \mathcal{F} \to A$ such that $u(g(u), \bar{\nu}) \geq u(A, \bar{\nu})$ for μ-a.e., $u \in \mathcal{F}$ and $\bar{\nu} = \mu o g^{-1}$. So, define τ by letting $\tau(V) = \mu\{u \in \mathcal{F} : (u, g(u)) \in V\}$ for every Borel set V. This is our CN distribution. Q.E.D.

References

Aumann, R., 1963, "Economies with a Continuum of Agents," *Econometrica.*

Cournot, A., 1929, *Recherches Sur Les Principes Mathématiques de la Théorie des Richesse*, Hachette, Paris. Translated as *Researches into the Mathematical Principles of the Theory of Wealth*, Macmillan, New York.

Debreu, G., 1952, "A Social Equilibrium Existence Theorem," *Proc. Natl. Acad. Sci. USA* **38**, 886–893.

Dubey, P. and Shapley, L., 1977, "Non-Cooperative Exchange with a Continuum of Traders," Cowles Foundation Discussion Paper No. 447.

Dubey, P. and Shubik, M., 1978, "Strategic Market Games and Market Mechanisms," Cowles Foundation Discussion Paper, forthcoming.

Gabszewicz, J. and Vial, J. P., 1971, "Oligopoly à la Cournot in General Equilibrium Theory," *J. Econ. Theory.*

Green, E., 1978, "Non-Cooperative Price Taking in Large Dynamic Markets," Working Paper No. 228, Princeton University.

Hammond, P., 1976, "Individual Incentive Compatibility in Large Economies," University of Essex Discussion Paper No. 88.

Hart, O., 1977, "Monopolistic Competition with Differentiated Commodities," Cambridge, mimeo.

Hart, S., Hildenbrand, W., and Kohlberg, E., 1974, "On Equilibrium Allocation as Distributions on the Commodity Space," *J. Math. Econ* **1**, 159–166.

Hildenbrand, W., 1974, *Core and Equilibrium of a Large Economy*, Princeton University Press.

Hurwicz, L., 1959, "Optimality and Informational Efficiency in Resource Allocation Processes," in *Mathematical Methods in the Social Sciences*, Arrow, Karlin and Suppes, eds., Stanford University Press.

Jaynes, J., Okuno, M., and Schmeidler, D., 1976, "Efficiency in an Atomless Economy with Fiat Money," *Int. Econ. Rev.*, 124–128.

Mas-Colell, A., 1975, "A Model of Equilibrium with Differentiated Commodities," *J. Math. Econ.* **2**.

Novshek, W. and Sonnenschein, H., 1978, "Cournot and Walras," Working Paper No. 224, Princeton University.

Pazner, E. and Schmeidler, D., 1976, "Non-Walrasian Equilibria and Arrow-Debreu Economies," University of Illinois, Urbana, Illinois, mimeo.

Postlewaite, A. and Schmeidler, D., 1978, "Approximate Efficiency of Non-Walrasian Nash Equilibria," *Econometrica* **46:1**, 127–137.

Schmeidler, P., 1973, "Equilibrium Points of Non-Atomic Games," *J. Stat. Phys.* **7:4**, 295–309.

Shapley, L., 1974, "Non-Cooperative General Exchange," RAND Corporation Report No. p-5286.

Shubik, M., 1972, "Commodity Money, Oligopoly, Credit and Bankruptcy in a General Equilibrium Model," *West. Econ. J.* **10**.

Thomson, W., 1978, "Nash Equilibria of Walras and Lindhal Mechanism," University of Minnesota, mimeo.

Yosida, K., 1971, *Functional Analysis*, Springer-Verlag, New York and Berlin.

On Symmetric Cournot-Nash Equilibrium Distributions in a Finite-Action, Atomless Game

M. Ali Khan and Ye Neng Sun

Abstract. We show that in a finite action, atomless game, every Cournot-Nash equilibrium distribution can be "symmetrized." This yields an elementary proof of a result of Mas-Colell.

1. Introduction

Mas-Colell [1984] showed the existence of a Cournot-Nash equilibrium distribution (CNED) as a consequence of the Fan-Glicksberg theorem. Mas-Colell also showed the existence of a symmetric CNED in finite-action, atomless games as a consequence of the Kakutani fixed point theorem and of results in the theory of integration of correspondences. These results consist, in particular, of Lyapunov's theorem on the range of a vector measure, Aumann's measurable selection theorem, and his theorem on the upper hemicontinuity of the integral of a correspondence with upper-hemicontinuous values; on all of this [Hildenbrand, 1974] is a standard reference.

In this note, we show that in a finite-action, atomless game every CNED can be "symmetrized" to yield a symmetric CNED. This allows us to deduce Mas-Colell's result on the existence of a symmetric CNED from his first result on the existence of a CNED. The proof of our result is elementary in the sense that it uses only Lyapunov's theorem on the convexity of the range of a *scalar* measure; see [Jamison, 1974].

Section 2 recalls the model and presents the results. Section 3 gives the basic idea of the proof and Section 4 is devoted to the formalities of the proof. Section 5 concludes with a remark.

2. The Model and Results

We recall for the reader's convenience the basic definitions from Mas-Colell [1984]. Let A be a compact, metric space of actions, $\mathcal{M}$ the set of

Borel probability measures on A endowed with the weak* topology and $\mathcal{U}_A$ the space of continuous functions from $A \times \mathcal{M}$ into $\mathbb{R}$ and endowed with the supremum-norm topology. A *game* is a Borel probability measure on $\mathcal{U}_A$. A Borel probability measure τ is said to be a *Cournot-Nash equilibrium distribution (CNED)* of the game μ if the marginal of τ on $\mathcal{U}_A$, $\tau_{\mathcal{U}}$, is μ and $\tau(B_\tau) = 1$ where $B_\tau = \{(a,u) \in A \times \mathcal{U}_A : u(a, \tau_A) \geq u(x, \tau_A)$ for all $x \in A\}$ and τ_A denotes the marginal of τ on A. τ is said to be a *symmetric Cournot-Nash equilibrium distribution* if τ is a CNED and there exists a measurable function $h : \mathcal{U}_A \to A$ such that τ (graph h) $= 1$. We shall say that every CNED τ can be *symmetrized* if there exists as symmetric CNED τ^s such that $B_{\tau^s} = B_\tau$.

We can now state

Theorem. *Every Cournot-Nash equilibrium distribution of a game μ with action set A can be symmetrized if μ is atomless and A is finite.*

This yields as a corollary

Corollary (Mas Colell). *A symmetric Cournot-Nash equilibrium distribution exists for a game μ with action set A whenever μ is atomless and A is finite.*

The Corollary is an easy consequence of our theorem and Theorem 1 of Mas-Colell [1974].

3. Heuristics of the Proof

We illustrate the basic idea of the proof of our theorem by considering an action set with two elements. The reader may wish to keep Figure 1 in mind as we go through the argument.

Let τ be the CNED of a game μ with action set $\{a_1, a_2\}$. Let the set B_τ of all pay-offs and corresponding pay-off maximizing actions be denotes by the set $(a_1 \times U_1) \cup (a_2 \times U_2)$. Unlike Figure 1, U_1 and U_2 need not necessarily be connected sets. Suppose, again unlike Figure 1, that $U_1 \cap U_2 = \emptyset$. Since $U_1 \cup U_2 = \mathcal{U}_A$, τ can be shown to be symmetric CNED simply by letting $h(u) = a_i$ for all $u \in U_i$, for all $i = 1, 2$. Certainly h is measurable and τ (graph h) $= 1$. Thus, in the case $U_1 \cap U_2 = \emptyset$, there is nothing to prove.

Suppose $U_1 \cap U_2 \neq \emptyset$. The basic idea in this case is to "disjointify" U_1 and U_2, i.e., to construct measurable subsets $U_i^* \subset U_i$ for all $i = 1, 2$, such that $U_1^* \cap U_2^* = \emptyset$. Since μ is atomless, this can be done in a number of ways but the important consideration is to do this in such a way that the marginal of τ on A, τ_A, does not change. Since B_τ depends only on τ_A, this ensures that B_τ does not change. We now briefly spell out the mechanics of such a procedure.

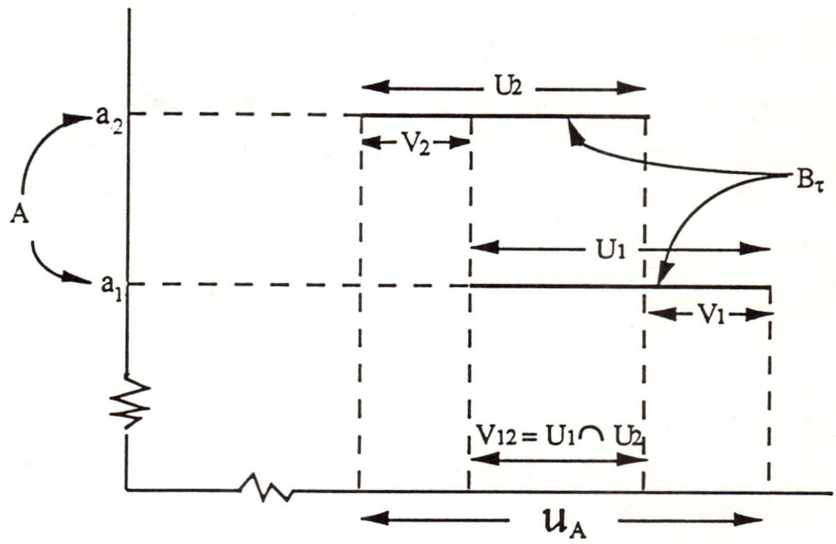

Figure 1

Let $V_i = U_i - U_j$, $i = 1, 2$, $j \neq i$, and $V_{12} = U_1 \cap U_2$. Find measurable subsets V_{12}^1, V_{12}^2 of V_{12} such that $V_{12}^1 \cap V_{12}^2 = \emptyset, V_{12}^1 \cup V_{12}^2 = V_{12}$ and $\mu(V_{12}^i) = \tau(a_i \times V_{12})$, $i = 1, 2$. Since $\sum_{i=1}^2 \tau(a_i \times V_{12}) = \tau(\bigcup_{i=1}^2 (a_i \times V_{12})) = \tau(\{a_1, a_2\} \times V_{12}) = \tau_u(V_{12}) = \mu(V_{12})$, Lyapunov's theorem on the range of an atomless scalar measure guarantees that V_{12}^1 and V_{12}^2 can be found; see Lemma 2 below. Now let $U_i^* = V_i \cup V_{12}^i$, $i = 1, 2$. These are the sets that work by letting $h : \mathcal{U}_A \to A$ be a function such that $h(u) = a_i$ for all $u \in U_i^*$, for all $i = 1, 2$. Now let $\tau^s(B) = \mu\{u \in \mathcal{U}_A : (h(u), u) \in B\}$ for any measurable subset B of $A \times \mathcal{U}_A$. τ^s is the symmetric CNED. The only point which needs to be checked is that $\tau_A^s = \tau_A$. But $\tau_A(\{a_i\}) = \tau(a_i \times \mathcal{U}_A) = \tau(a_i \times U_i) = \tau(a_i \times V_i) + \tau(a_i \times V_{12}) = \mu(V_i) + \mu(V_{12}^i) = \mu(V_i \cup V_{12}^i) = \mu(U_i^*) = \mu\{u \in \mathcal{U}_A : (h(u), u) \in (a_i \times \mathcal{U}_A)\} = \tau_A^s(\{a_i\})$.

4. Proof of the Theorem

We begin with an elementary lemma.

Lemma 1. *Let A_i $(i = 1, \dots, k)$ and B be arbitrary sets. Then*

$$\bigcup_{i=1}^{k}(A_i \times B) = \left(\left(\bigcup_{i=1}^{k} A_i\right) \times B\right).$$

Proof. Straightforward. □

Our next lemma is a simple consequence of Lyapunov's theorem on the range of a scalar measure.

Lemma 2. *Let $(S, \mathcal{S}, \mu)$ be an atomless measure space. If $V \in \mathcal{S}$, $\mu(V) = \sum_{i=1}^{n} \lambda_i$ with $\lambda_i \geq 0$ for all i, there exist for all $i = 1, \dots, n$, $V^i \in \mathcal{S}$ such that $V^i \cap V^j = \emptyset$ $(i \neq j)$, $\bigcup_{i=1}^{n} V_i = V$ and $\mu(V^i) = \lambda_i$.*

Proof. We shall prove the lemma by induction. The lemma is trivially true for $n = 1$. Assume it to be true for $n = k$ and let $V \in \mathcal{S}$ with $\mu(V) = \sum_{i=1}^{k+1} \lambda_i$, $\lambda_i \geq 0$ for all $i = 1, \dots, k+1$. If $\lambda_i = 0$ for any i, we are reduced to the case of $n = k$ and the proof is completed by letting $V_i = \emptyset$ for that i. Thus, suppose $\lambda_i > 0$ for all i. Let $\lambda(1) = \sum_{i=1}^{k} \lambda_i / \sum_{i=1}^{k+1} \lambda_i$ and $\lambda(2) = 1 - \lambda(1)$. By Lyapunov's theorem (see Hildenbrand [1974, p. 45]), we can find $V^{k+1} \in \mathcal{S}$ such that $\mu(V^{k+1}) = \lambda_{k+1}$. Since $(V - V^{k+1}) \in \mathcal{S}$, and $\mu(V - V^{k+1}) = \sum_{i=1}^{k} \lambda_i$, we use the induction hypothesis to complete the proof. □

Before we present the proof of Theorem, we develop some notation. Let I denote the set $\{1, 2, \dots, n\}$ and $P(I)$ the set of subsets of I, including the empty set. For any $\pi \in P(I)$, let π^c denote the complement of π in I. Let $P^m(I) = \{\pi \in P(I) : m \in \pi\}$. We shall use the convention that a union over the empty set is the empty set. We also use the same notation for a point and a set consisting solely of that point.

Proof of Theorem. Let τ be the Cournot-Nash equilibrium distribution of the game μ. Let $U_i = \text{proj}_{\mathcal{U}_A}(B_\tau \cap (a_i \times \mathcal{U}_A))$ for all $i \in I$.

$$\bigcup_{i=I} U_i = \mathcal{U}_A. \tag{1}$$

Certainly $U_i \subset \mathcal{U}_A$ for $i \in I$. On the other hand, let $u \in \mathcal{U}_A$. Certainly there exists $k \in I$ such that $u(a_k, \tau) \geq u(a_i, \tau)$. Then $(a_k, u) \in B_\tau$ and hence $u \in U_k$.

$$B_\tau = \bigcup_{i \in I} (a_i \times U_i). \tag{2}$$

Certainly $(a_i \times U_i) \subset B_\tau$ for all $i \in I$. Now any element x of B_τ can be written as (a_i, u) for some $i \in I$ and some $u \in \mathcal{U}_A$. Hence $u \in U_i$ and $x \in (a_i \times U_i)$.

$$\tau(a_i \times U_i) = \tau(a_i \times \mathcal{U}_A). \tag{3}$$

Since $(a_i \times U_i) \subset (a_i \times \mathcal{U}_A)$, certainly $\tau(a_i \times U_i) \leq \tau(a_i \times \mathcal{U}_A)$. Suppose there exists $i \in I$ such that strict inequality holds for that i. Then $1 = \tau(B_\tau) = \tau\left(\bigcup_{i \in I}(a_i \times \mathcal{U}_A)\right) = \tau(A \times \mathcal{U}_A)$, a contradiction to the fact that τ is a probability measure.

For any $\pi \in P(I)$, let $V_\pi = \left(\bigcap_{i \in \pi} U_i\right) - \left(\bigcup_{i \in \pi^c} U_i\right)$.

$$\bigcup_{\pi \in P(I)} V_\pi = \mathcal{U}_A, \tag{4a}$$

$$V_\pi \cap V_\sigma = \emptyset \quad (\pi, \sigma \in P(I), \pi \neq \sigma), \tag{4b}$$

$$\bigcup_{\pi \in P^i(I)} V_\pi = U_i. \tag{4c}$$

For (a), pick $u \in \mathcal{U}_A$. Let $\sigma = \{i \in I : u \in U_i\}$. By (1), $\sigma \neq \emptyset$. Then $u \in V_\sigma$. On the other hand, $u \in \bigcup_{\pi \in P(I)} V_\pi$ implies that there exists $\sigma \in P(I)$, $\sigma \neq \emptyset$ such that $u \in V_\sigma$. Hence $u \in U_i$ for all $i \in \sigma$ and hence, by (1), $u \in \mathcal{U}_A$. For (b), suppose there exists π, σ in $P(I)$ such that $\pi \neq \sigma$ and $V_\pi \cap V_\sigma \neq \emptyset$. Since V_π and V_σ are nonempty, π and σ are nonempty. Then there exists $i \in \pi$, $i \notin \sigma$. Now $u \in V_\pi \cap V_\sigma$ implies $u \in U_i$. Since $i \in \sigma^c$, $u \notin V_\sigma$ which is a contradiction. For (c), pick $u \in \bigcup_{\pi \in P^i(I)} V_\pi$. Then there exists $\pi \in P^i(I)$ such that $u \in V_\pi$. Since $i \in \pi$, $u \in U_i$. On the other hand, for any $u \in U_i$, let $\sigma = \{j \in I, u \in U_j\}$ and $\pi = \{i\} \cup \sigma$. Certainly $u \in V_\pi$ and $\pi \in P^i(I)$.

For any $\pi \in P(I)$, there exist measurable V_π^i $(i \in I)$,

$$V_\pi^i \cap V_\pi^j = \emptyset \quad (i \neq j), \quad \bigcup_{i \in \pi} V_\pi^i = V_\pi, \quad \text{and} \quad \mu(V_\pi^i) = \tau(a \times V_\pi). \tag{5}$$

Observe that $\mu(V_\tau) = \tau_{\mathcal{U}_A}(V_\pi) = \tau(A \times V_\pi) = \tau\left(\left(\bigcup_{i\in I} a_i\right) \times V_\pi\right)$ which, by Lemma 1, equals $\tau\left(\left(\bigcup_{i\in I} a_i \times V_\pi\right)\right) = \sum_{i\in I} \tau(a_i \times V_\pi)$. We can now apply Lemma 2 to complete the proof of (5).

Now let $U_i^* = \bigcup_{\pi\in P^i(I)} V_\pi^i$. For all $i \in I$,

$$U_i^* \subset U_i, \tag{6a}$$

$$U_i^* \cap U_j^* = \emptyset \quad (i \neq j), \tag{6b}$$

$$\bigcup_{i\in I} U_i^* = \mathcal{U}_A. \tag{6c}$$

To see (a), pick $u \in U_i^*$. Then there exists $\pi \in P^i(I)$ such that $u \in V_\pi^i$. This implies $u \in V_\pi$. Since $i \in \pi$, $u \in U_i$. (b) follows from the fact that for $i \neq j$, $V_\pi^i \cap V_\pi^j = \emptyset$ on the other hand, and from $V_\pi \cap V_\sigma = \emptyset$ for $\pi \neq \sigma$ on the other. For (c), note that

$$\begin{aligned}\bigcup_{i\in I} U_i^* &= \bigcup_{i\in I} \bigcup_{\pi\in P^i(I)} V_\pi^i \\ &= \bigcup_{i\in I} \bigcup_{\pi\in P(I)} V_\pi^i \\ &= \bigcup_{\pi\in P(I)} \bigcup_{i\in I} V_\pi^i \\ &= \bigcup_{\pi\in P(I)} V_\pi \\ &= \mathcal{U}_A,\end{aligned}$$

the last step from (4a).

$$\mu(U_i^*) = \tau(a_i \times U_i) \quad \text{for all} \quad i \in I. \tag{7}$$

The left hand side equals $\mu\left(\bigcup_{\pi\in P^i(I)}(V_\pi^i)\right)$. Since $V_\pi^i \subset V_\pi$ by (5), and $V_\pi \cap V_\sigma = \emptyset$ for $\pi \neq \sigma$ by (4c), this equals $\sum_{\pi\in P^i(I)} \mu(V_\pi^i)$. By (5), this equals $\sum_{\pi\in P^i(I)} \tau(a_i \times V_\pi)$ which equals $\tau\left(\bigcup_{\pi\in P^i(I)}(a_i \times V_\pi)\right)$. By Lemma 1, this can be written as $\tau\left(a_i \times \bigcup_{\pi\in P^i(I)} V_\pi\right)$ and hence by (4b) as $\tau(a_i \times U)i)$.

We are now ready to construct our symmetric Cournot-Nash equilibrium distribution. Let $h : \mathcal{U}_A \to A$ be such that $h(u) = a_i$ for all $u \in U_i^*$, for all $i \in I$. Since V_π^i are measurable, U_i^* are measurable. Moreover, from (6), h is a well-defined function. Now let τ^s be a measure on $A \times \mathcal{U}_A$ such that for any measurable B, $\tau^s(B) = \mu\{u \in \mathcal{U}_A : (h(u), u) \in B\}$. Given the measurability of h and of the identity map, τ^s is well-defined. Also

$$\tau^s(\text{graph } h) = \mu\{u \in \mathcal{U}_A : (h(u), u) \in (\text{graph } h)\} = \mu\{u \in \mathcal{U}_A\} = 1.$$

All that remains to be shown is that τ^s is a Cournot-Nash equilibrium distribution. Towards this end, we first show that $\tau^s_{\mathcal{U}_A} = \mu$. Pick any measurable subset W of $\mathcal{U}_A$. Then $\tau^s_{\mathcal{U}_A}(W) = \tau^s(A \times W) = \mu\{u \in \mathcal{U}_A : (h(u), u) \in A \times W\} = \mu\{u \in (\mathcal{U}_A \cap W)\} = \mu(W)$.

Next, we show $\tau^s_A = \tau_A$. Pick any measurable subset of A. If this set is empty, there is nothing to be shown. Hence, let this set be $\bigcup_{i\in\pi} a_i$ for some $\pi \in P(I)$. Now $\tau^s_A\left(\bigcup_{i\in\pi} a_i\right) = \tau^s\left(\bigcup_{i\in\pi} a_i \times \mathcal{U}_A\right) = \mu\left\{u \in \mathcal{U}_A : (h(u), u) \in \left(\left(\bigcup_{i\in\pi} a_i\right) \times \mathcal{U}_A\right)\right\} = \mu\left(\bigcup_{i\in\pi} h^{-1}(a_i)\right) = \sum_{i\in\pi} \mu(U_i^*)$. Now

$$\begin{aligned}
\sum_{i\in\pi}(U_i^*) &= \sum_{i\in\pi} \tau(a_i \times U_i) && \text{(by (7))} \\
&= \sum_{i\in\pi} \tau(a_i \times \mathcal{U}_A) && \text{(by (2))} \\
&= \tau\left(\bigcup_{i\in\pi}(a_i \times \mathcal{U}_A)\right) \\
&= \tau\left(\left(\bigcup_{i\in\pi} a_i\right) \times \mathcal{U}_A\right) && \text{(by Lemma 1)} \\
&= \tau_A\left(\bigcup_{i\in\pi} a_i\right).
\end{aligned}$$

We are done.

Since $\tau^s_A = \tau_A$ and since B_τ depends only on τ_A, $B_{\tau^s} = B_\tau$. Thus to show $\tau^s(B_{\tau^s}) = 1$. But by the definition of h, graph $h \subset B_\tau$. Since $\tau^s(\text{graph } h) = 1$, $\tau^s(B_{\tau^s}) = \tau^s(B_\tau) = 1$. The proof of the theorem is complete. □

5. Concluding Remark

In Khan [1989] and Khan and Sun [1990], the authors present an alternative formulation of Mas-Colell's result in games where pay-offs are represented by preference relations or by functions which are upper-semicontinuous in actions. We remark that the theorem proved here applies to that generalized set-up.

References

Hildenbrand, W., 1974, *Core and Equilibria of a Large Economy*, Princeton University Press, Princeton, New Jersey.

Jamison, R. E., 1974, "A Quick Proof for a One-Dimensional Version of Liapunoff's Theorem," *Amer. Math. Monthly* **81**, 507–508.

Khan, M. Ali, 1989, "On Cournot-Nash Equilibrium Distributions for Games with a Non-Metrizable Action Space and Upper Semi-Continuous Payoffs," *Trans. Amer. Math. Soc.* **315**, 126–146.

Khan, M. Ali and Sun, Y., 1990, "On a Reformation of Cournot-Nash Equilibria," *J. Math. Anal. Appl.* **146**, 442–460.

Mas-Colell, A., 1984, "On a Theorem of Schmeidler," *J. Math. Econ.* **13**, 210–206.

Equilibria in Random and Bayesian Games with a Continuum of Players

Erik J. Balder and Nicholas C. Yannelis

Abstract. We prove random Nash equilibrium existence theorems as well as Bayesian Nash equilibrium existence results for games with a measure space of players.

1. Introduction

The main purpose of this paper is to prove the existence of a random (Nash) equilibrium for a game with a continuum of players. Moreover, we show how such a random equilibrium existence result can be used to obtain a Bayesian equilibrium existence theorem for a game with a continuum of players.

In a seminal paper, Nash (1951) introduced the notion of a noncooperative equilibrium for a game with a finite number of players. In particular, according to Nash, a game consists of a finite number players, each of whom is characterized by a strategy set and a payoff (utility) function, i.e., a real-valued function defined on the Cartesian product of the strategy sets of the players. A noncooperative equilibrium for such a game is a strategy vector having the property that no player can deviate from his/her optimal strategy and increase his/her payoff. Nash (1951) and subsequently Debreu (1952) proved the existence of such an equilibrium, using finite-dimensional fixed point theorems of the Brouwer-Kakutani type.

Three main extensions of the Nash-Debreu results have been obtained in the literature. The first one is due to Glicksberg (1952), who allowed the strategy set of each player to be a subset of an infinite-dimensional linear topological space. This equilibrium result necessitated an infinite-dimensional version of the Kakutani fixed point theorem [see also Fan (1952) or Browder (1968)]. The second extension is due to Schmeidler (1973). It allowed for the set of players to be an atomless measure space. This development was motivated by economic problems [see for instance Aumann (1964) among others]. In particular, economists are interested in perfectly competitive outcomes, that is, in situations where each player's effect is "negligible" (which means that he/she is assigned measure zero in the model). In Schmeidler's approach the strategy sets are finite-dimensional. Khan (1986) extended this to the infinite-dimensional case. This work, together with that of Khan-Papageorgiou (1988) and Yannelis (1987), allowed each player in addition to have a preference correspondence (instead of the original utility function) which need not be transitive or complete and therefore may not be representable by a utility function.

The present paper is involved with the third of the extensions mentioned above. The value of such an extension is supported by empirical studies, which show that in many instances players do not behave in a transitive way [see also Shafer-Sonnenschein (1975) or Yannelis-Prabhakar (1983)]. We present results which do not only include the three main extensions of the work of Nash and Debreu, but which also allow for incomplete information. In particular, our first and main result is an equilibrium existence theorem which allows the preference correspondence of each agent to depend on the states of natures of the world, that is, it allows for random preference correspondences. This result is then used to obtain an equilibrium existence theorem for a Bayesian game with a continuum of players.

Our paper is organized as follows: Section 2 contains some preliminary notation and definitions. In Section 3 we state the main theorem, whose proof, which involves new ideas and techniques, can be found in Section 5. In Section 4 we discuss the assumptions of the main theorem. Section 6 contains an equilibrium existence result for a Bayesian game with a continuum of players. Some concluding remarks can be found in our closing section 7.

2. Preliminaries

We begin by introducing some notation:

2^A denote the set of all nonempty subsets of the set A,

con A denotes the convex hull of A,

$\setminus$ denotes the set theoretic subtraction,

int denotes interior,
dom denotes the domain.
If X is a linear topological space, its dual is the space X' of all continuous linear functionals on X, and if $p \in X'$ and $x \in X$ the value of p at x is denoted by $\langle p, x \rangle$.

Let X, Y be topological spaces. The set-valued function (or correspondence) $\phi : X \to 2^Y$ is said to be *upper-semicontinuous* (u.s.c.) if the set $\{x \in X : \phi(x) \subset V\}$ is open in X for every open subset V of Y. Let (T, τ) be a measurable space and $\phi : T \to 2^X$ be a correspondence. We say that the *graph* of ϕ, i.e., the set of all $(t, x) \in T \times X$ with $x \in \phi(t)$, is *measurable* if it belongs to the product σ-algebra $\tau \otimes \beta(X)$, where $\beta(X)$ denotes the Borel σ-algebra on X. Moreover, $\phi : T \to 2^X$ is said to be *lower measurable* if for every V open in X the set $\{t \in T : \phi(t) \cap V \neq \emptyset\}$ belongs to τ. If ϕ has closed values then lower measurability of ϕ implies that its graph is measurable, [Castaing-Valadier (1977, III)]; conversely, if ϕ has a measurable graph and τ is the σ-algebra of all universally measurable subsets of T (in particular, if τ is complete with respect to some σ-finite measure on T) then ϕ is lower measurable if it has a measurable graph, [Castaing-Valadier (1977, III)]. Let $(E, \|\cdot\|)$ be a separable Banach space and let E' be its topological dual. The weak topology $\sigma(E, E')$ on E will be referred to as the w-topology; thus, we speak of w-closed, w-compact, etc. There exists a countable subset $\{x'_i\}$ which is dense in E' for the topology $\sigma(E', E)$, [Castaing-Valadier (1977, III.32)]. Correspondingly, we define the *weak metric* d on E by

$$d(x, y) := \sum_{i=1}^{\infty} 2^{-i} \frac{|\langle x - y, x'_i \rangle|}{1 + |\langle x - y, x'_i \rangle|}.$$

Note that the d-topology, induced by d on E, is weaker than the w-topology. Hence, it coincides with the w-topology of any w-compact subset of E. Note also that the Borel σ-algebras $\beta(E, d)$, $\beta(E, w)$ and $\beta(E, \|\cdot\|)$ coincide, since

$$\|x\| = \sup_{i \in N} \frac{|\langle x, x'_i \rangle|}{\|x'_i\|'},$$

where $\|\cdot\|'$ stands for the dual norm on E'. Let (T, τ, μ) be a finite measure space and let $X : T \to 2^E$ be a correspondence. The set of (equivalence classes of) all μ-integrable functions from (T, τ, μ) into $R[E]$ is denoted by $L^1_R[L^1_E]$, [cf. Diestel-Uhl (1977)].[1] We say that the correspondence X is *μ-integrably bounded* if there exists a μ-integrable function $g \in L^1_R$ such that for μ-a.e. $t \in T$

$$\|x\| \leq g(t) \text{ for all } x \in X(t).$$

Correspondingly, we define

$$L_X := \{x \in L^1_E : x(t) \in X(t)\mu\text{-a.e.}\}.$$

The usual L^1-norm on L^1_E is defined by

$$\|x\|_1 := \int_T \|x(t)\|\mu(dt).$$

The topological dual of $(L^1_E, \|\cdot\|_1)$ is homeomorphic to the space $L^\infty_{E'}[E]$ of all scalarly measurable essentially bounded (equivalence classes of) functions from (T, τ, μ) into $(E', \|\cdot\|')$, [see for instance Ionescu-Tulcea, (1969)]. The topology $\sigma(L^1_E, L^\infty_{E'}[E])$ will be referred to as the weak topology on $L^1_{E'}$ [Diestel-Uhl (1977)].

3. The Main Theorem

Below we introduce the notion of a random game with a continuum of players. This notion of a game extends the ones of Khan (1986), Khan-Papageorgiou (1988), Schmeidler (1973), Yannelis (1987) by allowing the preference correspondence of each player to depend on the (random) state of nature. The random game with a continuum of players is described as follows:

Let (T, τ, μ) be a complete finite measure space, where T is the *set of players*. τ is the set of all possible coalitions, and μ is the set-function assigning to each coalition its "weight" for the game. Let E be a separable

[1] Throughout the paper the usual abuse of notation regarding L-spaces, where one does not distinguish between equivalence classes and their representations, will be in force. We thank Dr. A. Nowak (Silesian University, Karowice, Poland) for some remarks on this point.

Banach space, the *set of possible decisions* (or moves) for the players. The players are restricted in making their decisions as follows: Let $X : T \to 2^E$ be a given correspondence; then we require that μ-almost every player t selects his/her decision from the set $X(t)$, the *strategy set* of player t. (The exceptional set would represent a null coalition of players, whose erratic behavior does not carry any weight.) Let $(\Omega, \mathcal{A}, p)$ be a complete probability space, where Ω stands for *the possible states of nature*, $\mathcal{A}$ for the set of all the outcomes, and p for the probability distribution of the outcomes. Let L_X denote the set $\{x \in L^1_E : x(t) \in X(t) \mu\text{-a.e.}\}$. Let $P : T \times \Omega \times L_X \to 2^E$ be a correspondence revealing the *individual preferences* of the players. We require that $P(t, \omega, x) \subset X(t)$ for all $t \in T$ and $\omega \in \Omega$. For μ-a.e. player $t \in T$ the set $P(t, \omega, x)$ consists of the decisions which he/she strictly prefers to his/her own decision $x(t)$, given that ω is the state of nature and given that the decisions of all participating players modulo null coalitions are represented by $x \in L_X$ (the implicit assumption that the players take their individual decisions in a measurable way is standard in this context). Thus, each player's preference pattern is influenced by the decisions of the other players (modulo null coalitions) and by the realized state of nature. However, each player must make his/her decision independently after having observed the realized state ω of nature. Thus, the resultant of the players' actions (even though they act independently and noncooperatively!) can be modelled as a *decision rule* $f : \Omega \to L_X$, which prescribes, for each possible state of nature, the decisions of all players, modulo null coalitions. For reasons of analytical tractability we require that the decision rule f be $(\mathcal{A}, \beta(L_X))$-measurable. Summing up, a *random game with a continuum of players* is formally a quadruple $\Gamma = [(T, \tau, \mu), (\Omega, \mathcal{A}, p), X, P]$, where the measure spaces (T, τ, μ), $(\Omega, \mathcal{A}, p)$ and the correspondences X, P are as described above. The game Γ is said to have a *random* (Cournot-Nash) *equilibrium* if there exists a decision rule $f^* : \Omega \to L_X$ such that for p-a.e. $\omega \in \Omega$

$$P(t, \omega, f^*(\omega)) = \emptyset \text{ for } \mu\text{-a.e. } t \in T.$$

Thus, with probability one there is at most a powerless null coalition of players having "something left to be desired" under the equilibrium rule f^*; no player t outside the null coalition disposes of a decision which he/she would strictly prefer to his/her actual decision $f^*(\omega)(t)$

prescribed by f^*. Clearly, the above definition is a generalization of the usual notion in economics and game theory, [see, e.g., Khan (1986), Khan-Papageorgiou (1988), Schmeidler (1973), Yannelis (1987)]. [We especially recommend the excellent survey of Khan (1985)].

We now state the conditions needed for the proof of our main theorem. A detailed discussion of these is given in Section 4.

(C0) the σ-algebra τ is countably generated,

(C1) X has nonempty convex w-compact values,

(C2) X is μ-integrably bounded and has a $\tau \otimes \beta(E)$-measurable graph,

(C3) $\text{dom}(\text{con}\, P)$ is a $\tau \otimes \mathcal{A} \otimes \beta(L_X)$-measurable subset of $T \times \Omega \times L_X$,

(C4) there exists no decision rule $f : \Omega \to L_X$ such that for p-a.e. $\omega \in \Omega$, $f(\omega)(t) \in \text{con}\, P(t, \omega, f(\omega))$ for μ-a.e. $t \in T$.

We also require the existence of a correspondence $\alpha : \text{dom}(\text{con}\, P) \to 2^E$ with measurable graph and nonempty values, such that for every $t \in T$, $\omega \in \Omega$,

(C5) $\alpha(t, \omega, x) \subset \text{con}\, P(t, \omega, x) \subset X(t)$ for every $x \in L_x$,

(C6) $\alpha(t, \omega, \cdot) : L_X \to 2^E$ is u.s.c. with w-closed convex values,

(C7) $\text{dom}(\text{con}\, P(t, \omega, \cdot))$ is w-open.

Our main result, whose proof is deferred to Section 5, can now be stated.

Main Theorem. *Let $\Gamma = [(T, \tau, \mu), (\Omega, \mathcal{A}, p), X, P]$ be a random game satisfying the conditions (C0)–(C7). Then Γ has a random equilibrium.*

As a corollary of our Main Theorem, we can obtain an extension of the results of Khan (1986) and Schmeidler (1973) by allowing the utility function of each player to be random. In particular, let $G = [(T, \tau, \mu), (\Omega, \mathcal{A}, p), X, u]$ be a random game with a continuum of players as defined above, with the exception that each player t in T is now equipped with a random utility function $u_t : \Omega \times X(t) \times L_X \to R$. The game is said to have a *random Cournot-Nash equilibrium* if there exists an $(\mathcal{A}, \beta(L_X))$-measurable function $f^* : \Omega \to L_X$ such that

$$u_t(\omega, f_t^*(\omega), f^*(\omega)) = \max_{y \in X(t)} u_t(\omega, y, f^*(\omega))$$

for μ-a.e. $t \in T$ and p-a.e. $\omega \in \Omega$. Now we can state the following corollary of our main theorem:

Corollary 3.1. *Let $G = [(T,\tau,\mu),(\Omega,\mathcal{A},p),X,u]$ be a random game with a continuum of players satisfying the conditions (C0)–(C2) and in addition:*

(N1) The set $\{t,\omega,y) \in T \times \Omega \times E : y \in X(t),\ u_t(\omega,y,x) \leq \delta\}$ belongs to $\tau \otimes \mathcal{A} \otimes \beta(E)$ for every $\delta \in R$, $x \in L_X$,

(N2) $u_t(\omega,\cdot,x)$ is quasi-concave on $X(t)$ for every $t \in T$, $\omega \in \Omega$, $x \in L_X$,

(N3) $u_t(\omega,\cdot,\cdot)$ is weakly continuous on $X(t) \times L_X$ for every $t \in T$, $\omega \in \Omega$.

Then G has a random Cournot-Nash equilibrium.

Proof. Define the correspondence $P : T \times \Omega \times L_X \to 2^E$ by

$$P(t,\omega,x) := \{y \in X(t) : u_t(\omega,y,x) > u_t(\omega,x(t),x)\}.$$

Then in view of Remarks 4.4, 4.5 in the next section it is easily seen (given the assumptions (N1)–(N3)) that the correspondence P satisfies all the conditions of the Main Theorem. The resulting random equilibrium is easily seen to form a random equilibrium for G.

The above corollary will be used in Section 6 to prove the existence of a symmetric Bayesian equilibrium. In the next section we will discuss the conditions used in the Main Theorem.

4. Discussion of the Assumptions

In this section we discuss a number of cases where the technical conditions of the Main Theorem are fulfilled. The conditions of the first two cases presented here are not attractive from a more practical standpoint, but in the third and fourth case the conditions are of a rather standard nature. The key instrument there is formed by recent Carathéodory selection results of Kim-Prikry-Yannelis (1987, 1988).

Remark 4.1. Condition (C4) is obviously weaker than

(C4′) for p-a.e. $\omega \in \Omega$ there does not exist $x \in L_X$ such that $x(t) \in \operatorname{con} P(t,\omega,x)$ for μ-a.e. $t \in T$.

Condition (C3) is weaker than

(C3′) $\operatorname{con} P : T \times \Omega \times L_X \to 2^E$ is a measurable correspondence.

Remark 4.2. Suppose that

(E1) $\operatorname{con} P : T \times \Omega \times L_X \to 2^E$ has a $\tau \otimes \mathcal{A} \otimes \beta(L_X \times E)$-measurable graph,

(E2) $\operatorname{con} P(t, \omega, \cdot) : L_X \to 2^E$ is u.s.c. and has nonempty w-closed values for every $t \in T$, $\omega \in \Omega$.

Then conditions (C5)–(C7) hold.

Proof. Define $\alpha := \operatorname{con} P$; then (C5)–(C7) hold trivially.

Remark 4.3. Suppose that (E1) holds and that

(E3) $\operatorname{con} P(t, , \cdot) : L_X \to 2^E$ is l.s.c. and has w-closed values (possibly empty) for every $t \in T$, $\omega \in \Omega$,

(E4) the σ-algebra $\tau \otimes \mathcal{A}$ is complete with respect to $\mu \times p$.

Then conditions (C5)–(C7) hold.

Proof. By the definition of lower semicontinuity, (E3) implies that (C7) holds. Also, it follows that from (E3)–(E4) that the Carathéodory selection result of Kim-Prikry-Yannelis (1987, Theorem 3.1) obtains. Hence, there exists a $(\tau \otimes \mathcal{A} \otimes \beta(L_X), \beta(E))$-measurable function $a : \operatorname{dom}(\operatorname{con} P) \to E$ such that for all $t \in T$ and $\omega \in \Omega$

$a(t, \omega, \cdot)$ is continuous on $\operatorname{dom}(\operatorname{con} P(t, \omega, \cdot))$ and
$a(t, \omega, x) \in \operatorname{con} P(t, \omega, x)$ for all $x \in \operatorname{dom} \operatorname{con} P(t, \omega, \cdot)$.

Therefore $a(t, \omega, x) := \{a(t, \omega, x)\}$ satisfies (C5), (C7).

In (E2) and (E3)the correspondence $\operatorname{con} P$ is required to have w-closed values. In view of the condition (C4) this is hardly satisfactory, since $P(t, \omega, x)$ represents for player t the decisions which he/she would strictly prefer over $x(t)$ under the state of nature ω. Fortunately, in the following cases the values of $\operatorname{con} P$ need not be closed.

The following case is a variant of the one above. It follows by applying the variant in Kim-Prikry-Yannelis (1987, Theorem 3.2) of the Carathéodory selection result used above. The proof in this case remains exactly the same.

Remark 4.4. Suppose that (E1) and (E4) hold and

(E5) $\operatorname{con} P(t, \omega, \cdot) : L_X \to 2^E$ is weakly l.s.c. for every $\tau \in T$, $\omega \in \Omega$, and at least one of the following two conditions are satisfied:

(E6) E is finite-dimensional,

(E6′) $\mathrm{int}(\mathrm{con}\, P(t, \omega, x))$ is nonempty for every $(t, \omega, x) \in \mathrm{dom}(\mathrm{con}\, P)$.

Then conditions (C5)–(C7) hold.

Remark 4.5. Suppose that (E1), (E4) hold and that for all $t \in T$ and $\omega \in \Omega$

(E7) $\mathrm{con}\, P(t, \omega, \cdot)^{-1}(x) := \{y \in L_X : x \in \mathrm{con}\, P(t, \omega, y)\}$ is weakly open for every $x \in E$,

(E8) rel int $\mathrm{con} P(t, \omega, x)$ is nonempty for every $x \in \mathrm{dom}(\mathrm{con}\, P(t, \omega, \cdot))$, where the relative interior is taken with respect to $X(t)$.

Then conditions (C5)-(C7) hold.

Proof. The proof is entirely similar to the proof of Remark 4.3; only this time we invoke to the Carathéodory selection result of Kim-Prikry-Yannelis (1988, Main Theorem).

5. Proof of the Main Theorem

We begin by proving some preparatory results that are needed for the proof of our main theorem.

The compactness part of the following result is commonly referred to as *Diestel's theorem.* This was given by Diestel (1977) for a "dominating" correspondence $X(t)$ which did not vary with t. In its present form the theorem was first stated by Byrne (1978, Theorem 3), [see also Balder (1990) for an extension involving a.e. convergence of arithmetic averages]. Note also that the nonemptiness part of the result below is a direct consequence of the von Neumann-Aumann measurable selection theorem, [Castaing-Valadier (1977, III.22)].

Theorem 5.1. *Suppose that conditions (C1)–(C2) hold. Then L_X is a nonempty convex and weakly compact subset of L^1_E.*

Proposition 5.2. *Suppose that conditions (C0)–(C2) hold. Then the weak topology of L_X coincides with the topology induced by the weak metric D of L^1_E.*

Proof. By (C0) the Banach space $(L^1_E, \|\cdot\|_1)$ is separable. Thus, L^1_E has a well-defined weak metric D (see the definition given in Section 2). By (C1), (C2) L_X is a weakly compact subset of L^1_E (apply Theorem 5.1), so by what was said following the introduction of the weak metric, the weak topology and the D-topology coincide on L_X.

Let (Y, ρ) be a separable metric space, and let $\gamma : T \times \Omega \times Y \to 2^E$ be a given correspondence such that $\gamma(t, \omega, y) \subset X(t)$ for every $t \in T$, $\omega \in \Omega$. Correspondingly, we define $\psi : \Omega \times Y \to 2^{L_X}$ by

$$\psi(\omega, y) := \{x \in L_X : x(t) \in \gamma(t, \omega, y) \mu\text{-a.e.}\}.$$

The first part of the next result is well-known [see for instance Khan-Papageorgiou (1987) or Yannelis (1987, 1989)]. We given a new proof, which matches the proof of its second part.

Proposition 5.3. *Suppose that (C0), (C1), and (C2) are valid. If*

$$\gamma(t, \omega, \cdot) : Y \to 2^E$$

is w-u.s.c. with w-closed, convex values for every $t \in T$, $\omega \in \Omega$, *then*

$$\psi(\omega, \cdot) : Y \to 2^{L_X}$$

is weakly u.s.c. for every $\omega \in \Omega$. *If in addition*

$$\gamma \text{ has a } \mathcal{T} \otimes \mathcal{A} \otimes \beta(Y \times E)\text{-measurable graph},$$

then there exists a correspondence $\psi' : \Omega \times Y \to 2^{L_X}$ *such that*

$$\psi'(\omega, \cdot) = \psi(\omega, \cdot) \text{ for } p\text{-a.e. } \omega \in \Omega,$$

and

$$\psi' \text{ has a } \mathcal{A} \otimes \beta(L_X)\text{-measurable graph.}$$

Proof. To prove the first statement, it is enough, in view of Theorem 5.1, to prove that for arbitrary fixed $\omega \in \Omega$ the correspondence $\psi(\omega, \cdot)$ has a closed graph in $Y \times L_X$ [Aubin-Cellina (1984), Corollary 1.1.1)]. To this end, let $\{y_k\}$ converge in Y to $\bar{y}$, and let $\{x_k\}$ converge weakly to $\bar{x}$ in L_X, $x_k \in \psi(\omega, y_k)$. Define $m : T \times \Omega \times Y \times E \to \{0, +\infty\}$ by

$$m(t, \omega, y, x) := \begin{cases} 0 & \text{if } x \in \gamma(t, \omega, y) \\ +\infty & \text{if not.} \end{cases}$$

Since $\omega \in \Omega$ is fixed, we shall abbreviate as follows:

$$\ell(t, y, x) := m(t, \omega, y, x).$$

The desired conclusion $\bar{x} \in \psi(\omega, \bar{y})$ follows now immediately from applying a classical lower semicontinuity theorem to the outer integral functional $I_\ell : Y \times L_X \to \{0, +\infty\}$, given by

$$I_\ell(y, x) := \int_T^\sim \ell(t, y, x(t))\mu(dt).$$

Note that for every $t \in T$ the function $\ell(t, \cdot, \cdot)$ is l.s.c. on $Y \times (E, w)$, since the graph of $\gamma(t, \omega, \cdot)$ is a closed subset of $Y \times X(t)$. Note also that the function $\ell(t, y, \cdot)$ is convex. Thus, all the conditions of the lower semicontinuity result in Balder (1984, Theorem 3.1) hold, and we obtain

$$I_\ell(\bar{y}, \bar{x}) \leq \liminf_k I_\ell(y_k, x_k) = 0.$$

(Note the y_k's act as constant functions on T, which converge to the constant function $\bar{y}$.) In view of the definition of outer integration it follows immediately that μ-a.e. $\ell(t, \bar{y}, \bar{x}(t)) \leq 0$, i.e., $\bar{x}(t) \in \gamma(t, \omega, \bar{y})$.

For the proof of the second part we employ a very similar argument, which is based on the key observation that the Borel σ-algebras $\beta(L^1_E, \|\cdot\|_1)$ and $\beta(L^1_E, D)$ coincide (as was noted following the definition of the weak metric). Note first that measurability of the graph of γ is actually equivalent to $\tau \otimes \mathcal{A} \otimes \beta(Y \times E)$-measurability of m, defined above. Also, as we already saw above, $\ell(t, \cdot, \cdot) := m(t, \omega, \cdot, \cdot)$ is l.s.c. on $Y \times (E, w)$—hence a fortiori on $Y \times (E, \|\cdot\|)$ for every $t \in T$, $\omega \in \Omega$. Thus, m is a so-called normal integrand on $T \times \Omega \times Y \times (E, \|\cdot\|)$. By the construction given in Balder (1984, Appendix) there exist a nondecreasing sequence $\{m_n\}$ of $\tau \otimes \mathcal{A} \otimes \beta(Y \times E)$-measurable functions $m_n : T \times \Omega \times Y \times E \to [0, +\infty)$ and a $\tau \otimes \mathcal{A}$-measurable subset N of $T \times \Omega$, $(\mu \times p)(N) = 0$, such that for every $(t, \omega) \in T \times \Omega$, $n \in N$

$$|m_n(t, \omega, y, x) - m_n(t, \omega, y', x')| \leq n\rho(y, y') + n\|x - x'\|$$

for all $y \in Y$, $x \in E$ and for every $(t, \omega) \in (T \times \Omega) \setminus N$, $n \in N$

$$\lim_n \uparrow m_n(t, \omega, y, x) = m(t, \omega, y, x) \text{ for all } y \in Y,\ x \in E.$$

From the second property it follows immediately, by the monotone convergence that for p-a.e. $\omega \in \Omega$ for all $y \in Y$ and $x \in L_X$

$$\lim_n \uparrow I_{m_n}(\omega, y, x) = I_m(\omega, y, x),$$

where the integral functionals $I_m, I_{m_n} : \Omega \times Y \times L_X \to [0, +\infty]$ are defined by

$$I_m(\omega, y, x) := \int_T m(t, \omega, y, x(t))\mu(dt),$$

etc. (note that there is no longer need for outer integration). By the Lipschitz continuity property of the $\{m_n\}$ it follows elementarily that for every $n \in N$

$$I_{m_n}(\omega, \cdot, \cdot) \text{ is continuous on } Y \times (L^1_E, \|\cdot\|_1) \text{ for every } \omega \in \Omega.$$

Also, it is a basic fact, [e.g., see Neveu (1964, III)] that for every $n \in N$

$$I_{m_n}(\cdot, y, x) \text{ is } \mathcal{A}\text{-measurable for every } y \in Y,\ x \in L_X.$$

Therefore, it follows from Castaing-Valadier (1977, III.14), in view of the separability of $Y \times (L^1_E, \|\cdot\|_1)$, that for every $n \in N$

$$I_{m_n} \text{ is } \mathcal{A} \otimes (Y \times L_X)\text{-measurable.}$$

Hence, by (5.1)

$$I_m \text{ is } \mathcal{A} \otimes \beta(Y \times L_X)\text{-measurable.}$$

Finally, it remains to define $\psi' : \Omega \times Y \to 2^{L_X}$ by specifying its graph to be the set

$$\{(\omega, y, x) \in \Omega \times Y \times L_X : \lim_n \uparrow I_{m_n}(\omega, y, x) \leq 0\};$$

then the proof is over, in view of (5.1) and the definition of m.

Remark 5.4. An alternative proof of the measurability part of Proposition 5.3 can be given using Castaing-Valadier (1977, III.15). In contrast to the proof given above, one then has to exploit the fact that γ has convex values.

We are now ready to complete the proof of our Main Theorem.

Proof of the Main Theorem. To begin with, note that by Theorem 5.1 and Proposition 5.2 the space (L_X, D) is metrizable, compact and hence separable for the weak topology. (This space will play the role of (Y, ρ) in the previous section.) We define the correspondence $F : T \times \Omega \times L_X \to 2^E$ by

$$F(t,\omega,x) := \begin{cases} \alpha(t,\omega,x) & \text{if } x \in \operatorname{dom}(\operatorname{con} P(t,\omega,\cdot)) \\ X(t) & \text{if not.} \end{cases}$$

From the definition of upper semicontinuity it follow from (C5), (C6) that for every $t \in T$, $\omega \in \Omega$, $F(t,\omega,\cdot) : L_X \to 2^E$ is upper semicontinuous; also, $F(t,\omega,\cdot)$ has w-compact convex values in $X(t)$ for every $t \in T, \omega \in \Omega$ by (C1), (C5) and the properties of α. Therefore, by Proposition 5.3 the convex-valued correspondence $B : \Omega \times L_X \to 2^{L_X}$, defined by

$$B(\omega, y) := \{x \in L_X : x(t) \in F(t,\omega,y) \text{ for } \mu\text{-a.e. } t \in T\},$$

is such that for every $\omega \in \Omega$

$$B(\omega,\cdot) : L_X \to 2^{L_X} \text{ is weakly u.s.c.}$$

Also, for every $\omega \in \Omega$, $y \in L_X$ the correspondence $F(\cdot,\omega,y)$ has a measurable graph and nonempty values, by (C3) and the definitions of α, F. Hence, the values of B are nonempty by the von Neumann-Aumann measurable selection theorem [Castaing-Valadier (1977, III.22)]. By Theorem 5.1, L_X is a nonempty convex weakly compact subset of L^1_E. Hence, it follows from the Fan-Glicksberg fixed point theorem [Fan (1952), Glicksberg (1952)] that for every $\omega \in \Omega$

(5.2) there exists $x \in L_X$ such that $x \in B(\omega, x)$.

By (C3) and the definitions of α, X the correspondence F is seen to have a $\tau \otimes \mathcal{A} \otimes \beta(L_X \times E)$-measurable graph. Hence, by Proposition 4.3 there exists a correspondence $B' : \Omega \times L_X \to 2^{L_X}$ with $\mathcal{A} \otimes \beta(L_X \times L_X)$-measurable graph such that $B'(\omega,\cdot) = B(\omega,\cdot)$ p-a.e. Therefore, it is immediate that the graph

$$G := \{(\omega, y, x) \in \Omega \times L_X \times L_X : y = x,\ x \in B'(\omega, y)\}$$

of the correspondence $\Phi \cap B'$ is also $\mathcal{A} \otimes \beta(L_X \times L_X)$-measurable, where $\Phi : \Omega \times L_X \to 2^{L_X}$ is defined by $\Phi(\omega, y) := \{y\}$ (note that the graph of Φ is measurable by virtue of the fact that L_X is separable and metric). By (5.2) we have that for p-a.e. $\omega \in \Omega$ the section of G at ω is nonempty. Hence, by the von Neumann-Aumann measurable selection theorem [Castaing-Valadier (1977, III.22)] there exists a $(\mathcal{A} \otimes \beta(L_X), \beta(L_X \times L_X))$-measurable function $h : \Omega \to L_X \times L_X$ such that

$$(\omega, h_1(\omega), h_2(\omega)) \in G \text{ for } p\text{-a.e. } \omega \in \Omega,$$

where h_1, h_2 stand for the coordinate functions of h. In particular, this implies the following

$$h_2(\omega) \in B'(\omega, h_2(\omega)) \text{ for } p\text{-a.e. } \omega \in \Omega.$$

By the definition of B' and B, this implies that for p-a.e. $\omega \in \Omega$

$$h_2(\omega)(t) \in F(t, \omega, h_2(\omega)) \text{ for } \mu\text{-a.e. } t \in T.$$

If there was a set $C \in \mathcal{A}$, $p(C) > 0$, such that $\operatorname{dom}(\operatorname{con} P(t, \omega, h_2(\omega))) \neq \emptyset$ μ-a.e. for every $\omega \in C$, then by the definition of F for every $\omega \in C$

$$h_2(\omega)(t) \in \alpha(t, \omega, h_2(\omega)) \in \operatorname{con} P(t, \omega, h_2(\omega)) \text{ for } \mu\text{-a.e. } t \in T.$$

This would contradict (C4). Thus we conclude that for p-a.e. $\omega \in \Omega$

$$P(t, \omega, .h_2(\omega)) \subset \operatorname{con} P(t, \omega, h_2(\omega)) = \emptyset \text{ for } \mu\text{-a.e. } t \in T,$$

which proves that h_2 is the desired rule to achieve a random equilibrium for the game Γ.

6. The Existence of a Symmetric Bayesian Equilibrium

We now show how our main result can be used to prove the existence of an equilibrium for a Bayesian game with a continuum of players. For somewhat similar finite player Bayesian games, existence results have been obtained by Balder (1988), Harsanyi (1967), Milgrom-Weber (1985) and Yannelis-Rustichini (1991).

A *symmetric Bayesian game with a continuum of players* is a sextuple $B = [(T,\tau,\mu),(\Omega,\mathcal{A},p),X,u,\mathcal{S},q]$, where (T,τ,μ) is the *measure space of players.* $(\Omega,\mathcal{A},p)$ a probability space denoting all the *possible states of nature*, whose probability distribution p may be unknown, $X : T \to 2^E$ the *decision correspondence* from T into the separable Banach space E, $u_t : \Omega \times X(t) \times L_X \to R$ the *random utility function* of player t in T, $\mathcal{S}_t = \mathcal{S}$ a partition of $(\Omega,\mathcal{A})$ representing the *information pattern available* to the player t (supposed to be the same for all players; hence the adjective *symmetric* for the game), and $q_t : \Omega \to \mathbb{R}_{++}$ is the *prior* of player t, i.e., q_t is a Radon-Nikodym derivative having the property that $\int_{\omega\in\Omega} q_t(\omega)d\mu(\omega) = 1$. Denote by $E(\omega)$ the event in $\mathcal{S}$ containing the realized state of nature $\omega \in \Omega$ and suppose that $\int_{\omega'\in E_i(\omega)} q_t(\omega')d\mu(\omega') > 0$. Given $E(\omega)$ in $\mathcal{S}$ define the *conditional expected utility* of player t, $v_t : \Omega \times X(t) \times L_X \to \mathbb{R}$ by

$$v_t(w,y,x) = \int_{\omega'\in E(\omega)} u_t(w',y,x)q_t(\omega' \mid E(\omega)d\mu(\omega'),$$

where

$$q_t(\omega' \mid E(\omega)) = \begin{cases} 0 & \text{if } \omega' \in E(\omega) \\ \dfrac{q_t(\omega')}{\int_{\omega'\in E(\omega)} q_t(\omega')d\mu(\omega')} & \text{if } \omega' \notin E(\omega). \end{cases}$$

A *symmetric Bayesian equilibrium* for B now consists of an $\mathcal{S}$-measurable function $f^* : \Omega \to L_X$ such that

$$v_t(\omega, f_t^*(\omega), f^*(\omega)) = \max_{y\in X(t)} v_t(\omega, y, f^*(\omega))$$

for μ-a.e. $t \in T$ and p-a.e. $\omega \in \Omega$.

The result below may be seen as an extension of Theorem 3.3 in Yannelis-Rustichini (1991) to Bayesian games with a continuum of players.

Corollary 6.1. *Let $B = [(T,\tau,\mu),(\Omega,\mathcal{A},p),X,u,\mathcal{S},q]$ be a Bayesian game with a continuum of players satisfying the conditions (C1)–(C2), (N1)–(N3). Moreover, suppose that for every $t \in T$, $\omega \in \Omega$, $u_t(\omega,\cdot,\cdot)$ is integrably bounded and $u_t(w,\cdot,x)$ is concave on $X(t)$ for every $t \in T$, $\omega \in \Omega$, $x \in L_X$. Then B has a symmetric Bayesian equilibrium.*

Proof. By the dominated convergence theorem it follows from (N3) that for every $t \in T$, $\omega \in \Omega$, $v_t(\omega, \cdot, \cdot)$ is weakly continuous on $X(t) \times L_X$. Moreover, it is easily seen that v is measurable in the sense that the set $\{(t, \omega, y) \in T \times \Omega \times E : y \in X(t), u_t(\omega, y, x) \leq \delta\}$ belongs to $\tau \otimes \mathcal{S} \otimes \beta(E)$ for every $\delta \in R$, $x \in L_X$. It follows from (N2) that $v_t(\omega, \cdot, x)$ is quasi-concave on $X(t)$ for every $t \in T$, $\omega \in \Omega$, $x \in L_X$. We can now consider the Bayesian game B as a random game $[(T, \tau, \mu), (\Omega, \mathcal{S}, p), X, v]$. This random game satisfies all the conditions of Corollary 3.1, so there exists an $\mathcal{S}$-measurable equilibrium decision rule $f^* : \Omega \to L_X$ for the random game. This rule is precisely the desired symmetric Bayesian equilibrium rule for B.

7. Concluding Remarks

Remark 7.1. The Main Theorem as well as Corollary 3.1 can be extended in a straightforward manner to random abstract economies; that is, abstract economies as defined in Khan-Papageorgiou (1988) or Yannelis (1987), with the only exception that preference correspondences as well as constraint correspondences are now allowed to depend on the states of nature of the world. Obviously, such results can be used to obtain equilibrium existence results for either random or Bayesian exchange economies.

Remark 7.2. The form of the Bayesian game with a continuum of players described in Section 6 can be generalized by replacing the random utility function $u_t : \Omega \times X(t) \times L_X \to R$ of each player by a random preference correspondence $P : T \times \Omega \times L_X \to 2^E$. In this new setting the *a posteriori preference correspondence* of player t is now defined by

$$\Pi(t, \omega, x) := \int_\Omega q_t(\omega; d\omega') P(t, \omega', x),$$

where the integral of the correspondence $P(t, \cdot, x)$ is defined in the usual way [see for instance Yannelis (1990)]. By setting in Theorem 6.1, $E = \mathbb{R}^n$ and replacing the assumptions (N1)–(N3) by:

(N1′) $\operatorname{con} \Pi(\cdot, \cdot, \cdot)$ is lower measurable,

(N2′) for each measurable function $x : \Omega \to L_X$, $x_t(\omega) \notin \operatorname{con} \Pi(t,\omega,x(\omega))$ for almost all t in T and for almost all ω in Ω,

(N3′) for each fixed t in T and ω in Ω, $P(t,\omega,\cdot)$ is l.s.c., P is integrably bounded and it has a measurable graph,

then one can prove the existence of a symmetric Bayesian equilibrium for this more general form of a Bayesian game. In particular, by Theorem 3.3 in Yannelis (1990) for each fixed $t \in T$ and $\omega \in \Omega$, $\Pi(t,\omega,\cdot)$ is l.s.c. Hence, (in view of Remark 4.4) it follows from the Main Theorem that there exists an $\mathcal{S}$-measurable function $f^* : \Omega \to L_X$ such that for almost all t in T, $\Pi(t,\omega,f^*(\omega)) = \emptyset$ for almost all $\omega \in \Omega$.

References

Aubin, J. P. and Cellina, A., 1984, *Differential Inclusions*, Springer-Verlag, Berlin.

Aumann, R. J., 1964, "Markets with a Continuum of Traders," *Econometrica* **32**, 39–50.

Balder, E. J., 1984, "A General Approach to Lower Semicontinuity and Lower Closure in Optimal Control Theory," *SIAM J. Control Optim.* **22**, 570–599.

Balder, E. J., 1988, "Generalized Equilibrium Results for Games with Incomplete Information," *Math. Oper. Res.* **13**, 265–276.

Balder, E. J., 1990, "New Sequential Compactness Results for Spaces of Scalarly Integrable Functions," *J. Math. Anal. Appl.* **151**, 1–16.

Browder, F. E., 1968, "The Fixed Point Theory of Multivalued Mappings in Topological Vector Spaces," *Math. Ann.* **177**, 283–301.

Byrne, C. L., 1978, "Remarks on the Set-Valued Integrals of Debreu and Aumann," *J. Math. Anal. Appl.* **62**, 243–246.

Castaing, C. and Valadier, M., 1977, "Convex Analysis and Measurable Multifunctions," *Lect. Notes in Math.* **580**, Springer-Verlag, New York.

Debreu, G., 1952, "A Social Equilibrium Existence Theorem," *Proc. Natl. Acad. Sci. USA* **38**, 886–893.

Diestel, J., (1977), "Remarks on Weak Compactness in $L_1(\mu, X)$," *Glasgow Math. J.* **18**, 87–91.

Diestel, J. and Uhl, J., (1977), *Vector Measures*, Mathematical Surveys, No. 15, American Mathematical Society, Providence, Rhode Island.

Fan, K., 1952, "Fixed Point and Minimax Theorems in Locally Convex Topological Linear Spaces," *Proc. Natl. Acad. Sci. USA* **38**, 131–136.

Glicksberg, I. L., 1952, "A Further Generalization of the Kakutani Fixed Point Theorem, with Applications to Nash Equilibrium Points," *Proc. Amer. Math. Soc.* **3**, 170–174.

Harsanyi, J. C., 1967, "Games with Incomplete Information Played by Bayesian Players," Parts I, II, II, *Management Sci.* **14**, 155–182, 320–334, 486–502.

Himmelberg, C. J., 1975, "Measurable Relations," *Fund. Math.* **87**, 53–72.

Ionescu-Tulcea, A. and C., 1969, *Topics in the Theory of Lifting*, Springer-Verlag, Berlin.

Khan, M. Ali, (1986), "Equilibrium Points of Nonatomic Games Over a Banach Space," *Trans. Amer. Math. Soc.* **29**, 737–749.

Khan, M. Ali, 1985, "On Extensions of the Cournot-Nash Theorem," in *Advances in Equilibrium Theory*, C. Aliprantis et al, eds., Lecture Notes in Economics and Mathematical Systems No. 244, Springer-Verlag, Berlin.

Khan, M. Ali and Papageorgiou, N. S., (1987), "On Cournot-Nash Equilibria in Generalized Quantitative Games with an Atomless Measure Space of Agents," *Proc. Amer. Math. Soc.* **100**, 505–510.

Kim, T., Prikry, K. and Yannelis N. C., 1987, "Carathéodory-Type Selections and Random Fixed Point Theorems," *J. Math. Anal. Appl.* **122**, 393–407.

Kim, T., Prikry, K. and Yannelis, N. C., 1988, "On a Carathéodory-Type Selection Theorem," *J. Math. Anal. Appl.* **135**, 664–670.

Milgrom, P. and Weber, R., 1985, "Distributional Strategies for Games with Incomplete Information," *Math. Oper. Res.* **10**, 619–632.

Nash, J., 1951, "Non-Cooperative Games," *Ann. Math.* **54**, 286–295.

Neveu, J., (1964), *Bases Mathematiques du Calcul des Probabilites*, Masson, Paris.

Schmeidler, D., (1973), "Equilibrium Points of Non-Atomic Games," *Journal of Statistical Physics* **7**, 295–300.

Shafer, W. and Sonnenschein, H., 1975, "Equilibrium in Abstract Economies Without Ordered Preferences," *J. Math. Econ.* **2**, 345–348.

Yannelis, N. C., 1987, "Equilibria in Noncooperative Models of Competition," *J. Econ. Theory*, **41**, 96–111.

Yannelis, N. C., 1990, "On the Upper and Lower Semicontinuity of the Aumann Integral," *J. Math. Econ.* **19**, 373–389.

Yannelis, N. C. and Prabhakar, N. D., 1983, "Existence of Maximal Elements and Equilibria in Linear Topological Spaces," *J. Math. Econ.* **12**, 233–245.

Yannelis, N. C. and Rustichini, A., 1991, "Equilibrium Points of Noncooperative Random and Bayesian Games," in *Positive Operators, Riesz Spaces, and Economics*, C. D. Aliprantis, K. C. Border and W. A. J. Luxemburg, eds., Springer-Verlag, forthcoming.

PART 7

SEQUENTIAL EQUILIBRIA

Recursive Utility Under Uncertainty

Soo H. Chew and Larry G. Epstein*

Abstract. This paper provides an axiomatization of recursive utility functions in an infinite horizon stochastic setting. In addition, some recently developed atemporal non-expected utility theories are integrated axiomatically into an intertemporal framework. The key axioms deal with intertemporal consistency and attitudes towards the temporal resolution of uncertainty.

1. Introduction

Consider intertemporal utility functions defined for consumption programs which extend over an infinite horizon. In deterministic models, the specification which dominates the capital theory literature is the intertemporally additive function with a constant rate of time preference, while generally in stochastic models the latter specification is adopted for the von Neumann-Morgenstern index and expected utility theory is assumed. For a framework of certainty, Koopmans (1960) has provided an axiomatic basis for a class of utility functions which weaken additivity over time. In this paper, we extend his axiomatic framework to admit uncertainty and a broad new class of intertemporal utility functions is characterized. These functions are called *recursive* and a key axiom is called recursivity, because of the recursive functional relation which defines intertemporal utility. Various subclasses of recursive utility are identified in Figure 1, which is clarified below.

Recursive utility functions need not conform with expected utility theory even in ranking restricted pairs of consumption programs, such as those in which all uncertainty is resolved immediately. Rather, the ranking of such "timeless gambles" may conform with one of several atemporal non-expected utility theories which have recently been proposed (e.g., Chew (1983) and (1989), Dekel (1986), Chew, Epstein and Segal (1990)).

---

* We are grateful to the Social Sciences and Humanities Research Council of Canada and to the National Science Foundation for financial support and to Tan Wang for pointing out an error in an earlier draft of the paper.

Indeed, the paper provides an axiomatic integration of the Chew and Dekel theory into an infinite horizon temporal framework.[1]

Two limiting features of the (expected) additive utility model which have been identified in the literature are: (i) the constancy of the rate of time preference (see Lucas and Stokey (1984) and Epstein and Hynes (1983) for recent discussions), and (ii) the fact that the two conceptually distinct aspects of preference, intertemporal substitutability and risk aversion, are intertwined in the within-period felicity function. Koopman's generalization of additivity endogenizes the rate of time preference and thus rectifies (i). The recursive utility functions developed here go further and also permit the disentangling of substitution from risk aversion. Moreover, this is accomplished in a framework where intertemporal consistency of choice prevails and dynamic programming techniques may be applied to solve optimization problems. (For an example of such an application see Epstein and Zin (1989).) The property of the expected additive utility model which is dropped in order to make the above separation possible is indifference to the way in which uncertainty resolves over time, in the sense of Kreps and Porteus (1978). We propose two weaker postulates regarding attitudes towards the timing of resolution, which are pivotal in the characterization of the subclasses of recursive utility considered below.

The stationarity provided by the infinite horizon framework plays an important simplifying role in our representation theorems (e.g., contrast with Chew and Epstein (1989)). But the infinite horizon and the need to distinguish between consumption programs which differ only in the way some common uncertainty resolves over time, requires that we adopt a domain for utility that has a complicated mathematical structure. The domain resembles the space of the infinite hierarchy of beliefs of players in Bayesian games (for example, see Mertens and Zamir (1985) and Myerson (1985)). In the literature on intertemporal utility theory, related domains have appeared in Kreps and Porteus (1978) in the finite horizon case and in Epstein and Zin (1989) for the case where consumption in the initial period is deterministic.

We proceed as follows: The domain is described in Section 2. The

---

[1] For a related analysis in a two-period model see Chew and Epstein (1989).

general class of recursive utility functions is defined and characterized in Section 3. A number of subclasses are explored in Section 4. Proofs are collected in an appendix.

2. Consumption

Adopt the following notation: For any metric space Y, $\mathbf{B}(Y)$ denotes the Borel σ-algebra and $M(Y)$ is the space of Borel probability measures on Y endowed with the weak convergence topology. The probability measure which assigns unit mass to $\{y\}$ is denoted $\delta[y]$. As a result of the map $y \to \delta[y]$, Y may be identified as a subspace of $M(Y)$. We write $Y' \subseteq Y$ if Y' is homeomorphic to a Borel subspace of Y. In that case $M(Y')$ can be identified with a subspace of $M(Y)$ via the map which takes $m' \in M(Y')$ into $m \in M(Y)$, $m(B) \equiv m'(B \cap Y')\ \forall B \in B(Y)$.

Consumption in each period t, $t = 0, 1, \ldots$, is restricted to lie in a compact metric space X.[2] Deterministic programs $(c_0, c_1, \ldots, c_t, \ldots)$ lie in Ω, the infinite Cartesian product of X. Under the product topology, Ω is also a compact metric space.

The domain D of consumption programs is constructed inductively. Let $D_{-1} \equiv \Omega = X \times \Omega$ and then for each $t \geq 0$ define[3]

$$D_t \equiv M(X \times D_{t-1}). \tag{2.1}$$

By Parthasarathy (1967, p. 43), each D_t is a compact metric space. Elements of D_1 are probability measures on Ω and can be interpreted as consumption programs in which the gamble underlying the probability measure is played out, and all uncertainty is resolved, at $t = 0$. Similarly, elements of D_t can be interpreted as programs in which all uncertainty is resolved at or before time t. Since $X \times \Omega \subset M(X \times \Omega)$, it follows by induction that

$$D_t \subset D_{t+1}, \quad t = -1, 0, \ldots.$$

---

[2] If "compact metric" is everywhere replaced by "separable metric," the principal result (Theorem 2.1) remains valid. Compactness is, however, convenient for the subsequent utility analysis.

[3] The counterpart definition in the construction of belief spaces (see references in the introduction) has the form $D_0 = M(X)$ and $D_t = M(X \times D_{t-1})$ for $t \geq 1$.

The set $\bigcup_0^\infty D_t$ contains all consumption programs for which uncertainty persists only for finitely many periods. But we would like D to contain also programs in which uncertainty is resolved only asymptotically. For that purpose proceed as follows: Given any $d_1 \in D_1$, we can "collapse" the uncertainty in d_1 so that it is resolved completely by $t = 0$ rather than $t = 1$. Formally, define the map

$$f_0 : D_1 \to D_0 = M(\Omega), \quad f_0(d_1)(B) \equiv E_{d_1} T_B(\cdot\,,\cdot), \quad B \in \mathbf{B}(\Omega),$$

where $T_B : X \times M(\Omega) \to \mathbb{R}^1$,

$$T_B(c, \nu) \equiv \nu\{w \in \Omega : (c, w) \in B\}.$$

We inductively define

$$f_t : D_{t+1} \to D_t, \quad t \geq 1$$

by $f_t(d_{t+1})(B) \equiv d_{t+1}\{(c, d_t) \in X \times D_t : (c, f_{t-1}(d_t)) \in B\}$, where $d_{t+1} \in M(X \times D_t)$ and $B \in \mathbf{B}(X \times D_{t-1})$. Then d_{t+1} and $f_t(d_{t+1})$ induce the identical probability measure $f_0 f_1 \ldots f_t(d_{t+1})$ on Ω, but they differ in the temporal resolution of the common uncertainty. Of course, if d_{t+1} already lies in D_t, then $f_t(d_{t+1}) = d_{t+1}$; in fact, for each $t \geq 0$ and $d_{t+1} \in D_{t+1}$,

$$f_t(d_{t+1}) = d_{t+1} \Leftrightarrow d_{t+1} \in D_t. \tag{2.2}$$

We are now ready to define the space of consumption programs D. Let

$$D \equiv \{(d_0, d_1, \ldots) : d_t \in D_t \text{ and } d_t = f_t(d_{t+1})\ \forall t \geq 0\}. \tag{2.3}$$

The following intuition underlies this definition: Elements of D are intended to represent infinite probability trees in which each branch corresponds to an element in Ω. Picture such a tree d and for each t imagine "collapsing" everything beyond t in the sense that all uncertainty which in d resolves at t or later is now completely resolved at t. This transformation generates a new tree d_t. As t increases, d_t provides a better approximation to the initial tree d and the approximation error vanishes asymptotically. Thus the infinite sequence of such approximations $(d_1, \ldots, d_t, \ldots)$ accurately represents d.

Each D_t is a compact metric space and thus so is $X_0^\infty D_t$. Endow D with the relative topology it inherits as a subspace of $X_0^\infty D_t$. Then we can prove (by adapting the arguments in Epstein and Zin (1989)) the following result:

Theorem 2.1. *The space D is a compact metric space such that D is homeomorphic to $M(X \times D)$. Moreover, $\bigcup_0^\infty D_t$ is homeomorphic to a dense subset of D.*

As a result of the indicated homeomorphism each $d \in D$ can be identified with a probability measure on $X \times D$. This is a reflection of the fact that as one moves along an infinite probability tree, the "future" remaining conditional on information received at time 0 is also an infinite tree in D. Such "stationarity" of the domain is essential for the investigation of recursive utility functions (see the stationarity and recursivity axioms and the functional structure in Theorem 3.1).

We interpret the denseness of $\bigcup_0^\infty D_t$ in D as the statement that for programs in D all uncertainty is resolved asymptotically.

3. Recursive Utility

We begin with a (complete and transitive) preference ordering $\succsim$ on D. A number of axioms are proposed. They imply a utility function representation for $\succsim$ which has a recursive structure.

By Theorem 2.1 we can identify each element of D with a measure on $X \times D$. By $(c, d) \in D$ we mean the degenerate measure $\delta[c, d]$ in which initial consumption c is certain and the uncertain future is represented by d. Of course, deterministic programs $(c_0, c_1, \ldots)$ may be identified as elements of D.

First we impose continuity.

Continuity. *For each $d \in D$, the sets $\{d' \in D : d' \succsim d\}$ and $\{d' \in D : d \succsim d'\}$ are closed.*

The next two axioms parallel Koopmans' Postulates 3b and 4 respectively.

Risk Separability. *For all $(c, c') \in X^2$ and $(d, d') \in D^2$, $(c, d) \succsim (c, d') \Leftrightarrow (c', d) \succsim (c', d')$.*

Stationarity. *For some $\bar{c} \in X$ and all $(d, d') \in D^2$, $(\bar{c}, d) \succsim (\bar{c}, d') \Leftrightarrow d \succsim d'$.*

Consider the comparison between two programs sharing a common deterministic period 0 consumption. Risk separability requires that the rankings of such programs and the uncertainty about the future which they embody, be independent of the level of initial consumption. If stationarity is also adopted, then the relative ranking of any pair of programs (c, d) and (c, d') is not only independent of c, but is also the same as would prevail if $\gtrsim$ were applied at $t = 1$ as though time began then. In this sense the passage of time and past consumption do not affect preferences.

The situation dealt with in the stationarity axiom is special in that there is no uncertainty resolved between $t = 0$ (when the choice between (c, d) and (c, d') is made) and $t = 1$ when the choice between d and d' is possibly reconsidered. Typically, some new information is forthcoming to an agent in the interval between two instants at which decisions are taken. Thus in a model with uncertainty the above axioms are not sufficient to imply the intertemporal consistency of preferences. The latter is guaranteed by the following important axiom:

Recursivity. *For all* $\alpha_i \in (0,1)$ *and* (c_i, d_i) *and* (c'_i, d'_i) *in* $X \times D$, $i = 1, \ldots, n$, *such that* $\sum \alpha_i = 1$, *if* $(c_i, d_i) \gtrsim (c'_i, d'_i)$ *for all* i, *then* $\sum \alpha_i \delta[c_i, d_i] \gtrsim \sum \alpha_i \delta[c'_i, d'_i]$. *Moreover, the latter preference is strict if* $(c_i, d_i) > (c'_i, d'_i)$ *for some* i.

The numbers $\alpha_1, \ldots, \alpha_n$ represent the probabilities corresponding to an experiment conducted at $t = 0$. If the ith outcome of the experiment occurs, then (c_i, d_i) or (c'_i, d'_i) will follow depending upon the choice made at $t = 0$ between the probability mixtures $\sum \alpha_i \delta[c_i, d_i]$ and $\sum \alpha_i \delta[c'_i, d'_i]$. If the former leads to a preferred program ex post regardless of the outcome which is realized, then recursivity requires that the former lottery should be chosen ex ante. Otherwise, the ex ante choice would be regretted ex post with probability 1 and would be revised if possible.[4]

If $\gtrsim$ satisfies all of the above axioms, we refer to it as a *recursive preference ordering.* Any utility function which represents $\gtrsim$ is called a *recursive utility function.* We turn now to the functional structure of recursive utility.

---

[4] Recursivity is essentially identical to the notion of consistency explored by Johnsen and Donaldson (1985). For an alternative view of consistency see Machina (1989).

Our representation theorem requires the following definition and notation. Let $\hat{M} \subset M(\mathbf{R}^1)$ and let $\mu : \hat{M} \to \mathbf{R}^1$. Say that μ is a *certainty equivalent* if (i) μ is increasing in the sense of first degree stochastic dominance, and (ii) $\mu(\delta[v]) = v$ for all $\delta[v]$ in $\hat{M}$. Secondly, for any $V : D \to \mathbf{R}^1$ and $d \in D$, denote by $m_V(d)$ that probability measure on $V(D)$ defined by

$$m_V(d)(B) \equiv d\{(c, d') \in X \times D : V(c, d') \in B\}, \quad B \in \mathbf{B}(V(D)). \tag{3.1}$$

We have identified d with a probability measure on $X \times D$ under the homeomorphism between D and $M(X \times D)$. Thus $m_V(d)$ describes the probability distribution of utility $V(c, d')$ induced by d.

Theorem 3.1. *$\succsim$ satisfies continuity, risk separability, stationarity and recursivity if and only if it can be represented numerically by a continuous function V which satisfies*

$$V(d) = \mu(m_V(d)) \tag{3.2a}$$

and

$$V(c, d) = W(c, V(d)) \tag{3.2b}$$

$\forall (c, d) \in X \times D$, where $m_V(d)$ is defined in (3.1), $\mu : \hat{M}(V(D)) \to \mathbf{R}^1$, $\hat{M}(V(D)) \equiv \{m_V(d) : d \in D\}$, μ is continuous and is a certainty equivalent, $W : X \times V(D) \to \mathbf{R}^1$ is continuous and $W(c, \cdot)$ is increasing on $V(D)$ for every $c \in X$.

The functional representation of V has two components—a certainty equivalent function μ and an *aggregator* W.[5] They define the following recursive relation, obtained by combining (3.2a) and (b), which V must satisfy:

$$V(c, d) = W(c, \mu(m_V(d))). \tag{3.3}$$

[5] Both μ and W are degenerate if $V(D)$ consists of a single point, which occurs if and only if all programs in D are indifferent according to $\succsim$. Such degeneracy could be ruled out by a sensitivity axiom similar to Postulate 2 of Koopmans (p. 291). Note also that W and μ change if V is replaced by an ordinally equivalent utility function. Thus there exist many (W, μ) pairs that represent the identical ordering in the sense of (3.2).

The recursive relation (3.3) is readily interpreted. Given a program (c, d), period 0 consumption c is nonrandom but the future, represented by d, is uncertain. Consequently, the value of intertemporal utility at $t = 1$ is uncertain from the perspective of the initial period. According to (3.3), $V(c, d)$ is computed in two stages: (i) the certainty equivalent of random future utility is computed, and then (ii) it is combined with current consumption via the aggregator W. If there is no uncertainty, μ drops out and (3.3) reduces to the recursive relation derived by Koopmans:

$$V(c_0, c_1, c_2, \ldots) = W(c_0, V(c_1, c_2, \ldots)).$$

One desirable feature of the structure of recursive utility functions, particularly of (3.3), is that dynamic programming techniques may be applied to solve optimization problems (see Epstein and Zin (1989)). The other important feature is that a degree of separation is achieved between intertemporal substitutability (encoded in W) and risk aversion (encoded in μ) in the sense which we now describe.

Definition. *If $\succsim^*$ and $\succsim$ are preference orderings on D, $\succsim^*$ is more risk averse than $\succsim$ if any gamble rejected by $\succsim$ is also rejected by $\succsim^*$, i.e., $\forall d \in D$ and $\forall C = (c_0, c_1, \ldots) \in \Omega$,*

$$C \succsim d \Rightarrow C \succsim^* d.$$

For the result regarding comparative risk aversion we need one additional assumption.

Postulate 1. *For every $d \in D$ $\exists C$ and C' (deterministic programs) in Ω, such that $C \succsim d \succsim C'$.*

Theorem 3.2. *Let $\succsim$ and $\succsim^*$ be two recursive preference orderings on D which also satisfy Postulate 1. Then $\succsim^*$ is more risk averse than $\succsim$ if and only if there exist corresponding utility functions V^* and V satisfying: (i) $V^* \mid \Omega = V \mid \Omega$; (ii) $W^* = W$ and $\mu^* \leq \mu$, where (W^*, μ^*) and (W, μ) satisfy the appropriate forms of (3.2a) and (b) for $\succsim^*$ and $\succsim$ respectively.*

Roughly speaking, given a recursive utility function V, we can increase risk aversion without changing the rankings of deterministic programs, by keeping the same aggregator and adopting a new certainty equivalent function μ^*; the latter should assign lower certainty equivalents to probability measures in its domain than does μ.

Besides Koopmans (1960), other papers which have studied aggregators include Lucas and Stokey (1984) and Boyd (1990). For examples of aggregator functions, see Koopmans, Diamond and Williamson (1964) and Epstein (1983); for the latter example see also (4.1) below. The next section describes a number of classes of certainty equivalent functions and also relates the general recursive utility specification to the standard expected additive utility form and another specification ((4.3) below) which has appeared in the literature.

4. Attitudes Towards Temporal Resolution

We will consider a number of subclasses of recursive utility corresponding to different hypotheses about attitudes towards the way in which uncertainty resolved over time, in the sense first formalized by Kreps and Porteus (1978). It is convenient to define the projection π from D onto D_0,

$$\pi(d) = \pi(d_0, \ldots, d_t, \ldots) \equiv d_0. \tag{4.1}$$

Interpret $\pi(d) \in M(\Omega)$ as representing the "marginal" distribution of consumption inherent in the program d, where information about the temporal resolution of uncertainty has been eliminated.

The first and most common hypothesis is that temporal resolution is a matter of indifference.

Timing Indifference. *For all $\alpha \in [0,1]$, $c \in X$ and $(d, d') \in D^2$,*

$$\alpha\delta[c,d] + (1-\alpha)\delta[c,d'] \sim \delta[c, \alpha d + (1-\alpha)d'].$$

The two programs in the statement of the axiom involve the same uncertainty about the future in the sense that they have identical images under the projection π. But in $\delta[c, \alpha d + (1-\alpha)d']$ one learns only at $t = 1$, after the realization of the random variable corresponding to the $(\alpha, 1-\alpha)$ probability distribution, whether it is d or d' that is to be faced. In the other lottery, that information is forthcoming at $t = 0$. In the absence of an ability to exploit earlier information to improve planning, and planning advantages are not an issue in this section, one may wish to hypothesize timing indifference.

The timing indifference axiom has strong implications for recursive preferences.

Theorem 4.1. *The preference ordering $\succsim$ is recursive and satisfies timing indifference if and only if it can be represented by a continuous utility function V for which the aggregator and certainty equivalent functions of Theorem 3.1 take the form:*

$$W(c, v) = u(c) + B(c)v, \tag{4.1}$$

for some $u : X \to \mathbb{R}^1$ and $B : X \to \mathbb{R}^1_{++}$, and

$$\mu(m) = E(m), \tag{4.2}$$

the expected value of m, for $m \in \hat{M}(V(D))$.

The aggregator (4.1) is the discrete-time version of the function proposed by Uzawa (1968). In conjunction with (4.2) it implies the expected utility model

$$V(d) = E_{\pi(d)} \sum_0^\infty u(c_t)B(c_0)\cdots B(c_{t-1}), \tag{4.3}$$

where $E_{\pi(d)}$ is the expected value with respect to the measure $\pi(d) \in M(\Omega)$. (An alternative axiomization of (4.3), under the maintained hypothesis of expected utility theory, may be found in Epstein (1983).) The specification (4.3) is the most general recursive utility function consistent with expected utility theory. But it does not permit comparative risk aversion in the sense of Definition 3.1 and Theorem 3.2, since if $W^* = W$ (= (4.1) without loss of generality), then $\mu^* = \mu$ (= (4.2)).

For completeness we also describe an axiomatic basis for the standard additive model which consists of (4.1)–(4.3) with B constant. It is straightforward to show that the following additional axiom, similar to Postulate (3′a) of Koopmans (p. 307), will suffice.

Future Independence. *For all $(c_0, c_1, c_0', c_1') \in X^4$ and deterministic programs C and C' in Ω, $(c_0, c_1, C) \succsim (c_0', c_1', C) \Leftrightarrow (c_0, c_1, C') \succsim (c_0', c_1', C')$.*

This axiom deals only with deterministic programs and requires that trade-offs between consumptions in periods 0 and 1 be independent of consumption levels in later periods.

In view of the unfortunate consequence of timing indifference noted above, we are led to reconsider that axiom. We would argue that it is perfectly "rational" for an individual to care about the temporal resolution of uncertainty. For example, early resolution might be preferred by a "nervous" or "edgy" person who does not like living with uncertainty. On the other hand, an affinity for surprises or the pleasure derived from hope, for, or anticipation of, favorable events which have some chance of occurring in the future, could lead to a preference to defer the resolution of uncertainty.[6] Thus we turn to a number of axioms which admit limited forms of nonindifference to timing. In all cases, the implied utility functions are sufficiently flexible that comparative risk aversion analysis in the sense of Definition 3.1 becomes possible. The subclasses of recursive utility obtained in this way and their interrelationships are indicated in Figure 1.

Suppose that the uncertainty to be resolved is whether d or d' will be faced in the future and suppose further that d and d' are indifferent to one another. Then the psychic costs or benefits of early resolution are less apparent and timing indifference is plausible. More precisely, consider the following axiom:

Quasi-Timing Indifference. *For all $\alpha \in [0,1]$, $c \in X$ and $(d,d') \in D^2$, if $d \sim d'$ then $\alpha\delta[c,d] + (1-\alpha)\delta[c,d'] \sim \delta[c, \alpha d + (1-\alpha)d']$.*

Next suppose that $d > d'$ and that

$$\alpha\delta[c,d] + (1-\alpha)\delta[c,d'] \sim \delta[c, \beta d + (1-\beta)d']$$

---

[6] It is difficult to find direct evidence on attitudes towards timing, since people's observed choices invariably reflect both the planning advantages of early resolution and the psychic costs or benefits upon which we focus here. But revealed preference for late resolution, in spite of the planning cost that entails, would constitute an a fortiori case for psychic preference for late resolution. An example would be a preference for not resolving early uncertainty about date of death. Some experimental evidence regarding attitudes towards timing is provided in Cook (1989).

for $\beta > \alpha$. Then the fact that indifference holds only when the preferred prospect d is given a large weight β in the late resolution case, reflects a preference for early resolution. In fact, the difference between β and α, or alternatively the normalized expression $[\beta(1-\alpha)/\alpha(1-\beta)]-1$, can be interpreted as a probability premium which would be demanded if late resolution were substituted for early resolution. It is intuitive that the premium should be unaffected if d and d' are replaced by respectively indifferent programs. Thus consider the following axiom:

Constant Timing Premium. *For all* $(\alpha,\beta) \in [0,1]^2$, $c \in X$ *and* $(d,d',e,e') \in D^4$ *with* $d \sim e$ *and* $d' \sim e'$, *if*

$$\alpha\delta[c,d] + (1-\alpha)\delta[c,d'] \sim \delta[c,\beta d + (1-\beta)d'],$$

then

$$\alpha\delta[c,e] + (1-\alpha)\delta[c,e'] \sim \delta[c,\beta e + (1-\beta)e'].$$

The above axioms have no implications for the aggregator function of a recursive ordering, but they do restrict the certainty equivalent function μ, albeit not as much as does (4.2). We now describe the implied functional forms for μ, all of which have been studied in the atemporal literature on non-expected utility theories.

Let μ be defined on $M(S)$ where $S \subset \mathbb{R}^1$. Say that μ is a *betweenness* function if $\exists$ continuous $\phi : S \times \mathbb{R}ng(\mu) \to \mathbb{R}^1$ such that $\phi(s,s) \equiv 0$, ϕ is increasing in its first argument and $\forall m \in M(S)$, $\mu(m)$ is the unique solution to

$$\int_S \phi(s,\mu(m))dm(s) = 0. \tag{4.4}$$

(See Dekel (1986) and Chew (1989).) The special case where $\phi(s,\cdot)$ is linear in $\mu(\cdot)$ leads to an explicit expression for μ of the following form:

$$\mu(m) = u^{-1}\left[\int u(s)w(s)dm(s) \Big/ \int w(s)dm(s)\right], \tag{4.5}$$

for suitable u and w. Such μ's are called *weighted utility* functions (Chew (1983)). If w is constant, the latter specializes to the *expected utility* uncertainty equivalent

$$\mu(m) = u^{-1}\left(\int u(s)dm(s)\right). \tag{4.6}$$

Our final result relates these functional forms to the timing axioms (see also Figure 1).[7]

↓ ordering, continuity

$V : D \to \mathbb{R}^1$
continuous

↓ risk separability, stationarity and recursivity

recursive utility:
$V(d) = \mu(m_V(d))$
$V(c, d) = W(c, V(d))$

↓ quasi-timing indifference

μ is a betweenness function

↓ constant timing premium

μ is expected utility;
Kreps-Porteus structure

↓ timing indifference

$V(d) = E_{\pi(d)} \sum u(c_t) B(c_0) \cdots B(c_{t-1})$
intertemporal expected utility

↓ future independence

$V(d) = E_{\pi(d)} \sum \beta^t u(c_t)$

Figure 1

Theorem 4.2. *The preference ordering $\succsim$ is recursive and satisfies respectively*

---

[7] A timing axiom characterization of the weighted utility certainty equivalent is not included here. See Chew and Epstein (1989) for a characterization in a two-period model.

(i) quasi-timing indifference,

(ii) quasi-timing indifference and constant timing premium,

if and only if it can be represented by an aggregator W and certainty equivalent μ as in Theorem 3.1, where in addition μ lies in the following functional form classes respectively:

(i′) betweenness,

(ii′) expected utility.

The last case corresponds to the functional structure first explored by Kreps and Porteus (1978). Note that even though μ is expected utility based, the corresponding intertemporal utility function V does not satisfy the independence axiom on D and does not conform with (4.3).

Both of the intertemporal utility theories described in the theorem are sufficiently flexible to model comparative risk aversion. For example, in the expected utility case, if in the appropriate forms of (4.6) u^* is more concave than u, then $\mu^* \leq \mu$. For the betweenness case, let μ and μ^* be represented by ϕ and ϕ^* respectively as in (4.4). Suppose that ϕ^* is a concave transform of ϕ in their first arguments, i.e.,

$$\phi^*(s,z) \equiv h(\phi(s,z),z),$$

for (s,z) in the domain of ϕ, where h is defined on an appropriate domain and is an increasing and concave function of its first argument there. (The function h must also satisfy $h(0,z) \equiv 0$ in order that $\phi(s,s) \equiv 0$ and $\phi^*(s,s) \equiv 0$.) Then, by Jensen's inequality applied to (4.4), $\mu^* \leq \mu$.

It would clearly be of interest to exploit the flexibility of the intertemporal utilities described in the Theorem, and indeed of the general recursive utilities in Theorem 3.1, to reexamine standard issues in capital theory, such as asset pricing or optimal stochastic growth. Some results in the asset pricing context may be found in Epstein (1988) and Epstein and Zin (1989).

Appendix

Proof of Theorem 3.1. The necessity of the axioms is clear. We prove their sufficiency.

By Debreu (1954), $\succsim$ can be represented numerically by a continuous real-valued function V defined on D. Define W on $X \times V(D)$ by

$$W(c,v) \equiv V(c,d) \quad \text{for any} \quad d \in V^{-1}(v). \tag{A1}$$

Risk separability and stationarity imply that W is well-defined and that $W(c,\cdot)$ is increasing on $V(D)$ for each $c \in X$. Since D is compact and V is continuous, we can show that W is continuous on $X \times V(D)$. Evidently, (3.2b) is satisfied.

Let ψ be the map which takes $d \in D$ into $m_V(d) \in M(V(D))$. If f is any continuous (and therefore also bounded) real-valued function on $V(D)$ then $f(V(\cdot))$ is continuous (and bounded) on D. It follows that ψ is a continuous map.

Define μ on $\hat{M}(V(D))$ by

$$\mu(m) \equiv V(d), \quad \text{for any} \quad d \in D \quad \text{such that } m = m_V(d).$$

We need to show that μ is well-defined, i.e., that

$$m_V(d) = m_V(d') \Rightarrow V(d) = V(d'). \tag{A2}$$

The functions ψ and V are continuous and the subset of $M(X \times D)$ consisting of measures having finite support is dense in $M(X \times D)$. Therefore, it suffices to prove (A2) for the case where d and d', identified as elements of $M(X \times D)$, each has finite support. In that case, if $m_V(d) = m_V(d')$, then $\exists \alpha_i, c_i, d_i, c_i'$ and d_i', $i = 1, \ldots, n$, such that $V(c_i, d_i) = V(c_i', d_i')\ \forall i$, $d = \sum \alpha_i \delta[c_i, d_i]$ and $d' = \sum \alpha_i \delta[c_i', d_i']$. Thus recursivity implies that $V(d) = V(d')$.

Since D is compact and ψ is continuous, we can show that μ is continuous. Recursivity implies that μ is increasing in the sense of first degree stochastic dominance. The definition of μ immediately implies that $\mu(\delta[v]) = v\ \forall v \in V(D)$, and so μ is a certainty equivalent. Finally, it is clear that (3.2a) is satisfied. Q.E.D.

Proof of Theorem 3.2. Suppose $\succsim^*$ is more risk averse. Then $\succsim^*$ and $\succsim$ must rank deterministic programs identically. Thus the representations V and V^*, provided by Theorem 3.1, can be chosen so that

$$V \mid \Omega = V^* \mid \Omega. \tag{A3}$$

By Postulate 1, $V(D) = V^*(D)$. By the construction of the aggregator (see (A2)), $W = W^*$. In light of (A3), $\succsim^*$ being more risk averse amounts to $V^* \leq V$ on D. Thus $\mu^* \leq \mu$ follows from the appropriate forms of (3.2a).

Consider the converse. We need only show that

$$V^* \leq V \quad \text{on } D. \tag{A4}$$

Prove the inequality first on D_0 (recall (2.1)). Any $d \in D_0$ can be viewed as a measure on Ω. Since $V \mid \Omega = V^* \mid \Omega$, $m_V(d) = m_{V^*}(d)$. Therefore, we can use (3.2a) and $\mu^* \leq \mu$ to show that $V^*(d) \leq V(d)$. Proceed inductively, (exploiting also (3.2b)), to prove that $V^* \leq V$ on $\bigcup_0^\infty D_t$. Since the latter is dense in D, (A4) follows. Q.E.D.

Proof of Theorem 4.1. Let V represent $\succsim$ on $M(X \times D)$ as provided by Debreu (1954). We show first that V satisfies the independence axiom, i.e., $\forall \alpha \in [0,1]$,

$$V(d) = V(d') \Rightarrow V(\alpha d + (1-\alpha)e) = V(\alpha d' + (1-\alpha)e).$$

Consider the following four programs, where $c \in X$ is arbitrary:

$$d^1 = \alpha\delta[c,d] + (1-\alpha)\delta[c,e], \quad d^2 = \alpha\delta[c,d'] + (1-\alpha)\delta[c,e],$$
$$d^3 = \delta[c, \alpha d + (1-\alpha)e], \qquad d^4 = \delta[c, \alpha d' + (1-\alpha)e].$$

Then

$$\begin{aligned} V(d^1) &= V(d^3) && \text{by timing indifference,} \\ V(d^1) &= V(d^2) && \text{by recursivity,} \\ V(d^2) &= V(d^4) && \text{by timing indifference,} \\ \Rightarrow V(d^3) &= V(d^4) \Rightarrow && \text{by (3.2b)} \end{aligned}$$

$V(\alpha d + (1-\alpha)e) = V(\alpha d' + (1-\alpha)e)$, as desired.

We conclude that, after redefining V if necessary,

$$V(d) = E_d U(\cdot) \quad \forall d \in M(X \times D), \tag{A5}$$

where $U : X \times D \to \mathbb{R}^1$ is a von Neumann-Morgenstern utility index. Since $U(c,d') = V(\delta[c,d'])$, we see that (4.2) is a restatement of (3.2a).

To show that W defined in (A1) satisfies (4.1), i.e., is linear in its second argument, apply (3.2b), the mixture linearity of V represented by (A5) and timing indifference as follows:

$$\begin{aligned}\alpha W(c,V(d))+(1-\alpha)W(c,V(d')) &= \alpha V(c,d)+(1-\alpha)V(c,e)\\ &= V(\alpha\delta[c,d]+(1-\alpha)\delta[c,d'])\\ &= V(c,\alpha d+(1-\alpha)d')\\ &= W(c,\alpha V(d)+(1-\alpha)V(d')).\end{aligned}$$

Q.E.D.

Proof of Theorem 4.2. The sufficiency of the functional forms is readily verified. For necessity, adapt the proof of Theorem 4.1. For example, show that (i) implies that V satisfies the betweenness axiom of Chew (1989) and Dekel (1986) and then invoke their representation results. In the case of (ii), show that V satisfies the independence axiom. More details for the two-period context may be found in Chew and Epstein (1989). Q.E.D.

References

Boyd, J., 1990, "Recursive Utility and the Ramsey Problem," *J. Econ. Theory* **50**, 326–345.

Chew, S. H., 1983, "A Generalization of the Quasilinear Mean with Applications to the Measurement of Income Inequality and Decision Theory Resolving the Allais Paradox," *Econometrica* **51**, 1065–1092.

Chew, S. H., 1989, "Axiomatic Utility Theories with the Betweenness Property," *Ann. Oper. Res.* **19**, 273–298.

Chew, S. H. and Epstein, L. G., 1989, "The Structure of Preferences and Attitudes Towards the Timing of the Resolution of Uncertainty," *Int. Econ. Rev.* **30**, 103–117.

Chew, S. H., Epstein, L. G., and Segal, U., 1990, "Mixture Symmetry and Quadratic Utility," *Econometrica*, to appear.

Cook, V. G., 1989, "The Effects of Temporal Uncertainty Resolution on the Overall Utility and Suspense of Risky Monetary and Survival Gambles," Ph.D. dissertation, Department of Psychology, McGill University.

Debreu, G., 1954, "Representation of a Preference Ordering by a Numerical Function," in *Decision Processes*, R. Thrall, C. Coombs and R. David, eds., New York, John Wiley.

Dekel, E., 1986, "An Axiomatic Characterization of Preferences Under Uncertainty," *J. Econ. Theory* **40**, 304–318.

Epstein, L. G., 1983, "Stationary Cardinal Utility and Optimal Growth Under Uncertainty," *J. Econ. Theory* **31**, 133–152.

Epstein, L. G., 1988, "Risk Aversion and Asset Prices," *J. Monetary Econ.* **22**, 179–192.

Epstein, L. G. and Hynes, A. J., 1983, "The Rate of Time Preference and Dynamic Economic Analysis," *J. Pol. Econ.* **91**, 611–625.

Epstein, L. G. and Zin, S. E., 1989, "Substitution, Risk Aversion and the Temporal Behavior of Consumption and Asset Returns: A Theoretical Framework," *Econometrica* **57**, 937–969.

Johnsen, T. H. and Donaldson, J. B., 1985, "The Structure of Intertemporal Preferences Under Uncertainty and Time Consistent Plans," *Econometrica* **53**, 1451–1458.

Koopmans, T. C., 1960, "Stationary Ordinal Utility and Impatience," *Econometrica* **28**, 287–309.

Koopmans, T. C., Diamond, P., and Williamson, R., 1964, "Stationary Utility and Time Perspective," *Econometrica* **32**, 82–100.

Kreps, D. M. and Porteus, E. L., 1978, "Temporal Resolution of Uncertainty and Dynamic Choice Theory," *Econometrica* **46**, 185–200.

Lucas, R. E. and Stokey, N., 1984, "Optimal Growth with Many Consumers," *J. Econ. Theory* **32**, 139–171.

Machina, M. J., 1988, "Dynamic Consistency and Non-Expected Utility Models of Choice Under Uncertainty," *J. Econ. Lit.* **27**, 1622–1668.

Mertens, J. F. and Zamir, S., 1985, "Formulation of Bayesian Analysis for Games with Incomplete Information," *Int. J. Game Theory* **14**, 1–29.

Myerson, R. B., 1985, "Bayesian Equilibrium and Incentive Compatibility: An Introduction," in *Social Goals and Social Organizations, Essays in Memory of Elisha Pazner*, L. Hurwicz, D. Schmeidler, and H. Sonnenschein, eds., Cambridge, Cambridge University Press.

Parthasarathy, K. R., 1967, *Probability Measures on Metric Spaces*, New York, Academic Press.

Uzawa, H., 1968, "Time Preference, the Consumption Function, and Optimum Asset Holdings," in *Value, Capital and Growth: Papers in Honour of Sir John Hicks*, J. N. Wolfe, ed., Chicago, Aldine.

Consistency and Continuity of Choice in a Sequence of Spot and Futures Markets

David C. Nachman and Robert P. Kertz*

Abstract. This paper is the first of a competitive analysis of an exchange economy where markets are open at each of an infinite sequence of dates for spot trading and unconditional futures contracting. In the absence of institutional arrangements for handling bankruptcy, the consistency (determinateness) and continuity of agent choice becomes an issue. If an agent's probabilistic opinions (expectations) regarding prices are consistent in an appropriate sense, then choice is consistent and demand is upper hemi-continuous for important price-action histories. In the second part of this analysis [Nachman, 1980], commonness and compatibility assumptions regarding agents' opinions imply a specific support structure of these opinions. This structure entails that for important histories at a given date individual and aggregate demand for futures contracts are bounded below by resources at the subsequent date. Existence of a sequence of temporary equilibria then follows in a routine fashion.

1. Introduction

In recent years, considerable attention has been focused on the equilibrium analysis of incomplete market economies [Radner, 1974] with particular emphasis on temporary equilibria in economies that evolve in time [Grandmont, 1977]. The objective of this research is a competitive analysis of an economy where markets are open at each of an infinite sequence of dates for spot trading and limited unconditional futures trading, and where agents at each date are uncertain only about prices that will prevail at future dates. The problem is the viability of a purely competitive exchange mechanism in this context of sequential trading under uncertainty.

The problem is really twofold, consisting of one problem of an essentially static nature and one of a dynamic nature. The static problem

---

* This research was supported by the National Science Foundation under Grant SOC75-14663 to the Georgia Institute of Technology. Typing support was given by the Graduate School of Business, Columbia University. The authors benefitted from discussions with James S. Jordan, Richard E. Kihlstrom, and Frederic B. Shipley on an earlier version of this work.

concerns the existence of a temporary equilibrium for markets open at a given date, i.e., at one stage of sequential trading. The usual method of demonstrating existence of a competitive equilibrium is to apply a market equilibrium theorem, e.g., the theorem of Debreu [1956]. The application of such a theorem requires that aggregate demand exhibit appropriate behavior over approaches to the boundary of the set of admissible prices (c.f. [Grandmont, 1977: Section 3.1]). This behavior can be deduced if aggregate demand is bounded below independently of prices. Similar boundedness requirements are also needed for application of the more recent results of Mas-Colell [1974], Gale and Mas-Colell [1975], and Shafer and Sonnenschein [1975]. In the usual case, either no uncertainty [Debreu, 1959: Chapter 5] or a complete finite system of contingent claims markets [Debreu, 1959: Chapter 7], an individual consumer's choice set, and hence demand, are bounded below independently of prices by a priori but natural minimum consumption constraints. In an economy with markets for unconditional forward commitments, individual and aggregate demand for forward contracts need not be bounded below in the appropriate sense unless bounds of an institutional character are imposed. Such bounds are imposed by Stigum [1969: (3), p. 541, (2), p. 545; 1972: (2.3), (2.8)] in a model with spot markets for currently deliverable goods and for consumer and entrepreneurial debt, and by Radner [1972: (2.1), (5.2)] in a model with an incomplete system of contingent claims markets.

In contrast, Green [1973] addresses the determinateness of agent choice and boundedness of aggregate demand directly in an exchange model that is the prototype for the one considered here. There are two market dates in this model with spot and unconditional futures markets at the initial date and spot markets at the second or final date. Green [1973: Theorem 2.1] characterizes price systems for the initial date for which the choice behavior of an agent at that date is determinate.

Moreover, Green shows that the desired behavior of aggregate demand in this model can be obtained without institutional bounds provided agent's opinions about prices exhibit some degree of commonness.[1] Commonness of opinions in an ordinary sense of existence of common price forecasts (based on current prices) is a necessary condition for aggre-

[1] See the comments in [Green, 1973: p. 1114 and Remark 4.5].

gate demand to be well defined, i.e., to have a non-empty domain [Green, 1973: (4.1)]. Beyond this, Green's condition [1973: (4.2)] requires that agents share an open set of price forecasts for the second date that is independent of initial date prices.

The dynamic problem is posed at the end of [Green, 1973]. The problem is that of determining conditions, if any, under which a history of temporary equilibrium actions and prices up through one stage of sequential trading gives rise to initial conditions at the succeeding stage that ensure existence of a temporary equilibrium at that stage. At each stage of trading, agents must honor contractual obligations incurred at previous stages. Thus the dynamic problem is one of determining conditions under which temporary equilibrium actions at one stage entail contracts that can be honored at subsequent stages. This is the general problem of bankruptcy.

At the date in question in [Stigum, 1969], there are preexisting contractual obligations in the form of maturing consumer and entrepreneurial loans. Stigum establishes existence of a temporary equilibrium [1969: Proposition III] under conditions that assume away a possible bankruptcy [1969: (1), (2), p. 548]. These conditions are relaxed considerably in [Stigum, 1972, Propositions 1, 2] to essentially the same effect. There is no guarantee, however, that these conditions would or could obtain as a consequence of a history of temporary equilibria.[2]

In [1971: Theorem T.5.7], Arrow and Hahn establish the existence of a compensated equilibrium with bankruptcy for an economy with preexisting personal or household debt. They point out the difficulty in defining a corresponding notion of competitive equilibrium with bankruptcy [1971: Remark 1, p. 121]. Grandmont [1970] and Green [1974] avoid this issue altogether by investigating equilibrium in competitive type models augmented by institutional arrangements that may be interpreted as bankruptcy laws. Agents take into account the bankruptcy law in deciding to become debtors or creditors [Grandmont, 1970] or in making unconditional futures contracts for sale or delivery of goods [Green, 1974]. The outcomes of these augmented mechanisms reflect then not only the action of the bankruptcy law in case of bankruptcies but they also reflect

[2] See the comments at the end of [Stigum, 1972: Section 2].

the influence of the bankruptcy law on agents' decisions.

While it is desirable to study alternative institutional arrangements for handling bankruptcies, such investigations may shed little light on the circumstances in which these arrangements may be required. Some understanding of why a competitive mechanism fails to avoid bankruptcies is needed. In the context of sequential trading, the burden of avoiding bankruptcies must be carried by agents' opinions. In the tradition of general competitive analysis, a step toward such understanding is made by answering the question, are there conditions on agents' opinions that imply the existence of a temporary equilibrium path in a sequential trading model with no institutional arrangements for handling bankruptcy? "In attempting to answer the question 'Could it be true?,' we learn a good deal about why it might not be true."[3]

This question is addressed here and in a subsequent paper [Nachman, 1980] in the context of an extension of Green's model [1973] to an infinite sequence of market dates. The question is broken into two parts. The first, the subject of this paper, concerns the consistency and continuity of individual agent choice at each date and over the infinite horizon. Assumptions made regarding an agent's preferences and endowments are more or less standard in the literature of temporary equilibrium theory. In addition, two assumptions are made regarding an agent's opinion. The first consists of four hypotheses, three of which parallel assumptions in the literature. The fourth is a new (to the best of our knowledge) continuity hypothesis that requires the boundary of the support of an agent's (date n) opinion to have subjective probability zero. The second assumption also has no counterpart in the extant literature, though it is consistent with the interpretation of futures prices as forecasts of future spot prices. This assumption and the new continuity hypothesis imply that at each date and history at the date the set of prices for the subsequent date at which an agent's set of feasible actions is bounded has subjective probability one.

With regard to consistency (c.f. [Kertz and Nachman, 1979]) and even continuity of agent choice, these assumptions are clearly of a sufficiency character and no attempt has been made to investigate their

[3] [Arrow and Hahn, 1971: p. vii].

necessity. For the sake of convenience, however, and at the risk of abusing the language, opinions that satisfy these assumptions are referred to simply as *consistent*. The assumptions are discussed further in Section 2 where they are presented.

In Section 3, the feasible action relations for a typical agent are defined and the regularity properties of these relations are derived. Included here are some remarks on the concept of economic bankruptcy.

In Sections 4 and 5, the agent's choice problem is cast in the framework of (non-stationary) dynamic programming. The approach, as in [Kertz and Nachman, 1979], builds on the work of Jordan [1977]. The results of Jordan [1977] and Kertz and Nachman [1979], however, cannot be applied here directly owing to the possibility of empty values of the feasible action relations and the lack of continuity of these relations at some state (price)-action histories. In Section 4, the relation between histories and attainable futures (probabilities on posterities) is defined and the needed regularity properties of this relation are derived. In Section 5, these results are used to establish existence of solutions of an agent's infinite horizon choice problem and to derive continuity, concavity/convexity, and monotonicity properties of derived utility and single period demand relations.

The second part of the above question, dealt with in [Nachman, 1980], concerns the consistency (in the aggregate sense) of individually optimal sequential choice decentralized through the price mechanism at each market date. Two assumptions are made concerning agents' opinions that ensure the existence of appropriate common price forecasts. The first is necessary for aggregate demand to be well defined while the second can be viewed as a dynamic analog of Green's commonness of expectations condition. A third assumption of a compatibility nature is made on opinions to obtain a set of admissible prices suitable for application of a market equilibrium theorem.

These assumptions, together with those of this paper, imply a specific support structure of agent's opinions. As a consequence of this specific structure, at important histories each agent's demand for futures contracts on current markets is bounded below by the agent's known endowment at the subsequent market date. This result solves at once both the static and dynamic problems mentioned earlier. At any candidate for temporary equilibrium at a given date, agents individually choose actions that entail contracts they can honor at the subsequent market date. Aggregate demand for such contracts is bounded below by the resources of the economy available at the next market date, and the existence of a sequence of temporary equilibria for the economy follows in a routine fashion.

We begin with some notation and terminology. Results, definitions, remarks, important conventions, etc., are numbered consecutively within each subsection of the paper.

2. The Model and Assumptions

2.1 Notation and Terminology. Let $\mathbb{R}$ denote the set of real numbers, $\mathcal{N}$ the set of positive integers, and for m a positive integer, let $\mathbb{R}^m$ denote the m-fold Cartesian product of $\mathbb{R}$ with itself. If $x = (x_1, \ldots, x_m) \in \mathbb{R}^m$ and $y = (y_1, \ldots, y_m) \in \mathbb{R}^m$, $x \leqq y$ (or $y \geqq x$) means $x_i \leq y_i$, $i = 1, \ldots, m$, $x \leq y$ ($y > x$) means $x \leqq y$ and $x \neq y$, and $x < y$ ($y > x$) means $x_i < y_i$, $i = 1, \ldots, m$. We let $\mathbb{R}^m_+ = \{x : x \in \mathbb{R}^m, x \geqq 0\}$, $\mathbb{R}^m_{+0} = \{x : x \in \mathbb{R}^m, x \geq 0\}$, and $\mathbb{R}^m_{++} = \{x : x \in \mathbb{R}^m, x > 0\}$, where $0 \in \mathbb{R}^m$. These relations and sets are defined in an analogous coordinatewise fashion on $\mathbb{R}^\infty = \mathbb{R} \times \mathbb{R} \times \cdots$. If $x = (x_1, \ldots, x_m) \in \mathbb{R}^m$, $\|x\|$ denotes the Euclidean norm of x, while $\tilde{x} = x\left(\sum_{i=1}^m |x_i|\right)^{-1}$ provided $x \neq 0$. Similarly, for $B \subset \mathbb{R}^m$, $\tilde{B} = \{z : z = \tilde{x}, x \in B, x \neq 0\}$.

For a topological space X, $\mathcal{B}(X)$ denotes the σ-algebra of Borel subsets of X, and $\mathcal{P}(X)$ denotes the set of probability measures defined on $\mathcal{B}(X)$, endowed with the topology of weak convergence.[4] Unless specifically stated to the contrary, products of topological spaces are given the product topology and products of measurable spaces are given the product σ-algebra [Ash, 1972: 2.6.1, 2.7.1]. Notation and terminology concerning functions, relations, and correspondences follows that in [Hildenbrand, 1974: pp. 4–5, 21–28] except that we use the notation $g : X \to Y$ to denote the former and $g : X \Rightarrow Y$ to denote the latter, where X

[4] All spaces X in this paper for which the topology of weak convergence for $\mathcal{P}(X)$ is of interest are metrizable, and the appropriate references are [Billingsley, 1968; Parthasarathy, 1967].

and Y are sets. Throughout, the abbreviations "u.h.c." and "l.h.c." stand for "upper hemi-continuous" and "lower hemi-continuous," respectively [Hildenbrand, 1974: pp. 21–28].

For two measurable spaces $(\Omega, \mathcal{F})$ and $(\Omega', \mathcal{F}')$, by a transition probability from Ω to Ω' we mean the function $p : \Omega \times \mathcal{F}' \to [0,1]$ such that for each ω in Ω, $p(\omega, \cdot)$ is a probability measure on $\mathcal{F}'$ and for each A in $\mathcal{F}'$, $p(\cdot, A)$ is $\mathcal{F}$-measurable ($\mathcal{F}/\mathcal{B}([0,1])$-measurable). Alternatively, if $\mathcal{P}(\Omega', \mathcal{F}')$ denotes the set of probability measures on $\mathcal{F}'$, a transition probability from Ω to Ω' is a function $p : \Omega \to \mathcal{P}(\Omega', \mathcal{F}')$ such that for each A in $\mathcal{F}'$, $p(\cdot)(A)$ is $\mathcal{F}$-measurable.

Some basic sets and spaces of interest in this paper are listed here. Their intended interpretations will become clear as the analysis develops. Let ℓ be a positive integer, $\ell \geq 2$ (the number of commodities). For each positive integer n, let $C_n = \mathbb{R}^\ell_+$, $F_n = \mathbb{R}^\ell$, $A_n = C_n \times F_n$, $S_n = \mathbb{R}^{2\ell}$, $H_n = A_{n-1} \times S_n$, $n \geq 2$, and $H_1 = S_1$. The Cartesian product of any of these sets through n is indicated with a subscript "(n)." Thus $S_{(n)} = S_1 \times \cdots \times S_n$ and $H_{(n)} = H_1 \times \cdots \times H_n$. The Cartesian product of any of these sets from $n+1$ on is indicated with a superscript "(n)." Thus $C^{(n)} = C_{n+1} \times C_{n+2} \times \cdots$ and $H^{(n)} = H_{n+1} \times H_{n+2} \times \cdots$. The symbol for a space without a sub- or superscript denotes the infinite product space, e.g., $C = C_1 \times C_2 \times \cdots$ and $H = H_{(n)} \times H^{(n)}$ for each n. For any product space having $S_n(A_n)(C_n)(F_n)$ as a factor, $\xi_n(\alpha_n)(\alpha_n^1)(\alpha_n^2)$ will denote the projection of the product onto $S_n(A_n)(C_n)(F_n)$. The map $\xi_n^1(\xi_n^2)$ denotes the projection of any product space with S_n as a factor onto the first (second) ℓ coordinates of S_n.

2.2 Markets, Commodities, and Prices.

We consider an exchange economy where markets are open at each of an infinite sequence of dates, indexed by $\mathcal{N}$, for spot trading and limited futures trading. For simplicity, it is assumed that there are $\ell \geq 2$ elementary commodities traded at each date. Elementary commodities are those distinguishable by their physical characteristics and perhaps location but not by date or state of nature. At each date, futures contracts may be executed for unconditional receipt or delivery of each elementary commodity one period hence.[5] Here a period is simply the time elapsed between

[5] The extension of the model here to futures contracts with varying but

successive market dates.

The terms of exchange at each date n are expressed by a price system, in units of account, that assigns to each elementary commodity j two real numbers s_{nj} and $s_{n(\ell+j)}$, where s_{nj} is the spot price and $s_{n(\ell+j)}$ is the futures price of commodity j. To say that at date n the price system $s_n = (s_{n1}, \ldots, s_{n2\ell})$ prevails means the following. To obtain a unit of commodity j an agent will in general have to trade other commodities or claims to other commodities. To obtain delivery at date n of one unit of commodity j in terms of current (spot) delivery of commodity k, an agent must deliver to the spot market at n s_{nj}/s_{nk} units of commodity k, provided $s_{nk} \neq 0$. If $s_{nk} = 0$, exchange for commodity j in terms of current delivery of commodity k is not possible. To obtain delivery at date n of one unit of commodity j in terms of a future claim on commodity k, an agent must contract to deliver to the spot market at date $n+1$ $s_{nj}/s_{n(\ell+k)}$ units of commodity k, provided $s_{n(\ell+k)} \neq 0$. If $s_{n(\ell+k)} = 0$, exchange for commodity j in terms of future delivery of commodity k is not possible. The exchange ratios $s_{n(\ell+j)}/s_{nk}$ and $s_{n(\ell+j)}/s_{n(\ell+k)}$ have similar interpretations when they are defined. If $s_{nj} = 0$, exchange in terms of commodity j if $j \leq \ell$ or in terms of future claims on commodity $j-\ell$ if $j > \ell$ is not possible.

It appears from these interpretations that what is important for agents' trade decisions is relative prices. This is in fact the case in standard general equilibrium models [Debreu, 1959] primarily because there is no primitive data of these models that depend on prices. In models of temporary general equilibrium, however, agents' opinions are data and these opinions at any date depend, in general, on the past history of prices and on the prevailing price system. The past history and prevailing price system enter an agent's derived utility function through conditional expectation (see Section 5). In this case, the all importance of relative prices comes into question.

From an economic modeling point of view, there are two sides to this question. First, one must determine the set of price histories, including current or prevailing prices, for which each agent must be assumed to re-

---

bounded contract length appears feasible though complicated. Such an extension is of interest in developing a term structure of futures contracts but is beyond the scope of this analysis.

spond by the formation of an opinion regarding future prices. Secondly, one must specify the range of these opinions. In models of temporary equilibrium, there is every reason not to restrict consideration on either side to normalized or relative prices. Not only is demand, in general, not positively linear homogeneous in prices, but such restrictions preclude studying price level dynamics of sequences of temporary equilibria and formulating and studying hypotheses of inflationary and deflationary expectations. While these price level issues are not immediate objectives of this work, the model developed here may provide the foundation for such investigations.

The price space for each date n is therefore taken to be S_n. Although in principle agents will be assumed to have a well defined opinion regarding future prices at date n for every history $s_{(n)}$ in $S_{(n)}$, for purpose of analysis, only price systems in $\mathbb{R}^{2\ell}_{+0}$ will matter. The role played by normalized prices in the sequel will be strictly a technical one.

2.3 Agent Characteristics. An agent is viewed as an idealized decision making unit that engages in trade at each date, and hence lives forever, and faces uncertainty at each date only regarding prices that will prevail at future market dates. The typical agent is identified by a 4-tuple $\langle b_0, \omega, \precsim, q\rangle$, where $b_0 = (b_{01}, \ldots, b_{0\ell}) \in \mathbb{R}^\ell$, $\omega = \{\omega_n\}_{n\in\mathcal{N}} \in C$, $\precsim \subseteq \mathcal{P}(C) \times \mathcal{P}(C)$, and $q = \{q_n\}_{n\in\mathcal{N}}$ is a sequence of transition probabilities $q_n : H_{(n)} \times A_n \to \mathcal{P}(S_{n+1})$, each n in $\mathcal{N}$.

The vector b_0 represents the preexisting contracts of the agent that must be honored at date 1. If $b_{0j} < 0$, the agent has contracted to deliver $-b_{0j}$ units of commodity j at date 1 and if $b_{0j} > 0$, the agent has contracted to receive b_{0j} units of commodity j at date 1.

The sequence ω is a naturally occurring endowment posterity, with ω_n interpreted as a vector of elementary commodities made available to the agent at date n. In general, at any date prior to n, an agent would be uncertain regarding ω_n. For simplicity however, we assume that ω is known with certainty at date 1. A more realistic point of view would be to assume that an agent's endowment sequence is a predictable stochastic process or to assume predictability of some lower bounds for the stochastic process of endowments (c.f. [Radner, 1967]). These generalizations may form the basis of research on sequences of random temporary equilibria and their asymptotic behavior.

Assumption (A.1). *$\omega_1 + b_0 \in \mathbb{R}^\ell_{+0}$ and $\omega_n \in \mathbb{R}^\ell_{++}$, $n \geq 2$.*

Remarks 2.3.1. The quantity $\omega_1 + b_0$ is the agent's naturally occurring endowment for date 1 augmented by the vector of preexisting contracts. The assumption that $\omega_1 + b_0 \geq 0$ is an initializing condition. This assumption together with strict positivity of ω_n, $n \geq 2$, is needed in obtaining lower hemicontinuity of feasible action relations (Section 3). Some such positivity or semi-positivity conditions are common in general equilibrium models.

The relation $\precsim$ is a preference ordering that is assumed to satisfy the usual version of the expected utility hypothesis [Grandmont, 1977: Assumption 1], and a risk aversion and monotonicity hypothesis [Green, 1973: 2.4(b), (c)].

Assumption (A.2). *There exists a bounded continuous function $u : C \to \mathbb{R}$ such that (i) if $\nu^1, \nu^2 \in \mathcal{P}(C)$, $\nu^1 \precsim \nu^2$ if and only if $\int u d\nu^1 \leq \int u d\nu^2$;*[6] *(ii) u is concave on C; and (iii) u is strictly increasing on C, i.e., if $c^1, c^2 \in C$ and $c^1 \leq c^2$, then $u(c^1) < u(c^2)$.*

The sequence $q = \{q_n\}_{n \in \mathcal{N}}$ of transition probabilities is referred to as an opinion and its nth component q_n as a date n opinion. For each history $(h_{(n)}, a_n)$, $q_n(h_{(n)}, a_n)$ is the agent's subjective probability measure over date $n+1$ (equilibrium) price systems. The date n opinion q_n is the analog here of the agent's "expectation function" [Grandmont, 1977: p. 539].

Definitions (2.3.2). *For each integer n, define the correspondence $\sigma_n : H_{(n)} \times A_n \Rightarrow S_{n+1}$ by $\sigma_n(h_{(n)}, a_n) = \mathrm{supp}(q_n(h_{(n)}, a_n))$, where $\mathrm{supp}(\mu)$ denotes the support of the measure μ [Parthasarathy, 1967: p. 28]. While σ_n has closed values, these values need not be bounded. For technical purposes, it will suffice to work with a bounded transformation of σ_n. For $j = 1, 2$, let $e^j = (1, \ldots, 1) \in \mathbb{R}^{j\ell}$ and let $\Omega^j = \{x \in \mathbb{R}^{j\ell} : x \cdot e^j = 1\}$, where as usual $x \cdot y = \sum_{k=1}^{j\ell} x_k y_k$. For each n, define the relation $\bar{\sigma}_n : H_{(n)} \times A_n \Rightarrow \Omega^2$ by $\bar{\sigma}_n(h_{(n)}, a_n) = \mathrm{cl}(\tilde{\sigma}_n(h_{(n)}, a_n))$, where "cl" denotes the closure.*[7] *Then $\bar{\sigma}_n$ is compact valued and $\bar{\sigma}_n(h_{(n)}, a_n) = \emptyset$ if*

---

[6] Throughout, when the range of integration is unspecified, it is understood to be the whole space in question, in this case C.

[7] The notation "cl" and "int" denote closure and interior relative to the ambient factor space of H in which the set lies. In the case in (2.3.2) this space

and only if $q_n(h_{(n)}, a_n)(\{0\}) = 1$, *i.e.,* $q_n(h_{(n)}, a_n)$ *is degenerate at 0 in* $\mathbb{R}^{2\ell}$.

Conventions (2.3.3). *Henceforth, unless specifically stated otherwise, the quantifier "for each n in* $\mathcal{N}$*" is understood in all definitions, assumptions, theorems etc., in the sequel. Also, if the range of a variable is left unspecified in such statements it is understood to be the relevant projection or factor space of H. For example, in (A.3)(i) below, the range of* $(h_{(n)}, a_n)$ *and* $(h'_{(n)}, a'_n)$ *is the set* $H_{(n)} \times A_n$.

Assumption (A.3). *(i) If* $\xi_k(h_{(n)}, a_n) = \xi_k(h'_{(n)}, a'_n)$, $k = 1, \ldots, n$, *then* $q_n(h_{(n)}, a_n) = q_n(h'_{(n)}, a'_n)$*; (ii)* q_n *is continuous and the values of* σ_n *are convex subsets of* $\mathbb{R}^{2\ell}_+$*; (iii)* $\bar{\sigma}_n$ *is u.h.c. on* $H_{(n)} \times A_n$*; and (iv)* $q_n(\operatorname{int} \sigma_n(h_{(n)}, a_n) | h_{(n)}, a_n) = 1$.

Remark (2.3.4). Assumption (A.3)(i) states simply that opinions do not depend on the history of past and current actions. This assumption is implicit in most models of temporary competitive equilibrium reflecting the underlying assumption that agents are price takers, who, by definition, believe that their actions have no effect on price formation. We will alternately write q_n and objects derived from it, such as σ_n and $\bar{\sigma}_n$, as functions of the entire history or as functions defined on $S_{(n)}$ as convenience dictates.

Remark (2.3.5). The continuity assumption of (A.3)(ii) is also standard in temporary equilibrium models [Grandmont, 1977: Assumption 2], [Green, 1973: (3.1)]. As in [Green, 1973: Remark 3.1], this continuity assumption implies that σ_n is l.h.c. It then follows from (A.3)(ii)–(iv) that $\bar{\sigma}_n$ is non-empty ((iii) says this implicitly, but so does (iv)), compact, and convex valued and continuous on $H_{(n)} \times A_n$, since the mapping $x \to \tilde{x}$ is continuous on $\mathbb{R}^{2\ell}_{+0}$ and preserves convexity.

Remarks (2.3.6). From a strictly mathematical point of view, the convexity assumption of (A.3)(ii) is probably unnecessary since most of the results of this paper would hold without this assumption if everywhere σ_n is replaced by $\operatorname{co} \sigma_n$, the convex hull of σ_n. This greater generality, however, leads to the possibility (in [Nachman, 1980]) of a temporary

---

is S_{n+1} $(= \mathbb{R}^{2\ell})$, which is equivalent to taking the closure in Ω^2 since Ω^2 is closed in $\mathbb{R}^{2\ell}$. The relative interior of a convex set is denoted by "ri."

equilibrium price system, say at date $n \geq 2$ for a given history, for which for some agent this price system belongs to $\operatorname{co}\sigma_{n-1}$ but not to σ_{n-1} at that history. Such a possibility seems inconsistent with the interpretation of agent opinions as probabilistic forecasts of future price equilibria and precludes the possibility that opinions are even in the weakest sense realized or fulfilled at equilibrium. The convexity assumption simply avoids this issue and simplifies the analysis as well. The non-negativity assumption of (A.3)(ii) is consistent with (A.2)(iii) that implies that all commodities are desired [Green, 1973: (2.3)(ii)].

Remarks (2.3.7). The convexity assumption of (A.3)(ii) also rules out date n opinions with finite non-degenerate support, as does (A.3)(iv), which implies that $\operatorname{int}\sigma_n$ is non-empty valued. Equation (A.3)(iv) is a continuity hypothesis similar in spirit to those made about consumer preferences [Debreu, 1959: Section 4.6]. It is used in establishing lower hemi-continuity of the relation studied in Section 4. Opinions absolutely continuous with respect to Lebesgue measure or opinions with atoms that form a countably dense subset of some open convex set are consistent with (A.3)(iv). Assumption (A.3)(iii) is also a continuity hypothesis analogous to [Green, 1973: (3.2)].

Remark (2.3.8). Let $\sum_n^0$ denote the graph of $\operatorname{int}\sigma_n$. Under (A.3)(ii), (iv), $\sum_n^0$ is open in $H_{(n+1)}$. For by (2.3.5), $\operatorname{int}\sigma_n$ is a l.h.c. correspondence. It then follows that the triple $(H_{(n)} \times A_n, S_{n+1}, \operatorname{int}\sigma_n)$ satisfies [Cornwall, 1972: CST, p. 772] and by the remark following [Cornwall, 1972: Theorem 2], $\sum_n^0$ is open in $H_{(n)} \times A_n \times S_{n+1} = H_{(n+1)}$.

Definitions (2.3.9). *Price systems s_{n+1} in $\operatorname{int}\sigma_n(s_{(n)})$, in light of (A.3)(iv), are referred to as* forecasted price systems, price forecasts, *or simply as forecasts (at the price history $s_{(n)}$). If $x \in \mathbb{R}^\ell$, x is a* spot (futures) price forecast *if $x = \xi_{n+1}^1(s_{n+1})(\xi_{n+1}^2(s_{n+1}))$ for some price forecast s_{n+1}. Similarly, if $x = \tilde{s}_{n+1}$ for a price forecast s_{n+1}, then x is referred to as a* relative price forecast. *For such x, $\gamma\xi_{n+1}^1(x)$ is a spot price forecast and $\gamma\xi_{n+1}^2(x)$ is a futures price forecast for some scalar γ.*

Definitions (2.3.10). *Of particular interest in analyzing agent choice is the set of current price systems whose futures price component is a spot price forecast for the subsequent date, appropriately scaled. For $B \subseteq \mathbb{R}^m$,*

$B \neq \emptyset$, let $\Gamma(B)$ denote the smallest cone containing B. For $n = 1$, define

$$Q_1 = \{s_1 : \xi_1^1(s_1) \in \mathbf{R}^\ell_{++}, \xi_1^2(s_1) \in \xi_2^1(\Gamma(\operatorname{int} \sigma_1))\},$$

and for $n \geq 2$, let $Q_n : S_{(n-1)} \Rightarrow S_n$ be defined by

$$Q_n(s_{(n-1)}) = \{s_n : \xi_n^1(s_n) \in \mathbf{R}^\ell_{++}, \xi_n^2(s_n) \in \xi_{n+1}^1(\Gamma(\operatorname{int} \sigma_n(s_{(n-1)}, s_n)))\}.$$

Then Q_n associates to a price history $s_{(n-1)}$ the set of date n price systems s_n that are positive and whose futures price component $\xi_n^2(s_n)$, perhaps after some scaling, is a spot price forecast for date $n+1$ at the history *$(s_{(n-1)}, s_n)$. A similar interpretation applies to the set Q_1, which is the analog here of the set S in [Green, 1973: p. 116].*

Remark (2.3.11). It follows from (2.3.8) by a straight forward argument that Q_1 is an open subset of S_1 and that for $n \geq 2$, Q_n is open valued and has an open graph in $S_{(n)}$.

The importance of the price systems in $Q_n(s_{(n-1)})$ is that at these prices and only at these prices is an agent's set of feasible actions at date n bounded (Theorem (3.2.2)). In light of this result, it seems reasonable to require that $Q_1 \neq \emptyset$ and that for $n \geq 2$ and each $s_{(n-1)}$, $q_{n-1}(Q_n(s_{(n-1)}) \mid s_{(n-1)}) = 1$. If this latter condition holds, then $\operatorname{int} \sigma_{n-1}(s_{(n-1)}) \subseteq \operatorname{int}(\operatorname{cl} Q_n(s_{(n-1)}))$ by (A.3)(iv). For technical reasons it is convenient to have $\operatorname{int} \sigma_{n-1}(s_{(n-1)}) \subseteq Q_n(s_{(n-1)})$. This would be the case under the assumption that $Q_n(s_{(n-1)})$ has subjective probability one if this set is a regular open set, e.g., if it is convex. These conditions, however, are not necessary or interpretable, and we assume the desired result.

Assumption (A.4). *$Q_1 \neq \emptyset$ and for $n \geq 2$ and $s_{(n-1)}$ in $S_{(n-1)}$, $\operatorname{int} \sigma_{n-1}(s_{(n-1)}) \subseteq Q_n(s_{(n-1)})$.*

Remark (2.3.12). In the presence of (A.3)(i), the non-negativity and convexity parts of (A.3)(ii), and (A.3)(iv), the inclusion assumed in (A.4) is implied by a version of the expectations hypothesis that, for positive current futures prices, conditional expected spot prices equal current futures prices. To formulate this hypothesis, let $q = \{q_n\}_{n \in \mathcal{N}}$ be an opinion satisfying the parts of (A.3) just mentioned, and let $q_0 \in \mathcal{P}(S_1)$ be some (subjective) distribution for initial date prices. The sequence $\{q_n\}_{n \geq 0}$

determines a unique probability measure on $(S, \mathcal{B}(S))$ [Ash, 1972: Theorem (2.7.2)], call it P, and for each $n \geq 1$, q_n is a regular conditional distribution for P of ξ_{n+1} given $\xi_1, \ldots, \xi_n$ [Breiman, 1968: p. 79], where these functions are the projections of the infinite product space S onto the factors S_{n+1} and $S_1, \ldots, S_n$, respectively. Thus a version of the (vector of) conditional expectation(s) under P of ξ_{n+1} given $\xi_1, \ldots, \xi_n$ is given by the composition of the vector integral $\int s_{n+1} q_n(ds_{n+1} \mid s_1, \ldots, s_n)$ (which exists by non-negativity of the support $\sigma_n(s_1, \ldots, s_n)$) with the mapping $s \to (\xi_1(s), \ldots, \xi_n(s))$. Suggestively, let $E(\xi_{n+1} \mid \xi_1, \ldots, \xi_n)$ denote this version. Clearly, the projection of $E(\xi_{n+1} \mid \xi_1, \ldots, \xi_n)$ onto its first ℓ coordinates is a version of the conditional expectation of date $n+1$ spot prices, ξ^1_{n+1}, given $\xi_1, \ldots, \xi_n$, which we also denote suggestively by $E(\xi^1_{n+1} \mid \xi_1, \ldots, \xi_n)$. The expectations hypothesis is that $E(\xi^1_{n+1} \mid \xi_1, \ldots, \xi_n)(s) = \xi^2_n(s)$ for every $s \in S$ such that $\xi^2_n(s) > 0$ (note the integrability assumption implicit here). (More generally, one could have $E(\xi^1_{n+1} \mid \xi_1, \ldots, \xi_n) = \lambda \xi^2_n$ for some positive scalar function λ defined on S and measurable with respect to $\xi_1, \ldots, \xi_n$.) But under the convexity assumption of (A.3)(ii) and (A.3)(iv), it follows that $E(\xi_{n+1} \mid \xi_1, \ldots, \xi_n)(s) \in \operatorname{int} \sigma_n(\xi_1(s), \ldots, \xi_n(s))$ for every $s \in S$. Thus from the expectations hypothesis, $\xi^2_n(s) \in \xi^1_{n+1}(\operatorname{int} \sigma_n(\xi_1(s), \ldots, \xi_n(s)))$ if $\xi^2_n(s) > 0$ (here using ξ^1_{n+1} as the projection of S_{n+1} onto its first ℓ coordinates). In particular, if $\xi_n(s) \in \operatorname{int} \sigma_{n-1}(\xi_1(s), \ldots, \xi_{n-1}(s))$ and $n \geq 2$, then $\xi_n(s) \in Q_n(\xi_1(s), \ldots, \xi_{n-1}(s))$, as assumed in (A.4).

Remark (2.3.13). The expectations hypothesis just formulated violates the continuity assumption of (A.3)(ii) if the parts of (A.3) assumed in (2.3.12) are maintained. For suppose that $(s^k_1, s^k_2, \ldots) = s^k \in S$, $k = 0, 1, \ldots$, with s^k converging to s^0, $s^k_n = \xi_n(s^k) > 0$, $k = 1, 2, \ldots$, and $\xi^2_{nj}(s^0) = 0$, for some $j = 1, \ldots, \ell$, where ξ^2_{nj} is the jth coordinate of ξ^2_n. Let $q^k_n = q_n(s^k_1, \ldots, s^k_n)$, $k = 0, 1, \ldots$, and let ξ^1_{n+1j} denote the jth coordinate of ξ^1_{n+1}. The expectations hypothesis entails that $\lim_k \int \xi^1_{n+j} dq^k_n = \lim_k \xi^2_{nj}(s^k) = 0$, and hence, by the non-negativity in (A.3)(ii), that the sequence of functions $f_k \equiv \xi^1_{n+1j}$ on the measure spaces $(S_{n+1}, \mathcal{B}(S_{n+1}), q^k_n)$, $k = 1, 2, \ldots$, is uniformly integrable [Hildenbrand, 1974: (40), p. 52]. But under the continuity assumption of (A.3)(ii), q^k_n converges weakly to q^0_n. It follows that $\int \xi^1_{n+1j} dq^0_n = \lim_k \int \xi^1_{n+1j} dq^k_n = 0$ [Hildenbrand, 1974: (42), p. 52]. But this is impossible under the rest of (A.3)(ii) unless the marginal distribution of ξ^1_{n+1j} under q^0_n is degenerate at zero, which violates (A.3)(iv).

The dilemma posed by these last remarks is a dramatic example of an ex ante version of a fundamental problem raised by Jordan [1976: pp. 455-456]. In the present case this problem amounts to the choice between positivity of subjective opinions about equilibrium prices and the continuity of these opinions on the boundary of positive prices on the one hand and the ex ante unbiasedness of current futures prices as forecasts of future spot prices on the other hand. If one insists on the former, one cannot have the latter, i.e., expectations about (the unbiased estimates of) future spot prices must differ from current futures prices at least in some neighborhood of each boundary point of positive current futures prices.

While the expectations hypothesis has considerable intuitive appeal and it does explicate the inclusion assumed in (A.4), it is by no means compelling either as an a priori hypothesis, the relevant case here, or as a condition of equilibrium in a competitive setting with or without rational expectations.[8] One might avoid ruling out the expectations hypothesis in the context here by foregoing continuity of q_n on the boundary of $\mathbb{R}^{2\ell}_{++}$ while maintaining lower hemi-continuity of σ_n on this boundary, but we have not explored this possibility. Alternatively, one might modify the hypothesis so that it holds, for date n, only for those price systems in $\operatorname{int}\sigma_{n-1}(\cdot)$, for this is all that is required to produce (A.4). In anticipation of [Nachman, 1980: Theorem (3.2.2)], however, the contradiction produced in Remark (2.3.13) would remain.

Finally, we note that (A.4) is itself a weak form of a restricted expectations hypothesis. It states that the futures component of every price forecast for date n is, up to scale change, a forecast of spot prices for date $n+1$, where the term "forecast" is used in the weak sense of (2.3.9)

[8] The well known and ongoing controversy over whether or not futures prices are or should be unbiased estimates of spot prices is at the heart of theories of speculation and hedging [Cootner, 1967; Gray and Rutledge, 1971]. There is also a growing literature on the so-called "martingale" or unbiasedness property of asset prices in the rational expectations setting that indicates that this property need not and in general will not hold in such equilibria [Leroy, 1979].

as opposed to conditional mean forecasts. This provides sufficient intuition for this work to proceed on the basis of (A.3) and (A.4). That these assumptions are consistent can be seen by a trivial example. Let $q_n \equiv \nu \in \mathcal{P}(\mathbf{R}^{2\ell})$ with $\nu(\mathbf{R}^{2\ell}_{++}) = 1$ and $\text{supp}(\nu) = \mathbf{R}^{2\ell}_{+}$. Then (A.3) holds, $Q_1 \equiv Q_n(s_{(n-1)}) \equiv \mathbf{R}^{2\ell}_{++}$, and consequently (A.4) holds as well.

3. Feasible Actions

3.1 Bankruptcy and Feasibility. At each date n, when feasible, an agent chooses a vector c_n in C_n of elementary commodities and a vector $b_n = (b_{n1}, \ldots, b_{n\ell})$ of futures contracts, where $b_{nk} > (<)\ 0$ indicates a contract to receive (deliver) $|b_{nk}|$ units of commodity k at date $n+1$. To determine feasibility, agents use the prevailing price system at date n to present value their known endowment augmented by previous contractual obligations.

Conventions (3.1.1). *For each n, let $f_{n-1} = \omega_n + b_{n-1}$. Then f_{n-1} is a vector of net futures contracts made at date $n-1$ corresponding to the vector of futures contracts b_{n-1}, and (f_{n-1}, ω_{n+1}) is the part of the agent's known endowment, augmented by preexisting contracts, relevant for trade at date n. The sense in which f_n represents net futures contracts made at date n is explained below. Since f_n is determined when b_n is and vice versa, we can focus on f_n as the futures part of the agent's action at date n. Formally, an action for an agent at date n is a vector $a_n = (c_n, f_n)$ in A_n, where c_n denotes consumption and f_n denotes net futures contracts. A history $h_{(n)}$ in $H_{(n)}$ for the agent is then a sequence of prices and actions up through prices at date n. For such a history $h_{(n)}$, $\alpha^2_{n-1}(h_{(n)})$ is the vector of net futures contracts made at date $n-1$ with the convention that $\alpha^2_0(h_{(1)}) \equiv \omega_1 + b_0 \equiv f_0$.*

Definitions (3.1.2). *Define $r_n : H_{(n)} \to \mathbf{R}$ by $r_n(h_{(n)}) = \xi_n(h_{(n)}) \cdot (\alpha^2_{n-1}(h_{(n)}), \omega_{n+1})$. Then r_n is agent specific and $r_n(h_{(n)})$ is the present value at prices $\xi_n(h_{(n)})$ of the agent's known augmented endowment at the history $h_{(n)}$. If $r_n(h_{(n)}) \geq 0$, the agent is solvent at $h_{(n)}$, and in this case the agent may execute spot trades and futures contracts subject to the usual budgetary restriction, i.e., the agent may choose an action from the budget set $\hat{D}^1_n(h_{(n)}) \equiv \{a_n \in A_n : \xi_n(h_{(n)}) \cdot a_n \leq r_n(h_{(n)})\}$. If*

$r_n(h_{(n)}) < 0$, *the agent is (defined to be) bankrupt at* $h_{(n)}$, *and in order to avoid institutional arrangements for handling bankruptcy, the budgetary relation is defined to be empty at* $h_{(n)}$. *Formally, the budgetary relation* $D_n^1 : H_{(n)} \Rightarrow A_n$ *is defined by*

$$D_n^1(h_{(n)}) = \begin{cases} \hat{D}_n^1(h_{(n)}), & \text{if } r_n(h_{(n)}) \geq 0, \\ \emptyset, & \text{if } r_n(h_{(n)}) < 0. \end{cases}$$

Remark (3.1.3). Clearly r_n is a continuous function and $\operatorname{dom} D_n^1 = \{h_{(n)} : r_n(h_{(n)}) \geq 0\}$ is a closed set as is any section of this set.

If there is to be any hope for determinateness of intertemporal choice with the specifications of (3.1.2), an agent must plan to be solvent with subjective certainty.

Definition (3.1.4). *Define the relation* $D_n^2 : H_{(n)} \Rightarrow A_n$ *by*

$$D_n^2(h_{(n)}) = \{a_n \in A_n : q_n(\operatorname{dom} D_{n+1}^1(h_{(n)}, a_n) \mid h_{(n)}, a_n) = 1\}.$$

Then $D_n^2(h_{(n)})$ *is the set of date n actions where with subjective probability one the agent will be solvent at date* $n+1$.

Remark (3.1.5). $D_n^2(h_{(n)}) = \{a_n : r_{n+1}(h_{(n)}, a_n, s_{n+1}) \geq 0$, for all $s_{n+1} \in \sigma_n(h_{(n)}, a_n)\}$. This follows from the fact that the section $\operatorname{dom} D_{n+1}^1(h_{(n)}, a_n)$ is closed and $\sigma_n(h_{(n)}, a_n)$ is the smallest closed set with $q_n(h_{(n)}, a_n)$-measure one [Parthasarathy, 1967: Theorem 2.1, p. 27].

Definition (3.1.6). *Feasible actions for the agent at date n are those that satisfy the budgetary relation* D_n^1 *and the planning relation* D_n^2, *i.e., the feasible action relation* $D_n : H_{(n)} \Rightarrow A_n$ *is defined by*

$$D_n(h_{(n)}) = D_n^1(h_{(n)}) \cap D_n^2(h_{(n)}).$$

We let $\Delta_n = \text{graph } D_n = \{(h_{(n)}, a_n) : a_n \in D_n(h_{(n)})\}$.

Bankruptcy, as we have defined it, is synonymous with negative net worth, and is, as Stigum [1974: c10.1 1.2] has noted, somewhat arbitrary from an economic theory perspective. According to this point of view an agent should be declared bankrupt only when he cannot meet his maturing contractual obligations by trading on current markets. The appropriate formulation of the budgetary relation in this case would be simply the budget set relation $\hat{D}_n^1$. An agent would be bankrupt at $h_{(n)}$ in this formulation if and only if $\hat{D}_n^1(h_{(n)}) = \emptyset$, irrespective of the sign of $r_n(h_{(n)})$. For intertemporal consistency then, one would define $\hat{D}_n^2(h_{(n)})$ as in (3.1.4) with dom $\hat{D}_{n+1}^1$ replacing dom D_{n+1}^1.

The problem with this formulation is that under (A.3)(i), if $\Gamma(\Omega^1 \times \{0\}) = \{s_{n+1} : \xi_{n+1}^1(s_{n+1}) \geq 0 = \xi_{n+1}^2(s_{n+1})\}$ has measure zero under $q_n(h_{(n)}, a_n)$, which holds under (A.3)(ii), (iv), then $\hat{D}_n^2(h_{(n)}) = A_n$. Thus for $\hat{D}_n^2$ to impose some constraint on choice at date n and history $h_{(n)}$, it is necessary that $\Gamma(\Omega^1 \times \{0\})$ have positive $q_n(h_{(n)}, a_n)$-measure, for some and hence all a_n. Establishing existence of temporary competitive equilibrium in this case by the methods employed here and in [Nachman, 1980] appears difficult. By these methods, the set $\Gamma(\Omega^1 \times \{0\})$ must, in a sense spelled out in [Nachman, 1980], constitute part of the boundary of $\Gamma(\sigma_n(h_{(n)}, a_n))$ for appropriate $h_{(n)}$.

The need for $\hat{D}_n^2$ to impose a constraint on date n actions stems from the fact that if $\hat{D}_n^1(h_{(n)}) \neq \emptyset$, this set is not bounded and is unbounded in the direction of increasing preferences (increasing c_n) unless $\xi_n^2(h_{(n)}) = 0 < \xi_n^1(h_{(n)})$. This follows also for D_n^1, but as will be shown below, D_n^2 imposes the needed bounds for appropriate histories. In this regard, the definition of bankruptcy in (3.1.2) seems less arbitrary. We leave for further study the formulation based on $\hat{D}_n^1$.

As a final comment before turning to the analysis of D_n, note that the accounting inequality $\xi_n(h_{(n)}) \cdot a_n \leq r_n(h_{(n)})$, in one sense, entails that the agent sell his entire date $n+1$ endowment ω_{n+1} on the futures markets at date n. For if $f_{n-1} = \alpha_{n-1}^2(h_{(n)})$ and $a_n = (c_n, f_n)$, then the inequality can be written as $\xi_n^1(h_{(n)}) \cdot c_n + \xi_n^2(h_{(n)}) \cdot b_n \leq \xi_n^1(h_{(n)}) \cdot (\omega_n + b_{n-1})$, where of course $b_{n-1} = f_{n-1} - \omega_{n+1}$. This is the sense in which f_n represents net futures contracts, total futures contracts b_n net of the endowment $-\omega_{n+1}$. Since we impose no restrictions on the choice of f_n that would not be imposed on the quantity $\omega_{n+1} + b_n$ and vice versa, i.e., $f_n \equiv \omega_{n+1} + b_n$ is a true identity throughout our analysis, whether or not the agent must sell his future endowment is a matter of interpretation.

3.2 Regularity of Feasible Actions. In this section we are concerned with regularity of the relation D_n defined in (3.1.6). Throughout this section and the sequel, Assumptions (A.1)–(A.4) are maintained. The first result concerns closedness and convexity of D_n.

Lemma (3.2.1). *Δ_n is a non-empty closed subset of $H_{(n)} \times A_n$ and D_n is closed and convex valued on $H_{(n)}$.*

Proof. Clearly $0 \in D_n(h_{(n)})$ for every $h_{(n)}$ in $\operatorname{dom} D_n$. By (A.1), $\mathbb{R}^{2\ell}_+ \subseteq \operatorname{dom} D_1$, and for $n \geq 2$, $\{h_{(n)} : \alpha^2_{n-1}(h_{(n)}) \in \mathbb{R}^\ell_+, \xi_n(h_{(n)}) \in \mathbb{R}^{2\ell}_+\} \subseteq \operatorname{dom} D_n$. Thus $\Delta_n \neq \emptyset$. The remainder of the lemma follows essentially as in [Green, 1973: Lemma 3.3] using continuity of ξ_n and r_n and lower hemi-continuity of σ_n. □

The interest in Q_n stems from the following characterization of histories $h_{(n)}$ for which $D_n(h_{(n)})$ is bounded.

Theorem (3.2.2). *If $h_{(n)} \in \operatorname{dom} D_n$, then $D_n(h_{(n)})$ is bounded if and only if $\xi_n(h_{(n)}) \in Q_n(\xi_1(h_{(n)}), \ldots, \xi_{n-1}(h_{(n)}))$ ($= Q_1$, for $n = 1$).*

Proof. Suppose that $\xi_n(h_{(n)}) \in Q_n(\xi_1(h_{(n)}) \ldots, \xi_{n-1}(h_{(n)}))$ and $h_{(n)} \in \operatorname{dom} D_n$. The proof that $D_n(h_{(n)})$ is bounded is by contradiction, essentially as in [Green, 1973: Lemma 2.2]. If $D_n(h_{(n)})$ is not bounded, there exists a sequence $\{a^k\}_{k\in\mathcal{N}} \subseteq D_n(h_{(n)})$ such that $\|a^k\| \to \infty$. It follows that either $\|\alpha^1_n(a^k)\| \to \infty$ or $\|\alpha^2_n(a^k)\| \to \infty$. Since $a^k \in D_n(h_{(n)})$ for every k, the valuation inequalities $\xi^2_n(h_{(n)}) \cdot \alpha^2_n(a^k) \leq r_n(h_{(n)})$ and $r_{n+1}(h_{(n)}, a^k, (\gamma\xi^2_n(h_{(n)}), p)) \geq 0$ hold for some scalar $\gamma > 0$ and some p in $\mathbb{R}^\ell$ and all $k \in \mathcal{N}$. If $\|\alpha^2_n(a^k)\| \to \infty$, then using these inequalities one can find a subsequence $\{a^{k'}\}$ of $\{a^k\}$ and a price system s_{n+1} in $\operatorname{int}\sigma_n(h_{(n)}, a^k)$, all k in $\mathcal{N}$, such that $\xi^1_{n+1}(s_{n+1}) \cdot \alpha^2_n(a^{k'}) \downarrow -\infty$ as $k' \to \infty$. But then $r_{n+1}(h_{(n)}, a^{k'}, s_{n+1}) < 0$ for k' sufficiently large, in contradiction of the fact that $a^k \in D^2_n(h_{(n)})$ for all k.

Thus it must be the case that $\|\alpha^1_n(a^k)\| \to \infty$. But $a^k \in D^1_n(h_{(n)})$ for every k implies that $0 \leq \xi^1_n(h_{(n)}) \cdot \alpha^1_n(a^k) \leq r_n(h_{(n)}) - \xi^2_n(h_{(n)}) \cdot \alpha^2_n(a^k) \leq M$ for some $M < \infty$. By definition, $\xi^1_n(h_{(n)}) \in \mathbb{R}^\ell_{++}$ and $\alpha^1_n(h_{(n)}) \in \mathbb{R}^\ell_+$, and the contradiction ensues.

To prove the converse, let $h_{(n)}$ be in $\operatorname{dom} D_n$ but assume that $\xi_n(h_{(n)}) \notin Q_n(\xi_1(h_{(n)}), \ldots, \xi_{n-1}(h_{(n)}))$. Clearly, if $\xi^1_n(h_{(n)}) \not> 0$, then $D_n(h_{(n)})$ is not bounded. Therefore, assume that $\xi^1_n(h_{(n)}) > 0$. The proof in this case follows [Green, 1973: Lemma 2.5]. Since $h_{(n)}$ is fixed, let $\Gamma = \Gamma(\sigma_n(\xi_1(h_{(n)}), \ldots, \xi_n(h_{(n)})))$. Then Γ is a convex cone and $\operatorname{int}\Gamma = \Gamma(\operatorname{int}\sigma_n(\xi_1(h_{(n)}), \ldots, \xi_n(h_{(n)}))) \neq \emptyset$. By assumption, for every $\gamma > 0$

and p in $\mathbb{R}^\ell$, $(\gamma\xi_n^2(h_{(n)}), p) \notin \operatorname{int}\Gamma$. Let $\Gamma' = \{x \in \mathbb{R}^\ell : (x, y) \in \Gamma$, some $y \in \mathbb{R}^\ell\}$. By [Rockafeller, 1970: Theorem 6.8] and openness of the projection map of $\mathbb{R}^{2\ell}$ onto $\mathbb{R}^\ell$, it follows that for every $\gamma > 0$, $\gamma\xi_n^2(h_{(n)}) \notin ri\Gamma' = \operatorname{int}\Gamma' \neq \emptyset$.

By the usual separation arguments [Rockafeller, 1970: Theorem 11.6], there exists a vector y in $\mathbb{R}^\ell$ such that $y \neq 0$, $\xi_n^2(h_{(n)}) \cdot y = 0$, and $x \cdot y \geq 0$ for all $x \in \Gamma'$. It is then easy to show from these properties that $(0, \lambda y) \in D_n(h_{(n)})$ for all λ in $\mathbb{R}$. Thus $D_n(h_{(n)})$ is unbounded. □

Let $Q_1^* = Q_1$ and for $n \geq 2$, let Q_n^* denote the graph of Q_n considered as a subset of $H_{(n)}$, that is, $Q_n^* = \{h_{(n)} \in H_{(n)} : \xi_n(h_{(n)}) \in Q_n(\xi_1(h_{(n)}), \ldots, \xi_{n-1}(h_{(n)}))\}$.

Theorem (3.2.3). *D_n is u.h.c. and compact valued at each point of* dom $D_n \cap Q_n^*$.

Proof. By Lemma (3.2.1), (i) Δ_n is closed in $H_{(n)} \times A_n$, (ii) D_n is convex valued on dom D_n, and (iii) $0 \in D_n(h_{(n)})$ for each $h_{(n)}$ in dom D_n. By Lemma (A.I) in the Appendix, D_n is u.h.c. at each $h_{(n)}$ in dom D_n where $D_n(h_{(n)})$ is compact. The result then follows from Theorem (3.2.2). □

Definition (3.2.4). *For each n, let $\bar{r}_{n+1} : H_{(n)} \times A_n \to \mathbb{R}$ be defined by $\bar{r}_{n+1}(h_{(n)}, a_n) = \min\{r_{n+1}(h_{(n)}, a_n, x) : x \in \bar{\sigma}_n(h_{(n)}, a_n)\}$. Then $\bar{r}_{n+1}(h_{(n)}, a_n)$ is the minimum present value, in terms of relative price forecasts and their limits, of the agent's wealth at date $n+1$ given the history $h_{(n)}$ and action a_n.*

Lemma (3.2.5). *$\bar{r}_{n+1}$ is continuous and for each $h_{(n)}$, $\bar{r}_{n+1}(h_{(n)}, \cdot)$ is concave on A_n and $a_n \in D_n^2(h_{(n)})$ if and only if $r_{n+1}(h_{(n)}, a_n) \geq 0$.*

Proof. Follows directly from Remarks (2.3.5) and (3.1.3) and the usual maximum theorems, e.g., [Hildenbrand, 1974: Corollary, p. 30]. □

In establishing where D_n is l.h.c., one encounters a problem analogous to the minimum wealth problem of standard general equilibrium analysis [Debreu, 1959: Section 4.8]. As one might expect from this analogy, D_n is l.h.c. wherever r_n is positive. Let $D_n^+ = \{h_{(n)} : r_n(h_{(n)}) > 0\}$.

Theorem (3.2.6). *D_n is l.h.c. at each point of D_n^+.*

Proof. Let $h_{(n)}$ be in D_n^+ and let $\{h_{(n)}^k\}_{k\in\mathcal{N}}$ be such that $\lim_k h_{(n)}^k = h_{(n)}$. Since D_n^+ is open, we may assume that $h_{(n)}^k \in D_n^+$ for each k. If $a_n \in D_n(h_{(n)})$, choose f in $\mathbb{R}_{++}^\ell$ such that $\xi_n^2(h_{(n)}) \cdot f < r_n(h_{(n)})$, and let $a = (0, f)$. Then $a \in D_n^1(h_{(n)})$. Also, $(f, \omega_{n+2}) > 0$ and hence $\bar{r}_{n+1}(h_{(n)}, a) > 0$. By Lemma (3.2.5), $a \in D_n(h_{(n)})$. For each scalar λ with $0 \leq \lambda \leq 1$, let $a(\lambda) = \lambda a_n + (1-\lambda)a$. By Lemma (3.2.1), $a(\lambda) \in D_n(h_{(n)})$. In particular, for $0 \leq \lambda < 1$, $\xi_n(h_{(n)}) \cdot a(\lambda) < r_n(h_{(n)})$ and by Lemma (3.2.5) again, $\bar{r}_{n+1}(h_{(n)}, a(\lambda)) > 0$. It is then straight forward, as in [Green, 1973: Lemma 3.3], to construct a subsequence $\{h_{(n)}^{k'}\}$ of $\{h_{(n)}^k\}$ and a corresponding sequence $\{a^{k'}\}$ with $a^{k'}$ in $D_n(h_{(n)}^{k'})$ such that $\lim_{k'} a^{k'} = a_n$. By [Hildenbrand, 1974: Theorem 2, p. 27], this completes the proof. □

Remarks (3.2.7). Certainly $\mathbb{R}_+^\ell \times \mathbb{R}_{+0}^\ell \subseteq D_1^+$, and for $n \geq 2$, $\{h_{(n)} : \alpha_{n-1}^2(h_{(n)}) \in \mathbb{R}_+^\ell, \xi_n(h_{(n)}) \in \mathbb{R}_+^\ell \times \mathbb{R}_{+0}^\ell\} \subseteq D_n^+$. The important histories with regard to regularity of D_n can then be identified as follows. Recall the definition of $\sum_n^0$ in (2.3.8). Define $H_1^* = Q_1^*$, and for $n \geq 2$, define $H_n^* = (\Delta_{n-1} \times S_n) \cap \sum_{n-1}^0$. By Lemma (3.2.1), $H_n^* \neq \emptyset$ for each n.

Lemma (3.2.8). $H_n^* \subseteq D_n^+ \cap Q_n^*$.

Proof. By (A.4) it suffices to show that $H_n^* \subseteq D_n^+$. For $n = 1$ and $s_1 \in Q_1$, $s_1 > 0$ and hence $Q_1 \subseteq D_1^+$. For $n \geq 2$, let $h_{(n)} = (h_{(n-1)}, a_{n-1}, s_n)$ be in $H_{(n)}^*$. Then $a_{n-1} \in D_{n-1}(h_{(n-1)})$ and hence $r_n(h_{(n)}, a_{n-1}, s_n') \geq 0$ for all s_n' in $\sigma_{n-1}(h_{(n-1)}, a_{n-1})$. If $s_n' \in \operatorname{int} \sigma_{n-1}(h_{(n-1)}, a_{n-1})$, then $s_n' > 0$, and if $r_n(h_{(n-1)}, a_{n-1}, s_n') = 0$, then $\xi_n^1(s_n') \cdot \alpha_{n-1}^2(a_{n-1}) = -\xi_n^2(s_n') \cdot \omega_{n+1} < 0$. By altering an appropriate coordinate of $\xi_n^1(s_n')$ one can produce s_n'' in $\operatorname{int} \sigma_{n-1}(h_{(n-1)}, a_{n-1})$ such that $\xi_n^2(s_n'') = \xi_n^2(s_n')$ and

$$\xi_n^1(s_n'') \cdot \alpha_{n-1}^2(a_{n-1}) < \xi_n^1(s_n') \cdot \alpha_{n-1}^2(a_{n-1}).$$

But then $r_n(h_{(n-1)}, a_{n-1}, s_n'') < 0$, a contradiction. Since it follows that $r_n(h_{(n-1)}, a_{n-1}, s_n) > 0$, the proof is complete. □

4. Attainable Futures

4.1 The Dynamic Programming Problem.

In general, an agent's choice of an action at any market date n can depend on the entire history $h_{(n)}$ experienced by the agent up to the date n. As is common in formulations of sequential decision processes, it is convenient to allow the agent to make this choice by randomizing over feasible actions.

Definitions (4.1.1). *A* date n strategy *is any function* $\pi_n : H_{(n)} \to \mathcal{P}(A_n)$ *such that* π_n *is a transition probability from* $H_{(n)}$ *to* A_n. *In the context here (see Lemma (A.II)), such a function* π_n *is a transition probability if and only if* π_n *is* $\mathcal{B}(H_{(n)})/\mathcal{B}(\mathcal{P}(A_n))$*-measurable. A date n strategy* π_n *is said to be* feasible *if* $\pi_n(D_n(h_{(n)}) \mid h_{(n)}) = 1$ *for all* $h_{(n)}$ *in* dom D_n. *Since* D_n *has closed values,* π_n *is feasible if and only if* $\text{supp}(\pi_n(h_{(n)})) \subseteq D_n(h_{(n)})$, *each* $h_{(n)}$ *in* dom D_n. *The set of all feasible date n strategies is denoted by* Π_n.

Remark (4.1.2). For each n, $\Pi_n \neq \emptyset$. To see this, let $\bar{D}_n = D_n$ on dom D_n and $\bar{D}_n = A_n$, otherwise. It is easy to check that the correspondence $\bar{D}_n$ has a measurable graph and σ-compact values. By [Brown and Purves, 1973: Theorem 1], there exists a $\mathcal{B}(H_{(n)})$-measurable function $\pi_n : H_{(n)} \to A_n$ that selects from $\bar{D}_n$. Identifying π_n with the function whose value at $h_{(n)}$ is the probability measure degenerate at $\pi_n(h_{(n)})$ makes π_n a transition probability and clearly then $\pi_n \in \Pi_n$.

Definitions (4.1.3). *A* (feasible) date n plan *is a sequence* $\pi^n = \{\pi_m\}_{m \geq n}$, *where* π_m *is a (feasible) date m strategy for each* $m \geq n$. *The set of feasible date n plans is denoted by* Π^n. *A date 1 (feasible) plan is referred to simply as a (feasible) plan, and* Π *denotes the set of feasible plans.*

Given the agent's opinion $q = \{q_n\}_{n\in\mathcal{N}}$ and a date n plan $\pi^n = \{\pi_n\}_{m\geq n}$, there is a transition probability $\pi^n q \equiv \pi_n q_n \pi_{n+1} q_{n+1} \cdots$ from $H_{(n)}$ to $H^{(n)}$ given by the standard (conditional) product measure theorem [Ash, 1972: Theorem 2.7.2]. Similarly, for $n \geq 2$ there is a transition probability $q\pi^n \equiv q_{n-1}\pi_n q_n \pi_{n+1} \cdots = q_{n-1}\pi^n q$ from $H_{(n-1)} \times A_{n-1}$ to $S_n \times H^{(n)}$. For a plan π, we let $\pi q = \pi_1 q_1 \pi_2 q_2 \cdots$.

Expected Utility Maximization (4.1.4). The infinite horizon choice problem for the typical agent satisfying (A.1)–(A.4) is to find $\pi^* \in$

Π, if it exists, such that

$$\int_{H^{(1)}} u(\mathrm{proj}_C(h^{(1)}))\pi q(dh^{(1)} \mid h_{(1)}) \\ \leq \int_{H^{(1)}} u(\mathrm{proj}_C(h^{(1)}))\pi^* q(dh^{(1)} \mid h_{(1)}),$$

for every $h_{(1)}$ in H_1^* and every π in Π, where proj_C denotes the projection of $H^{(1)}$ onto the set C of consumption histories and u is the utility function of the agent given in (A.2). In words, the agent seeks a feasible plan that maximizes his expected utility (the integral above) for each initial date price system in Q_1. This last restriction of the problem arises because of the characterization of Theorem (3.2.2).

4.2 Attainable Futures: Continuity and Compactness.

In Section 5, we show that the problem of (4.1.4) does indeed have a solution and that the corresponding demand relations for this solution have the regularity properties needed for the equilibrium analysis of [Nachman, 1980]. To prepare the way for this solution, we consider an important relation between histories and posterities at a given date.[9]

Definitions (4.2.1). *For each n in $\mathcal{N}$, let $\mathcal{F}_n : H_{(n)} \times A_n \Rightarrow \mathcal{P}(S_{n+1} \times H^{(n+1)})$ be defined by*

$$\mathcal{F}_n(h_{(n)}, a_n) \\ = \{\nu \in \mathcal{P}(S_{n+1} \times H^{(n+1)}) : \nu = q\pi^{n+1}(h_{(n)}, a_n), \quad \pi^{n+1} \in \Pi^{n+1}\}.$$

The relation $\mathcal{F}_n$ associates with a history $(h_{(n)}, a_n)$ through date n the set of probability measures on posterities at $(h_{(n)}, a_n)$ that are attainable by following a feasible date $n+1$ plan. The elements of $\mathcal{F}_n(h_{(n)}, a_n)$ are referred to as attainable futures. *The relation $\mathcal{F}_n$ is analogous to Jordan's future decision rule relation [Jordan, 1977: 2.5] and the relation F^n of [Kertz and Nachman, 1979: (2.6)] was modeled on $\mathcal{F}_n$ with the current action variable included as part of the future at n.*

As we show in Section 5, at each date n and history $h_{(n)}$ in dom D_n, the agent can be viewed as selecting for each feasible action a_n an attainable future ν in $\mathcal{F}_n(h_{(n)}, a_n)$ to maximize expected utility conditional

---

[9] c.f. Definition (4.4.1). The term "posterity" is borrowed from [Sobel, 1975: p. 968].

on $(h_{(n)}, a_n)$, and then choosing a_n in $D_n(h_{(n)})$ to maximize this maximum expected utility conditional on $h_{(n)}$. The agent's demand relation is derived from this second stage of optimization.

Application of the usual maximum theorems is crucial in this two stage optimization process. The regularity required for the first stage is given in the following theorem. The proof of this result is involved and is given in Section 4.4.

Theorem (4.2.2). $\operatorname{dom} \mathcal{F}_n = H_{(n)} \times A_n$, *and* $\mathcal{F}_n|_{\Delta_n}$ *is continuous and compact valued.*

4.3 Attainable Futures: Convexity and Monotonicity.

To obtain concavity and monotonicity of the derived utility function of an agent, it is necessary to have a particular convexity property and a monotonicity property of the correspondence $\mathcal{F}_n$. The convexity property, the prototype of which is due to Jordan [1974: Proposition 2.33], involves the following setting. For $i = 1, 2$, let $\delta_n^i = (h_{(n)}, a_n^i)$ be an element of Δ_n, and let ν_1 be in $\mathcal{F}_n(\delta_n^i)$, $\nu_i = q_n \pi_{n+1}^i q_{n+1} \pi_{n+2}^i \cdots (\delta_n^i)$, where $\pi_{n+k}^i \in \Pi_{n+k}$ for each k in $\mathbb{N}$. For β given $0 < \beta < 1$, let $\delta_n = \beta\delta_n^1 + (1-\beta)\delta_n^2$, It follows from Lemma (3.2.1) that δ_n belongs to Δ_n. It is not the case necessarily, however, that $\beta\nu^1 + (1-\beta)\nu^2$ belongs to $\mathcal{F}_n(\delta_n)$, i.e., the graph of $\mathcal{F}_n|_{\Delta_n}$ need not be convex.

There is, however, a method of combining ν^1 and ν^2 so that the resulting combination belongs to $\mathcal{F}_n(\delta_n)$ and this combination is all that is needed (Lemma (5.3.1)) to establish concavity of the derived utility function.

Notation and Definitions (4.3.1). *Let* $\hat{H}_1 = H_1$ *and for* $n \geq 2$, *let* $\hat{H}_n = A_{n-1} \times A_{n-1} \times S_n$. *Then as in Section 2.1,* $\hat{H}_{(n)} = \hat{H}_1 \times \cdots \times \hat{H}_n$ *and* $\hat{H}^{(n)} = \hat{H}_{n+1} \times \hat{H}_{n+2} \times \cdots$. *If* $0 < \beta < 1$, *let* $\hat{\beta}_n : S_{n+1} \times \hat{H}^{(n+1)} \to S_{n+1} \times H^{(n+1)}$ *be defined by*

$$\hat{\beta}_n(s_{n+1}, \hat{h}^{(n+1)}) = (s_{n+1}, \beta a_{n+1}^1 + (1-\beta)a_{n+1}^2, s_{n+2}, \beta a_{n+2}^1 + (1-\beta)a_{n+2}^2, \ldots),$$

where $\hat{h}^{(n+1)} = (a_{n+1}^1, a_{n+1}^2, s_{n+2}, a_{n+2}^1, a_{n+2}^2, \ldots)$, *with* a_{n+k}^i *in* A_{n+k}, *all* k. *Since* A_{n+k} *is convex,* $\hat{\beta}_n$ *is well defined and is clearly continuous on* $S_{n+1} \times \hat{H}^{(n+1)}$. *For each* k *in* $\mathbb{N}$, *let* $\hat{H}_{(n+k)}^{(n)} = S_{n+1} \times \hat{H}_{n+2} \times \cdots \times \hat{H}_{n+k}$

with $\hat{H}^{(n)}_{(n+1)} = S_{n+1}$, *and define* $\hat{\pi}_{n+k} : \hat{H}^{(n)}_{(n+k)} \to \mathcal{P}(A_{n+k} \times A_{n+k})$ *by*

$$\begin{aligned}\hat{\pi}_{n+k}(s_{n+1}, a^1_{n+1}, a^2_{n+1}, s_{n+2}, \ldots, s_{n+k}) \\ &= \pi^1_{n+k}(\delta^1_n, s_{n+1}, a^1_{n+1}, s_{n+2}, \ldots, s_{n+k}) \\ &\quad \times \pi^2_{n+k}(\delta^2_n, s_{n+1}, a^2_{n+1}, s_{n+2}, \ldots, s_{n+k}),\end{aligned}$$

where $\times$ *here denotes the classical product measure [Ash, 1972: Theorem (2.6.2)]. The function* $\hat{\pi}_{n+k}$ *so defined is a transition probability from* $\hat{H}^{(n)}_{(n+k)}$ *to* $A_{n+k} \times A_{n+k}$. *We obtain a measure* $\hat{\nu}$ *on* $S_{n+1} \times \hat{H}^{(n+1)}$ *by piecing the* $\hat{\pi}_{n+k}$ *together (using the conditional product measure theorem [Ash, 1972: Theorem (2.7.2)]) with the* q_{n+k} *evaluated at* δ_n, *i.e.,* $\hat{\nu} = q_n \hat{\pi}_{n+1} q_{n+1} \hat{\pi}_{n+2} \cdots (\delta_n) \in \mathcal{P}(S_{n+1} \times \hat{H}^{(n+1)})$. *Finally, the map* $\hat{\beta}_n$ *can be used to induce* $\hat{\nu}$ *onto* $S_{n+1} \times H^{(n+1)}$, *i.e., define* $\nu(B) = \hat{\nu}(\hat{\beta}_n^{-1}(B))$, *for each* B *in* $\mathcal{B}(S_{n+1} \times H^{(n+1)})$.

Intuitively, one can think of the actions in $\hat{H}^{(n+1)}$ as being selected by independent date $n+k$ strategies π^1_{n+k} and π^2_{n+k} and the prices as being selected by the opinions in the usual sense. The resulting probability law on sequences of price-action-action triples is $\hat{\nu}$. The induced measure ν in essence represents the selection of actions that are β-convex combinations of the independently chosen actions in $\hat{H}^{(n+1)}$. The convexity result states that the measure ν is an attainable future at δ_n.

Lemma (4.3.2). *If* $0 < \beta < 1$, $\delta^i_n = (h_{(n)}, a^i_n) \in \Delta_n$ *and* $\nu^i \in \mathcal{F}_n(\delta^i_n)$, $i = 1, 2$, *then for* $\delta_n = \beta\delta^1_n + (1-\beta)\delta^2_n$ *and* ν *defined in (4.3.1),* $\nu \in \mathcal{F}_n(\delta_n)$.

Proof. Let β, δ^i_n, and ν^i, $i = 1, 2$, be as hypothesized, and let ν be defined as in (4.3.1). Let ν^i_{n+k} and ν_{n+k} denote the marginals of ν for $H^{(n)}_{(n+k)} = S_{n+1} \times A_{n+1} \times \cdots \times S_{n+k}$ and $H^{(n)}_{(n+k)} \times A_{n+k}$, respectively, $k = 1, 2, \ldots$. Also for each k let π_{n+k} be a regular conditional distribution [Breiman, 1968: Theorem 4.34] of ν for (the projection onto) A_{n+k} given (the projection onto) $H^{(n)}_{(n+k)}$. Using the properties of these distributions one can show by induction that $\nu = q_n \pi_{n+1} q_{n+1} \pi_{n+2} \cdots (\delta_n)$, and that for each k in $\mathcal{N}$, $\nu^1_{n+k}(H^*_{n+k}(\delta_n)) = 1 = \nu_{n+k}(\Delta_{n+k}(\delta_n))$. It follows that the set

$$\begin{aligned}B_k = \{h^{(n)}_{(n+k)} : (\delta_n, h^{(n)}_{(n+k)}) \in \operatorname{dom} D_{n+k}, \\ \pi_{n+k}(D_{n+k}(\delta_n, h^{(n)}_{(n+k)}) \mid h^{(n)}_{(n+k)}) < 1\}\end{aligned}$$

belongs to $\mathcal{B}(H^{(n)}_{(n+k)})$ and has ν^1_{n+k}-measure zero. Then as in Lemma (4.4.8), π_{n+k} can be modified and extended to an element of Π_{n+k} so that the representation $\nu = q_n\pi_{n+1}q_{n+1}\pi_{n+2}\cdots(\delta_n)$ remains valid. It follows that $\nu \in \mathcal{F}_n(\delta_n)$. □

The desired monotonicity property is more easily stated.

Lemma (4.3.3). *If* $\delta^i_n = (h_{(n)}, a^i_n) \in \Delta_n$, $i = 1,2$, *and* $a^1_n \le a^2_n$, *then* $\mathcal{F}_n(\delta^1_n) \subseteq \mathcal{F}_n(\delta^2_n)$.

Proof. Let $\delta^i_n = (h_{(n)}, a^i_n)$, $i = 1,2$, be as hypothesized, and let ν^1 be in $\mathcal{F}_n(\delta^1_n)$, $\nu^1 = q_n\pi^1_{n+1}q_{n+1}\pi^1_{n+2}\cdots(\delta^1_n)$ where $\pi^1_{n+k} \in \Pi_{n+k}$, $k = 1,2,\ldots$. Define π^2_{n+1} by

$$\begin{aligned}\pi^2_{n+1}(\delta^1_n, s_{n+1}) &= \pi^1_{n+1}(\delta^1_n, s_{n+1}), \quad \delta_n = \delta^2_n, s_{n+1} \in H^*_{n+1}(\delta^1_n),\\ &= \pi^1_{n+1}(\delta^2_n, s_{n+1}), \quad \delta_n = \delta^2_n, s_{n+1} \notin H^*_{n+1}(\delta^1_n),\\ &= \pi^1_{n+1}(\delta_n, s_{n+1}), \quad \delta_n \ne \delta^2_n.\end{aligned}$$

Then π^2_{n+1} is a transition probability from $H_{(n+1)}$ to A_{n+1} since π^1_{n+1} is. For $s_{n+1} \in H^*_{n+1}(\delta^1_n) = H^*_{n+1}(\delta^2_n)$, $a^1_n \le a^2_n$ implies that $D_{n+1}(\delta^1_n, s_{n+1}) \subseteq D_{n+1}(\delta^2_n, s_{n+1})$. Since $\pi^1_{n+1} \in \Pi_{n+1}$, it follows that $\pi^2_{n+1} \in \Pi_{n+1}$.

For $k > 1$, define π^2_{n+k} by

$$\begin{aligned}\pi^2_{n+k}(\delta_n, h^{(n)}_{(n+k)}) &= \pi^1_{n+k}(\delta^1_n, h^{(n)}_{(n+k)}), \quad \delta_n = \delta^2_n\\ &= \pi^1_{n+k}(\delta_n, h^{(n)}_{(n+k)}), \quad \delta_n \ne \delta^2_n.\end{aligned}$$

Since D_{n+k} does not vary with δ_n for $h^{(n)}_{(n+k)}$ fixed, we have that $\pi^2_{n+k} \in \Pi_{n+k}$.

For these definitions, it follows that for every s_{n+1} in $H^*_{n+1}(\delta^i_n)$,

$$\begin{aligned}&\pi^2_{n+1}q_{n+1}\pi^2_{n+2}q_{n+2}\cdots(\delta^2_n, s_{n+1})\\ &\qquad = \pi^1_{n+1}q_{n+1}\pi^1_{n+2}q_{n+2}\cdots(\delta^1_n, s_{n+1}).\end{aligned}$$

Clearly for $\nu^2 = q_n\pi^2_{n+1}q_{n+1}\pi^2_{n+2}\cdots(\delta^2_n)$, $\nu^2 \in \mathcal{F}_n(\delta^2_n)$, and since $q_n(\delta^1_n) = q_n(\delta^2_n)$, it follows that $\nu^1 = \nu^2$. □

Intuitively, if $a^1_n \le a^2_n$, then

$$r_{n+1}(h_{(n)}, a^1_n, s_{n+1}) \le r_{n+1}(h_{(n)}, a^2_n, s_{n+1})$$

for each $s_{n+1} \in \mathbb{R}_+^{2\ell}$, and consequently the set of actions feasible at date $n+1$ following $(h_{(n)}, a_n^2)$ is at least as large as the set following $(h_{(n)}, a_n^1)$. Since the feasible action sets beyond date $n+1$ are unaffected by the action at date n, it seems intuitive that any future attainable from $(h_{(n)}, a_n^1)$ would also be attainable from $(h_{(n)}, a_n^2)$, and this is precisely what Lemma (4.3.3) states.

Based on this argument, one would expect $\mathcal{F}_{n+1}$ to be independent of the action taken at date n. The final result of this section states this independence formally.

Lemma (4.3.4). *Let $\delta_n^i = (h_{(n)}, a_n^i)$ be in Δ_n, $i = 1,2$, and suppose $s_{n+1} \in \operatorname{int}\sigma_n(\delta_n^i)$. If $h_{(n+1)}^i = (\delta_n^i, s_{n+1})$, $i = 1,2$, and if $a_{n+1} \in D_{n+1}(h_{(n+1)}^1) \cap D_{n+1}(h_{(n+1)}^2)$, $\mathcal{F}_{n+1}(h_{(n+1)}^1, a_{n+1}) = \mathcal{F}_{n+1}(h_{(n+1)}^2, a_{n+1})$.*

Proof. Let $\delta_{n+1}^i = (h_{(n+1)}^i, a_{n+1})$, where $h_{(n+1)}^i$ and a_{n+1} are as hypothesized, $i = 1,2$. Let $\nu^1 = q_{n+1}\pi_{n+2}^1 q_{n+2}\pi_{n+3}^1 \cdots (\delta_{n+1}^1)$ be in $\mathcal{F}_{n+1}(\delta_{n+1}^1)$. For each $k \geq 2$, let $\pi_{n+k}^2(\delta_{n+1}^2, \cdot) = \pi_{n+k}^1(\delta_{n+1}^1, \cdot)$ and $\pi_{n+k}^2(\delta_{n+1}, \cdot) = \pi_{n+k}^1(\delta_n, \cdot)$, all $\delta_{n+1} \neq \delta_{n+1}^2$. Since $D_{n+k}(\delta_{n+1}^1, \cdot) = D_{n+k}(\delta_{n+1}^2, \cdot)$ for $k \geq 2$, it follows that $\pi_{n+k}^2 \in \Pi_{n+k}$ for $k \geq 2$, and that $\nu^2 \equiv q_{n+1}\pi_{n+2}^2 q_{n+2}\pi_{n+3}^2 \cdots (\delta_{n+1}^2) = \nu^1$. Since the argument is symmetric in δ_{n+1}^1 and δ_{n+2}^2, the result follows. □

4.4 Proof of Theorem (4.2.2).

First note that $\operatorname{dom}\mathcal{F}_n = H_{(n)} \times A_n$ by Remark (4.1.2). It remains to show that $\mathcal{F}_n$ restricted to Δ_n is continuous and compact valued. This will be done through a series of lemmas.

Definition (4.4.1). *For each n, let $E_n : H_{(n)} \times A_n \Rightarrow S_{n+1} \times H^{(n+1)}$ be defined by*

$$E_n(h_{(n)}, a_n) = \{(s_{n+1}, h^{(n+1)}) : \alpha_{n+k}(h^{(n+1)}) \\ \in D_{n+k}(h_{(n)}, a_n, s_{n+1}, \ldots, \xi_{n+k}(h^{(n+1)})),\ k \in \mathcal{N}\}.$$

Then $E_n(h_{(n)}, a_n)$ is the set of posterities at date n and history $(h_{(n)}, a_n)$ (c.f. [Jordan, 1977: 2.4]).

Lemma (4.4.2). *$\Delta_n \subseteq \operatorname{dom} E_n$, E_n has a closed graph in H, and* $\operatorname{supp}(\nu) \subseteq E_n(\delta_n)$ *if $\delta_n \in \Delta_n$ and $\nu \in \mathcal{F}_n(\delta_n)$.*

Proof. The first two statements follows from Lemma (3.2.1). To prove the last statement, suppose that $\delta_n \in \Delta_n$ and that $\nu \in \mathcal{F}_n(\delta_n)$,

$\nu = q\pi^{n+1}(\delta_n)$, some $\pi^{n+1} = \{\pi_m\}_{m\geq n+1}$ in Π^{n+1}. Suppose also that $(s_{n+1}, h^{(n+1)}) \in \mathrm{supp}(\nu)$ and let $U \subseteq S_{n+1} \times H^{(n+1)}$ be an open set containing $(s_{n+1}, h^{(n+1)})$. We may take $U = V^1_{n+1} \times V^2_{n+1} \times \cdots \times V^1_t \times V^2_t \times S_{t+1} \times H^{(t+1)}$, for some $t > n+1$, V^1_k open in S_k and V^2_k open in A_k, $k = n+1, \ldots, t$. Let $\hat{V}^1_{n+1} = \{s_{n+1} : \pi^{n+1}q(U(s_{n+1}) \mid \delta_n, s_{n+1}) > 0\}$. Since $\nu(U) > 0$, it follows that $U^1_{n+1} \equiv \hat{V}^1_{n+1} \cap V^1_{n+1} \cap \sigma_n(\delta_n) \neq \emptyset$. Let $\bar{s}_{n+1}$ be in U^1_{n+1} and let $\hat{V}^2_{n+1} = \{a_{n+1} : q\pi^{n+2}(U(\bar{s}_{n+1}, a_{n+1}) \mid \delta_n, \bar{s}_{n+1}, a_{n+1}) > 0\}$. Then $U^2_{n+1} \equiv \hat{V}_{n+1} \cap V^2_{n+1} \cap \mathrm{supp}(\pi_{n+1}(\delta_n, \bar{s}_{n+1})) \neq \emptyset$. Let $\bar{a}_{n+1}$ be in U^2_{n+1}. Continuing in this way, one constructs a sequence $(\bar{s}_{n+1}, \bar{a}_{n+1}, \ldots, \bar{s}_t, \bar{a}_t)$ in $V^1_{n+1} \times V^2_{n+1} \times \cdots \times V^1_t \times V^2_t$ such that $\bar{s}_k$ is in $\sigma_{k-1}(\delta_n, \ldots, \bar{s}_{k-1}, \bar{a}_{k-1})$ and $\bar{a}_k$ an element of $\mathrm{supp}(\pi_k(\delta_n, \bar{s}_{n+1}, \ldots, \bar{s}_k))$, $k = n+1, \ldots, t$ For $k > t$, choose $\bar{s}_k$ in $\sigma_{k-1}(\delta_n, \bar{s}_{n+1}, \ldots, \bar{s}_{k-1}, \bar{a}_{k-1})$ and $\bar{a}_k$ in $\mathrm{supp}(\pi_k(\delta_n, \bar{s}_{n+1}, \ldots, \bar{s}_k))$ arbitrarily. Let $(\bar{s}_{n+1}, \bar{h}^{(n+1)}) = (\bar{s}_{n+1}, \bar{a}_{n+1}, \ldots)$, and observe that $(\bar{s}_{n+1}, \bar{h}^{(n+1)}) \notin U \cap E_n(\delta_n)$. Thus every open set containing $(s_{n+1}, h^{(n+1)})$ contains a point of $E_n(\delta_n)$ and $(s_{n+1}, h^{(n+1)})$ is a point of closure of $E_n(\delta_n)$. □

The next three results deal with specific properties of opinions and with essential sets of finite dimensional distributions of measures of the form $q\pi^{n+1}(\cdot)$ formed from feasible plans.

Lemma (4.4.3). *If $\delta_n \in H_{(n)} \times A_n$, there is a sequence $\{K_m\}_{m\in\mathcal{N}}$ of non-empty convex and relatively compact subsets of $\mathbb{R}^{2\ell}$ such that $\mathrm{cl}\, K_m \subseteq K_{m+1}$ for each m and $\cup_{m\in\mathcal{N}} K_m = \mathrm{int}\, \sigma_n(\delta_n)$.*

Proof. By [Dugundji, 1966: Theorem 7.2], $\mathrm{int}\, \sigma_n(\delta_n) = \cup_{m\in\mathcal{N}} U_m$, where U_m is non-empty, open and relatively compact. Let $K_m = \mathrm{co}\, U_m$ and the result follows. □

Lemma (4.4.4). *If $\delta_n \in H_{(n)} \times A_n$ and $\varepsilon > 0$, there is a compact set $K \subseteq \mathbb{R}^{2\ell}$ and an open set $U \subseteq H_{(n)}$ such that $\delta_n \in U \times A_n$ and if $\delta'_n \in U \times A_n$, then $K \subseteq \mathrm{int}\, \sigma_n(\delta'_n)$ and $q_n(K \mid \delta'_n) > 1 - \varepsilon$.*

Proof. By Lemma (4.4.3), there is a compact set $K \subseteq \mathrm{int}\, \sigma_n(\delta_n)$ such that $q_n(\mathrm{int}\, K \mid \delta_n) > 1 - \varepsilon/2$. By continuity of q_n, there is an open set $\hat{U} \subseteq H_{(n)}$ such that $\delta_n \in \hat{U} \times A_n$ and if $\delta'_n \in \hat{U} \times A_n$, then $q_n(\mathrm{int}\, K \mid \delta'_n) > q_n(\mathrm{int}\, K \mid \delta_n) - \varepsilon/2 > I - \varepsilon$.

Since $\sum^0_n$ is an open set (Remark (2.3.8)), if $s \in K$, there exists a pair of open sets (V, W) with $V \subseteq H_{(n)}$ and $W \subseteq \mathbb{R}^{2\ell}$ such that $\delta_n \in V \times A_n$,

$s \in W$, and if $\delta'_n \in V \times A_n$, then $W \subseteq \operatorname{int}\sigma_n(\delta'_n)$. Since the W cover K, there is a finite number of points $s^1, \ldots, s^m$ in K and corresponding pairs $(V_1, W_1), \ldots, (V_m, W_m)$ such that $K \subseteq \bigcup_{i=1}^m W_i \equiv W$. For $V = \bigcap_{i=1}^m V_i$, $V \subseteq H_{(n)}$ is open, $\delta_n \in V \times A_n$, and if $\delta'_n \in V \times A_n$, then $K \subseteq W \subseteq \operatorname{int}\sigma_n(\delta'_n)$. Let $U = \hat{U} \cap V$, and the proof is complete. □

Lemma (4.4.5). *If $\pi = \{\pi_n\}_{n\in\mathcal{N}} \in \Pi$, for each $n \in \mathcal{N}$ and $k \geq 0$, if $\delta_n \in \Delta_n$, then*

$$q_n\pi_{n+1}\cdots\pi_{n+k}q_{n+k}(H^*_{n+k+1}(\delta_n) \mid \delta_n) = 1; \tag{4.4.6}$$

$$q_n\pi_{n+1}\cdots q_{n+k}\pi_{n+k+1}(\Delta_{n+k+1}(\delta_n) \mid \delta_n) = 1. \tag{4.4.7}$$

Proof. By definition, if $\delta_n \in \Delta_n$, then $H^*_{n+1}(\delta_n) = \operatorname{int}\sigma_n(\delta_n)$, and (4.4.6) for $k = 0$ follows from the assumption (A.3)(iv). Also, if $s_{n+1} \in \operatorname{int}\sigma_n(\delta_n)$, then $(\delta_n, s_{n+1}) \in H^*_{n+1} \subseteq \operatorname{dom} D_{n+1}$, and hence $\pi_{n+1}(\Delta_{n+1}(\delta_n, s_{n+1}) \mid \delta_n, s_{n+1}) = 1$. Thus

$$\begin{aligned} &q_n\pi_{n+1}(\Delta_{n+1}(\delta_n) \mid \delta_n) = \\ &\qquad \int_{\operatorname{int}\sigma_n(\delta_n)} \pi_{n+1}(\Delta_{n+1}(\delta_n, s_{n+1}) \mid \delta_n, s_{n+1})q_n(ds_{n+1} \mid \delta_n) \\ &\qquad = q_n(\operatorname{int}\sigma_n(\delta_n) \mid \delta_n) = 1, \end{aligned}$$

and (4.4.7) holds for $k = 0$.

Assume that (4.4.6) and (4.4.7) hold for some $k > 0$. If $(s_{n+1}, \ldots, a_{n+k+1}) \in \Delta_{n+k+1}(\delta_n)$, then it follows that $H^*_{n+k+2}(\delta_n, s_{n+1}, \ldots, a_{n+k+1}) = \operatorname{int}\sigma_n(\delta_n, s_{n+1}, \ldots, a_{n+k+1})$. Again by (A.3)(iv), (4.4.7) for k implies (4.4.6) holds for $k+1$. By an argument identical to the one for $k = 0$, if (4.4.6) holds for $k+1$, then so does (4.4.7). □

The strategy in proving that $\mathcal{F}_n$ is u.h.c. and compact valued on Δ_n involves showing that $\mathcal{F}_n$ restricted to Δ_n has a closed graph and then showing that from $\mathcal{F}_n$ over a convergent sequence from Δ_n, only tight sequences of measures can be selected. The result then follows from Prohorov's Theorem.

Lemma (4.4.8). *$\mathcal{F}_n|_{\Delta_n}$ has a closed graph.*

Proof. Assume that (δ_n, ν) is a point of closure of the graph of $\mathcal{F}_n|_{\Delta_n}$. Then there is a sequence $\{(\delta^k_n, \nu^k)\}_{k\in\mathcal{N}}$ such that for each k, $\delta^k_n \in \Delta_n$

and $\nu^k \in \mathcal{F}_n(\delta_n^k)$, and such that $\lim_k \delta_n^k = \delta_n$ and $\lim_k \nu^k = \nu$. For each k, let $\{\pi_r^k\}_{r\geq n+1}$ denote an element of Π^{n+1} such that $\nu^k = m^k(\delta_n^k) \equiv q_n\pi_{n+1}^k q_{n+1}\pi_{n+2}^k \ldots (\delta_n^k)$. Since Δ_n is closed, it suffices to show that there exists $\{\pi_r\}_{r\geq n+1}$ in Π^{n+1} such that $\nu = q_n\pi_{n+1}q_{n+1}\pi_{n+2}\ldots(\delta_n)$.

For each positive integer j, let ν_{n+j}^1 and ν_{n+j} denote the marginals of ν for $H_{(n+j)}^{(n)} = S_{n+1} \times A_{n+1} \times \cdots \times S_{n+j}$ and $H_{(n+j)}^{(n)} \times A_{n+j}$, respectively. Also, let π_{n+j} be a regular conditional distribution for (the projection onto) A_{n+j} given (the projection onto) $H_{(n+j)}^{(n)}$, [Breiman, 1968: Theorem 4.34], i.e., π_{n+j} is a transition probability from $H_{(n+j)}^{(n)}$ to A_{n+j} satisfying

$$\nu_{n+j}(B_1 \times B_2) = \int_{B_1} \pi_{n+j}(B_2 \mid h_{(n+j)}^{(n)})\nu_{n+j}^1(dh_{(n+j)}^{(n)}),$$

for all B_1 in $\mathcal{B}(H_{(n+j)}^{(n)})$ and B_2 in $\mathcal{B}(A_{n+j})$.

By continuity of projections, $m^k(\delta_n^k) \to \nu$ implies that for each j,

$$q_n\pi_{n+1}^k \cdots \pi_{n+j-1}^k q_{n+j-1}(\delta_n^k) \to \nu_{n+j}^1$$

and

$$q_n\pi_{n+1}^k \cdots q_{n+j-1}\pi_{n+j}^k(\delta_n^k) \to \nu_{n+j}.$$

Using these results and the above formula for ν_{n+j} it can be shown by a straightforward but tedious induction argument that

$$\nu_{n+j}^1 = q_n\pi_{n+1}\cdots\pi_{n+j-1}q_{n+j-1}(\delta_n)$$

and

$$\nu_{n+j} = q_n\pi_{n+1}\cdots q_{n+j-1}\pi_{n+j}(\delta_n),$$

for each j (here the product measures are formed by using [Ash, 1972: Theorem 2.7.2]) and $q_n(\delta_n)$, $q_{n+1}(\delta_n, \cdot), \ldots$.

We now use the conditional distributions π_{n+j} to construct the desired feasible date $n+1$ plan. Note first that if $(s_{n+1}, h^{(n+1)}) \in \mathrm{supp}(\nu)$ and if $U \subseteq S_{n+1} \times H^{(n+1)}$ is open and $(s_{n+1}, h^{(n+1)}) \in U$, then $m^k(\delta_n^k) \to \nu$ implies that $\underline{\lim}_k\, m^k(U \mid \delta_n^k) \geq \nu(U) > 0$. It then follows by a straightforward argument that $\mathrm{supp}(\nu) \subseteq \mathrm{Li}(\mathrm{supp}(m^k(\delta_n^k)))$, where "Li" denotes the topological limit inferior [Hildenbrand, 1974: p. 15]. By Lemma (4.4.2), $\text{supp}(m^k(\delta_n^k)) \subseteq E_n(\delta_n)$. For each j, let

$$B_j = \{h_{(n+j)}^{(n)} : (\delta_n, h_{(n+j)}^{(n)}) \in \text{dom}\, D_{n+j},$$
$$\pi_{n+j}(D_{n+j}(\delta_n, h_{(n+j)}^{(n)}) \mid h_{(n+j)}^{(n)}) < 1\}.$$

Then $B_j \in \mathcal{B}(H_{(n+j)}^{(n)})$ and it follows that $\nu_{n+j}^1(B_j) = 0$ for each j.

Let $\bar{\pi}_{n+j}$ be any element of Π_{n+j}, and extend π_{n+j} by defining $\pi_{n+j}(\delta_n', h_{(n+j)}^{(n)})$ to be $\pi_{n+j}(h_{(n+j)}^{(n)})$ if $\delta_n' = \delta_n$ and $h_{(n+j)}^{(n)} \in B_j^c$, and to be $\bar{\pi}_{n+j}(\delta_n', h_{(n+j)}^{(n)})$ otherwise. Then clearly π_{n+j} so extended is in Π_{n+j}, and it follows that $\nu = q_n\pi_{n+1}q_{n+1}\pi_{n+2}\cdots(\delta_n)$. □

Theorem (4.4.9). *$\mathcal{F}_n$ is u.h.c. and compact valued on Δ_n.*

Proof. Suppose that $\{\delta_n^k\}_{k\in\mathcal{N}} \subseteq \Delta_n$ with $\delta_n^k \to \delta_n^0$, and that $\nu^k \in \mathcal{F}_n(\delta_n^k)$ for each k. Let $\{\pi_r^k\}_{r\geq n+1}$ be an element of Π^{n+1} such that $\nu^k = m^k(\delta_n^k)$, where $m^k(\delta^n) \equiv q_n\pi_{n+1}^k q_{n+1}\pi_{n+2}^k\cdots(\delta_n)$. By Lemma (4.4.8) and [Hildenbrand, 1974: Theorem 1, p. 24], the theorem will be proved if it can be shown that $\{m^k(\delta_n^k)\}_{k\in\mathcal{N}}$ has a convergent subsequence. To do this, we show that this sequence is tight.

Let $\varepsilon > 0$ be given. By Lemma (4.4.4), there is a positive integer k_0 and a compact set K_0 such that for $k \geq k_0$, $K_0 \subseteq \text{int}\,\sigma_n(\delta_n^k)$ and $q(K_0 \mid \delta_n^k) > 1 - \varepsilon 2^{-1}$. Also, by Lemma (4.4.3), for $k = 1,\ldots,k_0 - 1$, there is a compact set K_0^k such that $K_0^k \subseteq \text{int}\,\sigma_n(\delta_n^k)$ and $q_n(K_0^k \mid \delta_n^k) > 1 - \varepsilon 2^{-1}$. For $k \geq k_0$ let $K_0^k = K_0$, and let $L_1 = \cup_{k\geq 1} K_0^k$. For $k \geq 0$, let $T_1^k = \{\delta_n^k\} \times K_0^k$ and $J_1^k = \{(s_{n+1}, a_{n+1}) : s_{n+1} \in K_0^k, a_{n+1} \in D_{n+1}(\delta_n^k, s_{n+1})\}$, and let $T_1 = \cup_{k\geq 0} T_1^k$ and $J_1 = \cup_{k\geq 0} J_1^k$. Then $T_1 \subseteq H_{n+1}^*$, T_1 is closed, and since $T_1 \subseteq \bar{J}_0 \times L_1$, T_1 is compact, where $\hat{J}_0 = \{\delta_n^k\}_{k\geq 0}$. By Theorem (3.2.3), $D_{n+1}(T_1)$ and J_1^k, for each k, are compact. Thus J_1 is measurable and for each $k \geq 1$, $q_n\pi_{n+1}^k(J_1 \mid \delta_n^k) \geq q_n\pi_{n+1}^k(J_1^k \mid \delta_n^k) = q_n(K_0^k \mid \delta_n^k) > 1 - \varepsilon 2^{-1}$. Let $\bar{J}_1 = \cup_{k\geq 0}\{\delta_n^k\} \times J_1^k$. One can verify that $\bar{J}_1$ is closed, and since $\bar{J}_1 \subseteq \bar{J}_0 \times L_1 \times D_{n+1}(T_1)$, $\bar{J}_1$ is compact.

The proof now proceeds by induction. Suppose that for some integer $r > 1$, there exist compact sets $\bar{J}_{r-1} \subseteq \Delta_{n+r-1}$, $L_r \subseteq \mathbb{R}_{++}^{2\ell}$, and $T_r \subseteq H_{n+r}^*$, and for every $k \geq 0$, there is a compact set J_r^k such that (a) $\{\delta_n^k\} \times J_r^k \subseteq \Delta_{n+r}$, (b) $q_n\pi_{n+1}^k\cdots q_{n+r-1}\pi_{n+r}^k(J_r^k \mid \delta_n^k) > (1 -$

$\varepsilon 2^{-r})(1-\varepsilon 2^{-r+1})\ldots(1-\varepsilon 2^{-1})$, and (c) $\bar{J}_r \equiv \cup_{k\geq 0}\{\delta_n^k\} \times J_r^k \subseteq \bar{J}_{r-1} \times L_r \times D_{n+r}(T_r)$ and $\bar{J}_r$ is compact.

By Lemma (4.4.4), if $\delta_{n+r} \in H_{(n+r)} \times A_{n+r}$, there is a compact set $K \subseteq \mathbb{R}^{2\ell}$ and an open set $U \subseteq H_{(n+r)}$ such that $\delta_{n+r} \in U \times A_{n+r}$ and if $\delta'_{n+r} \in U \times A_{n+r}$, then $K \subseteq \operatorname{int} \sigma_{n+r}(\delta'_{n+r})$ and $q_{n+r}(K \mid \delta'_{n+r}) > 1 - \varepsilon 2^{-r-1}$. Since $H_{(n+r)}$ is locally compact [Dugundji, 1966: Theorem 6.5(4), p. 239], we may assume that $\operatorname{cl} U$ is compact and that these properties hold with U replaced by $\operatorname{cl} U$. The U cover $\bar{J}_r$, which is compact by hypothesis (c). Then there is a finite set $\{\delta_{n+r}^i : i = 1,\ldots,i^*\} \subseteq \bar{J}_r$ and corresponding open sets U_i and compact sets K_i, $i = 1,\ldots,i^*$, with $J_r \subseteq \bigcup_{i=1}^{i*} U_i$. Let $L_{r+1} = \bigcup_{i=1}^{i*} K_i$, and define, for $k \geq 0$, the sets

$$T_{r+1}^{ik} = \{(h_{(n+r)}^{(n)}, a_{n+r}, s_{n+r+1}) : ((h_{(n+r)}^{(n)}, a_{n+r}) \in J_r^k, \\ (\delta_n^k, h_{(n+r)}^{(n)}) \in \operatorname{cl} U_i, s_{n+r+1} \in K_i\},$$

$$J_{r+1}^{ik} = \{(h_{(n+r+1)}^{(n)}, a_{n+r+1}) : h_{(n+r+1)}^{(n)} \in T_{r+1}^{ik}, \\ a_{n+r+1} \in D_{n+r+1}(\delta_n^k, h_{(n+r+1)}^{(n)})\}.$$

Let $\hat{T}_{r+1}^k = \bigcup_{i=1}^{i*} T_{r+1}^{ik}$, $T_{r+1}^k = \{\delta_n^k\} \times \hat{T}_{r+1}^k$, and let $T_{r+1} = \cup_{k\geq 0} T_{r+1}^k$ and $J_{r+1} = \cup_{k\geq 0} J_{r+1}^k$.

It is easily verified that $\hat{T}_{r+1}^k$ is closed, and since $\hat{T}_{r+1} \subseteq J_r^k \times L_{r+1}$, both $\hat{T}_{r+1}^k$ and T_{r+1}^k are compact. One can also verify that T_{r+1} is closed, $T_{r+1} \subseteq \bar{J}_r \times L_{r+1}$, and hence by (c), T_{r+1} is compact. Finally, by construction $T_{r+1} \subseteq H_{n+r+1}^*$. By Theorem (3.2.3), $D_{n+r+1}(T_{r+1})$ and J_{r+1}^k, each $k \geq 0$, are compact. Thus J_{r+1} is measurable and for each $k \geq 1$,

$$\begin{aligned} q_n\pi_{n+1}^k \cdots \pi_{n+r}^k q_{n+r}\pi_{n+r+1}^k(J_{r+1} \mid \delta_n^k) \\ &\geq q_n\pi_{n+1}^k \cdots \pi_{n+r}^k q_{n+r}\pi_{n+r+1}^k(J_{r+1}^k \mid \delta_n^k) \\ &= q_n\pi_{n+1}^k \cdots \pi_{n+r}^k q_{n+r}(\hat{T}_{r+1}^k \mid \delta_n^k) \\ &\geq (1-\varepsilon 2^{-r-1}) q_n\pi_{n+1}^k \cdots \pi_{n+r}^k(J_r^k \mid \delta_n^k) \\ &> (1-\varepsilon 2^{-r-1})(1-\varepsilon 2^{-r})\ldots(1-\varepsilon 2^{-1}), \end{aligned}$$

where the last inequality follows from (b) of the induction hypothesis. Let $\bar{J}_{r+1} = \cup_{k\geq 0}\{\delta_n^k\} \times J_{r+1}^k$. It can be shown that $\bar{J}_{r+1}$ is a closed subset of

Δ_{n+r+1}. Since $\bar{J}_{r+1} \subseteq \bar{J}_r \times L_{r+1} \times D_{n+r+1}(T_{r+1})$, it follows that $\bar{J}_{r+1}$ is compact.

The induction hypothesis thus holds for $r+1$ and hence for every $r \in \mathcal{N}$. Note that by definition of $\bar{J}_r$, the set J_r is compact and $\bar{J}_{r+1} \subseteq \bar{J}_r \times L_{r+1} \times D_{n+r+1}(T_{r+1})$, for each r. The set $J_{(r)} \equiv J_r \times S_{n+r+1} \times H^{(n+r+1)}$ is thus closed in $S_{n+1} \times H^{(n+1)}$ and $J_{(r+1)} \subseteq J_{(r)}$. Thus, $J \equiv \cap_{r\in\mathcal{N}} J_{(r)}$ is closed and $J \subseteq L_1 \times D_{n+1}(T_1) \times L_2 \times D_{n+2}(T_2) \times \cdots$, implying that J is compact. But for $k \geq 1$,

$$\begin{aligned} m^k(J \mid \delta_n^k) &= \lim_r m^k(J_{(r)} \mid \delta_n^k) \\ &= \lim_r q_n \pi_{n+1}^k \cdots q_{n+r-1} \pi_{n+r}^k (J_r \mid \delta_n^k) \\ &\geq \lim_r (1 - \varepsilon 2^{-r})(1 - \varepsilon 2^{-r+1}) \cdots (1 - \varepsilon 2^{-1}) \\ &\geq 1 - \lim_r \sum_{i=1}^{r} \varepsilon 2^{-i} \\ &= 1 - \varepsilon. \end{aligned}$$

Since ε was arbitrary, the sequence $\{m^k(\delta_n^k)\}_{k\in\mathcal{N}}$ is tight. By Prohorov's Theorem [Billingsley, 1968: Theorem 6.1], $\{m^k(\delta_n^k)\}_{k\in\mathcal{N}}$ is relatively compact, and the proof is complete. □

As in [Jordan, 1977: 5.3–5.7], the strategy in proving that $\mathcal{F}_n$ is l.h.c. on Δ_n involves showing that $\mathcal{F}_n$ is generated by continuous selections. Here, however, continuity of selections is limited by the restricted continuity of D_n.

Lemma (4.4.10). *If $\varepsilon > 0$, $\pi_n \in \Pi_n$, and $\nu \in \mathcal{P}(H_{(n)})$ with $\nu(H_n^*) = 1$, then there exists π_n^* in Π_n such that $\pi_n^* \mid_{H_n^*}$ is continuous and for every bounded continuous function $g : H_{(n)} \times A_n \to \mathbb{R}$, $|\int g d\nu\pi_n^* - \int g d\nu\pi_n| < 2\varepsilon\|g\|$, where $\|g\| = \text{supp}\{|g(\delta_n)| : \delta_n \in H_{(n)} \times A_n\}$.*

Proof. Let ε, π_n, and ν be as hypothesized. By Lemma (A.III), there is a closed set $B' \subseteq H_{(n)}$ such that $\nu(B') > 1-\varepsilon$ and $\pi_n \mid_{B'}$ is continuous. For $B = B' \cap H_n^*$, B is a closed subset of H_n^*, $\nu(B) = \nu(B')$ and $\pi_n \mid_B$ is continuous. Define $\mathcal{D}_n(h_{(n)}) = \{\mu \in \mathcal{P}(A_n) : \text{supp}(\mu) \subseteq D_n(h_{(n)})\}$. By Lemma (A.IV), dom $\mathcal{D}_n$ = dom D_n and $\mathcal{D}_n \mid_{H_n^*}$ is continuous, compact and convex valued. Since $\pi_n \mid_B$ is a continuous selection for $\mathcal{D}_n \mid_B$, it follows from [Michael, 1959: Theorem 1.5(a)] that $\pi_n \mid_B$ can be extended to a continuous selection $\hat{\pi}_n$ for $\mathcal{D}_n |_{H_n^*}$. Let $\pi_n^* = \hat{\pi}_n$ on H_n^* and $\pi_n^* = \pi_n$, otherwise. Since $H_n^* \in \mathcal{B}(H_{(n)})$, $\pi_n^* \in \Pi_n$ and $\pi_n^* |_{H_n^*}$ is continuous.

Finally, if $g : H_{(n)} \times A_n \to \mathbb{R}$ is bounded and continuous, then

$$\left|\int g d\nu\pi_n^* - \int g d\nu\pi_n\right| = \left|\int_{B^c \times A_n} g d\nu\pi_n^* - \int_{B^c \times A_n} g d\nu\pi_n\right|$$
$$\leq 2\|g\|\nu(B^c) < 2\|g\|\varepsilon,$$

where B^c is the complement in $H_{(n)}$ of B. □

Definition (4.4.11). *For each n, let $\Pi_n^* = \{\pi_n : \pi_n \in \Pi_n, \pi_n |_{H_n^*}$ is continuous$\}$, and let $\Pi^{*n} = \{\pi^n = \{\pi_m\}_{m \geq n} : \pi_m \in \Pi_m^*, m \geq n\}$. Analogous to (4.2.1), let $\mathcal{F}_n^* : H_{(n)} \times A_n \Rightarrow \mathcal{P}(S_{n+1} \times H^{(n+)})$ be defined by*

$$\mathcal{F}_n^*(h_{(n)}, a_n) =$$
$$\{\nu \in \mathcal{P}(S_{n+1} \times H^{(n+1)}) : \nu = q\pi^{n+1}(h_{(n)}, a_n), \pi^{n+1} \in \Pi^{*n+1}\}.$$

By Lemma (4.4.10), $\Pi_n^* \neq \emptyset$ for each n, and consequently $\operatorname{dom} \mathcal{F}_n^* = H_{(n)} \times A_n$.

The next result shows that $\mathcal{F}_n^*$ is dense in $\mathcal{F}_n$ on Δ_n.

Lemma (4.4.12). *If $\delta_n \in \Delta_n$, then $\mathcal{F}_n(\delta_n) = \operatorname{cl} \mathcal{F}_n^*(\delta_n)$.*

Proof. By Theorem (4.4.9), if $\delta_n \in \Delta_n$, then $\operatorname{cl} \mathcal{F}_n^*(\delta_n) \subseteq \mathcal{F}_n(\delta_n)$. Suppose then that $\nu \in \mathcal{F}_n(\delta_n)$, $\nu = q_n\pi_{n+1}q_{n+1}\pi_{n+2}\cdots(\delta_n)$, where $\pi_{n+k} \in \Pi_{n+k}$, each k. Let ν_{n+k}^1 denote the marginal of ν for $H_{(n+k)}^{(n)}$, i.e., if $B \in \mathcal{B}(H_{(n+k)}^{(n)})$, then $\nu_{n+k}^1(B) = q_n\pi_{n+1}\cdots q_{n+k-1}(B \mid \delta_n)$. Let $\hat{\delta}_n$ be the element of $\mathcal{P}(H_{(n)} \times A_n)$ degenerate at δ_n, i.e., $\hat{\delta}_n(\{\delta_n\}) = 1$. If $B \in \mathcal{B}(H_{(n+k)})$, then $\hat{\delta}_n\nu_{n+1}^1(B) = \nu_{n+k}^1(B(\delta_n)) = \hat{\delta}_n\nu(B \times H^{(n+k)})$. In particular, $\hat{\delta}_n\nu_{n+k}^1(H_{n+k}^*) = \nu_{n+k}^1(H_{n+k}^*(\delta_n)) = 1$ by (4.4.6).

Let $\varepsilon > 0$ be given. By Lemma (4.4.10), for each k there exists π_{n+k}^* in Π_{n+k}^* and a closed subset $B_{n+k} \subseteq H_{n+k}^*$ such that $\pi_{n+k} = \pi_{n+k}^*$ on $B_{n+k} \cup {H_{n+k}^*}^c$ and $\hat{\delta}_n\nu_{n+k}^1(B_{n+k}) > 1 - \varepsilon 2^{-k}$. Let $\nu^* = q_n\pi_{n+1}^*q_{n+1}\pi_{n+2}^*\cdots(\delta_n)$, and define $B = \cap_{k\in\mathbb{N}}B_{n+k} \times H^{(n+k)}$. Then $B \in \mathcal{B}(H)$, $\nu(B(\delta_n)) > 1 - \varepsilon$, and if $B' \in \mathcal{B}(S_{n+1} \times H^{(n+1)})$ with $B' \subseteq B(\delta_n)$, then $\nu(B') = \nu^*(B')$. But then if $g : S_{n+1} \times H^{(n+1)}$ is bounded and continuous, then $|\int g d\nu - \int g d\nu^*| \leq 2\|g\|\nu(B(\delta_n)^c) < 2\|g\|\varepsilon$. Since

ε was arbitrary and $\nu^* \in \mathcal{F}_n(\delta_n)$, it follows that every basic neighborhood [Billingsley, 1968: (5), p. 236] of ν in $\mathcal{P}(S_{n+1} \times H^{(n+1)})$ contains an element of $\mathcal{F}_n^*(\delta_n)$, and hence $\nu \in \mathrm{cl}\,\mathcal{F}_n^*(\delta_n)$. □

If $\pi^{n+1} \in \Pi^{*n+1}$, then $q\pi^{n+1}$ is a selection for $\mathcal{F}_n^*$ and hence also for $\mathcal{F}_n$. These selections are continuous on Δ_n.

Lemma (4.4.13). *If $\pi^{n+1} \in \Pi^{*n+1}$, then $q\pi^{n+1}|_{\Delta_n}$ is continuous.*

Proof. Suppose $\pi^{n+1} = \{\pi_m\}_{m \geq n+1} \in \Pi^{*n+1}$. Since Δ_n and $\mathcal{P}(S_{n+1} \times H^{(n+1)})$ are metrizable, sequential convergence determines continuity. By an argument similar to [Billingsley, 1968: p. 30], it suffices to show that the finite dimensional distributions of $q\pi^{n+1}$ are continuous on Δ_n.

This is true by assumption for q_n. To show it for $q_n\pi_{n+1}$, let $\hat{g} : S_{n+1} \times A_{n+1} \to \mathbb{R}$ be bounded and continuous, and let $g : \Delta_n \times S_{n+1} \to \mathbb{R}$ be given by

$$g(\delta_n, s_{n+1}) = \int_{A_{n+1}} \hat{g}(s_{n+1}, a_{n+1})\pi_{n+1}(da_{n+1} \mid \delta_n, s_{n+1}).$$

Then g is bounded and measurable and by the usual mapping theorems [Billingsley, 1968: Theorems 5.4, 5.5], $g|_{H^*_{n+1}}$ is continuous since $\pi_{n+1}|_{H^*_{n+1}}$ is. Let $\{\delta_n^k\}_{k \in \mathcal{N}} \subseteq \Delta_n$ with $\lim_k \delta_n^k = \delta_n^0$, and for each $k \geq 0$, define $g_k(s_{n+1}) = g(\delta_n^k, s_{n+1})$. If $s_{n+1}^0 \in \mathrm{int}\,\sigma_n(\delta_n^0)$ and $\{s_{n+1}^k\}_{k \in \mathcal{N}} \subseteq S_{n+1}$ with $\lim_k s_{n+1}^k = s_{n+1}^0$, then $\lim_k g_k(s_{n+1}^k) = g_0(s_{n+1}^0)$. For by Lemma (4.4.4) and its proof, there is an open set $K \subseteq \mathrm{int}\,\sigma_n(\delta_n^0)$ with compact closure and an open set $V \subseteq \Delta_n$ such that $(\delta_n^0, s_{n+1}^0) \in V \times K$, and if $\delta_n \in V$, then $K \subseteq \mathrm{int}\,\sigma_n(\delta_n)$. Thus for k sufficiently large, $(\delta_n^k, s_{n+1}^k) \in V \times K \subseteq H^*_{n+1}$, and the claimed convergence follows. By the uniform boundedness of $\{g_k\}_{k \in \mathcal{N}}$ and [Billingsley, 1968: Theorem 5.4, 5.5], it follows that $\lim_k \int \hat{g}\,dq_n\pi_{n+1}(\delta_n^k) = \int \hat{g}\,dq_n\pi_{n+1}(\delta_n^0)$ and thus that $\lim_k q_n\pi_{n+1}(\delta_n^k) = q_n\pi_{n+1}(\delta_n^0)$. Hence, $q_n\pi_{n+1}$ is continuous on Δ_n.

By way of induction, suppose $q_n\pi_{n+1}\cdots q_{n+k-1}\pi_{n+k}$ is continuous on Δ_n for some $k > 1$. By essentially the same arguments as above, one can show that $q_n\pi_{n+1}\cdots\pi_{n+k}q_{n+k}$ is continuous on Δ_n, that $q_{n+k}\pi_{n+k+1}$ is continuous on Δ_{n+k}, and finally that $q_n\pi_{n+1}\cdots q_{n+k}\pi_{n+k+1}$ is continuous on Δ_n. □

Lower hemi-continuity of $\mathcal{F}_n$ is now easy.

Theorem (4.4.14). *$\mathcal{F}_n^* |_{\Delta_n}$ and $\mathcal{F}_n |_{\Delta_n}$ are l.h.c.*

Proof. By [Hildenbrand, 1974: 4, p. 28] and Lemma (4.4.12), $\mathcal{F}_n$ is l.h.c. on Δ_n if and only if $\mathcal{F}_n^*$ is. To show this, suppose $\delta_n^0 \in \Delta_n$ and $\{\delta_n^k\}_{k\in\mathcal{N}} \subseteq \Delta_n$ with $\lim_k \delta_n^k = \delta_n^0$, and suppose $\nu \in \mathcal{F}_n^*(\delta_n^0)$, $\nu = q\pi^{n+1}(\delta_n^0)$ for some π^{n+1} in Π^{*n+1}. Then for each $k \geq 1$, $q\pi^{n+1}(\delta_n^k) \in \mathcal{F}_n^*(\delta_n^k)$, and by Lemma (4.4.13), $\lim_k q\pi^{n+1}(\delta_n^k) = q\pi^{n+1}(\delta_n^0) = \nu$. By [Hildenbrand, 1974: Theorem 2, p. 27], $\mathcal{F}_n^*$ is l.h.c. at δ_n^0. □

Theorems (4.4.9) and (4.4.14) complete the proof of Theorem (4.2.2).

5. Intertemporal Choice

5.1 Derived Utility and Demand.

Definition (5.1.1). *For each positive integer n, define the function $u_n : H_{(n)} \times A_n \times \mathcal{P}(S_{n+1} \times H^{(n+1)}) \to \mathbb{R}$ by setting*

$$u_n(h_{(n)}, a_n, \nu) = \int u(\text{proj}_C(h_{(n)}, a_n, s_{n+1}, h^{(n+1)}))\nu(d(s_{n+1}, h^{(n+1)})).$$

Then $u_n(h_{(n)}, a_n, \nu)$ gives the agent's expected utility at date n when the future is governed by ν and experience to date is $(h_{(n)}, a_n)$, It is clear from (A.2) that u_n is bounded and continuous in the product topology.

Definitions(5.1.2). *The agent's* derived utility function *v_n at date n is simply the supremum of expected utility u_n over attainable futures, i.e., $v_n : H_{(n)} \times A_n \to \mathbb{R}$ is defined by*

$$v_n(h_{(n)}, a_n) = \sup\{u_n(h_{(n)}, a_n, \nu) : \nu \in \mathcal{F}_n(h_{(n)}, a_n)\}.$$

Associated with this supremum is the set of measures that attain it: $\zeta_n : H_{(n)} \times A_n \Rightarrow \mathcal{P}(S_{n+1} \times H^{(n+1)})$ given by

$$\zeta_n(h_{(n)}, a_n) = \{\nu : \nu \in \mathcal{F}_n(h_{(n)}, a_n), v_n(h_{(n)}, a_n) = u_n(h_{(n)}, a_n, \nu)\}.$$

Lemma (5.1.3). *v_n is defined and bounded on $H_{(n)} \times A_n$, $v_n |_{\Delta_n}$ is continuous, and $\zeta_n |_{\Delta_n}$ is non-empty, compact valued and u.h.c.*

Proof. Follows directly from Theorem (4.2.2) and [Hildenbrand, 1974: Corollary, p. 30]. □

Remarks (5.1.4). Since we are not interested in the values of v_n off Δ_n, but it would be convenient to have v_n bounded and continuous on all of $H_{(n)} \times A_n$, we simply extend $v_n |_{\Delta_n}$ to a bounded continuous function on all of $H_{(n)} \times A_n$. By Lemma (3.2.1), the existence of such an extension is guaranteed (c.f. [Dugundji, 1966: Theorem 5.1, p. 149]). We fix one such extension and refer to it as v_n throughout the sequel.

The first stage of the two stage optimization process mentioned in Section 3.2 is depicted in (5.1.2). It consists of choosing a best attainable future at each date. The second stage consists of choosing a best current action that is feasible, where "best" refers to the derived utility function v_n.

Definition (5.1.5). *For each n, let* $v_n^* : \operatorname{dom} D_n \to \mathbb{R}$ *be defined by* $v_n^*(h_{(n)}) = \sup\{v_n(h_{(n)}, a_n) : a_n \in D_n(h_{(n)})\}$. *The function* v_n^* *is analogous to the optimal value function in dynamic programming. The agent's demand relation* $d_n : \operatorname{dom} D_n \Rightarrow A_n$ *is then given by*

$$d_n(h_{(n)}) = \{a_n : a_n \in D_n(h_{(n)}), v_n^*(h_{(n)}) = v_n(h_{(n)}, a_n)\}.$$

Lemma (5.1.6). v_n^* *is bounded on* $\operatorname{dom} D_n$, $v_n^* |_{H_n^*}$ *is continuous, and* $d_n |_{H_n^*}$ *is non-empty, compact valued, and u.h.c.*

Proof. Follows directly from Theorems (3.2.3) and (3.2.6), Lemmas (3.2.8) and (5.1.3), and [Hildenbrand, 1974: Corollary, p. 30]. □

5.2 Optimal Plans.

An agent's intertemporal choice behavior, as depicted in (5.1.2) and (5.1.5), is consistent if it is equivalent to following an optimal plan, i.e., a solution to the problem (4.1.4). Such a solution is constructed here from measurable selections for the relations ζ_n and d_n.

Lemma (5.2.1). *There exists a transition probability* $m_n : \Delta_n \to \mathcal{P}(S_{n+1} \times H^{(n+1)})$ *such that*

(i) $m_n(\delta_n) \in \zeta_n(\delta_n)$;

(ii) m_n *is* $\mathcal{B}(\Delta_n)/\mathcal{B}(\mathcal{P}(S_{n+1} \times H^{(n+1)}))$*-measurable;*

(iii) for every B in $\mathcal{B}(S_{n+1})$, $m_n(\delta_n)(B \times H^{(n+1)}) = q_n(B \mid \delta_n)$.

Proof. The existence of m_n satisfying (i) and (ii) follows from Lemma (5.1.3) and [Engelking, 1968: Theorem 1]. By (ii) and Lemma (A.II), m_n is a transition probability. By (i), for each δ_n in Δ_n, there exists a date $n+1$ feasible plan π^{n+1} in Π^{n+1} such that $m_n(\delta_n) = q\pi^{n+1}(\delta_n)$, and (iii) follows. □

Remarks (5.2.2). In general, the π^{n+1} in the last sentence of the above proof may depend upon the δ_n in Δ_n. In this case, though m_n selects from ζ_n, m_n itself need not be the tail of an optimal plan. Even if m_n were of the form $m_n(\delta_n) = q\pi^{n+1}(\delta_n)$ for some π^{n+1} in Π^{n+1} and every δ_n in Δ_n, and this held for every n, there is no guarantee in general that π^{n+1} would be the tail of π^n for every n. This is the essence of the existence question.

Lemma (5.2.3). *There exists a function $\pi_n^* : H_{(n)} \to A_n$ such that (i) $\pi_n^*(h_{(n)}) \in D_n(h_{(n)})$, $\forall\, h_{(n)} \in \operatorname{dom} D_n$; (ii) $\pi_n^*(h_{(n)}) \in d_n(h_{(n)})$, $\forall\, h_{(n)} \in H_n^*$; (iii) π_n^* is $\mathcal{B}(H_{(n)})/\mathcal{B}(A_n)$-measurable. Moreover, for any $h_{(n)}^\circ$ in $H_{(n)}^*$ and a_n° in $d_n(h_{(n)}^\circ)$, there exists a function $\pi_n^\circ : H_{(n)} \to A_n$ satisfying (i)–(iii) such that $\pi_n^\circ(h_{(n)}^\circ) = a_n^\circ$.*

Proof. By Lemma (5.1.6) and [Kuratowski and Ryll-Nardzewski, 1965: Corollary 1], there exists a function $\hat{\pi}_n : H_n^* \to A_n$ that is $\mathcal{B}(H_n^*)/\mathcal{B}(A_n)$-measurable and that selects from $d_n\,|_{H_n^*}$. Let $\pi_n^* \equiv \hat{\pi}_n$ on H_n^* and let $\pi_n^* \equiv 0$ (the zero vector in $\mathbb{R}^{2\ell}$) on the complement of $H_{(n)}^*$ (in $H_{(n)}$). Since $H_n^* \in \mathcal{B}(H_{(n)})$ and $0 \in D_n(h_{(n)})$ for all $h_{(n)}$ in $\operatorname{dom} D_n$, π_n^* satisfies (i)–(iii). The second statement of the Lemma follows from the fact that π_n^* can be modified on any singleton subset of H_n^* in the desired manner, preserving (i)–(iii). □

Conventions (5.2.4). *The need to modify selectors for d_n for particular histories and actions and still have a measurable selection stems from the fact that equilibrium actions must be capable of being chosen by agents following feasible strategies. We identify any function π_n^* satisfying (5.2.3)(i)–(iii) with the transition probability degenerate at the values of π_n^*. With this identification it is clear that $\pi_n^* \in \Pi_n$. For any sequence of such functions $\{\pi_n^*\}_{n\in\mathcal{N}}$, define $m_n^* : H_{(n)} \times A_n \to \mathcal{P}(S_{n+1} \times H^{(n+1)})$ by $m_n^*(h_{(n)}, a_n) = q_n\pi_{n+1}^* q_{n+1}\pi_{n+2}^* \cdots (h_{(n)}, a_n)$. Then m_n^* is a transition probability [Ash, 1972: Theorem 2.7.2] and hence a measurable selection for $\mathcal{F}_n$ (Lemma A.II). It will follow from the next theorem that m_n^* also* *selects from* ζ_n *on* Δ_n*. In proving this result it is convenient to have the selections* m_n *of Lemma (5.2.1) defined on all of* $H_{(n)} \times A_n$*. One easy way to do this is to let* $m_n = m_n^*$ *on the complement of* Δ_n*, where* m_n^* *is defined above. Henceforth, we assume the* m_n *of (5.2.1) are extended in this fashion.*

Theorem (5.2.5). *If* $\{\pi_n^*\}_{n\in\mathcal{N}}$ *is a sequence each component of which satisfies Lemma (5.2.3)(i)–(iii), then for each* n *in* $\mathcal{N}$ *and* δ_n *in* Δ_n*,*

$$
\begin{aligned}
u_n(\delta_n, m_n^*(\delta_n)) &= v_n(\delta_n) \\
&= \int_{H_{n+1}^*(\delta_n)} v_{n+1}^*(\delta_n, s_{n+1}) q_n(ds_{n+1} \mid \delta_n) \qquad (5.2.6) \\
&= \int_{\Delta_{n+1}(\delta_n)} v_{n+1}(\delta_n, s_{n+1}, a_{n+1}) q_n \pi_{n+1}^*(d(s_{n+1}, a_{n+1}) \mid \delta_n).
\end{aligned}
$$

Proof. Fix n and let δ_n be in Δ_n. By Lemma (5.1.6) the first integral in (5.2.6) is well defined. By definition of π_{n+1}^*, $v_{n+1}^*(\delta_n, \cdot) = v_{n+1}(\delta_n, \cdot, \pi_{n+1}^*(\delta_n, \cdot))$ on $H_{n+1}^*(\delta_n)$. The last equality in (5.2.6) then follows from (4.4.6) and (4.4.7).

To prove the first two equalities, let ν be in $\mathcal{F}_n(\delta_n)$, $\nu = q\pi^{n+1}(\delta_n)$, some $\pi^{n+1} = \{\pi_m\}_{m\geq n+1}$ in Π^{n+1}. It follows from (5.1.2) and (5.1.5) and from (4.4.6) and (4.4.7) that

$$
\begin{aligned}
&u_n(\delta_n, \nu) \\
&\quad \leq \int_{\Delta_{n+1}(\delta_n)} v_{n+1}(\delta_n, s_{n+1}, a_{n+1}) q_n \pi_{n+1}(d(s_{n+1}, a_{n+1}) \mid \delta_n),
\end{aligned}
$$

and for every s_{n+1} in $H_{(n+1)}^*(\delta_n)$, that

$$
\begin{aligned}
\int_{\Delta_{n+1}(\delta_n, s_{n+1})} & v_{n+1}(\delta_n, s_{n+1}, a_{n+1}) \pi_{n+1}(da_{n+1} \mid \delta_n, s_{n+1}) \\
&\leq v_{n+1}^*(\delta_n, s_{n+1}).
\end{aligned}
$$

Integrating both sides of this last inequality with respect to $q_n(\delta_n)$ and using the last inequality of (5.2.6) gives that

$$
\begin{aligned}
&u_n(\delta_n, \nu) \\
&\quad \leq \int_{\Delta_{n+1}(\delta_n)} v_{n+1}(\delta_n, s_{n+1}, a_{n+1}) q_n \pi_{n+1}^*(d(s_{n+1}, a_{n+1}) \mid \delta_n).
\end{aligned}
$$

Since ν was arbitrary and $m_n^*(\delta_n) \in \mathcal{F}_n(\delta_n)$, we conclude that

$$\begin{aligned} u_n(\delta_n, m_n^*(\delta_n)) &\leq v_n(\delta_n) \\ &\leq \int_{\Delta_{n+1}(\delta_n)} v_{n+1}(\delta_n, s_{n+1}, a_{n+1}) q_n \pi_{n+1}^*(d(s_{n+1}, a_{n+1}) \mid \delta_n). \quad (*) \end{aligned}$$

Let $\{m_{n+k}\}_{k\geq 0}$ be a sequence of functions satisfying Lemma (5.2.1) (extended as in (5.2.4)). Let $\lambda_n = m_n(\delta_n)$ and for each k in $\mathcal{N}$, let $\lambda_{n+k} = q_n\pi_{n+1}^* \cdots q_{n+k}\pi_{n+k}^* m_{n+k}(\delta_n)$ (recall that m_{n+k} is a transition probability and use [Ash, 1972: Theorem 2.7.2]). Then $\lambda_{n+k} \to m_n^*(\delta_n)$ in $\mathcal{P}(S_{n+1} \times H^{(n+1)})$ since the finite dimensional distributions of λ_{n+k} converge to those of $m_n^*(\delta_n)$ (c.f. [Billingsley, 1968: p. 30]). Also for each $k = 0, 1, \ldots$, define

$$w_{n+k} = \int u(\text{proj}_C(\delta_n, s_{n+1}, h^{(n+1)}))\lambda_{n+k}(d(s_{n+1}, h^{(n+1)})).$$

Since u is bounded and continuous, $\lim_k w_{n+k} = u_n(\delta_n, m_n^*(\delta_n))$. Since $m_n(\delta_n) \in \zeta_n(\delta_n)$, $w_n = v_n(\delta_n)$. Similarly, for $k > 0$ and $t \in \Delta_{n+k}(\delta_n)$, $u_{n+k}(\delta_n, t, m_{n+k}(\delta_n, t)) = v_{n+k}(\delta_n, t)$, and consequently (4.4.7) implies that

$$w_{n+k} = \int_{\Delta_{n+k}(\delta_n)} v_{n+k}(\delta_n, t) q_n \pi_{n+1}^* \cdots q_{n+k-1}\pi_{n+k}^*(dt \mid \delta_n).$$

It follows from this representation and $(*)$ that $w_n \leq w_{n+1}$. Using this representation and an argument similar to that leading to $(*)$, one can show that $w_{n+k} \leq w_{n+k+1}$ for every $k = 0, 1, \ldots$, and hence that

$$\begin{aligned} v_n(\delta_n) = w_n &\leq w_{n+1} \\ &= \int_{\Delta_{n+1}(\delta_n)} v_{n+1}(\delta_n, s_{n+1}, a_{n+1}) q_n \pi_{n+1}^*(d(s_{n+1}, a_{n+1}) \mid \delta_n) \\ &= \lim_k w_{n+k} \\ &= u_n(\delta_n, m_n^*(\delta_n)) \leq v_n(\delta_n). \end{aligned}$$

Thus equality holds throughout, proving (5.2.6). □

Remarks (5.2.7). Equation (5.2.6) is an optimality type equation for the problem (4.1.4). The second equality in (5.2.6) produces a version of the optimality criterion for non-stationary dynamic programming [Kertz and Nachman, 1979: (5.1)]. Existence of optimal non-randomized plans follows easily from this result.

Theorem (5.2.8). *If $\pi^* = \{\pi_n^*\}_{n\in\mathcal{N}}$ is any sequence of functions each component of which satisfies Lemma (5.2.3)(i)–(iii), then $\pi^* \in \Pi$ and if $\pi \in \Pi$ and $h_{(1)} \in H_1^*$, then*

$$\int_{H^{(1)}} u(\mathrm{proj}_C(h^{(1)}))\pi q(dh^{(1)} \mid h_{(1)}) \leq \int_{H^{(1)}} u(\mathrm{proj}_C(h^{(1)}))\pi^* q(dh^{(1)} \mid h_{(1)}).$$

Proof. Apply (5.2.6) for $n = 1$. □

Remark (5.2.9). Any sequence $\pi^* = \{\pi_n^*\}_{n\in\mathcal{N}}$ as hypothesized in Theorem (5.2.8) solves the problem (4.1.4). The interpretation of the components of such a plan as demand functions derives from the optimality of this plan. Similarly, the interpretation of d_n as the agent's demand relation derives from this optimality property. The behavior of π_n^* off H_n^* is irrelevant so long as it selects from D_n on dom D_n, since, as will be demonstrated in the next section (Theorem (5.3.5)), d_n is empty valued off Q_n^*.

5.3 Concavity and Monotonicity.

The concavity and monotonicity of u assumed in (A.2) is preserved to some extent in the derived utility function v_n. The concavity result is due to Jordan [1974: Proposition 2.33].

Lemma (5.3.1). *If $h_{(n)} \in \mathrm{dom}\, D_n$, then $v_n(h_{(n)}, \cdot)$ is concave on $D_n(h_{(n)})$. If $h_{(n)} \in H_{(n)}^*$, then $d_n(h_{(n)})$ is convex.*

Proof. Suppose $h_{(n)} \in \mathrm{dom}\, D_n$ and $a_n^i \in D_n(h_{(n)})$, $i = 1, 2$. Then $\delta_n^i = (h_{(n)}, a_n^i) \in \Delta_n$ and there exists $\nu^i \in \zeta_n(\delta_n^i)$, $i = 1, 2$, (Lemma (5.1.3)). If $0 < \beta < 1$, let $\hat{\beta}_n$, $\hat{\nu}$, and ν be as in (4.3.1). For $\delta_n = \beta\delta_n^1 + (1-\beta)\delta_n^2$, $\nu \in \mathcal{F}_n(\delta_n)$ by Lemma (4.3.2). Thus

$$\begin{aligned}
v_n(\delta_n) &\geq u_n(\delta_n, \nu) \\
&= \int_{S_{n+1}\times \hat{H}^{(n+1)}} u(\mathrm{proj}_C(\delta_n, \hat{\beta}_n(s_{n+1}, \hat{h}^{(n+1)}))\hat{\nu}(d(s_{n+1}, \hat{h}^{(n+1)})) \\
&\geq \int \{\beta u(\mathrm{proj}_C(\delta_n^1, s_{n+1}, a_{n+1}^1, \ldots)) \\
&\quad + (1-\beta)u(\mathrm{proj}_C(\delta_n^2, s_{n+1}, a_{n+1}^2, \ldots))\}\hat{\nu}(d(s_{n+1}, \hat{h}^{(n+1)})) \\
&= \beta u_n(\delta_n^1, \nu^1) + (1-\beta)u_n(\delta_n^2, \nu^2) \\
&= \beta v_n(\delta_n^1) + (1-\beta)v_n(\delta_n^2).
\end{aligned}$$

If $h_{(n)} \in H_n^*$, the convexity of $D_n(h_{(n)})$ and concavity of $v_n(h_{(n)}, \cdot)$ imply that $d_n(h_{(n)})$ is convex. □

The monotonicity result is the analog here of [Green, 1973: Lemma 3.4(iii)]. Though the result is standard, as in the case of Lemma (5.3.1), the context is not and a proof is required.

Lemma (5.3.2). *If $h_{(n)} \in \operatorname{dom} D_n$ and $a_n^i \in D_n(h_{(n)})$, $i = 1, 2$, and if $a_n^1 \leq a_n^2$, then $v_n(h_{(n)}, a_n^1) < v_n(h_{(n)}, a_n^2)$.*

Proof. Let $h_{(n)}$, a_n^1, a_n^2 be as hypothesized and let $\delta_n^i = (h_{(n)}, a_n^i)$, $i = 1, 2$. By Lemma (4.3.3), $\mathcal{F}_n(\delta_n^1) \subseteq \mathcal{F}_n(\delta_n^2)$. Thus for $\nu^1 \in \zeta_n(\delta_n^1)$,

$$\begin{aligned} v_n(\delta_n^1) &= u_n(\delta_n^1, \nu^1) \\ &\leq \int u(\operatorname{proj}_C(\delta_n^2, s_{n+1}, h^{(n+1)}))\nu^1(d(s_{n+1}, h^{(n+1)})) \\ &\leq v_n(\delta_n^2). \end{aligned}$$

If $a_n^i = (c_n^i, f_n^i)$ and $c_n^1 \leq c_n^2$, then the first inequality is strict. Thus $v_n(h_{(n)}, \cdot)$ is non-decreasing on $D_n(h_{(n)})$ and strictly increasing in c_n.

By Lemma (4.3.4), $v_{n+1}(\delta_n^1, s_{n+1}, a_{n+1}) \leq v_{n+1}(\delta_n^2, s_{n+1}, a_{n+1})$, for every s_{n+1} in $H_{n+1}^*(\delta_n^1) = H_{n+1}^*(\delta_n^2)$ and for every a_{n+1} in $D_{n+1}(\delta_n^1, s_{n+1}) \cap D_{n+1}(\delta_n^2, s_{n+1})$. Since $a_n^1 \leq a_n^2$, it follows that if $s_{n+1} \in H_{n+1}^*(\delta_n^i)$, then $D_{n+1}(\delta_n^1, s_{n+1}) \subseteq D_{n+1}(\delta_n^2, s_{n+1})$ and $(f_n^2 - f_n^1, 0) + D_{n+1}(\delta_n^1, s_{n+1}) \subseteq D_{n+1}(\delta_n^2, s_{n+1})$. Assume that $f_n^1 \leq f_n^2$, and let π_{n+1}^* satisfy Lemma (5.2.3)(i)–(iii). It follows from the strict monotonicity of $v_{n+1}(\delta_n, s_{n+1}, \cdot)$ in c_{n+1} and the results just derived that

$$v_{n+1}(\delta_n^1, s_{n+1}, \pi_{n+1}^*(\delta_n^1, s_{n+1})) < v_{n+1}(\delta_n^2, s_{n+1}, \pi_{n+1}^*(\delta_n^2, s_{n+1})),$$

for every s_{n+1} in $H_{n+1}^*(\delta_n^i)$. From this inequality and (5.2.6) we have that

$$\begin{aligned} v_n(\delta_n^1) &= \int_{H_{n+1}^*(\delta_n^1)} v_{n+1}(\delta_n^1, s_{n+1}, \pi_{n+1}^*(\delta_n^1, s_{n+1}))q_n(ds_{n+1} \mid \delta_n^1) \\ &< \int_{H_{n+1}^*(\delta_n^2)} v_{n+1}(\delta_n^2, s_{n+1}, \pi_{n+1}^*(\delta_n^2, s_{n+1}))q_n(ds_{n+1} \mid \delta_n^2) \\ &= v_n(\delta_n^2). \square \end{aligned}$$

Corollary (5.3.3). *If $h_{(n)} \in H_n^*$, then $\xi_n(h_{(n)}) \cdot d_n(h_{(n)}) = r_n(h_{(n)})$.*

Proof. Follows directly from Lemmas (5.1.6) and (5.3.2). □

The next result is the analog here of [Green, 1973: Theorem 3.5] and will be needed in [Nachman, 1980].

Lemma (5.3.4). *Let* $\{h^k_{(n)}\}_{k\in\mathcal{N}} \subseteq H^*_n$ *with* $h^k_{(n)} \to h^0_{(n)}$, *some* $h^0_{(n)}$ *in* $H_{(n)}$. *If* $a^k_n \in d_n(h^k_{(n)})$, *for each* k *in* $\mathcal{N}$, *and* $a^k_n \to a^0_n$, *and if* D_n *is l.h.c. at* $h^0_{(n)}$, *then* $a^0_n \in d_n(h^0_{(n)})$.

Proof. Follows from Lemmas (3.2.1) and (5.1.3) essentially as in [Green, 1973: Theorem 3.5]. □

Theorem (3.2.2) states that the feasible action relation is unbounded at any history $h_{(n)}$ for which $\xi_n(h_{(n)}) \notin Q_n(\xi_1(h_{(n)}),\ldots,\xi_{n-1}(h_{(n)}))$ in $\operatorname{dom} D_n$. This result, however, does not preclude $D_n(h_{(n)})$ from being unbounded only in directions in which $v_n(h_{(n)},\cdot)$ decreases, and hence does not preclude $d_n(h_{(n)})$ being non-empty at boundary points $h_{(n)}$ of H^*_n. This possibility is cleared up in our final result which makes the analogy with fundamental characterization [Green, 1973: Theorem 2.1] complete.

Theorem (5.3.5). *If* $h_{(n)} \in \operatorname{dom} D_n$ *but* $\xi_n(h_{(n)})$ *is not a member of* $Q_n(\xi_1(h_{(n)}),\ldots,\xi_{n-1}(h_{(n)}))$, *then* $v^*_n(h_{(n)}) > v_n(h_{(n)}, a_n)$ *for all* a_n *in* $D_n(h_{(n)})$.

Proof. Let $h_{(n)}$ be as hypothesized. If $\xi^1_n(h_{(n)}) \not> 0$, the result follows from Lemma (5.3.2). Therefore assume $\xi^1_n(h_{(n)}) > 0$. As in the proof of Theorem (3.2.2), there exists a vector y in $\mathbb{R}^\ell$, $y \neq 0$, such that $\xi^2_n(h_{(n)}) \cdot y = 0$ and $x \cdot y \geq (>)\ 0$ for all x in Γ' ($\operatorname{int}\Gamma'$), where Γ' is defined in the proof of Theorem (3.2.2). Thus, in particular, if $s_{n+1} \in \sigma_n(h_{(n)},\cdot)(\operatorname{int}\sigma_n(h_{(n)},\cdot))$, then $\xi^1_{n+1}(s_{n+1}) \in \Gamma'$ ($\operatorname{int}\Gamma'$) and $\xi^1_{n+1}(s_{n+1})\cdot y \geq (>)\ 0$.

Let $\hat{a}_n = (\hat{c}_n, \hat{f}_n)$ be in $D_n(h_{(n)})$ and suppose by way of contradiction that $v^*_n(h_{(n)}) = v_n(h_{(n)}, \hat{a}_n)$. Let $\bar{a}_n = (\bar{c}_n, \bar{f}_n)$ be such that $\bar{c}_n = \hat{c}_n$ and $\bar{f}_n = \hat{f}_n + y$. It is easily verified that $\bar{a}_n \in D_n(h_{(n)})$. Let $\hat{\delta}_n = (h_{(n)}, \hat{a}_n)$ and $\bar{\delta}_n = (h_{(n)}, \bar{a}_n)$. Then $H^*_{n+1}(\hat{\delta}_n) = H^*_{n+1}(\bar{\delta}_n) = \operatorname{int}\sigma_n(\hat{\delta}_n) = \operatorname{int}\sigma_n(\bar{\delta}_n)$, and if $s_{n+1} \in H^*_{n+1}(\hat{\delta}_n)$ then $D_{n+1}(\hat{\delta}_n, s_{n+1}) \subseteq D_{n+1}(\bar{\delta}_n, s_{n+1})$. In particular, if $a_{n+1} \in D_{n+1}(\hat{\delta}_n, s_{n+1})$, then $s_{n+1}\cdot a_{n+1} \leq s_{n+1}\cdot(\hat{f}_n, \omega_{n+2}) < s_{n+1}\cdot(\bar{f}_n, \omega_{n+2})$. Since $\hat{c}_n = \bar{c}_n$, it follows from

Lemma (4.3.4) that for every $a_{n+1} \in D_{n+1}(\hat{\delta}_n, s_{n+1})$, $v_{n+1}(\hat{\delta}_n, s_{n+1}, a_{n+1}) = v_{n+1}(\bar{\delta}_n, s_{n+1}, a_{n+1})$.

But by the above strict inequality in the budget constraint, Lemma (5.3.2) implies that

$$\begin{aligned} v^*_{n+1}(\hat{\delta}_n, s_{n+1}) &= \max\{v_{n+1}(\hat{\delta}_n, s_{n+1}, a_{n+1} : a_{n+1} \in D_{n+1}(\hat{\delta}_n, s_{n+1})\} \\ &= \max\{v_{n+1}(\bar{\delta}_n, s_{n+1}, a_{n+1} : a_{n+1} \in D_{n+1}(\hat{\delta}_n, s_{n+1})\} \\ &< \max\{v_{n+1}(\bar{\delta}_n, s_{n+1}, a_{n+1} : a_{n+1} \in D_{n+1}(\bar{\delta}_n, s_{n+1})\} \\ &= v^*_{n+1}(\bar{\delta}_n, s_{n+1}). \end{aligned}$$

Integrating the extremes in this inequality and using (5.2.6) gives

$$\begin{aligned} v^*_n(h_{(n)}) = v_n(h_{(n)}, \hat{a}_n) &= \int_{H^*_{n+1}(\hat{\delta}_n)} v^*_{n+1}(\hat{\delta}_n, s_{n+1}) q(ds_{n+1} \mid \hat{\delta}_n) \\ &< \int_{H^*_{n+1}(\bar{\delta}_n)} v^*_{n+1}(\bar{\delta}_n, s_{n+1}) q(ds_{n+1} \mid \bar{\delta}_n) \\ &= v_n(h_{(n)}, \bar{a}_n), \end{aligned}$$

a contradiction. □

6. Conclusion

This concludes the first part of a competitive analysis of a sequential exchange model with spot trading and unconditional futures contracting. The consistency and continuity of agent choice have been established in the absence of institutional arrangements for handling bankruptcy. These results are employed in the second part of this analysis [Nachman, 1980] concerned with the existence of temporary competitive equilibria.

Appendix

The results collected in this appendix are used in the text. They are variants of or similar to published results, but they require proof or annotated references.

Lemma(A.I). *Let r and s be positive integers, $B \subseteq \mathbb{R}^r$, and $\phi : B \to \mathbb{R}^s$ with $\emptyset \neq \operatorname{dom}\phi \subseteq B$. If (i) the graph of ϕ is closed in $B \times \mathbb{R}^s$, (ii) ϕ is convex valued, and (iii) there exists y in $\mathbb{R}^s$ such that $y \in \phi(x)$ for each x in $\operatorname{dom}\phi$, then ϕ is u.h.c. at each x in $\operatorname{dom}\phi$ where $\phi(x)$ is compact.*

Proof. Let $\bar{x}$ be in $\operatorname{dom}\phi$ and assume that $\phi(\bar{x})$ is compact. Let $\bar{y}$ be such that $(x, \bar{y}) \in \operatorname{graph}\phi$, for all x in $\operatorname{dom}\phi$. By (i), if $y \in \mathbb{R}^s$ but $y \notin \phi(\bar{x})$, there exists sets $V \subseteq \operatorname{dom}\phi$ and $U \subseteq \mathbb{R}^s$ such that V is open in $\operatorname{dom}\phi$ and $\bar{x} \in V$, U is open in $\mathbb{R}^s$, $y \in U$, and $\phi(V) \subseteq U^c$ (the complement of U) [Hildenbrand, 1974: (b), p. 24].

Let $\varepsilon > 0$ be given and let $D = \{y : y \in \mathbb{R}^s, d(y, \phi(\bar{x})) = \varepsilon\}$, where $d(y, \phi(\bar{x})) = \inf\{\|y - y'\| : y' \in \phi(\bar{x})\}$. Then D is compact and clearly $D \cap \phi(\bar{x}) = \emptyset$. Thus for each y in D there is a pair of open sets (V, U) with the properties mentioned above. Since the U cover D, there is a finite number of points $y_1, \ldots, y_k$ in D and corresponding pairs of open sets $(V_1, U_1), \ldots, (V_k, U_k)$ such that $D \subseteq \bigcup_{i=1}^k V_i \equiv U$. For $V \equiv \bigcap_{i=1}^k V_i$, $V \subseteq \operatorname{dom}\phi$, V is open in $\operatorname{dom}\phi$, and $\bar{x} \in V$. Also U is open in $\mathbb{R}^s$ and $\phi(V) \subseteq U^c \subseteq D^c$.

Let $D^- = \{y : d(y, \phi(\bar{x})) < \varepsilon\}$ and let $D^+ = \{y : d(y, \phi(\bar{x})) > \varepsilon\}$. Then $D^c = D^- \cup D^+$, $\phi(\bar{x}) \subseteq D^-$, and if $x \in V$, then by (ii) either $\phi(x) \subseteq D^-$ or $\phi(x) \subseteq D^+$. But $\bar{y} \in \phi(\bar{x}) \subseteq D^-$ and $\bar{y} \in \phi(x)$ for all x in V. This implies that $\phi(x) \subseteq D^-$ for all x in V, and hence ϕ is u.h.c. at $\bar{x}$ [Hildenbrand, 1974: p. 22]. □

Lemma (A.II). *Let $(X, \mathcal{B})$ be a measurable space and Y a metric space. If $\phi : X \to \mathcal{P}(Y)$ is $\mathcal{B}/\mathcal{B}(\mathcal{P}(Y))$-measurable, then ϕ is a transition probability. Conversely, if ϕ is a transition probability from X to Y and $\mathcal{P}(Y)$ is second countable, then $\phi : X \to \mathcal{P}(Y)$ is $\mathcal{B}/\mathcal{B}(\mathcal{P}(Y))$-measurable.*

Proof. The basic results along this line are [Dubins and Freedman, 1965: Theorems 2.1 and 3.1]. Indeed, according to [Dubins and Freedman, 1965: Theorem 2.1], if $\mathcal{W}$ is the σ-algebra of subsets of $\mathcal{P}(Y)$ generated by the mappings $\nu \to \nu(B)$, B in $\mathcal{B}(Y)$, then ϕ is $\mathcal{B}/\mathcal{W}$-measurable if and only if ϕ is a transition probability. In [Dubins and Freedman, 1965: Theorem 3.1], the equality of $\mathcal{W}$ and $\mathcal{B}(\mathcal{P}(Y))$ is asserted for Y a compact metric space. Since Y is then separable, which is equivalent to $\mathcal{P}(Y)$ being second countable [Billingsley, 1968: p. 239], this is a special case of the lemma. The coincidence of $\mathcal{W}$ with $\mathcal{B}(\mathcal{P}(Y))$ when $(Y, \mathcal{B}(Y))$ is a standard

Borel space is established in [Rieder, 1975: Lemma 6.1] but the proof uses only the fact that $\mathcal{P}(Y)$ has a countable base. □

Lemma (A.III). *Let X be a topological space and Y a separable metric space. If ν is a regular probability measure on $\mathcal{B}(X)$ ([Ash, 1972: 7.3.1]) and if ϕ is a transition probability from X to Y, then for every $\varepsilon > 0$ there is a closed set $B \subseteq X$ with $\nu(B) > 1 - \varepsilon$ such that $\phi|_B: B \to \mathcal{P}(Y)$ is continuous.*

Proof. This is a generalization of Lusin's theorem [Ash, 1972: 4.3.17(b)]. A proof when X is a metric space is given in [Jordan, 1977: Lemma 5.4]. The general case of the lemma follows from Lemma (A.II) and [Schaerf, 1947: Theorem 3.1(b), p. 35]. □

Lemma (A.IV). *Let X and Y be metric spaces and let $\phi : X \Rightarrow Y$. Define $\gamma : X \Rightarrow \mathcal{P}(Y)$ by $\gamma(x) = \{\nu : \nu \in \mathcal{P}(Y), \mathrm{supp}(\nu) \subseteq \phi(x)\}$. Then $\mathrm{dom}\,\phi = \mathrm{dom}\,\gamma$. If $B \subseteq \mathrm{dom}\,\phi$ and $\phi|_B$ is u.h.c. and compact valued, then $\gamma|_B$ is u.h.c. and compact valued. If Y is separable and complete and $\phi|_B$ is continuous and compact valued, then $\gamma|_B$ is continuous and compact valued. If Y is a Hilbert space and $\phi|_B$ is l.h.c. with closed convex values, then $\gamma|_B$ is l.h.c. with closed convex values.*

Proof. The first conclusion is clear. The proof in [Jordan, 1977: Lemma 5.5] can be relativised to $B \subseteq \mathrm{dom}\,\phi$ to obtain the second and third conclusions. If Y is a Hilbert space, the relation u_n defined in the proof of [Jordan, 1977: Lemma 5.5] can be shown to be a continuous function if $\phi|_B$ has closed convex values. The remainder of this proof then goes through. □

References

Arrow, K. J. and Hahn, F. H., 1971, *General Competitive Analysis*, San Francisco, Holden-Day.

Ash, R. B., 1972, *Real Analysis and Probability*, New York, Academic Press.

Berge, C., 1963, *Topological Spaces*, New York, Macmillan.

Billingsley, P., 1968, *Convergence of Probability Measures*, New York, John Wiley and Sons.

Breiman, L., 1968, *Probability*, Reading, Mass., Addison Wesley.

Brown, L. D. and Purves, R., 1973, "Measurable Selections of Extrema," *Ann. Stat.* **1**, 902–912.

Cootner, P. H., 1967, "Speculation and Hedging," *Food Res. Inst. Stud.* **7**, 65–106, supplement.

Cornwall, R. R., 1972, "Conditions for the Graph and the Integral of a Correspondence to be Open," *J. Math. Anal. Appl.* **39**, 771–792.

Debreu, G., 1956, "Market Equilibrium," *Proc. Natl. Acad. Sci. USA* **42**, 876–878.

Debreu, G., 1959, *Theory of Value: An Axiomatic Analysis of Economic Equilibrium*, New Haven, CT, Yale University Press.

Dubins, L. and Freedman, D., 1965, "Measurable Sets of Measures," *Pacific J. Math.* **14**, 1211–1222.

Dugundji, J., 1966, *Topology*, Boston, Allyn and Bacon.

Engelking, R., 1968, "Selectors of the First Baire Class for Semi-Continuous Set-Valued Functions," *Bull. de l'Academie Polonasie des Sciences*, séries des sciences math., astr., et phy. **1**, 277–282.

Gale, D. and Mas-Colell, A., 1975, "An Equilibrium Existence Theorem for a General Model without Ordered Preferences," *J. Math. Econ.* **2**, 9–15.

Grandmont, J. M., 1970, "On the Temporary Competitive Equilibrium," unpublished Ph.D. dissertation, CRMS Working Paper, University of California, Berkeley.

Grandmont, J. M., 1977, "Temporary General Equilibrium," *Econometrica* **45**, 535–572.

Gray, R. G. and Rutledge, D. J. S., 1971, "The Economics of Commodity Futures Markets: A Survey," *Rev. Marketing Agri. Econ.* **39**, 57–108.

Green, J. R., 1973, "Temporary General Equilibrium in a Sequential Trading Model with Spot and Futures Transactions," *Econometrica* **41**, 1103–1123.

Green, J. R., 1974, "Preexisting Contracts and Temporary General Equilibrium," in *Essays on Economic Behavior under Uncertainty*, M. S. Balach, D. McFadden, and S. Wu, eds., Amsterdam, North-Holland.

Hildenbrand, W., 1974, *Core and Equilibria of a Large Economy*, Princeton, NJ, Princeton University Press.

Jordan, J. S., 1974, "Temporary Competitive Equilibrium and the Existence of Self-Fulfilling Expectations," Ph.D. dissertation, Northwestern University, Evanston, IL.

Jordan, J. S., 1976, "Temporary Competitive Equilibrium and the Existence of Self-Fulfilling Expectations," *J. Econ. Theory* **12**, 455–471.

Jordan, J. S., 1977, "The Continuity of Optimal Dynamic Decision Rules," *Econometrica* **45**, 1365–1376.

Kertz, R. P. and Nachman, D. C., 1979, "Persistently Optimal Plans for Nonstationary Dynamic Programming: The Topology of Weak Convergence Case," *Ann. Prob.* **7**, 811–826.

Kuratowski, K. and Ryll-Nardzewski, C., 1965, "A General Theorem on Selectors," *Bull. de l'Academie Polonaise des Sciences*, (séries des sciences math., astr., et phy.) **13**, 397–403.

LeRoy, S., 1979, "Expectations' Models of Asset Prices: A Survey of Theory, Report 7957, Center for Mathematical Studies in Business and Economics, University of Chicago.

Mas-Colell, A., 1974, "An Equilibrium Existence Theorem without Complete or Transitive Preferences," *J. Math. Econ.* **1**, 237–246.

Michael, E., 1959, "Convex Structures and Continuous Selections," *Canadian*

J. Math. **11**, 556–575.

Nachman, D. C., 1980, "Temporary Competitive Equilibrium in a Sequence of Spot and Futures Markets," Working Paper, College of Management, Georgia Institute of Technology, Atlanta, GA.

Parthasarathy, K. R., 1967, *Probability Measures on Metric Spaces*, New York, Academic Press.

Radner, R., 1967, "Equilibre des Marchés à Terme et au Comptant en Cas d'Incertitude," *Cahiers d'Econometrie*, CNRS, Paris, 35–52, (translated as "Equilibrium of Spot and Futures Markets under Uncertainty," CRMS Technical Report **24**, University of California, Berkeley, 1967).

Radner, R., 1972, "Existence of Equilibrium of Plans, Prices, and Price Expectations in a Sequence of Markets," *Econometrica* **40**, 289–303.

Radner, R., 1974, "Market Equilibrium and Uncertainty: Concepts and Problems," in *Frontiers of Quantitative Economics*, Vol. II, M. D. Intriligator and D. A. Kendrick, eds., Amsterdam, North-Holland.

Rieder, U., 1975, "Bayesian Dynamic Programming," *Adv. Appl. Prob.* **7**, 330–348.

Rockafeller, R. T., 1970, *Convex Analysis*, Princeton, NJ, Princeton University Press.

Shafer, W. and Sonnenschein, H., 1975, "Equilibrium in Abstract Economies without Ordered Preferences," *J. Math. Econ.* **2**, 345–348.

Schaerf, H. M., 1947, "On the Continuity of Measurable Functions in Neighborhood Spaces," *Portugaliae Mathematica* **6**, 33–44.

Sobel, M. J., 1975, "Ordinal Dynamic Programming," *Management Sci.* **21**, 967–975.

Stigum, B. P., 1969, "Competitive Equilibrium under Uncertainty," *Q. J. Econ.* **83**, 533–561.

Stigum, B. P., 1972, "Resource Allocation under Uncertainty," *Int. Econ. Rev.* **13**, 431–459.

Stigum, B. P., 1974, "On Preexisting Contracts and Temporary Equilibria," comments on Chapter 10 in *Essays on Economic Behavior under Uncertainty*, M. S. Balach, D. McFadden, and S. Wu, eds., Amsterdam, North-Holland.

PART 8

REFERENCES

REFERENCES

Aliprantis, C. D. and Brown, D. J., 1983, "Equilibria in Markets with a Riesz Space of Commodities," *J. Math. Econ.* **11**, 189–207.

Aliprantis, C. D., Brown, D. J., and Burkinshaw, O., 1985, "Edgeworth Equilibria," Cowles Foundation Discussion paper.

Aliprantis, C. D., Brown, D. J. and Burkinshaw, O., 1986, "Edgeworth Equilibria in Production Economies," Cowles Foundation Discussion paper.

Aliprantis, C. D., Brown, D. J. and Burkinshaw, O., 1987, "Edgeworth Equilibria," *Econometrica* **55**, 1109–1138.

Aliprantis, C. D., Brown, D. J. and Burkinshaw, O., 1989, *Existence and Optimality of Competitive Equilibria*, Springer-Verlag, New York.

Aliprantis, C. D. and Burkinshaw, O., 1978, *Locally Solid Riesz Spaces*, Academic Press, New York.

Aliprantis, C. D. and Burkinshaw, O., 1985, *Positive Operators*, Academic Press, New York.

Aliprantis, C. D. and Burkinshaw, O., 1988, "The Fundamental Theorems of Welfare Economics without Proper Preferences," *J. Math. Econ.* **17**, 41–54.

Anderson, R., 1978, "An Elementary Core Equivalence Theorem," *Econometrica* **46**, 1483–1487.

Araujo, A., 1985, "Lack of Pareto Optimal Allocations in Economies with Infinitely Many Commodities: The Need for Impatience," *Econometrica* **53**, 455–461.

Araujo, A. and Monteiro, P. K., 1989, "Equilibrium without Uniform Conditions," *J. Econ. Theory* **48**, 416–427.

Armstrong, T. and Richter, M. K., 1984, "The Core-Walras Equivalence," *J. Econ. Theory* **33**, 116–151.

Armstrong, T. and Richter, M. K., 1986, "Existence of Non-atomic Core-Walras Allocations," *J. Econ. Theory* **38**, 137–159.

Arrow, K. J., 1953, "Le Rôle des Valeurs Boursières pour la Répartition la meilleure des Risques," *Econometrie*, CNRS, Paris, 41–47.

Arrow, K. J., 1951, "An Extension of the Basic Theorems of Classical Welfare Economics," in *Proc. Second Berkeley Symp. Math. Stat. Probab.*, J. Neyman, ed., University of California Press, Berkeley and Los Angeles, 507–532.

Arrow, K. J. and Debreu, G., 1954, "Existence of an Equilibrium for a Competitive Economy," *Econometrica* **22**, 265–290.

Arrow, K. J. and Hahn, F. H., 1971, *General Competitive Analysis*, San Francisco, Holden-Day.

Artstein, Z., 1979, "A Note on Fatou's Lemma in Several Dimensions," *J. Math. Econ.* **6**, 277–282.

Ash, R. B., 1972, *Real Analysis and Probability*, New York, Academic Press.

Aubin, J. P. and Cellina, A., 1984, *Differential Inclusions*, Springer-Verlag, Berlin.

Aumann, R., 1963, "Economies with a Continuum of Agents," *Econometrica*.

Aumann, R. J., 1964, "The Core of a Cooperative Game Without Side Payments," *Trans. Amer. Math. Soc.*, 539–552.

Aumann, R. J., 1964, "Markets with a Continuum of Traders," *Econometrica* **32**, 39–50.

Aumann, R. J., 1965, "Integrals of Set-Valued Functions," *J. Math. Anal. Appl.* **12**, 1–12.

Aumann, R. J., 1966, "Existence of a Competitive Equilibrium in Markets with a Continuum of Traders," *Econometrica* **34**, 1–17.

Aumann, R. J., 1967, "Measurable Utility and the Measurable Choice Theorem," in *La Decision*, 15–26, CNRS, Aix-en-Provence.

Aumann, R. J., 1974, "Subjectivity and Correlation in Randomized Strategies," *J. Math. Econ.* **1**, 67–96.

Aumann, R. J., 1976, "An Elementary Proof that Integration Preserves Uppersemicontinuity," *J. Math. Econ.* **3**, 15–18.

Aumann, R. J., 1987, "Correlated Equilibrium as an Expression of Bayesian Rationality," *Econometrica* **55**, 1–18.

Back, K., 1988, "Structure of Consumption Sets and Existence of Equilibria in Infinite Dimensional Commodity Spaces," *J. Math. Econ.* **17**, 88–99.

Balder, E. J., 1984, "A General Approach to Lower Semicontinuity and Lower Closure in Optimal Control Theory," *SIAM J. Control Optim.* **22**, 570–599.

Balder, E. J., 1984, "A Unifying Note on Fatou's Lemma in Several Dimensions," *Math. Oper. Res.* **29**, 267–275.

Balder, E. J., 1987, "More on Fatou's Lemma in Several Dimensions," *Canadian Math. Bull.* **30**, 334–339.

Balder, E. J., 1988, "Fatou's Lemma in Infinite Dimensions," *J. Math. Anal. Appl.* **136**, 450–465.

Balder, E. J., 1988, "Generalized Equilibrium Results for Games with Incomplete Information," *Math. Oper. Res.* **13**, 265–276.

Balder, E. J., 1990, "New Sequential Compactness Results for Spaces of Scalarly Integrable Functions," *J. Math. Anal. Appl.* **151**, 1–16.

Balder, E. J. and Yannelis, N. C., 1990, "Equilibria in Random and Bayesian Games with a Continuum of Players," this volume.

Beals, R. and Koopmans, T. C., 1969, "Maximizing Stationary Utility in a Constant Technology," *SIAM J. Appl. Math.* **17**, 1001–1015.

Becker, R. A., 1981, "The Duality of a Dynamic Model of Equilibrium and an Optimal Growth Model: the Heterogeneous Capital Goods Case," *Q. J. Econ.* **96**, 271–300.

Becker, R. A., Bercovici, H. and Foias, C., 1989, "Weak Pareto Optimality and the Approximate Support Property," working paper, Indiana University.

Berge, C., 1963, *Topological Spaces*, New York, Macmillan.

Berninghaus, S., 1977, "Individual and Collective Risks in Large Economies," *J. Econ. Theory* **15**, 279–294.

Bewley, T., 1969, "Equilibrium Theory with an Infinite Dimensional Commodity Space," working paper, CORE.

Bewley, T., 1972, "Existence of Equilibria in Economies with Infinitely Many Commodities," *J. Econ. Theory* **4**, 514–540.

Bewley, T., 1973, "The Equality of the Core and the Set of Equilibria in Economies with Infinitely Many Commodities and Continuum of Agents," *Int. Econ. Rev.* **14**, 383–393.

Bewley, T., 1982, "An Integration of Equilibrium Theory and Turnpike Theory," *J. Math. Econ.* **10**, 233–267.

Bewley, T., 1990, "A Theorem on the Existence of Equilibria in a Market with a Finite Number of Agents and whose Commodity Space is L_∞," this volume.

Bewley, T., 1990, "A Very Weak Theorem on the Existence of Equilibria in Atomless Economies with Infinitely Many Commodities," this volume.

Bhaskara Rao, K. P. S. and Bhaskara Rao, M., 1983, *Theory of Charges*, Academic Press, New York.

Bhattacharya, R. N. and Majumdar, M., 1973, "Random Exchange Economies," *J. Econ. Theory* **6**, 37–67.

Billingsley, P., 1968, *Convergence of Probability Measures*, New York, John Wiley and Sons.

Bonnisseau, J. M. and Cornet, B., 1988, "Valuation Equilibrium and Pareto Optimality in Non-Convex Economies," *J. Math. Econ.* **17**, 293–308.

Border, K., 1989, "Stochastic Dominance and Choice of Lotteries," mimeo.

Border, K. C., 1984, "A Core Existence Theorem for Games Without Ordered Preferences," *Econometrica* **52**, 1537–1542.

Borglin, A. and Keiding, H., 1976, "The Existence of Equilibrium Actions and of Equilibrium: A Note on the 'New' Existence Theorems," *J. Math. Econ.* **3**, 313–316.

Boyd, J. H., 1986, *Preferences, Technology and Dynamic Equilibria*, Ph.D. Dissertation, Indiana University.

Boyd, J. H., 1990, "Recursive Utility and the Ramsey Problem," *J. Econ. Theory* **50**, 326–345.

Breiman, L., 1968, *Probability*, Reading, Mass., Addison Wesley.

Brock, W. A., 1982, "Asset Prices in a Production Economy," *The Economics of Information and Uncertainty*, J. McCall, ed., University of Chicago Press, Chicago, 1–42.

Browder, F., 1968, "The Fixed Point Theory of Multivalued Mappings in Topological Vector Spaces," *Math. Ann.* **177**, 283–301.

Brown, D. J. and Lewis, L. M., 1981, "Myopic Economic Agents," *Econometrica* **49**, 359–368.

Brown, D. J. and Khan, M. A., 1980, "An Extension of the Brown-Robinson Equivalence Theorem," *Appl. Math. Comp.* **6**, 167–175.

Brown, D. J. and Robinson, A., 1975, "Nonstandard Exchange Economies," *Econometrica* **43**, 41–55.

Brown, L. D. and Purves, R., 1973, "Measurable Selections of Extrema," *Ann. Stat.* **1**, 902–912.

Byrne, C. L., 1978, "Remarks on the Set-Valued Integrals of Debreu and Aumann," *J. Math. Anal. Appl.* **62**, 243–246.

Castaing, C., 1979, "Sur l'existence des Sections Séparément Continues d'une Multi-Application," in *Travaux du Seminaire d'analyse Convexe*, Univ. des. Sci. et Techniques du Languedoc **5**, 14.

Castaing, C., 1988, "Quelques Resultats de Convergence des Suites Apaptees," *Seminaire D'Analyse Convexe*, Montpellier, Vol. 17, Exposés 1 á 12.

Castaing, C. and Valadier, M., 1977, "Convex Analysis and Measurable Multifunctions," *Lect. Notes Math.* **580**, Springer-Verlag, New York.

Champsaur, P. and Laroque, G., 1971, "Notes Sur Les Mechanismes de Blocage," unpublished manuscript, Paris.

Cheng, Harrison H. C., 1986, "The Coalitional Approach to the Core Theory," *J. Math. Econ.*, forthcoming.

Cheng, Harrison H. C., 1987a, "Arbitrage Theory and Equilibrium: The Case of Unconstrained Consumption," MRG Working Paper M8719, Department of Economics, University of Southern California.

Cheng, Harrison H. C., 1987b, "The Existence of Arbitrage-Free Equilibria in Banach Spaces," MRG Working Paper M8712, Department of Economics, University of Southern California.

Cheng, Harrison H. C., 1987c, "Asset Market Equilibrium in Infinite Dimensional Economies," *J. Math. Econ.*, to appear.

Cheng, Harrison H. C., 1987d, "Dynamic Hedging, Arbitrage Pricing, and the Efficient Market Hypothesis: An Axiomatic Approach," Department of Economics, University of Southern California.

Chew, S. H., 1983, "A Generalization of the Quasilinear Mean with Applications to the Measurement of Income Inequality and Decision Theory Resolving the Allais Paradox," *Econometrica* **51**, 1065–1092.

Chew, S. H., 1989, "Axiomatic Utility Theories with the Betweenness Property," *Ann. Oper. Res.* **19**, 273–298.

Chew, S. H. and Epstein, L. G., 1989, "The Structure of Preferences and Attitudes Towards the Timing of the Resolution of Uncertainty," *Int. Econ. Rev.* **30**, 103–117.

Chew, S. H., Epstein, L. G., and Segal, U., 1990, "Mixture Symmetry and Quadratic Utility," *Econometrica*, to appear.

Coles, J., 1985, "Equilibrium Turnpike Theory with Constant Returns to Scale and Possibly Heterogeneous Discount Factors," *Int. Econ. Rev.* **26**, 671–679.

Coles, J., 1986, "Equilibrium Turnpike Theory with Time-Separable Utility," *J. Econ. Dyn. Control* **10**, 367–394.

Cook, V. G., 1989, "The Effects of Temporal Uncertainty Resolution on the Overall Utility and Suspense of Risky Monetary and Survival Gambles," Ph.D. dissertation, Department of Psychology, McGill University.

Cootner, P. H., 1967, "Speculation and Hedging," *Food Res. Inst. Stud.* **7**, 65–106, supplement.

Cornwall, R. R., 1972, "Conditions for the Graph and the Integral of a Correspondence to be Open," *J. Math. Anal. Appl.* **39**, 771–792.

Cotter, K., 1989, "Correlated Equilibria with Payoff Uncertainty," CMSEMS Discussion Paper #840, Northwestern University.

Cotter, K., 1990, "Correlated Equilibria with Exogenous Uncertainty," mimeo.

Cotter, K., 1990a, "Correlated Equilibria in Games with Type-Dependent Strategies," *J. Econ. Theory*, to appear.

Cotter, K., 1990b, "Similarity of Games with Incomplete Information," *J. Math. Econ.*, to appear.

Cournot, A., 1929, *Recherches Sur Les Principes Mathématiques de la Théorie des Richesse*, Hachette, Paris. Translated as *Researches into the Mathematical Principles of the Theory of Wealth*, Macmillan, New York.

Dasgupta, P. and Maskin, E., 1986, "The Existence of Equilibrium in Discontinuous Economic Games, I: Theory," *Rev. Econ. Stud.* **53**, 1–26.

Dasgupta, P. and Maskin, E., 1986, "The Existence of Equilibrium in Discontinuous Economic Games, II: Applications," *Rev. Econ. Stud.* **8**, 27–41.

Datko, R., 1973, "On the Integration of Set-Valued Mappings in a Banach Space," *Fund. Math.* **78**, 205–208.

Debreu, G., 1951, "The Coefficient of Resource Utilization," *Econometrica* **19**, 273–292, reprinted in *Mathematical Economics: Twenty Papers of Gerard Debreu*, Cambridge University Press, New York, 1983, 30–49.

Debreu, G., 1952, "A Social Equilibrium Existence Theorem," *Proc. Natl. Acad. Sci. USA* **38**, 886–893.

Debreu, G., 1954, "Representation of a Preference Ordering by a Numerical Function," in *Decision Processes*, R. Thrall, C. Coombs and R. David, eds., New York, John Wiley.

Debreu, G., 1954, "Valuation Equilibrium and Pareto Optimum," *Proc. Natl. Acad. Sci. U.S.A.* **40**, 588–592. Reprinted in *Mathematical Economics: Twenty Papers of Gerard Debreu*, Cambridge University Press, New York, 1983, 98–104.

Debreu, G., 1956, "Market Equilibrium," *Proc. Natl. Acad. Sci. USA* **42**, 876–878.

Debreu, G., 1959, *Theory of Value*, John Wiley and Sons, New York.

Debreu, G., 1962, "New Concepts and Techniques for Equilibrium Analysis," *Int. Econ. Rev.* **3**, 257–273.

Debreu, G., 1967, "Integration of Correspondences," *Proc. Fifth Berkeley Symp. Math. Stat. Prob.*, University of California Press, Berkeley, Vol. II, Part I, 351–372.

Debreu, G., 1967a, "Preference Functions on Measure Spaces of Economic Agents," *Econometrica* **35**, 111–122.

Debreu, G., 1986, "Theoretic Models: Mathematical Form and Economic Content," *Econometrica* **54**, 1259–1270.

Debreu, G. and Scarf, H., 1963, "A Limit Theorem on the Core of an Economy," *Int. Econ. Rev.* **4**, 235–246.

Debreu, G. and Schmeidler, D., 1972, "The Radon-Nikodým Derivative of a Correspondence," *Proc. Sixth Berkeley Symp. Math. Stat. Prob.*, Vol. II, L. Lecam, J. Neyman and E. Scott, eds., University of California Press, 41–56.

Dekel, E., 1986, "An Axiomatic Characterization of Preferences Under Uncertainty," *J. Econ. Theory* **40**, 304–318.

Diestel, J., 1977, "Remarks on Weak Compactness in $L_1(\mu, X)$," *Glasgow Math. J.* **18**, 87–91.

Diestel, J. and Uhl, J., 1977, *Vector Measures*, Mathematical Surveys **15**, American Mathematical Society, Providence, Rhode Island.

Dinculeanu, N., 1973, "Linear Operations on L_p-Spaces," in H. Maynard and D. Tucker, eds., *Vector and Operator Valued Measures and Applications*, Academic Press, New York.

Dubey, P. and Shapley, L., 1977, "Non-Cooperative Exchange with a Continuum of Traders," Cowles Foundation Discussion Paper No. 447.

Dubey, P. and Shubik, M., 1978, "Strategic Market Games and Market Mechanisms," Cowles Foundation Discussion Paper, forthcoming.

Dubins, L. and Freedman, D., 1965, "Measurable Sets of Measures," *Pacific J. Math.* **14**, 1211–1222.

Duffie, D., 1986, "Competitive Equilibria in General Choice Spaces," *J. Math. Econ.* **14**, 1–23.

Duffie, D. and Huang, C. F., 1985, "Implementing Arrow-Debreu Equilibria by Continuous Trading of Few Long-lived Securities," *Econometrica* **53**, 1337–1357.

Dugundji, J., 1966, *Topology*, Allyn and Bacon, Boston.

Dunford, N. and Schwartz, J. T., 1958, *Linear Operators Part I: General Theory*, Wiley Interscience Publishers, New York.

Edgeworth, F., 881, *Mathematical Psychics*, Kegan Paul, London.

Edwards, R. E., 1965, *Functional Analysis: Theory and Applications*, Holt, Rinehart and Winston, New York.

Engelking, R., 1968, "Selectors of the First Baire Class for Semi-Continuous Set-Valued Functions," *Bull. de l'Academie Polonasie des Sciences*, séries des sciences math., astr., et phy. **1**, 277–282.

Epstein, L. G., 1983, "Stationary Cardinal Utility and Optimal Growth Under Uncertainty," *J. Econ. Theory* **31**, 133–152.

Epstein, L. G., 1988, "Risk Aversion and Asset Prices," *J. Monetary Econ.* **22**, 179–192.

Epstein, L. G. and Hynes, A. J., 1983, "The Rate of Time Preference and Dynamic Economic Analysis," *J. Pol. Econ.* **91**, 611–625.

Epstein, L. G. and Zin, S. E., 1989, "Substitution, Risk Aversion and the Temporal Behavior of Consumption and Asset Returns: A Theoretical Framework," *Econometrica* **57**, 937–969.

Fan, K., 1952, "Fixed Point and Minimax Theorems in Locally Convex Topological Linear Spaces," *Proc. Natl. Acad. Sci. USA* **38**, 131–136.

Fan, K., 1953, "Minimax Theorems," *Proc. Natl. Acad. Sci. USA* **39**, 42–47.

Fan, K., 1956, "On Systems of Linear Inequalities," in *Linear Inequalities and Related Systems*, H. W. Kuhn and A. W. Tucker, eds., Princeton University Press, 99–156.

Fan, K., 1962, "A Generalization of Tychonoff's Fixed Point Theorem," *Math. Ann.* **143**, 305–310.

Fan, K., 1969, "Extensions of Two Fixed Point Theorems of F. E. Browder," *Math. Z.* **112**, 234–240.

Federer, H., 1969, *Geometric Measure Theory*, Springer-Verlag, New York.

Florenzano, M., 1983, "On the Existence of Equilibria in Economies with an Infinite Dimensional Commodity Space," *J. Math. Econ.* **12**, 207–219.

Fryszkowski, A., 1977, "Carathéodory-type Selectors of Set-Valued Maps of Two Variables," *Bull. Acad. Polon. Sci.* **25**, 41–46.

Gabszewicz, J., 1968, "Coeurs et Allocations Concurrentielles dans des Economies d'Echange avec un Continu de Biens," Librarie Universitair, Louvain.

Gabszewicz, J. and Vial, J. P., 1971, "Oligopoly à la Cournot in General Equilibrium Theory," *J. Econ. Theory*.

Gale, D. and Mas-Colell, A., 1975, "An Equilibrium Existence Theorem for a General Model without Ordered Preferences," *J. Math. Econ.* **2**, 9–15.

Gerard-Varet, L. A. and Moulin, H., 1978, "Correlation and Duopoly," *J. Econ. Theory* **19**, 123–149.

Gilles, C. and Leroy, S. T., 1989, "Bubbles and Charges," working paper, University of California at Santa Barbara.

Glicksberg, I. L., 1952, "A Further Generalization of the Kakutani Fixed Point Theorem, with Applications to Nash Equilibrium Points," *Proc. Amer. Math. Soc.* **3**, 170–174.

Grandmont, J. M., 1970, "On the Temporary Competitive Equilibrium," unpublished Ph.D. dissertation, CRMS Working Paper, University of California, Berkeley.

Grandmont, J. M., 1977, "Temporary General Equilibrium," *Econometrica* **45**, 535–572.

Gray, R. G. and Rutledge, D. J. S., 1971, "The Economics of Commodity Futures Markets: A Survey," *Rev. Marketing Agri. Econ.* **39**, 57–108.

Green, E., 1978, "Non-Cooperative Price Taking in Large Dynamic Markets," Working Paper No. 228, Princeton University.

Green, J. R., 1973, "Temporary General Equilibrium in a Sequential Trading Model with Spot and Futures Transactions," *Econometrica* **41**, 1103–1123.

Green, J. R., 1974, "Preexisting Contracts and Temporary General Equilibrium," in *Essays on Economic Behavior under Uncertainty*, M. S. Balach, D. McFadden, and S. Wu, eds., Amsterdam, North-Holland.

Gretsky, N. and Ostroy, J., 1985, "Thick and Thin Market Non-Atomic Exchange Economies" in *Advances in Equilibrium Theory*, C. D. Aliprantis, O. Burkinshaw and N. J. Rothman, eds., Springer-Verlag, New York.

Grodal, B., 1972, "A Second Remark on the Core of an Atomless Economy," *Econometrica* **40**, 581–583.

Halmos, P. R. and Von Neumann, J., 1941, "Operator Methods in Classical Mechanics, II," *Ann. Math.* **43:2**.

Hammond, P., 1976, "Individual Incentive Compatibility in Large Economies," University of Essex Discussion Paper No. 88.

Hansen, T., 1969, "A Note on the Limit of the Core of an Exchange Economy," *Int. Econ. Rev.* **10**, 479–483.

Harris, M., 1987, *Dynamic Economic Analysis*, Oxford University Press, New York-Oxford, UK.

Harrison, J. M. and Kreps, D., 1979, "Martingales and Arbitrage in Multiperiod Securities Markets," *J. Econ. Theory* **20**, 381–408.

Harsanyi, J. C., 1967, "Games with Incomplete Information Played by Bayesian Players," Parts I, II, II, *Management Sci.* **14**, 155–182, 320–334, 486–502.

Hart, O., 1974, "On the Existence of Equilibrium in a Securities Model," *J. Econ. Theory* **9**, 293–311.

Hart, O., 1977, "Monopolistic Competition with Differentiated Commodities," Cambridge, mimeo.

Hart, S., Hildenbrand, W., and Kohlberg, E., 1974, "On Equilibrium Allocation as Distributions on the Commodity Space," *J. Math. Econ* **1**, 159–166.

Hart, S. and Schmeidler, D., 1989, "Existence of Correlated Equilibria," *Math. Oper. Res.* **14**, 18–25.

Hiai, F. and Umegaki, H., 1977, "Integrals Conditional Expectations and Martingales of Multivalued Function," *J. Multivar. Anal.* **7**, 149–182.

Hildenbrand, W., 1968, "The Core of an Economy with a Measure Space of Economic Agents," *Rev. Econ. Stud.* **35**, 443–452.

Hildenbrand, W., 1970, "On Economies with Many Agents," *J. Econ. Theory* **2**, 161–168.

Hildenbrand, W., 1971, "Random Preferences and Equilibrium Analysis," *J. Econ. Theory* **3**, 414–429.

Hildenbrand, W., 1974, *Core and Equilibria of a Large Economy*, Princeton University Press, Princeton, New Jersey.

Hille, E. and Phillips, R. S., 1957, *Functional Analysis and Semi-Groups*, American Mathematical Society, Providence.

Himmelberg, C. J., 1975, "Measurable Relations," *Fund. Math.* **87**, 53–72.

Holmes, R., 1975, *Geometric Functional Analysis and Its Applications*, Springer-Verlag, New York.

Huang, C. and Kreps, D., 1987, "On Intertemporal Preferences with a Continuous Time Dimension I: The Case of Certainty," working paper, Massachusetts Institute of Technology.

Hurwicz, L., 1959, "Optimality and Informational Efficiency in Resource Allocation Processes," in *Mathematical Methods in the Social Sciences*, Arrow, Karlin and Suppes, eds., Stanford University Press.

Ichiichi, T., 1981, *Game Theory for Economic Analysis*, Academic Press, New York.

Ichiichi, T., 1981a, "On the Knaster-Kuratowski-Mazurkiewicz-Shapley Theorem," *J. Math. Anal. Appl.* **81**, 297–299.

Ichiichi, T. and Schaffer, S. T., 1983, "The Topological Core of a Game without Side Payments," *Econ. Stud. Q.* **34**, 1–8.

Ionescu-Tulcea, A. and C., 1969, *Topics in the Theory of Lifting*, Springer-Verlag, Berlin.

Itoh, S., 1979, "Random Fixed Point Theorems with Applications to Random Differential Equations in Banach Spaces," *J. Math. Anal. Appl.* **67**, 261–273.

James, R., 1964, "Weakly Compact Sets," *Trans. Amer. Math. Soc.* **113**, 129–140.

Jameson, C., 1970, *Ordered Linear Spaces*, Springer-Verlag, New York.

Jamison, R. E., 1974, "A Quick Proof for a One-Dimensional Version of Liapunoff's Theorem," *Amer. Math. Monthly* **81**, 507–508.

Jaynes, J., Okuno, M., and Schmeidler, D., 1976, "Efficiency in an Atomless Economy with Fiat Money," *Int. Econ. Rev.*, 124–128.

Johnsen, T. H. and Donaldson, J. B., 1985, "The Structure of Intertemporal Preferences Under Uncertainty and Time Consistent Plans," *Econometrica* **53**, 1451–1458.

Jones, L. E., 1984, "A Competitive Model of Commodity Differentiation," *Econometrica* **52**, 507–530.

Jones, L. E., 1986, "Special Problems Arising in the Study of Economies with Infinitely Many Commodities," in *Models of Economic Dynamics*, H. F. Sonnenschein, ed., Springer-Verlag Lecture Notes in Economics and Mathematical Systems #264, Berlin-New York, 184–205.

Jones, L. E., 1987, "Existence of Equilibria with Infinitely Many Commodities: Banach Lattices Reconsidered," *J. Math. Econ.* **16**, 89–104.

Jordan, J. S., 1974, "Temporary Competitive Equilibrium and the Existence of Self-Fulfilling Expectations," Ph.D. dissertation, Northwestern University, Evanston, IL.

Jordan, J. S., 1976, "Temporary Competitive Equilibrium and the Existence of Self-Fulfilling Expectations," *J. Econ. Theory* **12**, 455–471.

Jordan, J. S., 1977, "The Continuity of Optimal Dynamic Decision Rules," *Econometrica* **45**, 1365–1376.

Kajii, A., 1989, "A Generalization of Scarf's Theorem: An α-Core Existence Theorem without Transitivity," Harvard University, mimeo.

Kelley, J. L., 1955, *General Topology*, van Nostrand, New York.

Kelley, J. and Namioka, I., 1963, *Linear Topological Spaces,* Springer, New York.

Kertz, R. P. and Nachman, D. C., 1979, "Persistently Optimal Plans for Nonstationary Dynamic Programming: The Topology of Weak Convergence Case," *Ann. Prob.* **7**, 811–826.

Khan, M. Ali, 1974a, "Some Remarks on the Core of a 'Large Economy'," *Econometrica* **42**, 633–642.

Khan, M. Ali, 1974b, "Some Equivalence Theorems," *Rev. Econ. Stud.* **41**, 549–565.

Khan, M. Ali, 1982, "On the Integration of Set-Valued Mappings in a Reflexive Banach Space," Johns Hopkins University Working Paper.

Khan, M. Ali, 1984, "An Alternative Proof of Diestel's Theorem," *Glasgow Math. J.* **25**, 45–46.

Khan, M. Ali, 1985, "On Extensions of the Cournot-Nash Theorem," in *Advances in Equilibrium Theory*, Lecture Notes in Economics and Mathematical Systems **244**, C. D. Aliprantis et al, eds., Springer-Verlag, New York.

Khan, M. Ali, 1985a, "On the Integration of Set-Valued Mappings in a Nonreflexive Banach Space II," *Simon Stevin* **59**, 257–267.

Khan, M. Ali, 1986, "Equilibrium Points of Nonatomic Games Over a Banach Space," *Trans. Amer. Math. Soc.* **29**, 737–749.

Khan, M. Ali, 1987, "Ioffe's Normal Cone and the Foundations of Welfare Economics: The Infinite Dimensional Theory," working paper, University of Illinois, *J. Math. Anal. Appl.*, to appear.

Khan, M. Ali, 1988, "Ioffe's Normal Cone and the Foundations of Welfare Economics: An Example," *Econ. Lett.* **28**, 15–19.

Khan, M. Ali, 1989, "On Cournot-Nash Equilibrium Distributions for Games with a Non-Metrizable Action Space and Upper Semi-Continuous Payoffs," *Trans. Amer. Math. Soc.* **315**, 126–146.

Khan, M. Ali and Majumdar, M., 1986, "Weak Sequential Convergence in $L_1(\mu, X)$ and an Approximate Version of Fatou's Lemma," *J. Math. Anal. Appl.* **114**, 569–573.

Khan, M. Ali and Papageorgiou, N. S., 1987, "On Cournot-Nash Equilibria in Generalized Quantitative Games with an Atomless Measure Space of Agents," *Proc. Amer. Math. Soc.* **100**, 505–510.

Khan, M. Ali and Peck, N. T., 1989, "On the Interiors of Production Sets in Infinite Dimensional Spaces," *J. Math. Econ.* **18**, 29–39.

Khan, M. Ali and Sun, Y., 1990, "On a Reformation of Cournot-Nash Equilibria," *J. Math. Anal. Appl.* **146**, 442–460.

Khan, M.Ali and Vohra, R., 1984, "Equilibrium in Abstract Economies without Ordered Preferences and with a Measure Space of Agents," *J. Math. Econ.* **13**, 133–142.

Khan, M. Ali and Vohra, R., 1985, "On the Existence of Lindahl Equilibria in Economies with a Measure Space of Nontransitive Consumers," *J. Econ. Theory* **36**.

Khan, M. Ali and Vohra, R., 1985a, "Approximate Equilibrium Theory in Economics with Infinitely Many Commodities," working paper, Brown University.

Khan, M. Ali and Vohra, R., 1985b, "Pareto Optimal Allocations of Non-Convex Economies in Locally Convex Spaces," working paper, University of Illinois, published in *Nonlinear Analysis* **12**, 943–950, 1988.

Khan, M. Ali and Vohra, R., 1988, "On Approximate Decentralization of Pareto Optimal Allocations in Locally Convex Commodity Spaces," *J. Approx. Theory* **52**, 149–161.

Khan, M. Ali and Yannelis, N. C., 1990, "Existence of a Competitive Equilibrium in Markets with a Continuum of Agents and Commodities," this volume.

Kim, T., 1990, "The Subjective Expected Utility Hypothesis and Revealed Preference," *Econ. Theory*, to appear.

Kim, T., Prikry, K. and Yannelis N. C., 1987, "Carathéodory-Type Selections and Random Fixed Point Theorems," *J. Math. Anal. Appl.* **122**, 393–407.

Kim, T., Prikry, K. and Yannelis, N. C., 1988, "On a Carathéodory-Type Selection Theorem," *J. Math. Anal. Appl.* **135**, 664–670.

Kim, T., Prikry, K. and Yannelis, N. C., 1989, "Equilibria in Abstract Economies with a Measure Space of Agents and with an Infinite Dimensional Strategy Space," *J. Approx. Theory* **56**, 256–266.

Kim, T. and Richter, M. K., 1986, "Nontransitive, Nontotal Consumer Theory," *J. Econ. Theory* **38**, 324–363.

King, R. G., Plosser, C. I. and Rebelo, S. T., 1988, "Production, Growth and Business Cycles I: The Basic Neoclassical Model," *J. Monetary Econ.* **21**, 195–232.

Kingman, J. and Robertson, A., 1968, "On a Theorem of Lyapunov," *J. London Math. Soc.* **43**, 347–351.

Kluvanek, I., 1973, "The Range of a Vector Valued Measure," *Math. Syst. Theory* **7**, 44–54.

Kluvanek, I. and Knowles, G., 1975, "Vector Measures and Control System," *Math. Stud.* **20**, North Holland.

Knowles, G., 1974, "Lyapunov Vector Measures," *SIAM J. Control* **13**, 294–303.

Koopmans, T. C., 1960, "Stationary Ordinal Utility and Impatience," *Econometrica* **28**, 287–309.

Koopmans, T. C., Diamond, P., and Williamson, R., 1964, "Stationary Utility and Time Perspective," *Econometrica* **32**, 82–100.

Kreps, D., 1981, "Arbitrage and Equilibrium in Economies with Infinitely Many Commodities," *J. Math. Econ.* **8**, 15–36.

Kreps, D. M. and Porteus, E. L., 1978, "Temporal Resolution of Uncertainty and Dynamic Choice Theory," *Econometrica* **46**, 185–200.

Kuratowski, K., 1966, *Topology*, Vol. I, Academic Press, New York.

Kuratowski, K. and Ryll-Nardzewski, C., 1965, "A General Theorem on Selectors," *Bull. Acad. Polon. Sci. Ser. Sci. Marsh. Astronom. Phys.* **13**, 397–403.

LeRoy, S., 1979, "Expectations' Models of Asset Prices: A Survey of Theory, Report 7957, Center for Mathematical Studies in Business and Economics, University of Chicago.

Lewis, L., 1977, Ph.D. Thesis, Yale University.

Lindenstrauss, L., 1966, "A Short Proof of Lyapunov's Convexity Theorem," *J. Math. Mech.* **15**, 971–972.

Loeb, P., 1971, "A Combinatorial Analog of Lyapunov's Theorem for Infinitesimal Generated Atomic Vector Measures," *Proc. Amer. Math. Soc.* **39**, 585–586.

Lucas, R. E. and Stokey, N., 1984, "Optimal Growth with Many Consumers," *J. Econ. Theory* **32**, 139–171.

Lucchetti, R., Papageorgiou, N. S. and Patrone, F., 1987, "Convergence and Approximation Results for Measurable Multifunctions," *Proc. Amer. Math. Soc.* **100**, 551–556.

Lyapunov, A. A., 1940, " Sur les Fonctions-Vecteurs Complèment Additives," *Izvestija Akademii Nauk SSSR*, 465–478.

McKenzie, L. W., 1959, "On the Existence of General Equilibrium for a Competitive Market," *Econometrica* **27**, 54–71.

McKenzie, L. W., 1981, "The Classical Theorem on Existence of Competitive Equilibrium," *Econometrica* **49**, 819–841.

Machina, M. J., 1988, "Dynamic Consistency and Non-Expected Utility Models of Choice Under Uncertainty," *J. Econ. Lit.* **27**, 1622–1668.

Magill, M., 1981, "An Equilibrium Existence Theorem," *J. Math. Anal. Appl.* **84**, 162–169.

Maharam, D., 1942, "On Homogeneous Measure Algebras," *Proc. Natl. Acad. Sci.* **28**, 108–111.

Majumdar, M., 1975, "Some Remarks on Optimal Growth with Intertemporally Dependent Preferences," *Rev. Econ. Stud.* **42**, 147–153.

Malinvaud, E., 1952, "Capital Accumulation and Efficient Allocation of Resources," *Econometrica* **30**, 233–268.

Marimon, R., 1989, "Stochastic Turnpike Property and Stationary Equilibrium, *J. Econ. Theory* **47**, 282–306.

Masani, P., 1978, "Measurability and Pettis Integration in Hilbert Spaces," *J. Reine Angew. Math.* **297**, 92–135.

Mas-Colell, A., 1974, "An Equilibrium Existence Theorem Without Complete or Transitive Preferences," *J. Math. Econ.* **1**, 237–246.

Mas-Colell, A., 1975, "A Model of Equilibrium with Differentiated Commodities," *J. Math. Econ.* **2**, 263–296.

Mas-Colell, A., 1978, "A Note on the Core Equivalence Theorem: How Many Blocking Coalitions Are There?" *J. Math. Econ.* **5**, 207–215.

Mas-Colell, A., 1982, "Perfect Competition and the Core," *Rev. Econ. Stud.* **49**, 15–30.

Mas-Colell, A., 1984, "On a Theorem of Schmeidler," *J. Math. Econ.* **13**, 210–206.

Mas-Colell, A., 1986, "The Price Equilibrium Existence Problem in Topological Vector Lattices," *Econometrica* **54**, 1039–1054.

Mas-Colell, A., 1986b, "Valuation Equilibrium and Pareto Optimality Revisited, in *Contributions to Mathematical Economics*, W. Hildenbrand and A. Mas-Colell, eds., North-Holland, New York, 317–331.

Mas-Colell, A. and Richard, S. F., 1987, "A New Approach to the Existence of Equilibria in Vector Lattices," working paper, Harvard University.

Mehra, R., 1988, "On the Existence and Representation of Equilibrium in an Economy with Growth and Nonstationary Consumption," *Int. Econ. Rev.* **29**, 131–135.

Mertens, J. F., 1990, "An Equivalence Theorem for the Core of an Economy with Commodity Space $L_\infty - \tau(L_\infty, L_1)$," this volume.

Mertens, J. F. and Zamir, S., 1985, "Formulation of Bayesian Analysis for Games with Incomplete Information," *Int. J. Game Theory* **14**, 1–29.

Meyer, P. A., 1966, *Probability and Potentials*, Blaisdell Publishing Company, Waltham, London.

Michael, E., 1956, "Continuous Selections I," *Ann. Math.* **63**, 363–382.

Michael, E., 1959, "Convex Structures and Continuous Selections," *Canadian J. Math.* **11**, 556–575.

Milgrom, P. and Weber, R., 1985, "Distributional Strategies for Games with Incomplete Information," *Math. Oper. Res.* **10**, 619–632.

Moulin, H., 1981, *Theorie des Jeux pour l'Economie et la Politique*, Herman,

Paris.

Moulin, H. and Vial, J. P., 1978, "Strategically Zero-Sum Games: The Class of Games Whose Completely Mixed Equilibria Cannot be Improved Upon," *Int. J. Game Theory* **7**, 201–221.

Myerson, R. B., 1983, "Bayesian Equilibrium and Incentive Compatibility: An Introduction," CMSEMS Discussion Paper #548, Northwestern University.

Myerson, R. B., 1985, "Bayesian Equilibrium and Incentive Compatibility: An Introduction," in *Social Goals and Social Organizations, Essays in Memory of Elisha Pazner*, L. Hurwicz, D. Schmeidler, and H. Sonnenschein, eds., Cambridge, Cambridge University Press.

Nachman, D. C., 1980, "Temporary Competitive Equilibrium in a Sequence of Spot and Futures Markets," Working Paper, College of Management, Georgia Institute of Technology, Atlanta, GA.

Nash, J. F., 1951, "Noncooperative Games," *Ann. Math.* **54**, 286–295.

Negishi, T., 1960, "Welfare Economics and Existence of an Equilibrium for a Competitive Economy," *Metroeconomica* **12**, 92–97.

Neveu, J., (1964), *Bases Mathematiques du Calcul des Probabilites*, Masson, Paris.

Novshek, W. and Sonnenschein, H., 1978, "Cournot and Walras," Working Paper No. 224, Princeton University.

Nowak, A. S., 1990, "Existence of Correlated Weak Equilibria in Discontinuous Games," this volume.

Ostroy, J., 1984, "The Existence of Walrasian Equilibrium in Large-Square Economies," *J. Math. Econ.* **13**, 143–163.

Ostroy, J. and Zame, W. R., 1988, "Non-Atomic Exchange Economies and the Boundaries of Perfect Competition," mimeo.

Owen, G., 1982, *Game Theory*, Academic Press, New York.

Papageorgiou, N. S., 1985, "Representation of Set-Valued Operators," *Trans. Amer. Math. Soc.* **292**, 557–572.

Parthasarathy, K., 1967, *Probability Measures on Metric Spaces*, Academic Press, New York.

Pazner, E. and Schmeidler, D., 1976, "Non-Walrasian Equilibria and Arrow-Debreu Economies," University of Illinois, Urbana, Illinois, mimeo.

Peleg, B. and Yaari, M. E., 1970, "Markets with Countably Many Commodities, *Int. Econ. Rev.* **11**, 369–377.

Phelps, R. R., 1964, "Weak* Support Points of Convex Sets in E^*," *Isr. J. Math.* **2**, 177–182.

Postlewaite, A. and Schmeidler, D., 1978, "Approximate Efficiency of Non-Walrasian Nash Equilibria," *Econometrica* **46:1**, 127–137.

Prescott, E. C. and Lucas Jr, R. E., 1972, "A Note on Price Systems in Infinite Dimensional Space," *Int. Econ. Rev.* **13**, 416–422.

Prescott, E. C. and Mehra, R., 1980, "Recursive Competitive Equilibrium: The Case of Homogeneous Households," *Econometrica* **48**, 1365–1379.

Pucci, P. and Vitillaro, G., 1984, "A Representation Theorem for Aumann Integrals," *J. Math. Anal. Appl.* **102**, 86–101.

Radner, R., 1967, "Efficiency Prices for Infinite Horizon Production Programs, *Rev. Econ. Stud.* **34**, 51–66.

Radner, R., 1967, "Equilibre des Marchés à Terme et au Comptant en Cas d'Incertitude," *Cahiers d'Econometrie*, CNRS, Paris, 35–52, (translated as "Equilibrium of Spot and Futures Markets under Uncertainty," CRMS Technical Report **24**, University of California, Berkeley, 1967).

Radner, R., 1972, "Existence of Equilibrium of Plans, Prices, and Price Expectations in a Sequence of Markets," *Econometrica* **40**, 289–303.

Radner, R., 1974, "Market Equilibrium and Uncertainty: Concepts and Problems," in *Frontiers of Quantitative Economics*, Vol. II, M. D. Intriligator and D. A. Kendrick, eds., Amsterdam, North-Holland.

Radner, R. and Rosenthal, R., 1982, "Private Information and Pure Strategy Equilibria," *Math. Oper. Res.* **7**, 410–409.

Ramsey, F., 1928, "A Mathematical Theory of Saving," *Econ. J.* **38**, 543–559.

Rashid, S., 1979, "The Relationship Between Measure-Theoretic and Non-Standard Exchange Economies," *J. Math. Econ.* **6**, 195–202.

Ricceri, B., 1982, "Sur l'Approximation des Selections Mesurables," *C. R. Acad. Sc. Paris* **295**, 527–530.

Richard, S. F., 1986, "Competitive Equilibrium in Riesz Spaces," working paper, Carnegie-Mellon University.

Richard, S. F., 1989, "A New Approach to Production Equilibria in Vector Lattices," *J. Math. Econ.* **18**, 41–56.

Richard, S. F. and Zame, W. R., 1986, "Proper Preferences and Quasi-Concave Utility Functions," *J. Math. Econ.* **15**, 231–247.

Richter, H., 1963, "Verallgemeinerung eimer in ser Startistik benötigten Satzes der Masstheorie," *Math. Annalen* **150**, 85–90.

Richter, M. K., 1971, "Coalitions, Core and Competition," *J. Econ. Theory* **3**, 323–334.

Rieder, U., 1975, "Bayesian Dynamic Programming," *Adv. Appl. Prob.* **7**, 330–348.

Robertson, A. P. and Kingman, J. F. C., 1968, "On a Theorem of Lyapunov," *J. London Math. Soc.* **43**, 347–351.

Rockafeller, R. T., 1970, *Convex Analysis*, Princeton, NJ, Princeton University Press.

Rustichini, A., 1989, "A Counterexample and an Exact Version of Fatou's Lemma in Infinite Dimension," *Archiv der Mathematic* **52**, 357–362.

Rustichini, A. and Yannelis, N. C., 1986, "An Elementary Proof of Fatou's Lemma in Finite Dimensional Spaces," Department of Economics, University of Minnesota, Discussion Paper No. 237.

Rustichini, A. and Yannelis, N. C., 1989, "Commodity Pair Desirability and the Core Equivalence Theorem," University of Illinois at Urbana-Champaign, mimeo.

Rustichini, A. and Yannelis, N. C., 1990, "What is Perfect Competition?" this volume.

Rustichini, A. and Yannelis, N. C., 1991, "Edgeworth's Conjecture in Economies with a Continuum of Agents and Commodities," *J. Math. Econ.*, to appear.

Rybiński, L., 1985, "On Carathéodory Type Selections," *Fund. Math.* **125**, 187–193.

Samuelson, P. A., 1958, "An Exact Consumption-Loan Model of Interest with or without the Social Contrivance of Money," *J. Pol. Econ.* **66**, 467–482.

Scarf, H., 1962, "Analysis of Markets with a Large Number of Participants," *Recent Advances in Game Theory*, Princeton University Press, Princeton, NJ.

Scarf, H., 1967, "The Core of an N-Person Game," *Econometrica* **35**, 50–69.

Scarf, H., 1971, "On the Existence of a Cooperative Solution for a General Class of N-Person Games," *J. Econ. Theory* **3**, 169–181.

Schaefer, H. H., 1974, *Banach Lattices and Positive Operators*, Springer-Verlag, Berlin.

Schaefer, H. H., 1986, *Topological Vector Spaces*, Springer-Verlag, New York.

Schaerf, H. M., 1947, "On the Continuity of Measurable Functions in Neighborhood Spaces," *Portugaliae Mathematica* **6**, 33–44.

Schecter, E., 1989, "Closure and Other Properties of the Aumann Integral in Infinite Dimensions," Vanderbilt University.

Schmeidler, D., 1969, "Competitive Equilibrium in Markets with a Continuum of Traders and Incomplete Preferences," *Econometrica* **37**, 578–585.

Schmeidler, D., 1970, "Fatou's Lemma in Several Dimensions," *Proc. Amer. Math. Soc.* **24**, 300–306.

Schmeidler, D., 1972, "A Remark on the Core of an Atomless Economy," *Econometrica* **40**, 579–580.

Schmeidler, D., 1973, "Equilibrium Points of Non-Atomic Games," *J. Stat. Phys.* **7**, 295–300.

Shafer, W. J., 1974, "The Nontransitive Consumer," *Econometrica* **42**, 913–919.

Shafer, W. J. and Sonnenschein, H., 1975, "Equilibrium in Abstract Economies Without Ordered Preferences," *J. Math. Econ.* **2**, 345–348.

Shapley, L. S., 1973, "On Balanced Games without Side Payments," in *Mathematical Programming*, T. C. Hu and S. M. Robinson, eds., Academic Press, New York.

Shapley, L., 1974, "Non-Cooperative General Exchange," RAND Corporation Report No. p-5286.

Shubik, M., 1972, "Commodity Money, Oligopoly, Credit and Bankruptcy in a General Equilibrium Model," *West. Econ. J.* **10**.

Sion, M., 1958, "On General Minimax Theorems," *Pacific J. Math.* **8**, 171–176.

Sobel, M. J., 1975, "Ordinal Dynamic Programming," *Management Sci.* **21**, 967–975.

Sonnenschein, H., 1971, "Demand Theory without Transitive Preferences with Applications to the Theory of Competitive Equilibrium," in *Preferences, Utility, and Demand*, J. Chipman, L. Hurwicz, M. K. Richter and H. Sonnenschein, eds., Harcourt Brace Jovanovich, New York.

Stigum, B. P., 1969, "Competitive Equilibrium under Uncertainty," *Q. J. Econ.* **83**, 533–561.

Stigum, B. P., 1972, "Resource Allocation under Uncertainty," *Int. Econ. Rev.* **13**, 431–459.

Stigum, B. P., 1974, "On Preexisting Contracts and Temporary Equilibria," comments on Chapter 10 in *Essays on Economic Behavior under Uncertainty*, M. S. Balach, D. McFadden, and S. Wu, eds., Amsterdam, North-Holland.

Thomson, W., 1978, "Nash Equilibria of Walras and Lindhal Mechanism," University of Minnesota, mimeo.

Toussaint, S., 1984, "On the Existence of Equilibria in Economies with Infinitely Many Commodities and without Ordered Preferences," *J. Econ. Theory* **33**, 98–115.

Uhl, J., 1969, "The Range of a Vector-Valued Measure," *Proc. Amer. Math.*

Soc. **23**, 158–163.

Uzawa, H., 1968, "Time Preference, the Consumption Function, and Optimum Asset Holdings," in *Value, Capital and Growth: Papers in Honour of Sir John Hicks*, J. N. Wolfe, ed., Chicago, Aldine.

Vind, K., 1964, "Edgeworth Allocations in an Exchange Economy with Many Traders," *Int. Econ. Rev.* **5**, 165–177.

Vind, K., 1973, " A Third Remark on the Core of an Atomless Economy," *Econometrica* **40**, 585–586.

Von Neumann, J., 1950, "Functional Operators," *Ann. Math. Stud.* **22**, Princeton University Press.

Weller, P. A., 1982, "The Speed of Convergence of Prices in Random Exchange Economies," *J. Econ. Theory* **28**, 71–81.

Yannelis, N. C., 1985, "On a Market Equilibrium Theorem with an Infinite Number of Commodities," *J. Math. Anal. Appl.* **108**, 595–599.

Yannelis, N. C., 1987, "Equilibria in Noncooperative Models of Competition," *J. Econ. Theory* **41**, 96–111.

Yannelis, N. C., 1988, "Fatou's Lemma in Infinite Dimensional Spaces," *Proc. Amer. Math. Soc.* **102**, 303–310.

Yannelis, N. C., 1989, "Weak Sequential Convergence in $L_p(\mu, X)$," *J. Math. Anal. Appl.* **141**, 72–83.

Yannelis, N. C., 1990, "On the Upper and Lower Semicontinuity of the Aumann Integral," *J. Math. Econ.* **19**, 373–389.

Yannelis, N. C., 1990a, "Set-Valued Functions of Two Variables in Economic Theory," this volume.

Yannelis, N. C., 1990b, "Integration of Banach-Valued Correspondences," this volume.

Yannelis, N. C., 1990c, "The Core of an Economy with Differential Information," *Econ. Theory*, to appear.

Yannelis, N. C., 1990d, "The Core of an Economy without Ordered Preferences, this volume.

Yannelis, N. C. and Prabhakar, N. D., 1983, "Existence of Maximal Elements and Equilibria in Linear Topological Spaces," *J. Math. Econ.* **12**, 233–245.

Yannelis, N. C. and Rustichini, A., 1990, "On the Existence of Correlated Equilibria," this volume.

Yannelis, N. C. and Rustichini, A., 1991, "Equilibrium Points of Noncooperative Random and Bayesian Games," in *Positive Operators, Riesz Spaces, and Economics*, C. D. Aliprantis, K. C. Border and W. A. J. Luxemburg, eds., Springer-Verlag, forthcoming.

Yannelis, N. C. and Zame, W. R., 1984, "Equilibria in Banach Lattices without Ordered Preferences," Preprint no. 71, Institute for Mathematics and Its Applications, University of Minnesota, Minneapolis, MN.

Yannelis, N. C. and Zame, W. R., 1986, "Equilibria in Banach Lattices without Ordered Preferences," *J. Math. Econ.*, **15**, 85–110.

Yano, M., 1984, "Competitive Equilibrium on Turnpikes in a McKenzie Economy, I: A Neighborhood Turnpike Theorem," *Int. Econ. Rev.* **25**, 695–718.

Yi, G., 1989, "Classical Welfare Theorems in Economies with the Overtaking Criterion," *J. Math. Econ.* **18**, 57–75.

Yosida, K., 1980, *Functional Analysis*, Sixth Edition, Springer-Verlag, New York.

Yosida, K. and Hewitt, E., 1956, "Finitely Additive Measure," *Amer. Math.*

Soc. Trans. **72**, 46-66.

Zame, W. R., 1986, "Markets with a Continuum of Traders and Infinitely Many Commodities," Department of Mathematics, SUNY at Buffalo.

Zame, W. R., 1987, "Competitive Equilibria in Production Economies with an Infinite Dimensional Commodity Space," *Econometrica* **55**, 1075–1108.